12-25-89

Best wishes,

Ned Whelan

CLEVELAND

SHAPING ▲ THE ▲ VISION

"Cleveland's Enterprises" by Betsy Tabac
Produced in cooperation with the Greater Cleveland Growth Association

Cleveland
GREATER CLEVELAND GROWTH ASSOCIATION
THE CHAMBER OF COMMERCE FOR GREATER CLEVELAND

Windsor Publications, Inc.
Chatsworth, California

CLEVELAND

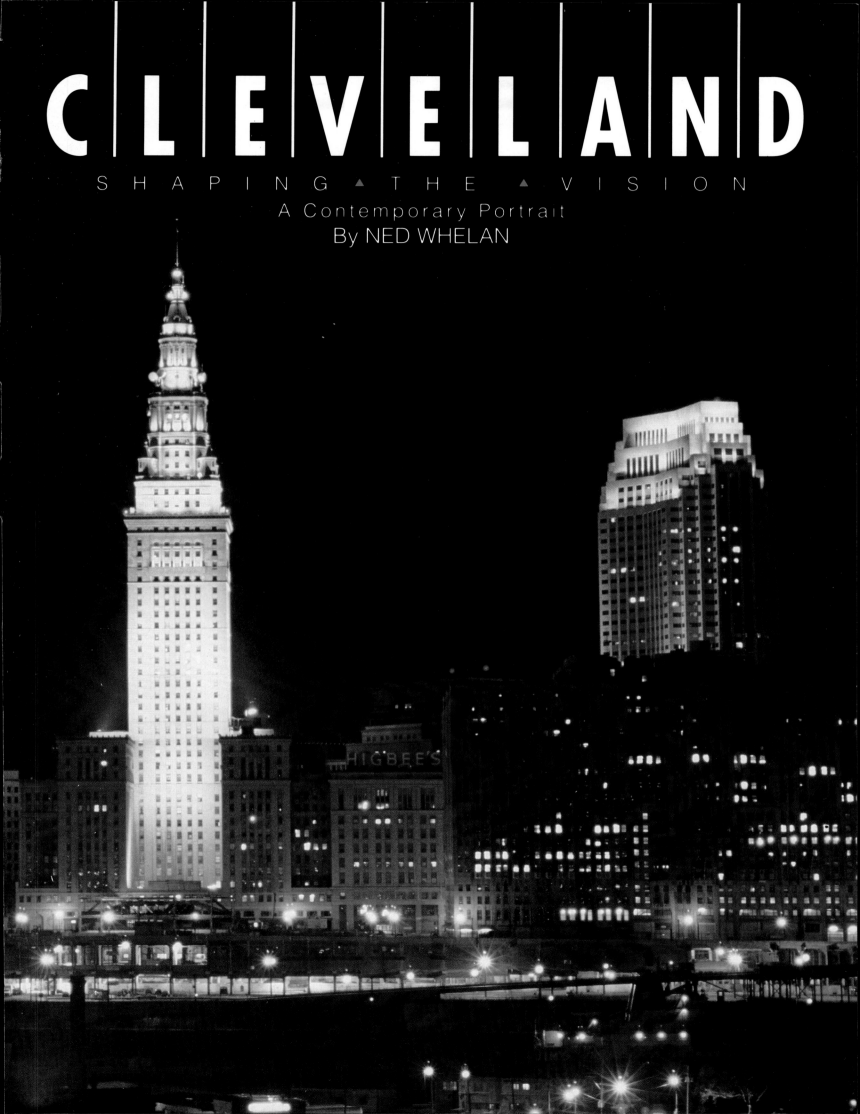

SHAPING ▲ THE ▲ VISION

A Contemporary Portrait

By NED WHELAN

Windsor Publications, Inc.—Book Division
Managing Editor: Karen Story
Design Director: Alexander D'Anca
Photo Director: Susan L. Wells
Executive Editor: Pamela Schroeder

Staff for *Cleveland: Shaping the Vision*
Manuscript Editor: Douglas P. Lathrop
Photo Editor: Cameron Cox
Senior Editor, Corporate Profiles: Judith L. Hunter
Editor, Corporate Profiles: Lin Schonberger
Senior Production Editor, Corporate Profiles: Phyllis Gray
Customer Service Manager: Phyllis Feldman-Schroeder
Editorial Assistants: Kim Kievman, Michael Nugwynne, Kathy B. Peyser, Theresa Solis
Publisher's Representatives, Corporate Profiles: Henry Hintermeister, Robert Lahn, Dale Palmer
Layout Artist, Corporate Profiles: Bonnie Felt
Production Assistant: Deena Tucker

Layout Artist, Editorial: Christina L. Rosepapa
Designer: Thomas Michael McTighe

Library of Congress Cataloging-in-Publication Data
Whelan, Ned, 1943-
Cleveland : shaping the vision : a contemporary portrait /
by Ned Whelan. -- 1st ed.
p. 512 cm. 23 x 31
Bibliography: p.
Includes index.
ISBN 0-89781-320-0
1. Industrial promotion—
History. 3. Cleveland (Ohio)—Economic conditions. 4. Cleveland
(Ohio)—Social conditions. I. Title.
HC108.C7W54 1989
338.6'042'0977132—dc20 89-33035
CIP

Published 1989
Printed in the United States of America
First Edition

Windsor Publications, Inc.
Elliot Martin, Chairman of the Board
James L. Fish III, Chief Operating Officer
Michele Sylvestro, Vice President/Sales-Marketing

Title page: The Terminal Tower and the BP America building stand out from within a blossoming Cleveland skyline. Photo by Barbara Durham

Facing page: The lakefront continues to attract residents and tourists alike for its beauty and for the variety of activities it offers. Photo by Roger Mastroianni

To my parents, Edward J. and Margaret H. Whelan, who always will be the wind beneath my wings, and my children, Colleen and Matthew, the love and inspiration of my life.

CONTENTS

FOREWORD

Greater Cleveland—a vital, vigorous metropolitan area on the Great Lakes and a national symbol of progress and determination. A city where business, labor, government, and proud citizens have cooperated in a partnership that has resulted in a new, vibrant urban region.
Greater Cleveland today takes center stage, with economists and urban experts pointing to it as the "Comeback City" of the 1980s—and as the progressive, forward-looking city of the 1990s that other cities are now emulating.

Look at Greater Cleveland and you'll see a community working together. A community where, over the past decade, leaders from the public and private sectors have taken stock of the challenges facing this urban center and have resolved to turn matters around. A community where cooperation and a keen vision of what the city must and could accomplish have set the stage for achieving goals.

This teamwork has paid dividends. Greater Cleveland has come back full throttle and is one of the nation's great metropolitan areas—a model of progress, achievement, and cooperation.

The economic development climate is strong and healthy, as witnessed by a record number of business locations and expansions in recent years. Investment is at an all-time high. New jobs have been created. The area is nationally recognized as a hotbed for entrepreneurship and small business growth. Downtown Cleveland's skyline changes almost daily as construction of new office buildings, hotels, and retail outlets sets a record pace. At the same time, steady and substantial progress is made daily in developing Cleveland's inner-city neighborhoods, housing, and retail opportunities.

Colorful hot air balloons color the sky at the Cuyahoga Valley Annual Festival. Photo by Barbara Durham

Partnerships between the city's leaders and its citizens have shaped Greater Cleveland's comeback. Working together, the Cleveland "team" has streamlined government operations by increasing the mayor's term from two to four years and reducing the city council's size by one-third. That, and countless other wins, have resulted in Cleveland's being named an All-America City three times within five years—the only city so distinguished.

Like other urban centers, Greater Cleveland has many unmet challenges. But the city and its people have in place the mechanism for winning these challenges. Partnerships will continue to focus on such critical issues as downtown revitalization, education, community development, housing, and business growth.

Greater Cleveland—its assets are the envy of many other cities. An excellent location on Lake Erie—a skilled labor force unafraid of tomorrow's technology—top-ranked education, research, and health-care facilities—recreational amenities, cultural institutions, and sports teams with world-class reputations. They add up to an unparalleled quality of life.

Cleveland is a big-league city in every way. But it's not too big for its people to become involved. And to care. And to choose this city as the home for their businesses, their families, and themselves.

Shaping the vision—to Clevelanders it embodies the vitality of the past decade and the momentum to carry the city into the next century. Teamwork, hard work, and dedication are the hallmarks of any great city, and the foundation for Cleveland's future.

George V. Voinovich
Mayor
City of Cleveland (1979-1989)

Virgil E. Brown
President
Cuyahoga County Board of Commissioners

William J. Williams
Chairman
Greater Cleveland Growth Association
Chairman and Chief Executive Officer
Huntington National Bank

PREFACE

Scripture says that without vision the people will perish. For those of us who have grown up in Greater Cleveland, current local events are a dramatic prelude to our vision of the future. When we open our eyes and look around, we see that the promise of Cleveland at long last is being realized.

Cleveland hardly is without warts—just like every other major American city—but it is determined to overcome past trauma and prevail economically and socially. Accomplishments over the past years have been extraordinary: a soaring skyline; a transformed, thriving business foundation increasingly secured by advanced technology; a major role in America's aggressive space program; expanding world-class recreational opportunities; and challenges in higher education and medicine not dreamed of a decade ago.

Shaping the Vision is an account of the evolution—some would say revolution—that has taken place in Greater Cleveland over the past few years. It also is a glimpse of what the twenty-first century holds for us. As the city prepares to celebrate its 200th anniversary in 1996—surely the greatest civic event in its history—Cleveland bids us all to share in the promise and the vision.

Certainly not every worthy civic leader, place, or event could be mentioned in *Shaping the Vision*. That would take volumes. Rather, I have tried to spotlight areas of our everyday lives that are undergoing the most compelling changes: civic activities and spirit, business and research, sports and recreation, higher education, medicine, the arts, and our downtown renaissance. Alas, the protean nature of current events precluded certain personnel and program changes from being corrected.

Business and government united on a common goal and restored Playhouse Square Center in their successful attempt to revive the arts. Photo by Don Snyder

What do I see for the future? I see a city going through a second great revolution, reclaiming the excitement, strength, character, and national and international dominance that made it a leader in business and culture a century ago.

More important, I see an initiative and commitment by racial, business, civic, political, and religious leaders to make a great city—and the surrounding Greater Cleveland—an even better community for those of us who live here. At the same time, I see them drawing new economic investment here and fostering a positive spirit of accomplishment so that others can share in the same excitement.

That openness beckoned the first pioneers two centuries ago. That same spirit beckons again today.

—Ned Whelan

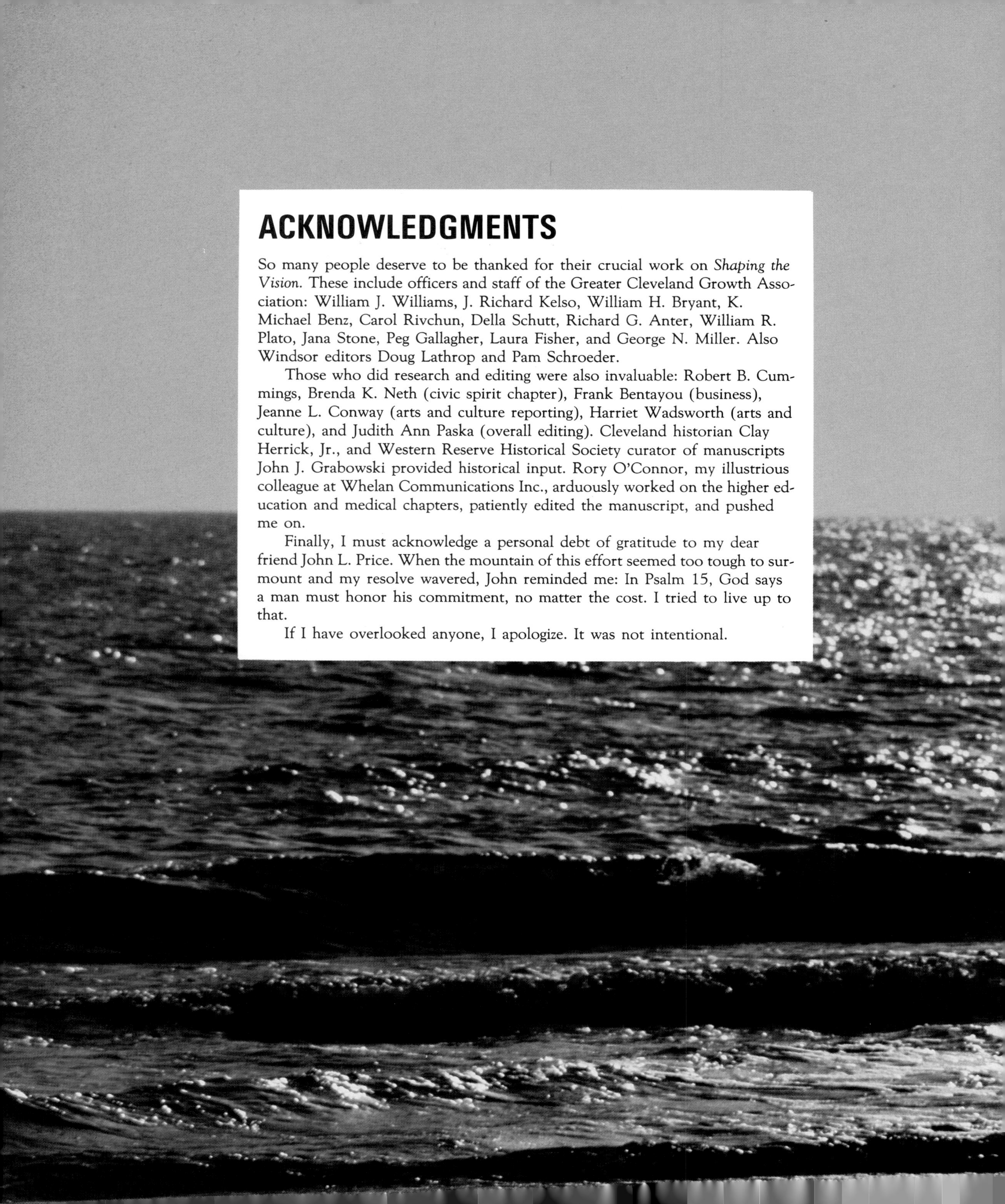

ACKNOWLEDGMENTS

So many people deserve to be thanked for their crucial work on *Shaping the Vision.* These include officers and staff of the Greater Cleveland Growth Association: William J. Williams, J. Richard Kelso, William H. Bryant, K. Michael Benz, Carol Rivchun, Della Schutt, Richard G. Anter, William R. Plato, Jana Stone, Peg Gallagher, Laura Fisher, and George N. Miller. Also Windsor editors Doug Lathrop and Pam Schroeder.

Those who did research and editing were also invaluable: Robert B. Cummings, Brenda K. Neth (civic spirit chapter), Frank Bentayou (business), Jeanne L. Conway (arts and culture reporting), Harriet Wadsworth (arts and culture), and Judith Ann Paska (overall editing). Cleveland historian Clay Herrick, Jr., and Western Reserve Historical Society curator of manuscripts John J. Grabowski provided historical input. Rory O'Connor, my illustrious colleague at Whelan Communications Inc., arduously worked on the higher education and medical chapters, patiently edited the manuscript, and pushed me on.

Finally, I must acknowledge a personal debt of gratitude to my dear friend John L. Price. When the mountain of this effort seemed too tough to surmount and my resolve wavered, John reminded me: In Psalm 15, God says a man must honor his commitment, no matter the cost. I tried to live up to that.

If I have overlooked anyone, I apologize. It was not intentional.

Beach visitors enjoy the splendor of a lakefront sunset. Photo by Don Snyder

PART 1

Shaping The Vision

Proud symbols of Cleveland's rich history and prosperous future, stone silhouettes of the Soldiers and Sailors Monument contrast boldly with today's Terminal Tower. Photo by Barbara Durham

The Resurgence Of A Modern City

Richard Pogue will not forget that morning in December 1978—the morning after Cleveland hit bottom. He was walking to his office downtown along a bitterly cold Euclid Avenue, depressed by headlines that had shaken the city and stunned the nation. The media from coast to coast had bannered the discouraging news: Cleveland was the first major city to default since the Depression.

"I thought to myself, 'Is this what I am part of?'" recalls Pogue, national managing partner of Jones, Day, Reavis & Pogue, the enormous Cleveland-based international law firm.

Pogue was not alone. On this gray morning the headstrong young mayor, Dennis Kucinich, and the city's business establishment were shouting at each other over $14.5 million in short-term municipal notes that the city could not repay to local banks.

The crisis stemmed from a shortfall of revenue provoked by an eroding tax base and years of fiscal neglect at city hall, and was intensified by the palpable animosity that the mayor and civic leadership held for each other.

Yet at that chaotic moment, amid the din of strident charges and countercharges, when the future of the city seemed grim at best, a quiet miracle began taking place. For Pogue, and other civic leaders, that miracle was manifested through a unity of purpose. "From one point of view, the default was beneficial," says Pogue. "Business leaders came together—some for the first time."

Determined to reclaim their besieged city, these civic leaders rose above the political discord and joined in an effort to urge George Voinovich, then lieutenant governor of Ohio, to run for mayor. Fulfilling pledges made to Voinovich, they loaned the services of hundreds of top executives to the city after the election. "This started the public-private partnership that transformed Cleveland and has been working successfully ever since," Pogue observes.

This unique business-government relationship also has helped write one of the most seemingly implausible urban success stories of the 1980s—a story that continues to unfold into the dawn of the twenty-first century.

The Cleveland skyline is seen here reflected in local waters. Photo by Jim Baron. Courtesy, Image Finders, Inc.

Not only has the partnership helped make city hall solvent again, but it has encouraged broad-based confidence in Greater Cleveland as a place to work and live.

Nowhere is this more evident than in downtown Cleveland. When the vision is fully shaped, the city will boast a central business district of gleaming new skyscrapers, world-class hotels, upscale retail plazas, a renovated convention center, a university convocation center, an elegant apartment district carved from converted nineteenth-century lofts and warehouses, and the prized possession: a new leisure-time waterfront that someday will be home to a technology museum and enormous aquarium.

For on-land entertainment, the $38-million restoration of three magnificent vaudeville theaters—the Ohio, Palace, and State—hardly can be topped. Anywhere. With 7,000 seats, the Playhouse Square Center is larger than any American theater complex outside of New York and San Francisco.

The Playhouse Square area is undergoing dramatic change with construction of a new hotel and office building—not to mention various structures planned by nearby Cleveland State University to strengthen its ties to the city.

The heart of Cleveland's renaissance is beating where the city's history began—on Public Square. On one quadrant of the square, sheathed in Italian marble, sits the new 46-floor BP America Building, headquarters for one of the city's largest multinational corporations.

When the ambitious $400-million Tower City project, catty-corner to the BP Building, is fully completed, it will include a three-level concourse with 150 shops and 16 multitheaters, a glass-enclosed rapid-transit station accessible by escalators and elevators, a six-story office building with a seven-floor, 207-room Ritz-Carlton Hotel above it, several new department stores (including a Neiman-Marcus that will open in 1990), and a food court overlooking the Cuyahoga River and the proposed Rock and Roll Hall of Fame. All this will surround the renovated 52-floor Terminal Tower, Cleveland's most recognizable landmark for the past 60 years.

North of Tower City is the $375-million Society Center, which will open by 1992 with the 57-story Society Tower office headquarters for Society National Bank, a 424-room Marriott Hotel, and a 900-car garage. The same developers, brothers Richard and David Jacobs, are planning a $400-million, 60-story office building and 484-room Hyatt Regency on the square's southwest quadrant.

The Ameritrust Center, the new headquarters for Ameritrust Bank, will open in the mid-1990s. "The timing is right," says Richard Jacobs, whose company, JVJ Incorporated, is the nation's fourth-largest shopping center developer. "The executive and legislative branches of city government and the business community are determined to work in harmony. The result is the advancement of Cleveland."

The Jacobs brothers, who also own the Cleveland Indians baseball team, developed the Galleria at Erieview, a two-floor, glass-enclosed promenade of retail shops and restaurants. If all this were not enough, they also are planning several other structures downtown, including two additional large office buildings and an expansion of the Galleria at Erieview.

In the first half of the 1980s alone, Cleveland could claim more development than the combined total of downtown Detroit, Milwaukee, and Indianapolis. During the full decade more than $4 billion was funneled into downtown Cleveland development.

The turnaround, however, is not just marked by bricks and mortar. It has come in recreation, education, health care, the arts, housing, cooperative race relations in recent years (as espoused by the white mayor and black city council president), and perhaps most importantly the economy.

Greater Cleveland is the nation's 12th-largest consumer and retail market and the ninth-largest industrial market. It ranks among the top five regions in the country in the number of *Fortune* 500 corporate headquarters. The city is a transportation hub; half the population of North America is within 600 miles.

An overriding factor in Cleveland's rejuvenation has been its economic diversity. In the shifting emphasis from manufacturing to service industries, the makeup of the economy of Greater Cleveland is beginning to mirror the national economy. Manufacturing now comprises less than one-quarter of the economic output—only slightly higher than the national average. Among the fastest growing nonmanufacturing segments is health care, in which one out of 10 Greater Cleveland workers is employed.

Each year 3,000 Greater Cleveland plants ship more than $30 billion in goods across the globe. By the close of the decade, Greater Cleveland unemployment had dropped to 6 percent, the lowest since the late 1970s.

"The reality of our economic vitality is reflected in the bottom-line employment statistics," says Peg Gallagher, director of research for the Greater Cleveland Growth Association. "We are experiencing growth in both the manufacturing and nonmanufacturing sectors, which has put more people to work in Greater Cleveland than at any time in the area's recent history."

Area steel mills and other heavy industries are making a remarkably strong comeback because of advanced technology, the escalating cost of foreign imports, and productivity contracts hammered out by labor leaders and management in a new spirit of enlightened self-interest and cooperation.

It is hardly a secret that Greater Cleveland ranks only behind Detroit in the production of automobiles;

the Big Three have made more than one billion dollars in capital investments in plants here since 1980.

A study by the Greater Cleveland Growth Association, the chamber of commerce for Northeast Ohio, found that more than one- third of the area's fastest growing companies are manufacturers. While manufacturing is growing, the service industry is expanding even faster, producing many thousands of new jobs since the late 1970s.

Cleveland Tomorrow, a blue-ribbon economic planning group composed of some 50 chief executive officers from Greater Cleveland's biggest companies and nonprofit employers, projects that the so-called "high end" of the service economy—health care, law, and finance—will continue to grow by almost 15 percent into the 1990s.

The city also is creating a fertile climate for new entrepreneurship, nurtured by many public-private partnerships. Each year more than half of the business start-ups in the state are in Greater Cleveland. In turn, the area's increase in new businesses is far ahead of the national average.

The Council of Smaller Enterprises (COSE), a division of the Greater Cleveland Growth Association, is considered the most successful small-business advocacy organization in America. Through numerous seminars and training programs, it has helped thousands of companies to get started and to grow. Greater Cleveland has 60,000 businesses, 97 percent of which have fewer than 100 employees.

The Primus Capital Fund, a venture capital fund established to advance the technology base of Northeastern Ohio, has put dozens of new high-tech and health-care firms into business with hundreds of millions of dollars in financing.

At the same time, the new public-private cooperation is extending to foundations and universities. Enterprise Development, Inc., established by the State of Ohio, the Cleveland Foundation, George Gund Foundation, Cleveland Tomorrow, the Growth Association, and the Weatherhead School of Management of Case Western Reserve University, is helping to create new companies. EDI even provides subsidized start-up space in its office "incubators." Local universities also are participating in the Cleveland Advanced Manufacturing Program (CAMP) to provide millions of dollars in research for new business technology.

Along with an infusion of venture capital and advanced technology, the public-private partnerships are enhancing Cleveland's reputation as one of the world's leading scientific and biomedical centers. Much of this effort is focused on or near University Circle, a square-mile area five miles east of downtown.

The Circle encompasses one of the largest concentrations of academic, cultural, and medical facilities in the world—from the multifacility University Hospitals, to Severance Hall, ornate home of the internationally acclaimed Cleveland Orchestra, to the renowned Cleveland Museum of Art.

The Circle's academic anchor, Case Western Reserve University, is undertaking a master plan for redeveloping the campus, including a 12-story biomedical center that will double its research capacity. When the center opens in the early 1990s, it will create 300 jobs and attract $25 million annually in contracts and grants, largely for advanced work on infectious diseases.

The nearby Cleveland Clinic Foundation is erecting its own new biomedical research building. The clinic is one of the largest and most important diagnostic, treatment, research, and teaching medical facilities in the world.

Each year the Cleveland Clinic handles almost 700,000 outpatient visits and 32,000 hospital admissions from 80 countries and all 50 states. Many foreign dignitaries regularly check into the clinic.

With 9,000 employees, including 450 physicians, the clinic is the largest nongovernmental employer in the city proper. Not long ago the clinic also opened the Cleveland Clinic Florida, an outpatient facility in Fort Lauderdale. It plans to build a full-scale hospital and clinic on the edge of the Everglades in Broward County to attract patients from the expanding population of Florida's east and west coasts.

While the clinic provides the ultimate in high-tech medicine, Cleveland's claim as a high-tech scientific center is bolstered by NASA's Lewis Research Center, adjacent to Cleveland Hopkins International Airport on the city's far west side. Lewis is the only facility of its kind north of the Sun Belt. Its $1.6-billion contract to formulate the power system for the permanent space station, *Freedom*, is infusing hundreds of millions of dollars annually into the local economy and energizing Cleveland's expanding high-tech and aerospace industries.

A private organization, the Great Lakes Space Technology Association, is lobbying for additional Lewis funding and encouraging public awareness of Cleveland's expanding role in America's space program. It also assists local firms in applying for Lewis contracts.

As much as space is now a ***cause celebre*** among the business leadership, so is a down-to-earth program that is stimulating inner-city education—the Cleveland Initiative for Education.

The Greater Cleveland Roundtable—a coalition of religious, minority, and business leaders—is raising $16 million from corporations and foundations to complete funding for the Initiative's Scholarship-in-Escrow, School-to-Work, and Cleveland Education Partners programs.

The Scholarship-in-Escrow program allows Cleveland public-school students between grades 7 and 12 to earn upwards of $4,800 for attaining course grades of A, B, or C. The money is held in escrow until graduation and paid as tuition to the college where the graduate enrolls. The School-to-Work program helps qualified Cleveland school graduates prepare for employment through work in local corporations. The Cleveland Education Partners are 12 major employers whose employees volunteer their skills at individual high schools.

"What's really made these public-private partnerships work is that people believe in the city again," says J. Richard Kelso, former chairman of the East Ohio Gas Company and former chairman of the Greater Cleveland Growth Association.

"Newcomers take Cleveland for what it is, without any baggage," adds Kelso, a former Pittsburgher. "They find it marvelous—a great place to live, work, invest, and raise a family."

That Clevelanders are passionately proud of their city can be seen in the overflow crowds at theaters, museums, and concert halls. It also is obvious in the devotion to their electrifying professional sports teams—the Browns in football, the Indians in baseball, and the Cavaliers in basketball—who have attracted record attendance in recent years.

Such enthusiasm has not been dimmed by the inner-city population loss. The city population peaked in 1950 at 914,000 and today is something over 500,000. The Cuyahoga County population is around 1.5 million, also down from a high of 1.7 million.

While the population has pushed into once-rural outlying counties, projections for Cleveland and Cuyahoga County anticipate a turnaround. Middle-class home owners are moving back into gentrified city neighborhoods and downtown apartment and condominium complexes. Meanwhile, suburban housing developments keep going up at a near-record pace.

Since 1981 city and suburban county neighborhoods have been bolstered by the $2-billion Build Up Greater Cleveland program, which has lobbied for discretionary federal and state dollars to rehabilitate roads, bridges, sewage and water facilities, and mass-transit systems.

Under the auspices of the Greater Cleveland Growth Association, Build Up Greater Cleveland—one of the city's first public-private partnerships—enlists executives to support legislation of community interest and to petition government officials to fund needed infrastructure projects, from sewers to bridges to highways.

"Because this private-public cooperation is innovative, Build Up Greater Cleveland has become a national model," says Carlton Schnell, the original chairman of the program and partner in the law firm of Arter & Hadden. "The effort will encourage development and make Greater Cleveland attractive for new business."

Another key undertaking to invigorate both downtown and working-class city neighborhoods has been Civic Vision 2000, a citywide land-use and zoning modernization plan that is the crowning touch to George Voinovich's decade in office, and a vehicle that will help smooth the way for the new mayor.

A guideline for assisting future development of office buildings, retail space, housing, and municipal improvements, Civic Vision—a public-private partnership—has been funded largely by the Cleveland and George Gund foundations, BP America, the Building Owners and Managers Association, the Growth Association, and Cleveland Tomorrow.

When fully implemented in the 1990s, the new Civic Vision codes will allow for mixed uses of buildings—particularly those downtown—open up space for retail districts, stimulate townhouse development, and control neighborhood deterioration.

"Our biggest city hall accomplishment was providing an environment where community resources, including professional people, could come together and make progress," says Voinovich, who in 1989 opted not to seek reelection as mayor but to run for governor.

In one of his first moves at city hall, Voinovich formed a waterfront task force that led to the North Coast Harbor development. "Our water is our greatest resource," Voinovich says. "It was neglected for years. We knew by developing it, we could stimulate the economy and make Cleveland competitive while giving people a place to enjoy themselves."

"The direction of the town turned away from the lakefront when the Terminal Tower was built," says Ruth Miller, president of Tower City Center and former chairman of the Convention and Visitors Bureau. "Now, with the extraordinary waterfront development, the circle is complete.

"Cleveland is becoming a regional center for work, recreation, commerce, and entertainment," Miller adds. "We are taking on a whole new identity."

EXTRACT
VANILLA
LEMON
15c
TOMATO CATSUP
SMALL BOTTLE
10c
LARGE BOTTLE
15c
CORN STARCH
8c
BUTTER
25c

CHAPTER 1

The Struggle To Survive and Prevail

Much of Cleveland's renaissance is springing up along its lakefront, from the same waters that provided food and transportation for Indians—Senecas and Eries—for hundreds of years before white explorers were drawn to America's North Coast.

Historians believe that French missionaries explored our land in the early seventeenth century before LaSalle traveled along Lake Erie on his way to discovering the Mississippi River. "LaSalle's return trip, by land, may have taken him along the southern shore of the lake and through the future site of Cleveland," wrote George E. Condon, newspaperman and raconteur, in his popular book, *Cleveland: Prodigy of the Western Reserve.*

A century later the British already were making their presence strongly felt. Major Robert Rogers in 1760 headed out after—who else?—the French. He confronted a combative Chief Pontiac at the mouth of the Cuyahoga, an Indian word meaning "crooked" that aptly describes the river's tortuous course. "Apparently the great chief was open to argument and presents," notes Condon. "The Rogers party was allowed to resume its journey."

At the end of the French and Indian War, the territory became British. After the American Revolution and the opening of the Northwest Territories, the way was paved for white settlers.

Some tried but could not persevere against the forbidding winters and sometimes-hostile Indians. A small band of Moravian Christians, fleeing from an Indian massacre 100 miles south of Lake Erie, settled only 10 miles from the shore of the lake in 1786 and 1787. After they were harassed by marauding tribes, the Moravians hurriedly packed up and scurried west to Sandusky Bay.

For well over 100 years pioneers like the Fisher Brothers, seen here in 1915 in their store on Cedar Road, have helped build Cleveland. Courtesy, Western Reserve Historical Society

This detail from 1796 reveals the nature of the lakefront topography that greeted pioneers in the earliest years of the city. Courtesy, Western Reserve Historical Society

Notwithstanding such perils, the land barons who controlled this western territory from Connecticut were visionaries. They foresaw the fortunes that could be made by forging out to the frontier and beyond; Indians would not long stand in their way.

This Connecticut Yankee presence—stamped on our land and psyches more than 300 years ago—is still felt socially, spiritually, and architecturally. The Connecticut connection came as a result of King Charles II rewarding his Connecticut colonists for braving the harsh New England territory. He granted them the 80 miles between the 41st and 42nd parallels—the width of present-day Connecticut—from the western border of Pennsylvania to the Pacific Ocean. This became known as the Western Reserve.

After the War of Independence, the Connecticut legislature decided to cash in on the king's promise, at least partially. In arguing to Congress that the state was too small and needed more land, the politicians asked for the width of the Western Reserve 120 miles westward from the

western Pennsylvania line.

Today this is still called the Western Reserve, and a prep school, university, and scores of businesses and institutions include "Western Reserve" in their titles.

The Western Reserve was hardly considered choice real estate before the Revolution, but it became a coveted location with the opening of the Northwest Territories. The far western acreage of the Reserve—the Firelands—was given to Connecticut residents "who had suffered losses by fire or otherwise during the Revolution," writes knowledgeable Cleveland historian Clay Herrick, Jr., in his abbreviated history *Cleaveland's Rich Heritage.*

No better judge than George Washington predicted an auspicious future for this "New Connecticut." In 1784, while surveying western Pennsylvania and poring over maps of pioneering traders, Washington wrote to William Henry Harrison, then governor of the Virginia Territory, "Let the courses and distances be taken from the mouth of the Muskingum and up that river to the carrying place of the Cuyahoga to Lake Erie . . . the object in my estimation is of vast commercial importance."

Washington's forecast was right on the mark, and these prophetic words are carved at the base of his statue in Washington Square at the new Federal Building downtown. "It's another way of saying the best location in the nation," Herrick says.

The father of our country was foretelling how America would grow—that the Cuyahoga, via other waterways and portage trails, would open commerce from Lake Erie to the Ohio and Mississippi rivers and beyond.

Eleven years after Washington's prophecy, the Connecticut government authorized the sale of the 3 million Western Reserve acres, excluding the Firelands, to the Connecticut Land Company. This syndicate of wealthy investors picked it up at a "fire sale" for 40 cents an acre.

One of those privileged investors, Moses Cleaveland, became the company's field superintendent and was charged with surveying the land and preparing it for sale. A severe and swarthy lawyer and former general in the state militia, Cleaveland was a Yale graduate. Even today the tradition of sending their progeny to Yale is carried on by many of the city's prominent families.

Part of Cleaveland's band of 40 pioneers came by land, but the boss led a group by boat from western New York, pausing in Buffalo to con-

Without a doubt one of the more significant citizens in Cleveland's rich history, it was Moses Cleaveland who first surveyed the flats and the land that would give birth to one of the nation's strongest cities. Courtesy, Western Reserve Historical Society

firm title to the Western Reserve with the Indians. Cleaveland appeased the Indians with $1,500, two cows, and some whiskey. He and his advance party sailed up the sand-choked Cuyahoga on July 22, 1796.

"What they saw in the flats of the river valley was an unprepossessing sight," Condon observed in *Cleveland: Prodigy of the Western Reserve.* "A marshy growth of wild vegetation concealed most of the riverside . . . a more cheerful vista awaited the party at the top of the 80-foot-high hillside on the eastern edge of the valley."

Cleaveland was not one for celebration. Without much ado, he ordered the woods atop the hill surveyed. Thus Cleveland—the city, its Public Square, and downtown—was born.

Three months after Moses had stepped foot in the promised land, he turned back for Connecticut, disenchanted by the primitive conditions and confounded by the vulgarity of his crew. He never returned, leaving only his name—minus the first *a*—three men, and one woman to stay among the Indians.

By the 1820s and 1830s not only had settlers arrived, but they had formed a government and established an assortment of churches and hotels. This view depicts Euclid Avenue near Public Square in 1833. Courtesy, Western Reserve Historical Society

The next spring, however, new Connecticut Land Company surveyors arrived, including Lorenzo Carter, the first permanent settler. They finished plotting the land in the same grid pattern as the traditional Connecticut commons, with a 10-acre public square.

By the late 1820s early settlers had formed a government and built hotels and churches. But they were still cutting paths to the outlands and eking out a living through farming. The city had experienced only modest growth; development was hampered by poor access over land and through the mosquito-breeding Cuyahoga.

"Throughout the first 30 years there was no harbor," observes the *Encyclopedia of Cleveland History*, "because the entrance to the river was blocked by sandbars that forced goods and passengers to be off-loaded on to smaller vessels."

Though the Cuyahoga was difficult to negotiate, the lake already had become vital to the security of the adolescent nation. Commodore Oliver Hazard Perry defeated a mighty British fleet only 60 miles west of Cleveland off South Bass Island in 1813. This crucial Battle of Lake Erie in the War of 1812 saved the United States from becoming British again. In commemoration, the city's Early Settlers' Association convenes each year on the September 10 anniversary.

The toasts to Perry were still being raised when, less than 15 years after his return, America's territorial and commercial imperative found an outlet on Cleveland's waterways. The Erie Canal, linking the Atlantic to Lake Erie, was completed in 1825. Even before it opened, financiers were mounting political pressure to build the next logical extension to commercial riches, the Ohio Canal.

Leading Clevelanders underwrote the monumental Ohio Canal project, which, as George Washington had predicted, joined the Cuyahoga along various water routes to the Ohio River and beyond. The disappearance of the American frontier was hastened when the two canals were finally linked via Lake Erie.

It was the skillful judgment and determination of Alfred Kelley, pictured, that made the Ohio Canal a reality. The opening of the canal ushered in a new age of growth for Cleveland. Courtesy, Western Reserve Historical Society

By any definition, the Ohio Canal—built under the guidance of Alfred Kelley, Cleveland's first lawyer—was epochal. In 1825, as the digging started, the city population was a mere 600; when the canal opened seven years later, the population had mushroomed to nearly 6,000.

Cleveland's future was assured by winning the political battle against other towns for the canal's northern terminus. It guaranteed that the hamlet would become a thriving center of commerce and trade. In no time, mule-drawn barges were arriving and departing day and night.

Along with prosperity, however, the boom brought squalor. Slums were choked with diseased and impoverished Irish, who, along with native farm labor, dug the canal with picks and shovels, muscle and sweat, and nightly rations of whiskey.

It also brought political feuding. Even today few local political clashes can match the intensity of the pitched battles of 150 years ago that divided Cleveland and Ohio City, the smaller town that had sprouted up on the west bank of the Cuyahoga. Convinced that Cleveland was siphoning off Ohio Canal commerce, Ohio City residents threatened to burn down the bridges across the Cuyahoga. To settle the conflict, the sister cities agreed to merge in 1854, with the Ohio City mayor becoming mayor of Cleveland.

Geographic jealousies do not die easily. Many of the subtle barriers and rivalries that divided East Siders and West Siders more than a century ago are still deeply engraved in the Cleveland psyche. Suburbanites have inherited this dispute, and many continue to hold passionate territorial views about where they live in relation to the Cuyahoga.

Oliver H. Perry's victory over the British in the Battle of Lake Erie helped turn the tide in the War of 1812. Courtesy, Western Reserve Historical Society

The Ohio and Erie canals have played equally significant roles in charting Cleveland's history. This painting from 1860 shows the lockhouse on the Ohio Canal at the foot of Seneca Street Hill. Courtesy, Western Reserve Historical Society

Facing page, top: Hot on the heels of the canals came the railroads. But it was the introduction of the "iron horse" that would ultimately render the canals obsolete. This image from the Cleveland lakefront is from 1850. Courtesy, Western Reserve Historical Society

Facing page, bottom: By the late 1800s railroads, shipping, and the steel industry had forever changed the Cleveland lakefront. Courtesy, Western Reserve Historical Society

The Ohio City-Cleveland merger of the mid-nineteenth century was aimed at ending neighborhood chauvinism and brutal trade wars, but the railroads were more successful at the task than the civic peacemakers. By the 1850s the iron horse was rendering the Ohio Canal obsolete.

After tracks were laid and the canal shipping dried up, the canal tragically fell into disrepair. Today a few locks have been restored within the scenic Cuyahoga Valley National Recreation Area between Cleveland and Akron.

Just as quickly as one waterborne era came to a close, another welled up. America's industrial revolution, which changed the course of world history, was spawned on Cleveland's water.

It started in 1846, when a Western Reserve University medical professor, chemist, and geologist, Dr. James Lang Cassels, a Scottish immigrant, discovered copper and iron ore in the Michigan Upper Peninsula on the southern shore of Lake Superior. He called his serendipity Cleveland Mountain.

Shortly afterward, Cleveland financiers backed the search for ore deposits in the Minnesota Messabi Range and in no time were building big ships to tote their precious cargo through the Great Lakes back home to the shores of Lake Erie, where it was smelted in steel mills fired by Appalachian coal hauled north by rail.

Shipping, railroading, and steelmaking may have produced environmental problems—the newly industrialized Cuyahoga Valley was often veiled in black soot—but such raw capitalism was powering a growing city dominated by a civic elite.

This Gilded Age of cheap wages and no taxes also gave rise to great family corporations. Today many of those same companies remain vital to our economy and carry the names of their founders.

These early industrial captains were not shy about displaying their wealth, generally believing that they were favored by God for their enterprise and intellect. They chose the city's main thoroughfare, Euclid Avenue—the original Indian trail and later stagecoach route to Buffalo—to show off their blessings.

By the Civil War Euclid Avenue, just east of downtown, was becoming "Millionaires Row." The city's tycoons erected fashionable mansions with lawns and ballrooms on the scale of *The Great Gatsby*. Within two generations, commercial sprawl from downtown began to intrude on the privileged neighborhood. As World War I dawned, the first families were riding off to the suburbs, leaving behind empty mansions, stables, and servants' quarters.

Only a few of the palaces have survived the wrecker's ball. Among them are the sprawling Beckwith home, now the private University Club; the Mather mansion, which houses administrative offices for Cleveland State University; and the Carlin house, which served as a union headquarters for many years.

To see upper Euclid Avenue today—a mixture of stores, university buildings, office buildings, restaurants, and rooming houses—it is hard to fathom that a century ago the richest man in the world lived here.

John D. Rockefeller arrived in Cleveland as a teenager from western New York State in 1853. After graduating from Central High School in 1855, he went to work as a bookkeeper for a commission merchant who bought and sold commodities ranging from marble to grain.

By the age of 19 the enterprising Rockefeller, with an older partner, had formed their own commission business. In 1864, five years after the discovery of oil in Titusville, Pennsylvania (a mere 100 miles east of Cleveland), Rockefeller opened an oil refinery in the Flats along the Cuyahoga River. He organized the Standard Oil Company in 1870 with his brother and three other partners, changing the course of world history.

In her informative book, *John D. Rockefeller: The Cleveland Years*, Cleveland historian Grace Goulder notes: "Neither Rockefeller nor any of his partners glimpsed the future in store for them: 'None of us ever dreamed of the magnitude of what proved to be the later expansion,' Rockefeller said 40 years later, and even then, he could not quite believe it."

The growth of Standard Oil from its million-dollar capitalization into the most formidable corporation on earth forced John D. to move to New York City in 1884. He maintained Forest Hill, a summer estate in East Cleveland, for the next 20 years, but stayed away after the county tried to tax him as a full-time resident. Still, Rockefeller never truly left Cleveland. He

As the city grew and citizens prospered, lavish homes began to dot the landscape. Here, the sprawling Beckwith home lends a touch of class to what soon became known as "Millionaires Row." Courtesy, Western Reserve Historical Society

The enterprising John D. Rockefeller, the man behind Standard Oil, is seen here at the turn of the century. Courtesy, Western Reserve Historical Society

Tom L. Johnson, who made his fortune with streetcar railways, was also mayor of Cleveland for three terms in the early twentieth century. Courtesy, Western Reserve Historical Society

is buried in Lake View Cemetery, not far from his beloved Forest Hill.

In 1905 Rockefeller erected a 17-story local headquarters in downtown Cleveland that he unashamedly called the Rockefeller Building. He sold it, but then bought it back when the new owner changed its name; Rockefeller did not want the city establishment to forget him—as if they could.

Rockefeller's decision to relocate to New York may have been dictated by his gargantuan oil trust, but he also had been shunned by Cleveland's old guard. Putting his philanthropy aside, their argument was simple: Rockefeller and his partners had built Standard Oil unethically by demanding kickbacks from railroads transporting their crude oil, thereby destroying the competition. "When Rockefeller . . . later offered a large bequest to Western Reserve University, the trustees refused the money and it went to the University of Chicago," observes Clay Herrick, Jr., in *Cleaveland's Rich Heritage.*

Rockefeller and his money may be missed today, but they certainly were not at the turn of the century. Cleveland was prospering without John D. The premier civic, political, and business leader was Marcus Alonzo Hanna. In his own way, Hanna was as incredible as Rockefeller.

Hanna founded the M.A. Hanna Company—an international mining and shipping firm whose business has evolved largely into polymers—and soon became consumed with Republican politics as a means of furthering the interests of big business.

In 1894 he began a two-year drive to gain Canton's William McKinley the Republican nomination for president. As chairman of the Republican National Committee, Hanna ran the presidential campaign. Four years later, he did the same thing and was responsible for McKinley's reelection.

The Ohio governor appointed Hanna to the U.S. Senate in 1897, and the state legislature elected him to a full term in 1898. Shortly after his reelection in 1904, he died unexpectedly at the age of 66.

Hanna also was the principal founder of the Union Club, the city's paramount business club. An oil portrait of him hangs on the west wall of the stately reading room, gazing toward the city's east side—where the turn-of-the-century establishment lived and from where they controlled the city.

If Hanna stood for business control in politics, another magnate used his fortune at the turn of the century to speak politically for the anxieties and aspirations of the common man. Tom L. Johnson, whose own streetcar railways had rivaled Hanna's for dominance in the 1890s, was elected mayor in 1901 on a populist platform that included pledges of reform and a three-cent streetcar fare.

Johnson pushed a municipal light system that fought with the private electric company for city customers—a battle that continues today. Municipal ownership of utilities was controversial, but Johnson's grand scheme for a downtown public building district, the Group Plan resulted in architect Daniel Burnham's designing the city hall, public auditorium, federal courthouse, county courthouse, library, Federal Reserve Bank, and board of education building all with a distinctive classical motif, surrounding a mall with an open vista to Lake Erie.

While not all of Johnson's reforms worked, nor did all of his plans come to fruition, he opened an era of change where the swelling tide of immigrants from Europe—the Irish, Germans, and Slavs—could hope for a share in the American dream. Ironically, the Germans helped vote Johnson out of office after three two-year terms in favor of a German-American.

Johnson died broke and brokenhearted, but he still is revered and considered Cleveland's greatest mayor. His formidable bronze statue dominates the northwest quadrant of Public Square.

In calling for reform, Johnson and his disciples, including Newton D. Baker, Democratic mayor and later Secretary of War under Woodrow Wilson, were preaching to a growing populace. In 1900 the city population was 360,000. It had exploded to 900,000 by 1930.

By the 1920s the immigrants were becoming assimilated into American society and eager to participate in the post-World War I boom. Cleveland was a model for what a twentieth-century American city should be. The government was efficient; the economy was churning.

In an effort to capitalize on the affluence created by these good times, the bachelor Van Sweringen brothers—Oris Paxton and Mantis James—developed Shaker Heights as an exclusive executive suburb. To assure home sales in an area considered remote at the time, they purchased a railroad right-of-way and built a streetcar line between Shaker Heights and downtown.

The reclusive Vans possessed fabulous wealth. Their holdings included the Nickel Plate, Chesapeake & Ohio, and numerous other railroads. Determined to bring their railroad and rapid-transit passengers under one roof, they began building the Cleveland Union Terminal, with the Terminal Tower office building above it. At 708 feet, the Terminal Tower was, the *Encyclopedia of Cleveland History* contends, "the tallest building in the world outside New York City until 1967."

The terminal opened in 1930 amid a whooping celebration, but the stock market already had crashed. In the next few years the Vans lost everything, dying within months of each other far from the glare of the public eye.

It is often said that Cleveland did not recover from the Great Depression until recently. There is some truth in this. Many of the great families lost their fortunes. Their companies were forced to make massive layoffs. Others simply shut down. After such abundance in the 1920s, the next decade was dismal.

Seen here under construction in the 1920s, the Terminal Tower would soon become, at 708 feet, one of the tallest buildings in the nation. Courtesy, Western Reserve Historical Society

In search of some comfort from the soup lines and unemployment, the city fathers were intent upon celebrating Cleveland's 100th year of incorporation, and successfully lobbied for the 1936 Republican National Convention at the Public Auditorium. Alf Landon was nominated, but was run over by the steamroller of Franklin D. Roosevelt and his New Deal.

By the early summer of 1936, and into the following year, the Great Lakes Exposition at the mall and waterfront drew millions of people to futuristic industrial displays, aquatic exhibitions, style shows, fountains, horticultural gardens, farms, art exhibits, and promenades. The 80,000-seat Cleveland Municipal Stadium, still used today, was erected in anticipation of the Exposition.

While the Exposition afforded some diversion from the grim reality of the Depression, it was not until World War II and after that the city began to rebound. In this new industrial era, family-owned companies gave way to large corporations dominated by professional managers.

The war also brought racial change. Blacks continued moving to Cleveland from the South in great numbers, taking jobs abandoned by whites going off to fight. Peace, however, brought with it a housing shortage. Veterans coming home to start families took their cheap mortgages to the open suburbs, while blacks generally settled for what inner-city housing—including new public projects—they could find.

Until 1950 the population of Cleveland had steadily expanded. With a revived industrial economy and a housing boom, Clevelanders started fleeing

Growth in the wake of the Industrial Age and an influx of new residents soon led to the suburb movement. Clevelanders moved outward to new neighborhoods and affordable housing. Courtesy, Western Reserve Historical Society

to the new suburbs. The city's population was peaking just as Cleveland was reaching its postwar industrial pinnacle.

Parma, on Cleveland's southern boundary, and other once-obscure suburbs turned into popular working-class havens, their growth hastened by economic realities, new freeways, and racially changing city neighborhoods.

Cleveland city officials had not foreseen the impact of the suburban migration. They failed to use their control of municipal services as an inducement to annex the suburbs. The result: a mother city and more than 60 Balkanized suburbs in Cuyahoga County.

Left behind in this suburban atomization was a growing black underclass, whose frustration exploded in 1966 in the Hough ghetto. Four residents were killed during riots ostensibly started over the refusal of a white bartender to give a black woman a glass of water.

But the Hough riots had deeper roots—pent-up anger over jobs, housing, schools, and perceived political unresponsiveness. The business establishment listened, and turned in the following year to Carl B. Stokes, a handsome and charming Democratic state legislator who narrowly defeated Seth Taft, descendant of President William Howard Taft, to become the first black mayor of the city.

Even Stokes, with much business support and the black electorate behind him, could not change everything. On July 23, 1968, black nationalist extremists opened fire with high-powered rifles in the Glenville ghetto and ambushed policemen. When the smoke and rubble cleared, three

The local canals soon became popular attractions as residents discovered the utility of the waterways. Courtesy, Western Reserve Historical Society

police officers and eight blacks had been killed in the city's second race riot.

The Glenville riots threw cold water on the excitement and promise generated by Stokes' mayoralty. Stokes won another two-year term, but he opted not to continue battling with his political adversaries and declined to seek a third term.

Though Stokes went off to New York to become a television newsman, he returned to Cleveland and, as an elected municipal judge, again became involved in local politics in the 1980s. Stokes' name and charisma helped his brother, Louis Stokes, easily to become the first black congressman in Ohio. By the late 1980s Louis Stokes had more seniority than any other Ohio member of Congress.

The city hall exodus of Carl Stokes brought a temporary defusing of political contention, but within a few years Cleveland's troubles seemed to multiply; a declining tax base, industrial closings, loss of jobs, and forced school busing continued to accelerate middle-class flight.

Republican Ralph J. Perk, a former county auditor, devoted his three terms trying to keep the decline in check. To balance the city budget without raising taxes, he was forced to sell city assets to regional agencies and to borrow from various bond funds.

The forces that began to pull Cleveland into a vortex of trouble congealed with the defeat of Perk and election—by a mere 2 percent of the vote—of a 31-year-old former newspaper copyboy and city councilman, Dennis J. Kucinich. Kucinich rose to power on a "populist" agenda appealing to the lower-middle-class whites living in old city neighborhoods.

In the name of his concern for the "little people," Kucinich seemingly clashed with anyone—city employees, councilmen, the media, and the civic establishment—he perceived as standing in the way of his reforms. During a televised news conference, Kucinich fired Police Chief Richard Hongisto, whom he had handpicked with much fanfare only months before. More than any of Kucinich's other pronouncements, the firing mobilized a popular groundswell for a recall election.

The Democratic mayor survived it by only 236 votes out of 120,000 cast, but a short time later stood front and center at the ignominious default. Many business leaders claimed that the financial debacle resulted from Kucinich's fiscal mismanagement, including his refusal to sell the deficit-plagued municipal light plant to help pay off more than $14.5 million in short-term municipal notes. The ill-concealed feelings of contempt between Kucinich and his adversaries further heightened the negative national publicity surrounding the default, eventually leading to Kucinich's defeat in 1979 at the hands of Republican George V. Voinovich.

If default was not enough, Cleveland also was facing another serious challenge. In the late 1970s U.S. District Judge Frank J. Battisti, in response to a suit filed by the NAACP, ordered Cleveland schools to desegregate.

His controversial decision, which still provokes heated argument, led to forced crosstown school busing. It also accelerated the flight of middle-class blacks and whites from the city and intensified the struggle—one that still persists—over the ability of the Cleveland public schools to deal with high dropout rates, resegregation in the classroom, inner-city poverty, and other ills that plague big-city systems.

Along with educational quality and city hall turmoil, the Greater Cleveland economy was also a burning issue in the 1970s. In the late 1940s the city could claim more than 200,000 manufacturing jobs. By 1977 that fig-

The early 1900s were a time for growth, change, and fun. These women were pictured on Broadway Avenue. Courtesy, Western Reserve Historical Society

ure had plunged to 120,000, and a few years later it was 90,000.

The job picture in surrounding Northeast Ohio remained rosier, as some of the departing jobs had only moved to the suburbs. Many more, however, had flown to the Sun Belt. Others were phased out by international competition and changing technology. A number of Cleveland-headquartered companies were sold, merged, or moved out of town.

Yet the scope of today's rebirth has been as remarkable as the past years were tragic. The renaissance is economic in that the job loss has been forcefully reversed in an atmosphere that encourages business and labor-management cooperation. It is political in that the ascerbic city hall confrontations are largely over. Perhaps more than anything, it is deeply emotional. The comeback has satisfied Clevelanders' deep longing for positive change.

Voinovich himself set the tone for this new spirit. "I say that the history of free man is not written by chance, it is determined by choice," he declared at his inauguration. "Today I choose to say that I believe in the future of Cleveland."

From the start, Voinovich realized that the renewal had to start at city hall or it could not start at all. Voinovich and his staff trimmed unnecessary jobs, increased productivity, adopted stringent new auditing measures, cleared up $100 million in lingering debt, improved the bond rating, and resolved the default. The state had taken control of city finances. With volunteer help from Cleveland corporations, the books were straightened out and local control was soon restored.

With renewed confidence in city government, voters hiked the city income tax and passed a charter amendment to increase the mayoral term from two to four years and to reduce the unwieldy 33-member council to 21.

To foster racial harmony in a city that has become slightly more than half black, Voinovich formed an alliance with George L. Forbes, the long-time city council president. Among their efforts was the establishment of a Minority Business Enterprise program to assure that blacks obtained a share of city contracts.

Though Voinovich is a Republican and Forbes a Democrat like the rest of the city council, the relationship worked. "This has been the golden era of cooperation," says Voinovich. "We wanted to win, not fight. Without that together-we-can-do-it attitude, it wouldn't have worked."

Forbes has told civic gatherings on many occasions that their deep feeling of "friendship has worked to move the city forward." Both Forbes and Voinovich credit the business leadership for its commitment to Cleveland. "There is no city where private business has been more involved," Forbes told a gathering of Leadership Cleveland, an intensive yearlong program designed to develop future Greater Cleveland leaders that is sponsored by the Greater Cleveland Growth Association.

Washington also has helped with millions of dollars in federal Urban Development Action Grants. Selective tax abatement and federal loans are enabling developers to build new downtown hotels and skyscrapers, thereby creating new jobs and stimulating the economy. Though tax abatement for

Stone cutters on the Lorain-Carnegie bridge pose in front of the guardian of transportation they created. Courtesy, Western Reserve Historical Society

downtown projects is opposed by some neighborhood groups, it also is used for appropriate commercial and industrial development in once-decaying neighborhoods.

Buttressed by the new political and business harmony, many companies are opening new operations or increasing their work force in Greater Cleveland. As the 1980s come to a close, the number of jobs—upwards of one million—in Cuyahoga and the six surrounding counties is the highest in a decade.

Considering its scope, this dramatic reversal—from downtown to the neighborhoods and beyond—has prompted the national media to look favorably upon Cleveland. Coverage by *Fortune, The Washington Post*, the *Detroit Free Press, Reader's Digest, Time, Newsweek, The New York Times*, the *Christian Science Monitor*, and other major national media has been effusive. ABC's "Good Morning America" produced an entire live show from Cleveland.

The fallout has touched Clevelanders as well as non-Clevelanders. The New Cleveland Campaign, which serves to promote the city nationally, conducted an opinion survey of Greater Clevelanders in which 79 percent of the respondents said they expected their city to improve in the near future. Nearly half of the national opinion leaders who were questioned felt Cleveland was improving.

"Our goal," says Voinvoich succinctly, "was to make Cleveland rank with other major cities in the world. And we accomplished it."

CHAPTER 2

High Quality And Low Cost

One of the attractions of Greater Cleveland is that residents can work in the city and still maintain a country lifestyle. Photo by Jim Baron. Courtesy, Image Finders, Inc.

When he returned to Cleveland in November 1987, Joel Hyatt was only 37 years old but already among the best-known multimillionaires in the country. Through personal television advertising for his low-cost storefront legal clinics, Hyatt had gained national recognition while building Hyatt Legal Services into one of the biggest law firms in the United States in terms of clients.

With more than 600 lawyers and a support staff of another 1,000 in some 200 neighborhood offices across the country, Hyatt easily could have established himself and his company anywhere in America. He chose Cleveland, where he grew up and went to high school.

After graduating from Yale Law School and spending a year as an associate at a large New York law firm, Hyatt made his first return to Cleveland to start his mass-marketed, low-fee law firm. Three years later he moved to Kansas City and joined forces with another high-profile firm, H&R Block. In March 1987 Hyatt purchased the Block interest in a management consulting company and on the same day announced he was moving back to Cleveland.

"Cleveland has a larger well-trained labor pool here than most other comparable big cities," says Hyatt. "In short, the business environment is good . . . the place for our company to grow."

Hyatt is not alone in debunking the dictum, "You can't go home again." The list of active Clevelanders who have left only to return is growing. Among them are Kevin O'Donnell, former director of the Peace Corps, who returned to run SIFCO Industries; songwriter Eric Carmen; and

Downtown office workers head home at the close of the day. Photo by Jack Van Antwerp

Dr. Frederick Robbins, a Nobel Prize winner, who came back to teach in the medical school at Case Western Reserve University, where he was dean in the 1970s.

A more direct impact on the economy will be felt when Figgie International, Inc., a billion-dollar *Fortune* 500 manufacturer of safety, fire-fighting, and sports equipment, finishes developing its corporate headquarters on a portion of 630 acres owned by the city of Cleveland in suburban Warrensville Township.

Chairman Harry E. Figgie, Jr., moved operations from the Cleveland area to Virginia in the mid-1980s but decided to return here because of Cleveland's business environment, cost of living, and availability of land at a reasonable cost. When the full project is completed, it will include an additional 3.5 million square feet in corporate office space, a retail mall, and two 250-room hotels. Figgie International alone will bring thousands of jobs to Greater Cleveland.

Harry Figgie and the others who have come back certainly would agree with a poll conducted by the Citizens League, in which an overwhelming majority of Greater Clevelanders—76 percent—said they are optimistic about the future of their hometown. A wide majority in the same poll believed that the quality of life and the national image of the city had improved during the late 1980s.

An important part of downtown Cleveland is the financial district along East Ninth Street. Photo by Roger Mastroianni

Such confidence in the area is one reason that it is not just returning Clevelanders who are happy with the quality of life here. The number of upper-middle-income families moving to Greater Cleveland and becoming entrenched in the community continues to increase.

Part of this is due to companies and institutions, especially those with white-collar work forces, that are relocating or establishing regional offices here. For one thing, they have discovered that office operating costs and rentals are considerably less than in most major American cities.

Surveys by local industrial and commercial real-estate firms have found that class-A office space in Cleveland is renting at roughly half the price

(including taxes and operating expenses) as in New York City, Philadelphia, and Chicago.

The low cost of first-class office space is one reason that Robert L. Edgell, chairman of Edgell Communications, Inc., an international publishing, trade show, and school supply conglomerate, anchors his company here.

Facing page: Cleveland's business environment, which incorporates One Cleveland Center, is growing strong. Photo by Jim Baron. Courtesy, Image Finders, Inc.

As vice-chairman of Harcourt Brace Jovanovich Incorporated, Edgell in 1982 moved HBJ's magazine division to an underutilized office building in Middleburg Heights, a suburb near Hopkins International Airport.

In late 1987 Edgell directed a leveraged buy-out of HBJ's 110 magazines and related interests. At $334 million, it was the largest transaction involving business publications in America. Since then Edgell has increased the number of magazines, expanded its trade show division, and enlarged Beckley-Cardy, a huge national school and office supply dealer. Edgell Communications has some 400 employees here and more than 2,000 nationwide, and publishes the largest number of business and professional publications in America. New York tycoon Donald Trump called on Edgell's bicycling magazines and trade show division in 1989 to promote the 10-day "Tour de Trump" bicycle race from Albany to Atlantic City.

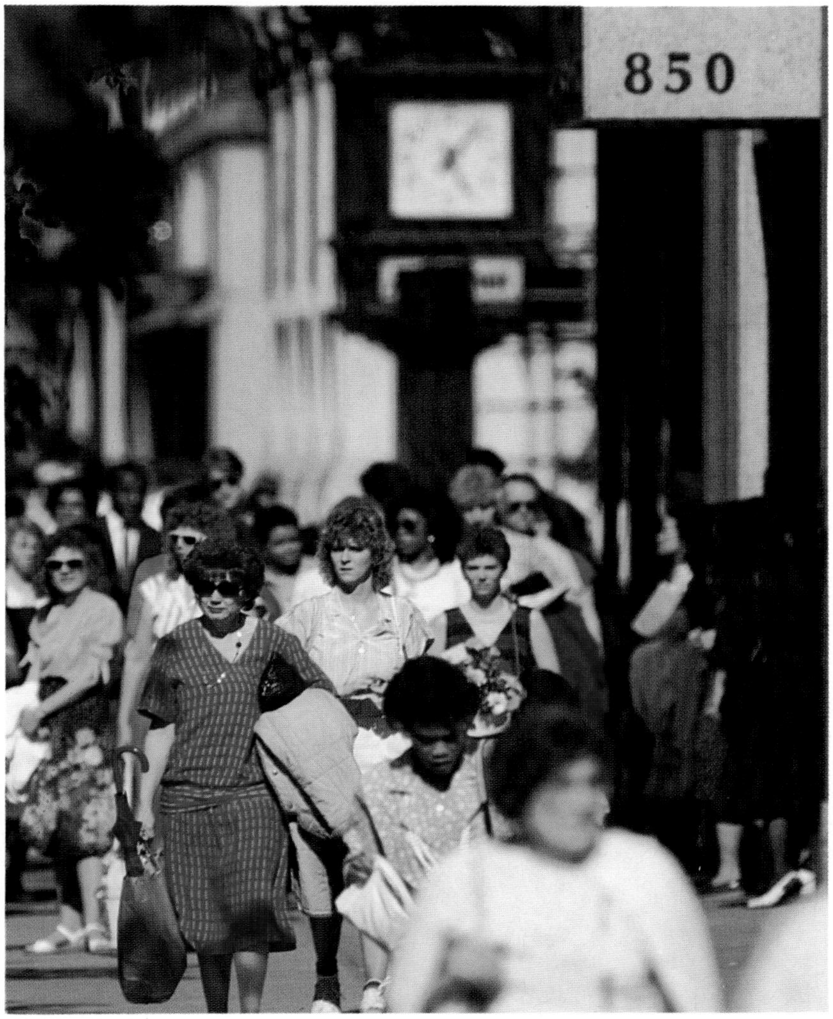

Above: Workers can leave downtown in the late afternoon and still have time for daylight activities. Photo by Roger Mastroianni

"I'm a midwesterner and love the midwestern work ethic," says Edgell, who had lived in New York since 1945. "We moved here because Cleveland is rich in human resources. When you draw a concentric circle of 500 miles around Cleveland, you have the ideal location for our business—only minutes from the airport and our markets.

"The quality of life is terrific," Edgell adds. "Since we're on the western edge of the Eastern Time Zone, we have an hour extra daylight than in New York. Our employees love it. They can go boating, play tennis, and golf later on summer evenings.

"Housing values are also outstanding. Many of our employees moved here from New York and bought mansions for what they sold their Monopoly houses in the East. And they instantly became part of the community."

Russell Reynolds Associates, Inc., an executive recruiting consultant firm, reports that salaries of top and middle management in Cleveland's

NCB

One of the things that attracts businesses to Cleveland is class-A office space at competitive prices. Photo by Jim Baron. Courtesy, Image Finders, Inc.

leading corporations are equal to their *Fortune* 500 counterparts across the country.

"In some cases, Cleveland's fastest growing service firms are paying salaries above national averages," says Steven J. Kurdziel, a Cleveland-based Russell Reynolds recruiter. "These include beginning associates at the city's two largest law firms, Jones, Day, Reavis & Pogue and Squire, Sanders & Dempsey.

"Among candidates we contact nationwide," Kurdziel adds, "the word is getting out about Cleveland's renaissance and what its corporations can offer in salaries and quality of life."

"Clevelanders are eager to welcome newcomers and help them get assimilated into neighborhoods, clubs, volunteer groups, and churches," says Cindy Denney, a former Junior League officer who teamed up in 1978

This police officer is just one of many of Cleveland's public servants. Photo by Barbara Durham

with Flo Pollack, a former volunteer with the Cleveland Orchestra, to start Executive Arrangements.

Corporations and professional firms hire Executive Arrangements to introduce prospective executives to the quality and scope of life in Greater Cleveland. Each program is tailored to the interests of the executive and his or her family; there is even a special program for teenagers.

Executive Arrangements introduces candidates for major corporate positions to business and civic leaders. If the executive's or spouse's interest is in the arts, one of Cleveland's cultural leaders will be on the daylong agenda, which includes tours of downtown, the suburbs, and the lakefront.

"The warmth of the Midwest seeps through," says Pollack. "We introduce newcomers to people who ultimately become their friends."

Cleveland corporations are intensifying their recruiting programs to dual-career couples. In fact, a study on the relocation of dual-career couples, sponsored by the Cleveland Foundation and Case Western Reserve University Weatherhead School of Management, resulted in a firm known as Resource: Careers.

"Some 90 percent of those surveyed concluded that Cleveland should have a service to help trailing spouses in their careers," says Marjorie B. Shorrock, who with her partner, Cathy Lewis, established Resource: Careers to provide such a service.

"Today many couples won't move unless the impact on both careers is considered," Shorrock says. "Because the business climate in Cleveland is increasingly welcome to professional women, the percentage of men—15—following their wives here is higher than the national average, which is 11 percent.

"Companies that assist trailing spouses in their careers can usually guarantee getting the executive they want," Shorrock adds. "In our follow-up evaluations, we find that trailing spouses feel very positive about the city and their employer. When both husband and wife are satisfied with their careers, they rave about being here."

Deborah and Jim Iacoponi bear this out.

After BP America transferred Jim into strategic planning at its Cleveland headquarters, the company referred Deborah, a marketing support representative for a computer firm, to Resource: Careers. In turn, Resource directed Deborah to Ameritrust, one of the city's major banks.

"The career opportunities here are wonderful," says Deborah, who is ascending the executive ladder at the bank. "We also were accepted here right away, unlike in other cities where we lived. Cleveland not only has great cultural assets, it has a spirit and a comfort level we had not found elsewhere.

"Our house in Shaker Heights is the best we've ever had," says Deborah, who grew up on Long Island. "The neighborhood has personality. We have friends on the East Coast living in shacks for what we can afford here."

"Even if we get transferred," adds Jim, who grew up in New Jersey, "we'll always call Cleveland home and hope that we get transferred back."

Above: Prospective home buyers have a variety of well-kept neighborhoods to choose from. Photo by Roger Mastroianni

Right: This industrial building in the revitalized Flats area has been converted to apartments. Photo by Barbara Durham

Prospective home buyers have a constant refrain about what they want—and ultimately find—in Greater Cleveland: affordable suburban housing; quality schools; trustworthy day care; a short commute to work; well-paved highways; low-cost utilities; good public transportation; minimal real estate and payroll taxes; low crime rates; access to recreation, sports, culture, and churches; and the ability to become part of a social organization.

The greatest—but most serendipitous—shock to newcomers is the affordability of housing. And the availability.

"The willingness of people to put their money in new homes reflects the overall confidence in the Greater Cleveland economy," says Robert J. Farling, president of Centerior Energy Corporation, which operates the Cleveland Electric Illuminating Company.

Tree-lined streets in the West Side community of Brooklyn sport their fall foliage. Photo by Barbara Durham

"Greater Clevelanders spend only 20 percent of their annual income on mortgage payments, while the national average is 28 percent," says Thomas Bier, director of the Housing Policy Program of Cleveland State University's Urban Center.

"In quality of construction we can match any city in quality and affordability," adds Thomas LaRochelle, executive director of the Cleveland Area Board of Realtors. "Yet builders are also holding costs down more than in other areas of the country."

Most of Greater Cleveland's new homes are going up in growing suburbs on the edge of Cuyahoga County and in abutting counties—areas such as Mentor, Concord Township, and Willoughby in Lake County; Medina and Brunswick in Medina County; and Solon, Brecksville, Strongsville, Chagrin Falls, and Westlake on the farthest edges of Cuyahoga County.

Among the fastest growing communities is Hudson, a charming touch of New England in northern Summit County between Akron and Cleveland. Here, in one of the oldest towns in the Western Reserve, new subdivisions complement the early nineteenth-century gingerbread architecture of churches, stores, and homes near the Village Green and its historic clock tower.

This picture-postcard setting of restored white homes with black shutters was a location for a television movie, "The Gathering" (as was Chagrin Falls). Hudson also is home to Western Reserve Academy, a leading prep school. Students come from all over the world to WRA,

whose campus was patterned after the Yale Green.

"Increasingly, corporations are smoothing the relocation of executives and their families into Greater Cleveland," says Patricia Mead, president of Corporate Relocation/Realty One.

"People are impressed with the low prices and different styles of housing, and that most of our communities are only a half-hour from downtown," says Mead. "After prospective buyers see so many neighborhoods across town, the Metroparks, Lake Erie, downtown, University Circle, and even the countryside—all in two hours—they are so overwhelmed that sometimes they can't make up their minds.

"We have a 100-percent capture rate," Mead boasts. "We've never had anyone turn down a transfer, job, or home after seeing Greater Cleveland. Their dilemma is, they don't want to move away after they get here."

Lucius B. McKelvey, president of Smythe, Cramer Company, one of Greater Cleveland's largest residential real-estate firms, believes "our conservative midwestern roots have created a sense of price stability over the years."

"We also have been blessed with excellent land planners, zoning laws, building codes, architects, developers, and builders over the years," McKelvey adds. "These have served to create the desirable variety and quality of housing stock."

Facing page: A short drive south of Cleveland takes one to the peaceful farm country of Medina County. Photo by Barbara Durham

Below: This beautiful fountain graces the grounds of the Cleveland Museum of Art at University Circle. Photo by T. Williams. Courtesy, Image Finders, Inc.

One reason Christine Belz did not want to move away again after she came back to her native Cleveland from Dallas in 1980 was housing value. Thus, she turned down a transfer and promotion and started her own human resources consulting firm, Belz & Associates, Inc. "I don't know of any other city in the U.S. where you can live at such a high level of fashion and standard of living," says Belz, who lives in a 2,000-square-foot lakefront condominium in Bratenahl, a few miles east of downtown. Belz bought the condominium for $100,000, one-third of the cost at the time for a similar place in Texas.

Above: In the face of tremendous growth in the housing market, Cleveland homes, such as this one in Ohio City, continue to retain their individuality. Photo by Roger Mastroianni

Facing page: The Cleveland Metroparks System maintains a taste of the country on the edge of the city. Photo by Barbara Durham

Bratenahl, a community along Lake Erie that resembles Newport, Rhode Island, is an enclave of modern high-rise condominiums and formidable nineteenth-century estates. Because of its proximity to Cleveland's expanding downtown, Bratenahl is attracting downtown professionals in search of convenient and secure affluent housing. Developer John Domo is putting up more than 80 town-house condominiums, as well as cluster and single-family houses, on 100 acres of choice lakefront property. Surrounded by stately oak, maple, beech, black gum, and ginkgo trees, the $60-million project—aptly called Newport—includes two private marinas and the conversion of a nineteenth-century mansion into a posh private club with athletic facilities and guest rooms.

A suburb that does an exceptional job of attracting newcomers is Shaker Heights, originally a colony founded by religious Shakers in 1822. With a population of 32,000, a rapid-transit line to downtown, four scenic lakes, a regional nature center, and a nationally recognized school system, Shaker is probably the best-known Cleveland suburb.

Each Shaker neighborhood is named after the grade school at its center and has a distinctive architectural look, with a mixture of Tudors, Georgians, Colonials, and contemporaries. Home prices generally range from $60,000 to $600,000—half of what they would be in comparable suburbs of most other major cities. Still, Shaker has a higher concentration of expensive homes than any other Cleveland suburb.

"Many capable people live here and demand good schools, recreational facilities, quality housing, and municipal services, including backyard garbage pickup," says Mayor Steven Alfred.

The suburb has won governmental and foundation awards for its schools, its community effort against drugs, and its Fund for the Future of Shaker Heights, an innovative housing program that seeks to attract minority home buyers to other areas in Cleveland's eastern suburbs where minorities are underrepresented.

With a black population of 25 percent, Shaker also has instituted a housing program to allay concerns over integration and provides limited secondary mortgage financing to help whites and blacks move into certain areas.

"Integration is just another factor, which many folks are open to if the quality of life and surroundings impress them," says Donald L. DeMarco, director of Community Services and administrator of the housing program. "Shaker started the first program in the 1950s, and it's worked ever since. All properties are well maintained, and values continue to increase."

Adjacent to Shaker is Cleveland Heights, another community that stresses the quality and affordability of its housing. Many Cleveland Heights residents are attracted to the community by its accessibility to downtown and its proximity to the cultural and educational institutions of nearby University Circle.

Some 15 miles east of Shaker Heights and Cleveland Heights is the rolling horse country of the Chagrin Valley. In the center of the valley lies the village of Chagrin Falls, named for the Chagrin River Falls along Main Street. On summer evenings the village is crowded with suburbanites who buy ice-cream cones at the old-fashioned parlor overlooking the falls and who window-shop at the boutiques along Main Street. Just outside Chagrin Falls it is not uncommon to see horses and riders virtually any time of the year on the tree-lined roads that meander past the grand estates of Hunting Valley, Gates Mills, or beyond in the more rural townships of Geauga County.

Above: Waterfront living in Shaker Heights is just one of the many options open to Greater Cleveland home buyers. Photo by Roger Mastroianni

Left: Sunlight highlights the striking architecture of Enterprise Place in Beachwood. Photo by Barbara Durham

Left: Fire hydrant "people" brighten the streets of the West Side suburb of Brooklyn. Photo by Barbara Durham

Left: One of the attractions on Cleveland's west side is Olmsted Falls Park. Photo by Barbara Durham

Facing page: Residents enjoy a friendly game of volleyball. Courtesy, Luce Photography, Inc.

Below: Horses and riders are a familiar sight in the rolling country of the Chagrin Valley. Photo by Robert French. Courtesy, Tony Stone Worldwide

Country pleasures abound at the Cuyahoga Valley National Recreation Area Festival. Photo by Barbara Durham

Geauga is the most affluent county in Ohio. Here Amish farmers with their horses and buggies readily mix with their "Yankee" neighbors driving Broncos and Blazers.

On the other side of Cleveland, the western and southwestern suburbs have their own unique appeal. Lakewood, with superb schools, stately homes, lakefront condominiums, and apartments on the Gold Coast, is only a 15-minute drive from Hopkins International Airport and 10 minutes from downtown.

The opening of Interstate 90, from downtown to the far western edge of Cuyahoga County and beyond, has contributed mightily to the growth of such suburbs as Westlake, Bay Village, and Rocky River. All abut the Metroparks, with their miles of wooded jogging and bicycling paths.

Berea, adjacent to Hopkins Airport in southwest Cuyahoga County, is home to Baldwin-Wallace College, and the right place for anyone who wants to live in an ivy-covered small college town that has all the urban amenities. Farther south into Summit County are the restored country towns of Hudson, Bath, Peninsula, and Richfield, which adjoin the Cuyahoga Valley National Recreation Area and its 32,000 acres of ski areas, picnic groves, and rock ledges.

Such exurban escapes are only 30 to 40 minutes by interstate from the city of Cleveland, which has its own residential appeal, thanks in part to the nonprofit marketing organization, Living in Cleveland. The group attracts home buyers with extraordinary housing bargains. The median sale price for a single-family house in the city is incredibly low—half of what it is in the Cuyahoga County suburbs.

"We have been effective in persuading prospective home buyers, as well as real-estate brokers and lenders, to view city housing as a viable option to the suburbs," says Ray Schmidt, executive director of Living in Cleveland.

"Almost 80 percent of those we help are young couples without kids," Schmidt adds, "and increasingly they are out-of-towners. We generally point people with different interests to different neighborhoods. Families with a suburban life-style we might send to Kamms or Old Brooklyn on the Southwest Side; urban pioneers to Ohio City, Tremont, and Archwood-

Denison on the near West Side or Shaker Square on the East Side. Often the shell of a Victorian home can be picked up for from $10,000 to $15,000 and rehabilitated into a fantastic place for only $35,000 more."

Schmidt also can direct home buyers to any number of small ethnic enclaves that still survive in the city proper, the most notable of which is Little Italy, on the lip of Case Western Reserve University and University Circle.

Little Italy is a pastiche of neatly preserved old homes with finely manicured postage-stamp lawns, where elderly Italians blend in with professionals and university people, many of whom live in nearby dormitories, apartments, and new condominiums.

Art galleries, antique shops, and popular Italian restaurants dot Little Italy. In mid-August, on the Feast of the Assumption of the Blessed Virgin Mary, thousands from all over Greater Cleveland gather for a procession of the Virgin's statue through the narrow, winding streets, and for the three-day carnival that follows.

While Little Italy is enjoying a renaissance, so is Slavic Village, on the edge of an industrial mill area where Poles, Czechs, and other Eastern Europeans began settling more than a century ago. Urban pioneers are restoring old houses and moving in. Ethnic shops and restaurants cater to neighborhood people and to younger Slavic-Americans, who live in the suburbs but who return regularly to this city neighborhood to shop.

On the other side of town is Ohio City, one of the oldest sections of the city, where ex-suburbanites are buying splendid Victorian homes at low prices and refurbishing them.

Ohio City is anchored by St. Ignatius High School for boys, founded by the Jesuits in 1886 and considered one of the area's leading academic institutions. Down the street from St. Ignatius' century-old Gothic structure is another colorful landmark, the West Side Market, one of the largest food markets in the world.

On any given day Eastern European women in babushkas literally rub elbows with suburban yuppies as they roam through scores of stalls amply stocked with a wide array of fresh produce, fish, meats, exotic cheeses, and other ethnic and gourmet delicacies.

Cleveland's Old-World legacy is also preserved in restaurants, churches, and festivals. Each summer the area-wide All Nations Festival draws thousands of people downtown for the food, music, and dancing of nationalities ranging from Chinese to Croatian.

Delectable pastries are just one of the highlights of Little Italy's annual feast. Photo by Roger Mastroianni

Generations of Clevelanders have long enjoyed the annual mid-August Feast of the Assumption in Little Italy. Photo by Roger Mastroianni

Renewed interest in heritage has breathed life into some 300 ethnic organizations, representing 60 nationality groups, that sponsor dances, festivals, and even language classes. Often these organizations are dominated by young people, many of whose ancestors came here as long as a century ago. The largest include clubs for Germans, Hungarians, Slovenians, Poles, Czechs, Slovaks, and Irish.

"When Europeans came here, they tended to cluster together for support," says Dr. Thomas F. Campbell, an Irish immigrant, professor of history at Cleveland State University, and author of several books on Cleveland history. "With the post-World War II move to the suburbs, ethnic solidarity seemed to be dying off, even with the influx to Cleveland of tens of thousands of Hungarians who fled the Budapest uprising in 1956.

"In the 1960s, however, the black pride movement helped rekindle ethnic pride," adds Campbell. "Some city communities stayed relatively

A German band entertains visitors during the Octoberfest celebration at the Lake County Fairgrounds. Photo by Jim Baron. Courtesy, Image Finders, Inc.

intact, while new ethnic communities sprang up in blue-collar suburbs such as Parma, where, as in the city, the church is still the center of the community, just as it was a century ago. That's also true with the new immigrants—including the Vietnamese, Hispanics, and Koreans."

The nonprofit Nationalities Services Center continues to resettle immigrants, just as it has done for generations.

Generations of immigrants have found Cleveland so hospitable because of the opportunity for work, a close association with family and church, and affordable living.

In two categories alone, real-estate taxes and utilities, Greater Clevelanders pay far less than residents in comparable communities across the nation. As much as low taxes and utilities have been an inducement for companies to relocate and remain here, they also have been attracted by the extraordinary availability of quality day care, which is an issue for the increasing number of Cleveland's working couples.

"Cleveland is very innovative," says Mary Kerrigan, director of the Child Care Resource Center, an umbrella social-service agency that matches the amenities that parents seek in a nursery or day-care center and provides training for day-care personnel.

"We work with more and more Cleveland corporations that have child care at the workplace or provide some kind of day-care assistance, including family seminars," Kerrigan adds.

The Child Care Resource Center maintains listings of some 2,000 programs related to day care and the more than 200 day-care and nursery centers in Greater Cleveland. Among them is the internationally known English Nannies School and its placement service, English Nannies and Governesses, which were recently featured in the *Times* of London.

Cleveland day-care facilities recognize the need for well-trained professionals. Photo by Julie Houck. Courtesy, Tony Stone Worldwide

Started in 1984 by the English-born Sheilagh Roth, wife of a Case Western Reserve University history professor, the school has trained hundreds of child-care specialists for upscale families with working mothers.

After background and health checks, the postulant nannies—who range from recent high-school graduates to widows—are trained at institutions around University Circle, the city's cultural center, in everything they will need to teach and rear children properly, including art history, music appreciation, literature, safe driving, and CPR.

The graduates are in demand for jobs nationwide that provide substantial benefits, including salary, room and board, and paid taxes. "Executives come from all over the country, some on private jets, looking for nannies," says Roth. "Often they're astounded at what we have, and they always leave with a good impression."

The surging demand for nannies also has occasioned the start-up of a similar school, the Nannies School of Cleveland, across town in Lakewood. It also is run by a woman from England, Monica Bassett, and likewise has received increasing numbers of requests for its graduates.

As much as Greater Clevelanders demand quality day care, so, too, they insist on quality primary and secondary education.

To assist newcomers, the Growth Association distributes a regularly updated guide to public and private schools in Cuyahoga and sections of surrounding counties.

It points out, for example, that Shaker Heights seniors annually finish first or second in the National Merit competition among Ohio's public schools and in the top 25 nationally. Further, Shaker schools rank among the highest in the nation in the number of National Achievement scholars.

The guide shows that Greater Cleveland has private secondary schools that rank among the best in the nation, including University School, St. Ignatius, and St. Edward for boys; Hawken School and Gilmour Academy, which are coed; and Andrews, Laurel, and Hathaway Brown for girls.

The U.S. Department of Education recently chose Chagrin Falls High School as one of the nation's 218 best secondary schools. It was one of only six schools in Ohio so honored, and the only school in Northeast Ohio.

"Greater Cleveland is second to none in the nation in terms of quality secondary education," says John F. Lewis, managing partner of the Cleveland office of Squire, Sanders & Dempsey, Ohio's second-largest law firm, and chairman of the education committee of the Greater Cleveland Roundtable. "We have some of the top public and private schools anywhere. And that quality is greatly enhanced because of cooperation among school districts."

As important as education is to the quality of Greater Cleveland life, religion also plays a role.

The ecumenical spirit among Catholics, Protestants, and Jews was a major reason the United Church of Christ, formed here in 1957 at a synod of three Protestant denominations, has decided to move its national headquarters to Cleveland along with several hundred jobs.

"One of Cleveland's strengths is the cooperative environment that exists between the public and private sectors of the metropolitan community," declared the UCC headquarters report recommending the move to Cleveland.

"There is a spirit of confidence and optimism that is very evident and contagious," it continued. "New alliances incorporating leaders from business, government, and church, and crossing racial and ethnic lines, are pursuing strategic objectives to enhance the city's long-range future.

"We were impressed with the overall quality of life," says the Reverend John Krueger, chairman of the UCC Committee on National Headquarters Location and pastor of Peace United Church of Christ in Fort Wayne, Indiana. "Perhaps most notable is the abundance of affordable housing, the quality of health-care facilities, the availability of quality shopping and schools, the wide range of cultural and recreational opportunities, and

Facing page: Perhaps nothing exemplifies Greater Cleveland's ethnic diversity more than its multiplicity of churches. Shown here is St. Theodosius Russian Orthodox cathedral. Photo by Don Snyder

the purchasing power because of the low cost of living."

The UCC is a member of the Interchurch Council of Greater Cleveland, composed of 16 Protestant denominations, 700 congregations, and numerous agencies providing an array of services—from the funding and staffing of hunger centers, to adult literacy programs, to a center for homeless women and children.

Particularly important is the Faith and Order Commission, which holds ecumenical dialogues with Jews and Catholics.

In its eight counties, the Cleveland Catholic Diocese has some 250 parishes and makes up nearly 30 percent of the population of Northeastern Ohio. The diocese supports 150 social-service agencies largely through its annual Catholic Charities campaign.

With 175 elementary and high schools, the diocese also operates the largest school system in the state and the seventh-largest system of private schools in the country. In recent years, while the number of school-age children has decreased in the metropolitan area, Catholic school enrollment has increased.

Through its Inner-City School Fund, supported by foundations, corporations, and a coalition of Catholic, Protestant, and Jewish business leaders, the diocese operates 11 inner-city grade schools, whose pupils are overwhelmingly non-Catholic. A survey discovered that *all* graduates from a recent class of one inner-city Catholic school went on to graduate from high school—an astonishing accomplishment.

"The Catholic Church has been very much a part of the development of Cleveland and the Western Reserve," says Bishop Anthony M. Pilla, the first Catholic bishop of Cleveland born and raised in the city. "The history and tradition of the diocese, along with its present-day wealth of cultures and peoples, is a source of pride for us all."

Another source of Cleveland pride is the Jewish Community Federation, which also is active in civic affairs. Though the Jewish community is

Jewish community activities are well served by the Mandel Jewish Community Center. Photo by Jack Van Antwerp

Left: A $100-million renovation will transform the Shaker Rapid system into the most modern rail system in the nation. Photo by Barbara Durham

Above: In 1987 Cleveland Hopkins International Airport handled 338,000 commercial and private flights without an operational error. Photo by Jim Baron. Courtesy, Image Finders, Inc.

relatively small—65,000—90 percent of Greater Cleveland Jews live in a group of contiguous East Side suburbs and attend more than 30 temples and synagogues.

Such cohesion and organization has helped make Cleveland's Jewish community among the most active and philanthropic in the country. The annual Jewish Community Federation fund-raising drive eclipses all other major Jewish communities in the United States in per capita giving.

"The original rationale for the federation—consolidating fundraising for eight charities—has developed into a sophisticated system of campaigning, planning, and budgeting for various human service agencies as well as many national and overseas agencies," says Stephen H. Hoffman, executive director of the JCF.

"In putting up our building in downtown in the 1960s," he adds, "we made a commitment to emphasize our identification with the total fabric of Greater Cleveland. That commitment to the general community is just as strong today."

Religious cooperation often extends to intergovernmental cooperation. While Northeast Ohio has many suburbs, each with its own community services, in recent years there has been increasing governmental cooperation on "mega" projects that transcend boundary lines and layers of government.

Through the cooperation of Cleveland with more than 60 suburbs in Cuyahoga County, the Ohio Bell Telephone Company has been able to set up a 911 emergency telephone service for most of Northeast Ohio.

The $2-billion Build Up Greater Cleveland program—an innovative partnership put together largely through the cooperation of the Growth Association, Cuyahoga County Commissioners, City of Cleveland, Regional Transit Authority, Northeast Ohio Regional Sewer District, and other foundations and corporations—is reconstructing the area infrastructure, from roads and bridges, to rail and bus transportation, to wastewater treatment plants.

In recent years the Build Up Greater Cleveland campaign also has helped the area receive its fair share of federal tax dollars from Washington. In transportation alone, Greater Cleveland now gets back some 85 percent of federal gasoline taxes paid into the Highway Trust Fund, up from 50 percent only a few years ago.

"This has come about because of the close cooperation between our program and the area's congressional delegation and two U.S. senators," Ted Olson, director of Build Up Greater Cleveland, observes.

The campaign has been particularly resourceful in directing federal funds into the Regional Transit Authority (RTA), the transit system that also receives one percent of the Cuyahoga County sales tax—more than $80 million annually.

The RTA recently completed a $100-million renovation of its Shaker Rapid system, including tracks, signals, cars, and stations. When fully remodeled in the early 1990s, the downtown transit stop in the Tower City Center will be the most modern rail station in the country.

The rapid transit system, which crosses the city from the West Side to the East Side, is a boon not only for Clevelanders but for visitors as well. Cleveland was the first city to connect its airport to downtown by rail. The 12-mile, 24-minute ride to the airport costs only a dollar and will be made even smoother when a $40-million upgrading of the Red Line track from Hopkins to the East Side is completed.

Easy accessibility (via rapid transit and interstates 71 and 480) is a reason that Hopkins International Airport is one of the busiest and most convenient airports in the nation. Upwards of 8 million passengers use Hopkins each year, traveling on more than 500 daily departures and arrivals between more than 350 worldwide locales on 20 airlines.

Moreover, the frequency of flight delays is among the lowest of major American airports. The Hopkins tower won the FAA National Facility of the Year Award in 1987, beating out more than 200 other airport towers. Hopkins handled 338,000 commercial and private flights that year without an operational error, while cutting overtime and keeping morale high.

Hopkins also serves as a regional hub for Continental and USAir, which provide nonstop flights to 50 cities. In fact, Continental now bases hundreds of employees, including flight crew members, in Cleveland. With $30 million in tax-exempt bonds to finance expansion of its local facilities, Continental is expected to more than double its flights into and out of Hopkins in the 1990s.

Because Hopkins is so accessible by freeway or rail and only 20 minutes from downtown, and since delays have been minimized by a new 210-foot, $5-million control tower, companies and governmental agencies increasingly are setting up or expanding offices nearby. Many of these are aerospace firms increasing their spin-off work from NASA's Lewis Research Center adjacent to the airport.

"Greater Cleveland's economic future depends heavily on its ability to provide services to companies considering relocating here," says William R. Plato, vice president of economic development for the Growth Association. "One way Cleveland meets these needs is to provide convenient access to markets and centers of commerce through superior air service."

The growth in activity at Hopkins is a result, in part, from the low cost of travel in Greater Cleveland. According to Michael Sturgess, a partner with the Cleveland office of Laventhol & Horwath who helps prepare the accounting firm's annual corporate travel index, Cleveland restaurant, hotel, and travel costs are among the lowest in the nation.

This may be one reason Clevelanders are dining out more than ever. According to *Cleveland Magazine*'s noted food editor, Patricia Weitzel, the quality and quantity of restaurants have increased greatly.

"Cleveland has witnessed a change in its restaurants that is nothing short of dramatic," according to Weitzel. This culinary revolution has been staged by a new breed of restauranteur whose enthusiasm and unrelenting demand for quality have sent positive shock waves through the food community.

"The steak houses in large part have been replaced by an eclectic assortment of eateries catering to a wide variety of tastes—-Mexican, Thai, Cajun, Vietnamese, Spanish, and Californian, to name but a few."

Dining on a sunlit terrace is just one of the options available to shoppers at the Galleria. Photo by Roger Mastroianni

Facing page: The new Terminal Tower and the striking BP America Building dominate the night in this downtown image. Photo by Barbara Durham

Unique dining opportunities can be found from Nighttown in Cleveland Heights—which resembles an upper East Side New York restaurant—to Johnny's, tucked-away in a West Side Italian neighborhood, to Parker's—in an old ethnic enclave on the East Side—which utilizes Ohio fruits, vegetables, fresh herbs, fish, chicken, and lamb.

Cleveland Magazine, a leading city magazine, annually publishes a poll of the most popular restaurants selected by readers. Year after year, top billing goes to Sammy's in the Flats, with a commanding view of the Cuyahoga River, and Ristorante Giovanni's, on a section of Chagrin Boulevard in the Eastern suburbs known as "Restaurant Row."

Others often included in the survey are the Watermark in the Flats, Z Contemporary Cuisine on Restaurant Row in Shaker Heights, Baricelli Inn in Little Italy, the Wintergarten in the Marriott near the airport, and three restaurants operated by Cleveland-based Stouffer Corporation: the Top of the Town and French Connection, both downtown, and Pier W, overlooking Lake Erie on the Gold Coast.

In her annual "Pat's Picks," Weitzel cites her favorites, which have included a tiny adjunct to Sammy's called the Tenth Street Cafe, Gourmet of China, Szechwan Garden on Restaurant Row, and Shujiro, a Japanese restaurant in Cleveland Heights.

One factor that makes dining out increasingly popular in Greater Cleveland is the low cost and the high availability of parking. "Low and stable real-estate taxes keep parking costs moderate. Cleveland rates compare to those of Columbus and Cincinnati and are in median range nationwide," says John P. Coyne, president of Coyne-Kangesser, the city's largest parking-lot concern.

"We have nearly 60,000 private and city-operated parking spaces in the central business district downtown," adds Coyne. "The $4 average for a full day downtown is less than half of Chicago and Boston, a third of New York. Since there is no shortage, everyone can readily find a space. Furthermore, valet parking at shopping areas encourages people to come downtown."

Though 250,000 cars commute into the central business district daily, the crime rate for downtown remains relatively low. Over the years the four-county metropolitan area has had a lower rate of overall crime—violent and property crime included—than most other large metropolitan areas in the country.

The low crime rate was just one reason Heather Roulston came back to Cleveland from Boston, where she had worked for an investment firm after graduation from Dartmouth.

She is now a broker with her father's investment advisory firm, Roulston & Company. Her decision was based on Greater Cleveland's quality of life and affordability, including what may be the most important aspect—civic involvement.

"Civic involvement is important in Cleveland," observes Roulston. "People are willing to help out. Here I might get two calls a day from someone asking me to assist an organization or a project. On the East Coast, you have to search for a place to volunteer."

CHAPTER 3

Catching Cleveland's Community Spirit

No community in America has the reputation for civic involvement—giving time and money—as does Cleveland. It is a rich history, dating to a century ago, when the railroad, steel, and shipping barons took seriously their private responsibility to bestow a portion of their largess on the less fortunate.

In the final decades of the nineteenth century, when Cleveland was one of the fastest growing cities in America, civic and charitable organizations were dominated by the likes of John D. Rockefeller and his bitter rival, Amasa Stone, whose railroad fortune helped Western Reserve University move to Cleveland from Hudson.

Such families as the Mathers, Wades, Severances, and Blossoms established settlement houses for the surging flood of European immigrants. They also put their great wealth behind the formation of the city's preeminent cultural institutions, including the Cleveland Orchestra and the Cleveland Museum of Art.

By the first decades of the twentieth century, Frederick H. Goff, a corporate lawyer and head of Cleveland Trust, the predecessor of Ameritrust, believed that community philanthropy needed to be broadened.

He reasoned that narrowly focused trusts set up by wealthy families often were unresponsive to new societal demands generations later. Goff also wanted to tap the money of the middle class, who had no real means with which to leave something to the community.

In 1914, with first-year contributions of $40,000 from a wide range of benefactors, Goff

The spacious Blossom Music Center grounds are perfect for pre-concert picnics. Photo by Roger Mastroianni

The Cleveland Orchestra enjoys strong financial support from area patrons, just one example of the importance placed on cultural amenities.
Photo by Jack Van Antwerp

A prominent city institution, the Cleveland Museum of Art is widely supported by those with an interest in the arts. Courtesy, Cosgray Photography

set up the Cleveland Foundation, the first community trust in the United States. Since then it has spawned more than 300 community foundations across the country.

Goff's idea was novel at the time, but today it is the accepted system of American philanthropy. He encouraged as many people as possible to leave their money in a pooled fund. Under the vigilant guidance of bankers, civic leaders, and professional workers, it would be prudently invested and distributed where it was most needed.

Today the Cleveland Foundation has an endowment of some $500 million—second in size only to the New York Community Trust—and, thanks to Goff's vision, 80 percent of its funds have a large degree of flexibility.

Often with the support of the George Gund Foundation—set up by George Gund, Goff's successor at Cleveland Trust—the Cleveland Foundation has pioneered innovative programs that have become models for other community foundations.

"The Cleveland Foundation has been a little more daring in dealing with public issues than other community foundations," says Homer Wadsworth, its former director. "This grows out of a belief that public and private issues often are inseparable."

Among the programs the foundation has funded are the mayor's Civic Vision; the restoration of three old vaudeville theaters at Playhouse Square Center; Lexington Village, a 277-unit low- and moderate-income rental housing project (a public-private partnership that has brought many middle-class professionals back to the inner city to live); and lakefront redevelop-

Playhouse Square Center's renovation is a result, in part, of the Cleveland Foundation's concern for the city. Other projects funded by the Foundation include low- and moderate-income housing projects. Photo by Don Snyder

ment, including the transfer of city-owned parks to the state.

The adjacent Foundation Center library in the Hanna Building downtown also serves as a far-reaching resource for data on other local and out-of-town foundations. It is down the hall from the unique Grantmakers Forum, which is supported by the Cleveland Foundation. The forum regularly brings together Greater Cleveland corporations, foundations, and individuals to discuss common issues that their philanthropy might address.

The Cleveland Foundation concentrates its giving in six major areas: health, social welfare, education, culture and arts, economic development, and civic issues. "The Foundation has always met the needs of its time," notes Steven A. Minter, the current director, who was the first black appointed to head a major community foundation in the United States.

"Beginning in the 1960s it became solidly proactive in its grant making, funding programs for housing, race relations, and improving public education. In the 1970s we moved aggressively into cultural affairs. In the 1980s our emphasis turned to regional economic issues and public education. The two are related, because the quality of the Greater Cleveland labor force and our economic revitalization depends in part on improving inner-city education."

The project drawing national attention in recent years is the Cleveland Initiative for Education, which the foundation established with two grants totaling almost $4 million, its largest award ever.

Developed by Cleveland school superintendent Alfred D. Tutela and sponsored by the Greater Cleveland Roundtable, the initiative is the most far-reaching public-private effort mounted by a major city to stem the urban

The Memorial Day Weekend is time for the Blossom Time Festival with its five-mile run and carnival in Chagrin Falls. Photo by Jennie Jones

Concern for preserving the lakefront has prompted the Cleveland Foundation to fund redevelopment along its shores. Courtesy, Luce Photography, Inc.

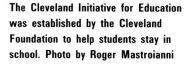

St. Thomas More Elementary School is one of the many private schools in Greater Cleveland. Photo by Barbara Durham

drop-out rate. It also strives to improve the overall education and quality of life for urban students.

Many top business and civic leaders have spent countless hours raising corporate and foundation funds for the initiative, which, through its Scholarship-in-Escrow program, offers students financial incentives to get good grades and to graduate. The money is applied to college tuition. More than a score of colleges and universities are matching or exceeding students' earnings and applying it toward the cost of attending the institution.

The counterpart School-to-Work program commits employers to helping find entry-level work for qualified Cleveland public high-school graduates. Career specialists also meet with juniors and seniors to help them gain skills necessary to obtain and retain employment after graduation.

School-to-Work grew out of Youth Opportunities Unlimited (YOU), which for many years had pledged employers to provide part-time,

The Cleveland Initiative for Education was established by the Cleveland Foundation to help students stay in school. Photo by Roger Mastroianni

Volunteers aid the educational work force in providing Cleveland children with a motivational school environment. Courtesy, Luce Photography, Inc.

summer, and entry-level employment for eligible city students.

Attention is increasingly centering on the initiative's long-term Cleveland Education Partners program, which encourages corporations, banks, and other major employers to form alliances with individual schools. Each partnership is unique. Top school and corporate management set the agenda for each school. Employees—from the top down—volunteer to share their skills at the individual school, including tutoring and coaching.

"Public education is Cleveland's critical issue, and private business is addressing it on a full-scale level," says John F. Lewis, chairman of the education committee of the Greater Cleveland Roundtable and a driving force behind the initiative. "The program is important because it offers motivation for kids to stay in school and produce, and it makes business realize it can increase profits through a more literate, well-trained, and motivated work force."

Supplementing the Cleveland Initiative for Education is the Greater Cleveland Literacy Coalition, which works to increase literacy skills. The coalition, supported with foundation and corporate grants, has brought thousands of volunteers and learners together, assists employers in upgrading work-related literacy skills, and provides a clearinghouse and literacy hot line to identify the growing number of literacy programs in Northeast Ohio.

Another remarkable effort attracting national attention is the Cleveland Scholarship Programs, Inc., which was set up in 1967 to help high-school graduates from low-income families to receive a college education. Since its inception, 80 percent of the program's participants have graduated from college, far above the national average of 50 percent for students who start college.

In many ways the commitment of the Cleveland Foundation to urban education, and the establishment of the Greater Cleveland Roundtable to address racial, employment, and social issues, is in keeping with Cleveland's capacity to set up civic organizations to meet pressing needs.

The Greater Cleveland Roundtable was formed in the early 1980s to establish a formal dialogue between leaders of the black and white communities, relating especially to the economic progress of Greater Cleveland.

"Over the years our mission has expanded," says Edward F. Bell, chairman of the roundtable and president and chief executive officer of Ohio Bell Telephone Company. "While race relations are still at the core, minority business development, labor-management relations, and education issues have become increasingly important."

The roundtable board has expanded to 70 members—one-third Asian, Hispanic, and black—including religious leaders, representatives from the city's leading law firms, heads of major hospitals, chief executive officers of large corporations, and public officials.

Many of the roundtable's undertakings have been trailblazing. Its labor-management committee, composed of labor officials and corporate executives, meets regularly to create a better management-union understanding and endeavors to head off serious labor disputes. Another program is geared toward minority business development.

The roundtable may be a relatively new organization, but the city's commitment to such civic causes crystallized as far back as 1913, when the local United Way was established as the Federation for Charity and Philanthropy.

"Cleveland invented the allocation process whereby volunteers determined the needs of a community and established a budget and raised money to meet them," says Jack Costello, president and chief professional officer of the Cleveland area United Way Services, which encompasses three counties and part of a fourth. "That complex process, while more sophisticated, still goes on today."

Indeed it does. The Cleveland United Way is the seventh largest in the nation in total dollars raised, though it draws from only a portion of the Cleveland Consolidated Metropolitan Statistical Area (the country's 12th largest). Even more incredibly, the per capita giving to the local United Way from the population base (about $33 per person in recent years) is the highest of any major area in the country and third among all United Way campaigns. The only cities of any size with higher figures are Hartford, Connecticut, and Rochester, New York.

The annual take in the late 1980s was around $50 million from a base of 1.57 million people. Greater Cleveland also leads the nation in the number of people—upwards of 250—who donate more than $10,000 to the United Way.

After covering campaign and operating expenses of less than 12 percent—among the lowest in the nation—the money is distributed to some 175 agencies that provide services as diverse as day care, AIDS education, literacy programs, and contributions to the Red Cross and the American Cancer Society.

Care for the elderly is a major concern for the LakeEast Hospital in Painesville. Photo by Jim Baron. Courtesy, Image Finders, Inc.

"I've worked at nine United Ways and the national office, and never have I seen a philosophy of giving so embedded in the community conscience," Costello adds. "In large part, what once was the province of the city's leading families has been adopted by the corporate sector. The top corporations in Greater Cleveland do a fantastic job in corporate and employee giving.

"We also are helped by the top-drawer volunteer leadership, including many loaned executives, donated to United Way from business, labor, and community groups—right from allocation to fund raising."

United Way estimates that it distributes funds to 70 percent of all human-service programs in the area, and that 500,000 people—one in three—directly benefit from its recipient agencies. Among its many in-house services, United Way has a round-the-clock answering service, First Call for Help, which makes 3,000 referrals weekly to callers looking for various types of assistance.

The Donated Goods Clearinghouse of United Way distributes large gifts-in-kind—from refrigerators to automobiles—to needy agencies. And its Volunteer Action Center recruits, trains, and places volunteers for nonprofit agencies. A Management Assistance Program provides corporate executives to help agencies with financial and administrative problems.

The United Way also is breeding its own corps of volunteer leadership through its Associate Cabinet, composed of accountants, lawyers, investment bankers, and other professionals between the ages of 25 and 35. The members, who are urged to volunteer for various programs, come together for an annual rollicking volleyball tournament. The success of the Associate Cabinet has instigated similar programs in other major cities.

The largest recipient of United Way funds is the Center for Human Services, which, among its many programs, provides family and employee assistance counseling, child care, and a unique adolescent drug and truancy counseling service known as the RAPArt program.

Apart from agencies funded by United Way, numerous other social service organizations raise their own private and public money. One such nonprofit organization has been helping the aging for more than 80 years. The Benjamin Rose Institute was set up by the estate of philanthropist Benjamin Rose, who died in 1908. The terms of his will stipulated that a board made up of women operate the institute, because of Rose's belief in women's sensitivity to the aged.

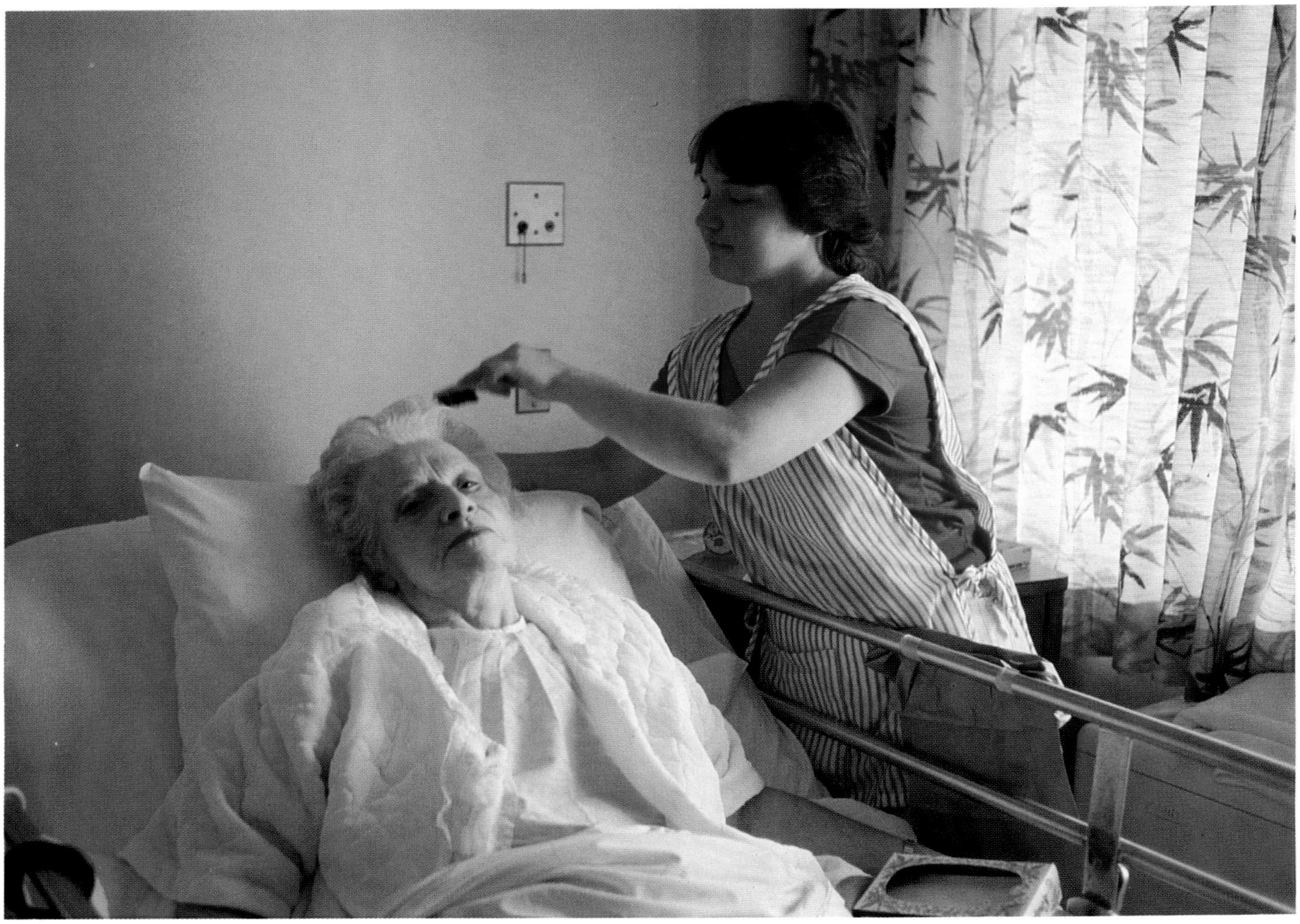

The LakeWest Hospital in Willoughby is one of several important institutions which helps to meet the medical and social needs of the elderly. Photo by Jim Baron. Courtesy, Image Finders, Inc.

For years research conducted by the institute has been on the cutting edge of aging issues. The institute uses part of the interest from its $65-million endowment to help finance this research, while running a nursing home and numerous other community services. Along with University Hospitals and other social service agencies, the Benjamin Rose Institute has refurbished an old state mental-health hospital, renamed the Fairhill Institute for the Elderly. Among Fairhill's multitude of services are fitness programs, a geriatric outpatient clinic, and volunteer programs.

Volunteering also plays a major role in various government agencies. Among the more active groups is the Mayor's Operation Volunteer Effort (MOVE), which appeals to private business and institutions to loan their experts to the city—with annual savings of millions of dollars of public money.

"The recruitment and placement of loaned executives, volunteers, and faculty fellows has resulted in enhanced and extended services to the city, and also has helped streamline government operations," says Joan H. Ainsworth, Project MOVE coordinator.

MOVE's projects have included loss prevention control and customer service training programs for the Utilities Department through the East Ohio Gas Company, an internal auditing plan for utilities developed by an

Eaton Corporation executive, Ohio Bell Telephone Company executives cooperating with the Safety Department to develop 911 emergency calling procedures, an erosion reduction plan for the Division of Urban Forestry developed with a TRW executive, and a study on Cleveland's Chinese community by a John Carroll University professor assisting the city planning department.

One key volunteer organization that contributes a great amount of time and money to local projects is the Junior League of Cleveland. Established in 1912, the league today utilizes more than 1,200 trained female volunteers who donate more than 100,000 hours annually in public affairs, health, education, and culture.

The league also makes annual allocations to community groups and recently gave $75,000 to the Great Lakes Historical Society to renovate the William G. Mather ore boat for the North Coast Harbor.

Scores of effective volunteer groups in Greater Cleveland are also meeting specific social needs, ranging from the Christ Child Society—which, in some ways, has become a funding source of last resort for individuals and groups—to the well-established Catholic Charities, which funds the multifaceted Catholic Social Services, to the very proficient Jewish Family Service Association.

Many of the social needs in Greater Cleveland are identified through the Federation of Community Planning, which started with the United Way's predecessor in 1913. The federation, one of the few independent planning agencies in the United States with such a broad-based mission, serves as a planning agency for a wide variety of nonprofit and governmental entities, including schools, hospitals, the county human services department, juvenile court, and the United Way.

"We deal with cutting-edge issues, such as AIDS, health care for the homeless, teen pregnancy prevention, and guardianship legislation," says executive director Ralph Brody. "Our effort is problem-focused. It is not an academic exercise. We're in the business to see things happen—new legislation, funding, programs, and organizations."

Over the years the federation has been responsible for creating some 50 organizations and groups, including the Governmental Affairs Alliance, which brings together Protestant, Catholic, and Jewish charities in a united front to lobby for human services legislation.

Since Cleveland began its decade of renewal, new levels of civic leadership have emerged from diverse vocational backgrounds with a broad base of social interests.

In large part, this is the direct result of the Greater Cleveland Growth Association's Leadership Cleveland program, which has become a national model for similar programs in other major cities.

"Each year a new class of 50 men and women, selected from hundreds of applicants, meet monthly and attend two annual retreats with established business and government leaders to become immersed in community affairs—from urban education concerns to downtown development," says Judith Ruggie, director of Leadership Cleveland.

With help from the League of Women Voters Educational Fund,

The Ice Mutants volunteer their services outside the West Side Market. Photo by Roger Mastroianni

Leadership Cleveland also sponsors the Look Up to Cleveland program, in which 40 high-school juniors from Cuyahoga County schools participate in civic activities geared to prepare them to become future Greater Cleveland leaders.

"Not only does Leadership Cleveland form networks of people who otherwise might not ever meet each other, it provides a cadre of well-trained civic leaders who are thoroughly aware of community problems and committed to dealing with them," says Joseph T. Gorman, chairman of TRW, Inc., and chairman of Leadership Cleveland.

As much as Leadership Cleveland certainly is a dynamic program, one does not have to go beyond Northern Ohio Gives to see the impressive commitment of countless Greater Clevelanders to giving and volunteering.

Formed in the late 1980s as part of the Independent Sector, a national coalition of 650 foundations, individuals, organizations, and businesses, Northern Ohio Gives is composed of more than 50 educational, religious, business, cultural, and human-service organizations from a four-county area of Northeast Ohio. The steering committee includes the bishop of the Catholic Diocese of Cleveland, the president of the Federal Reserve Bank of Cleveland, the president of Case Western Reserve University, and the president of the Junior League.

Northern Ohio Gives has set an ambitious five-year goal for itself: to urge Greater Clevelanders to commit five hours per week to voluntary service and to donate 5 percent of their gross income to charity. Both efforts will greatly increase Greater Cleveland's philanthropy and volunteering.

"The focus of this activity can be anything, from assisting at a nursing home to selling daffodils downtown for the American Cancer Society to serving on the board of a treatment center," says Daniel J. Dougherty, executive director of Northern Ohio Gives.

This comprehensive effort, which started with a Cleveland Foundation grant, also includes a public relations campaign within Greater Cleveland schools to educate students on the importance of careers in nonprofit organizations.

Northern Ohio Gives also is helping to recruit better trained individuals for nonprofit boards of trustees, while serving as a resource center for data gathered about the extent of volunteering within and contributions to local nonprofit groups.

"Cleveland has a long tradition of a strong social conscience," says Cleveland Foundation's Steve Minter. "That tradition is carried on through the organizations set up years ago.

"The community's civic leaders have an ethic that says, 'Everybody should do their fair share and more.' There is a civic consensus on issues and a determination to try to involve as many people as possible in the process."

"Cleveland has the most dedicated civic leadership of any city in the United States," adds Richard W. Pogue, managing partner of Jones, Day, Reavis & Pogue, former chairman of the Greater Cleveland Roundtable, and chairman of the 1989 United Way Services campaign.

"I don't know of any other major city that can compare. This spirit has been maintained through economic ups and downs and become part of the fabric of the town. If you are a business leader, it's assumed you will participate in the civic life."

A strong sense of community prevails in Cleveland that should carry the city into the next century. Photo by Jennie Jones

NEW JERSEY

CHAPTER 4

America's Class Act

Not long ago on a beautiful spring night, at the edge of the spreading Cleveland State University campus downtown, thousands of elegantly attired patrons celebrated the completion of America's most ambitious theater restoration project.

They dined and danced at three opulent, interconnected 1920s vaudeville theaters—the State, Palace, and Ohio—amid crystal chandeliers, marble columns, with ceilings and walls ornamented in gold leaf hand-carved by skilled, Old-World craftsmen.

With 7,000 seats, Playhouse Square Center is the third-largest performing arts center in America, only slightly smaller than the San Francisco War Memorial and Lincoln Center in New York City. At 320 feet, the State has the longest theater lobby in the world.

This dazzling premier was the emotional crescendo of a remarkable civic commitment that had begun in the late 1970s as the city's first sizable public-private partnership. The alliance brought together the Cuyahoga County Commissioners, who purchased the deteriorating buildings with public funds and assistance from the Cleveland Foundation, numerous individual contributors, and corporations who anted up additional money.

Today Playhouse Square Center has 70 employees and an annual operating budget exceeding $10 million, and draws one million people a year to musicals, plays, lectures, and concerts. The center is pumping $15 million a year into the Greater Cleveland economy. It also is spawning new office buildings and restaurants while encouraging the continued expansion of nearby Cleveland State University. A $30-million, 216-room luxury hotel across

A statue of President James A. Garfield dominates the Garfield Monument at the Lake View Cemetery. Photo by T. Williams. Courtesy, Image Finders, Inc.

Above: The Ohio Theatre's glittering marquee recalls the glory of the 1920s. Photo by Jim Baron. Courtesy, Image Finders, Inc.

Right: The Playhouse Square Center restoration project includes fine artwork of yesteryear. Photo by Roger Mastroianni

Facing page: An elegant black-tie reception marked the opening of Playhouse Square Center, the nation's most ambitious theater restoration project. Photo by Roger Mastroianni

the street from the theater complex will open in the early 1990s.

"Playhouse Square Center is a symbol of what Cleveland can do when it really wants to," says John F. Lewis, managing partner of the Cleveland office of Squire, Sanders & Dempsey, who, as chairman of the Playhouse Square Foundation, spearheaded the $38-million restoration drive. "When the center reaches full maturity in the next decade, you will begin to see the whole Playhouse Square area taking on a life of its own around the clock."

"The project has become a psychological symbol for Cleveland's turnaround," Playhouse Square Foundation president Lawrence Wilker adds. "It was the first place where the whole community came together to make things happen. It unleashed tremendous development and gave Clevelanders the belief that we can make our city what we want it to be."

"Playhouse Square Center provides amenities that make Cleveland competitive with other cities," he says. "If we want to attract more jobs, we must have a major performing arts center that showcases the world's great artists. And we do!"

"No project has had more impact from $25,000," insists Lainie

The city's major art and cultural institutions attract more than half of Greater Cleveland's adult population. Photo by Roger Mastroianni

Hadden, who, as president of the Junior League of Cleveland in the early 1970s, guided the league into providing the initial seed money that saved the theaters from the wrecking ball.

Playhouse Square Center is only part of the cultural renewal marking Cleveland's second Golden Age of Arts. One hundred million dollars has been injected into building new cultural facilities and expanding old ones. The surge in attendance has invigorated existing arts organizations and has led to the creation of new ones.

One survey found that 55 percent of Greater Cleveland adults annually visit one or more of the area's major arts and cultural institutions. The survey thus recommended cooperative programming among the groups and joint marketing to the outer edge of Greater Cleveland—as far as two-and-a-half hours from downtown—east to Erie, Pennsylvania, west to Toledo, and south to Columbus.

Buoyed by growing regional interest in the city's arts and entertainment, the Cleveland Foundation helped set up the Cleveland Arts Consortium. It is composed of some 20 major museums and visual and performing arts institutions with a combined annual attendance of more than 3 million.

"We are a national model," says Harriet Wadsworth, the consortium's director. "Unlike other cooperative arts groups, which basically serve as clearinghouses, our agenda is set by the member institutions. We are streamlining costs, expanding audiences, and raising new money."

Directors of institutions as diverse as the Cleveland Museum of Art, Cleveland Opera, the Cleveland Health Education Museum, and SPACES, a downtown art gallery, comprise the other board members.

Much of the Arts Consortium's focus has been on downtown arts activities, especially at Playhouse Square Center, but it also has focused on Cleveland's longtime cultural nexus, University Circle, only five miles east of downtown. Within the Circle area are scores of celebrated institutions, including the Cleveland Orchestra and the Cleveland Museum of Art.

University Circle—concentrated in one square mile—also is home to Case Western Reserve University, one of America's top private research universities. Within the Circle are another 40 museums, cultural centers, and music halls, as well as religious, educational, social service, and health-care institutions. The physical investment alone is valued at more than $2 billion.

Immediately surrounding the borders of University Circle are two dozen related institutions. Collectively, they all employ nearly 30,000 people with a payroll approaching one billion dollars a year. More than 3 million people visit and work annually within University Circle and its surrounding environs.

Community leaders in 1957 formed the nonprofit University Circle, Incorporated (UCI) to coordinate administration of services in the area. Today UCI has a $10-million annual budget and operates parking lots and a free shuttle service between member institutions. UCI also has its own police department.

"University Circle is the only place in the world where the great bulk

One of the members of the Cleveland Arts Consortium is SPACES, an art gallery located downtown. Photo by Jack Van Antwerp

of a city's cultural institutions are on one campus," says former Harris Corporation chairman Richard Tullis, who moved back to Cleveland from Florida after his retirement to chair UCI. "It is the strongest base Cleveland has."

UCI also encourages appropriate development within the area. This has led to construction of new apartment buildings, an upscale shopping mall, and a posh 52-room bed-and-breakfast hotel in a converted mansion once owned by Clifford Glidden, son of the founder of the Glidden Paint Company.

The organization also is pushing plans for the Dual Hub Corridor, a proposed $500-million rapid-transit line that would operate above ground and underground from University Circle past the Cleveland Clinic to downtown—through what retired UCI president Joseph Pigott calls "the spine of the city."

The city's first Golden Era of Arts before World War I was galvanized at University Circle. Cleveland's ruling families, descendants of the city's original New England pioneers, felt obliged to return a part of their immense wealth to their city.

"With their own fortunes secure, Cleveland industrialists, like those in other American cities, turned to cultural philanthropy," writes Margaret Lynch in *The Birth of Modern Cleveland,* a collection of historical essays published by the Western Reserve Historical Society in cooperation with the Cleveland Heritage Program of the Cleveland Public Library. "Travel abroad made wealthy Americans feel acutely a lack of the culture that enriched European cities."

Cleveland patrons also saw this cultural undertaking as a way to afford poor immigrants an opportunity to become culturally Americanized, while providing them a respite from their often grim living conditions. Hence, the major cultural institutions were set off in sylvan University Circle, which was semirural at the time.

"For the convenience of workers, the orchestra scheduled Sunday concerts and the museum had Wednesday-evening hours and free Sunday admission," Lynch writes. "Extension exhibitions in schools and libraries and orchestra concerts in high-school auditoriums brought the arts to people in their own neighborhoods."

"Just as the great patrons responded to needs of their workers by building houses and churches, they also felt a commitment to add to their quality of life," adds Dr. Evan Turner, director of the Museum of Art.

In the Cleveland Cultural Gardens in Rockefeller Park, near University Circle on land granted to the city by the Rockefeller family, 21 nationalities commemorate leaders in the arts and literature from their homelands

Only five miles from downtown Cleveland is University Circle, the city's longtime cultural and educational center. Photo by Roger Mastroianni

with statues and plaques.

The United Labor Agency, the social-services arm of organized labor in Cleveland, continues to foster the arts among working men and women with its Cultural Arts and Education Committee, the only one of its kind in a union.

Cleveland lagged behind other major American cities in its cultural development, but once the building started, the pace was feverish. The opening thrust came in 1912, when proponents of social reform organized the City Club as a platform for debate on urban problems. The club, the oldest continuous public forum in America, carries on its legacy of free speech by inviting speakers—from presidents to preachers—to address its weekly luncheon. The forum airs on 150 radio stations coast to coast.

"We're an educational effort whose role is to heighten awareness of issues and help people keep up on social, economic, and political problems," says Alan Davis, the club's executive director.

As the City Club took root, community leaders turned toward cultural causes. The Cleveland Museum of Art opened in 1916 on University Circle land donated years earlier by Jeptha Wade, a onetime itinerant portrait painter, who changed careers and started the Western Union Telegraph Company.

Above: Today Clevelanders take great pride in the restoration of their city's art treasures. Photo by Roger Mastroianni

Top, right: The beauty of the Palace Theatre is reflected in its detailed ceiling. Photo by Roger Mastroianni

A year before the museum opened, the Musical Arts Association was established to form the Cleveland Orchestra. Three years later the orchestra played its first concert downtown at the fortress-like Gray's Armory.

Today the orchestra's principal home is the 2,000-seat Severance Hall, which contains design elements borrowed from classicism, art deco, Georgian, and Egyptian Revival to blend with the classical architecture of the nearby Museum of Art. Both buildings look out on the museum's beautiful Fine Arts Garden and Lagoon and the massive bronze cast of Rodin's *The Thinker* on the museum's south steps.

What has continued to keep these and other Cleveland cultural institutions so strong is the deep commitment of their patrons, who have devoted fortunes to operations and untold hours to fund raising. Just as important, these patrons insisted from the earliest days that the institutions hire top-notch administrators, many of whom had served at cultural institutions in New York or Boston and studied abroad.

Although the Depression somewhat dampened the city's cultural activity, it did not thwart wealthy donors from continuing their funding of the major institutions. This built the solid financial foundation on which they rest today. Because of this, the Cleveland Museum of Art has the second-highest published acquisition endowment of any museum in the country, behind only the Getty Museum in California. Moreover, it remains one of the very few major art museums in the United States with free admission.

The museum spends $7 million per year for purchases and $12 million for operations. Its combined endowment and trust funds are valued at nearly $300 million. More than 500,000 people annually visit the Art Museum. In recent years that figure has approached 800,000 because of popular international exhibitions.

Turner believes that the Cleveland Museum of Art has one of the world's finest collections of art because of cooperation—rather than competition—among local patrons. "Relative to its size and wealth our city has produced few art collectors," he notes. "This is an asset because so

A lilly pond enhances the splendor of the Garden Center of Greater Cleveland in University Circle. Courtesy, Cosgray Photography

The Cleveland Museum of Art resides on land in University Circle donated by Jeptha Wade, who founded the Western Union Telegraph Company. Photo by Jim Baron. Courtesy, Image Finders, Inc.

Facing page: The principal home of the world-famous Cleveland Orchestra is the 2,000-seat Severance Hall. Photo by Jim Baron. Courtesy, Image Finders, Inc.

many families of means have left fortunes to help the museum create its own collections."

Another reason has been management continuity. The art museum has had only four directors. Each has been determined to build a quality collection and effective support services, such as the Teachers Resource Center, which sets up school field trips, and an extensions division, which brings exhibitions to local schools, libraries, and community centers. The museum also holds summer and Saturday youth art classes.

One unique feature of the Cleveland Museum of Art is its greenhouse—presumably the only one in an art museum—which produces, among other things, orchids to provide a touch of summer to the Garden Court on gray winter days.

In spring and summer the museum grounds are bathed in a profusion of flowers. This is when visitors flock to the museum's annual May Show, which started in 1919 and is among the oldest continuous local juried art shows in the United States. Any artist 18 years old and over who lives, works, or was born in one of the counties of the Western Reserve is eligible to submit two works. Judged by outside professionals and museum personnel, the artists receive access to a showcase and market. The museum buys and displays many winners.

Each winter, for another popular exhibition called "The Year in Review," the art museum displays everything it has purchased over the previous 12 months.

Special shows draw large crowds, but it is the permanent collection

Each year more than a half-million people visit the Cleveland Museum of Art. Here a young visitor is enchanted by the medieval suits of armor in the Armor Court. Photo by Jim Baron. Courtesy, Image Finders, Inc.

which places the Cleveland Museum of Art among the great museums of the world. The 50,000-piece collection is considerably smaller than those institutions to which the museum is compared, but virtually every object is judiciously chosen and of superior quality.

When opening the heavy anodized aluminum doors at the north entrance designed by architect Marcel Breuer, one enters spacious galleries whose paintings, sculpture, pottery, textiles, and decorative arts are displayed together by period.

A visitor can trace the development of eastern or western civilization by walking through historically arranged galleries. These include an unparalleled collection of Asian art with masterpieces from the high points of Chinese, Indian, Southeast Asian, Korean, Himalayan, and Japanese cultures.

The European medieval collection, primarily of decorative arts, is one of America's best known. Other distinguished collections include the textiles, which span all ages, and the prints, with special emphasis on fifteenth- and sixteenth-century works.

Audiences find the American art, including works such as George Bellows's popular prize fight depiction, *Stag at Sharkey's,* especially appealing. Notable among the European paintings are the seventeenth-century works of Caravaggio and Poussin as well as a broad Impressionist and Post-Impressionist collection. This includes one of Monet's finest, *Water Lilies,* and works by Degas, van Gogh, and Gauguin. The Picasso collection charts the artist's changing career and includes his Blue Period masterpiece, *La Vie.*

For youngsters, however, nothing surpasses the medieval suits of armor in the Armor Court and the mummy cases in the Egyptian Gallery.

The Cleveland Institute of Art, across the street from the museum, was founded in 1882. More than 500 students from across the country are offered 15 majors in the fine arts, such as painting and sculpture, and the applied arts, including industrial, jewelry, and graphic design.

One of the most uncommon academic buildings anywhere is the Joseph McCullough Center for the Visual Arts, named after the man who served as president of the Cleveland Institute of Art for 36 years. This four-story loft "Art Factory" is a converted Ford Motor Company plant on the

Even the dinosaurs at the Cleveland Museum of Natural History are not immune to "Brownsmania." Photo by Barbara Durham

edge of Case Western Reserve University, where sculpture, painting, graphic design, glassblowing, and ceramics are taught.

Among the institute's graduates are William McVey, a prominent Cleveland sculptor; Viktor Schreckengost, an industrial designer and water colorist who teaches at the institute; Gerry Hirschberg, head of design for Nissan Corporation; and Richard Anuszkiewicz, a New York op artist.

The Cleveland Museum of Natural History also has a prominent role in the city's cultural affairs. In its *Places Rated Almanac,* Rand McNally & Company ranked the Cleveland Museum of Natural History—a short walk from the Institute of Art—among the six elite museums in America (along with the Cleveland Museum of Art). Only New York City and Cleveland placed two institutions on the exclusive list.

Equally important, Rand McNally listed Cleveland among the top 10 metropolitan areas for its range of cultural facilities. Chicago was the only midwestern city with a higher rating.

Excluding the American Museum of History and the Smithsonian Institution, which also made the Rand McNally list, the Cleveland Museum of Natural History is among the largest natural history museums in America. It has grown even bigger with its new four-floor, \$4-million, 59,000-square-foot wing that will house large-scale traveling exhibitions.

State-of-the-art climate control in the new wing allows for storage of delicate plants, insects, birds, and mammals, along with a large collection of rare books on natural history. A special "cold room" preserves research material and mounted animals.

Among its more priceless collections are Northeast Ohio flora and fauna, some of which were last extant a century ago, and fish fossils from the Devonian Age (300 million years ago), which include the largest shark fossils in the world. The museum also specializes in urban archaeology, and supervises regular digs in downtown Cleveland in search of Indian and early white settler sites.

The Museum of Natural History was one of the first of its kind to conduct classes for all age groups. In cooperation with Cleveland State University, the museum sponsors courses for science teachers. With Case Western Reserve University, it hosts an annual lecture series on astronomy in its planetarium and observatory.

When Dr. Donald Johanson was curator of physical anthropology, he unearthed in Ethiopia what are reputed to be the earliest known human bones. Today a replica of that famous discovery, known as "Lucy," is on display at the museum. The museum also exhibits several dinosaurs, including the only known Nanotyrannus ("pygmy tyrant") specimen, which had been excavated in the early 1940s but misidentified. In 1987 a visiting scholar discovered the skeleton at the museum and properly identified it.

Wildlife also is an overriding concern of the museum, which serves as steward of several natural preserves, including bogs and sand dunes, a marsh in suburban Mentor, and land on Kelleys Island, where each September the museum participates in the Monarch Butterfly Festival to track the winter migration of monarchs from Canada to Mexico. Museum staff members also nurse wounded birds of prey and breed bald eagles before reintroducing them into their natural habitat.

"We help people learn about nature and become better informed about making environmental decisions," says Dr. J. Mary Taylor, the museum director and former professor of zoology and director of the vertebrate museum at the University of British Columbia. With the assistance of William E. Scheele, museum director from 1949 to 1972, Taylor is making plans for the museum's 75th anniversary celebration in 1995. One

The Cuyahoga Valley National Recreation Area is part of the National Park System and reflects Greater Cleveland's commitment to wildlife and the outdoors. Photo by Barbara Durham

reason for the museum's success is its volunteers, who contribute more than 40,000 hours each year.

Another treasury of Cleveland history that relies heavily on volunteers is the Western Reserve Historical Society. Founded in 1867, the society is the oldest University Circle institution. It is housed in two early twentieth-century Italian Renaissance-style mansions with large formal gardens. One was the residence of Mrs. Leonard Hanna, sister-in-law of Senator Marcus A. Hanna, the other for Mrs. John Hay, whose husband was Secretary of State under President McKinley.

The 20 period rooms in the Hanna wing of the museum enclose a broad collection of American (particularly Western Reserve) and European decorative arts and furnishings dating from the mid-eighteenth century. The Napoleon Collection, an assortment of Napoleon's belongings and items commemorating his life, was left to the museum by shipping magnate David Z. Norton.

The Chisholm Halle Costume Wing contains more than 20,000 restored garments and accessories dating from the eighteenth century and preserved in special climate-controlled galleries. Clothing by major twentieth-century designers draws the most public interest.

The society's Frederick C. Crawford Auto-Aviation Museum—named for a pioneer in aviation and a chairman of the predecessor of TRW—is housed in its own wing. More than 150 classic automobiles, motorcycles, and early planes are on display.

The new Western Reserve Historical Society Library is not only a repository for the papers of civic leaders, businessmen, and government officials, but also a storehouse of genealogical research material and records relating to Cleveland's ethnic communities.

The Historical Society also maintains Lawnfield, home of President James A. Garfield, in suburban Mentor. Its most popular attraction may be Hale Farm and Village in the Cuyahoga Valley National Recreation Area. Hale Farm is a living history museum *a la* Greenfield Village, with authentically reconstructed early nineteenth-century homes and workplaces, including a sawmill and shops for blacksmiths, glassblowers, potters, spinners, and weavers. Hale Farm is open from May through October and in December. Guides in period costumes describe life in the early days of the Western Reserve.

Across the street from the Western Reserve Historical Society in University Circle is the Garden Center of Greater Cleveland, founded in 1930 as the nation's first civic garden center. It is dedicated to "horticultural enhancement and conservation."

The shrubs and seasonal plantings at its entrance serve as colorful introductions to the Garden Center's special exhibitions, including its popular spring and Christmas shows. The Garden Center has one of the largest gardening libraries in America, with 12,500 volumes. It also offers classes on flower arranging, growing, and garden advice. Much of its support comes from the popular "White Elephant Sale" of donated household items.

Less than a half-mile away from the Garden Center is Severance Hall, home of the Cleveland Orchestra, which *Time* magazine called the "best-

Facing page: Conductor Christoph von Dohnanyi leads the orchestra through a spirited rehersal. Photo by Roger Mastroianni

Below: A trip to Hale Farm and Village in the Cuyahoga Valley National Recreation Area is a trip through early nineteenth-century life. Photo by Barbara Durham

sounding orchestra in the country" and which the *San Francisco Examiner* stated "may well be the greatest orchestra in the nation."

Christoph von Dohnanyi, the orchestra's sixth music director, previously was artistic director and principal conductor of the Hamburg State Opera. Under Dohnanyi, the orchestra balances the great classics of the eighteenth, nineteenth, and twentieth centuries with adventuresome selections by more modern composers.

The Cleveland Orchestra, one of the most recorded in America, also plays an annual subscription series at Carnegie Hall and tours abroad regularly. To expand appreciation of the orchestra's repertoire, music scholars present educational talks prior to Severance Hall subscription concerts.

To interest young people in classical music, the orchestra sponsors a Youth Orchestra under the direction of its resident conductor, Jahja Ling, for which students between the ages of 12 and 20 audition. Youth Orchestra members are coached by Cleveland Orchestra members and present their own concerts.

The orchestra's Educational Activities Department presents the Musical Rainbow Series to introduce orchestral instruments to youngsters aged three to six. Each season it also holds two pairs of hour-long Key Concerts for children aged five to nine.

Through its Community Music Project, the orchestra presents a free concert of music by black artists in January to honor Dr. Martin Luther King's birthday. The orchestra also presents 20 educational matinee weekday concerts each year, attracting 50,000 high-school students. Supplemented with preconcert explanations, teacher curriculum guides, and educational brochures, these concerts are aimed at creating an audience of classical music lovers for the future.

In addition, the orchestra selectively opens its rehearsals, which are popular with senior citizen groups. It also has staged a free outdoor summer concert at Riverfest in the Flats along the Cuyahoga. This has attracted 200,000 people, the orchestra's largest audience.

Over the years the orchestra has

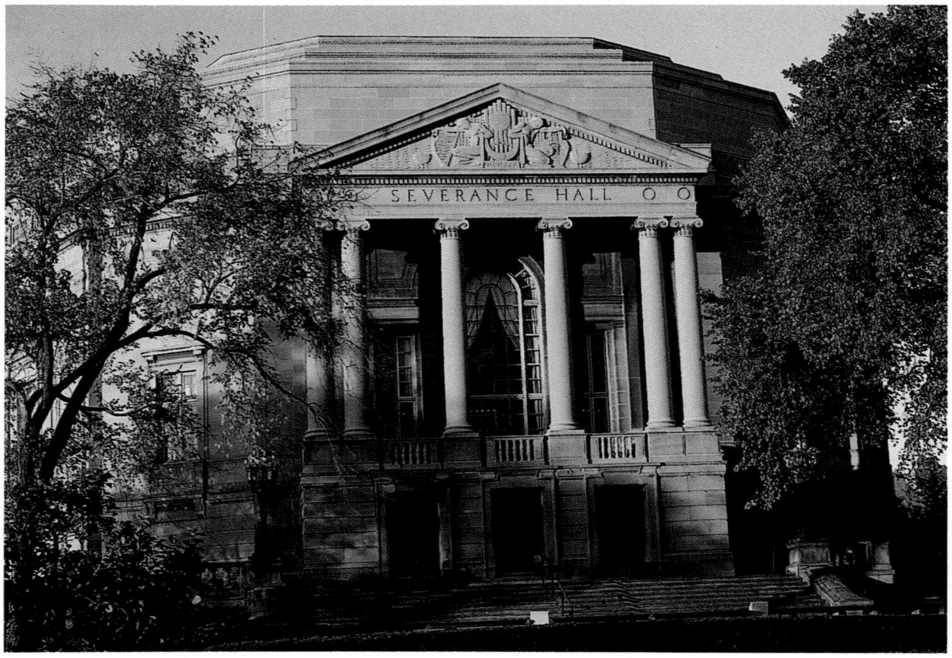
SEVERANCE HALL

increased its popularity through special Christmas concerts in Severance Hall. During the summer it moves to Blossom Music Center, on 800 unspoiled acres of woodlands between Akron and Cleveland near the Cuyahoga National Recreation Area. The Blossom pavilion can seat more than 5,200, and sloping lawn seating on a four-acre natural amphitheater can accommodate an additional 13,500.

Rock bands and popular singers often jam Blossom Music Center, as does the Blossom Festival Band, a wind and brass band composed of orchestra members and other musicians. The Festival Band puts on a resounding Fourth of July concert, which concludes with fireworks at the climax of "The Stars and Stripes Forever."

The Cleveland Orchestra balances its books through fund-raisers such as Scheherazade, a biennial black-tie auction that offers a potpourri of glamorous prizes, including New York theater tickets with a chic *pied-a-terre* and a regatta on the Thames with tickets to Wimbledon.

Cleveland's appreciation for classical music is heightened by the Cleveland Women's Orchestra. Formed in 1935 by Cleveland Orchestra member Hyman Chandler, it provides women ages 16 and up the chance to express their musical talent by performing for social service constituencies, including the elderly. The high point of the Cleveland Women's Orchestra schedule is its annual concert in Severance Hall.

Facing page, top: Members of the Cleveland Orchestra perform a free summer concert at the Sohio Riverfest in the Flats. Photo by Roger Mastroianni

Left: The Blossom Music Center, summer home of the Cleveland Orchestra, also hosts a wide variety of musical performances by contemporary artists. Photo by Roger Mastroianni

Facing page, bottom: The orchestra's regular concert season opens in the fall at Severance Hall. Photo by Roger Mastroianni

A variety of music can be heard in daytime and evening concerts at Nautica in the Flats. Photo by Roger Mastroianni

The community's appreciation for classical music also is enriched by the Cleveland Music School Settlement. The settlement is unique because it is both a social and a cultural institution established to provide "inexpensive or free musical training, and to help with personal problems."

Headquartered in a 42-room University Circle mansion called the Main School, the settlement provides nondegree voice, music, and dance instruction, regardless of age, ability, or financial means. Its innovative programs include music therapy for children with mental, social, and physical challenges. A Music School Settlement benefit brought together in concert—for the first time—the world-famous violinist Isaac Stern and his son Michael, an assistant conductor with the Cleveland Orchestra.

The settlement's educational work is buttressed by the nearby Cleveland Institute of Music, which, under president David Cerone, is becoming one of the best-known conservatories in the country. Donald Erb, professor of composition, has already established an international reputation for his contemporary orchestra, ensemble, and solo compositions. Donald Weilerstein, a founding member and first violinist of the distinguished Cleveland Quartet, has joined the institute's faculty, strengthening the institute's reputation as an outstanding string conservatory.

Students at the institute can major in voice, opera, and instruments. Enrollment includes 300 full-time college conservatory students, plus 1,700 children and adults who take preparatory and continuing education classes.

Each academic year is highlighted by one of two rotating biennial events—the Art Song Festival, which draws eminent singers and accompanists to teach master classes and conduct recitals, and the Robert Casadesus International Piano Competition (named after the late French pianist) in which 40 young artists from around the world compete for cash prizes and concert appearances.

The Institute of Music hosts summer performances of Lyric Opera Cleveland. This so-called "Opera Al Fresco" features intermission picnic suppers on the institute's grounds.

Lyric Opera Cleveland, which started in 1974 and performs in English, complements the Cleveland Opera, whose own season runs from fall through spring. Started in 1976 in a junior high school auditorium, the Cleveland Opera has become the 10th-largest opera company in the United States in terms of audience attendance. It presents a full range of works—from *Aida* to *West Side Story*—at the State Theatre in Playhouse Square Center.

With one of the largest and best-equipped stages in the world, the State can handle the largest opera companies, including the Metropolitan, which over the years has visited Cleveland on its spring tour. The Cleveland Opera keeps its ticket prices reasonable enough to make opera accessible to the broader community. It also sends touring singers and ensembles to schools, nursing homes, and hospitals.

Since its creation in 1975, the Cleveland Ballet, under the direction of its hard-driving cofounder Dennis Nahat, has had a similar educational commitment. The ballet, housed in the State Theatre, is augmented by its School of Cleveland Ballet, whose teachers formerly performed with Cleveland and other ballet companies.

Nahat, who also serves as dancer and resident choreographer, has helped the ballet gain an excellent national reputation for the performance of classic as well as modern works. In March 1987 the ballet set an American box-office record for a ballet performance other than *The Nutcracker* with its premier of *Swan Lake*. Some 42,000 people attended the lavish 10-day production at the State.

When not performing in Cleveland, the ballet has a second home and full season in San Jose, California. For many years prima ballerina Cynthia Gregory has been the ballet's permanent guest artist.

Behind its energetic director, Heinz Poll, the smaller Ohio Ballet, based in Akron, performs three weekends a year at the Ohio Theatre and tours throughout the nation. Its repertoire includes romantic period ballets, contemporary works, dance excerpts from opera, and pieces by Poll himself.

Both ballet companies have heightened interest in dancing. DANCECleveland, a modern dance presenting and educational organization, brings contemporary dance companies to the Ohio Theatre. It also hires instructors to conduct modern dance workshops.

Efforts to interest Cleveland in modern dance are bolstered by the Footpath Dance Company, which performs in Cleveland in the spring and summer and then tours the country, and the new Tom Evert Dance Company, headed by Tom Evert, a former Paul Taylor dancer who grew up in Cleveland and moved back from New York.

The versatile Ohio Chamber Orchestra plays for both the Cleveland Op-

The Great Lakes Theatre Festival stages productions at the Ohio Theatre. Photo by Roger Mastroianni

era and the Cleveland Ballet. Its music director, Dwight Oltman, has created a repertoire that ranges from the Baroque period to the twentieth century.

The Ohio Chamber Orchestra presents a summer series at Cain Park, an outdoor theater in suburban Cleveland Heights, and puts in an appearance at the annual Bach Festival at Baldwin-Wallace College. It also offers a winter series at the Cleveland Play House.

Classical music is just one of the many activities at the Play House. Founded in 1919, the Play House is the oldest professional repertory theater in the country.

Under new artistic director Josephine R. Abady, the Play House has taken a decidedly different direction. Abady utilizes playwrights, designers, directors, and actors who are relatively new to Cleveland, and concentrates on American plays. The Play House is attracting younger audiences while keeping its established patrons. "This theater continues to encourage young artists," Abady says.

Long before Abady's arrival, the Play House was known as a training ground for actors. Among its distinguished alumni are Joel Grey and Paul

Newman (who both grew up in Cleveland), as well as Margaret Hamilton, Alan Alda, and Daniel J. Travanti.

No one can argue that the new $15-million Play House complex, four miles east of downtown and near the Cleveland Clinic and University Circle, is not daunting. Designed by renowned Cleveland-born architect Philip Johnson, the Romanesque structure connects the smaller and older Drury and Brooks theaters to the new 612-seat Bolton Theatre.

A vital resource of the Play House is the 200,000-square-foot production center (once a Sears, Roebuck and Co. department store), where sets and costumes are built and props are stored. The center also houses a 5,000-volume theater archival library, three rehearsal halls, and the private 210-seat Play House Club, one of the most popular dining spots in Cleveland.

The Play House apprentice program for professional actors, playwrights, and directors is a nonprofessional effort at teaching acting to youngsters and adults, who are known as Curtain Pullers. It also conducts outreach classes at local schools and hosts an annual Midwestern Young Peoples' Playwrighting Festival and Conference.

The Cleveland Play House maintains an extensive apprentice program for theater professionals. Photo by Roger Mastroianni

Special needs are met by the Fairmount Theater of the Deaf, which performs plays simultaneously in sign language and English. Founded in 1975 by a hearing actor and a deaf actor, the Fairmount is one of the few professional resident theaters of the deaf. With performances at the Cleveland Play House, the Fairmount enriches the lives of the deaf and increases public awareness of the world of deafness.

Only a few blocks south of the Play House is Karamu House (Swahili for "a place of joyful meeting"), the oldest interracial metropolitan center for the arts in the United States. Here budding black playwrights and actors are given the opportunity to hone their skills in major theater productions. Art exhibitions that complement the productions are held in the Arena Gallery.

Karamu also offers senior citizen classes in choral singing, drama, and sewing, and children as young as two years old may attend its early childhood development center enrichment program. Karamu's mission is augmented by Accord Associates, which nurtures minority artists and brings leading national and international black performers to Cleveland. Langston Hughes, the internationally acclaimed author, poet, and playwright, had his early schooling in Cleveland. He was a significant contributor in the early days of community theater at Karamu House.

A few miles east of Karamu House in Cleveland Heights, Dobama, a well-known community theater, sponsors an amateur playwright competition that attracts upwards of 500 submissions. The theater stages several of the winning plays.

While many prominent actors perform at the Cleveland Play House, they also are drawn to the Great Lakes Theater Festival, whose home is at the Ohio Theatre in Playhouse Square Center. Founded in 1962 as the Great Lakes Shakespeare Festival, the scope of its spring-to-fall productions has broadened under artistic director Gerald Freedman. "The responsibility of classical theater is to preserve the heritage and traditions that make our culture unique," Freedman says.

Although it still stages the classics of Shakespeare, Moliere, Ibsen, Shaw, and Chekhov, the festival also brings musical comedies to Cleveland that often go on to New York and other large cities.

Many Cleveland traditions that are not specifically cultural are preserved in institutions such as the Cleveland Health Education Museum, which is near the Play House and the Cleveland Clinic. The Health Museum is the only one of its kind in the Western Hemisphere. It houses more than 200 major displays—including "Juno," the transparent electronic woman who explains the body's systems.

If the Health Museum is popular with children, so is the city's newest museum, the Cleveland Children's Museum in University Circle. The museum has been described as "child's play" because of its hands-on exhibits. Children can do artwork, build model homes, listen to the recorded sounds of Cleveland's bridges, or become amateur musicians for a day.

Much of Cleveland's cultural activity is in its highly visible museums, but the smaller arts organizations and galleries offer unusual alternatives. Among them is NOVA (New Organization for the Visual Arts), which provides professional development assistance to local artists through workshops on marketing and publicity. NOVA also brings artists and the community together through enrichment projects, notably Artists Open Studio Day and Art in Special Places.

SPACES, an unconventional artist-run gallery in a downtown Historic Warehouse District loft building, offers space for regional artists to show and sell their work. Another arts organization, the Cleveland Center for Contemporary Art, which celebrated its 20th anniversary in 1988, puts on exhibitions and sales of contemporary international and national artwork at both its University Circle gallery and its satellite showroom downtown in the Galleria at Erieview shopping center.

Other Greater Cleveland galleries that draw a steady stream of visitors include the American Crafts Gallery at Shaker Square, which has one of the largest displays of crafts in the United States and is along a row of galleries; the Malcolm Brown Gallery in Shaker Heights, which specializes in African art by major black artists; the Mitze Verne Gallery at the John Carroll

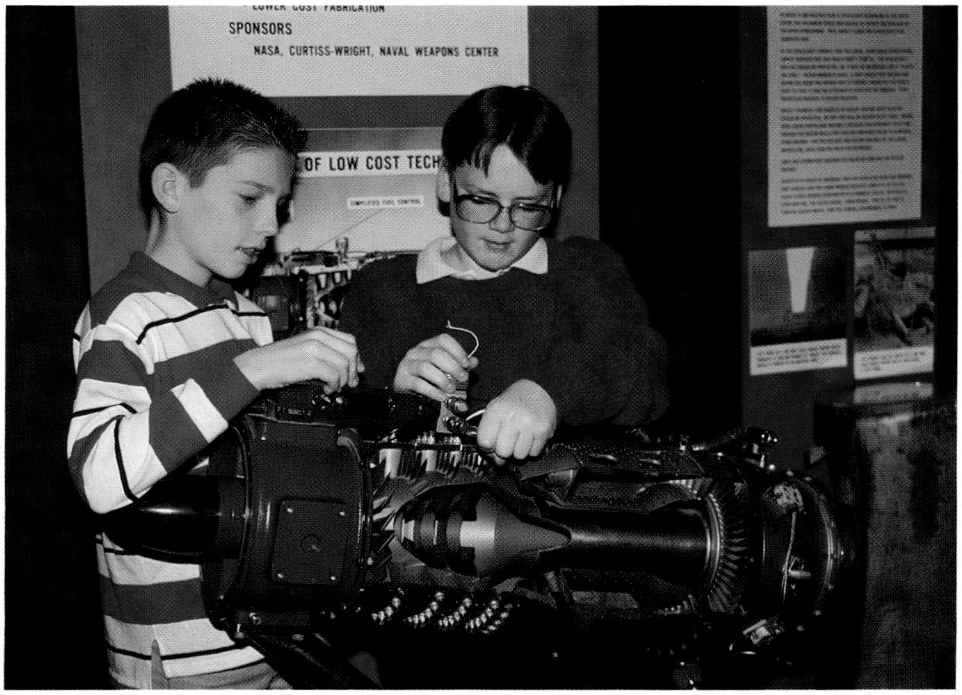

The visitors center at the NASA Lewis Research Center in Cleveland brings the wonders of the space age down to earth with its fascinating exhibits. Photo by Barbara Durham

University Library, which includes a collection of Japanese prints and folk arts; the Florence O'Donnell Wasmer Gallery at Ursuline College in suburban Pepper Pike; the Fenwick Art Gallery at Baldwin-Wallace College; the Allen Memorial Art Museum at Oberlin College; the Mather Gallery at Case Western Reserve University; and the Cleveland State University Gallery.

Other popular commercial art galleries include the Bonfoey Company at Playhouse Square, established in 1893, which also offers picture framing, appraisals, and restorations; Vixseboxse in Cleveland Heights, a gallery of distinguished fine art; the Ellen Stirn Galleries, with an emphasis on decorative arts, including ceramics, silver, and prints, in the Potter and Mellen store at University Circle; and the Colagrossi Gallery, a contemporary American crafts gallery in Rocky River.

The 12,000-square-foot Wolf's Auction Gallery, in the Warehouse District, conducts regular art and antique auctions and increasingly is making its mark in the world of high-quality expensive estate sales. A Wolf auction brought a record price for a Thomas Hart Benton painting, a Mary Cassatt print, and a Cézanne lithograph.

Only a few miles east of downtown, in Little Italy on the edge of Case Western Reserve University and University Circle, the Murray Hill Area Arts Association conducts art walks in June and December along the splurge of tiny new art studios and galleries. These include the popular Fiori Gallery and Murray Hill Market.

Neighborhood, ethnic, and amateur singing groups proliferate, too. The Singers Club, started in 1893 in a YMCA, is a popular all-male chorus that sings for benefits and produces annual shows in the spring and at Christmas. Cleveland has long had a tradition of private cultural organizations. The Hermit Club, tucked away behind Playhouse Square Center, is a private men's dining and performing club, whose members act, sing, play a musical instrument, or work backstage at its private theatrical productions.

Adults are not the only amateurs producing professional concerts. Apart from the Cleveland Orchestra Youth Orchestra, the Singing Angels, who range in age from 6 to 18, travel around the world. Bill Boehm, who founded the chorus in 1964, has taken the Angels to Israel, the White House, the Vatican, and the Great Wall in Peking. Tuition scholarships raised through community support allow children from all backgrounds the opportunity to qualify for the Singing Angels.

The Angels also entertain at Cleveland City Hall, hospitals, schools, and nursing homes, and present a spring benefit concert at the Music Hall, the intimate theater attached to the Cleveland Convention Center. (It was here that Jimmy Carter and Ronald Reagan debated during the 1980 presidential campaign.)

The Front Row Theater in the East Side suburb of Highland Heights—a theater-in-the-round—draws nearly 400,000 people a year to hear well-known singers, musicians, and speakers.

Since 1977 attendance at the Cleveland International Film Festival has grown steadily. Each spring upwards of 25,000 people attend two weeks of rare independent and foreign films. Celebrity actors and directors usually show up for a world premier at the festival's opening night at the Ohio Theatre in the Playhouse Square Center.

Music also is center stage at the downtown campus of Cuyahoga Community College. Each spring the college sponsors the Tri-C JazzFest at Playhouse Square Center, bringing to Cleveland many top national jazz musicians. The National Music Center at Cuyahoga Community College is also scheduled to become the educational component of the Rock and Roll Hall of Fame and Museum, providing on-site music courses, workshops, and lessons.

In addition, comedy is becoming big business locally. The new L.A. Improv at Nautica in the Flats books leading regional and national comedians in a familiar nightclub setting. Hilarities, on the other hand, operates from a large hall in the Warehouse District.

Most of Cleveland's cultural institutions are on the East Side, but on the West Side three key institutions are vigorously reaching out to growing constituencies.

The 246-seat Huntington Playhouse, on the Huntington Reservation of the Cleveland Metroparks System in Bay Village, stages well-known musicals and plays while providing summer acting lessons for children. Huntington's support comes strictly through the box office. A majority of its productions are bought out by nonprofit organizations for raising funds.

Cleveland Public Theatre, in an old Italian-Irish neighborhood at West 65th Street and Detroit Avenue, has converted an old warehouse into a two-story, 150-seat New York loft theater-in-the-round.

With support from foundations and corporations, Cleveland Public Theatre is helping renovate the area while bringing experimental works by Ohio playwrights to city dwellers who might not otherwise ever see a play. "Anyone can be involved, from producing the programs to working the concession stands or painting sets," says Amanda Shaffer, the theater's production manager. "If someone can't afford a ticket, they can come in and sweep the floor."

A few miles farther west in Lakewood, the Beck Center for the Cultural Arts, a kind of full-service cultural/arts/education facility, has been serving West Side suburbs since 1931. As the home of the popular Lakewood Little Theatre, Beck provides a training ground for actors, artists, and dancers. The Robert Page Singers, the only professional chorus in Northeastern Ohio, make their home at Beck. An integral part of Beck Center is its Museum Galleria, where local artists and craftsmen display and sell works at annual shows.

The Beck's nonprofit counterpart across town in semirural Geauga County, the Fairmount Center for Creative and Performing Arts, is a community arts and teaching center with a focus on dance, theater, painting, martial arts, and gymnastics for preschoolers through adults.

The center also has an art gallery for its monthly exhibits and sponsors two dance troupes, the Fairmount Spanish Dancers and Fairmount Dancin' Jazz Company. Pending construction of their own theater, Fairmount performers are using nearby community and college theaters.

Like the Lakewood Little Theatre and the Huntington Playhouse, the Fairmount Center is one of more than 40 suburban theaters and theater groups in Greater Cleveland. Others include the Chagrin Valley Little Theatre, the Gates Mills Players, and the Bratenahl Playhouse in the eastern suburbs, plus the Greenbrier Theatre, the Olde Towne Hall Theatre, the Dover Playhouse, the Clague Playhouse, and the Berea Summer Theater in the western suburbs. The 1,130-seat Carousel Dinner Theatre in Akron is the largest dinner theater in the United States.

The Broadway School of Music & the Arts has few trees and little grass, but it is an oasis for an old steel-mill neighborhood in the shadow of downtown. To a large degree Broadway serves children and adults who have had limited experience in the arts, offering opportunities in music, dance, theater, and visual arts.

Community theaters may be growing in popularity, but Greater Clevelanders also cherish public art. Works of William McVey, the city's most illustrious sculptor, are spread throughout Greater Cleveland. McVey also carved the figure of Winston Churchill for the English Speaking Union that stands in front of the British Embassy in Washington, D.C.

His prominent Cleveland works include a statue of the legendary Cleveland-born Olympic gold medalist, Jesse Owens, in Huntington Park near the Cleveland Stadium; George Washington as a surveyor, at the entrance to the new federal building; an enlarged bust of John Carroll, first Catholic bishop in the United States, on the suburban John Carroll University campus; Tom L. Johnson, the turn-of-the-century reform mayor; Ohio poet Hart Crane at Case Western Reserve University's Freiberger Library; and airplane pioneer Frederick Crawford at the Crawford Auto-Aviation Museum.

Other McVey works include *The Long Road,* a relief of the Jewish

This statue of Cleveland-born Olympic gold medalist Jesse Owens is one of William McVey's many outstanding works. Courtesy, Cosgray Photography

people in procession, at the Jewish Community Center in Cleveland Heights, and a limestone grizzly bear in the wildlife preserve at the Cleveland Museum of Natural History. He also has a bronze relief portrait of city manager William Hopkins at Cleveland Hopkins International Airport.

"He has given Cleveland artists a traditional approach in sculpture that is the highest quality," says his associate, Mike Moore, who signed a piece with McVey of legendary Clevelander John W. Heisman, for whom the Heisman Trophy was named, at the entrance of Georgia Tech stadium in Atlanta. "In many respects Bill's presence is subdued, but his work is there no matter where you go in Cleveland."

In a more avant-garde way, the Committee of Public Art, funded through government, foundations, and individuals, brings sculpture to public spaces. "The Hidden City Revealed" is a bold undertaking to create a mini-park with sculpture at a site along the Cuyahoga where the first Connecticut settlers lived.

Cleveland has other distinguished public sculpture, including a massive steel monument to David Berger, a Clevelander who was killed with Israeli athletes in the Munich Olympics massacre, by David E. Davis, a local sculptor.

An increasing number of the city's large corporations and office building developers are buying and displaying sculpture and paintings in their lobbies. These include Jacobs, Visconsi, & Jacobs, whose chairman, Richard Jacobs, personally selects his company's artwork; TRW, whose suburban Lyndhurst headquarters is filled with a wide variety of original artwork; National City Bank and BP America, which have small galleries in their downtown lobbies; and the Progressive Insurance Company, whose chairman, Peter Lewis, is a collector of modern art. Progressive is planning to attach an art museum to its proposed new downtown headquarters.

The Price Waterhouse accounting firm exhibits the Western Reserve Historical Society's artwork in exchange for financial and technical assistance. The Corporate Center in the massive Great Northern Shopping Center in suburban North Olmsted was built with a jazzy four-story atrium art gallery to showcase regional artists and provide space for cultural benefits.

Along with such visible displays, Greater Cleveland has an immeasurable number of tiny single-purpose museums with small but zealous devotees. The Cleveland Police Museum in the Justice Center downtown holds a collection of early police weaponry and crime-solving paraphernalia.

The George Rickey sculpture *Rectangles Vertical Gyratory IV* complements the National City Bank building at East Ninth and Euclid. Photo by Barbara Durham

While serving the community, the Mandel Jewish Community Center also houses different displays of Jewish art each month. Photo by Jack Van Antwerp

The Dunham Tavern Museum on Euclid Avenue between downtown and University Circle is the oldest structure in the city and offers a true-to-life glimpse of life in the early Western Reserve. The Shaker Historical Museum carries one back to the days of the Shakers, a celibate religious society that settled in what is now Shaker Heights in the early nineteenth century.

The Dittrick Museum of Medical History on the Case Western Reserve campus has one of the most extensive collections of early medical instruments and rare books. The Indian Museum of Lake County in Painesville, 30 miles east of Cleveland, displays artifacts of midwestern tribes. The Northeast Ohio Art Museum in University Circle displays art by Northeast Ohioans dating to the nineteenth century.

Forty miles west of Cleveland, in Vermilion, the Great Lakes Historical Society Marine Museum displays historic items of the Great Lakes, including a model of Commodore Oliver Perry's ship, the *Niagara,* which defeated the British in the War of 1812. In Milan, 17 miles southwest of Vermilion, the two-story brick birthplace and early home of Thomas Edison has been converted into a historical museum.

The Kent State University Museum, which houses the Higbee Gallery, exhibits clothing and items related to fashion from different eras. It was set up with donations by fashion designers Shannon Rodgers and Jerry Silverman.

The African American Museum, not far from University Circle, has exhibits of Afro-American and African culture. The Temple Museum at University Circle is a repository of priceless Jewish cultural and religious objects and ancient Israeli artifacts.

Why such an emphasis on the arts?

Patricia Jansen Doyle, who oversees arts grants for the Cleveland Foundation, attributes this interest in visual and performing arts to an increased standard of living, higher level of education, and more leisure, which have stimulated foundations and patrons to fund more arts activities.

"It's a national phenomenon," says Doyle, who has overseen grants of $25 million to local cultural organizations, "but when Cleveland picked up on it, quality was emphasized.

"This is due to the sophistication of our audiences, our strong volunteer tradition, and the caliber of trustees," Doyle says. "Unlike some other cities where a single powerful donor often funds everything, our volunteer base is broad, and our corporations have a firm philanthropic commitment."

The memory of what Cleveland almost lost when its great Playhouse Square vaudeville theaters were heading for the wrecking ball is burned deeply in the community psyche. In fact, the Playhouse Square Center's mission statement has a universal application: "A civilization must build upon its arts heritage instead of destroying the very foundations of its culture." Cleveland certainly has done that—and more.

Through the years the Cleveland Museum of Art has greatly contributed to the city's strong cultural heritage. Photo by Jim Baron. Courtesy, Image Finders, Inc.

Marlboro Country

CHAPTER 5

A Spectrum Of Seasonal Sensations

From a roomy office overlooking Lake Erie on East Ninth Street in Cleveland's financial district, lawyer Mark McCormack, who shuns pinstriped suits in favor of blue blazers and plaid slacks, coordinates a business empire that circles the globe.

To keep up with his jet-setting promotional activities, the man whom *Sports Illustrated* calls the "most powerful in sports" maintains separate offices, secretaries, homes, and clothes closets in Cleveland, New York, and London.

McCormack started his business in 1960 on a handshake with his golfing buddy, Arnold Palmer. From that one-client office in downtown Cleveland, International Management Group (IMG) has become, in less than three decades, the General Motors of sports marketing.

IMG continues to represent Palmer, the most famous golfer in the world, solely on the strength of his handshake with McCormack. McCormack also has added 500 other superstars, including golfers Gary Player, Curtis Strange, Jan Stephenson, and Nancy Lopez; tennis stars Andre Agassi, Ivan Lendl, Chris Evert, and Martina Navratilova; ex-Cleveland Browns coach Marty Schottenheimer; and acclaimed America's Cup winner Dennis Conner.

With more than 700 employees in 25 offices in 17 countries, IMG also promotes mammoth sporting events such as the British Open, the Nestlé World Championship of Women's Golf, and the Wimbledon Tennis Tournament.

The Catholic Church hired IMG to handle merchandising rights for Pope John Paul II's trip to

Fans enjoy the excitement of major league baseball at Cleveland Municipal Stadium, home of the Cleveland Indians and the NFL's Cleveland Browns. Photo by Roger Mastroianni

Great Britain. IMG also negotiated television rights for the Seoul Olympics and the Calgary Winter Olympics, and has forged an alliance with the Soviet Union to oversee construction and manage two 18-hole golf resorts in the U.S.S.R. IMG also represents a growing number of Russian athletes who are now competing in the United States, including the young tennis sensation Natalya Zvereva.

Cleveland-based Society Corporation works with IMG to provide financial planning services to the firm's clients.

Mark McCormack himself is an international celebrity who also is well known for his iconoclastic best sellers, *What They Don't Teach You at Harvard Business School* and *The Terrible Truth About Lawyers*.

As much as McCormack's work is international, IMG is becoming increasingly active in Cleveland. The firm handled promotion for the successful three-day opening of the North Coast Harbor (down the street from its world headquarters) and helped line up corporate sponsors for a Cleveland Orchestra tour of Europe.

"We've had lots of opportunities to move out of Cleveland," says McCormack, who started his career as a lawyer with Cleveland-based Arter & Hadden, "but we've never given thought to moving. So many people at the top of IMG have roots here. The life-style is especially appealing to young married couples. They are taken with the city and its heritage. Cleveland is part of our corporate heritage, and we are planning to promote more events here in the future."

It is fitting that IMG managed the North Coast Harbor opening. Clevelanders recognize that Lake Erie—shallowest and most unpredictable of the Great Lakes—has opened a new dimension in sports and recreational leisure activities unimagined only a few years ago.

"There's something magic about water," says Gary Conley, president of North Coast Development Corporation, the nonprofit public-private partnership that is revitalizing the downtown lakefront with funds from various sources, including $5.7 million from the Cleveland Foundation. "You can't think of San Francisco or Boston without envisioning their water. Now you can think of Cleveland as the jewel by the lake."

The first segment of the billion-dollar North Coast Harbor—an eight-acre safe harbor that is part of the Cleveland Lakefront State Park—was officially opened at a dedication attended by hundreds of thousands of Greater Clevelanders.

On land that was once nothing more than a parking lot, today there are day moorings for 60 pleasure boats, a 1,300-by-50-foot promenade with antique street lighting, eight acres of landscaped parks, and a terraced festival park with open plaza seating for 10,000.

The waterfront excitement has spilled over to rowing on the Cuyahoga in the Flats. During its first year of competition in 1988, the Flats Racing League attracted more than 1,200 men and women representing scores of teams sponsored by companies, riverside nightclubs, and restaurants.

A sister organization, the Cleveland Rowing Federation, competes in sculling races around the country and instructs local high-school students who have formed their own competitive rowing league.

Facing page: Rowing enthusiasts compete on the Cuyahoga River in the Flats. The Flats Racing League attracted more than 1,200 participants in 1988, its first year of competition. Photo by Jim Pickerell. Courtesy, Tony Stone Worldwide

Above: Cleveland beaches, among the busiest nationwide, draw more than 10 million visitors annually. Photo by Jim Baron. Courtesy, Image Finders, Inc.

Above, left: Cleveland's local waters attract millions of water sports enthusiasts each year. Photo by Don Snyder

From late spring to early fall, the riverside restaurants in the Flats are lined with downtown office workers cheering for men's, women's, and mixed nine-member crews sculling in 65-foot boats. Competition takes place two weekday evenings and on Saturday throughout the summer to prepare for the September championships. "We just went back to the original idea for rowing in London where people rowed from bar to bar along the Thames," says Jay Milano, a Flats Racing League organizer.

The waterfront revival is not limited to downtown. Only a few miles both east and west of the Flats, the state of Ohio has taken over city parks and integrated them into Cleveland Lakefront State Park. The state has spent $30 million to make these among the most active family-friendly urban parks in North America, with new fishing piers, boat launching ramps, and picnic areas.

Excluding Jones Beach in New York, the Cleveland Lakefront State Park beaches— Edgewater on the West Side, and Gordon Park, Euclid Beach, and Wildwood on the East Side—are considered the busiest public beaches in America, drawing more than 10 million people a year for swimming, picnicking, fishing, and boat launching. The numbers are up dramatically—from less than one million in the late 1970s.

In recognizing the enormous impact of the cleanup of Lake Erie and other Cleveland waterways in recent years, Governor Richard Celeste has created a special Lake Erie Redevelopment Task Force. Priorities are coastal management, environmental quality, shoreline protection, and creation of another state park between Cleveland and Sandusky, 60 miles to the west.

A side effect of the cleanup, which began in the 1970s under tightened state and federal environmental regulations, is that Lake Erie marinas are

Left: The *Goodtime II,* provides tours of Lake Erie for thousands of schoolchildren and adults each year. Photo by Barbara Durham

jammed to capacity. New docks are leased even before their construction. Membership in the many private yacht clubs along the lake is at its peak.

It is no wonder. Some 400,000 registered boaters are out on Lake Erie, and the largest indoor boat show in the country is held annually in Cleveland. The season, which runs from April into November for hearty boaters, culminates with numerous sailboat and powerboat races. Cleveland Race Week, a series of sailboat races in July at Edgewater Yacht Club just west of downtown, is one of Lake Erie's most popular events.

In September 1990 the Cleveland Yachting Club in Rocky River will host the Star Class World Championships, a week of races involving hundreds of boats and sailors from 25 countries. This is only the ninth time the races will have been held in the United States, and the first time on Lake Erie. Cleveland beat out Newport Harbor and San Francisco for the weeklong event. The Star Class is the oldest and most competitive one-design racing class in sailing.

Boating is just one aspect of the Lake Erie comeback. The Lake Erie shoreline, especially west of Cleveland, is now one of the busiest resort areas in the world. Vacationland, as it is known, draws 5 million tourists a year.

In a survey of its booking agents, Holiday Inns ranked Sandusky, in the heart of Vacationland, as the fifth busiest city in the United States for summer motel bookings. Only Holiday Inns in Orlando, Florida, Myrtle Beach, South Carolina, Washington, D.C., and San Francisco were busier.

The impact of tourism along Lake Erie is so pronounced that the Erie

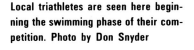

Local triathletes are seen here beginning the swimming phase of their competition. Photo by Don Snyder

Right: One of the most popular events on Lake Erie is Cleveland Race Week, a series of sailboat races held at Edgewater Yacht Club each July. Courtesy, Luce Photography, Inc.

County Visitors Bureau responds to 30,000 inquiries each year. The Ohio Travel and Information Center near Sandusky is the busiest in the state. One Rand McNally guide compares Vacationland to the Florida Panhandle as a vacation hotspot.

Expensive new Vacationland condominiums complement the growing number of summer homes along the lake and on picturesque islands only a few miles offshore. The most visible Vacationland landmark, the International Peace Monument on Put-in-Bay (the busiest island in Lake Erie), commemorates Oliver Hazard Perry's victory nearby over the British in the War of 1812.

Put-in-Bay, which lies just south of the international boundary line with Canada, draws thousands of vacationers—many on sailboats and yachts—to its large natural harbor. In early August hundreds of sailboats compete in the Inter-Lake Yachting Association's colorful annual regatta off Put-in-Bay.

Luxury motels and resorts, such as the New England-style Radisson Harbour Inn, near the entrance to Cedar Point and Sawmill Creek in Huron, are attracting business conferences that allow executives to bring along their families for swimming, boating, water skiing, golfing, waterfront dining, island cruises, and amusement parks.

One reason for Vacationland's popularity is simple to understand: the fish are jumpin'. From early spring to late fall Lake Erie, from Cleveland to Toledo, is dotted with thousands of fishing boats. The Ohio State University Sea Grant Program estimates the tourism value of Lake Erie fishing (largely perch, bass, and walleye), at more than $100 million per year with a haul of 25 million fish annually.

That is why western Lake Erie is called the Walleye Capital of the World. More than one million fisherman hook 5 million walleye each season. Lake Erie walleye tournaments offer more than one million dollars in prize money. A special attraction to fishermen are two new artificial reefs west of Cleveland that serve as storehouses of yellow perch, walleye, and smallmouth bass.

Lake Erie charter boats also are teeming—from a paltry 34 only a decade ago to more than a 1000 today. The U.S. Coast Guard has been licensing 50 new Lake Erie charter captains per week during fishing season. Charter boats on Lake Erie in Ohio alone have surpassed the total number on all the lakes in Michigan!

The area also is appealing to retirees because of the shoreline, which remains temperate into autumn. *U.S. News & World Report* called western

Top, left: Put-in-Bay, the busiest island on Lake Erie, is a popular fun-in-the-sun spot for Clevelanders. Photo by Barbara Durham

One of the more popular attractions at Cedar Point is the Big Wheel. Photo by Barbara Durham

Above: Cedar Point, in Sandusky is one of the country's busiest amusement parks. Photo by Barbara Durham

Facing page: Each year 2.75 million visitors enjoy Cedar Point's rides and attractions. The park celebrated its 120th birthday in 1989. Photo by Barbara Durham

Lake Erie one of the "Ten Great Places to Spend Your Retirement," along with Fort Lauderdale and Phoenix.

Cedar Point, in the heart of Vacationland, is among the nation's 10 busiest amusement parks, drawing 2.75 million visitors a year and offering more rides and roller coasters than any other American amusement park.

Among its biggest attractions is Soak City, a $3.5-million water park with 4,000 feet of twisting fiberglass chutes. Cedar Point also boasts the world's largest roller coaster, the Magnum XL-200, which has a 201-foot drop and can reach speeds of 70 miles per hour. The focal point of the park, which turned 120 years old in 1989, is the grand old 400-room Breakers Hotel on the lakefront. It was built in 1905 and recently refurbished.

The growth of Cedar Point—due in part to its accessibility to the Ohio Turnpike and Lake Erie—has had a positive fallout for two other Greater Cleveland amusement parks, Geauga Lake Park and Sea World, which face each other from either side of Geauga Lake, 25 miles southeast of Cleveland. Like Cedar Point, they are near an Ohio Turnpike interchange and open from mid-May through mid-September.

Geauga Lake Park, which celebrated its 100th anniversary in 1988, draws one million visitors annually to more than 100 wet and dry rides on 265 acres, including the Raging Wolf Bobs, a wooden roller coaster on a 25-acre lot, and the 2.5-million-gallon wave pool, one of the biggest pools in the nation.

A 90-acre marine life park, Sea World, also attracts one million visitors each year to its animal shows, which feature "Shamu" the killer whale,

CEDAR POIN

Each year nearly one million people visit the Cleveland Metroparks Zoo and its 3,300 animals. Photo by Jim Baron. Courtesy, Image Finders, Inc.

bottlenose dolphins, Pacific black whales, walrus, sea lions, and otters. The most distinctive Sea World exhibit is the Penguin Encounter, an antarctic facility housing more than 120 polar birds. Sea World, one of four such parks in the nation, also features live entertainment and water-ski shows, an evening laser light show, and a fireworks display.

The 165-acre Cleveland Zoo, with more than 3,300 animals, also has its own aquatic exhibit. It is one of the largest and oldest zoos in America and is closed only on Christmas and New Year's Day. Operated by the Cleveland Metroparks System, the zoo is a 10-minute ride southwest of downtown.

Through an injection of sorely needed money and management, along with new animal exhibits, annual zoo attendance doubled in the 1980s—from less than 500,000 to almost one million.

Special zoo attractions include one of the most extensive bear collections in the United States, from grizzlies to polars; African animals such as waterfowl, zebras, giraffes, and antelopes; a showcase of 200 rare birds in their natural settings; a unique rhino/cheetah exhibit; an island with 75 rhesus monkeys; a seal and sea lion display; and a Children's Farm with native Ohio farm animals.

Educational shows and musicals are presented at the Sohio Amphitheatre, which has lawn seating for nearly 3,000. Components of the Cleveland Orchestra have performed at the amphitheatre. BP America provided a $240,000 grant for the amphitheatre's construction.

In 1990 the zoo will open its $20-million Tropical Rain Forest, the costliest project ever undertaken by the Metroparks and one of the largest of a rare number of man-made rain forests.

The 85,000-square-foot, climate-controlled natural habitat building, topped by a geodesic dome, will hold 500 species of animals from tropical rain forests from around the world. Among them: orangutans, American crocodiles, colobus monkeys, siamangs, gibbons, rare birds (including screamers

Above: These Macaroni penguins, residents of the Cleveland Metroparks Zoo, live outdoors in a large, open area when the weather is cold and inside the bird building in warm weather. Photo by Barbara Durham

Left: A peacock flaunts its beautiful plumage at the Cleveland Metroparks Zoo. Photo by Barbara Durham

and tourocos), many rare or endangered salamanders, frogs and toads, and tree kangaroos.

"The combination of rare animals, exotic flora, rolling topography, and various educational and entertainment activities make the Cleveland Zoo one of the best in the nation," says Donald Kuenzer, the zoo's general curator.

Apart from amusement parks and the zoo, Northeast Ohio has innumerable outdoor recreational opportunities. The most accessible is the Metroparks system, which is within a 10-minute drive of virtually every Greater Cleveland resident.

Within the 18,000 acres of unspoiled Metroparks woodlands are biking, hiking, and jogging trails; golf courses; streams; swimming holes; boating and picnic areas; ball fields; sledding areas; boat rental and launching facilities; ice skating; ice fishing ponds; snowmobiling and cross-country skiing trails; sledding and tobogganing hills; and downhill ski slopes.

Above: The beautiful colors of fall are enjoyed by visitors to the Cleveland Metroparks System's 18,000 acres of unspoiled woodlands. Photo by Barbara Durham

Top, right: A hiker experiences the tranquility of late fall in the Cleveland Metroparks. Photo by Barbara Durham

The Metroparks, supported by fees and real-estate tax levies, are patrolled round-the-clock by specially trained deputy rangers. Wildlife preservation and education are stressed at the system's four public nature centers.

Park naturalists regularly conduct hikes, bird walks, backpacking demonstrations, forest adventure walks for children, and talks on nature photography. Popular educational programs also are conducted at the Schuele Planetarium at the Huntington Reservation in Bay Village and its nearby Lake Erie Nature and Science Center.

The Metroparks system is known as the Emerald Necklace because its 12 reservations form a green ring around Cuyahoga County. With only a few detours, one can drive from the far western suburbs to the far eastern

One of the many special programs hosted by the Cleveland Metroparks is Fall Fest, which features a camp-out. Photo by Barbara Durham

suburbs on more than 100 miles of Metroparks roadways.

Each reservation has a unique beauty. In the Rocky River Reservation on the West Side, the narrow Rocky River winds north from Strongsville to Lake Erie beneath steep shale cliffs and forests thick with white-tailed deer.

In the far eastern suburbs of Greater Cleveland, the Sunset Wildlife Preserve in the North Chagrin Reservation has evolved into a habitat for local wildlife with a two-acre marsh and pond for migrating birds. Children are fascinated by the turn-of-the-century Squire's Castle, erected as a gate house for an estate with locally quarried stone.

Among the most romantic settings in Greater Cleveland is the meandering maple- and oak-lined Chagrin River Road, stretching south from the North Chagrin Reservation through scenic Gates Mills and Hunting Valley astride the Chagrin River, where the autumn fox hunt formerly took place.

Along the many miles of neat, black-shuttered houses and rolling estates in the Chagrin Valley, horseback riders are as commonplace as station wagons and pickup trucks. Chagrin River Road runs past the Polo Field in the Metroparks' South Chagrin Reservation where Cleveland Polo Club teams compete from May through September against clubs from other major cities.

The prestigious Hunter-Jumper Classic, part of a 30-city nationally televised tour, is held each July at the Metroparks polo field. The highlight of the four-day event is the oldest equestrian Grand Prix in America, in which premier riders compete for local and national prize money.

Hinckley Reservation, at the southern tip of the Emerald Necklace on the border of Medina County, encloses 90-acre Ledge Lake. Each March 15 thousands of visitors show up at the Hinckley Reservation for the annual return of buzzards from the South.

The Metroparks—established in 1917 as Ohio's first metropolitan park district—were designed in part by naturalist and park planner Frederick Law Olmsted, who designed Manhattan's Central Park. The Metroparks System estimates that 24 million visits are made to its parks and zoo each year. Directly east of Cuyahoga County, the Lake County Metroparks encompass another 4,000 acres, attracting 800,000 park visits a year.

As popular as the Metroparks are, they are not Greater Cleveland's only nature preserve. Holden Arboretum, 10 miles east of the Cleveland Metroparks' North Chagrin Reservation in Lake and Geauga counties, is a unique 3,100-acre refuge of woodlands, display gardens, ponds, fields, and ravines.

Holden, the nation's largest arboretum, blooms with seasonal flora. In the spring, when sap pours from the thick stands of sugar maples, the Arboretum calls on a local Amish family to demonstrate to schoolchildren how maple syrup is distilled in the "Sugarbush."

Shortly after the sap stops running and the snow melts, crab apples and lilacs burst into full life at Holden. In early summer, rhododendrons and azaleas cover the grounds. The arboretum has more than 20 miles of trails—for short walks and lengthy hikes—that are particularly inviting in October, when the foliage turns brilliant orange, red, and yellow.

The nonprofit arboretum, dedicated "to the preservation and collection of woody plants for scientific and educational purposes," is operated through contributions and dues. It houses a horticulture reference library. So seriously does the arboretum take its commitment to preserve the environment that, while it provides picnic areas, it bans radios and sports playing on the grounds.

A short drive south of Holden Arboretum, near Burton in Geauga County, is Punderson State Park, whose large Tudor manor house (once a private residence) encloses 31 guest rooms overlooking a natural lake.

The highlight of the Hunter-Jumper Classic is the crowing of the Grand Prix Champion. Photo by Jennie Jones

Other park amenities include an 18-hole golf course, lighted tennis courts, cross-country skiing and snowmobiling trails, and tobogganing slopes. Punderson Lake is filled with small boats in the summer and ice fishermen in winter.

Twenty miles southwest of Punderson, the Cuyahoga National Recreation Area begins its long stretch from just south of Cleveland to north of Akron. The 33,000-acre recreation area was carved out in 1974 to preserve one of the last remaining unspoiled suburban green belts in America.

The Cuyahoga River snakes through the recreation area—past Dover Lake Park and its summer waterslides, Brandywine Ski Center and the Boston Mills Ski Resort, the 37-bed American Youth Hostel Stanford House, miles of winding trails and steep rock ledges in Virginia Kendall Park, Blossom Music Center, and the restored early nineteenth-century Hale Farm and Village.

Each year 7 million people visit the 33,000-acre Cuyahoga Valley National Recreation Area. Photo by Barbara Durham

Quaint towns with preserved century homes and decidedly English pastoral names—Bath, Peninsula, and Richfield—lie on the edge of the Cuyahoga Valley National Recreation Area. Richfield is home to the 20,500-seat Coliseum, where the Cleveland Cavaliers play their National Basketball Association home games. Greater Cleveland's contribution to indoor soccer, the Cleveland Crunch (which arose in place of the late Cleveland Force of the Major Indoor Soccer League), also plans to play its home games at the Coliseum.

Some 7 million people visit the recreation area annually, driving along the Cuyahoga and what remains of the Ohio Canal locks and towpath. Six regional parks within the recreation area are operated by the Metro Parks serving Summit County and the Cleveland Metroparks.

The Cuyahoga Valley National Recreation Area promotes organized activities, including a May Day Celebration, a 10-kilometer run in June, the Cuyahoga Valley Festival (a national folk music festival in September), an art and photo competition of valley sites in October, and a Friday-evening Lyceum speakers' series in January, February, and March at the Happy Days Visitors Center.

Also within the recreation area, the old Jaite Paper Mill is being converted into a 180,000-square-foot horseshoe palladium, with 60 indoor and outdoor pitching courts and a lounge and restaurant. When finished, it will include exhibits of the history and process of paper making.

The National Park Service and a private horsemen's group are working to expand existing bridle trails at Virginia Kendall Park and converting an old barn into an equestrian center.

Forests, ponds, streams, and marshes within the valley provide breeding grounds for wildlife. Rangers conduct bird-watching workshops, bird

A member of the Mask Theatre Workshop is shown during a performance at the Cuyahoga Valley Festival. Photo by Barbara Durham

walks, seasonal wildflower tours, and talks on prehistoric Indians of Northeast Ohio.

Popular attractions within the valley include the Inn at Brandywine Falls, a bed-and-breakfast with facilities for 12 guests, leased by the Park Service to private operators. The inn, built in 1846, is open year-round. Near the inn is the Brandywine Falls, one of the most scenic spots in the valley. Waterpower generated by the falls ran grist and woolen mills in the early nineteenth century.

Perhaps the favorite attraction within the Recreation Area is the nonprofit Cuyahoga Valley Railroad, a restored steam railroad that operates between mid-June and late October. It is the only regularly scheduled

The Cuyahoga Valley Festival is held each September at the Cuyahoga Valley National Recreation Area. Here a child has her face painted by a festival participant. Photo by Barbara Durham

steam-powered train running between two major metropolitan areas.

The 52-mile round trip begins at the north edge of the Cuyahoga Valley Recreation Area. After stopping at Hale Farm and Village, it terminates in Akron at Quaker Square, an old cereal factory converted into retail outlets, restaurants, and a hotel.

Rolling stock of the Cuyahoga Valley Line includes coaches from the Nickel Plate, Erie, and New York Central built between 1914 and 1926. The belching, chugging, and clanging steam engine, manufactured in 1918, also pulls a restored Pullman car, the "Mt. Baxter," which serves as the more expensive first-class service and does extra duty for private parties.

The beauty of the Cuyahoga Valley National Recreation Area has been captured in a national exhibit of photographs, first shown at the Akron Art Museum, by celebrated nature photographer Robert Glenn Ketchum.

Apart from the Cuyahoga and other major recreational areas, there is plenty more for any outdoorsman within an hour's drive of most of Greater Cleveland, including canoeing in Portage County on the east branch of the Cuyahoga River over the winding Hiram Rapids, and fishing on nearby La Due Reservoir in Geauga County. With its sparkling blue water edged by tall pines and spruce, La Due could be mistaken for a lake in the Rockies.

In the 300-acre Shaker Lakes Regional Nature Center in Shaker Heights, one of the few nature preserves operated by an American suburb, hikers can explore eight miles of trails. Not far from University Circle, the City of Cleveland Greenhouse houses botanical gardens and a talking garden for the blind with plants identified in Braille.

As much as Greater Clevelanders flock to their parks, they also jam festivals and county fairs. Among the most popular are the early summer Rib Burn-Off at the Cuyahoga County Fairgrounds and the Geauga County Fair in Burton over Labor Day weekend. Standing-room-only school and volunteer fire department pancake breakfasts in early spring when the maple sap runs are a longtime tradition in Geauga County.

From mid-June through late October the restored steam Cuyahoga Valley Railway provides a 52-mile tour through the Cuyahoga Valley National Recreation Area. Photo by Barbara Durham

Greater Cleveland's many parks and outdoor attractions have boosted widespread interest in personal fitness, particularly jogging. No one has been more responsible for this than Jess Bell, president and chief executive officer of Bonne Bell, the Greater Cleveland-based cosmetics manufacturer.

Bell credits his turning to running in the early 1970s in the Cleveland Metroparks' Rocky River Reservation with giving him a new lease on life, as well as reinvigorating his marriage and his company. As a consequence, Bell built a two-mile outdoor cinder jogging track at his cosmetics plant in suburban Westlake.

Since 1975 Bonne Bell also has sponsored 10-kilometer women's races throughout the United States and foreign countries, including New Zealand, Australia, South Africa, Sweden, England, and Canada. Each fall the company promotes a local fitness weekend that includes an 7.34-mile Open Run from Bonne Bell executive offices in Lakewood to the company plant in Westlake, a five-kilometer race, and a kids' race.

Bell, who also is an accomplished mountain climber, has finished numerous marathons along with 50- and 60-mile ultras. But his favorite pastime is running in the Metroparks where he logs between 40 and 60 miles a week, including two hours each Saturday and Sunday with his wife, Julie.

Each Wednesday at 6:45 A.M., no matter the weather, Bell is joined by various employees, suppliers, and friends for an hour run, starting at a Metroparks entrance near his office. Everyone is invited back to company headquarters for breakfast. "I never make an appointment before 9 A.M.

on Wednesday," says Bell. "The midweek run creates camaraderie." Among those who have participated in the Wednesday run are U.S. Olympic skier Betsy Frazier Youngman, former track star Jim Ryun, marathoner Frank Shorter, and Cleveland Browns star wide receiver Brian Brennan.

"I've run all over the world, but the Metroparks are second to none," says Bell. "You can enter the Rocky River Reservation and, without leaving, run 60 miles over trails, hills, woods, and roads. What is more, the Metroparks may be the safest place anywhere to run." Along with the Bonne Bell fitness runs, other popular running events include the annual May marathon and 10,000-meter races, which together draw 12,500 runners. They are sponsored by Revco, the national drugstore chain headquartered in Twinsburg between Cleveland and Akron.

Both races start simultaneously in front of Cleveland State University. The marathon zigzags through the western suburbs while the 10K twists through downtown. The Blossom Time Run, a 5.25-mile race through the countryside near Chagrin Falls on Memorial Day weekend, is attracting more and more runners every year.

Despite a fickle climate and lack of mountainous terrain, skiing also continues to grow in Greater Cleveland. The three ski areas—Brandywine and Boston Mills in the Cuyahoga Valley Recreation Area, and Alpine Valley in Geauga County—offer clinics, lessons, and night skiing.

Only a short drive east of Cleveland are such popular ski resorts as Peek 'n Peak and Holiday Valley in western New York and Seven Springs in Pennsylvania.

When the skiing shuts down—usually from mid-March through mid-December—most of Northeast Ohio's 225 public and 40 private golf courses come alive. According to the National Golf Foundation, the state of Ohio ranks sixth in the country in the number of courses and golfers.

"Greater Clevelanders are wild about golf, and our courses can compete in quality with any in America," says Al Mulberry, executive director of the Northern Ohio Golf Association, which represents private clubs in the area. "And I don't flinch when saying it."

In recent years a number of professional tournaments, including the

Both amateurs and pros can enjoy Northeast Ohio's 225 public and 40 private golf courses. Courtesy, Tony Stone Worldwide

REVCO
START
CLAIROL

Ameritech Seniors, have been held at the Canterbury Golf Club in Shaker Heights. Along with Firestone in Akron, where the World Series of Golf has been played since 1962, Canterbury regularly shows up on the *Golf Digest* list of the top 100 courses in America.

Cleveland has a legendary role in golf. In 1898 Coburn Haskell, who lived near the old Cleveland Golf Club in Bratenahl, one of the first golf courses in the Midwest, put a rubber-wound core inside a golf ball, an idea he got from baseball.

With help from the B.F. Goodrich Company, Haskell invented the modern golf ball. The local PGA sponsors the annual Mitchell-Haskell Trophy, named for Haskell and Joe Mitchell, an early club pro who helped test the new ball, which revolutionized golf.

Tennis is almost as popular as golf. The number of public courts is increasing, as is the number of year-round affordable tennis clubs. Among the premier private tennis clubs are the Cleveland Racquet Club and Cleveland Skating Club, which have both indoor and outdoor courts.

Each July the Northeastern Ohio Tennis Patrons sponsor the National Amateur Hardcourt Tennis Championships, limited to 64 men and 64 women. Winners of this prestigious event generally move up to the professional circuit.

"Cleveland is one of America's foremost tennis cities," says Robert Malaga, a fund-raiser for the Cleveland State University athletic department and head of the Greater Cleveland Tennis Association. "Tennis here is a tradition." Beyond the Hardcourt Championships, upwards of 30 club and public tournaments are held annually, including the Ohio Intercollegiate Tennis Championships—men's singles and doubles—and the *Plain Dealer* Junior Championships, which attract hundreds of teenagers in singles and doubles competition. The Greater Cleveland Tennis Association owns and maintains the 5,000-seat Harold Clark Tennis Center along Lake Erie on the edge of downtown, which hosts major tennis events. The courts may be moved to Cleveland State University, which is enlarging its sports facilities.

Tennis and golf are fashionable pastimes in Greater Cleveland, but it is hard to top softball for crowd fervor and overall participation. More than 40,000 Greater Clevelanders play on 3,000 men's, women's, coed, and youth softball teams in church, company, and community leagues. The number of specialty leagues seems limitless, such as the one for players 60 years and older in suburban Solon.

Over the past two decades Greater Cleveland has hosted nearly 15 na-

Facing page: Greater Cleveland running enthusiasts can enter the annual Revco marathon and 10K races held in May. Photo by Roger Mastroianni

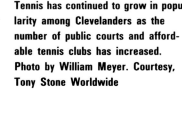

Tennis has continued to grow in popularity among Clevelanders as the number of public courts and affordable tennis clubs has increased. Photo by William Meyer. Courtesy, Tony Stone Worldwide

Cleveland has been called "the softball capital of the world." More than 40,000 people play on men's, women's, coed, and youth softball teams. Courtesy, Luce Photography, Inc.

tional major division softball tournaments. Cleveland's Pyramid Cafe won the Men's Major National Slow Pitch Tournament in the late 1970s, while Non-Ferrous Metals of suburban Euclid won it in 1985.

As *Time, People,* and *Sports Illustrated* have pointed out, the best softball players in the world compete for Steele's Sports Company, a softball and baseball equipment manufacturer and distributor, in Grafton, 25 miles southwest of downtown Cleveland.

Steele's Silver Bullets, organized in 1978, begin barnstorming the nation in February and do not finish until late September. The 18-man roster is rotated so that no more than 12 players are traveling at one time. A number of the Steele players are ex-major leaguers.

Coor's Light sponsors the Men of Steele, who average six feet four inches and a beefy 250 pounds. Players are considered "consultants" and are paid to endorse products and conduct softball clinics. The premier softball slugger, Clevelander Mike Macenko, set the world record by smashing an unbelievable 844 home runs in 1987 and another 830 in 1988.

Steele's in 1988 traveled more than 100,000 miles to 44 states and Canada and, because of the summer drought, played a record 120 days in a row, finishing the season with another incredible world record of 365-19-2, with 6,331 home runs and a team batting average of .682. The 1989 record was just as spectacular.

In winning the restricted 16-team United States Slow Pitch Association World Series of Softball Tournament in 1988, the Silver Bullets became the first team in slow-pitch softball to win all five major tournaments.

So popular are the Silver Bullets that 37,000 people once came to Seattle's Kingdome to see their hitting exhibition. They increasingly are hired to warm up major league teams, including the Cleveland Indians.

But it is the second weekend in June, at State Road Park in suburban Parma, that the Men of Steele anticipate each year as their homecoming. That is reserved for the 32-team Coor's Light Steele's Sports Invitational, which draws more than 40,000 fans over three days.

"I moved the team to Greater Cleveland because it's the softball capital of the world," says Steele's co-owner Dave Neale. "Our team is a good way of advertising our products."

In numbers alone, only bowling rivals softball in Greater Cleveland. According to the Bowling Proprietors of America, Ohio's 19th Congressional District, which rings the Cuyahoga County suburbs from east to west, has more bowling alleys than any other Congressional district in America. The biggest of these is the Stardust Lanes, with 78 alleys, in Brook Park near Hopkins Airport.

Cleveland has had few major college sports teams, but Cleveland State University has emerged as a top basketball school. In 1987 CSU went to the NCAA "final 16" play-offs before losing to the U.S. Naval Academy. Each year the university also hosts NCAA swimming competitions at its Olympic-size natatorium. Cleveland's Jesuit-run John Carroll University never shuns the opportunity to point out that its famous alumnus, Miami Dolphins Coach Don Shula, played football there.

A member of the Cleveland Sport Parachuting Club anticipates a safe landing at Parkman Field in Geauga County. Photo by Barbara Durham

High school sports also are very competitive. Several local scholastic football teams rank among the top in the United States. Throughout the 1980s St. Edward High School in Lakewood was ranked as the top scholastic wrestling team in America.

Of course, it is Cleveland professional sports—Indians, Cavaliers, and Browns—that elicit the loyalty and attract such huge, passionate crowds.

The Cleveland Indians, one of three charter teams in the American League, struggled through the 1960s, 1970s, and early 1980s, both on the field and in attendance. In late 1986, however, they were purchased by Richard E. Jacobs, the shopping center developer who built the Galleria at Erieview and is building the city's two tallest buildings, the Society Tower and Ameritrust Tower on Public Square.

Jacobs has made a commitment not only to keep the Indians in Cleveland, but to make them competitive again. More than one million fans filed through the turnstiles each season in the late 1980s, something that had not happened since the glory days of Indians baseball in the early 1950s.

In the late 1980s more than one million fans attended the Cleveland Indians games each season. Photo by Roger Mastroianni

Facing page, top: Located on the shores of Lake Erie, Cleveland Municipal Stadium, which seats 80,000 people, is one of the largest stadiums in professional sports. Photo by Richard L. Prochaska, Jr. Courtesy, Image Finders, Inc.

Facing page, bottom left: This young fan may someday play on a high school football team. Many Northeast Ohio high school football teams rank among the best nationwide. Photo by Don Snyder

Facing page, bottom right: From 1985 through 1987 quarterback Bernie Kosar led the Cleveland Browns through three straight AFC Central Division titles and two consecutive AFC championship games. Photo by Roger Mastroianni

The turnaround has been engineered in part by Hank Peters, whom Jacobs hired from Baltimore, where he had put the Orioles into two World Series. The new president and chief operating officer has already strengthened the Tribe's farm system, where such standouts as slugging outfielder Cory Snyder, pitchers Greg Swindell and John Farrell, and catcher Andy Allanson had been harvested.

The Indians now have 24 full-time scouts, as many as any club in the major leagues, and six minor-league teams, each with a three-man coaching staff and fielding and hitting instructors. Only two teams in professional baseball have more minor league affiliates.

"I wanted the joy and achievement in a field other than real estate and bought the team to make sure it stays and plays in Cleveland," says Richard Jacobs. "We're working at making the Indians a contender that Clevelanders will be proud to root for."

One reason for the new financial success of the Indians is the size of crowds they can attract in Cleveland Municipal Stadium, which seats 80,000 and is one of the largest stadiums in professional sports.

A midsummer series against the New York Yankees can bring in almost a quarter-million people. If a key civic proposal comes to fruition, Cleveland someday will have a modern baseball stadium capable of seating expansion for football.

Among the firms involved in the design of the proposed structure is Cleveland-based Osborn Engineering, which designed the Cleveland Municipal Stadium in the early 1930s and, a half-century later, was called upon to design the well-publicized lighting for Wrigley Field in Chicago, the last major-league stadium to install lights.

Cleveland Municipal Stadium is operated by Art Modell, principal owner of the Cleveland Browns, under a contract with the City of Cleveland. In 1987 the *Los Angeles Times* noted that "according to the individuals who run the clubs, the NFL's most respected owner is Art Modell."

The Browns, one of the top teams in professional football, have galvanized Cleveland sports fans for more than 40 years. Statistics alone express why every fall, virtually all sports talk centers enthusiastically on the Browns. They have won more division or conference titles than any other team in NFL history. Through 1988 the Browns had made the play-offs 19 of their 39 years in the league.

"The Cleveland Browns are one of the most important institutions in the city," says Art Modell, who bought the team in 1961. "They affect the spirit of the community. The Browns are our number-one social common denominator. Where else can people from different walks of life find

Marlboro
BROWNS

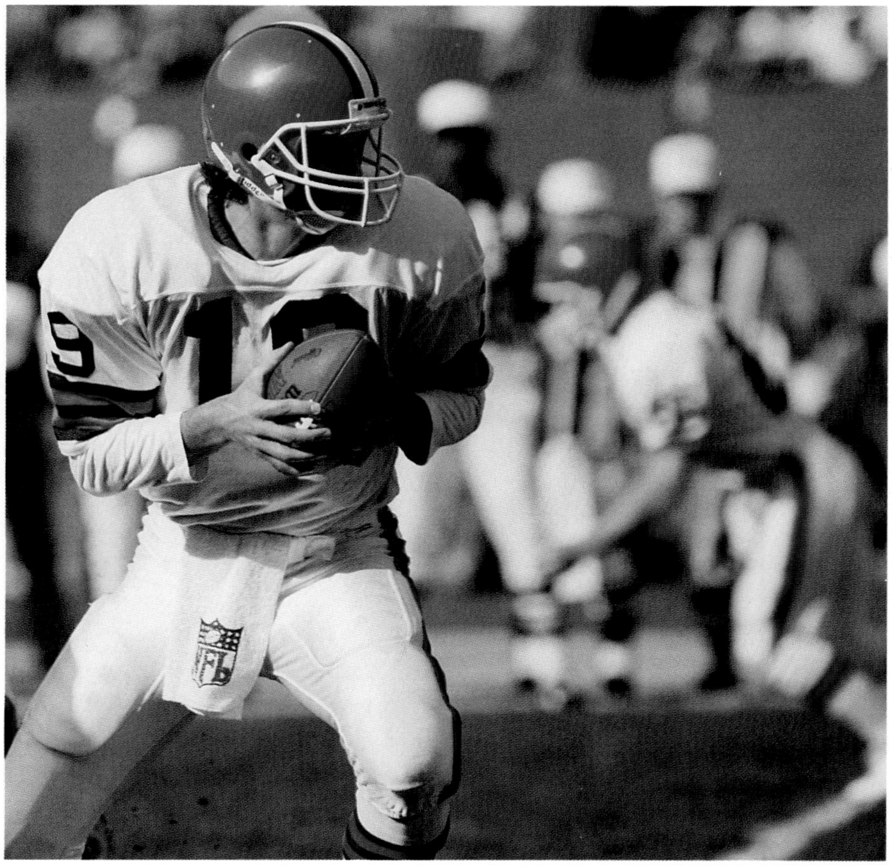
NFL

themselves sitting next to each other with a common rooting interest? The Browns help local commerce, but even more important, they instill civic pride, spirit, and togetherness into the town."

The Browns have placed 12 players in the National Football League Hall of Fame in Canton, the birthplace of professional football, only 50 miles south of Cleveland along Interstate 77.

The team is built around the electrifying young quarterback, Bernie Kosar, northern Ohio's number-one sports hero. Kosar first suited up for the Browns in 1985 at age 21, making him the youngest starting quarterback in the National Football League.

Kosar broke most passing records at the University of Miami, where he was an All-American and graduated with a double major after playing only two years and with two years of eligibility remaining. Moreover, he already holds many Browns and NFL passing records.

From 1985 through 1987 he led the Browns to three straight AFC Central Division titles and two consecutive AFC championship games through pinpoint passing with a sidearm release. Kosar also is much sought after on the speaking circuit and 64 charity drives. He is so popular that when he and several teammates appeared locally with then-Vice-President George Bush during the 1988 presidential campaign, the *Plain Dealer* bannered the story, "Bush Gets Kosar on His Team in Akron."

Yet Kosar is not the town's only superstar. The Cleveland Cavaliers of the National Basketball Association has a Mutt-and-Jeff combination that also is creating its own legends: Brad Daugherty, a seven-foot-one center from the University of North Carolina, and Mark Price, a point guard playmaker from Georgia Tech, who is only six-foot-one and 170 pounds.

Daugherty, the first player chosen in the 1986 draft, was selected for the NBA All-Star Game in only his second year in the NBA, while Price holds one of the best three-point field goal shooting percentages in NBA history.

It is only in the late 1980s, with a young team built around Daugherty, Price, shooting guard Ron Harper, and forward Larry Nance, that the Cavs have truly excelled. Under the ownership of brothers Gordon Gund and George Gund III, attendance increased 214 percent between 1983 and 1988. After winning 57 games in the regular 1989 season before record crowds, the Cavs went to the NBA playoffs.

The Gund brothers, whose late father, George Gund, Jr., was the longtime president of Cleveland Trust Bank, predecessor of Ameritrust, purchased the Coliseum in Richfield in 1981, two years before buying the Cavs. The Gunds blazed a sports trail by hiring both a black vice-president/general manager, Wayne Embry, and black coach, Lenny Wilkens.

Baseball, basketball, and football are not the only professional sports competing for fans.

Greater Clevelanders wage more than a total of one million dollars daily during daytime thoroughbred racing at Thistledown in North Randall (a small suburb southeast of Cleveland) and daytime and evening harness racing at Northfield Park in suburban Northfield between Cleveland and Akron. Thistledown stays open from late March until mid-December, while Northfield is open year-round.

Greater Clevelanders enjoy daytime thoroughbred racing at Thistledown in North Randall. The facility is open from late March until mid-December. Photo by Barbara Durham

Ever since it was built in 1925, Thistledown has had an interesting history. A fire partially destroyed the track during World War II, but it was rebuilt in 1953. Thistledown, which is owned by Edward J. DeBartolo of Youngstown (the nation's largest shopping center developer), has undergone a $28-million face-lift. Its major race, the $250,000 Ohio Derby in June, attracts top three-year-olds and is televised by ESPN.

Harness racing does not take a back seat to the thoroughbreds. More trotters and pacers are bred in Ohio than in any other state; 77 of the 88 county fairs host harness racing. The major race at Northfield Park is the $100,000 Battle of Lake Erie for four- and five-year-old pacers in early June. Northfield also is a host track for the prestigious Grand Circuit and Breeders' Crown races.

In a no less competitive sport, Cleveland has become a training center for top prizefighters. Don King, the world's leading professional fight promoter (with some 250 fights to his credit through the decade), grew up in Cleveland. He owns a 179-acre farm east of the city in rural Ashtabula County, complete with a mansion for him and his wife, Henri, and separate houses for his grown son and daughter.

Only a few miles beyond the elaborate compound is the ultramodern, 250-acre Don King Training Camp, where many of the world's top fighters regularly train and visit. They include heavyweight champion Mike Tyson, often seen with King in Cleveland; WBC-WBA lightweight champion Julio Cesar Chavez; and former lightweight champion Roberto Duran.

King is planning to develop another 1,600 acres nearby into a year-round family recreation center, which may include an outside arena for prizefights, a swim club, and a picnic area.

Right: The Air Force Thunderbirds perform at the Cleveland National Air Show. Held on Labor Day weekend, the show draws more than 250,000 people. Photo by Don Snyder

Below: Burke Lakefront Airport is the site of the Cleveland National Air Show, the nation's oldest air show. Courtesy, Luce Photography, Inc.

Cleveland's two biggest outdoor spectacles are held at Burke Lakefront Airport downtown. The larger of these, the Cleveland National Air Show, is the oldest air show in the nation. Begun in 1929 as the National Air Races, it has continued with a hiatus only during World War II and during the early 1950s.

The show is eclectic, and includes fliers from foreign countries, vintage airplanes (the Warbirds), and, on alternative years, the U.S. Navy Blue Angels or the U.S. Air Force Thunderbirds. Held on Labor Day weekend, it draws from 250,000 to 300,000 spectators. Because of its scope and historical significance, it is considered among the most prestigious air shows in the nation.

"Wing walker John Kazian always tells us, 'For an air show performer to be invited to Cleveland is like a musician playing Carnegie Hall,'" declares Jim Foster, assistant director of the show.

The newest extravaganza at Burke Lakefront Airport is the Budweiser Cleveland Grand Prix. Indy Car Grand Prix, Inc., a subsidiary of Penske Corporation, which is headed by international race car impresario Roger Penske, promotes the Grand Prix.

Upwards of 100,000 people show up each Fourth of July weekend for three days of auto racing, climaxing with the 188-mile Cart-PPG Indy Car World Series, when Burke is converted into a hairpin speedway. So popular are the Cleveland Grand Prix and the preliminary support races that only the Indianapolis 500 and three other CART-PPG World Series events surpass it in attendance.

Penske also enters his own Indy Car driving team in the Grand Prix, which has been composed of Indianapolis 500 winners Danny Sullivan and Rick Mears.

"The Cleveland Grand Prix is one of the best races in the nation," says Penske, who grew up in Shaker Heights. "Besides, it's an annual homecoming."

Another promising sports endeavor for Greater Cleveland is the Ohio Sports Festival State Games, which were held for the first time in the summer of 1989. The competition is part of the fastest growing amateur sports movement in the United States, with a long-range goal of having all 50 states sponsor games and send winners to a national championship.

In the Ohio finals in Cleveland, some 4,000 individual and team winners—from regional contests in Akron, Toledo, Cincinnati, and Columbus—competed in 10 sports: basketball, softball, soccer, cycling, swimming, wrestling, a five-mile run, track and field, gymnastics, and bowling. Categories were established for different age groups, beginning with youngsters. The opening and closing ceremonies, held at Finney Stadium at Baldwin-Wallace College in Berea, included an Olympic-like parade of athletes, parachutists descending into the stadium with American and Ohio state flags, and appearances by Olympic medal-winners from Ohio, including Cleveland's own Harrison Dillard.

The games took two years to plan because of Ohio's large population," says Buffy Filippell, who heads a search firm servicing sports organizations and who first suggested the games for Cleveland, "but it is another

Above: Each Fourth of July weekend Burke Lakefront Airport plays host to the Budweiser Cleveland Grand Prix, a 188-mile Cart-PPG Indy car race. Photo by Roger Mastroianni

Right: More than 100,000 people attend the three days of auto racing at the Budweiser Cleveland Grand Prix. Photo by Roger Mastroianni

opportunity for the city to demonstrate how enthusiastically it supports amateur athletics and how effectively it can organize major sporting events."

"By the mid-1990s we hope to have 25,000 athletes compete statewide and possibly 10,000 in the finals," says Bob Gries, chairman of the festival's steering committee. Gries also is an ultramarathon runner, mountain climber, venture capitalist, and minority-share owner of the Cleveland Browns.

Six Greater Cleveland and Ohio institutions paid upwards of $75,000 each to serve as official sponsors of the State Games: the Ohio Lottery, the Ohio Department of Development, Society Bank, Stouffer's/Nestlé Enterprises, Inc., University Hospitals, and BP America.

"This didn't come out of their philanthropy budgets," Gries points out. "It was a marketing cost. They saw the tremendous opportunity such sports sponsorship would have in helping themselves, and hence the economy and growth of Northeast Ohio. Greater Cleveland business today is more astute than ever."

Boaters enjoy a beautiful sunset on Lake Erie at the entrance to the Cleveland Harbor. Photo by Roger Mastroianni

960243 REV-E3

CHAPTER 6

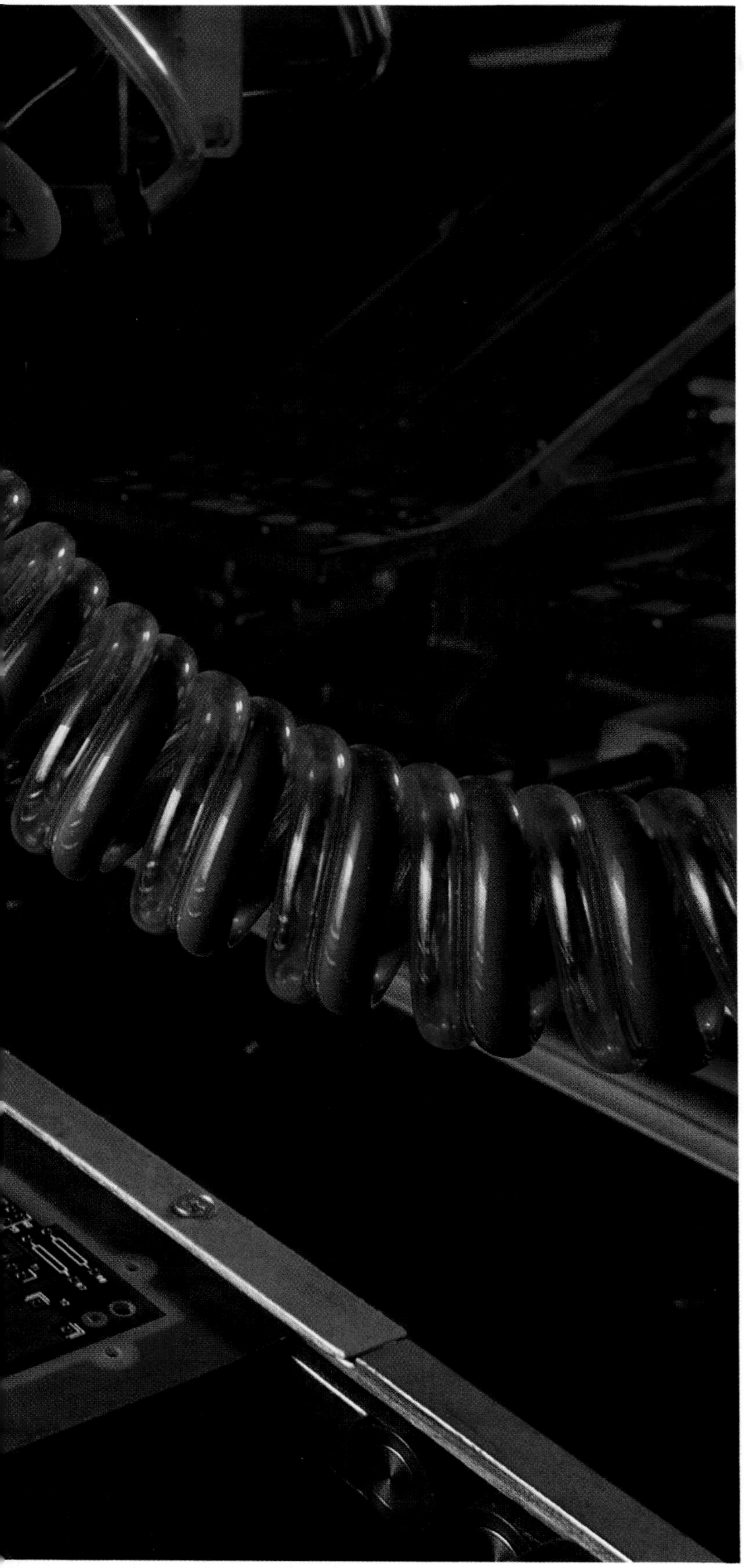

Rising to The Challenge

During the 1990s a new $500-million headquarters complex for Figgie International, one of the fastest growing conglomerates in America, will rise on 630 acres of fallow land owned by the City of Cleveland in suburban Warrensville Township on the eastern end of Cuyahoga County.

The full complex, known as Chagrin Highlands, will include a high-end retail mall and two 250-room luxury hotels. Buildings will be grouped around ponds, trees, hills, and wooded vistas with jogging trails and exercise stations.

Securing such a huge corporate headquarters is important to Cleveland. In the mid-1980s Figgie International, whose sales exceed one billion dollars annually, moved south from its headquarters in suburban Willoughby. The departure of this company—with its more than 16,000 employees and 40 divisions and subsidiaries worldwide—meant a substantial loss, financially and emotionally.

The return of Figgie International, made possible with the inducement of land and other considerations, will be completed by the first decade of the next century. It will do more than just reverse the loss. It will mean an economic impact of $1.7 billion per year on Greater Cleveland and a contribution of more than $15 million annually in local payroll and real-estate taxes.

Chagrin Highlands should produce 1,300 construction jobs and attract 5,000 permanent employees in the 1990s, with upwards of triple that 15 years beyond. What is more, Figgie International has pledged to involve minority business enterprises in the construction phase.

The Allen-Bradley programmable controller division assembly line is one of the area's expanding high-tech employers. Photo by Don Snyder

The master planner for the project is the firm of Wallace Roberts & Todd of Philadelphia, designer of Baltimore's Inner Harbor and author of a master plan for the U.S. Capitol. Not only will the City of Cleveland retain majority ownership of the property, but the state has agreed to widen access routes and build a new interchange to nearby Interstate 271.

"We welcome this as a great economic opportunity for the area and the corporation and are very happy to return to our roots," says Harry Figgie, Jr., chairman and founder of the *Fortune* 500 conglomerate, whose products include sports equipment, fire sprinklers, electrical products, aerospace research, and defense electronics.

As immense as it is, the Figgie project is just one of innumerable developments—many fostered by working partnerships of private enterprise and governmental agencies—that are contributing mightily to the resurgence of the Greater Cleveland economy.

This business renaissance has been a godsend, because in the 1980s the Northeast Ohio economy suffered severely. Thousands of jobs—primarily in steelmaking and other heavy industries—were liquidated by global competition, outmoded technology, sagging productivity, and high labor costs.

The area, however, is well on its way to turning around. Upwards of one million people are employed in the four counties—Cuyahoga, Lake, Geauga, and Medina—comprising the Primary Metropolitan Statistical Area. This is 50,000 more than in the early 1980s.

The unemployment rate has dipped to 6 percent, roughly the same as the national average. Even more important, the job mix is approaching that of the nation as a whole. Roughly 20 percent of Greater Cleveland is employed in manufacturing, down from 25 percent in the mid-1980s and 39 percent in 1964.

At the same time, Greater Cleveland heavy manufacturing, including steel, is staging an astonishing comeback, abetted by new labor-management agreements, a soaring increase in worker productivity, a drop

The medical industry in Cleveland continues to grow, offering local students and professionals a variety of career possibilities. Photo by Barbara Durham

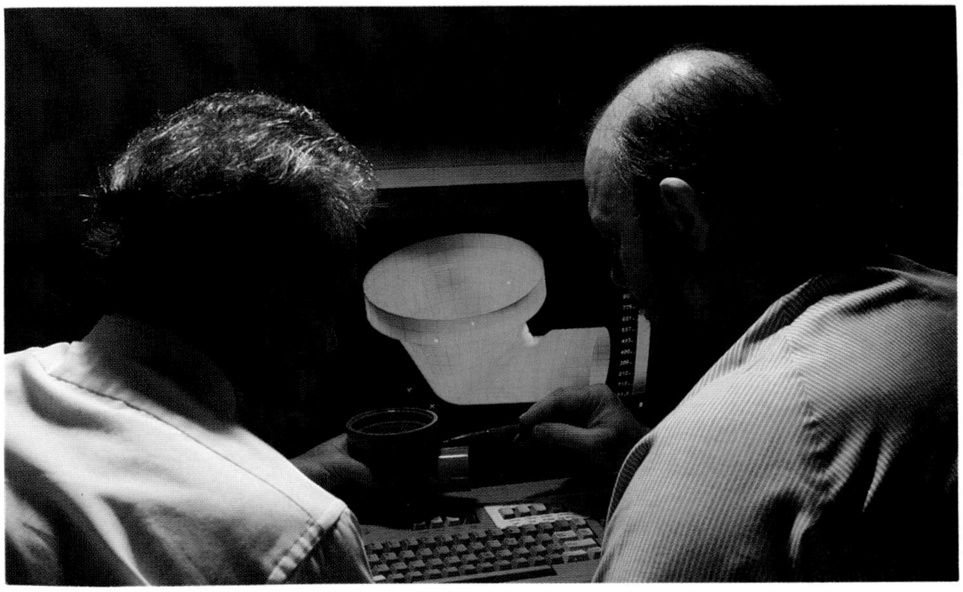

Structural dynamics research requires advanced computer technology at the B.F. Goodrich Research and Development Center in Brecksville. Photo by Don Snyder

in the dollar against foreign currencies, and sweeping technological advances.

The white-collar service economy continues to boom, particularly in law, accounting, and finance. Advanced high-end technology, largely in space, the biomedical field, and polymers, is creating whole new industries.

Health care is expanding so rapidly that it has become one of the area's leading employers. Almost one in 10 Northeast Ohio jobs is in the health-care industry—in hospitals, laboratories, and private clinics. In the 1980s the number employed in the health-care industry grew from 80,000 to 100,000, an increase of 25 percent. The Greater Cleveland and Akron health-care payroll is more than $2 billion a year.

A study by the Greater Cleveland Hospital Association concluded that the health-care industry attracts a vast amount of capital to the region. Much goes to such enormous medical institutions as University Hospitals and the Cleveland Clinic. The latter is the largest nongovernmental employer in the city of Cleveland, with 9,000 employees.

Another crucial economic asset is Greater Cleveland's proximity to the major markets of the East, Midwest, South, and Canada. Northeast Ohio, including Akron, is the 12th-largest market in the nation. Within 500 miles are 12 of the top 20 U.S. markets and 45 percent of the nation's households, along with 40 percent of all U.S. business and 80 percent of the top 500 industrial corporate headquarters.

Greater Cleveland ranks among the top five cities—behind only New York and Chicago—in the number of *Fortune* 500 industrial corporate headquarters. The area is also home to North American headquarters of innumerable European and other foreign multinationals.

Yet it is not just big business that is regenerating the economy. A new entrepreneurial spirit is sweeping across the region, powered by sizable venture capital funds that encourage the creation of advanced technology firms.

Cleveland, with its large population and rich industrial base, boasts a strong labor force which can meet the demands of any job. Photo by Roger Mastroianni

"Northeast Ohio's economic base is larger than that of all but a few of the nations of the world," says William H. Bryant, president of the Greater Cleveland Growth Association, the largest metropolitan chamber of commerce in the nation with some 9,000 member firms.

"Our future is exciting because of Cleveland's proximity to Lake Erie and its unlimited water, expertise of management and white-collar services, skilled labor, excellent higher education institutions, and the growing number of advanced technology firms. The free-trade agreement with Canada, only 50 miles across Lake Erie, makes us even more of a decision-making center for North America."

The diversity of the comeback is testimony to the ability of the Greater Cleveland economy to meet global changes and not only to survive but to prevail.

The M.A. Hanna Company illustrates this story of change. For more than a century the company, founded by industrialist Marcus A. Hanna, was one of Cleveland's preeminent iron-ore and shipping firms. When the Lake Erie shipping and mining business began drying up, Hanna largely shifted out of mining and shipping into polymers and specialty chemicals. "To survive we had to make severe changes," says Hanna chairman Martin D. "Skip" Walker. From 1986 through 1988 Hanna made key acquisitions, and its sales mushroomed from $130 million to well over one billion dollars. Hanna had the fastest growth of any company in the 1988 *Fortune* 500. In 1989 *Crain's Cleveland Business,* a highly respected weekly business newspaper, presented Walker and Hanna with its annual Award for Business Excellence.

In many ways, this adaptability and achievement parallels the same gritty determination that made Cleveland the center of America's industrial growth a century ago. The effort began in earnest in the mid-nineteenth century and struggled through the crippling Depression, only to experience deep vicissitudes through the 1980s.

The early days of the city's economic history were triumphant ones. Because of its Lake Erie port, Cleveland was the ideal point at which to combine iron ore shipped from Michigan and Minnesota with coal coming by

A rail worker clears the tracks at a fuel loading terminal near the Collinwood rail yards. Photo by Roger Mastroianni

rail from Appalachia. That combination powered the city's first steel mills.

Cleveland helped inaugurate the new Industrial Age that transformed America from a rural to an urban nation. Local steelmaking gave birth to foundries, casting shops, and a sophisticated machine-tool industry. In later years a determined management and skilled work force helped foster early automobile manufacturing and an auto parts industry, which still are important to the local economy.

Fortunes were also made in shipping and railroads. Thanks to John D. Rockefeller, Cleveland for a time was the nation's leading petroleum refiner, with pipelines stretching to the Pennsylvania oil fields.

Education also helped spin the wheels of industry. Case Institute of Technology, now combined into Case Western Reserve University, graduated metallurgists, engineers, and chemists to lead technological advances at the turn of the century. The paint making of the Sherwin-Williams Company—a *Fortune* 500 firm headquartered and thriving in Cleveland—benefited greatly from such chemical breakthroughs.

The Industrial Revolution helped the population to swell, primarily with Irish, German, and Slavic immigrants who worked in the mills and machine shops and lived near their jobs. Much of the manufacturing—and early city dwellings—sprang up in the neighborhoods of earliest commerce, along the Cuyahoga River banks known as the Flats.

Not only did the Cleveland topography offer easy access to Great Lakes shipping and provide more than ample water for industry, but it was rich in natural resources such as salt and lime. Salt companies still work active mines burrowed deep beneath Lake Erie on the edge of the Flats.

As much as steel, heavy manufacturing, shipping, and railroads made Cleveland one of the major industrial cities of the world, their crippling shutdown contributed to its woe during the Depression. The late Cleveland industrialist and railroad tycoon Cyrus Eaton, whose headquarters for his

Above: Lake Erie and the Cuyahoga River have sustained a lucrative shipping industry in Cleveland ever since the Industrial Revolution. Courtesy, Luce Photography, Inc.

Right: Conrail employees enjoy a moment's respite from work amid a never-ending procession of railcars. Photo by Roger Mastroianni

Chessie System and other holdings was in a posh suite in the Terminal Tower, often said that no American city was as hurt by the Depression as Cleveland.

Just as quickly as Cleveland fell on hard times, however, the city staged its first modern revival. Its manufacturing infrastructure was converted into a potent military machine during World War II.

Not far from Hopkins International Airport, the government erected a vast aviation assembly plant. It later was used to manufacture armored tanks. Today the structure is the 2.5-million-square-foot International Exposition Center, which the *Guinness Book of World Records* calls the largest single-building exhibition hall in the world. It annually draws hundreds of thousands of visitors to sporting events, banquets, conventions, and trade shows.

Cleveland's postwar years were marked by prosperity. Steel mills and other heavy industry were channeled into meeting the unslakable demand for consumer goods. Yet the seeds of social and economic change were already planted.

For one thing, the area's black population swelled during World War II to fill the wartime factories. By the early 1950s whites began moving to new suburbs. As Cleveland and other major American cities wrestled with social and racial change in the 1960s and 1970s—in the work force as well as in the neighborhoods and schools—the economy continued to expand. Despite high wages and near full employment, however, Greater Cleveland industry was largely competing in a national economy, not a global one.

The oil embargo in the early 1970s had a numbing impact. A few years later, with Japan and third-world countries producing steel and other products at a cost far less than that of Cleveland industry, the economic fiber that had kept the city resilient for so long began to shred. Our technology was no longer competitive. Nor were our wages or productivity.

By the mid-1980s Northeast Ohio had lost one- third—some 60,000, all told—of its manufacturing jobs. Most of these were at large facilities that had long employed the fathers, mothers, uncles, aunts, and children of many generations. Only the growing service sector kept business moving ahead.

Nonetheless, at the bleakest moment the Greater Cleveland turnaround started to ignite. It began as a modest effort in the political arena, when civic leaders came together to support George Voinovich's mayoral campaign. At the close of 1989, his 10th year at city hall, Voinovich could leave office proud that he had been mayor of Cleveland longer than anyone.

Buoyed by its success—and newfound unity—the same civic leadership turned its energy toward reversing the downward spiral of the economy. They prevailed upon the Cleveland Foundation to retain the Rand Corporation to determine what exactly they should do to accomplish their goal.

Rand's unmistakable conclusion: Greater Cleveland must have an organization to gather sophisticated economic data on which to base critical business decisions. The Rand study led to the creation of the Center for Regional Economic Issues. Once housed in the Cleveland Federal Reserve

Bank, REI is now a part of the Weatherhead School of Management at Case Western Reserve University.

REI serves as a kind of economic think tank. "We offer organizations that are making key development decisions sophisticated, reliable information about the economy," says REI director Michael Fogarty.

Another step in the the crucial turnaround was a pivotal 1981 McKinsey & Company study funded by the George Gund Foundation, entitled "Cleveland Tomorrow—A Strategy for Economic Vitality." The report called attention to the region's high labor costs and low productivity.

The study recommended the creation of Cleveland Tomorrow, composed of 50 chief executive officers of the largest Greater Cleveland corporations, professional firms, and nonprofit institutions. They would be commissioned to turn around established businesses and create high-tech companies to propel a revitalized economy into the twenty-first century.

Since its inception, Cleveland Tomorrow's mission has redoubled. It set up the Technology Leadership Council, composed of business, government, and research institution leaders.

Over the next 20 years the council intends to push Cleveland into the ranks of America's pacesetting cities in advanced technology research and development. "The foremost objective is for business, academia, and govern-

The sun sets peacefully over the Cleveland Electric Illuminating Company power plant in Eastlake. Photo by Jim Baron. Courtesy, Image Finders, Inc.

ment to pull together to expand the research capacity of medical institutions, universities, and NASA's Lewis Research Center," says Frank Mosier, vice chairman of BP America and chairman of the Cleveland Tomorrow Technology Leadership Council.

"Cities that are leaders in university research are leaders in high-tech start-ups," Mosier adds. "Advanced research also increases the business of established corporations. The bottom line is industrial growth, jobs, and development."

Realizing that jobs and neighborhoods are interconnected, Cleveland Tomorrow has established the Cleveland Housing Network, a coalition of nine neighborhood organizations that helps generate housing for low-income families. Other by-products of this Cleveland Tomorrow commitment are the Cleveland Neighborhood Partnership Program, which provides operating money for neighborhood groups, and Neighborhood Progress, an alliance of funders and grass-roots leaders who look for ways to make neighborhood groups more effective.

The original Cleveland Tomorrow study placed considerable emphasis on physical redevelopment. The result: the Cleveland Development Partnership, a real-estate venture of corporate partners, which is raising $60 million to spur large-scale, high-impact downtown and neighborhood building projects. These include hotels, housing, and sports facilities such as the proposed stadium and arena behind Public Square.

A Regional Economic Issues study for Cleveland Tomorrow concluded that, through the 1990s and into the twenty-first century, education—secondary and higher—also must be fortified to keep the economy competitive.

"This can be accomplished through improving our universities, attracting educated workers, upgrading research and technology capabilities, increasing productivity, and promoting the entrepreneurial spirit," says REI director Fogarty.

"Cleveland Tomorrow strives to identify significant ways corporations can support regional economic development," notes Richard Shatten, Cleveland Tomorrow executive director. "We are trying to make a difference."

Long before Cleveland Tomorrow was prodding the economy, the Greater Cleveland Growth Association was laying the groundwork for the city's recovery. Recognizing that economic development goals were out of reach until fundamental improvements were made, the association tackled two tough jobs—making Cleveland a better place to do business and assisting businesses to cope with the recession and remain competitive.

In an effort to help newly elected Mayor Voinovich streamline and improve the efficiency of city government, the Growth Association led a successful effort for city government reform. As a result of that effort, voters in 1981 approved a four-year term for mayor and city council representatives, ending the constant campaigning that came with two-year terms. Similarly, the city council was reduced from an unwieldy 33 members to 21.

The Growth Association also led a coalition of public officials and civic leaders to develop a coordinated plan to rehabilitate the city's deteriorating infrastructure. Titled the Community Capital Investment Strategy, the plan has been implemented as the Build Up Greater Cleveland program. In its first six years BUGC helped acquire more than $600 million in new capital funds for infrastructure renewal.

Recognizing that quality air service is a necessity for local businesses, the Growth Association, in cooperation with the city of Cleveland, set about to increase the number of daily flights at Hopkins Airport. Since the formation of the Air Service Committee, Continental Airlines and USAir have created regional hubs in Cleveland and flights at Hopkins are at an all-time high.

The Cleveland State University Communications Research Center, in a poll of area residents, discovered strong positive feelings toward the business community because of its determination to pursue economic growth and accomplish civic projects. One successful effort of the Growth Association has been in luring corporate headquarters of major corporations to Northeastern Ohio.

"Cleveland's strategic location, accessibility to key markets, our extensive and strong professional service network, our outstanding quality of life, and comparatively low cost of doing business make us an attractive headquarters city," says Robert J. Farling, president of Centerior Energy Corporation and chairman of the Cleveland Area Development Corporation, the business development arm of the Growth Association.

The association can count headquarters here of more than two dozen *Fortune* 500 industrial and service firms, including TRW, Eaton Corporation, Sherwin-Williams, Parker Hannifin, Reliance Electric, Lubrizol, Ferro Corporation, Cleveland Cliffs, Standard Products, and M.A. Hanna.

First National Supermarkets, Leaseway Transportation, and Centerior Energy are among Greater Cleveland's largest service firms. Large rubber companies—GenCorp, Goodyear, and B.F. Goodrich—continue to make their home in the nearby "Rubber City" of Akron, though they have expanded into high-technology products. Firestone Tire & Rubber Company, now owned by Bridgestone of Japan, still has almost 2,000 white-collar employees in Akron.

From its downtown Cleveland headquarters, Management Recruiters International, Inc. (MRI), the world's largest search and recruitment organization, operates a network of 600 offices, some 90 percent of which are franchised. Cofounded in 1965 by Clevelander Alan R. Schonberg, MRI spe-

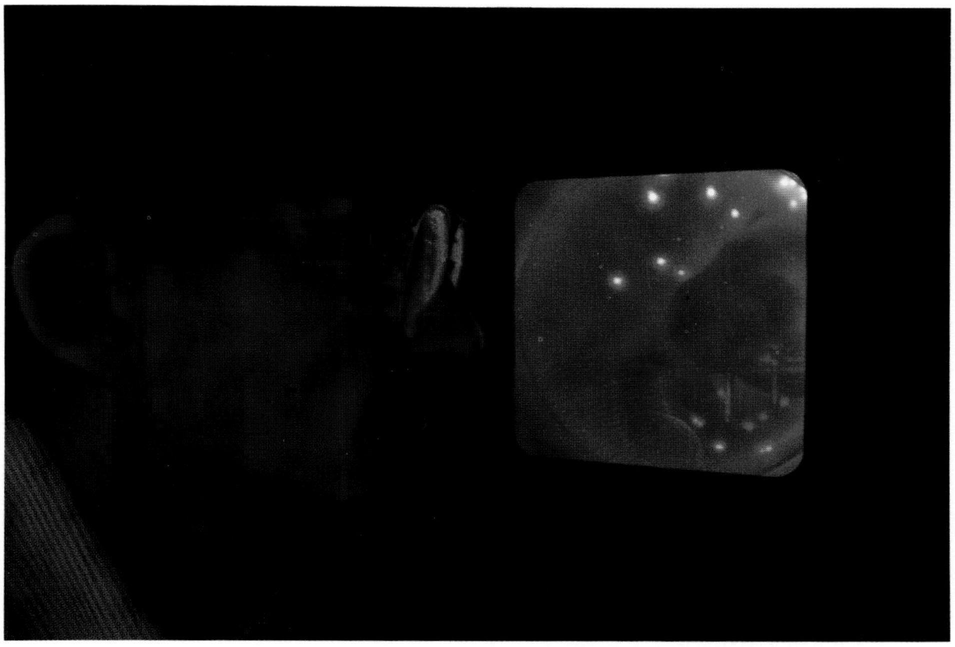

An engineer at B.F. Goodrich conducts "plasma" research at the giant rubber company's Brecksville facility. Photo by Don Snyder

cializes in middle management, information systems, office support, and sales recruitment.

MRI has expansion plans for more than 1,000 domestic and international offices by the year 2000. The company provides each new franchisee with an intensive three-week training program in Cleveland.

Other large companies have expanded their Cleveland presence or relocated here. Ohio Mattress has taken ownership of most Sealy Mattress licensee operations nationwide and has moved its headquarters into expanded downtown offices. The most recognizable name in American candy, Fanny Farmer, moved its corporate headquarters from Massachusetts to Cleveland in 1989 to be closer to its chocolate factory in Norwalk, 50 miles west of Cleveland.

Gould Incorporated, a large maker of electronics products and computers for information processing, will complete the move of its world headquarters from Chicago to suburban Eastlake in 1990. The company has sales of $500 million a year and dozens of plants in the United States and abroad. It is owned by Nippon Mining Company of Tokyo.

All told, some 140 foreign-owned companies—largely from West Germany, Switzerland, Japan, and Great Britain—have operations in the seven counties of Northeast Ohio. These companies and their 20,000 employees represent only a fraction of the area's business establishments and employment, but they are growing.

Among them are Vax Appliances, a British vacuum cleaner manufacturer which built a new manufacturing facility in suburban Solon; Cello-glas N.A., a British maker of laminated materials for the printing industry, that moved its United States headquarters to Twinsburg; AGA Gas, the Swedish bottled gas manufacturer; and Electrolux, a large manufacturer of household appliances based in Sweden.

The biggest foreign-owned firms with North American headquarters in

Cleveland are Swiss-owned Nestlé Enterprises, Inc., which oversees 4,000 Greater Cleveland employees and another 30,000 nationwide from its 60-acre office complex in suburban Solon, and BP America, with 2,500 employees at its headquarters building downtown.

Nestlé operates more than 35 Stouffer hotels nationwide, including the 500-room Tower City Plaza on Public Square. The company also manufactures frozen foods—more than one million packages a day, including Lean Cuisine—in Solon, and manages its huge restaurant chain from here. In the late 1980s Nestlé built a new $12.8-million office complex to further consolidate North American operations.

James M. Biggar, chairman and chief executive officer of Nestlé Enterprises and chairman of Cleveland Tomorrow, was born and reared in Cleveland. "It's a lot easier to start a business trip from Cleveland Hopkins than from a busy airport on the East or West coast," says Biggar in explaining one reason why Stouffer and Nestlé remain in Cleveland. "There is a huge cost of living benefit to living here, and office space is far less than in the East . . . and it seems that here there are more realistic down-to-earth people with solid values.

"We've passed the era when businesses could be separate from the community," Biggar adds. "Frankly a better community means a better total business market for everyone. Business must be an active participant in finding ways where our resources can speed up the process. This means bringing people together to work for quality education, physical development, and jobs."

London-based BP America, which purchased Standard Oil of Ohio—the backbone of John D. Rockefeller's oil trust—and took over its elaborate $200-million, 45-floor headquarters on Public Square, is (based on assets) the 13th-largest corporation in the United States.

BP has 40,000 employees in the U.S., including almost 6,000 in its various Greater Cleveland operations. The company also has a profound presence in Alaska, where it was the first oil company to drill on the North Slope.

In consolidating its North American operations in Cleveland, BP's leadership has made sizable contributions to community programs, including many in the field of secondary and higher education, such as the Cleveland Initiative for Education and Case Western Reserve University. It also sponsors national broadcasts of the Cleveland Orchestra.

TRW, which has 70,000 employees worldwide, is the largest American corporation to have its world headquarters in Greater Cleveland. The TRW office complex is on more than 100 rolling acres on the former Lyndhurst estate of the late Congresswoman Frances Payne Bolton. Amenities include athletic facilities, wooded jogging paths, and an elegant guest house for visiting dignitaries.

The company is a pioneer in aerospace and defense, and has adapted much of its "Star Wars" research (such as in laser technology) for scientific and medical use. TRW also is a leading manufacturer of automotive accessories, including engine components, steering and suspension systems, and electronic controls. Ford Motor Company has made TRW its sole

The soaring BP America headquarters adds dimension to the Cleveland skyline. Courtesy, Luce Photography, Inc.

supplier of occupant restraint systems (passive seatbelts and airbags), which are mandatory on all new cars sold in the United States beginning with the 1990 models. Another key part of TRW's worldwide activities is credit information reporting services.

The TRW foundation has contributed to numerous local causes, including the Cleveland Initiative for Education, the Weatherhead School of Management, low-income housing, student science programs, and various arts organizations.

Along with BP America and TRW, Eaton Corporation rounds out the Big Three corporate presence in Greater Cleveland. Eaton markets to the automotive, industrial, commercial, and defense industries. Principal products include truck transmissions and axles, engine components, electrical equipment, and a wide variety of control systems.

Headquartered in downtown Cleveland, Eaton has some 40,000 employees nationwide. Its larger corporate contributions to Greater Cleveland civic causes have come in health and social services, the arts, and education—including the Cleveland Initiative of Education, the Red Cross capital campaign, and the Playhouse Square Foundation.

The heads of all three corporations—James H. Ross of BP America, Joseph T. Gorman of TRW, and James R. Stover of Eaton—also are involved in important United Way and racial and educational concerns. Several other leading employers, including the Cleveland Clinic Foundation, Squire, Sanders & Dempsey, and Jones, Day, Reavis & Pogue, also have helped initiate the Cleveland Initiative for Education, which provides Cleveland public-school graduates with college tuition credits.

One enterprising aspect of the Initiative is the Cleveland Education Partners. The partners—corporations, financial firms, and nonprofit institutions—each have an alliance with an individual public high school. Volunteers, from the chief executive officer on down, offer their own expertise to students, including tutoring and mentoring. The program is

Rolled steel makes its way through production at LTV Steel. Photo by Roger Mastroianni

Through good times and bad, Cleveland's industrial economy has been profoundly influenced by steel production. Photo by Jack Van Antwerp

expanding into intermediate and elementary schools.

"Companies cannot thrive unless their community thrives, and the community cannot thrive unless neighborhoods and schools thrive," says Robert Gillespie, chairman of the Society Corporation and head of the Cleveland Education Partners. "Increasingly, Greater Cleveland corporations are becoming a national model by their commitment to confront critical social issues and to form public-private partnerships designed to improve the quality of urban life."

Indeed, the involvement of major employers in such activities as the Cleveland Initiative for Education could also be called "enlightened self-interest." To remain competitive in industries that increasingly demand advanced skills, high productivity, and solid reading ability, business leaders realize that the local work force must be suitably educated and trained.

Beyond their thrust at inner-city schools, business leaders are increasing their contributions to and alliances with local universities in efforts to create and to nurture new ventures. Start-up businesses created in the 1980s—upwards of 2,000—are responsible for one- fourth of all Greater Cleveland manufacturing jobs, most of which are in clean manufacturing and specialty firms that demand a higher educated and better trained work force.

The painful recession from 1980 to 1983 helped strip away obsolete, non-competitive facilities and paved the way for a much leaner and more produc-

Every day the sparks fly like fireworks at steel production facilities throughout Cleveland. Photo by Jim Baron. Courtesy, Image Finders, Inc.

tive manufacturing base. Nowhere is this more apparent than in steel making—once the backbone of the Cleveland economy and once crushed.

In the early 1980s, in the face of brutal competition from low-cost foreign steelmakers, inefficient Northeast Ohio mills made mass layoffs or, in some cases, shut down altogether.

Several developments, however, began to change the course of domestic steel production and the Cleveland economy along with it. Labor signed accords with management that cut high wages and obsolete work rules in return for preserving jobs. Foreign steelmakers agreed to voluntary restraint agreements. The drop in the dollar and advanced steelmaking technology made American prices more competitive.

In 1984 Cleveland-based Republic Steel merged with LTV Corporation's Jones & Laughlin Steel. Out of this marriage came LTV Steel Company, the third-largest steel manufacturer in America. After a gusher of red ink, LTV Steel filed for court protection to get itself moving again.

The effort has worked. With 8,000 hourly workers and salaried management at its Cleveland headquarters and plant, LTV is profitably operating the largest flat-rolled steelmaking complex in North America, producing high-

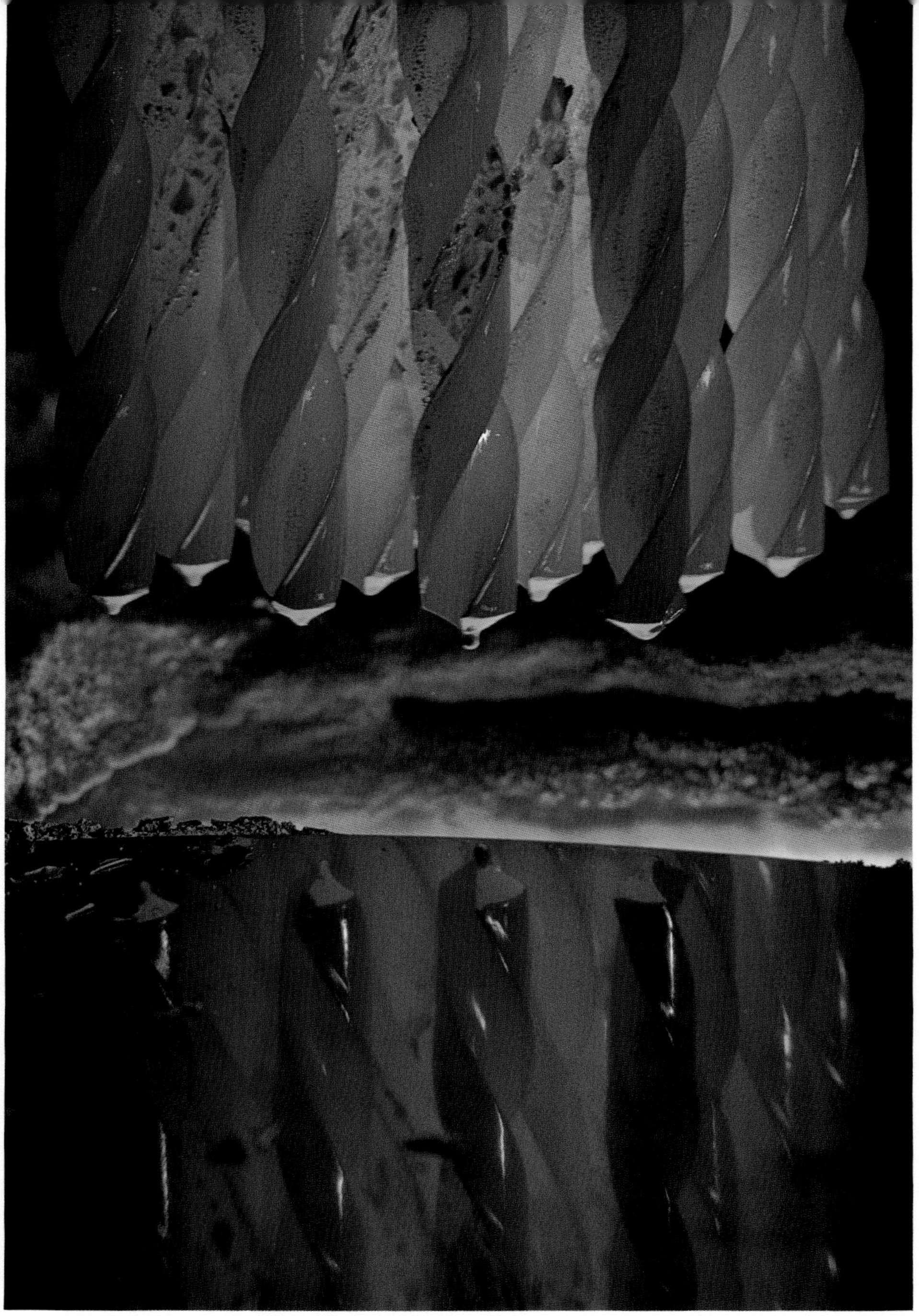

Above, right: Red-hot drill bits glow brightly during manufacturing at Cleveland Twist Drill. Photo by Don Snyder

quality steel for automotive and appliance markets.

Moreover, LTV Steel has cut operating costs and greatly boosted labor productivity. It also has obtained a 10-year, $690-million local tax abatement in return for investing $1.15 billion to upgrade the Cleveland Works through the mid-1990s.

LTV Steel and Sumitomo Metal Industries of Japan have formed a joint venture to create an enormous electrogalvanizing steel manufacturing facility in Cleveland. This state-of-the-art facility puts LTV Steel at the forefront of worldwide electrogalvanized steel.

"The Cleveland Works has a reputation for superior quality," says David H. Hoag, LTV Steel's president and chief executive officer. "With our investments in new technology and equipment, we will be in a better position to compete in the global marketplace."

The role of the Steelworkers Union in the LTV comeback was pivotal. "We logically looked at the problems of the company and went through the books," says Frank J. Valenta, director of District 28 of the United Steelworkers of America. "We took an initial 10.5-percent cut in benefits and wages and then another 9 percent in return for profit sharing. We helped develop a labor-management program geared toward customer satisfaction

"It paid off with new business," says Valenta, who represents some 26,000 union members in Northeast Ohio. "We are determined to continue our participation with management because we know everyone wins through cooperation rather than contention."

Many independent steel companies also have found success in Cleveland—largely through advanced technology and better productivity from a better-trained work force. Samuel Manu-Tech, based in Ontario, Canada, is building a new $12-million steel pickling plant on Cleveland's southeast side to burnish steel for appliances and automobile siding.

Perhaps the most telling example of how steel can be successfully manufactured in a participatory management environment is American Steel & Wire. As *Fortune* magazine gushed about this success story: "It is a steel company run like a high-tech Silicon Valley computer outfit and it takes modern management about as far as it will go."

At its three plants purchased from U.S. Steel (two in Cleveland and one in Illinois), the company produces high-quality steel for nuts and bolts manufacturers and for the welding rod industry.

Familiar to Cleveland residents are the sunset silhouettes formed by the LTV Steel mills. Photo by Don Snyder

All employees buy stock in the firm. Each quarter Tom Tyrrell, the president and chief executive officer, shuts down the plant for meetings. Financial information is openly discussed with employee-shareholders, and profit-sharing checks are passed out.

Executives and workers park in the same employee parking lot, and everyone is salaried. Absenteeism is less than one percent. Workers regularly meet with management to discuss ways to cut costs. Supervisors, even top management, must wear a uniform or a company jacket when in the plant.

In 1986, American Steel & Wire's first year, sales reached $90 million. Four years later they hit $250 million. Within two years of its start-up, ASW made a public stock offering and increased the number of employees from 220 to more than 500. "Our success has come about because Cleveland has a marvelous work ethic," Tyrrell says. "What we've done is give workers an active part in operating the business. We ask them—not tell them—how things should be done."

Just as steel is staging a comeback,

so are other heavy manufacturing sectors.

Among those with an exceptional international reputation is Lincoln Electric, a closely held public company that is the world's largest manufacturer of arc-welding products and a leader in the manufacture of industrial electric motors.

Lincoln, which is expanding rapidly worldwide through joint ventures and the purchase of foreign firms, compensates its overall management and local blue-collar work force of 2,500 on an incentive system. Every year since the merit system was instituted in 1934, Lincoln has paid employees at its two Greater Cleveland plants bonuses averaging nearly 90 percent of salaries. The company also pays bonuses to workers at its foreign subsidiaries when their plants are profitable.

The Harvard Business School has recognized the Lincoln Electric Company for its effective management practices. Harvard also maintains that its management case study of Lincoln Electric is among the most popular that it distributes to other universities worldwide.

Beyond Greater Cleveland's key role in steel, welding, machine tools, and heavy equipment, it can claim the distinction of being second only to metropolitan Detroit in domestic automobile production. All told, Ford, Chrysler, and General Motors pumped one billion dollars into Greater Cleveland plant modernization in the 1980s.

Chrysler has several thousand employees in Northeast Ohio. General Motors employs upwards of 8,000 at its various Greater Cleveland plants and dealerships. With 17,000 employees at six manufacturing facilities and 25 Ford and Lincoln-Mercury dealers, Ford Motor Company is the region's largest private employer. In fact, Greater Cleveland is the second-largest

Cleveland boasts a lucrative wire manufacturing industry, featuring state-of-the-art technology and innovative management. Photo by Jim Baron. Courtesy, Image Finders, Inc.

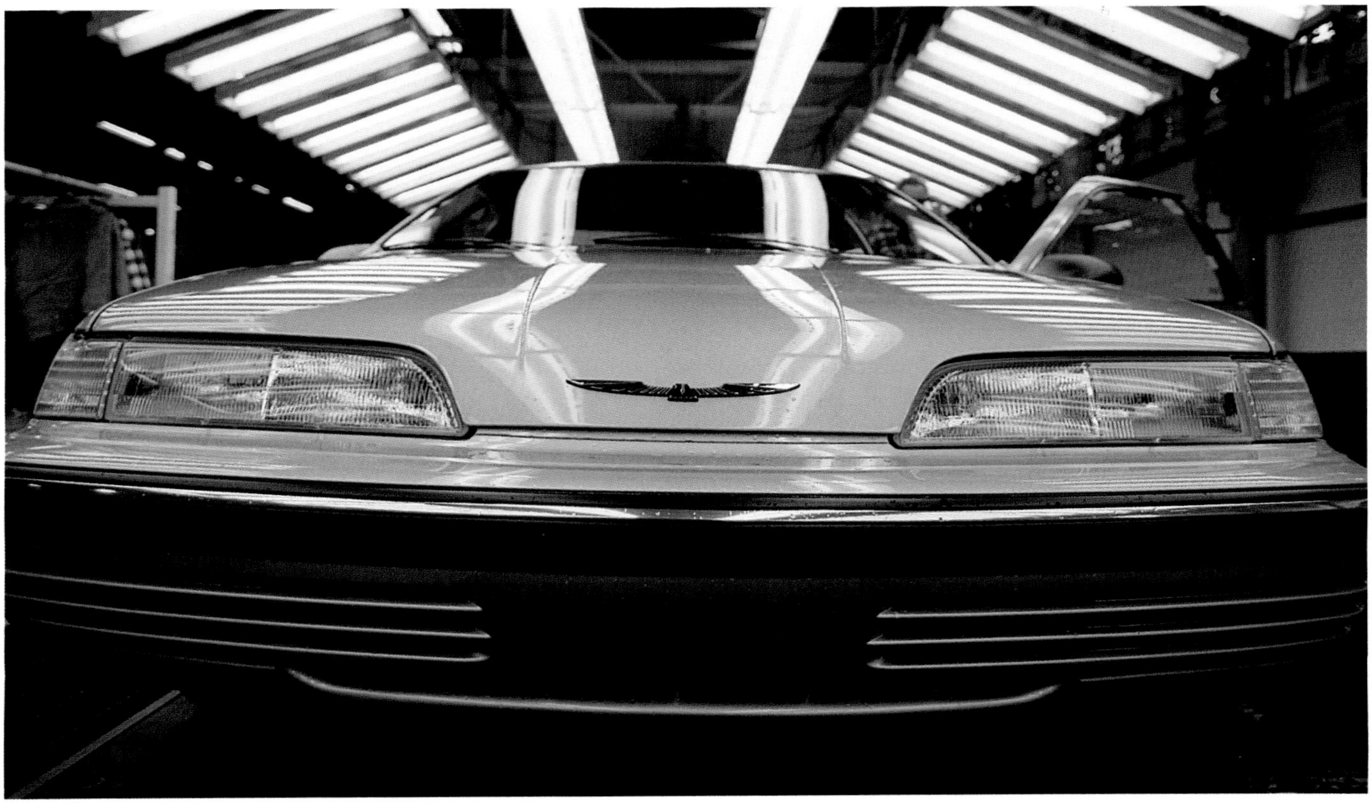

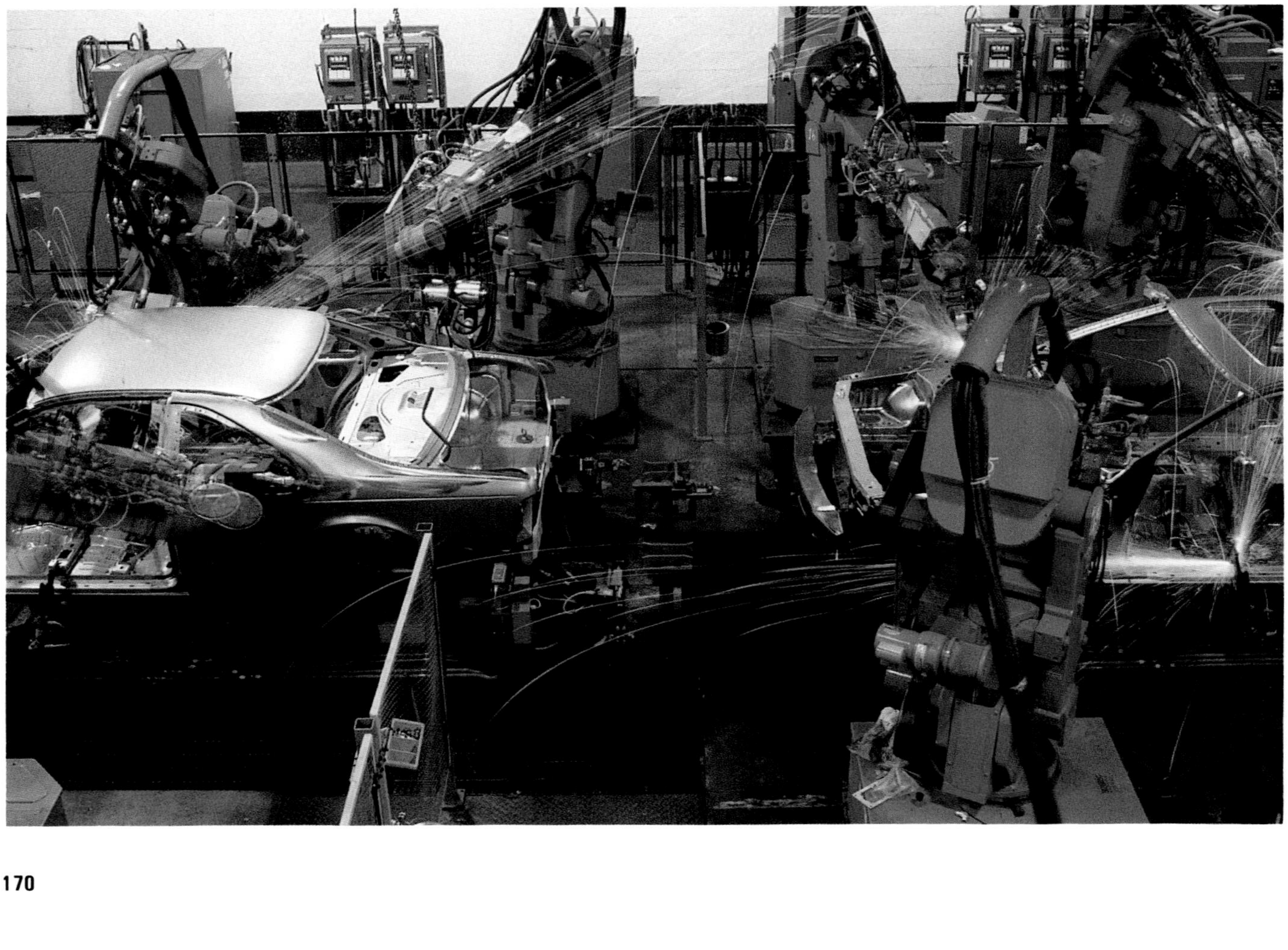

Facing page, top: A sleek Ford Thunderbird rolls off the assembly line in Lorain adding to the nation's growing number of Cleveland-built automobiles. Photo by Jack Van Antwerp

Facing page, bottom: Ford has taken advantage of the latest in mechanized manufacturing. Robotics has helped the Lorain assembly plant stay ahead in a very competitive industry. Photo by Jack Van Antwerp

center of Ford employment outside of Michigan.

In a joint venture with Nissan, Ford is investing one billion dollars to enlarge its truck plant in Avon Lake for building mini-vans. The project was made possible by tax abatement, state assistance to improve transportation access, on-site improvements, and job training.

Aggressive manufacturers such as Ford have been helped by the new business alliance between higher education and government. One successful project is the Cleveland Advanced Manufacturing Program (CAMP), set up through the state's Thomas Edison Program. CAMP is headquartered at Parker Hannifin, a *Fortune* 500 maker of components for automotive, aviation, and aerospace systems.

CAMP coordinates local university research to help companies stay competitive by utilizing advanced technology and equipment. It also administers a center, one of three in the United States, established by the National Institute of Standards and Technology to expedite the transfer of technology to industrial companies. The Great Lakes Manufacturing Technology Center is housed at the Unified Technologies Center on Cuyahoga Community College's Metro campus, which also provides job retraining for industry.

As much as the new union of advanced technology and higher education has helped rejuvenate Greater Cleveland, some ancient business methods are also accelerating the comeback. The rebirth of heavy industry has awakened the shipping industry. The ripples have not yet built to a flood tide, but they are causing economic waves, both in bulk shipments on the Great Lakes and in exports leaving the city's international port for Europe, Asia, and South America.

This turnaround is especially savory in the interlake bulk shipments of iron ore, coal, sand, limestone, and salt. In the early 1980s bulk shipments on the Great Lakes fell 42 percent from their high point of 215 million tons in 1979. The drop in iron ore shipments was even more precipitous, from 103 million to 43 million tons. Iron ore shipments to Cleveland docks fell from a high of 16 million tons in 1970 to 8 million in 1985.

Scores of vessels were put in reserve or carved up for scrap. American Ship Building in Lorain, owned by former Clevelander George M. Steinbrenner III (owner of the New York Yankees), shut down its local operations.

The large mining and bulk-cargo shipping firms—once the ballast of Cleveland's commerce—experienced a traumatic metamorphosis. M.A. Hanna shifted into polymers. Connecticut-based Moore-McCormack sold off its Cleveland-based Pickands Mather & Company, manager of iron ore and coal mines, as well as its Interlake Steamship Company, operator of a Great Lakes fleet.

Cleveland-Cliffs Inc purchased the iron ore and coal divisions of Pickands Mather. The Interlake Steamship Company and its 11 ships became an independent company. The other big Cleveland mining/shipping firm, Oglebay Norton, reduced its fleet to 13 from a high of 17 in 1982. Only the shipping companies' biggest, most efficient ships—those over 700 feet,

Right: Awaiting shipment to ports across the globe, goods from Cleveland are stowed on a foreign vessel moored at the Port of Cleveland on Lake Erie. Photo by Roger Mastroianni

Facing page, top: The Port of Cleveland finds favor with general cargo exporters and importers, who appreciate its reasonable fees, select facilities, and good labor relationships. Courtesy, Luce Photography, Inc.

equipped with self-unloaders—had a reasonable chance of work in the iron-ore trade.

Now, however, ships are coming out of mothballs, thanks to the resurgence in ore mining, steelmaking, and construction, which requires limestone, sand, and cement. The demand has been pressing the Great Lakes fleet to its fullest. Interlake greatly expanded in 1989, when the Ford Motor Company sold its three ore carriers to the Cleveland company.

From mid-March to as late as mid-January, the twisting Cuyahoga River is crowded with mammoth ore freighters. During good weather, these ships often must compete with pleasure boats for passage.

Companies along the Cuyahoga that receive or ship cargo on Great Lakes vessels employ almost 10,000 and have an annual payroll of $345 million. Today there are eight fleets based in Cleveland, with 32 vessels, half of all the carrying capacity on the Great Lakes.

The port turnaround has been especially evident in steel importing and exporting. In 1988 the Cleveland port exported 46,000 tons of steel, an increase of 58 percent over the previous year. In 1989 steel exports doubled again. Steel imports are even bigger business in Cleveland—more than 600,000 tons in 1989. To handle this growing enterprise, the port authority has built a new warehouse for steel.

The other key part of Cleveland shipping—general cargo—also has been affected. International exchange rates have trimmed imports but have precipitated a surge of exports from Cleveland. On any given day during the high summer season, foreign-flag vessels from several nations load and unload at the Port of Cleveland on Lake Erie. Many use the gargantuan Buckeye Booster, a crane with a 150-ton capacity.

A deckhand tends to one of the many ships that navigate the waters in and around Cleveland. Photo by Don Snyder

Though the harbor and docks can accommodate any vessel using the St. Lawrence Seaway, the Port of Cleveland is surrendering 4 berths, 2 warehouses, and 15 acres of open storage to the North Coast Harbor project. When the transition is completed, the port will have modern replacement facilities in a new dock area west of its current location.

The Port of Cleveland—operated by the independent Cleveland-Cuyahoga Port Authority and supported in part by a tax levy—is the choice of many general cargo importers-exporters because of affordable fees, select facilities (including storage docks and warehouses), and good labor relationships. Because of the St. Lawrence Seaway system, the port is closer to certain Northern European cities than are New York and Baltimore.

"We handle more than 600,000 tons of cargo a year," says port director Anthony Fugaro, a retired U.S. Coast Guard rear admiral. "The Cleveland port is cost-effective because of our proximity to the industrial center of North America."

"The Port of Cleveland can offer door-to-door one-stop shopping in trucking, stevedoring, warehousing, and vessel chartering," adds Thomas F. Coakley, chairman of Cleveland Stevedore Company, the largest stevedore and terminal operator on the Great Lakes. "It makes the port a key national transportation center."

The Cleveland World Trade Association, an arm of the Greater Cleveland Growth Association, supports the port operations. It expedites trade and creates new port- and trade-related jobs by providing overseas marketing data, information on tariffs, and export procedures. CWTA also helps companies set up foreign markets and sponsors a world trade conference each spring that attracts hundreds of participants.

Cleveland's role as a world center of trade has been further enhanced because of the new free trade agreement with Canada. Cleveland has a close relationship with Canada. The Canadians operate a busy tourist office in Cleveland, and an important role of the Canadian consulate here is to foster trade between Northeast Ohio and Canada.

The success of Cleveland in world trade also is due to improved labor-management relations. That critical undertaking is now a full-time mission of the Work in Northeast Ohio Council (WINOC), which strives to improve management-labor relations and to increase productivity at area companies.

WINOC was set up in the early 1980s as a result of studies that concluded that improved labor relations and heightened productivity are vital to the economy. Financed by business members, foundations, and state grants, WINOC is becoming a national model. The organization primarily targets the 2,000 manufacturing firms in Northeast Ohio with payrolls of from 50 to 500 workers.

"We work to improve productivity and quality by getting people to work together, so we stress communications and team building," says Bob Meyer, executive director of WINOC. "We also form problem-solving groups of management and labor."

The George Worthington Company, a hardware supplier whose roots go back to the nineteenth century, is one of more than 100 WINOC success stories. The firm had sought bankruptcy court protection but WINOC, with participation of the Teamsters Union, helped Worthington become profitable again by improving productivity. The effort saved some 200 hourly and salaried jobs.

"Organized labor is committed to the regeneration of the economy through development of advanced manufacturing systems and technology transfer strategies," says Richard D. Acton, executive secretary of the AFL-CIO Cleveland Federation of Labor.

As increased productivity recharges Greater Cleveland manufacturing, the positive fallout has given impetus to the service economy, particularly in high-end health care, accounting, law, and investment banking. Such growing firms include Jones, Day, Reavis & Pogue; Squire, Sanders & Dempsey, and Baker & Hostetler—among the largest law firms in the United States.

Jones, Day, Reavis & Pogue, with offices in many American and foreign cities, has 1,000 lawyers. It is now the second-largest law firm in the world. The firm represents such corporations as R.J. Reynolds, General Motors, and Eaton Corporation. Locally, the firm has 900 employees, including 275 lawyers at its modern headquarters in adjoining buildings overlooking Lake Erie downtown.

Squire, Sanders & Dempsey, with numerous offices in the United States and Europe (including Brussels, headquarters of the European Community), has more than 400 lawyers worldwide representing such clients as

BP America, Centerior Energy, Bridgestone Corporation, the Federal Home Loan Bank Board, and the National Collegiate Athletic Association. The oldest firm in Ohio with the same continuous name, Squire, Sanders & Dempsey celebrates its 100th anniversary in 1990. By 1992 it will move to its own technologically advanced headquarters in the Society Tower on Public Square.

Cleveland's other large national law firm is Baker & Hostetler, which has 400 lawyers. Baker represents such clients as baseball's American League, Progressive Insurance, and E.W. Scripps Company. Other Cleveland-based law firms that are growing rapidly include Arter & Hadden; Calfee, Halter & Griswold; Benesch, Friedlander, Coplan & Aronoff; and Thompson, Hine & Flory.

These big law firms prospered in Cleveland, and the biggest ones in recent years have opened offices across the globe to service their clients' own international growth. The same holds for the city's biggest accounting firm, Ernst & Young. With 36,000 employees worldwide, Ernst & Young is the largest of the Big Eight Worldwide accounting firms.

Ernst & Young represents most of Cleveland's *Fortune* 500 headquarters companies and keeps a significant portion of its national headquarters in Cleveland, including 1,100 employees from its local, regional, and national practices. Ernst & Young personnel from every nation regularly come for training at the firm's huge Richard T. Baker Education Center in suburban Middleburg Heights.

"We feel a duty to promote employee involvement in the community," says Earl F. Molloy, managing partner of the Cleveland office. "Our city is a great place for our employees to live and to do business."

Regional offices of other Big Eight accounting firms and two of America's top management consulting firms (McKinsey & Company and Booz • Allen & Hamilton, Inc.) continue to experience extraordinary growth. Greater Cleveland also has national or regional headquarters of several large consulting engineers, including MK-Ferguson Company; URS Corporation; the Austin Company; Middough Associates; HWH Architects, Engineers, and Planners; the Osborn Engineering Company; and Polytech (one of the nation's largest minority-owned engineering firms).

The growing service economy includes a sizable publishing business, which grew out of a once-thriving industry: the manufacture of heavy printing presses. The *Plain Dealer,* Cleveland's only major daily, is one of the nation's largest newspapers. *Plain Dealer* publisher and editor Thomas Vail has served as chairman of the promotional New Cleveland Campaign. Northeast Ohio is also the 10th-largest television market in the country.

Greater Cleveland is considered the second-largest center in the nation for business and trade publications. Among the prominent trade magazine publishers headquartered here are Edgell Communications, which purchased the magazine division of Harcourt, Brace, Jovanovich and now puts out more than 100 magazines, and a formidable competitor, Penton Publishing, which publishes more than 30 trade magazines.

The billion-dollar American Greetings Corporation, second-largest manufacturer of greeting cards in the world, started here in 1906 and is headquartered in a sprawling structure in suburban Brooklyn.

American Greetings converted some 200,000 square feet of warehouse space into a Creative Center. A staff of 550—one of the largest concentrations of artists, writers, and designers in America—design greeting cards and licensing characters such as Holly Hobbie, Strawberry Shortcake, the Care Bears, and Special Blessings. American Greetings, with 2,600 employees in Cleveland and another 20,000 worldwide, has a distribution network of 90,000 retail outlets worldwide for the 6 million greeting cards it produces each day.

In the creative world of advertising, Cleveland has many top-tier Midwest agencies along with regional offices of international firms. Wyse Advertising, headquartered in Cleveland and with a large office in New York, can show off annual billings exceeding $85 million while representing such clients as TRW, General Dynamics, and the J.M. Smucker Company. Wyse created the famous Smucker's slogan, "With a name like Smucker's,

Cleveland can lay claim to some successful publishers, among them Penton Publishing, which publishes more than 30 trade magazines. Photo by Don Snyder

it has to be good." Smucker's is located in Orrville, a small town less than 50 miles south of Cleveland. The family-run company is one of the largest makers of jams and jellies in America.

Other large advertising firms include Meldrum and Fewsmith, Liggett-Stashower, Griswold, Lowe Marschalk, the Jayme Organization, and Marcus. At more than $110 million in annual billings, the Cleveland-based Nationwide Advertising Service is the largest classified help-wanted ad agency in the nation.

Cleveland's central geographic location, its low cost of land, and its access to interstates also has made it increasingly appealing to national distributors. Among those are Premier Industries, an auto supply distributor; Harris Wholesale, one of the nation's largest pharmaceutical distributors; Revco Drug Stores; and Bearings, Inc., a distributor of bearings with sales of $500 million annually.

When the New England Mutual Life Insurance Company was searching for space for a national claims office, it chose the Great Northern Technology Park in North Olmsted for its 140 employees after considering 80 competing communities.

One exceptional service firm is Cleveland-based Progressive Corporation, a billion-dollar insurance empire with 5,000 employees nationwide. Progressive is best known for insuring high-risk drivers but has expanded into diverse insurance services. The company, headed by Peter B. Lewis, an avid collector of modern art, is planning to consolidate its numerous East Side suburban offices into a spectacular $300-million corporate campus downtown.

Headquartered downtown are many of Cleveland's biggest banks and savings-and-loan associations. Eastern, western, and southern banks have suffered from enormous third-world debts, but midwestern banks have been far less affected. This is especially true in Cleveland, which is emerging as a center of midwestern finance.

Servicing this widening financial nexus is the Federal Reserve Bank of Cleveland. With 800 employees in Cleveland, it is one of the largest in the 12-bank Federal Reserve system. The Fourth Federal Reserve District covers Ohio, western Pennsylvania, eastern Kentucky, and the West Virginia panhandle.

The Cleveland Fed has branches in Cincinnati and Pittsburgh and a check-processing center in Columbus. More than one million checks are processed daily out of the Cleveland Federal Reserve for Northeast Ohio banks alone. The bank also processes more than $9 trillion worth of wire transfers annually.

The president of the Cleveland Federal Reserve rotates every other year with the president of the Chicago Federal Reserve Bank for a seat on the Federal Open Market Committee, which sets the nation's monetary policy. "I'm optimistic about the Cleveland economy," says W. Lee Hoskins, president of the Federal Reserve Bank of Cleveland. "In manufacturing, there's been ongoing restructuring and productivity increases. The growth in service employment also makes Cleveland less vulnerable to recession.

"Financial institutions are bringing new dollars here as deregulation has allowed banks to extend markets beyond state borders," Hoskins adds. "This growth in services will help us to remain competitive as we move from a materials-processing economy to an information-processing economy."

Three of the state's largest bank holding companies—"superregional banks"—are headquartered in Cleveland: National City Corporation, Society Corporation, and Ameritrust. They have shown excellent growth and earnings in recent years.

Other major state banks, such as Huntington National Bank (the Cleveland-based bank of Huntington Bancshares of Columbus) and the state's largest, Bank One of Columbus, have a considerable presence here.

The mammoth three-story, L-shaped Huntington lobby on East Ninth and Euclid, with its 38-foot-high Corinthian marble columns and vaulted ceiling, is among the largest and most majestic banking rooms in the world. Star Bank, a growing three-state holding company based in Cincinnati, has moved into Greater Cleveland and is planning to expand throughout the area.

East Ninth and Euclid is home to the towering National City Bank Building. Photo by Barbara Durham

Big New York and foreign banks also have opened commercial loan offices in Cleveland in search of hefty business accounts. Ameritrust and Society Corporation will move their headquarters into the two tallest buildings in Cleveland when construction is finished on them in the early 1990s.

The Cleveland banks, often described as conservative, grew as the city's heavy industry grew. Today they are financing a more diverse economy, including advanced technology, health care, and service ventures. They also are moving aggressively into investment banking activities.

"Local business has experienced at least two rounds of restructuring in recent years," says Karen Horn, chairman of Bank One, Cleveland. "And they have left businesses here much stronger than they were before. No doubt, banks are benefiting from their success."

Northeast Ohio also is benefiting from its emerging role as a regional center for venture capital. Among such established Cleveland firms is Morgenthaler Associates, which has large-scale investments nationwide. Many other venture capital funds are serving as a catalyst in heating up Cleveland's hot new entrepreneurial climate.

These funds include Brantley Venture Partners, Gries Investment Company, National City Venture Corporation, Robinson/Medical Ventures, So-

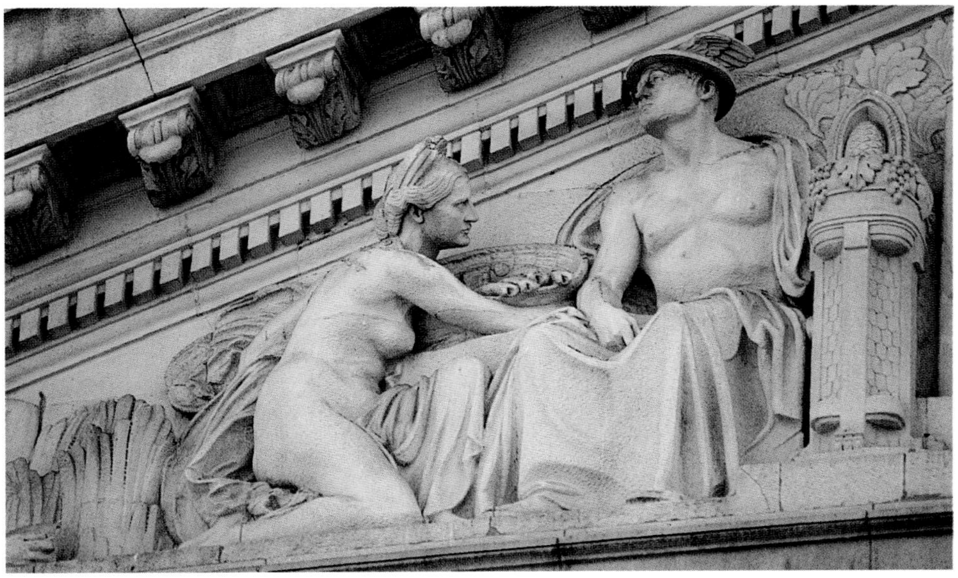

Karl Bitter's pediment, "Allegorization of the Main Springs of Wealth," graces the entrance to the Ameritrust headquarters in downtown Cleveland. Photo by Barbara Durham

Facing page: At the Cleveland Clinic medical technology provides solutions for ailing patients. Photo by Don Snyder

ciety Capital Corporation, Ameritrust Venture Capital Group, Basic Search, Inc., Clarion Capital Corporation, Kirtland Capital, and the Heartland Group. Lubrizol Enterprises, the large venture-capital arm of Lubrizol Corporation, a maker of oil additives, is housed in the company's Lake County offices, though most of its investments are spread across the country.

The venture capital effort started simmering in 1984, when Cleveland Tomorrow set up Primus Venture Partners with an initial $30 million from members and state pension funds. So successful was the first Primus fund that a second was established in 1987 with $74 million. Primus manages more than $100 million in capital available for investment and has more than 30 companies in its portfolio, the majority of which are in Ohio.

"Our role is to provide financial and business support for managers who want to start, build, or buy a company," says Loyal Wilson, managing partner of the Primus Fund. "Because Greater Cleveland has such an extraordinary amount of management talent and is so diverse, our investments include heavy industry, service, high tech, communications, and health care."

One Primus success story is Cleveland-based Action Auto Rental, which rents cars to the insurance replacement market. A start-up company in the late 1980s, today it has annual sales of more than $70 million. Otto Sensors Corporation, which makes micro-miniature medical sensors for blood analysis, is an example of a growing Cleveland high-tech biomedical firm financed by Primus.

Another Primus endeavor is the Trident Capital Fund, set up with various institutional investors to invest in biotechnology, advanced materials, and specialty chemicals.

"We view biotechnology as a growth opportunity in Greater Cleveland well into the next century," Wilson says. Forecasters predict that most of Greater Cleveland's economic expansion will continue to come from new ventures. Thousands of new businesses start up here each year—many of them run by families—and hundreds survive.

Perhaps Cleveland's best-known business consultant is Dr. Leon Danco, who travels worldwide to work with family businesses from his Center for Family Business in an East Side suburb. Danco also serves as a successful conference speaker, host of a public television series, and consultant to various domestic and international firms, including Smith Barney and Harris Upham & Company.

"The climate for family businesses has never been better in Greater Cleveland," Danco says. "Multigenerational family businesses today are in the forefront of the local business community's leadership."

Virtually 97 percent of all Greater Cleveland businesses have fewer than 100 employees, and the big net gain in employment has come from these developing new businesses. In many cases, the closing of major companies has prompted displaced employees to form their own firms. Many of these companies are in the early stages of growth.

This is what happened to Technicare, a pioneer in CT scanners and nuclear magnetic resonance. Johnson & Johnson bought Technicare and in

the late 1980s sold it off to General Electric. To consolidate operations, GE closed the Solon-based company. Numerous Technicare managers went on to start advanced technology spin-offs based on imaging technology.

Years before, Technicare had spun off its own Invacare division to private owners. They moved the company to Elyria in Lorain County and have built it into one of the largest manufacturers of home health-care supplies in the United States.

Not all advanced technology growth has been unplanned. Government agencies and business organizations are nurturing new enterprises with money and/or advice. These catalysts include Cleveland Tomorrow, Case Western Reserve University (through its Enterprise Development, Inc.), the state-financed Thomas Edison program, and the Greater Cleveland Growth Association's Council of Smaller Enterprises (COSE).

The most encompassing of the advisory organizations is COSE. Founded in 1972 by concerned business owners during a truckers' strike, COSE now has more than 8,000 members and is the largest locally based small business organization in America.

COSE provides affordable health coverage for more than 5,500 companies and 115,000 workers. It also offers a comprehensive array of education programs and advisory services, including management assistance, financial counseling, and sales training through volunteer entrepreneurs, lawyers, accountants, and academicians.

The organization lobbies local, state, and national government on issues affecting small businesses—from worker's compensation to health care to taxes. COSE publishes brochures and briefs on starting and managing a business and each year conducts more than 75 conferences and seminars, which attract thousands of participants with courses ranging from business and start-up planning to leadership training, tax reform, and hiring and firing practices.

One popular COSE program is a seminar where CEOs discuss issues affecting their businesses. Another is the annual entrepreneurship conference, which usually results in the creation of a dozen successful start-ups and scores of jobs. Through the Cuyahoga County Public Library system, COSE also offers a series of tape recordings on small businesses, which are accessed free of charge by telephone.

"Everyday COSE has something going on in Greater Cleveland to help businesspeople," says Growth Association vice-president John Polk. "COSE is an excellent environment for getting expert help from successful role models. It also is a place for building business contacts. The secret is the volunteers who are willing to share how they did it."

The Thomas Edison Program, sponsored by the State of Ohio Department of Development, helps to supplement COSE's efforts with advanced technology ventures. Among its many activities, the Edison Program helps worthy enterprises through research grants to accredited Ohio universities.

With corporate assistance, the Thomas Edison Program has established nine Centers for Excellence throughout the state to help commercialize new technology. Those in Greater Cleveland are the Edison Polymer Innovation Center (EPIC), located midway between Akron and Cleveland; the

Edison BioTechnology Center, at University Circle near Case Western Reserve University; and the Sensor Center on the CWRU campus. The Sensor Center is affiliated with the public-private Cleveland Advanced Manufacturing Program (CAMP).

The BioTechnology Center has a membership of 31 private companies and four medical institutions: the Cleveland Clinic Foundation, University Hospitals, Cleveland MetroHealth Medical Center, and CWRU Medical School.

Large companies, such as Picker International, and small ones, such as C-Bio Management Corporation (which produces serum for the growth of cell cultures), pay membership fees to the BioTechnology Center in exchange for research and development on projects for commercialization.

The Edison program also works hand in hand with Enterprise Development, Inc., which was formed in a merger of the public-private Center for Venture Development and the Entrepreneurial Assistance Group at CWRU Weatherhead School of Management.

EDI, a subsidiary of CWRU, receives both public and private financing. The nonprofit client assistance organization provides counseling to start-up companies, hosts entrepreneurial conferences, and conducts entrepreneurial management and marketing courses.

It also subleases low-cost "incubator" rental space at its University Circle headquarters for selected entrepreneurs. Among these are OttoSensors Corporation, whose laboratories produce micro-miniature liquid and gas sensors. Along with Prescott, Ball & Turben, a brokerage firm, EDI joins the Weatherhead School of Management in sponsoring an annual dinner honoring owners of the Weatherhead 100, the 100 fastest growing companies in Northeastern Ohio.

Technicians prepare an experiment in the wind tunnel at the NASA Lewis Research Center, which is involved in powering America's manned space station. Photo by Don Snyder

"Cleveland is ripe for starting a business," says Richard S. Gray, president of EDI. "It has all the needed services—venture capital, state- and university-supported technology, affordable standard of living, and great cultural opportunities . . . it's a strong market with a good supply of bright people who have a good work ethic."

One goal of local high-tech venture capitalists is making Cleveland to polymers what Northern California is to silicon—a kind of "Polymer Heights." Polymers are a class of materials—including adhesives and sealants—made by combining and rearranging various chemicals.

Polymer technology in Northeast Ohio is applied by more than 700 manufacturing firms. Greater Cleveland is third in the nation in the number of polymer research and development facilities. More than $500 million is spent each year at such facilities, including EPIC, whose research is conducted at CWRU and the University of Akron and at laboratories of member companies.

The greatest potential funnel of advanced technology activity is the 360-acre NASA Lewis Research Center adjacent to Cleveland Hopkins International Airport. Lewis is building the $2.3-billion on-board power system for the permanent manned space station, *Freedom*, that NASA expects to rocket into orbit in 1995.

"As the project intensifies, so will the number of engineering firms that supply our high-technology needs, possibly spawning a whole new industry in aerospace support services and specialized manufacturing," says John Klineberg, director of Lewis.

The spin-off in new companies from Lewis activities is due in part to efforts of the Growth Association and the Great Lakes Space Technology Association, composed of some 30 major Cleveland corporations. GLSTA is headed by Daniel Biskind, president of Biskind Development Company, owner of the 400-acre Great Northern Mall and Plaza in North Olmsted west of Hopkins Airport.

The Growth Association helped form GLSTA and its political action committee to encourage business and legislative leaders to support the expansion of Lewis Research Center and to promote private ventures to obtain work from Lewis.

"We're one element in an overall strategy to enhance the space program in Northeast Ohio," says Biskind. "Our target is to stimulate space technology businesses around Lewis like they have grown up around the space centers in Houston and Huntsville. We want to breed a new industry here."

Greater Cleveland has not yet benefited from its space center on the scope of Houston or Huntsville, but the coming years presage a boom in aerospace. Lewis has 2,700 civil-service employees and another 1,300 contract employees. In the late 1980s Lewis had a direct annual impact of more than $150 million on the Greater Cleveland economy, and that figure is expected to triple by the early 1990s.

For good reason. Beyond the permanent space station power system, Lewis is responsible for many other endeavors. The research center is working on advanced jet engine technology in hypersonic propulsion, which will lead to jets that can fly at four times the speed of sound. It is helping to design the propulsion system for the National Aero-Space Plane, whose purpose is to fly directly into low orbit upon takeoff.

As Klineberg and Biskind have predicted, spin-off work from Lewis is creating a new space community, largely in the suburbs surrounding the research center. Scientists and engineers are pouring into Greater Cleveland from all over the country. New office complexes, such as the 300-acre Aerospace Technology Park, are filled with Lewis contractors and subcontractors.

The Rocketdyne Division of Rockwell International, the major contractor on the space station power system, has been steadily expanding its local work force. So have other local and national space contractors, including Sverdrup Technology, Inc., TRW's Space and Defense

Corky and Lenny's at Cedar Center is one of the area's most popular New York-style delicatessens. Photo by Jack Van Antwerp

Group, Life Systems, Inc., Analex Corporation, and the Pratt & Whitney Aircraft Division of United Technologies.

An increasing number of contracts awarded each year by Lewis and Rocketdyne—several hundred—are going to Northeast Ohio companies. The Greater Cleveland Growth Association and Congressman Edward F. Feighan of Lakewood have held joint workshops for local contractors in an effort to increase their work.

All this activity has prompted the creation of the Cleveland Area Professional Research Association (CAPRA), composed of firms doing aerospace work. It also has heightened the profile of the Cleveland Technical Societies Council—a consortium of 48 far-ranging groups representing more than 21,000 engineering and scientific personnel.

As a result of Lewis' stepped-up role, area universities are also benefiting from millions of dollars in research stipends. The new Ohio Aerospace Institute, for college students seeking advanced aerospace degrees, opened in the fall of 1989 at Lewis. Lewis also is supporting private initiatives to create an aerospace museum and space camp.

As much as advanced technology is a concern of the Growth Association, so is minority entrepreneurship. It is a full-time effort for Jim Wade, director of Minority Business Development for the Growth Association and executive director of the Cleveland Regional Minority Purchasing Council, one of 50 regional councils of the National Minority Supplier Development Council.

The councils are composed of major corporations in large metropolitan areas that provide procurement opportunities for companies owned by minorities, including blacks, American Indians, Asians, and Hispanics.

"We bring together minority business owners and corporate purchasing representatives to help minorities get into the mainstream," Wade says. "This is not affirmative action, just an economically sound program."

The Development Council annually helps more than 50 companies gain hundreds of millions of dollars in contracts in Northeast Ohio. It also holds an annual trade fair, where corporate purchasing agents can explain their buying needs, and even a summer Lake Erie cruise to bring minority entrepreneurs and executives together socially.

Perhaps the most telling tasks are the educational seminars designed to eliminate misunderstandings and difficulties between big-business executives and minority business owners. That also is one purpose of the Matchmaker Program, coordinated by the Greater Cleveland Growth Association and the roundtable in an effort to put together buyers and specific minority vendors.

Most local governmental agencies also have minority business set-aside programs, including the Minority Business Development Center operated by the City of Cleveland in cooperation with the U.S. Department of Commerce. The center helps minority owners to package business plans for obtaining loans and gathering marketing assistance and to cut the red tape in bidding for city contracts.

Enterprise Development, Inc., also works with the Cuyahoga County Minority Assistance Program to foster minority businesses and participates in Success-Net, which holds monthly meetings for black business professionals on start-up and networking concerns.

Caesar Burkes is one of Greater Cleveland's most successful entrepreneurs of any color. With some 10 McDonald's franchises in Northeast Ohio, he is the largest minority operator in the McDonald's system. When employment is booming in the summer, he has upwards of 1,000 people on his payroll.

Burkes, who started his restaurant chain with a small family restaurant, is chairman of purchasing for the Northeast Ohio McDonald's Operators Association and is a member of the company's national advertising board. "The climate for black business is getting better in Greater Cleveland," says Burkes, "just like it is for everyone else."

While private organizations have sparked the growth of minority businesses, so has local government. The Cuyahoga County Department of Development helps by providing industrial revenue bonds for manufacturing concerns and creating enterprise zones in the suburbs for abating taxes. It also has a revolving low-cost loan fund for private economic development.

"Companies are impressed with the attitude toward government in helping them start or locate in Greater Cleveland," says Nancy Cronin, director of the Cuyahoga County Department of Development.

George Voinovich himself created the city Department of Economic Development, which now has 25 employees working to provide financial services to business. During the 1980s the department was able to leverage federal Urban Development Action Grants (UDAGs) of $152 million—more than any city of comparable size—into private investment of nearly one billion dollars.

These federal loans impelled new downtown and neighborhood development and generated millions in tax dollars. As the UDAGs are repaid, the money reverts to the Economic Development Department, which reloans it at below-market interest rates to small businesses.

The department requires its large loan recipients to hire minority companies on at least one-third of UDAG-financed work. This has helped pave the way for minority and female business enterprises to obtain special consideration in bidding on city contracts.

Significant undertakings of the department are in helping industries locate property within the city for development, resolving code problems, and establishing tax-abated enterprise zones. When necessary, the Economic Development Department also expedites capital improvement—bridges, roads, sidewalks, sewers, water lines, and street lighting—to foster large-scale development.

"All this has stimulated $3 billion in development downtown and in city neighborhoods," says Andi Udris, former director of the Economic Development Department and currently an investment specialist with AGR/Grubb & Ellis, a commercial realty firm. "We expect to duplicate this in the 1990s."

To encourage further development, the Growth Association also established its Economic Development Finance Incentives Task Force, composed of city, county, and business representatives. It devised alternatives to incentive financing for companies through tax-free Industrial Revenue bonds.

All told, more than a dozen ideas were produced by the task force. These included new state legislation to facilitate tax increment financing for construction projects and legislation to facilitate the assemblage of tax-delinquent inner-city property for development.

To keep such public-private partnerships churning well into the next century, the Growth Association, Cleveland Tomorrow, the Convention & Visitors Bureau, and the New Cleveland Campaign aided by the Cleveland Foundation called on McKinsey & Company to draw up an assessment of the region's strengths and to determine how these can be marketed. "The McKinsey report concluded that because so many new jobs have come in high-growth technology, Greater Cleveland must promote the continued expansion of these new businesses while encouraging out-of-town companies and headquarters of major corporations to relocate here," says Carol Rivchun, vice-president/marketing and communications for the Growth Association.

Because of the influence of British Petroleum in Cleveland and in London, the McKinsey report suggested that BP could "serve as a role model in persuading United Kingdom companies to locate or expand in Cleveland." The study also suggested stimulating new jobs through the promotion of Cleveland's burgeoning convention and tourism industry.

Implementation of the report's findings will continue through the 1990s. Efforts, however, have already begun and are paying off in increased tourism, conventions, and jobs.

"The idea is to concentrate Cleveland's promotional efforts in specific areas where the most can be accomplished," says Richard Gridley of McKinsey, who supervised the study. "The intended result is the benefit to all of Greater Cleveland."

"The marketing partnership formed by the New Cleveland Campaign, the Growth Association, and the Convention & Visitors Bureau will ensure a coordinated team effort to enhance economic development and tourism," says George N. Miller, executive director of the New Cleveland Campaign, the umbrella marketing program for Northeast Ohio.

"Greater Cleveland has had its ups and downs over the years," says William J. Williams, chairman of Huntington Bank and chairman of the Greater Cleveland Growth Association. "By implementing the study's recommendations, we should have an economic road map to shorten the downs and lengthen the ups. To ensure its success, it will take a continued commitment of the public-private partnerships that started the city's turnaround in the early 1980s."

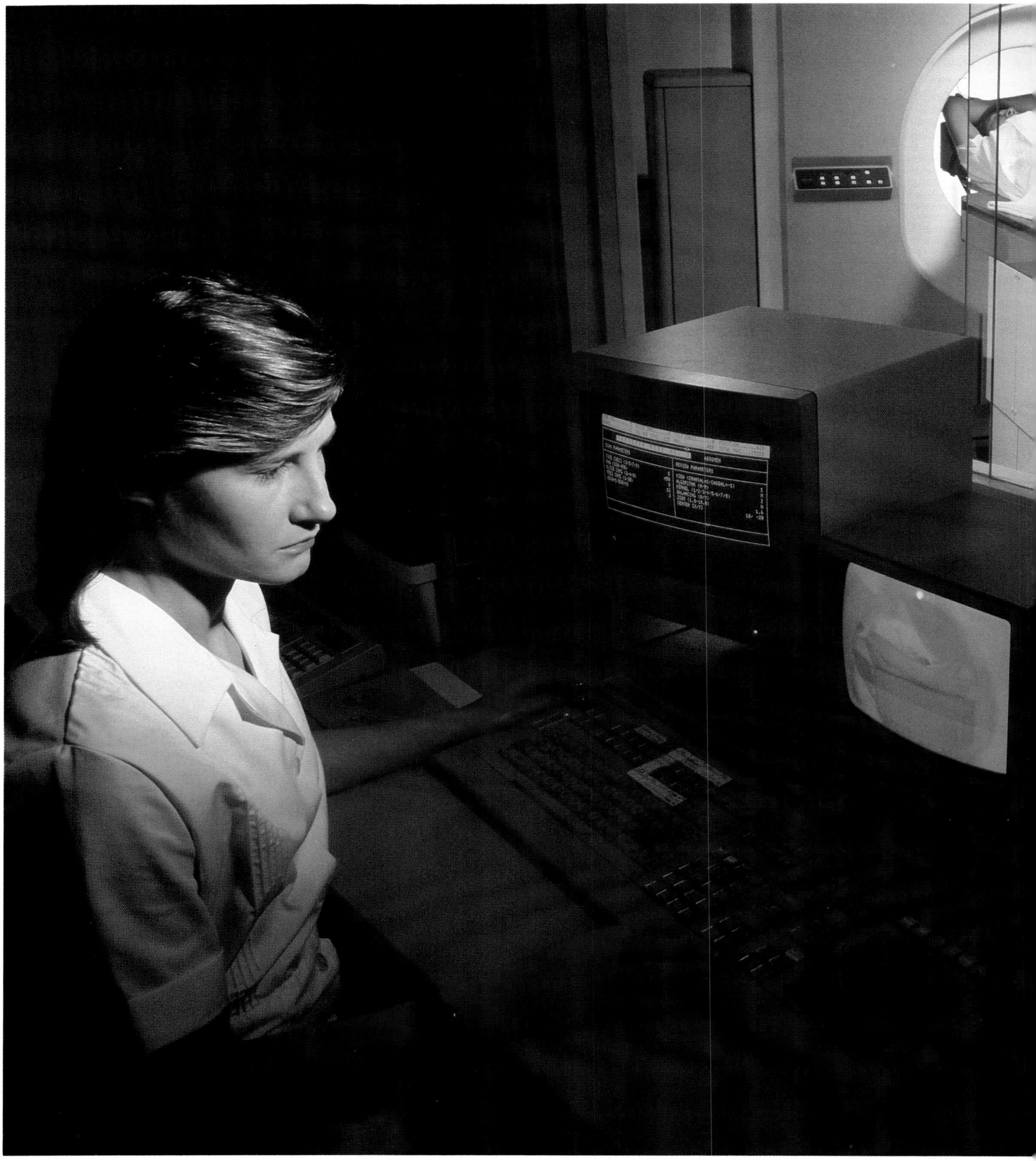

CHAPTER 7

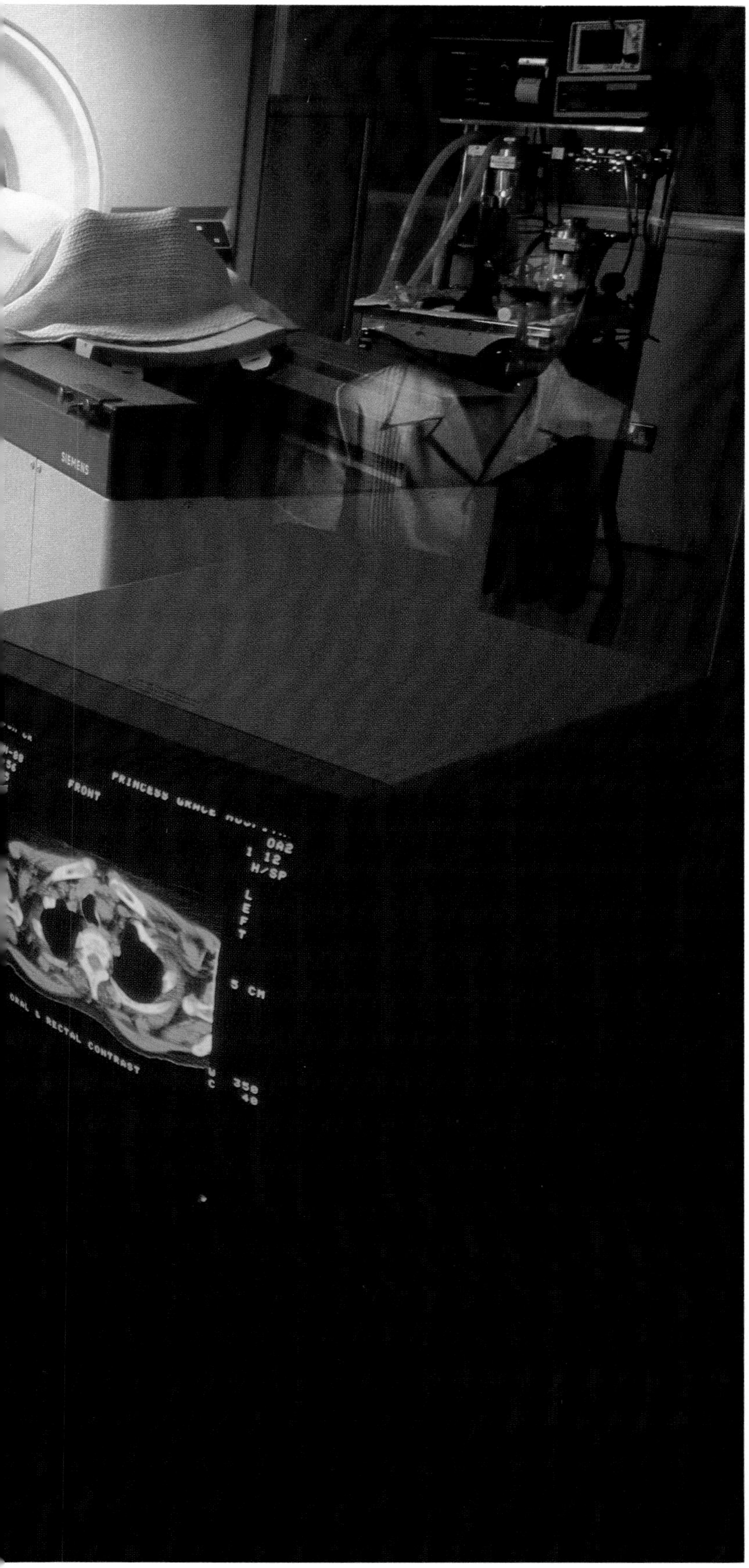

A World-Class Health-Care Community

Dr. Robert J. White, director of the Division of Neurosurgery and the Brain Research Laboratory at Cleveland MetroHealth Medical Center, is probably the Cleveland physician who is best known outside of Cleveland. A tireless lecturer, writer, and traveler, White is known by the ironic sobriquet of "Humble Bob." A graduate of Harvard University Medical School, White was the first medical scientist in the world to keep the brain of an experimental animal—a monkey—alive outside of the animal's body. As a result of his research, which he carried out in the laboratories at Metro, White developed techniques that are used in brain surgery worldwide, including methods for the treatment of spinal cord trauma.

White has written almost 500 articles on brain research, neurosurgery, and medical ethics, for publications ranging from arcane medical magazines to *Readers' Digest.* He has visited the Soviet Union 20 times as a consultant and speaker, and is well known throughout Europe, especially in Vatican City, where he instituted a bioethical committee for his friend Pope John Paul II and treated the superior general of the Jesuit order. He has been profiled in publications from the *Plain Dealer* to the influential French newspaper *Le Figaro.* "Meet our special envoy from Cleveland. Amazing!" read the photo caption in *Le Figaro.* In addition, the BBC did a half-hour television special on his activities.

Dr. White is the personification of Greater Cleveland's health-care industry—flamboyant, internationally recognized, pioneering, and highly competitive. Pacing in his small, book-lined office at Metro,

A wide spectrum of medical services and facilities provide the city of Cleveland with a rich and distinguished health-care community. Photo by Julian Calder. Courtesy, Tony Stone Worldwide

A part of Cleveland's medical community since the nineteenth century, St. Luke's Hospital has developed into one of Ohio's largest and most respected hospitals. Photo by Barbara Durham

White wears his operating blues as he oversees three different brain operations at once. Nevertheless, he takes a few minutes to recount his arrival in Cleveland in 1961.

"I was on the staff at the Mayo Clinic, and they told me that I had to do either full-time research or full-time surgery. I came here because the medical school at Case Western Reserve University, which has a say in the medical appointments at Metro, offered me the opportunity to do both research and surgery."

White, who can be controversial—the animal-rights movement considers him a bitter enemy for his strong defense of the use of animals in vital research—has a soft spot in his heart for the Cleveland medical industry, especially for the quality of care it provides. It was this commitment to quality that lured him here, along with many other renowned physicians.

Health care in Greater Cleveland is not merely one industry among

Fairview General Hospital is one of the many health-care institutions serving the growing west side suburbs. Photo by Barbara Durham

many; it is a way of life. The city and the region have come to be identified—perhaps more than anything else—as an international health-care center.

Cleveland's medical heritage is rich and distinguished and has contributed mightily to breakthroughs and discoveries in medical practice and research that have impacted medicine all over the world. Many of the important institutions—including Metro, University Hospitals, St. Vincent Charity Hospital and Health Center, Mount Sinai Medical Center, St. Luke's Hospital, and the Case Western Reserve University School of Medicine—can trace their origins to the nineteenth century.

The future is just as exciting. "As Cleveland becomes a medical mecca in the twenty-first century, it will be largely through a spirit of cooperation and collaboration," says Dr. William Kiser, chairman of the board of governors of the world-recognized Cleveland Clinic Foundation.

Cooperation among hospitals, especially in the booming field of biotechnological research, is becoming more and more of a necessity for the economic growth of the medical industry and, consequently, of the area as a whole. Cleveland's medical roots, however, are grounded in individual achievement. Many extraordinary physicians have crossed the pages of the city's medical archives.

One of the first of note is Peter Allen, patriarch of a long line of brilliant and influential Cleveland physicians. Allen came to Northeast Ohio in 1808 to practice medicine. He traveled a 12-county circuit on horseback, working out of the saddlebags in which he kept his instruments. Because there were no medical schools in the region at the time, Allen also served as a one-man private institution, most often with several students under his tutelage.

Dudley P. Allen, Peter Allen's grandson, followed in the footsteps of his grandfather—and father, Dudley Allen—to become perhaps the most notable of the family. He limited his practice to surgery and worked at both Lakeside Hospital (now a part of University Hospitals) and Charity Hospital (now St. Vincent Charity).

The younger Dudley was a Renaissance man, as befitted many intellectuals of the upper class in the early twentieth century. As an art lover, he was one of the first trustees of the Cleveland Museum of Art and was a lifetime member of the Western Reserve Historical Society. He also was the founder of the Cleveland Medical Library Association and the namesake of the Dudley P. Allen Memorial Medical Library on Euclid Avenue in University Circle.

The library association eventually joined with the health sciences libraries at Case Western Reserve University, and the Cleveland Health Sciences Library was formed to administer both the Allen collection and the university's collection.

The Howard Dittrick Museum of Historical Medicine, one of the city's great unsung museums, is the historical arm of the Cleveland Health Sciences Library. Founded in 1926, the museum is housed alongside the Allen library. One of the museum's most popular exhibits is the saddlebag and medical equipment used by Dudley's grandfather.

Even after Dudley P. Allen's death in 1915, his family continued to be

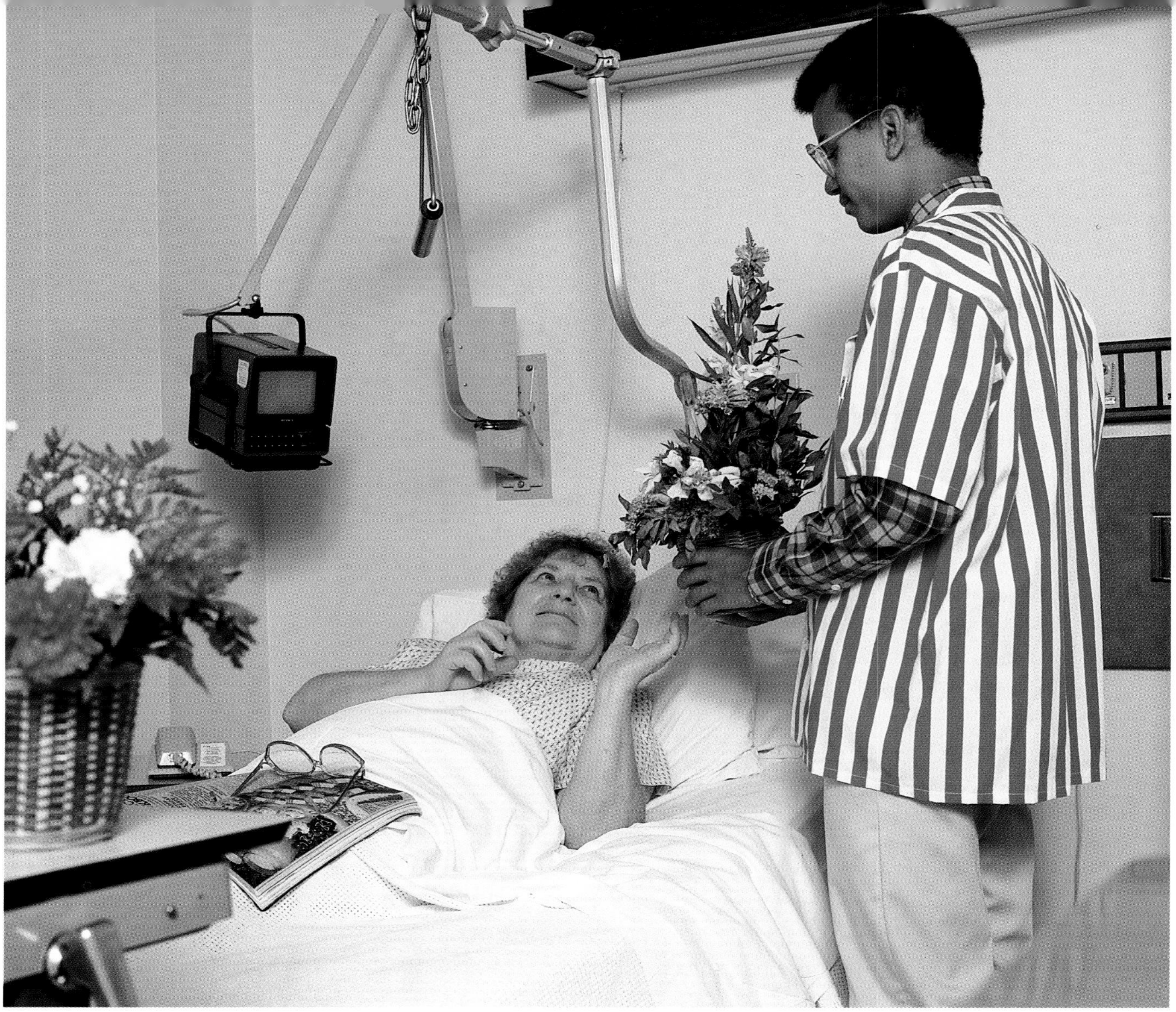

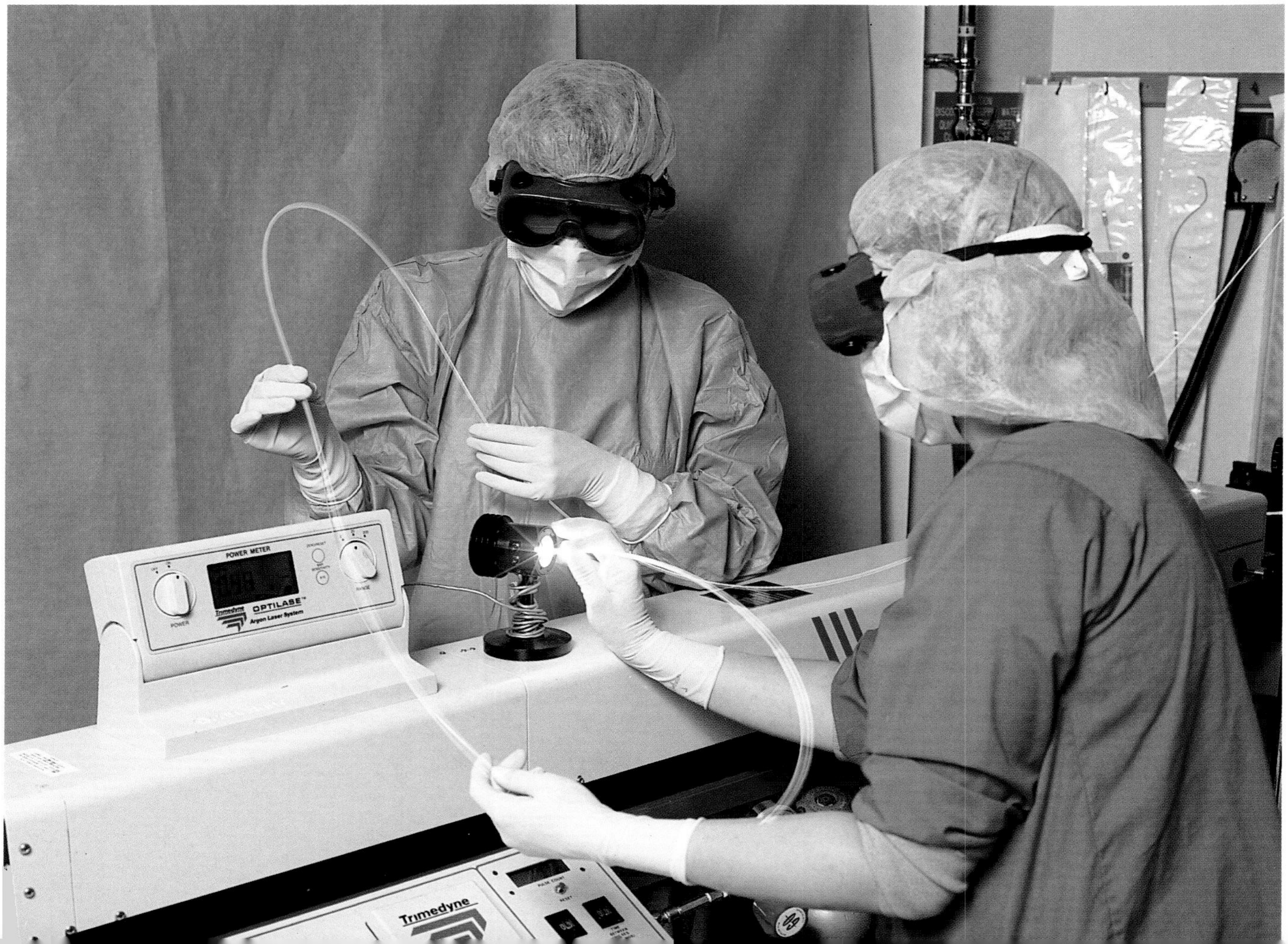
POWER METER
POWER
RANGE
OPTILASE™
Argon Laser System
Trimedyne

associated with the upper echelon of the medical field. Allen's widow, Elisabeth Severance Allen, married another legendary figure in Cleveland's medical lore, Francis F. Prentiss. Although not a doctor, Prentiss had a keen interest in health care. As a founder of the Cleveland Twist Drill Company, he was extremely wealthy and was one of the town's leading philanthropists.

Prentiss devoted a large part of his life to the solvency and growth of St. Luke's Hospital, donating more than $6 million over his life to the Methodist institution. Largely because of the Prentisses' financial support, St. Luke's was able to prosper and become one of the largest teaching hospitals in Ohio, affiliated with Ohio Wesleyan University, Kent State University, and Cuyahoga Community College.

Another well-known philanthropist who devoted himself to health care was Dudley P. Blossom, the city's director of public welfare in the 1920s, who saw MetroHealth Medical Center (then called City Hospital and owned by the City of Cleveland) through a major growth mode.

There is no institution with deeper roots in the community than Metro, located on the city's near south side in an old ethnic neighborhood called Tremont. It is the flagship hospital in the oldest public hospital system in the United States—the Cuyahoga County Hospital System. An institution contemporary with Cleveland's own origins, Metro celebrated its 150th anniversary in 1987.

A year after the city was incorporated in 1836, a poorhouse was designated as City Hospital to provide care for the indigent, a mission that is still carried out today.

Metro did not have a full-time medical staff until 1891, when it moved from the poorhouse to a new facility. It began an affiliation with the CWRU medical school in 1914, and, like University Hospitals, it is still a primary teaching hospital for the medical school.

In 1952 Dr. Frederick C. Robbins joined the staff of City Hospital. Two years later Robbins was awarded the Nobel Prize in medicine for polio research he had conducted in Boston. In that year, 1954, Metro won more honors and awards than any hospital in America.

The city transferred management of the hospital to Cuyahoga County in 1958. Included later as part of the county system were Highland View Hospital, Sunny Acres Skilled Nursing Facility, Kenneth W. Clement Center for Family Health (named for a prominent late black doctor), and the Chronic Illness Center.

As the twentieth century progressed and the Cleveland medical industry grew, the names of doctors and their contributions to world medicine grew along with it. Some made contributions in other areas as well—such as Dr. Charles Garvin, who helped break down racial barriers not just in medicine but, through his example, in all aspects of life.

Garvin was the first black physician in America to be commissioned in the U.S. Army (for service in France during World War I). When he settled in Cleveland after the war, he helped found the Cleveland Medical Reading Club, begun in 1925 by black doctors who took it upon themselves to prepare papers and lectures in order to update each other

Facing page, top: Volunteers foster a tradition of healing and caring at St. Vincent Charity Hospital & Health Center. Courtesy, St. Vincent Charity Hospital & Health Center

Facing page, bottom: Laser technology has revolutionized vascular surgery at St. Vincent Charity Hospital & Health Center. Courtesy, St. Vincent Charity Hospital & Health Center

Functioning under the oldest and finest public hospital system in the country, Metro General celebrated its 150th anniversary in 1987. Photo by Jennie Jones

on the latest developments in the health sciences.

Garvin went on to prosper as a physician, businessman, and civic leader. He became an international figure in the civil rights movement and was nearly 80 years old when he died in 1968 after a long and extraordinary career.

Significant breakthroughs in health care have occurred in the business arena as well. John Mannix, a Clevelander, was the designer of the Blue Cross/Blue Shield health insurance plan—the first third-party insurance payment plan ever developed. This led not only to reduced hospital costs for the average patient, but to the formation of an important segment of the insurance industry.

Dentistry also is big business in Cleveland. The dental school at Case Western Reserve University is one of the best in the country. In addition, the largest chain of Sears dental clinics in the United States, founded in Cleveland in 1981 by Dr. Edward Meckler and Dr. Stuart DuChon, is headquarted here.

Cleveland also is playing a role in the development of Health Maintenance Organizations (HMOs), which operate under a membership prepayment plan with the cooperation of area hospitals and other medical facilities. Between 1970 and 1985, seven HMOs were founded in Cleveland. Until 1970 there was only one—the Kaiser Community Health Foundation, part of the Kaiser Permanente Medical Care Program, the largest HMO in America. Its local hospital affiliates are St. Luke's, Fairview General Hospital, Lakewood Hospital, Akron City hospitals, and the Lake County Hospital System.

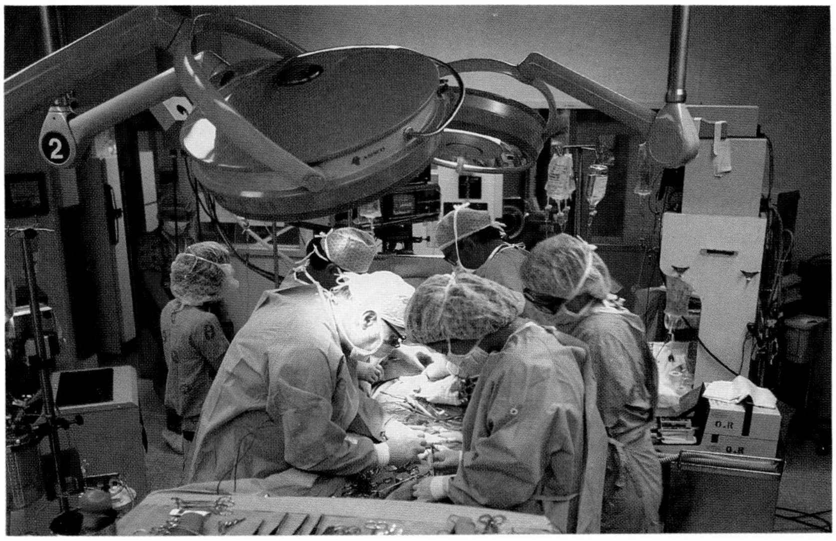

A patient undergoes surgery at the recently remodeled Mt. Sinai Medical Center. Courtesy, Mt. Sinai Medical Center

Greater Cleveland also boasts one of the largest health-care networks in the country, Meridia Health Systems. Founded in 1984, Meridia operates more than a dozen health-care facilities in the Cleveland area, including three acute care hospitals, a teaching hospital, a rehabilitation hospital, and a nursing school. Meridia, with 4,800 employees, is behind only the Cleveland Clinic and University Hospitals in its number of health-care workers, and has the highest volume of patient discharges in Northeast Ohio at 42,000 annually.

Another interesting feature of the Greater Cleveland health-care scene is the Ohio College of Podiatric Medicine, at East 105th Street and Carnegie Avenue near University Circle. It is one of only a handful of podiatric medical colleges in the nation. Founded in 1916 and graduating a mere 20 students the next year, the school over the years has developed a sophisticated four-year curriculum taught partially by medical doctors and osteopathic physicians. The college today has an enrollment of more than 500 students, and also operates the Cleveland Foot Clinic, which has 16 branches around Greater Cleveland.

This constant innovation and growth in diverse fields of medicine has begun to affect the area's economy in ways unforeseen even a generation ago, much less by the city's medical pioneers.

Health care is on its way to becoming the region's largest employer. According to a study conducted in 1988 by Cleveland State University for the Greater Cleveland Hospital Association, the number of health-care workers increased by more than 19,000 between 1980 and 1986, bringing the total to almost 100,000 employees.

The study was conducted for the seven-county region surrounding Cleveland, Lorain-Elyria, and Akron. Institutions included in the definition of health care were hospitals, research laboratories, nursing homes, private physicians, dentists, chiropractors, optometrists, and private outpatient clinics.

The study concluded that health services in the seven counties paid out more than $2 billion in salaries and wages, with the average worker being paid more than $20,000 a year.

Nearly 19,000 workers in the Akron area alone are on the health-care

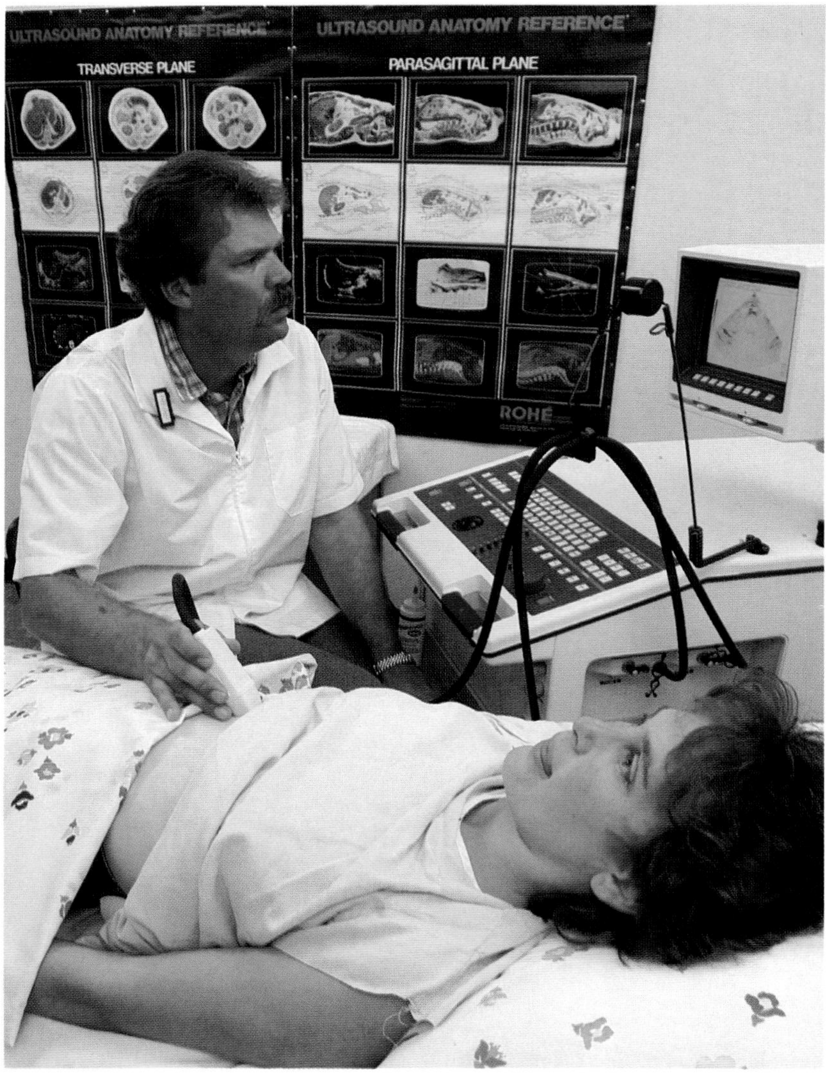

Ultrasound is just one of many procedures available through local hospitals. Photo by Jim Pickerell. Courtesy, Tony Stone Worldwide

payroll, with well over 7,000 in Lorain-Elyria. In Greater Cleveland, the number of health-care employees went from almost 10,000 in 1980 to more than 27,000 by 1986, with the figure increasing every year.

In the seven-county area, the sheer number of hospitals is amazing in itself. There are almost 50 general hospitals, along with six psychiatric hospitals, four children's hospitals, two rehabilitation hospitals, and several chemical dependency centers. These hospitals employ more than 50,000 people and have an annual payroll of more than one billion dollars.

Well over a half billion dollars are paid out in salaries and wages to the region's 4,000 private physicians. Overall, the study estimated the health-care industry's annual contribution to the region's economy to be an awesome $4 billion.

"That number was startling even to us," says Paul Lee, vice president for public affairs for the Center for Health Affairs and the Greater Cleveland Hospital Association. "We knew it was high, but not that high. It just shows how important the medical industry here really is.

"Obviously," Lee adds, "health care in this region has probably the largest impact in number of jobs. And in dollar impact it's also extremely significant. Our economy in Northeast Ohio is very much tied to health care, and certain actions—such as cuts in medicare—will affect the entire region."

The CSU study also cited the region's two medical schools, the Northeastern Ohio Universities College of Medicine in Rootstown (a six-year program at Akron, Kent, and Youngstown state universities) and especially the Case Western Reserve University School of Medicine in Cleveland, as having a strong influence on the region's health-care industry.

The influence of CWRU's medical school cannot be underestimated. Dr. White, also a professor of surgery at CWRU, says, "The school fosters a certain pride in the medical community. It is known internationally for its teaching methods. It trains students to be sensitive and concerned about patients from the minute they enter the school."

The school is located in the center of Greater Cleveland's medical neighborhood. University Circle is home to five of the city's biggest medical institutions: the CWRU medical school, University Hospitals of Cleveland, the

Dudley P. Allen, the man for whom the Allen Memorial Medical Library is named, pursued a brilliant surgical career in Cleveland and serves as a role model for today's physicians. Photo by Jim Baron. Courtesy, Image Finders, Inc

Cleveland Clinic Foundation on the west side of the Circle, Mount Sinai Medical Center, and a Veterans Administration hospital.

CWRU's School of Medicine was chartered as the Cleveland Medical College in 1843, at a time when the city's medical community was small but growing and gaining in national importance. The school, originally located downtown, served as a department of Western Reserve College, which was then in Hudson, 25 miles to the south.

More than 100 years later, under Dean Joseph T. Wearn, the school moved to University Circle and adopted the teaching system that put it ahead of the norm in American medical schools. Wearn, who joined the faculty in 1929, became dean in 1945. A brilliant man, his first order of business was bringing the school back from the verge of insolvency. That accomplished, in 1952 he instigated the pioneering teaching methods for which the school is internationally recognized.

"We were clearly the first, and we have been copied worldwide," Dr. Richard E. Behrman says. Behrman was the school's dean and CWRU's vice president for medical affairs through the 1980s until leaving to take a job with the Packard Foundation.

Behrman describes the teaching system as having three major aspects. The first is that students are introduced to live patients during their first year. "This is so they learn how to model themselves as doctors," Behrman says. "Many schools don't do this until the students are in their third year.

"The second aspect," Behrman says, "is attitude. They are treated as colleagues by the physicians on the faculty."

The third aspect is what Behrman calls "organ-system teaching." That is, students approach the human body as a series of systems rather than as

The Rainbow Babies & Childrens Hospital took its name from the Babies & Childrens Hospital and the Rainbow Hospital for Crippled & Convalescent Children, which merged in 1971. Photo by Barbara Durham

a conglomeration of isolated components. "This takes a lot of planning and work on the part of the faculty," Behrman says, "but this way, early on, we can show the student exactly how things go wrong."

In part, the high quality of Greater Cleveland's medical community emanates from the medical school. Because of its high standards and innovative policies, the school has attracted a superior faculty. Frederick C. Robbins, who was awarded the Nobel Prize, is a former dean of the medical school who still teaches and conducts research there.

Also, because the school attracts the best medical students from all over the world (competing toe-to-toe with premier institutions like Harvard and Columbia), it produces an enormous pool of medical talent—many of whom stay in the area to practice.

"Mount Sinai, University Hospitals, the Cleveland Clinic, you name it. A proportionately large share of the doctors practicing at the area's major hospitals come from our program," Behrman says.

The medical school has particularly strong ties to University Hospitals of Cleveland. The two institutions have been affiliated for almost 100 years—and their buildings are virtually side by side.

University Hospitals is a group of five facilities—Lakeside Hospital, Hanna House, Rainbow Babies and Childrens Hospital, MacDonald Hospital for Women, and the Hanna Pavilion, a psychiatric center—operating under one management. All told, the group has a work force of 5,500, putting it among Cleveland's 15 largest employers.

Ironically, its origins are humble. Lakeside, the first in the group, started during the Civil War as a hospital for refugees and displaced persons. The hospital began its association with Western Reserve University in 1897. By then both the university and the medical school had moved to land at University Circle donated by railroad magnate Amasa Stone. The university, through the School of Medicine, agreed to run the clinics in the hospital and to have its professors teach there. Today all members of UHC's medical staff—more than 1,000 doctors—have teaching appointments at the medical school.

Shortly after World War I, Maternity Hospital and Babies and Childrens Hospital were built, and in 1926 the two joined Lakeside in the University Hospitals complex. Hanna Pavilion was built in 1956.

Maternity Hospital, which goes back to 1891, became MacDonald House in 1936 and was later renamed MacDonald Hospital for Women. Babies and Childrens Hospital merged with the Rainbow Hospital for Crippled & Convalescent Children in 1971 to become Rainbow Babies and Childrens Hospital.

A poll in *Family Circle* magazine named UHC among the top 20 hospitals in America. UHC also was included, along with the Cleveland Clinic, in *The Best Hospitals in America* by Linda Sunshine and John W. Wright.

The first successful blood transfusion was carried out at University Hospitals in 1906. Likewise, University Hospitals developed an infant simulated-

Hanna House is just one of several facilities that comprise University Hospitals. Photo by Barbara Durham

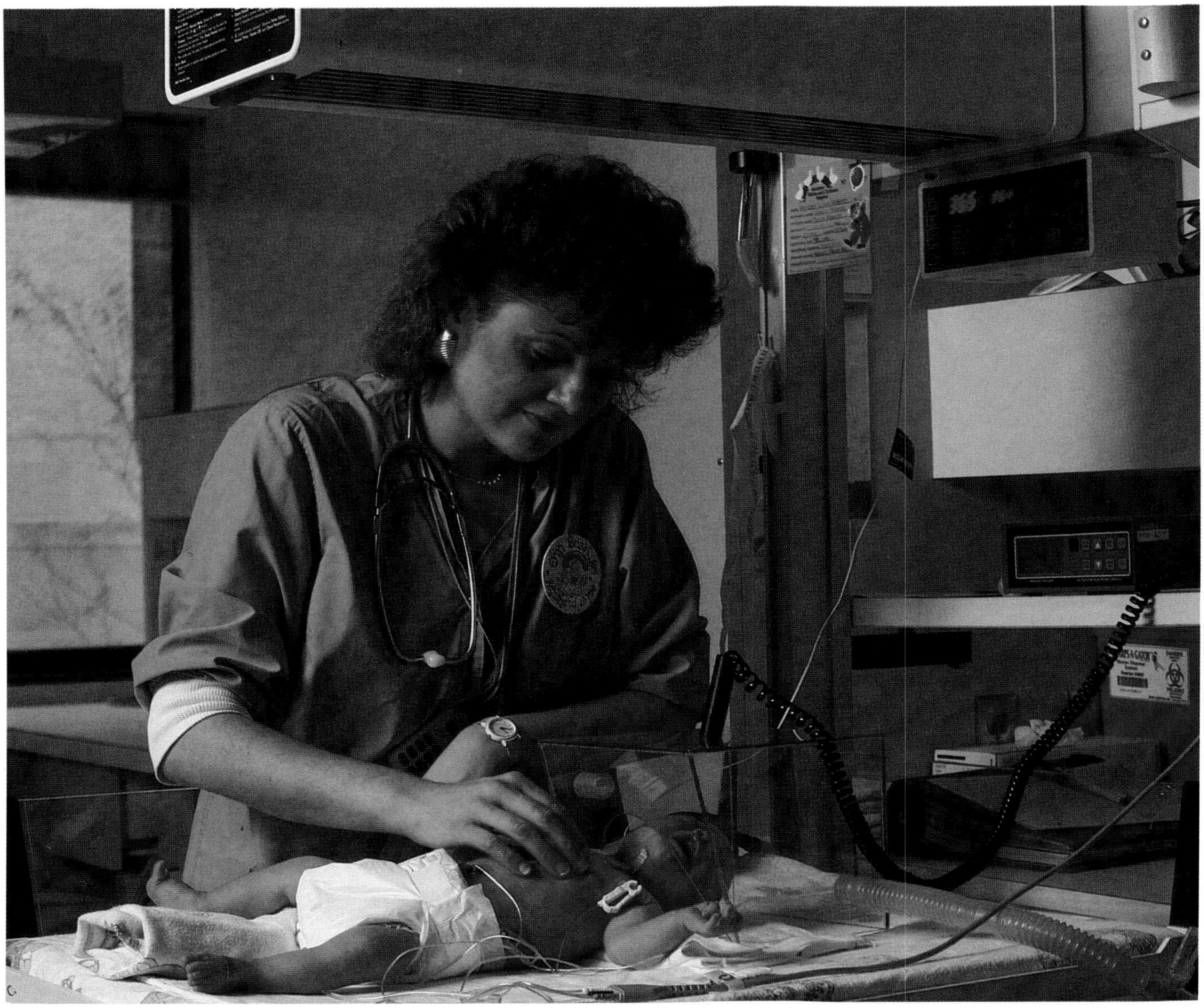

This young patient receives tender care at the Rainbow Babies & Childrens Hospital. Photo by Don Snyder

milk formula in 1915. It was the first hospital in America to have a whole-body Magnetic Resonance Scanner for diagnosis and treatment of cancer and heart disease.

Major areas of research, in conjunction with the CWRU medical school, include cancer at the Ireland Cancer Center, pulmonary disease, orthopedics, heart disease, geriatrics, and women's health. There are more than 100 research laboratories, under the banner of the Wearn Laboratory for Medical Research, making UHC Ohio's largest medical research center.

"We will continue to invest in people and facilities to remain one of the greatest academic medical centers in the United States," says Dr. James A. Block, UHC's president and chief executive officer.

Some of UHC's latest endeavors include the Alzheimer Center, the only state and federally designated facility of its kind in Ohio, and the One to One Fitness Center, a state-of-the-art health club. The main exercise area of the fitness center is 7,000 square feet, with skylights, greenery,

Left: With more than 5,000 employees, University Hospitals is one of Cleveland's top employers. A technician is pictured here reading magnetic resonance images during a CAT scan procedure. Photo by Henley and Savage. Courtesy, Tony Stone Worldwide

and more than 100 individual workout stations.

"We also will modernize our physical facilities," Block says, "and anticipate building a new medical/surgical hospital in University Circle over the next five years." The project, part of UHC's new master plan, is expected to cost $130 million. It will add 550,000 square feet and several hundred beds to UHC's clinical areas.

If cooperation is an important part of medicine in Cleveland, then University Hospitals holds the key to the future. One of the most significant cooperative programs—in medical-business partnerships as well as in partnerships among area hospitals—is the Edison Biotechnology Center.

Above: The spacious One to One Fitness Center has more than 100 individual workout stations and represents a continued effort on behalf of University Hospitals to provide quality facilities. Photo by Barbara Durham

Located in University Circle, the center's function is to help develop biotechnology as a business, utilizing the research done at University Hospitals, the Cleveland Clinic, The CWRU medical school, and Metro.

The program is part of the state's Thomas Edison Program, which was developed in 1983 to link universities and business with the support of government to maximize the economic benefits of advanced technology. Both CWRU and the Cleveland Clinic are building new multimillion-dollar biomedical research centers, which also will greatly benefit the Edison center and enhance the local economy.

"More than 140 businesses in Northeast Ohio alone deal in biotechnology," says the Edison Biotechnology Center's president, Dorothy Baunach. "And 70 percent of them are less than $10-million companies. It indicates that we have a lot of potential for growth in the industry. And we are here to assist the industry to grow."

One product, or system, at the forefront of the center's marketing thrust is Functional Electrical Stimulation (FES), a biomedical technique for helping victims of central nervous system disorders, including paralysis.

Two local doctors who have worked on the commercialization of FES are Hunter Peckham at CWRU's Department of Biomedical Engineering and E. Byron Marsolais, director of rehabilitation medicine at the Veterans Administration Hospital in University Circle. Nationally, the Veterans Administration has taken a strong interest in FES and will support an FES center in Greater Cleveland.

"FES is a marriage of engineering and medicine," says Cynthia S. Brogan, who is in charge of marketing the system. "The first commercial use to come to clinical fruition is a system that helps return hand movement to people with spinal cord injury."

The state put up the Edison Center's start-up money—$3.75 million. By the end of the center's first year, 32 local businesses and institutions came up with a combined matching total. Some of the center's charter members are BP America, Parker Hannifin Corporation, Ernst & Whinney, and Squire, Sanders & Dempsey, the second-largest law firm headquartered in Ohio.

"With such funding, we are able to bring some of our ideas to the marketplace that much quicker," says F.J. O'Neill, director of new enterprises for the Cleveland Clinic Foundation. "The clinic is proud to be a part of the biotechnology center."

Some of the projects the Cleveland Clinic Foundation is planning to market through the center include a special chair to provide pain relief for those who suffer from bone deterioration, a device for determining radiation doses for those undergoing radiation therapy, and a sensor that checks the glucose level in the blood.

The spirit of cooperation represented by the Edison Biotechnolgy Center extends deeper than it may appear on the surface. The effort marks the first time that the Cleveland Clinic and University Hospitals, two of the top research hospitals in America, have joined forces in a significant undertaking.

If University Hospitals represents Cleveland's old guard—the city's original medical establishment—then the Cleveland Clinic is symbolic of the new generation. The Cleveland Clinic has historic ties to University Hospitals. It was founded by a group of doctors who worked at Lakeside Hospital and served together in World War I.

These physicians put together what was known as the Army's Lakeside Unit and were among the first American forces to land in Europe after the U.S. entered World War I. They set up a hospital near Rouen, France, and later established a mobile hospital unit. When they returned from the war, these doctors—George W. Crile, Sr., Frank E. Bunts, and William E. Lower—got together with Dr. John Phillips, and the Cleveland Clinic was born.

The renowned Cleveland Clinic sits on 100 acres of inner-city land between downtown and University Circle. Photo by Jennie Jones

Among the most notable medical institutions in the world, the Cleveland Clinic is a complex of patient care facilities, research laboratories, and amenities like first-class hotels and restaurants sprawled across 100 acres between downtown and University Circle. Employing 9,000 people, it is one of the largest nongovernment employers in Greater Cleveland, and it brings an estimated $350 million in new money into the area each year.

With close to 700,000 outpatient visits and more than 30,000 hospital admissions annually, the Cleveland Clinic is also one of the busiest medical institutions in the world. Patients come from all 50 states, as well as from more than 78 foreign countries.

The Cleveland Clinic is affiliated with medical facilities in Turkey, England, Brazil, Japan, and West Germany, and operates a second clinic in Fort Lauderdale, where it is planning to build a $200-million ultramodern clinic.

The clinic was the first medical facility in America to be federally designated as a national referral center. "We are a national referral center and an international health resource for specialized and complex medical care," says Dr. William S. Kiser, who will be retiring at the end of 1989 after

13 years as chairman of the clinic. "As we grow and meet the challenges of the twenty-first century, health care represents a significant opportunity for the entire area."

Besides being among the most outstanding, the clinic is also one of the most glamorous medical institutions in the world. The Saudi royal family, Jordan's King Hussein, heads of government from Kuwait and Israel, congressmen, actors, and athletes all have availed themselves of the clinic's internationally known doctors and facilities. These facilities include VIP rooms for well-heeled patients in the new hospital wing. The VIP area features a conference room and 24-hour kitchen service. For nonpatients, the Clinic Center Hotel has suites that rent for as much as $1,000 a day, complete with butler. The hotel also is home to Classics, an elegant restaurant frequented by Cleveland's business community.

This clientele, however, represents only a tiny fraction of the clinic's business. More than 60 percent of the clinic's patients are from Northeast Ohio and the surrounding region. "Beyond many of the wealthiest and most powerful heads of state, the norm at the Cleveland Clinic is Everyman . . . and woman and child," Kiser says.

Designated by Congress in 1979 as a National Health Resource, the clinic is divided into three parts. "Our driving force is patient care, supported by research and education," Kiser adds. Research and education will get a tremendous boost over the next few years as the clinic embarks on a $160-million international fund-raising effort.

In education, the clinic boasts the largest independent postgraduate facil-

This magnetic resonance apparatus can be seen at the Cleveland Clinic. Courtesy, The Cleveland Clinic Foundation

ity in America. In research, the clinic is best-known for its trendsetting work in heart disease. Its hospital has a 351-room cardiovascular wing and sees 6,000 heart patients a year on average. The chairperson of the Department of Thoracic and Cardiovascular Surgery is Dr. Floyd Loop, while his wife, Dr. Bernadine Healy, is chairperson of the clinic's Research Institute.

Some of the most important advances in heart research and surgery have been developed at the clinic. Perhaps the most significant occurred on May 9, 1967, when Dr. Rene Favaloro, the international specialist from Argentina, performed the first successful coronary bypass operation.

One of the clinic's most notable medical scientists, and certainly one of its most interesting, was Dr. Willem Kolff, who invented the heart-lung machine (called the membrane oxygenator) and the kidney dialysis machine. Although the inventions were perfected in the 1950s at the clinic, Kolff had built the first dialysis machine in Nazi-occupied Holland in 1942.

From breakthroughs in kidney research to new epilepsy treatments, the Cleveland Clinic is on the leading edge of medical technology. Photo by Don Snyder

An energetic medical genius, Kolff split his time between the heart and the kidney, and between the operating room and the laboratory. He was on the surgical team that performed the first kidney transplant in 1963, after having helped develop the first intra-aortic balloon pump the year before.

Both Favaloro and Kolff were honored when their busts were put on permanent display at the Cleveland Health Education Museum, along with a dozen other doctors and medical scientists who have contributed to the understanding of heart disease through their work at Cleveland medical institutions. Another of the honorees was Dr. Irvine Page, for whom the clinic's Center for Creative Thinking in Medicine is named. The center is a think tank at which ethics, economics, politics, and social issues—any topic that affects medicine—are discussed.

More recent breakthroughs at the clinic include the study of a new agent used to dissolve blood clots. The federal Food and Drug Administration designated the clinic as one of only two centers in America to study the agent, called t-PA.

In another recent development, one of the clinic's prominent heart surgeons, Dr. Delos M. Cosgrove, invented a technique by which patients are administered drugs through a computerized "closed-loop system"—in other

A patient undergoes bypass surgery at the Cleveland Clinic. Courtesy, The Cleveland Clinic Foundation

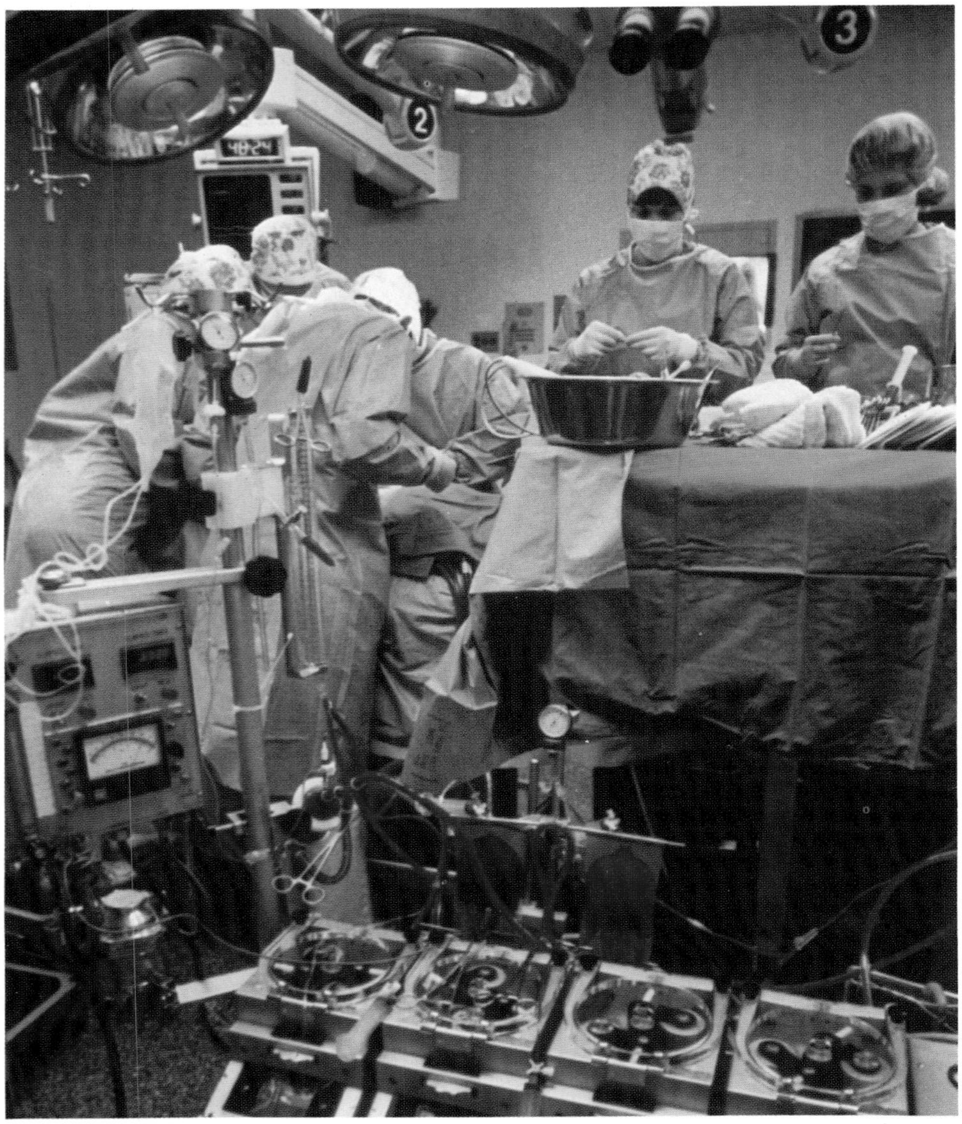

words, without the need for medical personnel.

The clinic also is at the forefront in epilepsy research. Its laboratories are testing sites for new drugs in epilepsy treatment and has helped to develop tests that allow surgeons to perform sophisticated operations for removing the source of seizures in the brain.

Overall, at any given time, the research laboratories at the clinic work on hundreds of projects in seven departments: artificial organs, biostatistics and epidemiology, brain and vascular research, general medical sciences, heart and hypertension research, immunology and cancer research, and musculoskeletal research.

But the clinic cannot lay claim to all of the top local research. One of the most important medical scientists ever to emerge from the Cleveland health-care field was Dr. Harry Goldblatt, who put Mount Sinai Medical Center on the map for his work with hypertension.

In the 1930s, while a professor at CWRU's medical school, Goldblatt, in what is considered one of the most famous medical experiments of all

Mount Sinai Medical Center traces its history to the late 1800s, and has gained a worldwide reputation through its advances in hypertension and fertility. Photo by Roger Mastroianni

time, discovered that high blood pressure resulted from stifling of the blood flow to the kidneys. The experiment was essential in helping researchers understand the causes and means of controlling hypertension and literally created an entirely new field of medical research.

In 1961 Goldblatt was named director of Mount Sinai's Louis D. Beaumont Research Laboratories, and in 1965, with Dr. Erwin Haas, he isolated renin, a hypertension-causing agent found in the kidneys. In 1976 he produced anti-renin in the Mount Sinai labs. For his work, Goldblatt was awarded the prestigious Scientific Achievement Award of the American Medical Association and received an appointment to the National Academy of Sciences.

The Mount Sinai Medical Center has established a reputation over the years as one of the most innovative medical institutions in America, with some nationally known surgeons attached to it—for instance, Dr. Bahman Guyuron, one of the country's foremost reconstructive surgeons, and Dr. Wulf Utian, who heads Mount Sinai's world-famous fertility clinic. Utian, who has accepted the chairmanship of the OB-GYN department at the CWRU School of Medicine, is moving his fertility clinic and staff to University Hospitals.

Mount Sinai is one of only a few Greater Cleveland hospitals actually to see a rise in admissions over the past several years, despite its having a comparatively small number of beds, at 450.

The hospital sprang from the Young Ladies' Hebrew Association in the late nineteenth century. The group's mission was to help the poor with medical care, and Mount Sinai is still known for its aid to the indigent. "We con-

St. Vincent Charity Hospital & Health Center first opened its doors in 1865, and continues to offer Cleveland modern medical care. Photo by Jennie Jones

sider it a moral responsibility," says Robert J. Shakno, Mount Sinai's president and chief executive officer.

"We are an agency of the Jewish Welfare Federation, and the federation provides money for indigent care," says Shakno. "The Jewish community that supports this hospital considers the hospital to be a source of tremendous pride."

The hospital, which has been affiliated with the CWRU School of Medicine since 1947, has become internationally famous for its work in aiding couples with childbirth problems.

The world's first in vitro surrogate baby, Shira Rudnitzky, was conceived at Mount Sinai in 1986. The Laboratory for In Vitro Fertilization and Embryo Transfer (the LIFE program), headed by Dr. Wulf Utian, has helped couples from across America succeed in having children, largely through surrogate mothers, who are implanted with an embryo conceived in a laboratory (in vitro) with the parents' eggs and sperm.

Mount Sinai's emphasis on family-oriented care led to the establishment of the Maternity Matters Center in Beachwood, which serves as an educational and informational source for young families, focusing on childbirth and parenting.

A generation ago, specialized programs such as the Maternity Matters Center would not have seemed within the realm of medical orthodoxy. But the needs of contemporary society have given rise to finely tuned treatment and counseling services, especially in the area of alcoholism and drug addiction.

One of the country's pioneer alcoholism treatment clinics, Rosary Hall, was established in 1952 at St. Vincent Charity Hospital and Health Center. Rosary Hall was started by Sister Mary Ignatia, a member of the Sisters of Charity of St. Augustine, who sponsor St. Vincent Charity Hospital. Sister Ignatia, who many area Catholics feel should be canonized, first worked closely with Alcoholics Anonymous cofounder Dr. Robert Smith at St. Thomas Hospital in Akron. In 1939 Smith and Sister Ignatia set up a clinic at St. Thomas for the treatment of alcoholism as a disease.

Hospitals all over the United States have used Rosary Hall as a model for their own alcoholism treatment centers. According to Mary Darrah, a Cleveland author who has written a biography of Sister Ignatia, "Rosary Hall was probably the most prominent alcoholism treatment center in the country when Sister Ignatia died in 1966."

St. Vincent Charity Hospital and Health Center itself occupies a prominent place in Cleveland's medical industry. Opened in 1865, it is the city's first permanent general hospital.

A number of medical firsts can be laid on the well-worn doorstep of St. Vincent, which remains a Catholic hospital. The first surgical amphitheater in the area was built there in 1872. The first open-heart surgery in the Midwest was performed there in 1956 by Dr. Earle B. Kay. The same year St. Vincent opened the world's first intensive care unit for heart surgery patients. The hospital still boasts one of the best heart programs in Ohio.

Located on the southeastern edge of downtown Cleveland, St. Vincent, aside from the quality of its medical care, is known for its civic efforts in taking the lead in the redevelopment of the 12-block inner-city neighborhood known as the St. Vincent Quadrangle.

In fact, as Cleveland's resurgence has expanded, most of the important medical institutions in the city have become involved in the redevelopment of their neighborhoods. Metro has a "campus development plan" for its South Side neighborhood. University Hospitals recently renovated a whole row of homes on East 115th Street in University Circle and is active in the preservation of Little Italy, which abuts its many buildings.

Neighborhood redevelopment is just one direction that the Cleveland health-care industry is facing as it shapes its vision for the future. Another important aspect of the future of health care is in geriatrics. Paul Lee of the Greater Cleveland Hospital Association says, "The basic demographics of the region tell us there is a growing number of elderly. We already have a high per capita of those 65 and over—and that trend will continue."

"Geriatrics is going to be very important, going to be *extremely* important, over the next 10 years," says Dr. Block of University Hospitals.

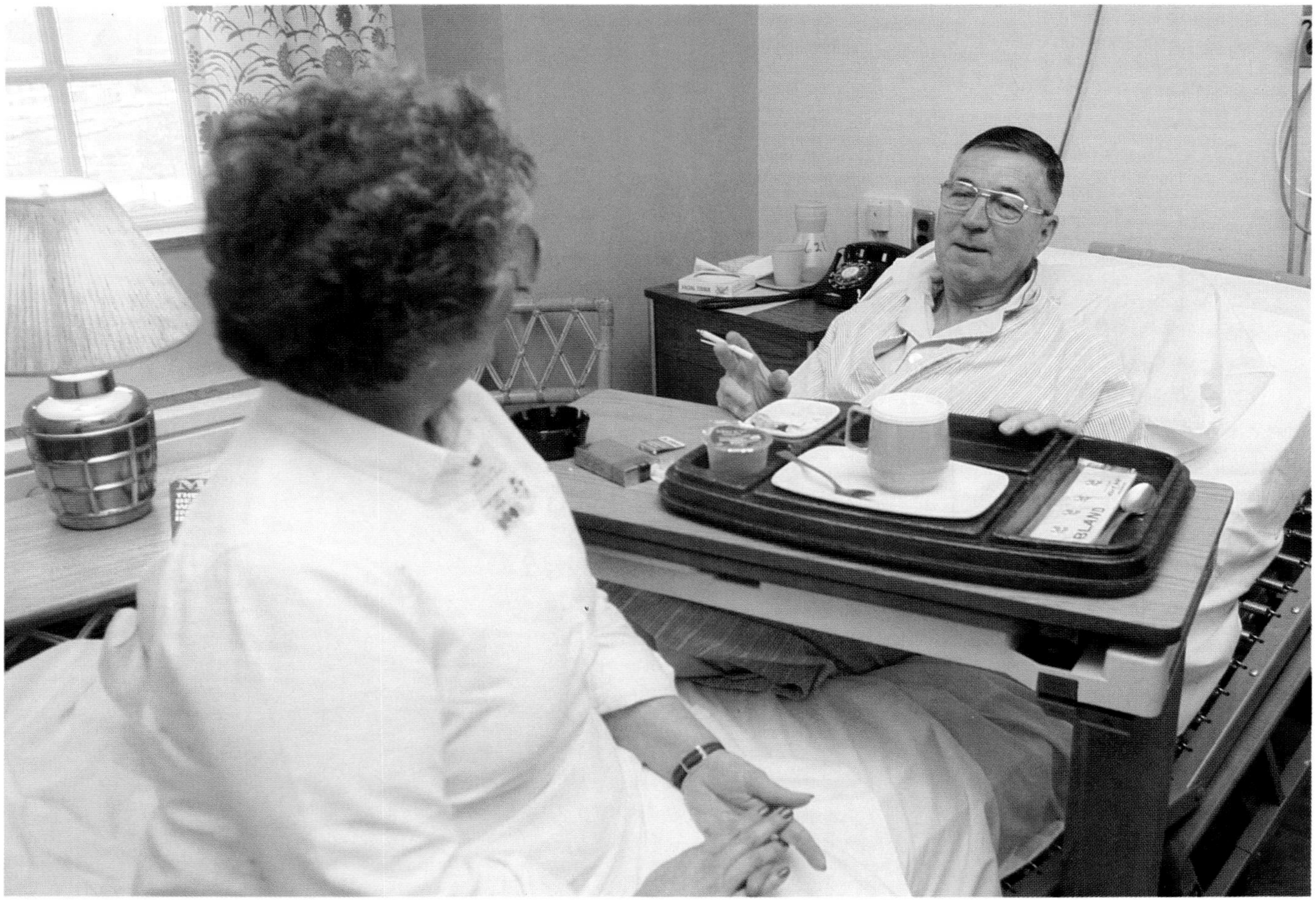

Geriatrics and related elderly-care programs are expected to increase dramatically as baby boomers reach maturity. Photo by T. Williams. Courtesy, Image Finders, Inc.

Facing page: The future looks bright for the health-care community in Cleveland. Photo by Barbara Durham

With that in mind, University Hospitals has helped turn the old Fairhill State Hospital on Fairhill Road into a facility for geriatric treatment.

But the health of the industry itself—and hence the economic health and quality of health care of all of Greater Cleveland—will depend perhaps more than anything else upon cooperative educational and research efforts. The Edison Biotechnology Center is just the first drop in the bucket.

"We need a well-trained, well-cultivated, well-educated work force," says Kiser at the Cleveland Clinic. "You will see us taking a more active role in education and in improving the quality of life in Cleveland."

The clinic's educational effort is already under way. It involves working with the Cleveland Board of Education in orienting the curriculum at nearby John Hay High School toward the health professions and regularly bringing the students to the clinic for field trips.

But as the Cleveland health-care industry gears up for the twenty-first century, the one component that every institution and facility is stressing is the most basic of all—putting the patient first.

"A patient in Cleveland has a unique opportunity," says Metro's White. "And that opportunity is that the level of care here is better than most of the rest of the country. The patient can feel very secure that he is going to be well cared for."

CHAPTER 8

Accelerating Cleveland's Future

A most symbolic development for the future of higher education in Greater Cleveland is unfolding in a seemingly unlikely place, unlikely yet logical: the NASA Lewis Research Center.

Cleveland's expanding space center adjacent to Hopkins Airport—the only such center in the northern United States—hardly has the sylvan setting of an Ivy League campus. But as a multibuilding facility responsible for designing the power system for America's first permanent space station, *Freedom*, which will be launched in the mid-1990s, Lewis is the ideal choice for Cleveland's newest addition to the challenging world of academia, the Ohio Aerospace Institute.

The institute opened its doors to its first class in the fall of 1989. All are graduate students at one of the nine Ohio universities that offer doctoral degrees in engineering, including Case Western Reserve University and Cleveland State University. The institute itself does not grant degrees, but offers Ph.D. candidates something just as important: the opportunity to study advanced aerospace engineering at the fountainhead.

The full impact of the institute on higher education in Ohio—and Greater Cleveland in particular—will be enormous.

"The institute is the only program of its kind outside of Marshall Space Center in Huntsville, Alabama," says Cleveland Congresswoman Mary Rose Oakar, who, along with Congressman Louis Stokes, has fought to increase the role of Lewis in the nation's space program even as the program itself has followed an unpredictable orbit around public opinion.

The State of Ohio was largely responsible for funding the institute in its formative years. In an ar-

This proud statue of President Lincoln stands at the entrance to the Cleveland Board of Education Administrative Building. Photo by Jennie Jones

rangement that Congress approved at Oakar's behest, the institute is housed on the sprawling Lewis complex under a 99-year lease. As the Aerospace Institute progresses, it will receive additional support from the participating universities.

"The institute also means that Ohio universities will have the opportunity to offer fellowships in aerospace engineering," says William Grimberg, who is working on the institute's development for Cleveland Tomorrow, a coalition of chief executive officers from Greater Cleveland's major corporations and professions. "We are ramping it up so eventually it will accommodate 150 people. It should be in full swing by 1994."

It is the hope of Cleveland's business leadership that the Ohio Aerospace Institute will not only attract top engineering students, but also tempt them to stay and work in the mushrooming aerospace and advanced technology industries.

The Ohio Aerospace Institute represents the heights to which higher education is rising here. Greater Cleveland's mandate for higher education is clear. Without higher education of the highest quality, there could be no cultural renaissance, no business boom, no sophisticated economic evolution into the next century.

With increased financial help from government and business, Cleveland's two major universities—Case Western Reserve University and Cleveland State University—are both undergoing profound periods of reevaluation. Both are guided by determined new presidents—Dr. Agnar Pytte at CWRU and Dr. John Flower at CSU—who are preparing their institutions for the changes of the next century.

The smaller institutions in Cuyahoga County—John Carroll University, Baldwin-Wallace College, Cuyahoga Community College, Dyke College, and the two Catholic women's colleges, Notre Dame and Ursuline—have made significant efforts to instill new life into programs and facilities. Enrollment at John Carroll and Notre Dame has risen. Though Notre Dame, a women's college, has fewer than 1,000 students, its increase in 1988 over enrollment in 1987 was somewhat astonishing—64 percent, largely a result of the school's personal outreach program to local high-school girls.

Two major organizations play strong supporting roles in strengthening higher education in Greater Cleveland: the Ohio Board of Regents, chaired by Cleveland businessman Alva T. "Ted" Bonda, and the Cleveland Commission on Higher Education, led until 1989 by William J. Williams, chairman and chief executive officer of the Huntington National Bank and chairman of the Greater Cleveland Growth Association.

The Ohio Board of Regents has developed a master plan to improve the quality of state-supported higher education. In an article written for the *Plain Dealer*, Bonda predicted that the plan will be one "under which our colleges and universities will rival any in the nation by the end of this century."

That is a tall order, but Bonda is confident. "We have implemented a variety of programs that are proving to be very successful," he says. In the Eminent Scholar program, for example, the Regents are given the financial wherewithal to lure the best teachers and researchers in their fields to

Ohio. "We have attracted more than two dozen prominent scholars," Bonda says. "We might go to a Harvard or a Stanford to lure somebody away. It's essentially a carrot on a stick. And it's working."

Closer to home, the Cleveland Commission on Higher Education provides colleges and universities in Cuyahoga County with a forum through which they can come together to address vital academic, financial, and promotional matters with business and civic leaders.

Founded in 1951, the commission at the time was unique in the country. It was responsible for the political lobbying efforts that established Cuyahoga Community College. It also helped establish Cleveland State University in 1964, thus giving Cleveland a major university that could reach out to both the business community and the center city.

The media is one environment which promises opportunity for tomorrow's graduates. Pictured here, local station WEWS broadcasts a diverse array of television programs to Cleveland's viewing audience. Photo by Jim Baron. Courtesy, Image Finders, Inc.

The commission is composed of the presidents of 10 institutions in Cuyahoga County (including the Cleveland Institute of Art and the Cleveland Institute of Music) and 10 prominent civic members. As chairman Williams sees it, the Cleveland Commission on Higher Education has two goals. "One is to get students to enroll here by getting them to recognize the resources and facilities that are available. The other is to get them to stay in the area after they are graduated."

A powerful inducement for top-level graduates to stay in Greater Cleve-

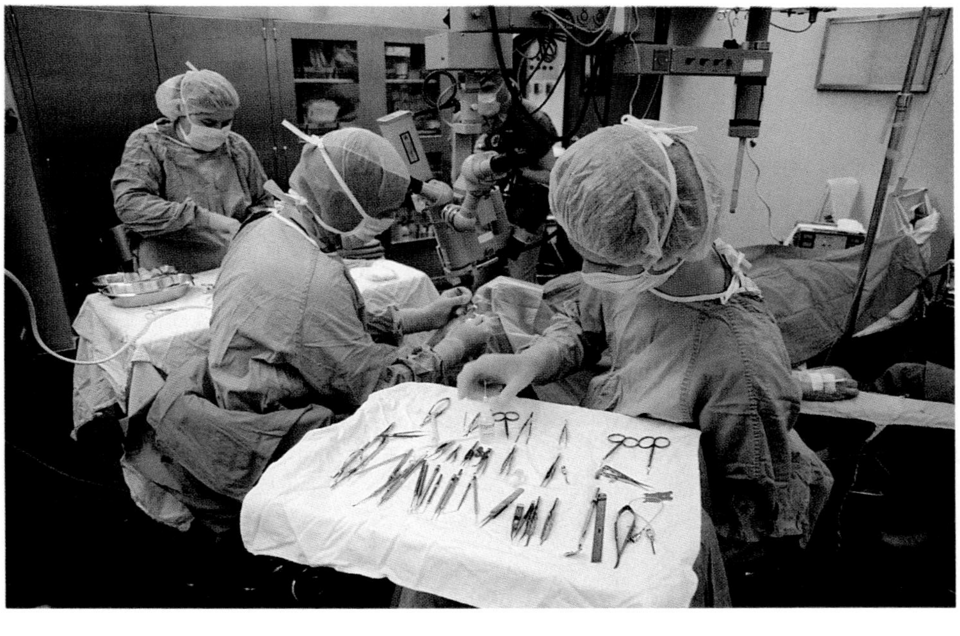

With some of the finest hospitals in the nation, there is little reason for a medical graduate to leave Cleveland. Courtesy, Luce Photography, Inc.

Government service represents still another avenue for advancement in Cleveland.

land once they have completed their undergraduate or postgraduate education are the emerging opportunities in advanced technology, manufacturing, and the service sector, including law, accounting, finance, and medicine.

Among the major goals in the growing alliance among higher education, government, and business in Greater Cleveland is the creation of promising high-tech companies to enhance the local economy. This commitment gives graduates the opportunities not just to practice their professions, but to become entrepreneurs if they so choose.

For instance, many graduates of the Case Western Reserve University School of Medicine stay in the area because of opportunities in sophisticated medicine and biomedical research that the medical school fosters.

In Northeast Ohio, perhaps more so than in other areas of the state, the move in higher education toward a marriage with advanced manufacturing and technology makes sense. The economic health of Cleveland's marketplace depends on the success of this marriage.

"Cleveland has always been a manufacturing center, and we have to take advantage of that," says George Sutherland, vice-president of the state-sponsored Cleveland Advanced Manufacturing Program (CAMP), which supports research, development, and training at area universities.

The marriage also is a response to the times. Gone are the days when local higher education meant an almost exclusive grounding in either the liberal arts or science.

"The marketplace is a factor in higher education in ways that it did not used to be," says Dr. John A. Flower, Cleveland State's fourth president. "Since the end of World War II, we have experienced an ever-increasing union of the traditional university and what were often considered trade school subjects—accounting, business, computers, engineering."

Perhaps the most important measure of the linkage between advanced technology/manufacturing and higher education are the commercial applications resulting from the research—in the creation of new companies, jobs, and skills. At the forefront of the effort to apply research to business is the Cleveland Advanced Manufacturing Program (CAMP).

CAMP is a public-private economic development and job training program that receives funding from the state's Thomas Edison Program, the federal government, and numerous corporations and nonprofit institutions. In turn, CAMP provides money for joint research efforts among education, business, and government, and marketing expertise for the commercialization of those research efforts. CAMP administers programs at Case Western Reserve University, Cleveland State University, and Cuyahoga Community College.

At Cleveland State, CAMP manages the Advanced Manufacturing Center. "The center primarily does project work for companies," Sutherland says. These companies include the Ford Motor Company, General Electric Company, Cleveland Pneumatic Company, Bendix Automation, and TRW.

Besides support from the Edison program, the Advanced Manufacturing Center also receives funding from a consortium of Cleveland corporations, including Parker Hannifin Corporation, Eaton Corporation, TRW, and Cleveland Pneumatic. "This is strictly generic support in that it does not go toward producing a specific product for a specific company," Sutherland says.

Some of the center's general projects include a system for using jets of water to cut materials, and research into the science of tribology—the study of the effects of friction on lubrication systems in machinery. The Advanced Manufacturing Center is studying ways to monitor the breakdown of lubrication systems.

Perhaps the most significant contribution CAMP has made to local higher education, however, is its role in convincing the National Institute of Standards and Technology (NIST) to set up a technology transfer program at the Unified Technologies Center at Cuyahoga Community College.

Cleveland's NIST center is only one of three such federally designated centers in the country. George Sutherland is the director of Cleveland's NIST facility, called the Great Lakes Manufacturing Technology Center.

"As I see it, there are two big projects that everyone in town got behind in recent years," Sutherland says. "One was the Rock and Roll Hall of Fame. The other was NIST."

Getting NIST to locate here was a coup not just for Cleveland and CAMP but for Cuyahoga Community College as well.

The two-year college was one of the first junior colleges set up in Ohio under the state's Community College Act of 1961. Cuyahoga Community College opened in 1963 with more than 3,000 students—the largest ini-

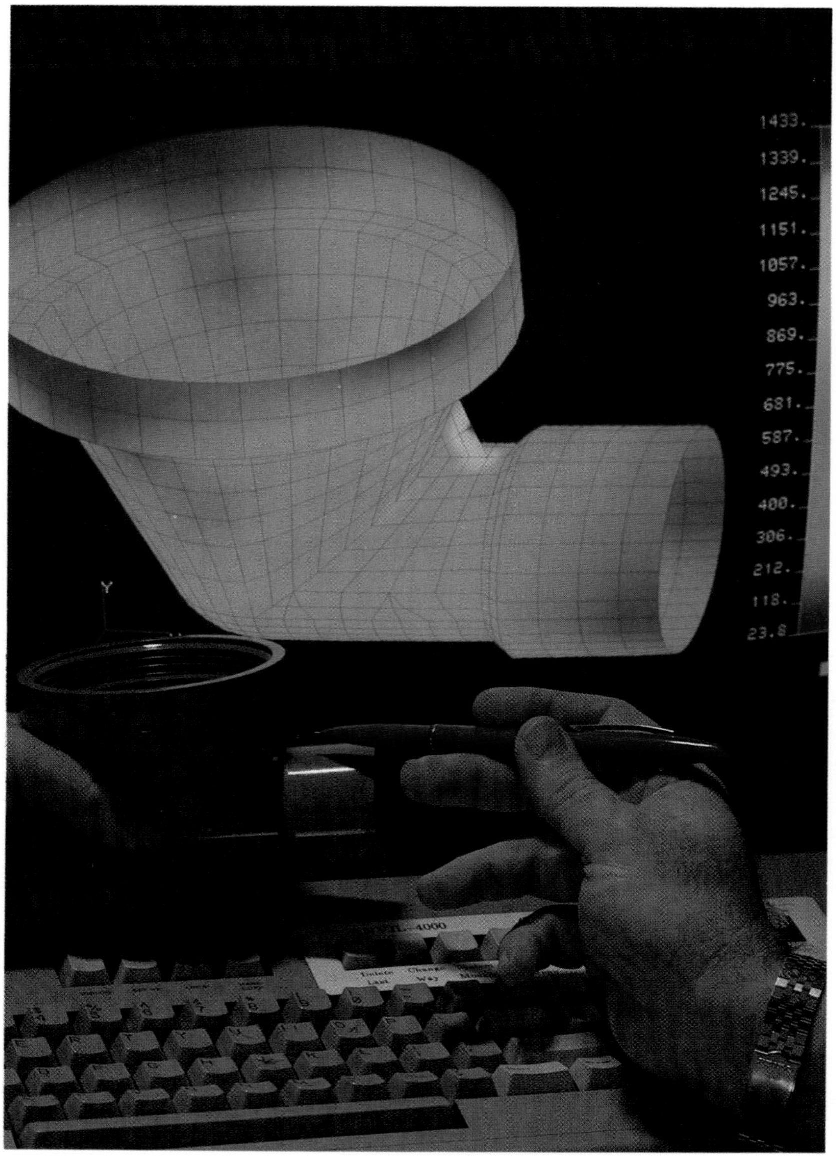

The United Technologies Center offers career training in, among other things, computer-aided design. This image shows engineers at the B.F. Goodrich facility in Brecksville. Photo by Don Snyder

tial enrollment of any two-year college in America. The Metropolitan Campus was established in 1966, the Western Campus in Parma in 1975, and the Eastern Campus in Warrensville Township in 1981.

CCC offers its students an academic track that can be transferred to four-year colleges, as well as remedial programs. In addition, it offers something vital to the community it serves—career-oriented programs in business, engineering, public service, and health care.

The Unified Technologies Center, which opened at the downtown Metropolitan Campus in 1986, is the jewel in the crown of the college's career-training program.

The center offers training in statistical processes, management, and advanced quality control, among other fields. But most of the programs are oriented toward training students and corporate employees in advanced manufacturing systems technologies, such as computer-aided design and manufacturing, instrumentation control, microcomputers, and robots.

In this light, the addition of NIST at the Unified Technologies Center is even more meaningful. Specifically, NIST does research into the impact of advanced technologies on small- to medium-size companies. "Our responsibility, Sutherland says, "will be to transfer the technology developed at NIST directly to those kinds of companies."

At CWRU there are two important programs under CAMP's aegis. One is the Center for Automation and Intelligent Systems Research, which does research into the burgeoning field of artificial intelligence. The other is the Edison Sensor Technology Center, the Edison-supported portion of CWRU's Electronics Design Center, which has concentrated on the development of sensor devices to direct the operation of machinery and equipment. Applications of these sensors in the biomedical field are of special interest to CAMP.

The Weatherhead School of Management at CWRU also has a CAMP-sponsored program: the Center for Management of Sciences and Technology, which investigates ways in which new technology can be put to use in companies.

Weatherhead recently moved into its large new quarters, Enterprise

Hall, marking the first time the school has had its own home. The building is dedicated to five area families and their companies, all of which have made key contributions to Weatherhead: the Keithley family of Keithley Instruments, the Mandel family of Premier Industrial Corporation, the Parker family of Parker Hannifin Corporation, the Tomsich family of NESCO, and the Wuliger family of the Ohio Mattress Company.

Weatherhead is very important not only to the university but to the community at large. One of its star programs is the Executive MBA Program (EMBA), whose curriculum is designed for experienced executives who want to delve deeply into the function of top management and learn from the best.

Cleveland's leading executives frequently lecture at the EMBA program, including Peter B. Lewis, chief executive officer of the Progressive Corporation; Dr. William S. Kiser, chairman of the Cleveland Clinic Foundation; and Frank E. Mosier, vice-chairman of BP America. The corporate sponsors of EMBA have included the biggest names in American industry, including the Goodyear Tire & Rubber Company, Coca-Cola Foods, Dun & Bradstreet Information Resources, TRW, and the Xerox Corporation.

Weatherhead is also one of the sponsors—along with the School of Law and the School of Applied Social Sciences—of the Mandel Center for Nonprofit Organizations, a program set up to educate future executives for the unique field of managing nonprofit organizations.

CWRU also has increasing initiatives in two affiliated companies: Enterprise Development, Inc., and University Technology.

University Technology is a wholly owned subsidiary of CWRU whose primary function is the commercialization of research. Enterprise Development is affiliated with Weatherhead and offers assistance and advice to entrepreneurs.

Since 1984 a multitude of advanced technology companies have been formed out of CWRU's technology initiatives. They include software companies such as Endot, STORM, ControlSoft, and BIOFOR. Clinical Instrumentation, Inc., sells fetal heartbeat monitors to hospitals, while Infantest markets tests to determine the learning ability of infants.

Yet the trends in higher education in Greater Cleveland consist of more than advanced manufacturing and technology. Adults—so-called "nontraditional" students—are going back to the classroom in droves. Cleveland State University has an enormous continuing education student population, as does Baldwin-Wallace College in Berea, a tree-lined college town only a few miles south of Hopkins Airport.

"Annually we enroll nearly 14,000 people in our continuing education programs, and that is 14,000 *apart* from the regular student body of 18,000," says CSU president John Flower.

A large portion—about 1,500—of Baldwin-Wallace's 4,500 students are nontraditional students enrolled in continuing education courses. On the average, 200 nontraditional students a year graduate from Baldwin-Wallace—a large number compared to the overall student body size.

Baldwin-Wallace president Dr. Neal Malicky feels that continuing educa-

Baldwin-Wallace College, which came about with the merger of Baldwin University and the German Wallace College, is recognized for its conservatory of music. Photo by Jim Baron. Courtesy, Image Finders, Inc.

tion is becoming more and more necessary as the twenty-first century draws closer. Even the license plates on his car read "BW 2001."

"In a rapidly changing age, how does one keep up?" Malicky asks rhetorically. "By keeping pace. By being a continual learner.

"We have not at all deemphasized the traditional students," Malicky says. "But education is much larger than the 18- or 19-year-old age group. Learning doesn't stop when you get a college degree."

Baldwin-Wallace is considered one of Ohio's most egalitarian liberal arts colleges. One reason is the large number of adults enrolled in continuing education classes. Another is because of the student fellowship fostered by the progressive Christian ethos it instills in the students through the school's affiliation with the United Methodist Church.

Baldwin-Wallace was formed in 1913 with the merger of Baldwin University and German Wallace College, which were founded in 1845 and 1863, respectively. The two schools had evolved from the Baldwin Institute, a Methodist educational institution named after John Baldwin, a religious educator who came here from New England.

The college has had only six presidents since its formation. The president emeritus, Alfred Bryan Bonds, Jr., served as president from 1956 to 1981, one of the longest terms of any college president in Ohio. He was succeeded by Malicky, who holds a theology degree from Southern Methodist University and a doctorate in international relations from Columbia University.

Baldwin-Wallace offers basic coursework in theology for seminary preparation, and is recognized by the American Association of Theological Schools. It also has strong graduate programs in education and business administration—including an MBA program for executives—and is known for its excellent undergraduate program in music.

The music school enjoys such a good reputation that its students have no trouble finding employment as extras with the Cleveland Orchestra and the Ohio Chamber Orchestra, or as church organists and choir directors. The music faculty is composed of some of the best musicians not just in Greater Cleveland but in the U.S. Members of the Cleveland Orchestra such as Ronald Bishop (tuba), William Herbert (piccolo and flute), and James Darling (trumpet) are on the faculty.

Baldwin-Wallace might be small, but it has graduated some very successful people, among them Arlene Saunders, a soprano with the Metropolitan Opera; Willard Carmel, former chief executive officer of McDonald & Company Securities; Steve Minter, director of the Cleveland Foundation; international tennis sportscaster Bud Collins; and George L. Forbes, longtime Cleveland City Council president.

Every academic, professional, and artistic discipline imaginable is represented within the framework of the 10 institutions of higher learning in Cuyahoga County—from law to lepidoptery, from public relations to physical therapy, from retail merchandising to religious studies.

Many of the programs within the overall framework enjoy national and even international reputations—the Mandel School of Applied Social Sciences, the School of Medicine and the Frances Payne Bolton School of Nursing at CWRU, and the Maxine Goodman Levin College of Urban Affairs at Cleveland State, for example.

But many other disciplines are also distinguished, such as the English program, department of theater arts, department of psychology, and law school at Case Western Reserve. The fashion design school at Ursuline College has come into its own in recent years, while John Carroll University—one of 28 Jesuit institutions of higher learning around the country—is noted for its Institute for Soviet and East European Studies and its Institute on Violence and Aggression.

Cleveland's leading research institution is Case Western Reserve University, one of the most competitive universities in the United States. In the University Athletic Association it competes with the likes of Brandeis, New York University, Emory, the University of Chicago, and Carnegie-Mellon, but it also competes with those eminent institutions nationwide for top students, faculty, and research dollars.

CWRU, the largest private university in Ohio, is located on 130 acres at University Circle. It is, in fact, the nerve center of the Circle, and the Circle in turn is the cultural nexus of Northeast Ohio.

The Cleveland Museum of Art abuts the campus, as does Severance Hall, home of the Cleveland Orchestra. In the same neighborhood are the Museum of Natural History and the Western Reserve Historical Society.

The southeast part of the campus touches Little Italy, with its diverse collection of excellent restaurants, bakeries, shops, and art galleries. Right next door, and virtually indistinguishable from the CWRU campus, is the complex of University Hospitals, one of America's major teaching and research medical facilities.

CWRU has 3,000 undergraduates, though the entire student body numbers more than 8,000, with 5,000 enrolled in postgraduate and professional programs in law, medicine, business administration, nursing, dentistry, applied social sciences, and the humanities.

Among its faculty, former faculty, and alumni, CWRU boasts eight Nobel Prize winners. The most recent is a former member of the medical school faculty, Dr. George Hitchings, who won the 1988 Nobel Prize in biochemistry for his work at the Wellcome Research Laboratory in North Carolina.

Prominent CWRU graduates include Herbert Henry Dow, class of 1888, founder of the Dow Chemical Company; Michael McCaskey, chief executive officer of the Chicago Bears, who received a master's degree in business; William Baker, president of WNET-TV in New York; James Biggar, president and chief executive officer of Nestlé Enterprises, Inc.; and best-selling author/psychiatrist M. Scott Peck, a graduate of the medical school.

Above: Located in University Circle near the Museum of Art and Severance Hall, the Western Reserve Historical Society preserves the past in its library and archives. Photo by Jennie Jones

Left: The student body at Case Western numbers more than 8,000 with 5,000 of these engaged in postgraduate or professional work. Photo by Jennie Jones

Facing page: Not far from CWRU is the Cleveland Museum of Art. Photo by Jennie Jones

Under Dr. Agnar Pytte, the university has embarked on an ambitious fund-raising program and has created a national network of alumni chapters. Pytte, a physicist and former provost at Dartmouth College, describes the school's new master plan as threefold: "We have an academic component—which drives the plan as a whole—we have a physical part, and we have a financial part."

The heart of the CWRU financial effort is a five-year, multimillion-dollar fund-raising campaign. Although CWRU receives more than $80 million a year in federal grants in addition to private contributions, it needs the campaign for its ambitious physical and academic proposals.

One of the most innovative and exciting parts of the overall plan is the campuswide TRW fiber-optic information and communications cable network that will link the library, dormitory rooms, faculty, and administrative offices. Students ultimately will be able to tap into library and other data services and transmit their work electronically to professors.

When the system—the most comprehensive intra-campus communications network using fiber optics in the United States—becomes fully operational in the mid-1990s, it also will allow the campuswide televising of campus activities, including classroom lectures. The university refers to the advanced network as an Electronic Learning Environment. "It pushes computer technology right up to the current moment," Pytte says.

As important as the Electronic Learning Environment is to the future of Case Western Reserve, so is the university's master development plan. In toto, the plan represents the most significant step the university has taken since Western Reserve University (founded in 1826 in Hudson and moved to Cleveland in the 1880s) merged in 1967 with the Case Institute of Technology (founded in 1880).

The plan involves an immense physical restructuring of the campus to give it a coherent look and thereby establish a sense of unity. One segment calls for the establishment of a campus "front door" on Euclid Avenue so that visitors entering University Circle from the west know unmistakably that they are also coming upon CWRU.

Another major component will be a campus "heart" courtyard on the north side of Euclid between the Thwing Student Center and Severance Hall. The Severance parking lot will be transformed into a courtyard and parking shifted to a new underground garage. To fill out the courtyard perimeter, the university will build a new library encompassing the present Freiberger Library along with a major new classroom building.

A new walkway, or "spine," with new lighting, landscaping, and benches, will traverse the campus diagonally across Euclid Avenue. Near Adelbert Hall, the university's historic granite administration building on the south side of the campus dedicated in 1882 by President Rutherford B. Hayes, a new courtyard is planned. The relocation of one building and the razing of another will serve to thoroughly integrate structures that once were distinctively Western Reserve or Case.

Plans for other buildings are under way as well. One of the new buildings will house the Mandel School of Applied Social Sciences. Morton, Joseph, and Jack Mandel, prominent Cleveland businessmen and civic leaders who founded Premier Industrial Corporation, contributed $3 million for the building's construction. A portion of the money needed also will come from the sale of Beaumont Hall to University Hospitals.

A new biomedical research facility also is in the works. This will be built next to the medical school and financed through the sale of tax-free long-term bonds. The medical school's expanding research activities require it, as does the region's economy. When completed, it will be the largest biomedical research facility in Ohio, complementing a new biomedical center planned for the nearby Cleveland Clinic.

When the master plan is fully implemented, it will improve the sense of campus unity and should enhance all of University Circle, including CWRU's prestigious allied institutions of higher education, the Cleveland Institute of Art and the Cleveland Institute of Music.

The Institute of Art (next to the Cleveland Museum of Art) is the larger of the two. It has 500 full-time students studying for a Bachelor of Fine Arts degree in a range of majors that include art education, graphics, medical illustrating, photography, and sculpture. Students also can work toward teacher certification.

The Cleveland Institute of Music, with some 300 full-time students, offers majors in various instruments as well as in audio recording, voice, and theory. More than a score of Cleveland Orchestra members are on the faculty, and much of the academic study is done through joint programs with Case Western Reserve.

Severance Hall, home of the Cleveland Orchestra, abuts the Case Western Reserve University campus. Photo by Roger Mastroianni

Mayfield City Schools offers art classes as part of their adult education curriculum. Photo by Jim Baron. Courtesy, Image Finders, Inc.

Four miles west of University Circle along Euclid Avenue, Cleveland State University has its own ambitious physical redevelopment plans, which also serve as downtown unification plans.

CSU's $47-million Convocation Center, scheduled for completion in 1991, is rising on property between Carnegie and Prospect avenues that was merely a conglomeration of urban eyesores. The Convocation Center (280,000 square feet, 13,000 capacity) will virtually meld three sections of the east end of downtown Cleveland: CSU, the St. Vincent Quadrangle, and Playhouse Square. It also will be home to CSU's nationally recognized NCAA Division I basketball team, the Vikings, which has been to the NCAA play-offs.

Since its establishment in 1964, CSU has been an integral part of downtown. The original Fenn Tower, where the university president has his office, has been surrounded by campus buildings that wind several blocks west from the Innerbelt to East 17th Street along Euclid and Chester avenues. The dominant structure, soaring through the downtown skyline, is the 25-story Rhodes Tower.

In the early 1990s new athletic fields—soccer, baseball, tennis, and a running track—will be built between Chester and Payne avenues, complementing the huge natatorium that is used for NCAA swimming and diving competitions.

The familiar facade of the 25-story Rhodes Tower at CSU has secured a place in a crowded Cleveland skyline. Photo by Barbara Durham

Some $90 million in construction projects are under way at CSU, representing the largest face-lift in the university's history. In addition to the Convocation Center, the other major project, scheduled for opening in the 1990-1991 academic year, is the $23-million Music and Communications Building, with recital rooms, auditorium, and radio and television studios.

Music is dear to CSU's new president, Dr. John A. Flower. He is a concert pianist, as well as one of Ohio's most respected academicians. Dr. Flower served as CSU's provost for 15 years until his appointment as president in 1988. He also was a fighter-bomber pilot in World War II. "CSU is inseparable from the community," Dr. Flower says. "The critical mass of Cleveland and CSU just cannot be separated."

As Cleveland State grows closer to the downtown community—economically as well as physically—the two will become even more intertwined. CSU is embarking on a campaign to vastly increase its endowment, and BP America has pledged one million dollars over five years to seed the effort. The research center of the Cleveland-based multinational corporation employs more graduates from CSU than it does graduates from any other university.

CSU is the city's largest university, with 18,000 students. Although CSU is entering only its second quarter of existence, its roots go back to

An integral part of the downtown cityscape, Cleveland State University is the region's largest university with some 18,000 students. Photo by T. Williams. Courtesy, Image Finders

These CSU students take a break from studying to "soak up some rays" on the campus grounds. Photo by Jennie Jones.

the 1880s, when the Cleveland YMCA started a night school. Forty years later the school was named the Cleveland Institute of Technology.

By 1929 the Cleveland Institute of Technology had become Fenn College, the name many Clevelanders remember fondly. The name was in honor of Sereno Peck Fenn, an early principal of the Sherwin-Williams Company and director of the Cleveland YMCA for 52 years (25 years as president).

Fenn College specialized in low-cost educational programs in engineering and business. It severed ties with the "Y" in 1951 and became Ohio's seventh state university in 1964 in a move that instilled the institution with a reason for being: stimulating Cleveland's urban educational and economic environment.

CSU continues to honor Fenn through its 2,000-student Fenn College of Engineering, which is gaining a national reputation for its Advanced Manufacturing Center, its Robotics Consortium, and its research work with the NASA Lewis Research Center.

The work of the Fenn College of Engineering mirrors the efforts of other colleges at the university to reach out to the community. In fact, CSU is one of only 13 universities in America that have official "urban university" status—a designation that focuses its mission.

More than 15 percent of CSU students are minorities, the second-highest minority enrollment at any state university in Ohio. CSU also has a commitment to affirmative action, creating a post of vice-president Minority Affairs and offering fellowships to minority postgraduate students

Cleveland State University enjoys an exceptional affirmative action program that allows minorities, among other things, the opportunity to study and conduct research at the NASA Lewis Research Center. Photo by Don Snyder

in computer science, engineering, and mathematics to study and direct research at Lewis Research Center. The university's LINK program also seeks to recruit and guide minorities majoring in business and engineering.

The student body is unique in other ways, too. "The vast majority are employed," president Flower says, "and therefore not programmed exclusively for the traditional academic life. We try to help the students make it, to realize their potential. It is one thing to have students who automatically live up to their potential. But it is a far more demanding teaching job to take a student and bring him or her up to excellence."

There is yet another way in which CSU is distinguished. "We have more than 55,000 CSU graduates, and most of them have stayed in the community to work here," Flower observes. "We are a training facility for Greater Cleveland's business community."

Not only for business, but for government as well. CSU estimates that its Cleveland-Marshall College of Law has 500 elected officials among its 6,000 living graduates—including Cleveland Congressman Louis Stokes. The CSU College of Law has graduated so many of Cleveland's lawyers that it can almost be said that CSU built the local justice system—from judges to bailiffs to prosecutors to defense lawyers. Many of the city's major law firms also employ CSU law graduates.

Baker & Hostetler, one of the nation's largest law firms, gave the College of Law one million dollars to endow the Joseph C. Hostetler/Baker & Hostetler chair. It was only the second endowed chair at Cleveland State. The College of Urban Affairs has the university's first chair, the Albert A. Levin Chair of Urban Studies and Public Service, named for the college's great benefactor.

In honor of Mrs. Levin, also a major benefactor, the university in 1989 renamed the College of Urban Affairs as the Maxine Goodman Levin College of Urban Affairs. The college is well known and respected because of its wide-ranging programs in urban policy analysis, planning, and management, which are directly oriented toward solving Cleveland's urban problems. "Part of our mission is linking CSU directly to the community," says Dr. David Sweet, dean of the college.

The college also is the flagship in the State of Ohio's Urban University Program (UUP), a funding body that provides eight universities across Ohio with financial assistance for their urban outreach programs.

One of the more notable programs funded by UUP for the College of Urban Affairs—undertaken in partnership with the Cleveland-Marshall College of Law and the Cleveland public schools—is the Law and Public Service Magnet High School in the inner city. State Representative Patrick Sweeney of Cleveland was instrumental in launching UUP and seeing that CSU played the lead role.

Also reaching out to the Cleveland schools is the College of Education, which has established an Urban Educational Research Center to bring together educators and other professionals to seek solutions to critical urban education issues.

Hands-on exhibits offer visitors a unique way to learn about aviation at the Lewis Research Center. Photo by Barbara Durham

The College of Law and the College of Urban Affairs, along with the James J. Nance College of Business Administration, are embarking on a large-scale building program on the western end of the campus. Several new buildings, to be constructed on the block between East Seventeenth and Eighteenth streets and Chester and Euclid avenues at a cost of more than $100 million, will expand and unify the resources of the colleges. Through covered walkways, they also will tie the complex into other parts of the campus and across East Seventeenth Street into Playhouse Square Center—and hence into all of downtown.

The Library of the Future, a joint project between the College of Urban Affairs and the College of Law, will house a law library and a large collection of documents relating to urban public policies. Also on the drawing board is the University Community Civic Forum, an all-purpose meeting hall partially funded by the Playhouse Square Foundation. The colleges will surround an enclosed graduate student commons that will include food-service facilities.

Another key institution of higher learning in downtown is Dyke College, headquartered in a renovated eight-story building on Prospect Avenue behind Public Square. Dyke has the distinction of being the city's first college—and the oldest college of its kind in the United States, focusing on commercial and occupational coursework and degrees. It was formed in 1942 with the merger of the Dyke School of Commerce, founded in 1894, and the Spencerian Business College, which goes back to 1848 under different names.

Before its merger with Spencerian, Dyke concentrated on the training of business clerks. It should be kept in mind that two of the school's more noteworthy graduates are John D. Rockefeller and Harvey S. Firestone. Spencerian, however, was more broad based, and a well-rounded curriculum grew out of the merger.

Dyke offers degrees in accounting, business administration, marketing, real estate, industrial management, paralegal training, information processing, and numerous other technical and occupational endeavors.

Under its longtime president, John C. Corfias, the commuter college has broadened its liberal-arts base, and also has courses in journalism, philosophy, and British literature. Although three-fourths of the college's 1,300 students are women, it has a men's basketball team, which plays an intercollegiate schedule using a rented school gymnasium as home court.

While liberal arts may not be the main focus at Dyke, it can be described as the cornerstone for the area's three Catholic colleges—John Carroll University, Notre Dame College, and Ursuline College. That cornerstone has been built upon over the years. The three schools have remained viable because they have laced their liberal-arts curricula with career accents while striving to retain their strong Catholic moral code. The histories of all three Catholic colleges are interconnected, closely tied to Cleveland's own varied past.

The establishment of the Catholic colleges can be directly attributed to the Cleveland Catholic Diocese's first two bishops, Amadeus Rappe and Richard Gilmour (for whom the highly acclaimed independent Catholic prep school, Gilmour Academy in Gates Mills, is named). Bishop Rappe initiated Catholic education in Cleveland when, in 1850, three years after the establishment of the diocese, he brought five Ursuline nuns from France to run parish schools. Twenty-one years later the nuns established Ursuline College.

The founding of Ursuline College coincided with a period of anti-Catholic prejudice around the country. It also coincided with the appointment of Rappe's successor, Richard Gilmour, as bishop. Gilmour is one of the more interesting and dynamic figures, lay or religious, in Cleveland history. Converting to Catholicism from Presbyterianism when he was still a teenager, he entered the priesthood. He was ordained in 1852 and named bishop in 1872.

Secondary education in Cleveland is represented by such fine institutions as St. Ignatius High School, pictured. Photo by Roger Mastroianni

With the zeal of a convert, Gilmour responded to the anti-Catholicism of the day by becoming proactive. He founded a newspaper, the *Catholic Universe,* in 1874 as a means of combating the anti-Catholic propaganda of the daily papers. That same year he asked the Notre Dame nuns in Germany to send a delegation to Cleveland to start a college.

In an incredibly bold move a few years later, he invited a handful of Jesuits from Buffalo to come to Cleveland and establish a college. In 1886 they established John Carroll University—named for the first Roman Catholic bishop in the United States—as well as St. Ignatius High School, one of the top academic and athletic secondary schools in Ohio. St. Ignatius won the state high-school football championship in 1988.

It was a bold move because Gilmour was in the middle of a six-year courtroom battle against the Cuyahoga County auditors. He was fighting to keep the county from selling Catholic school buildings at auction for alleged nonpayment of taxes. The diocese felt that the legal action was a thinly disguised anti-Catholic ploy.

John Carroll University, with 2,700 full-time students, has been in its upper-middle-class suburban setting in University Heights, adjacent to Shaker Heights, since it moved away from St. Ignatius on the near West Side in 1935. John Carroll is one of 28 Jesuit colleges and universities in America, linked to the Jesuit academic tradition that began in Europe over 400 years ago.

"The Jesuit philosophy is to cultivate what we call the education of the whole person," says Father Michael Lavelle, John Carroll's president. "Our students receive more than just academic instruction—they're encouraged to find ways to serve society, change society, better society."

Most of John Carroll's alumni take jobs in business and industry. Some of the exceptions are notable. One is Don Shula, famous head coach of the Miami Dolphins. Other prominent graduates include John F. Smith III, vice president of CBS News; John G. Breen, chairman of the Sherwin-Williams Company; and Cleveland Bishop Anthony M. Pilla.

John Carroll has a comfortable teacher-student ratio of 13 to 1, and most of its students live in dormitories or other nearby housing. It is ranked among the top 100 universities in America whose graduates go on to earn doctorate degrees. It has student exchange programs with schools in Tokyo and Nagoya, Japan. The seismological observatory, which measures the strength of world earthquakes, garners JCU local and national attention, as does the C.K. Chesterton collection housed in its library. The Cleveland Center for Economic Education, a nonprofit group that fosters economic skills among schoolchildren, also is housed at John Carroll.

"We actively involve our students in their education," says Father Lavelle. "We hope, by the time they graduate, that we have produced individuals who can think for themselves, who can approach a problem free from peripheral distractions and say, 'This is what the nub of the problem is,' who can make decisions, analyze, communicate, and deal with others."

Ursuline is the oldest chartered women's college in Ohio. Its roots go back to 1871. The current institution sits on 112 rolling acres a few miles east of John Carroll in Pepper Pike, one of Cleveland's most affluent suburbs. The college moved there in 1959 from older facilities near Case Western Reserve University.

Although Ursuline is not considered strictly a women's college, the student population is overwhelmingly female—more than 1,200 women and 100 men. Ursuline emphasizes the liberal arts and sciences, complementing them with strong programs in business, public relations, and health services, plus an effective internship program.

Fashion merchandising and design also are popular at Ursuline. Students who qualify spend a year studying at the Fashion Institute of Technology in New York City. Among Ursuline's more imposing structures are the Florence O'Donnell Wasmer Art Gallery and the Ralph M. Besse Library, both named in honor of prominent Cleveland civic leaders.

Notre Dame College, whose Tudor-Gothic-style campus has occupied 50 acres in the East Side suburb of South Euclid since 1928, is smaller than Ursuline, with fewer than 1,000 full-time students. The school encourages "independent thinking" in its students and puts a strong emphasis on Christian moral values.

However small the student body, Notre Dame offers 30 majors, and students can take some of their classes at 10 other colleges and universities. Notre Dame's Cooperative Education Program has affiliations with the NASA Lewis Research Center and the BP America research center in Warrensville Heights.

Some 85 percent of the students at Notre Dame receive financial aid and half the students live in college housing. Yet loans are a last resort. Notre Dame prefers that students apply for scholarships and grants, and strongly encourages outside employment through the cooperative education plan. Notre Dame's well-known alumnae include Clare M. Cavoli, a diplomat and economist with the U.S. Foreign Service, and Mary Strassmeyer, popular gossip columnist of the *Plain Dealer.*

Despite their relatively small enrollment, the women's parochial colleges have much significance in the community. "They are part of what makes Cleveland special," says Henry Eaton, chairman of Dix & Eaton, Cleveland's largest and best-known public relations firm. Eaton served on the board of trustees of Notre Dame College for 15 years.

"There are a growing number of young women who believe they will get a better education in a single-sex environment," Eaton says. "They will go to these schools because they feel they can function better in a single-sex environment. They can become more their own person, and can concentrate on the important role that women have in the world today."

Statistics show that women who graduate from single-sex colleges earn on the average $8,000 more a year than their coeducational counterparts. Further, they are more likely to do postgraduate work, and are more likely to be achievement oriented in their careers.

Congresswoman Mary Rose Oakar, a graduate of Ursuline College, explains why: "You get opportunities for leadership that you might not have elsewhere. Your self-confidence gets developed, and that is very important for women."

The women's colleges also represent something that has kept—and will keep—higher education in Northeast Ohio thriving: options.

Among other area colleges and universities that provide excellent options is Oberlin College, the first area college to contribute to the Cleveland Initiative for Education's Scholarship-in-Escrow Program, which provides college tuition credits to achieving Cleveland inner-city public school students.

A nationally acclaimed liberal-arts college founded in 1833, Oberlin is located on 440 acres in the small town of Oberlin (population, 8,600), 35 miles southwest of Cleveland. Since 1983 it has been headed by a lively and versatile president, S. Frederick Starr, a respected jazz musician, writer, and expert on the Soviet Union. Starr holds a master's degree in Slavonic languages and literature from Cambridge and a Ph.D. in history from Princeton.

Oberlin, which is one of the most competitive liberal arts colleges in America, has a number of other distinctions. More of its graduates earn doctoral degrees than the graduates of any other American liberal-arts college.

Facing page: Peters Hall at Oberlin College is framed through the Memorial Arch on Tappan Square. Photo by Jennie Jones

Students come from all over America and some 30 foreign countries.

Though it has fewer than 3,000 students, the college maintains an endowment of more than $250 million. Oberlin also has an exceptional college library and computer center.

The Allen Memorial Art Museum, the first college museum west of the Alleghenies, ranks among the leading college art museums in the country. Its collection includes paintings by Rubens, Monet, Cézanne, and Picasso, and prints by Dürer and Rembrandt.

The Oberlin Conservatory, where some 500 undergraduate music students are enrolled, is also a source of international attention and has served to stimulate musical exchange programs between the United States and Soviet Union.

One of Oberlin's newest academic efforts is the Project to Increase Mastery in Mathematics, a summer fellowship program for area high school mathematics teachers, made possible through grants from the General Electric Foundation.

Oberlin College has long had a reputation for liberal causes. It was the first college in the United States to admit women. Early in its history, Oberlin encouraged the admission of blacks and was a hotbed of the antislavery movement in the years before the Civil War and a drop-off point along the Underground Railroad. In those formative years the college had stronger church ties and sent abroad many of the early Protestant foreign missionaries.

Among Oberlin's prestigious graduates are Erwin Griswold, former U.S. Solicitor General and former dean of the Harvard Law School; screenwriter William Goldman (Butch Cassidy and the Sundance Kid); Johnnetta Cole, the first female black president of Spelman College; John H. Gutfreund, chairman of Salomon Brothers, a leading Wall Street brokerage firm; Jesse Philips, chairman of Philips Industries; Robert Krulwich, CBS television business reporter; and Cleveland City Councilman James Rokakis, who was first elected to his office while still a student.

How does Starr see the challenge of higher education into the next century?

"It will have to address a number of fundamental issues involving the curriculum," he says. "These include the need for internationalism . . . the demand for high expertise in science and technology, the need to educate citizens capable of adapting to an information economy, and the need for methods that satisfy requirements of a diverse student body."

Something of a counterpart to Oberlin is Hiram College, established in 1850 by the Disciples of Christ Church. The college is located on 145 tree-lined acres 35 miles to the southeast of Cleveland in Hiram, a crossroads town of 500. *U.S. News & World Report* ranked Hiram as one of the top liberal arts colleges in the country.

Forty percent of Hiram graduates go on to postgraduate study. The school believes in maintaining a strong sense of community among its faculty and students. Some 95 percent of the 1,200 students live in college-owned housing.

"A commitment to academic excellence, established during the early

Unique architecture and well-manicured school grounds attract the occasional visitor while providing a healthy environment for study at Oberlin College. Photo by Jennie Jones

years of the college, continues at Hiram as we compete for the nation's top students," says Edward Smerek, Hiram's dean and vice president.

Founded as the Western Reserve Eclectic Institute, one of its earliest students was James A. Garfield, who went on to become the 20th president of the United States. Garfield also served as Hiram's president, from 1857 to 1861, beginning his tenure when he was a mere 27 years old.

Other prominent Hiram graduates include Bill White, first black president of baseball's National League and former New York Yankees star; Andrew Stofan, former director of the NASA Lewis Research Center; and Galen Roush, the founder of Roadway Express Corporation.

While not within the boundaries of Cuyahoga County or under the purview of the Cleveland Commission on Higher Education, Oberlin and Hiram are nevertheless integral parts of Northeast Ohio's broad intellectual and cultural base.

So, too, are other leading institutions, such as Kent State University, only a few miles away from Hiram in Kent, which has 24,000 undergraduate and graduate students on the main campus—the preponderance of whom are from Northeast Ohio. Kent State has another 6,500 students at seven branch campuses in Northeast Ohio.

In recent years the College and Graduate School of Education at Kent State has established a strong reputation. So has the College of Fine and Professional Arts, which includes the School of Architecture and the School of Journalism and Mass Communication.

Also in the College of Fine and Professional Arts is the nationally known Shannon Rodgers/Jerry Silverman School of Fashion Design and Merchandising, which includes a fashion museum popular with visitors from around the country. Kent State also has erected a fitting memorial to the students who were killed or wounded in May 1970 during antiwar protests on campus.

Only a few miles west of Kent in downtown Akron (about 35 miles south of Cleveland) is the state-run University of Akron, which is the third-largest state university with 27,000 full- and part-time students and another 1,200 students at a branch in Orrville.

The University of Akron is spreading out from its 161-acre campus, spending $25.5 million to renovate an old downtown department store into a classroom and office complex. The university recently constructed a $17-million twin-tower complex for its College of Polymer Science and Polymer Engineering, the first college of its kind in the world.

The new academic center will allow the university to intensify its research into polymers, which include rubber and plastics. Akron and Case Western Reserve are engaged in joint research through the state-supported Edison Polymer Innovation Corporation (EPIC).

Some 30 miles east of Cleveland, Lake Erie College in Painesville has an enrollment of 700 full-time students. The great majority are women, as Lake Erie was founded in 1856 as a private women's college—actually a finishing school—and only began admitting men in the late 1980s.

Lake Erie is known for its unique equestrian program that combines a liberal-arts curriculum with studies that include breeding, stable management, and a rider-trainer program. Equestrian competitions are popular campus social events.

The MBA program at Lake Erie also is gaining momentum, and the college is conducting graduate business classes at the Cleveland Clinic and the nearby Perry Nuclear Power Plant in Lake County. Lake Erie also offers special scholarships for twins, allowing both to attend for the tuition of one.

In suburban Beachwood, the Cleveland College of Jewish Studies offers bachelor's and master's degrees in Jewish history and culture. Many unique language courses are taught at the college, including Hebrew and Arabic. The Jewish Community Federation and various foundations and donors support the college, which has 600 students and can trace its roots to the 1920s. Each year some 6,000 people attend its many lectures, workshops, and exhibitions.

Another private college with close ties to Greater Cleveland is the academically challenging College of Wooster (Presbyterian) on 320 acres in Wooster, a community 50 miles south of Cleveland. Wooster, with a student body of 2,000, offers a panoply of majors, including history, chemistry, and English. It also offers special foreign language programs and opportunities to study abroad.

Founded in 1878, Ashland University (Church of the Brethren) in Ashland, a town of 22,000 not far from Wooster and only 60 miles south of Cleveland, has a solid reputation for undergraduate programs in business and communications. Total undergraduate enrollment at Ashland, a liberal-arts school, is 1,600.

Ashland also is home to a highly respected Protestant seminary educating theology students from many denominations. The John M. Ashbrook Center for Public Affairs—a conservative policy institute—draws scholars and speakers from across the country. As president, Ronald Reagan dedicated the center, whose board of advisers has included William Rusher, publisher of the *National Review,* and William E. Simon, former U.S. Secretary of the Treasury. On the day before his presidential election in 1988, George Bush purposefully made a change in plans in order to campaign at a receptive Ashland University.

Also in Northeast Ohio are Youngstown State University, Mount Union College (United Methodist) in Alliance, and Malone College (Evangelical Friends Church) and Walsh College (Catholic) in Canton.

Back in downtown Cleveland, in a refurbished old elementary school on Sumner Court, one block south of Playhouse Square, Capital University of Columbus—affiliated with the Evangelical Lutheran Church—conducts classes for 200 part-time students in an Adult Degree Program leading to a bachelor of science or arts degree. Capital has operated its small Cleveland Center since the early 1980s.

"People relocating to Greater Cleveland have told me that they never realized that there are so many options in higher education," Henry Eaton says. "But there are!"

As these options expand to include aerospace, advanced technology, and manufacturing, along with the full complement of liberal arts and humanities, Greater Cleveland's future—in higher education and consequently, its economic base—will not only remain secure, but will flourish.

The Geauga County branch of Kent State University is a first choice for many local students. Photo by Jim Baron. Courtesy, Image Finders, Inc.

The Sophrenia Brooks Hall Auditorium at Oberlin College is pictured here amidst the color of spring. Photo by Jennie Jones

CHAPTER 9

Reaching For The Sky

In the early 1990s the focus of the music world, from London to Manhattan to Hollywood, will be riveted on Cleveland for what surely will be one of the most spectacular openings in American entertainment history. A galaxy of stars will descend here to dedicate the $48-million Rock and Roll Hall of Fame and Museum, which will rise 18 stories along the Cuyahoga River behind Tower City Center in the heart of downtown Cleveland.

World-famous architect I.M. Pei is designing the structure. Barry Howard, who won acclaim for his design of the Living Seas pavilion at the Walt Disney World Epcot Center, is coordinating design of the exhibits.

Trustees of the Rock and Roll Hall of Fame in New York—including many music industry leaders—chose Cleveland for the Hall of Fame because of the overwhelming outpouring of support from Northeast Ohio and across the country.

"From the outset we recognized the economic development opportunity represented by the Hall of Fame and Museum," says K. Michael Benz, executive vice president of the Growth Association, who coordinated the campaign to bring the hall here. "But we really won it because the entire community backed us 100 percent from the beginning."

Clevelanders logged 110,000 phone calls to *USA Today* in its nationwide straw poll for a museum site, almost 10 times more than the runner-up city. An additional 660,000 petitions were sent to the Hall of Fame Foundation in New York. Many reminded the foundation trustees that the term *rock and roll* was coined in the 1950s by Cleveland disk jockey Alan Freed.

To secure the Hall of Fame, Greater Cleveland corporations and state and local government pledged millions of dollars in seed money. The

In the early 1990s the 18-story Rock and Roll Hall of Fame and Museum will join the city's skyline. Photo by Roger Mastroianni

ongoing fund-raising campaign—a Cleveland-New York effort—has been chaired by Jann S. Wenner, editor and publisher of *Rolling Stone,* and Robert R. Broadbent, former chairman of the Higbee Company, the large Cleveland department store chain.

As envisioned, the building will be an entertainment and educational experience that should take at least two and a half hours to visit. It will pay tribute to the men and women inducted annually by the Rock and Roll Hall of Fame Foundation. These include performing artists and other industry representatives who have made a contribution to rock music as a cultural art form.

The Hall of Fame and Museum will encompass performance as well as production galleries, where visitors can learn something of the technical side of recording and see interactive multimedia presentations of artists' performances. Plans call for at least one small orientation theater and even a 1950s-style malt shop.

The rock complex is expected to draw more than 600,000 visitors annually and become a bigger attraction than Graceland in Memphis and the Country Music Hall of Fame and Museum in Nashville. It should bring some $20 million a year in tourism money to Cleveland.

Fans of all ages enjoy the excitement of Cleveland Indians baseball. Photo by Jim Baron. Courtesy, Image Finders, Inc.

"The impact on the city will be monumental," says Larry R. Thompson, the Hall of Fame director. "It will be a world-class attraction, both educational and exciting. Its economic effect will be geometric. It will serve as a catalyst for downtown shopping, dining, and business. The Rock and Roll Hall of Fame and Museum will manifest the pride Clevelanders have in their city."

That pride already is manifest in the growing amount of activity downtown. This includes ballet, opera, plays, musicals, and concerts at the Playhouse Square Center; a wide variety of conventions, exhibitions, and public shows at the Cleveland Convention Center, such as the popular late-winter Home and Flower Show; and an increasing number of classy nightclubs and restaurants.

Cleveland State University, Cuyahoga Community College, and Dyke College draw thousands of students and employees downtown every working day. Professional baseball and football at the stadium attract more than 2 million spectators annually.

Special events such as the Budweiser-Cleveland Grand Prix, the Revco Marathon, and the Cleveland National Air Show grow in popularity each year. Cleveland also hosts one of the largest St. Patrick's Day parades in the country.

Above: It takes a competent pit crew to stay on the track at the Budweiser Cleveland Grand Prix. Photo by Roger Mastroianni

Left: From wing-walkers to jets in formation, the Cleveland National Air Show sets an exciting pace for aviation enthusiasts. Courtesy, Luce Photography, Inc.

Facing page: Enterprise Place, in affluent Beachwood, lends a futuristic feel to the surrounding area with its modern design. Photo by Barbara Durham

Summer festivals are a distinctive downtown enticement, particularly the Sohio Riverfest in the Flats and the All Nations Festival. During good weather the early-evening Parties-in-the-Park, coordinated by the Downtown Business Council of the Greater Cleveland Growth Association at different downtown locations, draw thousands of office workers for conversation, music, food, and beverages.

The Business Council also coordinates Stop-in-Shop's Square to Square, a weekend family festival held each June on main downtown streets between Public Square and Playhouse Square. Most of the festivals are promoted through the city's Summerfare program, an umbrella marketing campaign that utilizes donated services from local public-relations and advertising agencies and free advertising time and space from the local media.

Developers also have been infected by the downtown fever. While downtown experienced more than $500 million in new building in the 1980s, the 1990s should be even more explosive. Richard Anter, director of downtown development for the Growth Association, predicts that more than $5 billion in new downtown building construction will take place before the end of 1995.

Planners foresee more than $5 billion in new downtown building development before the end of 1995. Photo by Don Snyder

"Other major cities are overbuilt," Anter observes. "Cleveland is ready. With a diverse economy, ranging from Fortune 500 service and industrial companies to small businesses to service jobs, the perception among national developers is that Cleveland is changing. With our recession and political confrontations behind us, we should be America's dynamic downtown of the '90s."

One pressing reason for the boom is that the vacancy rate of class-A downtown Cleveland office space dropped to 6 percent in the late 1980s—one of the lowest rates among major American cities.

"The sun is rising over Cleveland," says architect Richard Fleischman, who is designing a number of downtown buildings. "Developers are coming here because costs are low and political bottlenecks are fading away. Moreover, they are hiring architects to design imaginative, quality buildings."

Hunter Morrison, director of City Planning, has been expediting the downtown transformation as project manager of Civic Vision 2000, former mayor George Voinovich's updating of Cleveland land-use plans, development policies, design guidelines, and zoning codes.

Before asking the city council to adopt a comprehensive guideline for downtown development, Morrison and his associates spoke at numerous citizen meetings and met with government officials, architects, developers, and builders. They were able to get the city council to authorize the planning commission and its Fine Arts Committee to review all major downtown projects for aesthetic quality.

The last city plan for downtown was adopted in 1959. For the new

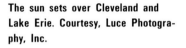

The sun sets over Cleveland and Lake Erie. Courtesy, Luce Photography, Inc.

Modernization of the 52-floor Terminal Tower marked the beginning of the Tower City Center expansion. Photo by Don Snyder

plan, Morrison divided downtown and its 2.8 square miles into 14 planning districts: east from West 25th Street to the eastern edge of the Innerbelt, and north from Lake Erie to the southern edge of the Innerbelt. This assured that property owners and others interested in a particular section could make their views known to the planning commission—and ultimately to the city council.

As part of the review process, the planning commission built an 18-by-24-foot model of downtown that is on display at the Cleveland Convention Center. "We were concerned about utilities, bridges and road conditions, transportation, employment, housing, parking, parks and landscaping, and architectural design," Morrison says.

The downtown planners also were concerned with finding ways to harmonize transportation, retail space, light industry, housing, public open space, office buildings, and cultural centers. To simplify his work Morrison started at the center of the city, Public Square. Several billion dollars in new con-

Facing page: Dressed in its holiday lights, Public Square attracts more than a half-million visitors each Christmas season. Photo by Barbara Durham

struction will take place at the square in the 1990s, including the Rock and Roll Hall of Fame and the adjacent Tower City Center, where some 125,000 people work or pass through each weekday.

The 34-acre Tower City complex has been undergoing expansion steadily since the early 1980s, shortly after it was purchased by Forest City Enterprises, a large Cleveland-based real-estate management and development firm. The first stage of the project was the modernization of the 52-floor Terminal Tower—the city's soaring landmark symbol—and its three-story lobby. Brass trimmings were shined, the marble columns polished, and vaulted ceilings regilded.

Forest City Enterprises is creating more than 350,000 square feet of new retail, dining, and entertainment space in the former Union Terminal train station beneath the Terminal Tower. The Regional Transit Authority is finishing the $55-million modernization of its underground climate-controlled rapid-transit station—downtown's only rapid-transit stop. The $20-million upgrading of vital streets and bridges was completed in the 1980s.

When Tower City Center is fully built, rapid-transit ridership should increase between Public Square and Cleveland Hopkins International Airport. Commuters will descend to the station on escalators. Buses and cabs will discharge and pick up passengers at the new Tower City Prospect Avenue south entrance.

More than 120 specialty stores, traditional shops, and sit-down restaurants will open on three retail levels. The English Oak Room, an historic restaurant that closed down in the 1970s, will be reopened with restored oak-paneled walls, inlaid teak columns, and glass and brass chandeliers.

An 80-foot-high skylight will cover one Tower City Center retail level. One and possibly two new major department stores, including a three-story Neiman-Marcus, will be open by the mid-1990s to complement Higbee's on the southeast corner of Public Square and the May Company across the street. By the turn of the century, downtown is expected to add

Visitors to Beachwood Place can choose from a variety of food outlets and dine in climate-controlled comfort. Photo by Jim Baron. Courtesy, Image Finders, Inc.

a total of some 1.5 million square feet of retail space.

Tower City's Riverview Marketplace, overlooking the Cuyahoga River, will feature cafes and specialty food stores. The food court ultimately will seat more than 2,000. A multiplex cinema will feature 10 to 12 screens.

The first of two new office buildings will incorporate a 207-room luxury Ritz-Carlton Hotel and an executive athletic club with a rooftop pool under a skylight dome. This 13-floor Ritz-Carlton building, including the hotel, should open in the summer of 1990.

The hotel will be connected to the Tower City retail area and to Stouffer Tower City Plaza, a 500-room hotel with a club floor of refurbished suites, a private lounge, a library, and a conference room. Stouffer's Grand Ballroom, which can accommodate 1,800 place settings, is the largest hotel ballroom in the state.

Tower City's second office building, the 12-floor Skylight Office Tower, should open in late 1990 and provide an entrance to the English Oak Room.

Another part of Tower City Center is the former U.S. Post Office building, which has been converted into office space. Architects are restoring the lobby, including its marble floors and walls, the ornamental bronze and stainless-steel trimming, and the original art deco postal windows and writing desks.

The preservation of what is now Post Office Plaza extends to the original marble wall medallions that relate the history of the U.S. Mail. Two five-story skylights will allow natural light into the interior. One of the two atriums will feature a 20-foot fountain.

"Tower City Center will help rekindle the confidence in Clevelanders in the city's vitality and return Cleveland to national prominence," says Albert B. Ratner, president of Forest City Enterprises.

The huge development complements the restoration of the four quadrants of Public Square, begun in the early 1980s with a public-private beautification project coordinated by Iris Vail—wife of Thomas Vail, publisher and editor of the *Plain Dealer*, and Herbert Strawbridge, retired chairman of the Higbee Company.

Standing confidently in the southwest quadrant is a statue of Moses Cleaveland. In planning the square, Cleaveland demanded wide cross streets patterned after grand European boulevards. These wide streets, especially Ontario and Superior, readily facilitate heavy traffic. This is particularly obvious during the Christmas season, when American Greetings Corporation and the General Electric Company lighting group (which has been headquartered since 1913 in East Cleveland's Nela Park, one of the nation's earliest industrial parks) contribute technical expertise for a huge downtown holiday lighting display that emanates from Public Square. More than a half-million people come downtown each year to enjoy the displays.

On the southeast quadrant is the Soldiers and Sailors Monument to Civil War dead, topped with a statue of Lady Liberty. Across the street from the monument is the pink marble BP America Building with its large atrium and gallery. The 45-story BP America Building is 50 feet shorter than the Terminal Tower.

The northeast quadrant of the square envelops an attractive water fountain. The northwest quadrant serves as the dwelling place for an imposing statue of Tom L. Johnson, the city's turn-of-the-century populist mayor. The area serves as a haven for political speeches and demonstrations.

Behind Johnson's statue is the front door of the Old Stone Church. Built in 1850, the Presbyterian church, with four original Tiffany windows, is the oldest structure on the square.

Immediately south of Public Square, not far from the proposed Rock and Roll Hall of Fame and Museum, is the site of what may be the city's most far-reaching proposal: a dual-use stadium for football or baseball. The structure or structures would be built on 28 acres purchased by the non-

The Soldiers and Sailors Monument, on the southeast quadrant of Public Square, was dedicated on July 4, 1894. Photo by Barbara Durham

profit New Stadium Corporation, which is supervising the public-private undertaking. Since the civic organization was formed, plans for a domed stadium have been scuttled because of cost, and because the owners of both the Indians and the Browns prefer playing fields of natural grass.

A number of developers, including Bert Wolstein, also want to erect a 20,000-seat arena on the land for basketball, hockey, and indoor soccer. "A stadium and arena could be the keystone to Cleveland's continuing major league status into the twenty-first century," says Frank Mosier, vice chairman of BP America and chairman of the civic committee behind the sports complex.

Across the street from the sports site, businessman George Maloof plans to put up a 24-story office building and a 1,000-car parking garage. If the sports project comes to fruition, Maloof's $75-million Ontario-Huron Center could be expanded to include a retail area and a 400-room hotel.

The center could connect by skywalk to a proposed 30-floor office building directly across Ontario Street in the Landmark Office Towers complex. The three-building Landmark Office Towers network is connected to Tower City via underground passageway.

While the stadium and arena and many of these proposed buildings nearby are still on the drawing board, two new buildings set for completion in the next few years will by themselves dramatically alter the vista of Public Square.

Construction of the 52-story Society Center will be completed by 1992, and the 60-story Ameritrust Center a few years after that. They will replace the Terminal Tower as the city's tallest building, a distinction the Tower has held since it was dedicated in 1930. (At 708 feet, it was then the tallest building in the country excluding New York's Woolworth Building.) The Ameritrust Center will be the tallest building in Ohio and the tallest between New York and Chicago.

Cleveland brothers Richard and David Jacobs, among the largest shopping center developers in America, are building these skyscrapers, which will serve as headquarters for two of Cleveland's largest banks, Society and Ameritrust.

World-famous architect Cesar Pelli is designing the Society Center on

The sun glows on the new downtown skyline. Photo by Don Snyder

In the near future the tall Cleveland skyline will get even taller. Photo by Roger Mastroianni

the northeast quadrant of the square. In addition to the office tower, the center also will contain a 424-room Marriott hotel and 900-car underground garage. They will be integrated with the century-old Society for Savings Building, whose exterior features a replica of the arc lamp that inventor Charles Brush first lighted on Public Square in 1879.

The 10-story Society for Savings Building, designed by architect John Root, is considered an architectural classic because of its five-foot-thick red sandstone walls. The prominent Cleveland architectural firm of van Dijk, Johnson & Partners is restoring the building's exterior, the richly carved, English oak-paneled boardroom on the mezzanine, and the marble banking room, which is dominated by a mural of a goose laying a golden egg. The banking room will lead into the lobby of the new office tower.

Facing the Society Center from the northwest will be the Ameritrust headquarters designed by the Chicago architectural firm of Kohn Pedersen Fox. Fourteen of the floors will enclose a 484-room Hyatt Regency and a huge banking room.

The Cleveland skyline glows at night. Photo by Roger Mastroianni

The Ameritrust complex will supplant a stretch of run-down older office buildings. Immediately west of the Ameritrust project and across Superior Avenue from Tower City, First Union Real Estate Investments (a large Cleveland-based real estate investment trust) has been making plans to erect an office tower with a connector at ground level. To meet increased parking needs, other developers are planning various parking structures, including a 3,000-car garage west of the square.

"When all the Public Square projects are complete, the area will come alive 24 hours a day and be transformed into one of the most attractive urban areas in the country," Richard Jacobs observes. "Our new modern skyline will serve as a signature for the city and heighten the sense of recognition nationwide about what is happening in Cleveland."

"Tower City Center, the Jacobs projects, and the others are examples of how the public sector can spur private development," says Andi Udris, former director of the city's Department of Economic Planning. "With selective tax abatement and UDAG grants, we were able to put together projects that otherwise would not have been developed."

What makes construction of these enormous projects so attractive is their proximity to the Cleveland Convention Center, which recently underwent a $28-million renovation. With more than a half-million square feet, it is the 14th-largest convention center in America.

Only 10 miles southwest of downtown near Hopkins International Airport is the enormous IX Center—at 1.8 million square feet, the world's largest exposition facility under one roof—to which the RTA may extend its airport rapid-transit line. This would connect the IX Center directly to downtown and expand the possibilities for huge multisite conventions.

The new Cleveland Convention Center ballroom—one of the largest ballrooms in the country—can seat 3,500 for food service. Four contiguous exhibition halls can handle up to four conventions and 1,500 exhibitors at the same time. Remodeled meeting rooms can accommodate groups of up to 1,000. There are 6,000 parking spaces nearby, including 1,500 in adjacent underground garages.

Cleveland lost 500 downtown hotel rooms with the razing of the Hollenden House a block away from the Convention Center. The Bank One Center, a $95-million, 28-story office building developed by John W. Galbreath & Company of Columbus and two Japanese partners as a regional headquarters for Bank One, will rise in its place.

Several new hotels are scheduled to open in downtown by the early 1990s, including the Ritz-Carlton, the Marriott, the Hyatt Regency, the 192-room Playhouse Square Center Hotel, and the $20-million, 252-room Radisson Suite Hotel, which will be fashioned from a section of the Reserve Square apartment building north of Playhouse Square at East Twelfth and Chester. Sheraton Hotels has taken over and renovated the Bond Court Hotel near the Convention Center.

A number of other hotels are also on the drawing board, including a 105-suite luxury hotel next to Sammy's, the popular restaurant in the Flats; a 416-room Westin in the proposed 23-floor Convention Plaza office tower just east of the Convention Center; and a 380-room addition to Stouffer's Tower City Plaza.

With retail space and a 1,000-car parking garage, the cost of Convention Plaza is expected to exceed $100 million. Irvin Chelm, a suburban office developer and manager, is building Convention Plaza. Architect Richard Fleischman is designing it.

Two major hotels are in the North Coast Harbor plans as well—one with 250 rooms at the harbor's edge, and the other with more than 400 rooms on the site of the proposed Progressive Corporation headquarters. Walkways will connect them to the harbor, the mall, and the Convention Center.

Atop the Convention Center is the 10,000-seat Public Auditorium, where in 1924 and 1936 the Republican national conventions were held. The space adjacent to the auditorium is taken up by the 3,000-seat Music Hall—where Jimmy Carter and Ronald Reagan staged the pivotal debate of the 1980 presidential election—and the 600-seat Little Theatre.

"Downtown Cleveland has a unique advantage for conventions because it is compact," says Dale Finley, president of the Greater Cleveland Convention and Visitors Bureau. "By 1994 we will have some 3,500 first-class hotel rooms all within a short walk to the Convention Center.

"Convention and visitor business is important because it is labor intensive and represents new jobs and new dollars," Finley adds.

The convention business, which has an annual impact of $80 million on Greater Cleveland, is expected to increase sizably in the 1990s. To assure conventioneers all-weather protection, the Convention and Visitors Bureau and the Growth Association are determined to link the Cleveland Convention Center and virtually all major downtown hotels and tourist attractions through a system of covered walkways and tunnels.

The $43-million Galleria at Erieview features two floors of upscale shops and restaurants. Courtesy, Cosgray Photography

The ultimate destination of these connectors will be the North Coast Harbor. On the doorstep of the harbor, between East Ninth and East 12 streets, sits the $43-million Galleria at Erieview, an enormous skylighted arcade with two floors of upscale shops and restaurants.

Richard Jacobs, who developed the Galleria, has plans for additional Galleria space, including a department store. A walkway will link the complex to two proposed Jacobs office buildings of 20 and 40 stories designed by internationally acclaimed architect Philip Johnson, who grew up in Cleveland. Johnson designed the new Cleveland Play House.

To handle the anticipated tourism explosion triggered by such attractions as the Galleria, Tower City, the Flats, North Coast Harbor, and the Rock and Roll Hall of Fame, the Convention and Visitors Bureau is erecting three additional street-level downtown visitor stations—at the Nautica entertainment area in the Flats, Playhouse Square, and North Coast Harbor. These will complement a travelers' aid station at Hopkins Airport and a visitor center in Tower City.

Conventioneers can avail themselves of the 10 bright red trackless motorized trolleys—or "Lolly the Trolley" as they are collectively called—that glide through downtown filled with inquisitive tourists. Sherrill D. Paul, owner of Trolley Tours of Cleveland, started her

Facing page: The lights of the city gleam through the skylighted arcade of the Galleria. Courtesy, Image Finders, Inc.

trolley service in 1985 with one Lolly escorting a handful of persons a day around downtown. Today, at peak season in the summer, her two-hour downtown/University Circle, shopping, and private tours attract 10,000 people per month.

Seventy percent of the tourists come from within 25 miles of Cleveland. The rest come from every state and almost every nation. "Cleveland is a surprise to most people who come here for the first time," says Paul. "Most don't realize the depth of our history, our recent development, and our cultural amenities."

The specialty Trolley Tours include a trip to Lake View Cemetery to visit the towering monuments of President James A. Garfield and John D. Rockefeller and an all-day shopping tour of several of the city's ethnic food stores—Spanish, German, Chinese, Italian, Greek, and Lebanese—that reflect much of the area's demographic diversity.

The highlight of the ethnic market tour is the city-owned West Side Market on West 25 Street and Lorain Avenue, directly across the art deco-style Hope Memorial Bridge from downtown. With its 137-foot clock tower and vaulted tile ceiling, the market, dedicated in 1912, is on the National Register of Historic Places. The Hope Memorial Bridge was named for Robert Hope (father of comedian Bob Hope), a stonemason who worked on its construction in the 1930s.

The market's 185 indoor and outdoor stands—many operated by the same families for several generations—proffer a seemingly endless assortment of vegetables, fruit, meats, cheese, fish, dairy products, spices, and specialty foods from nationalities as diverse as German, Greek, Irish, and Italian.

On Monday, Wednesday, Friday, and Saturday, when the market is open from 7 A.M. to 6 P.M., it bustles with a veritable crosscut of Greater Cleveland. City women in babushkas fill shopping bags with daily staples, while well-to-do suburbanites search for exotic delicacies, cheeses, and prime meats.

The West Side Market sits between two venerable old ethnic neighborhoods near downtown, Ohio City and Tremont. In recent years upscale urban pioneers have invested heavily in both areas by restoring Victorian homes, refurbishing brick apartment houses, and opening artists studios and chic restaurants. In Tremont, for example, developer Walter "Chick" Holtkamp III has converted the second floor of a former ethnic social club—Lemko Hall—into spacious loft apartments.

Adults may be infatuated with the Lolly the Trolley market tours, yet school groups are intrigued by the downtown/University Circle tour because of its strong emphasis on history. Beginning in the Historic Warehouse District, the tour takes careful note of the city's priceless architecture, especially the six buildings on the eastern edge of Public Square designed in 1903 as part of the Group Plan by architect Daniel Burnham.

Mayor Tom L. Johnson encouraged the 101-acre Group Plan as a visionary governmental complex surrounding a spacious mall—the most complete downtown plan outside of Washington, D.C.—to replace a

The pink Italian-marble Federal Reserve Bank Building is one of the city's foremost landmarks. Photo by Don Snyder

tenderloin of seedy stores, homes, and nightspots. Since then, fountains donated by the eminent Hanna family have enhanced the mall vista that sweeps north toward Lake Erie.

Inspired by the City Beautiful Movement growing out of the 1893 World's Columbian Exposition in Chicago, Burnham designed the buildings with hand-carved marble and woodwork in a kind of beaux-arts variation of ancient classicism. The first structure, the Federal Courthouse, opened in 1908.

Other buildings in the plan include Public Auditorium, Cleveland City Hall (where the large masterpiece version of Archibald Willard's *Spirit of '76* is displayed in the lobby), the Cuyahoga County Lakeside Courthouse, the Cleveland Board of Education, and the Cleveland Public Library.

The Main Library, as the Cleveland Public Library is officially designated, is embarking on a $67-million capital improvement, book preservation, and electronic document storage program. With a collection of 1.3 million circulating book titles, the Cleveland Public Library is the third-largest public research library system in the nation. It also is the largest library with open shelves in the country.

The full collection—one of the biggest in the world—swells to nearly 7 million items when reference volumes, sheet music, microforms, recordings, films, special research material, and periodicals are included.

The Main Library and its 30 neighborhood branches complement various independent suburban and county systems, including the 26 branches of the Cuyahoga County Public Library. They cooperate through the 43-member Cleveland Area Metropolitan Library System.

Across East Sixth Street from the Main Library is the august 13-story Federal Reserve Bank, constructed of pink Georgian marble and patterned after an Italian Renaissance fortress palace. The rotunda, with its gilded ceiling and ornate iron grillwork, resembles the interior of an Italian cathedral. Arched windows on the first floor are protected by heavy grilles of Swedish iron.

Listed on the National Register of Historic Places, the bank opened in 1923 with what was then the world's largest vault—two stories and 3,560 square feet with walls 6½ feet thick made of reinforced concrete. The main vault door is five feet thick with a 47-ton, 19-foot hinge. Yet the 100-ton door is so delicately balanced that one person can easily close it.

The Arcade, located between Euclid and Superior avenues, was built in 1890 and is often compared with the Galleria in Milan, Italy. Photo by Barbara Durham

The bank's ornate Early American executive floor, where a full-length portrait of Alexander Hamilton hangs, is paneled in American black walnut and English oak. The building has an employee gymnasium and firing range for its security guards. Francis X. Bushman, the early twentieth-century matinee idol, modeled for the three-ton bronze statue of *Energy in Repose* at the Superior Avenue entrance.

On the south side of Superior Avenue just east of Public Square is the north entrance of the Arcade, the most aesthetic of three downtown arcades that connect east-west thoroughfares. The Arcade, which opened in 1890, designed by architects John Eisenmann and George H. Smith as one of the first shopping malls in America, often is compared with the Galleria in Milan, Italy.

Twin nine-story stone office towers bolster the Arcade on either end. They are joined by a five-story iron and glass skylighted atrium—300 feet long, 60 feet wide, and almost 100 feet high—between Superior and Euclid avenues. Inside are four wrought-iron balconies filled with offices and shops, including a busy food court on the ground level where concert music is played at lunchtime.

Exiting the Arcade at its north entrance, a pedestrian is only a short walk east from two of downtown's most important buildings. The closer and older of these is St. John Cathedral, the central church of the Cleveland Catholic Diocese. Services are conducted daily at the beautiful sandstone Gothic Cathedral, which was built in 1852 on what was then the outer edge of downtown.

Two blocks north of the Cathedral is the 30-story Anthony J. Celebrezze Federal Building, named for the former Cleveland mayor and U.S. Court of Appeals judge. Government workers, many in formal military uniform, scurry in and out of the building daily. The U.S. Navy Finance Department, which processes checks for all naval personnel worldwide, is headquartered here.

Behind city hall—directly across Lakeside Avenue from the Federal Building—Progressive Corporation, one of the country's fastest growing insurance firms, is planning a 50-story, $400-million corporate office tower that will reflect the aesthetic tastes of the company president, Peter B. Lewis, a collector of modern art.

Included in the concept are a 100,000-square-foot art gallery, a scholar's library, a wellness center, a 3,200-car parking garage, and a large hotel. Designed by avant-garde Southern California architect Frank Gehry, the complex is slated to be built on a platform atop the railroad tracks behind city hall and the Lakeside Courthouse.

In the plans are an enormous steel C-clamp by artist/sculptor Claes Oldenburg, bracing the company cafeteria to the platform. It would be visible from the nearby four-lane Shoreway that runs through downtown along the Lakefront.

Across East Ninth Street from the proposed Progressive Project is North Point. The new seven-story building (five stories above ground, two below), on the site of the former *Cleveland Press* building, is headquarters of Jones, Day, Reavis & Pogue, the second-largest law firm in the world. North Point, developed by John Ferchill and Joseph Cole, is joined to a new 1,000-car parking garage by a glass-enclosed walkway.

The Jones, Day, Reavis & Pogue facilities are equipped with a mock courtroom, 1,000 phones, and 600 computer terminals connected by 50 miles of computer cable. The firm's expansion also has led it to lease part of the North Point Tower—scheduled to open in 1990—a 20-story, $85-million office building connected to North Point by a nine-story atrium.

North Point overlooks North Coast Harbor at the foot of East Ninth Street, where Cleveland will celebrate a yearlong 200th birthday party in 1996. The site is only one mile from where Moses Cleaveland alighted on the banks of the Cuyahoga River in 1796. "North Coast Harbor is the city's birthday gift to its citizens," George Voinovich says.

The cost of the full Progressive project and the adjacent 174-acre Harbor is estimated at more than $1 billion dollars. When finished, the harbor will be a self-contained city within a city that is expected to draw 10 million visitors annually.

William A. Behnke Associates, landscape architect, put together the master plan for the city's waterfront from the West Side to the East Side. Synthesis 20/20, an architectural consortium consisting of Robert Madison, Peter van Dijk, and Richard Fleischman, did the initial inner harbor design.

The North Coast Harbor Development Corporation is a nonprofit public-private partnership set up as a catalyst for development of the downtown lakeshore. Start-up grants came from major corporations as well as the George Gund Foundation, Cleveland Foundation, and the State of Ohio.

The harbor's $13.5-million Phase I, completed in 1988, includes a sloping eight-acre festival park, a 7.6-acre inner harbor with day mooring for 60 pleasure craft, and a 1,300-by-50-foot promenade with antique lighting and street furniture. The promenade, which borders the U.S. Coast Guard and Naval Reserve compounds, is paved with bricks engraved with the names of individuals who contributed to the project.

Slated for mooring is the *William G. Mather*, a 618-foot iron ore steamship donated by Cleveland Cliffs, Inc. The *Mather* will be open for tour groups. Business conferences also will be held in the luxuriously restored

The spires of St. Paul's Shrine are seen here silhouetted against an orange sky. Photo by Roger Mastroianni

captain's quarters and dining room. In the early 1990s construction will begin on Phase II, which includes the 90,000-square-foot, $35-million Great Lakes Museum. When completed it will include a natural history and environment wing and a science and technology hall.

A number of civic leaders want to integrate the proposed Aerospace Museum and space camp into the harbor, while others argue that the facility should be closer to NASA Lewis Research Center near Hopkins International Airport. The Aerospace Museum, which will be funded through private and public sources, should draw upwards of 600,000 people annually.

One of America's most elaborate aquariums also is proposed for Phase II of the North Coast Harbor. The $60-million structure will include not only aquatic displays but outstanding audiovisual simulations on the order of Epcot Center. "Such attractions will ensure that the harbor is Cleveland's foremost tourist attraction," says Gary Conley, president of North Coast Harbor Development Corporation.

A retail center of 40 to 60 shops and restaurants is included in the Phase II plan. So is the $60-million, 250-room Harborfront Hotel that will be integrated into the retail area along with a 1,200-car parking garage and office building. Additional public attractions at the harbor may in-

The downtown Cleveland skyline is seen here from the west bank of the Cuyahoga River. Photo by Barbara Durham

clude a sailing school, a floating restaurant, and concession boats to service pleasure craft and the growing number of excursion boats.

Phase III of North Coast Harbor, projected for completion at the turn of the century, could include a 400-boat marina and housing development near the docks of the U.S. Army Corps of Engineers and Burke Lakefront Airport, one of the few large downtown commuter and general aviation airports in the United States.

"We are mobilizing Cleveland's major resources for the celebration of the city's 200th anniversary at our greatest treasure—our waterfront," Conley says.

If North Coast Harbor reflects the pride of Cleveland's new urban environment, the 43-acre Historic Warehouse District on the western edge of downtown between Public Square and the Flats represents the best in preservation. When the restoration of the district is finished by the early part of the next century, it will be one of the largest projects of its kind in America.

Some 60 Victorian buildings are still standing in the district, which is on the National Register of Historic Places. Primarily built from 1849 through the turn of the twentieth century, the buildings are undergoing con-

Phase I of the harbor's development includes a 7.6-acre inner harbor that will accommodate 60 pleasure craft. Courtesy, Luce Photography, Inc.

version into living spaces, artist lofts, art galleries, antique shops, restaurants, and business offices.

Cleveland's first settlers built their log cabins here on bluffs at the mouth of the Cuyahoga River. Two generations later the district became the hub of the city's commerce, with office buildings, garment shops, and small factories.

"A new neighborhood is coming to life in the city's first neighborhood because of the great quality of nineteenth-century architecture and the creative people it is attracting," says Thomas J. Yablonsky, executive director of the nonprofit Historic Warehouse District Development Corporation, which is coordinating the neighborhood renovation.

Warehouse lofts converted into apartments with tall ceilings and high windows are making the Historic Warehouse District an increasingly popular place to live. More than 11,000 people are expected to live downtown by the close of century, about one-third of them in the district.

Among the first of these Warehouse District residential projects is the Hat Factory—the conversion of a millinery built in 1888 into 33 residential loft-style units. The Hat Factory has had a standing waiting list of hundreds of applicants since it opened in 1985.

The nearby mixed-use Bradley Building has had similar demand for its apartments and offices, which are inhabited by photographers, art consultants, and graphic design firms. The building also has an art gallery, a bookstore, a day-care center, and a chic cafe.

When it is finished in the early 1990s, the largest residential building in the district will be the $30-million conversion of the 11-story National Terminals Warehouse into 205 apartments, including 49 penthouse suites. Renamed Lighthouse Point because it is on the site of a lighthouse built in 1830, the apartment building will tower over the Flats and Cuyahoga River. Its attractions will include a grocery store, drugstore, health club, swimming pool, tennis court, and central courtyard.

Boyland Corporation, headed by developer Willis B. Boyer, Jr., has two key projects on the drawing board: the 425 Lakeside, which encloses 97 apartments, a health club, and retail space, and the 1913 L&N Gross Building, an office conversion.

Among the many other ventures in the district is the conversion by businessman Bruce B. Felder of the old Crown Building into Courthouse Square. The refurbished office building is across from the Justice Center and County Jail. A new county jail annex also will rise in the 1990s on the site of the Welfare Building.

Left: The Historic Warehouse District is being converted to accommodate living spaces, art galleries, antique shops, restaurants, and business offices. Photo by Jack Van Antwerp

Below: The Historic Warehouse District is seen here in an interesting view from West St. Clair Avenue. Photo by Jack Van Antwerp

In addition, developer John Ferchill is constructing Western Reserve II, a new office building. In the same vicinity, the proposed Crittenden Court will include apartments, a parking garage, and renovation of the existing Crittenden Building, built in 1868, into offices.

The district's restored structures, many with brick and stone facades and wrought-iron trim, also house new restaurants. Among them is the Burgess Grand Cafe—popular for its "power" business breakfast—fashioned out of what was a grocery store built in 1874.

Outlets for *objets d'art* in the district include Wolf's Gallery, auctioneers and appraisers in the Hat Factory; SPACES, a contemporary art gallery in the Bradley Building; and Metropolitan Antiques in the Lorenzo Carter Buildings.

After winning a competition sponsored by the Committee for Public Art (a group of urban artists, art professionals, and art advocates), Seattle artist Buster Simpson designed a paving pattern for the sidewalks of West Sixth Street, one of the area's main streets. He also created sandstone seating blocks for West Sixth resembling crates that once crammed the district's sidewalks.

The committee's walking tour, known as the Hidden City Revealed, offers a visual history of the district. Many of the district artifacts were catalogued during a research project sponsored by the committee and the Cleveland Museum of Natural History. These include an old storefront, steps of the old lighthouse, and retaining walls of a long-ago razed railroad station.

Out of this excavation has come a $300,000 effort to create a public green space—with wildflowers, meadow grass, and even birdhouses—on the surviving east abutment of the Old Superior Viaduct, the first high-level bridge to span the Cuyahoga. When complete in 1990, the half-acre Viaduct Gateway project will partially re-create a vision of how the bridge looked in the late nineteenth century.

Many of the business owners moving into the Historic Warehouse District are seeking an artistic atmosphere. Among them is architect Peter van Dijk, who shifted his studios from a modern downtown building into the Hoyt Block, which his firm restored.

The Hoyt Block, built in 1875, is part of West St. Clair, a block-long melange of Victorian warehouses owned by the Dalad Group, the district's major developer, headed by John Viny. "By pure luck, these buildings were left standing," says van Dijk. "They're constructed of timber, brick, cast iron, steel, and concrete, and they're all rugged."

When finished, West St. Clair will house offices, street-level shops, and 56 loft apartments, some fashioned on what once were covered walkways connecting brick warehouses. Apartments and offices with balconies will look out over a paved two-level central courtyard with a fountain, trees, cafe tables, and possibly a rathskeller. A walkway will span the courtyard.

"This room-without-a-roof, patterned after the Spanish Steps in Rome, will be the central social area in the district," says van Dijk, whose firm's offices overlook the courtyard. "It will be animated by the people on the walkway and apartment balconies, just like in a little Italian piazza."

Freighters haul materials to and from industries along the Cuyahoga River. Photo by Roger Mastroianni

The Historic Warehouse District serves as a link between Public Square's mushrooming skyscrapers and the flourishing business, entertainment, and recreation environs in the Flats—the oldest area of the city—along the Cuyahoga River.

At Heritage Park I, a minipark on the east bank of the river, the city's earliest roots are commemorated with a replica of the log cabin of the first permanent settler, Lorenzo Carter. The cabin is open in the summer for narrations about pioneer life and crafts.

When Moses Cleaveland stepped onto the banks of the Cuyahoga River, what he found was hardly the promised land; this flatland along the river, sheathed by steep hills on either side, was home to not much more than armies of squirrels and swarms of mosquitoes.

But it has gone through epic tranformations. Except in deepest winter, the first few miles of the coiling Cuyahoga are utilized by freighters delivering iron ore to upriver steel plants or hauling sand, cement, and grain to other businesses.

The winding narrow streets of the Flats are becoming diversified. Light and heavy industry—long the backbone of the area—is now elbow to elbow with entertainment, boating, businesses, and housing. Thousands of people work in the Flats, and more than one million flock here each year to nightclubs, concerts, festivals, and related water activities.

Rowing competitions—the Flats Racing League and the annual English Speaking Union Canoe Races "Queen's Cuyahoga Cup"—are popular in the summer. During good weather three excursion boats—the *Pride of*

Cleveland, Star of Nautica, and *Goodtime II*—ply the Cuyahoga and the lakefront, as do various fishing and tour charter boats. Waterskiing and parasailing charters are also available on the lakefront.

Pleasure boats often contend with freighters for space at the river's many hairpin curves. In fact, boaters meet periodically with local, state, and federal regulatory authorities to discuss ways to keep commercial shipping and pleasure boating orderly. The Flats Oxbow Association distributes a brochure to recreational boaters with lifesaving tips on how to make way for freighters and tugs.

Boaters also must make way, or take lengthy pauses, at the mouth of the Cuyahoga when the Conrail Iron Curtain Bridge, carrying a main Conrail line between New York and Chicago, is lowered. The 265-foot bridge is raised with cables and counterweights to almost 100 feet.

The most distinctive feature of the Flats is its varied bridges—many built in the nineteenth century by the railroads—including ones that raise up and down, jackknife, or swivel open and closed.

"The area is an adult Disney World," says Denise Fugo, who with her husband Ralph DiOrio operates Sammy's, Cleveland's tony contemporary American cuisine restaurant. Sammy's, located on the east side of the river, is frequently cited by food reviewers as one of the leading regional restaurants in the United States.

"There are bridges that swing and move, gravel pits that rise and fall, peach trees growing under concrete arches, a proliferation of wild herbs and plants, seagulls, trains and boats of all sizes, colorful restaurants and

Above: Pleasure craft and freighters often compete for space along the curves of the Cuyahoga River. Courtesy, Cosgray Photography

Facing page: This view of the Cuyahoga river from Settler's Landing shows the Conrail Lift Bridge and the Main Avenue Bridge of the Shoreway. Photo by Barbara Durham

MANTADOC

Above: A unique feature of the Flats area is its distinctive bridges. Courtesy, Luce Photography, Inc.

Left: A tugboat escorts a Thunder Bay freighter through the busy Cuyahoga River. Courtesy, Luce Photography, Inc.

nightclubs, small factories, and incredible sunrises and sunsets over the water," Fugo says. "For a jogger, there's no more spectacular scenery than what you see when running in the Flats."

On the east side of the Cuyahoga adjacent to Sammy's, Fugo is embarking on the construction of an eight-story, 100-room luxury hotel with a tent on the roof for year-round entertaining. Other nearby riverfront restaurants include Fagan's, complete with an outdoor swimming pool, and the warehouse-decor Watermark. The Samsel Supply Company, a marine supplier, also maintains a thriving business in the area.

Stouffer Restaurants, headquartered in suburban Solon, has drawn up blueprints for a 400-seat Parker's Lighthouse Restaurant at Settler's Landing on the river's east bank. Settler's Landing is near the River Bend Condominiums, among the newest housing projects in the Flats (on the spot where Moses Cleaveland reputedly debarked in 1796).

One of the most captivating proposals for the east side of the river is a trolley powered by an overhead electric wire. The 1924 double-decker English trolley, donated by Trolleyville U.S.A. (a museum in suburban Olmsted Falls), will be refurbished by the Cleveland Building Trades Association.

Fagan's is a popular riverfront restaurant in the Flats. Photo by Roger Mastroianni

As proposed, the trolley will run on an abandoned track along West Tenth Street between the transportation hub of the Flats and the nightclub district on Old River Road near the mouth of the Cuyahoga. The half-mile of track, which may be given by Conrail to the city, will be maintained by the RTA.

If city planners are successful, the system will be expanded to connect the trolley to another proposed rail link, the restored steam train from the Professional Football Hall of Fame in Canton to the Rock and Roll Hall of Fame and Museum at Tower City Center.

Part of the proposal calls for the downtown trolley to leave the Rock and Roll Museum and hook up with the Flats hub near Shorty's Delux Diner—a nostalgic 1950s-style grill—and eventually continue on through the nightclub district to the North Coast Harbor. A separate trolley extension has been proposed to link the Flats hub with the west bank of the river.

The west side of the Cuyahoga is just as active as the east side. Visitors can get there via a number of bridges or, from spring through fall, by one of the water taxis that crisscross the Cuyahoga.

Development on the west bank began in earnest in the mid-1980s, when developer Jeff Jacobs (son of Richard Jacobs) started assembling old industrial property into a mixed-use complex called Nautica. The first Nautica project, Shooter's Restaurant (part of a Fort Lauderdale chain), opened in 1987 in what was formerly a riverfront sugar warehouse. That same year—virtually overnight—Shooter's became the highest volume restaurant in Ohio and one of the highest in the nation.

Club Coconuts, a fashionable New York-style nightclub, opened after Shooter's in the glass-enclosed sugar warehouse. The converted warehouse houses a clothing store, a boat dealership, and the Boat Club, a private club on the Cuyahoga whose members can rent yachts and sailboats.

In addition to a half-mile wooden boardwalk along the Cuyahoga, Nautica facilities also include the Nautica Stage, a 4,000-seat outdoor riverfront amphitheater featuring jazz, rock, and popular musicians—even occasional prizefights—throughout the summer. The Cleveland Orchestra has played at the Nautica Stage during the annual Riverfest, drawing a spillover crowd of 200,000.

In late 1989 the four-story, 100,000-square-foot brick Powerhouse (built in 1892 to generate electricity for the city's first trolley system) opened after a $20-million restoration. The Powerhouse, with its enormous glass windows and galleries, encloses shops, offices, and restaurants, including a huge TGI Friday and the Improv theater from Chicago. In the early 1990s a large Quonset building occupied by a sign company will be converted into additional retail space and connected by a glass walkway to the Powerhouse and sugar warehouse.

Shooter's Restaurant, the first project at Nautica, has established itself as one of the busiest restaurants in the nation. Photo by Roger Mastroianni

Coors LIGHT
ENTER
ENTER

Facing page: A mixed-use complex called Nautica exists on the site of an old west bank industrial plot. Photo by Roger Mastroianni

Nautica developers also plan to open a restaurant in an abandoned U.S. Coast Guard station (a national historic landmark) on a breakwall at the mouth of the Cuyahoga. Ferryboats will transport diners from the Cleveland-Cuyahoga Port Authority property to the restaurant. The ground floor will cater to boaters. The second floor, reserved for fine dining, will be enclosed by glass, providing a 360-degree panorama of the Gold Coast along the lake on the west side, the downtown lakefront, river, and skyline.

Jeff Jacobs also has proposed a public marina for 850 boats west of the Coast Guard station on Whiskey Island, a mile-long stretch of lakefront land east of the Cuyahoga River so named for the distillery built there in the 1830s. Conrail, whose main line cuts through property in the same area, also has lakefront redevelopment plans that include a marina.

Additional property at the mouth of the Cuyahoga is owned by the Ontario Stone Corporation, an important cog in Cleveland's shipping business, which stores massive piles of crushed stone. Nearby, the Sterling and Morton salt companies own and operate huge mines that descend thousands of feet beneath the lake.

Jeff Jacobs has a number of proposals for future housing in the Flats, including apartments and expensive "boating condominiums"—boat docks beneath living quarters—south of Nautica at Irishtown Bend, an area named for an early nineteenth-century Irish immigrant settlement. He also has proposed additional apartments and condominiums at other Flats locations, including a unique partnership with residents of the Lakeview Terrace public housing project, which slopes up the west bluff of the Flats toward Ohio City.

Using a combination of public and private money, Jacobs' proposal involves building new housing in the area and rehabilitating the apartments at Lakeview Terrace. The goal of this plan is to bring upper-middle-income residents to the city while upgrading housing for low-income residents in the same projects.

As envisioned, Lakeview Terrace residents would have the option of staying in their upgraded apartments, moving to new units in the Flats, or selling their public housing units to buy private housing. "This could be a national model for improving the quality of housing for low-income families and serve as a catalyst for bringing middle-income property owners back into the city," Jacobs says.

Other residential plans for the Flats include 600 upscale condominiums and apartments on the 65-acre Collision Bend Peninsula across the Cuyahoga from Tower City. Among the interested developers is Forest City Enterprises (the developer of Tower City Center), which is planning a joint housing venture with another peninsula landowner, Scranton-Averell Limited. Bert Wolstein, head of Developers Diversified, Inc., also has housing plans on the peninsula.

Sam and Chuck Scaravelli, father-and-son wine importers, have opened a marina for 65 boats on the Scranton Road Peninsula. Known as Marina Bay, it stays open all year because of its location—a place on the river where the water does not freeze because of the current and steam from an LTV Steel plant upstream. The marina has berths for boats from 30 to 100 feet long.

After a nite at the Beach...there's always Lite!

Facing page: The Flats attract increasingly larger crowds every year. Courtesy, Cosgray Photography

Scranton Road Peninsula also is home to Jim Steak's House, one of Cleveland's most popular restaurants; a renovated city firehouse harboring heavy-duty fireboats that safeguard shipping and buildings along the Cuyahoga; an industrial ship repair yard; and one of the largest sawmills in Ohio.

While encouraging new housing, marinas, entertainment, and retail business, the Flats Oxbow Association, the area's nonprofit development corporation, is endeavoring to retain the gritty industrial character of the Flats. The group takes its name from the Flats—or flatlands—and Oxbow, an apt description of the hairpin turns in the river.

"With all the new entertainment outlets, marinas, artist lofts, and housing," Flats Oxbow executive director Genevieve Ray says, "it's important that we keep the industry. It still is the lifeblood of the Flats. We must have a balance."

Among the unique Flats enterprises are a medical equipment manufacturer, a wholesale fishery, a beverage distributor, a flour mill, a blacksmith shop, and many steel-related fabricators and finishers. Ray also is working to expand the greenbelts and open spaces in the Flats. "Our aim is to have a riverwalk system that affords public access to the Cuyahoga and links the various attractions in the Flats," she says.

To meet the crush of people descending on the Flats, the RTA now provides lunch-hour and weekend van service from Public Square in spring, summer, and fall. The RTA also has upgraded its loop bus service to reach locales east of Public Square because of the growing retail business along Euclid Avenue.

The increase in activity on Euclid, particularly at Playouse Square, has led to the conversion of the Halle Building, which once housed Halle's department store, into a select office complex with upscale clothing stores, a wine shop, a fine restaurant, and a roomy food court.

Across Euclid from the Halle Building, the Union Club has been affected by the downtown rejuvenation and has acid-cleaned the sandstone exterior of its four-story Renaissance-style building, constructed in 1905. Much of the city's principal business is conducted within the club's walnut-paneled formal dining room and private salons. Each year between Christmas and New Year's, the daughters of members of the socially exclusive Recreation League make their debuts down its steep red-carpeted stairway.

The restoration is extending beyond the Union Club to Playhouse Square, Cleveland State University, and the St. Vincent Quadrangle, where St. Vincent Charity Hospital and Health Center—the only downtown hospital—is the dominant institution.

"The $38-million refurbishing of the historic Ohio, Palace, and State theaters at Playhouse Square became a symbol of what Cleveland could accomplish," says Lawrence J. Wilker, president of the three-theater Playhouse Square Foundation. "Civic leaders saw that business and government could unite on a common goal to save these theaters from the wrecking ball. This opened the floodgates to other successful undertakings."

The Palace Theatre, with its enormous crystal chandeliers and marble columns, is the largest and most opulent of the three interconnected old vaudeville theaters that comprise the 7,000-seat Playhouse Square Center. All told, the center is the third-largest theater complex in the United States and second in attendance only to the Lincoln Center in New York City.

The Palace's opening-night black-tie gala also served a greater purpose: to demonstrate that the nation's largest theater restoration project would continue to expand far beyond the theaters themselves.

Spillover activity from the theaters has prompted construction of the $40-million, 15-story Renaissance on Playhouse Square office building (which will open in 1990) across the street from the center. Nearby, the 14-story, 216-room Playhouse Square Hotel, which is scheduled to open in the early 1990s, will accommodate many of the one million people who patronize Playhouse Square Center each year. Developers are building a $30-million luxury-suite hotel with a federal interest-free Urban Development Action Grant of $5 million. The Playhouse Square Development Corporation, the for-profit subsidiary of the foundation, is investing in both projects.

Much more is planned for Playhouse Square, including a $3-million public plaza at Euclid Avenue and East Fourteenth Street. A 750-car parking garage already has opened and soon will be connected to Playhouse Square Center by an enclosed walkway. The center also has ambitious plans for the fourth theater in the complex, the Allen, which will be converted into a comedy club and restaurant.

The Allen also may become home to an extraordinary private nightclub, the Magic Castle, which would be only the second of its kind in the United States. (The original Magic Castle in Hollywood serves as the clubhouse for the Academy of Magical Arts, and bills itself as "the most amazing private club in the world.") The Magic Castle includes galleries for intimate performances and various dining rooms—all with an ethereal decor and magic props.

Playhouse Square Center has moved beyond physical development and is now producing new American musicals for national touring companies. Among the shows developed and staged at Playhouse Square Center are *Big River, Gospel of Collonus,* and *Beehive.*

The center also is becoming increasingly important to the city's civic life. Charity fundraisers often are held in the center's spacious lobbies. Dr. John A. Flower chose to be installed as president of Cleveland State University at the 3,200-seat Palace.

Playhouse Square also serves as a link between Cleveland State University and the city's civic and social life. Expansion plans for the west end of Cleveland State show the university's College of Urban Affairs connected to Playhouse Square Center by a walkway over East Seventeenth Street. The center will build new offices on a second-story annex cantilevered over East Seventeenth.

Cleveland State University in the twenty-first century will be woven tightly into the fabric of downtown. The Maxine Goodman Levin College of Urban Affairs is designing the University-Community Civic Forum. Modeled after similar forums at the Kennedy School of Government at Harvard University and the Hubert H. Humphrey Institute of Public Affairs at the University of Minnesota, it will include large conference rooms where university faculty and students can hold dialogues with national and local political and civic leaders.

Attached to the Forum will be the Library of the Future, a joint facility of the College of Law and the College of Urban Affairs. Among its many missions, the library will house a vast law collection and material related to public policy issues. It also will serve as a federal depository for municipal, state, and federal documents.

Also in the planning, between East Seventeenth and East Eighteenth and between Euclid and Chester, is a new building for the James J. Nance College of Business. The three colleges—business, law, and urban affairs—will be tied together by a graduate student commons, which will include green space and new structures for offices, student lockers, a lounge, and a cafeteria.

"These major-league facilities will heighten the academic stature of Cleveland State," says David C. Sweet, dean of the College of Urban Affairs, "and strengthen the bond between the university and the community at large."

The Cleveland Play House is currently developing and staging new American musicals for national touring companies. Photo by Roger Mastroianni

When construction is finished north of Euclid Avenue, a covered walkway will link the $150-million Law, Urban Affairs, and Business complex not only to Playhouse Square but also to the new CSU Music and Communications Building.

The music building will house recital rooms and radio and television studios. From the music building, walkways will tie in other campus buildings, making it possible to go virtually anywhere on the main CSU campus by covered walkway.

New construction on the west end of the campus will not be finished before the late 1990s. The university, however, is already planning the 1993 grand opening of its $48-million Convocation Center.

With 13,000 seats, the Convocation Center is one of downtown's largest projects. Several city blocks of tenements, bars, and hotels were razed to make way for the center, which also will house workout rooms for men and women and conference rooms for community activities. The winning CSU Vikings basketball team, which competes against Division I colleges, will play its home games at the Convocation Center.

Perhaps it is ironic that so much of downtown and Cleveland State should be expanding along Euclid Avenue, for it was here more than a century ago that Cleveland's industrial titans built their showcase mansions in an array of architectural styles.

Only a handful of the enormous homes, with their expansive lawns, remain on what was once called "Millionaire's Row." Among them is the Mather Mansion, the Tudor home of Samuel Mather—a shipping and mining magnate once called "Cleveland's First Citizen"—which cost $1.2 million to build in 1910. The red-brick mansion, with an enormous third-floor ballroom, now houses CSU administrative offices.

Across the street from the Mather Mansion, the yellow-brick former home of George Howe—nephew of Elias Howe, inventor of the sewing machine—has gone through a number of metamorphoses since it was built in 1894. After serving as an art gallery for almost 70 years, it was purchased by the university. When fully restored, the Howe Mansion will open as the Joseph E. Cole Faculty Center, named after a Cleveland businessman who served as CSU chairman and is the faculty club's primary benefactor.

The Howe Mansion is among a handful of invaluable structures surrounding CSU that link modern Cleveland with its past. Among the others are three Euclid Avenue churches. The limestone Gothic Trinity Cathedral, central church of the Ohio Episcopal diocese, was designed by architect Charles Schweinfurth, who designed many of the Euclid Avenue mansions. Trinity was consecrated in 1907. Over the years, as the neighborhood has changed and Cleveland State has mushroomed, the beautiful oak-paneled church at East Twenty-second Street has become a campus focal point.

The St. Theodosius Russian Orthodox Cathedral displays beautifully preserved iconography. Photo by Don Snyder

The winter sun shines on the beautiful Garfield Monument. Photo by T. Williams. Courtesy, Image Finders, Inc.

Less than 10 blocks east of Trinity is First Church, a Methodist church that opened in 1905. First Church, like Trinity, has become increasingly cosmopolitan in its activities, and provides many social services for the university and the nearby inner-city community.

St. Paul's Shrine at East Fortieth and Euclid, on the outer eastern boundary of downtown, was built in 1876 as an Episcopal parish serving what was once Millionaire's Row. In 1931, after most of the mansions had come down and the residents had moved away, the Episcopal diocese sold the English Gothic church to the Catholic Diocese, which reconsecrated it as St. Paul's Shrine. Today St. Paul's also serves as a monastery for cloistered Poor Clare Franciscan nuns. Mother Angelica, the founder of Eternal World Television Network—among the largest Christian cable networks in America—was a novice at St. Paul's in the 1940s.

The three churches also function as gateways to the MidTown Corridor, which stretches from the east end of Cleveland State to East Seventy-ninth Street, and from Carnegie Avenue north to Perkins Avenue. The nonprofit MidTown Corridor, Inc., established in the early 1980s, is supervising an extraordinary rebirth of what was largely a deteriorating crime-ridden area of old factories and warehouses.

The first steps toward reclaiming the neighborhood began in late 1979 when Thomas H. Roulston, founder and chairman of Roulston & Company, purchased an old warehouse at East Fortieth and Chester. After full interior decoration and exterior rehabilitation, Roulston moved his firm into

Facing page: A clown entertains children of all ages at the Cuyahoga Valley National Recreation Area Festival. Photo by Barbara Durham

the building, which also included an indoor parking garage.

"The cost of the entire place was equal to two years rent where we were downtown," says Roulston, whose firm has 100 employees in Cleveland and offices in London and Hong Kong.

Subsequently, Roulston spurred the effort to rejuvenate the once-genteel University Club on Euclid Avenue, which had fallen into disrepair and had only 65 members left. In mid-1980 Roulston and 12 partners bought the antebellum mansion, closed it, pumped $1.5 million into renovations, and reopened it with modern facilities and parking for almost 200 cars.

The club now has 700 members—including political, business, and union leaders—and hosts upwards of 3,000 separate functions annually, from private luncheons to political receptions. It also has a full complement of athletic facilities, including outdoor tennis courts.

"We did it as a civic venture," Roulston says. "We knew it could be a central unifying force for the neighborhood."

On the heels of the University Club, several area business leaders joined Roulston in forming MidTown Corridor, Inc., including Morton L. Mandel, chairman of Premier Industrial Corporation, an international automotive and electronics supplier; John R. Cunin, chairman of Bearings, Inc., a leading bearings distributor; and G. Robert Klein, chairman of George R. Klein News Company, a magazine and book distributor.

One of MidTown Corridor's first tasks was cooperating with district police to curb prostitution and pressuring city hall to raze walk-up hotels and tenements that had contributed to prostitution. MidTown now has one of the lowest crime rates in the city.

With the goal of bringing in new residents, MidTown Corridor helped refurbish apartments, brownstones, and row houses. More than 2,000 people now live in the corridor, a mixture of low-income residents and middle-class professionals, including many CSU students and faculty.

A $950,000 Cleveland Foundation grant helped MidTown Corridor put together a land bank program. The first phase of the redevelopment program was the acquisition of a city-sponsored 20-acre industrial park. Designed by architect Keeva Kekst and located in an enterprise zone, MidTown Commerce Park offers security, low-cost land, accessibility to nearby interstates, and tax incentives for commercial and light-industrial enterprises.

More than 17,000 people work at 500 diverse businesses in the corridor, an increase of more than 200 companies in less than a decade. Among the more novel are Gust Gallucci Company, an Italian gourmet food store that attracts shoppers from all over Northeast Ohio, and Pierre's French Ice Cream Company, which makes and distributes high-quality ice cream throughout the Midwest.

The MidTown Corridor is home to 35 labor unions and two dozen government and social service agencies, including the new $11.5-million local Red Cross headquarters. When it opens in the early 1990s, the headquarters will be named after the late Joseph M. Bruening, founder of Bearings, Inc. Bruening's foundation contributed 1 million dollars to the project.

"MidTown is an example of what the public and private sector and organized labor can do together," Roulston says. "It is a better place to live and work, and the bottom line is businesses are making more money."

If anything, MidTown Corridor has variety. It also is home to several CSU fraternity houses and two venerable men's clubs. The Rowfant Club at East Thirtieth Street and Prospect focuses on various aspects of books, including book collecting. The comfortable clubhouse and private library have been in the same Victorian mansion since 1895, three years after the club was formed.

Not far away, at Prospect and East Thirty-sixth Street, is Cleveland's most exclusive men's social club, the Tavern Club, built in 1904, 12 years after the club was founded. Tavern Club membership is heavily composed of the descendants of Cleveland's first families. The four-story red-brick Tavern Club building—resembling a huge gingerbread house—has not changed much over the years. Its large rooms are trimmed in heavy oak, and the squash courts on the top floor are still used regularly.

"Time, talent, and resources of the entire area were thrust into reclaiming this neighborhood," says Margaret L. Murphy, executive director of MidTown Corridor. "Because of our pivotal placement between downtown and University Circle and proximity to nearby interstates and the low cost of land, MidTown is becoming a vital business center."

Among the many projects proposed for MidTown is the $33-million Municipal Center at East Fifty-fifth and Carnegie in what once was the Warner & Swasey tool-and-die company. The renovated complex will house several city services, including an Emergency Medical Service garage, a Third District police station, a 100-cell jail, an indoor police range, a fitness center, and a garage for municipal vehicles.

Not far away on Euclid Avenue between East Sixty-sixth and Sixty-ninth streets is the Dunham Tavern Museum, believed to be the oldest structure in the city. Built in 1824 by Rufus and Jane Dunham, the Tavern was an important inn on the Buffalo-Cleveland-Detroit Road.

Railroads replaced the stagecoach in the late 1850s, and Dunham Tavern became a private residence. In 1930 it was turned into studios for artists and architects, including Donald Gray, who designed the landscaping for the Great Lakes Exposition of 1936. Gray also designed gardens in the rear of the tavern and helped save it from becoming a used car lot in the late 1930s. For 50 years, until 1982, the old inn was used for nonprofit group meetings.

Restoration on the Tavern Museum began in the mid-1980s, and today it houses artifacts and furniture of early Cleveland and the Western Reserve, including the only early nineteenth-century tap room. Thousands of visitors—from schools to senior citizen groups—visit the Dunham Tavern each year.

By working with the Trust for Public Lands, the Dunham trustees hope to purchase abandoned parcels surrounding the property, expand the garden area and green space for use by community groups, and rebuild the original barn. "It's a slow process," says Bill Ruper, past president of the Dunham Museum board, "but eventually we will have a landmark Museum

Fireworks from the Fourth of July Festival of Freedom at Edgewater Park shower the downtown skyline. Photo by Roger Mastroianni

and private green space in the middle of the city."

CLEAN-LAND, OHIO, founded in 1981 by Lawrence C. Jones, chairman of the Van Dorn Company, also is helping to beautify MidTown. In less than a decade the organization planted almost 10,000 trees and 75,000 perennial flowers in city neighborhoods, including MidTown, and removed 5 million pounds of trash, much of it from the RTA rapid transit right-of-way.

Volunteers (along with adult criminal offenders working as a condition of their probation) perform the CLEAN-LAND tasks, which are funded by corporate, foundation, and public sources. "We elevate standards for how Clevelanders perceive their property," says founder and former chairman Jones.

CLEAN-LAND also is contributing to the rise in property values in the area known as Doan Center, between the eastern edge of MidTown at East Seventy-ninth Street and University Circle. Under the guidance of the nonprofit Doan Center Incorporated, this once-deteriorating inner-city neighborhood is rapidly changing with some $500 million in commercial and business development.

Gone are porno shops and strip joints, and in their place stores, office buildings, and housing are mushrooming. The $15-million MidTown Square Shopping Plaza, on 20 acres bordered by East Seventy-ninth, East Eighty-fourth, Euclid, and Chester, is scheduled to open in the early 1990s.

Partners in the shopping center are the nonprofit Neighborhoods Organized for Action and Housing (NOAH), Tri-Star Development Company, and Hannan Company. The project is only a few blocks west of the new Cleveland Play House complex.

NOAH also is working with neighborhood churches on a 150-suite moderate-income housing development in the area. Nearby, the Black Economic Union is hoping to develop a moderate-income apartment and condominium complex from East Eighty-fourth to East Eighty-seventh streets and from Euclid to Chester avenues.

The biggest Doan Center employer, the Cleveland Clinic Foundation, erected $200 million in new buildings in the late 1980s. These include the $14-million Clinic Guest House, a 200-unit hotel that serves patients and their families and complements the 390-suite Clinic Center Hotel across Euclid Avenue.

The clinic also is planning a new surgical wing and a $60-million biomedical research building on Carnegie Avenue on the southern edge of its vast complex. Doan Center Incorporated maintains a computerized data file on all properties in the area in an effort to coordinate development. The organization's most ambitious plans call for a medical conference center and a new gateway for University Circle near 107th and Euclid.

"A new gateway with green space and a circle visitor entry point would serve as a front door to an expanded University Circle and to the Dual Hub Corridor that leads downtown along Euclid Avenue," Doan Center president Kenneth W. McGovern says.

Like MidTown Corridor, Doan Center was modeled after University Circle, Inc. (UCI), the nonprofit group set up in 1957 to coordinate the services and development plans of some 35 member institutions at University Circle just east of Doan Center. UCI is facilitating upwards of one billion dollars in new University Circle construction through the 1990s, including new buildings for University Hospitals and Case Western Reserve University.

Richard B. Tullis, who became chairman of UCI in 1980 after his retirement as chairman of Harris Corporation, helped start MidTown and Doan Center. Admittedly, his effort was aimed at carrying out his vision to unite—through transportation and development—University Circle, the city's cultural nexus, with Public Square, the city's business and tourist center.

If Tullis' dream is fully realized, Cleveland by the late 1990s could have a combined downtown subway and low-platform light-rail transit system running from Public Square to University Circle. The five-mile Dual Hub Corridor system could cost $600 million in federal, state, local, and private funds. Starting downtown at Tower City Center—the western hub—it would burrow underground to East Ninth and Euclid, Playhouse Square, and Cleveland State University. From there the RTA train would return above ground and operate via rail down the middle of Euclid Avenue.

After making stops in the MidTown Corridor and Doan Center, it would stop at University Circle—the eastern hub—and link up with the main rapid-transit line at East 123rd Street. One proposal suggests a spur from University Circle along Fairhill and Martin Luther King Boulevard to the Shaker Rapid. "The economic spin-off would be tremendous," Tullis says. "It would help bring back the whole center of the city and, in effect, enlarge University Circle until it touches downtown."

The Dual Hub Corridor system, first presented in the early 1980s, must undergo numerous feasibility studies and gain the support of local government leaders who are divided over how to finance it.

"It's amazing that we have come this far," says J. Barry Barker, former assistant general manager for marketing and management of the RTA. Barker also believes that, even if the Dual Hub is not successful, commuter trains could someday utilize existing railroad tracks that extend from downtown to such outlying suburbs as Avon Lake, Mentor, Berea, Strongsville, Parma, Solon, and perhaps Hudson.

It is obvious that the downtown building boom has become the driving force behind progress throughout Northeast Ohio.

"Downtown sets the mood and creates the atmosphere for an entire urban region," says William Bryant, president of the Greater Cleveland Growth Association. "A metropolitan area rarely remains healthy if its downtown is not growing and vibrant.

"Downtown Cleveland is fast becoming all this and more," Bryant adds. "The revitalization is spurring neighborhood and suburban development. Cleveland is now the city to watch and emulate. We have taken our rightful place as one of the nation's great cities."

Following page: Downtown Cleveland stands ready to meet the challenges of the twenty-first century. Photo by Jim Baron. Courtesy, Image Finders, Inc.

A gentle explosion of floating color marks the climax of Balloon Fest in downtown Cleveland. Photo by Jim Baron. Courtesy, Image Finders, Inc.

PART 2

Cleveland's Enterprises

The Bell Building adds yet another touch of class to Cleveland's downtown business district. Photo by T. Williams. Courtesy, Image Finders, Inc.

CHAPTER 10

Networks

Cleveland's energy, communication, and transportation providers keep products, information, and power circulating inside and outside the area.

Courtesy, Cosgray Photography

THE EAST OHIO GAS COMPANY

One million. The East Ohio Gas Company took great pride in that number, when, in February 1987, the company welcomed its one-millionth customer. This milestone established The East Ohio Gas Company as one of the nation's largest gas utilities. Its growth has reflected the growth of Northeast Ohio for more than 90 years.

East Ohio Gas is, by any measure, a large company. It has 2,500 employees, 30 service centers or offices, 1,000 vehicles, 16,000 miles of underground pipeline, and sales of more than one billion dollars annually. Its corporate headquarters is in Cleveland, and there are offices in Akron, Ashtabula, Canton, Youngstown, Warren, Wooster, and New Philadelphia. East Ohio's 3,000-square-mile service area includes the major industrial centers of Northeast Ohio and the south shore of Lake Erie from the western suburbs of Cleveland to the Ohio-Pennsylvania border. The company serves 269 communities within a 20-county area.

ABOVE: By 1950 East Ohio was serving more than a half-million customers. The Home Service Department conducted on-site demonstrations for the homemaker of the 1950s. Courtesy, East Ohio Gas Historical Center

LEFT: At the turn of the nineteenth century, East Ohio's charge was to run a pipeline that would move natural gas from the oil fields of West Virginia to the growing industrial centers of Northeast Ohio. Courtesy, East Ohio Gas Historical Center

The East Ohio Gas Company functions as a natural gas distributor; it delivers the fuel to residential, commercial, and industrial customers. Natural gas is recognized as a safe, reliable, and affordable energy source. It has many applications, including heating homes, fueling blast furnaces used in steel production, and even generating electric power. However, the firm can trace its origins to a time when natural gas was regarded as a nuisance in the oil fields of West Virginia.

In the late 1800s drillers prayed

The Sunshine People are 2,500 employees working throughout Northeast Ohio. Employees at a Cleveland service center display their pride in the company with bumper stickers featuring the slogan "I'm Proud of the Company I Keep." Photo by Larry Joyner

first, to find oil, and second, to find it without natural gas. Most drillers burned off the gas, but John D. Rockefeller foresaw its bright future as a major energy source. Smokestacks were beginning to replace cornstalks in the Midwest in the 1890s, and Rockefeller formed two companies to supply booming new industrial centers with natural gas. One of those companies was East Ohio Gas.

Its charge was to run pipe from West Virginia, across the Ohio River into Ohio, and then north. Laying pipeline under rivers, around swamps, and through wilderness was a task that strained the technology of the times and the endurance of men, horses, and machines.

In Dennison, Ohio, in 1898 the firm officially incorporated as The East Ohio Gas Company and provided service to its first customer—train engineer Thomas Emmet Van Lehn.

When Rockefeller's original operation broke up in 1911, East Ohio came under the umbrella of The Standard Oil Company of New Jersey and remained there until 1943. Then, to avoid becoming a regulated utility under the Public Utility Holding Company Act, Jersey spun off its gas concerns. This resulted in the formation of Consolidated Natural Gas Company, East Ohio's parent firm. East Ohio Gas is the largest of Consolidated's five natural gas distribution subsidiaries. Headquartered in Pittsburgh, Consolidated has revenues of more than $3 billion per year.

In 1987 the Troy Black family entered East Ohio's history books as the company's one-millionth customer. East Ohio is one of only 13 natural gas distribution companies to hold this distinction. Photo by Larry Joyner

East Ohio's relationship with Consolidated aids the Cleveland-based utility in providing a competitively priced and reliable supply of natural gas and in developing new technologies. In addition, East Ohio invests in the future of its service area through corporate donations from the Consolidated Natural Gas Company Foundation.

One of Northeast Ohio's assets is the availability of a dependable, relatively inexpensive supply of natural gas. Consumers in Northeast Ohio pay less for natural gas than do residents of most of the country's 25 largest metropolitan areas. East Ohio Gas shops for the best-priced natural gas available, buying from suppliers in Ohio and throughout the United States. The firm, along with Consolidated, operates the largest natural gas storage system in the nation.

East Ohio's storage capacity enables the company to purchase inexpensive gas when it is available. Natural gas storage fields are actually depleted gas wells. New gas is injected into these porous sandstone cavities and stored until needed. The gas is usually stored in the summer when demand is low and drawn out in the winter when heating needs surge.

For many years East Ohio has worked closely with the Gas Research Institute to develop and test new technologies and applications for natural gas. The shifting economic base of Northeast Ohio, exemplified by changes in the steel industry and the growth of the polymer industry, has provided many opportunities to advance these technologies.

New industrial and commercial uses for natural gas are helping to give business in Northeast Ohio a competitive edge. One cost-effective method for producing electrical energy with natural gas is co-firing. This occurs when natural gas is added to the fuel mix in coal boilers. Co-firing reduces the sulfur dioxide and nitrogen oxide emissions, chief culprits in the formation of acid rain. East Ohio brought its first co-firing municipal power plant on line in 1987 and added another the following year.

Some of East Ohio's customers produce electricity on site with natural gas, using cogeneration technology, an alternative to more expensive traditional electric power. Cleveland's Deaconess Hospital, a cogeneration pioneer, has cut operating costs significantly by using this system.

In 1987 East Ohio launched an advertising campaign developed by and featuring employees. The campaign stressed the employees' commitment to customer service and the pride they take in their work.

New natural gas technology helps residential, commercial, and industrial customers operate more efficiently. East Ohio employees work with area businesses and industries in applying the new technology and helping them maintain the competitive edge. Courtesy, Consolidated Natural Gas

Gas injection, in which natural gas replaces a portion of coke in blast furnaces, helps steel manufacturers increase productivity and lower costs. Gas-fired, engine-driven chillers are used for industrial cooling processes. Natural-gas-fired central thermal fluid systems reduce costs in plastics, polymer, and rubber manufacturing.

East Ohio believes in its product so completely that 80 percent of its fleet is fueled by natural gas. The firm has been promoting natural-gas-powered vehicles for almost 10 years. They produce fewer emissions than gasoline-fueled vehicles and emit less particulate matter than diesel-powered vehicles. The technology is ideal for companies that operate heavy equipment and fleets of vehicles. School systems in Geneva, Cortland, and Hudson fuel their buses with natural gas; part of Cleveland's popular Lolly the Trolley tour fleet runs on natural gas; and the City of Cleveland is converting part of its fleet to natural gas.

Residential customers have also benefited from East Ohio's commitment to technology. The company recognizes that consumers have changed drastically in just 10 years. Because few customers can be at home when meter readers or service representatives visit, East Ohio is implementing CompuMatic Remote Meter Reading and Computer-Aided Radio Dispatching systems. The CompuMatic Remote Meter Reading device reads meters from outside the home. It speeds meter reading and is very efficient in older residential neighborhoods where indoor meters are common. Computer-Aided Radio Dispatching uses advanced computer communications to set up service calls, thus accommodating customers' schedules.

Most people in Northeast Ohio recognize the company and its employees as The Sunshine People. They are enthusiastic contributors to a wide variety of civic and charitable organizations, including the United Way, the United Negro College Fund, the Hispanic Community Forum, and the Salvation Army. Employees volunteer in almost 100 organizations and through the years have collectively contributed more than seven centuries of volunteer time to their community. East Ohio works closely with civic and business leaders to keep the region a place that businesses and residents will want to call home.

The East Ohio Gas Company has provided Northeast Ohio with a clean, competitively priced energy source for almost a century. The firm takes great pride in its history, a history that reflects the growth of the region. The story of East Ohio Gas is now on display in the company's Historical Center and Archives at its headquarters in Cleveland. In 1988 the grand opening of the center, which is open to the public, marked the company's 90th anniversary.

The Historical Center preserves The East Ohio Gas Company's past and demonstrates its role in shaping a dynamic vision of Northeast Ohio and the greater Cleveland area.

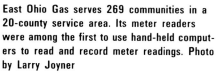

East Ohio Gas serves 269 communities in a 20-county service area. Its meter readers were among the first to use hand-held computers to read and record meter readings. Photo by Larry Joyner

Retired East Ohio chairman and former chairman of the Greater Cleveland Growth Association Dick Kelso (left) and other East Ohioans are working with leaders such as Greater Cleveland Growth Association president Bill Bryant, to help bring this civic vision model of Cleveland, closer to becoming a reality. Photo by Larry Joyner

OHIO BELL

The 9-1-1 emergency phone system in Cuyahoga County saves lives.

Twelve days after the Cuyahoga County 9-1-1 emergency telephone system became operational, it saved 14 people whose large, two-family home caught fire. Thanks to 9-1-1, the Cleveland Fire Department responded in less than three minutes to a call from a neighbor who noticed the fire. Eleven children and three adults were safely evacuated from the home.

An elderly woman whose illness tied her to an oxygen tank was frightened when the transformer on her house exploded and her appliances started to spark. She called 9-1-1. Before she finished talking with the dispatcher, a fire truck was at her door, and the power company had sent a service crew.

A 22-year-old woman was kidnapped, then bound, gagged, and assaulted at her kidnapper's apartment. He left her bound and unable to free her hands. With the tip of her nose, she pushed the telephone buttons and called 9-1-1. In minutes, she was on the way to the hospital, and the police were heading to her attacker's place of employment to arrest him.

The 9-1-1 emergency service network is used in many communities within Ohio Bell's service territory. Ohio Bell, in cooperation with the Cuyahoga County Commissioners, installed and maintains the countywide 9-1-1 service that provides 59 cities, villages, and townships with a single, easy-to-remember emergency phone number. In addition, calls to 9-1-1 can be dialed directly from public phones free of charge.

The 9-1-1 system relies heavily on sophisticated computers and communications systems. A computerized selective routing system connects any caller with one of 48 Public Safety Answering Points (PSAPs)—usually a police or fire station designated by each community. A computerized database matches the caller's phone number, the address Ohio Bell has for that number, and the nearest PSAP for that address. In less than three seconds from the time a caller dials 9-1-1, he or she is connected to the nearest PSAP.

For calls from mobile phones and phones where a specific answering point cannot be determined, such as a newly installed number, there is one countywide PSAP.

An additional level of information is available at most PSAPs in Cuyahoga County. Special equipment provides automatic number identification and automatic location identification. When the emergency dispatcher answers a call, the caller's phone number and address appear on a computer screen in front of the dispatcher. So even if the caller cannot speak or give the dispatcher any information about the emergency, help can still be sent.

Once a caller reaches the dispatcher and explains what is happening, he or she is either connected directly to the appropriate emergency service, or the dispatcher calls an emergency team and sends it to the proper address. Procedures depend on the nature of the call and the severity of the situation.

Telephone number and address changes and additions for new customers are usually entered into the computerized system within 48 hours of the change. Maintaining the 9-1-1 network and the master street address database costs one million dollars per year; the expense is covered by Ohio Bell subscribers at 12 cents per month per line.

It is not surprising that Ohio Bell is capable of installing and maintaining a sophisticated 9-1-1 emergency network with little downtime. The company has been at the forefront of communications technology for almost 70 years. Ohio Bell invests from $350 million to $400 million per year—every year—in new technology to remain a market leader. This dedication to advanced technologies and 24-hour operation has earned the company an enviable reputation for solving problems and responding to needs. The 9-1-1 emergency network is one of the best examples of how Ohio Bell earned this reputation.

CLEVELAND ELECTRIC ILLUMINATING COMPANY

The Cleveland Electric Illuminating Company provides electric power to nearly 730,000 customers in Northeast Ohio. The company serves a 1,700-square-mile area with a population of nearly 2 million people. Known locally as "CEI," the firm is one of Northeast Ohio's biggest promoters of area development. CEI's 5,000 employees today take pride in a tradition of service and excellence that dates back more than a century.

CEI's origins date back to 1881, when a local inventor named Charles Francis Brush founded the Brush Electric Light and Power Company. The fledgling firm sent line crews in horse-drawn wagons to string power lines over the rooftops of downtown Cleveland to light 88 street lamps. In 1883 Brush's operation merged with the Cleveland General Electric Company. The new enterprise served some 400 customers in an area of Cleveland less than one square mile. One year later the name became the Cleveland Electric Illuminating Company. By 1900 CEI was providing electric power to nearly 2,000 customers.

CEI's first generating facility was the Canal Road power plant located in Cleveland's industrial "flats" and completed in 1895. To avoid adding overhead power lines to what already was a congested area, CEI became one of the first utilities in the nation to distribute electricity through underground facilities. In 1911 CEI completed the first unit of its Lake Shore Plant to help accommodate a peak load of 27,000 kilowatts for 30,000 customers. A 1919 addition made Lake Shore the largest steam-powered electric plant in the world.

CEI promoted electric lamps and all-electric living to expand its customer base 500 percent between 1910 and 1920. By offering lower rates and more reliable service, CEI eventually acquired 36 local municipal electric systems and private generating plants to continue expanding its service area. By 1930 CEI was serving 310,000 customers in an area stretching beyond Cuyahoga County to include Lake, Geauga, Ashtabula, and part of Lorain County. By then the firm had completed building its Avon Lake Plant and was starting work on the Ashtabula Plant. Another coal-fired facility, the Eastlake Plant, was added in 1953.

During the late 1920s the firm pioneered many technological advances. Its innovations in high-voltage transmission systems made possible the beginnings of an interconnected "super power" system throughout Ohio. Company advances in coal pulverization and automation improved the efficiency of boiler operations at power plants.

CEI was one of the first utilities to have a department specifically dedicated to area development. Following World War II the firm launched an extensive marketing campaign to attract new enterprises. Promoting Northeast Ohio as "The Best Location in the Nation," CEI helped bring in nearly 900 new companies in the next four decades. Such giants as Ford, General Motors, NASA, and others constructed major facilities in Northeast Ohio, largely as a result of CEI efforts. In addition, CEI carried out a five-year land-use study with far-reaching consequences. It influenced highway planners to preserve large, empty sites in Northeast Ohio for industrial and commercial development. This prudent planning is providing benefits even today.

Meanwhile CEI has contributed to America's energy independence by continuing to bring the latest energy technology to Northeast Ohio. The company joined with partner utilities to build the Seneca Pumped Storage Hydroelectric Power Plant in Pennsylvania, the Davis-Besse Nuclear Power Station near Port Clinton, and the Perry Nuclear Power Plant located 35 miles east of

High-voltage transmission lines interconnect CEI's electric system with those of neighboring utilities to ensure a reliable supply of electric power to customers no matter how high the demand.

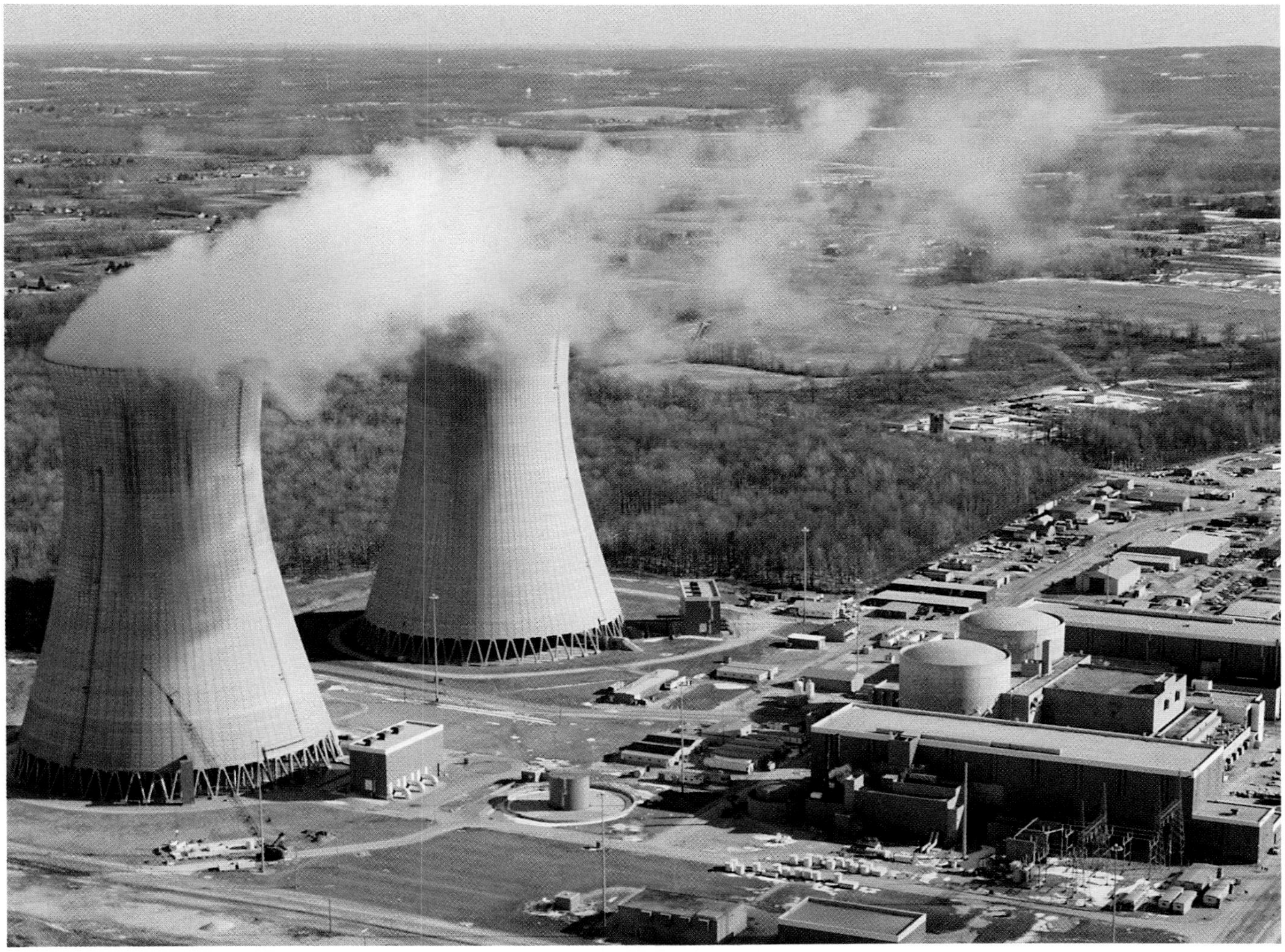

Cleveland. Operated by CEI, the Perry Plant went into service in 1987, representing state-of-the-art technology. Its electricity is distributed to some 7 million people in Ohio and western Pennsylvania. CEI also continues to run four coal-fired power plants, kept in operating condition by continuing maintenance programs.

CEI customers consume some 18 billion kilowatt-hours of electricity per year. The firm is now a wholly owned subsidiary of Centerior Energy Corporation, a holding company formed by the 1986 affiliation of CEI and the Toledo Edison Company. The combined generating capability of the two utilities ensures continued reliability of electric service to customers of both CEI and Toledo Edison. Centerior Energy ranks among the 20 largest electric utilities in the nation.

CEI prides itself on its commitment to the communities it serves. Employee volunteers give thousands of hours each year to community service projects and work with management to aid their favorite causes. The firm sponsors a wide variety of programs ranging from swimming classes for inner-city youths to the Senior Olympics for senior citizens. For more than a quarter-century CEI has sponsored "Academic Challenge," a weekly television quiz show featuring high school scholars. Civic beautification, educational television, consumer safety, and the fight against drug abuse are among other causes the company champions. Employee volunteers with the CEI Speakers Bureau reach some 40,000 people per year.

The Perry Nuclear Power Plant, built by CEI and co-owned with four other electric companies, went into service in 1987. The state-of-the-art facility helps serve the electricity needs of some 7 million people in Ohio and western Pennsylvania. Perry's cooling towers rise more than 500 feet and release pollutant-free water vapor into the air.

Since the first switch was thrown in 1881, electric power has brought comfort, convenience, and economic progress to Northeast Ohioans. As the twenty-first century approaches, Northeast Ohio is well positioned for further growth thanks to its many geographic, economic, and cultural assets, and to the reliable electric service assured by the electric company proud to serve "The Best Location in the Nation."

GE-REUTER-STOKES

When Reuter-Stokes started in 1956, its product line included ceramic-to-metal seals and components for the budding electronics industry. It was located in a 5,000-square-foot facility on Cleveland's east side. There were four employees: owners Fred Reuter and Art Stokes, and two other men.

Now the company is the world's largest manufacturer of radiation detectors. About one-half of its business is the manufacture of products to monitor neutron and gamma flux in nuclear reactors. These measurements are part of the control and safety system of the reactor. Other products include environmental monitoring and safeguards systems that are used around nuclear power plants, nuclear processing plants, and waste-storage sites to monitor radiation levels and nuclear material.

Reuter-Stokes also manufactures nuclear detectors for use in oil and gas exploration, industrial process control, and nuclear research. Special detectors have even gone to Mars, as part of the Viking Lander project.

The company's first order was placed by Oak Ridge National Laboratory. Many products designed and manufactured by Reuter-Stokes in those early years are still produced today, because their initial design set the standard for the industry. However, research has improved production and materials used in the detectors so they perform better, last longer, and are more reliable.

Other changes have occurred over time: The firm now employs more than 200 people. Total business volume in 1956 was less than one million dollars, and in 1987 it was $24 million.

Despite its growth, the corporation's dedication to quality and personal service to customers has not changed. Even today customers have easy access to engineering, manufacturing, and quality-control staff, as well as their highly trained sales contact. This open-door policy has helped Reuter-Stokes stay in touch with the customer, and thus respond more effectively to an ever-changing marketplace.

In 1984 the company was purchased by GE Nuclear Energy. This merger has given the firm a capability unmatched by its competitors. It can now draw upon the resources of the entire GE organization, as well as that of its own research and development department.

Reuter-Stokes recognizes that its most important resource is the tremendous knowledge and experience of its employees—nuclear physicists; electronic, mechanical, and nuclear engineers; skilled technicians; and machinists. Reuter-Stokes intends to continue the tradition begun by its founders: producing high-quality products, providing excellent service, and maintaining its position as a world leader in nuclear instrumentation.

Reuter-Stokes' facility at Edison Park.

AMERICAN GAS ASSOCIATION LABORATORIES

Visitors to the American Gas Association Laboratories (A.G.A. Labs) in Independence, Ohio, meander down a curving driveway lined with tall gas lamps, through a grove of trees, and finally arrive at the A.G.A. Laboratories main building.

The American Gas Association is a trade association for transmission and distribution companies in the gas industry. In addition to its Cleveland laboratory facilities, A.G.A. operates a smaller testing facility in Los Angeles, California.

The A.G.A. Labs were established in 1925 to meet three specific needs: to serve as an impartial agency to certify the designs of residential and commercial gas appliances for safety, to conduct a continuous factory inspection program to ensure that manufacturers' products complied with safety standards, and to develop new, safer, and more efficient appliances through research. To accomplish these tasks, the labs focus on three functions: appliance design certification, standards administration, and research and development.

The certification program is the most visible work at the A.G.A. Labs. Any manufacturer or individual who has developed a new gas appliance or accessory may submit it to the labs for testing. Since 1925 the two A.G.A. Labs have tested more than 57,000 models, submitted by more than 500 manufacturers, for compliance with national standards covering safety and performance. Those that pass are authorized to display the A.G.A. Blue Star Certification Seal. Manufacturers participate in the program because many local building codes require equipment certification from a nationally recognized agency.

The certification area at the Cleveland labs is as big as a football field and full of fascinating equipment. On any given day, 100 appliances might be on the floor in various stages of testing. To help ensure certified equipment continues to conform to standards, personnel from A.G.A. Labs perform announced and unannounced inspections at each manufacturing plant.

Certification is based on standards that have evolved in a national consensus procedure and are cleared through the American National Standards Institute (ANSI). The A.G.A. Labs do not write national standards, but serve as the administrative secretariat for three ANSI committees that develop the most widely used standards for gas equipment.

The third activity of the A.G.A. Labs is research and development. This work is funded by contracts with the Gas Research Institute or private firms and is aimed at providing new, innovative, and efficient equipment for customers of the natural gas industry.

Through these three primary activities, the American Gas Association Laboratories support the gas industry and contribute to its growth so that it can serve the needs of the public for space conditioning, cooking, water heating, manufacturing, transportation, and other services.

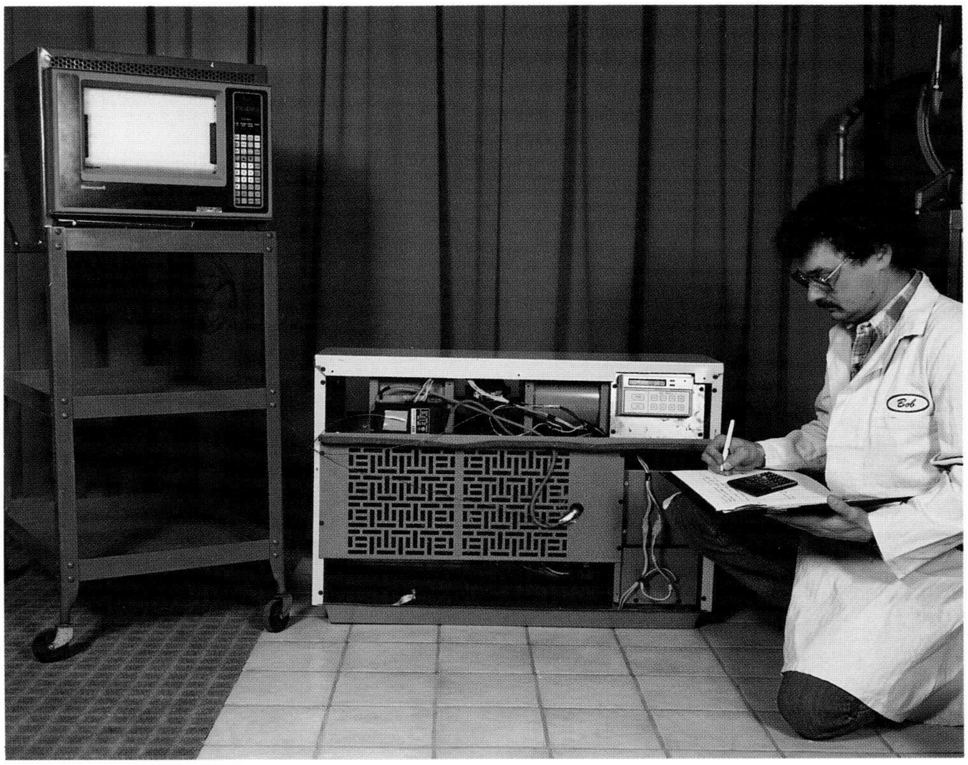

Since 1925 the A.G.A. Laboratories have tested the designs of more than 57,000 models under the A.G.A. Blue Star certification program, which requires that appliance designs comply with rigorous national standards. Today this testing program is among the most widely recognized in the United States. Photo by Stephen J. Romanik

Independence, Ohio, is home to the American Gas Association Laboratories, a trade association for transmission and distribution companies in the gas industry. Photo by Bernie Rich, Score Photography

THE GREATER CLEVELAND REGIONAL TRANSIT AUTHORITY

The Terminal Tower, Cleveland's most famous landmark, makes a perfect backdrop for the Heavy Rail Rapid Transit, which is the quickest and most economical way to get to the airport from downtown.

The Greater Cleveland Regional Transit Authority already is one of the largest multimodal transit systems in the United States, and it has plans that will make it even larger in the future.

The GCRTA employs 2,500 people and has an annual operating budget of $145 million. The transit system's capital program includes projects totaling $350 million. It has 740 buses, 150 railcars, and 129 other assorted vehicles.

GCRTA's physical plant also is considerable and includes 39 buildings, 47 rail stations, and more than 65 miles of track. In addition, the Authority owns 32 bridges, has 900 bus shelters, and is responsible for lots offering 8,000 parking spaces.

Obviously, there's a lot of prestige associated with being one of the largest transit systems, but not nearly as much as for being the best. And the GCRTA's future plans put it right on track to reach that goal.

But before finding out where the GCRTA is planning to go, it's necessary to find out where it has been.

Cleveland has been linked with some type of mass transportation since its first stagecoach service as far back as 1818. In more recent times the city's transit system was in the international spotlight when it featured the first airport rapid in North America in 1968.

Cleveland Transit System (CTS) was the last big-city public transportation service in the country to still be operating from the farebox in 1974. Legislation needed to establish a broader tax base in the name of regional transit was enacted by the formation of the GCRTA on December 30, 1974.

On May 21, 1975, a Memorandum of Understanding, setting forth the specifics of a proposed regional operation, was signed, and the voters of Cuyahoga County approved a one-percent increase in the sales tax to support transit on July 22, 1975.

It was agreed that the board of the GCRTA would be comprised of 10 trustees. Four are named by the City of Cleveland, three by the Cuyahoga County Commissioners, and three by the Cuyahoga County Mayors and City Managers Association. The board is responsible for overseeing the governing policies of the Authority. The day-to-day operation of the Greater Cleveland Regional Transit Authority is under the direct jurisdiction of the general manager.

Under the new county control, the GCRTA instituted a number of changes aimed at attracting more riders and presenting a positive attitude toward transit use, such as:

Developing a completely staffed, fully trained, and accredited police force that has jurisdiction over all transit property.

Establishing a specialized service for senior citizens and disabled persons called Community Responsive Transit (CRT).

Reconstructing the Light Rail—the Shaker Rapid then, but the Green/

The Authority's Light Rail Rapid Transit, shown at the architectural award-winning Shaker Square Station, originates from Tower City Center and carries passengers to the city's eastern suburbs.

Blue Line now—to better service East Side commuters traveling to downtown Cleveland.

Providing Color Loop Bus Service that offers riders frequent opportunities to travel throughout the downtown area over five routes for only 25 cents per trip.

The GCRTA's list of services has grown considerably through the years, and among the most popular is the 24-Hour RTAnswerline. For route and timetable information, the RTAnswerline is open for questions 24 hours per day, seven days per week.

The Authority's Customer Service Center at 2019 Ontario (just steps off Public Square) is another top attraction. Visitors can purchase tickets and passes there, and also can obtain route maps or timetables. For these service, the Center is open from 7:30 a.m. to 5 p.m. Monday through Friday. GCRTA tickets and passes are also available at more than 200 outlets through the county.

Persons 65 years of age or older and persons recognized as disabled who reside in GCRTA's service areas are eligible for a discount fare card. With proper registration through GCRTA, these passengers are entitled to ride all GCRTA buses, trains, and CRT vehicles for only 25 cents per trip.

CRT provides a prescheduled door-to-door service in 18 residential areas of Cuyahoga County. These services are designed to meet the special needs of elderly and severely disabled riders. It may be used for doctors' appointments, shopping, or visiting.

GCRTA provides regularly scheduled wheelchair-accessible bus service on seven major routes for people using wheelchairs or other aids, such as walkers, canes, and crutches. People with arthritis, heart problems, and other conditions that make it difficult to climb steps can also benefit from the lift-equipped buses because the lift stops at the ground level. In the future all new buses that are purchased by the Authority will be lift-equipped buses.

The Authority also runs a number of special services, such as the "Flyer" to the Flats, and a seasonal service to the Metroparks Zoo, the Browns' and Cavaliers' games, and other major attractions, such as the Home & Flower Show and the Air Show.

While the Authority has made great strides since becoming established, it still has much to do to modernize and rehabilitate the substantial public transit infrastructure that the area enjoys.

Currently, and over the next several years, GCRTA will be spending in excess of $100 million to upgrade and improve the Red Line Rapid Transit. It will be completing the new train control system, rebuilding the track structure, and modernizing its stations. Included in this effort is the $51 million the Authority will be spending to rebuild the Tower City Station—in its partnership with Tower City Development Corporation—scheduled to be completed in the spring of 1990.

The Authority also is teaming with other government forces to improve the quality, quantity, and efficiency of public transportation in the Dual Hub Corridor. The Dual Hub is Greater Cleveland's major transportation corridor between Downtown and University Circle.

GCRTA's main goal is to be the pride of Greater Cleveland. The Authority is working hard to become the premier public transportation system in the country. It intends to provide safe, accessible, clean, attractive services that are used by all sectors of the community.

Board trustees and management executives want the GCRTA to expand and grow while providing a full spectrum of transportation services throughout the entire region. In doing so, they recognize the need to maintain high-quality services to the Authority's traditional markets while aggressively pursuing new markets for its transportation services. They also recognize that the GCRTA is a service agency providing basic mobility to the disadvantaged people of the community.

Finally, they want the GCRTA to be a partner with business and local government, providing support for and transportation leadership in promoting the future growth and economic development of the region.

The Community Responsive Transit's family of specialized services for elderly and disabled persons is one of the longest running programs of its type in the country.

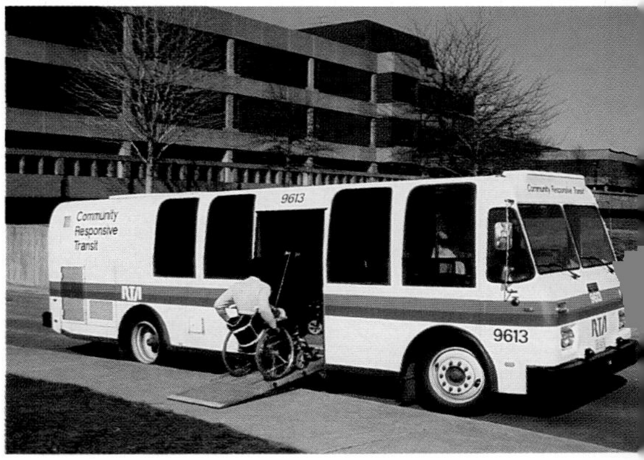

CLEVELAND PUBLIC POWER

The City of Cleveland's Department of Public Utilities, Division of Light and Power, more popularly known as Cleveland Public Power (CPP), is a municipally owned and operated electric power company. The CPP system supplies electricity to residential, commercial, industrial, and government users, primarily within the city. The city establishes rates for the power and services furnished by CPP and performs all functions necessary to operate the system. There are about 2,100 municipally owned power companies in the nation; CPP is one of the 100 largest in terms of power output and customers served.

Cleveland Public Power's roots are in the Populist Era—the early 1890s—when reformers first called for the city to build and operate an electric light plant. The establishment of a municipal power system was part of a national movement to provide essential public services, such as electricity and water, garbage collection, street cleaning, and public transportation, at a cost the urban poor could afford.

Throughout its long history CPP has been a center of controversy, since it has symbolized the struggle between those who believe the public good is better served by the private enterprise system and those who believe that certain services are so essential to the public's welfare that they must remain under public control. It has come close to being sold several times, but Cleveland citizens always vote to maintain it as a publicly owned utility.

Cleveland Public Power's customers represent a major portion of the public service facilities in the city. Its two largest customers are the City of Cleveland's Water Department, which consumes more than 11 percent of the power supplied by CPP, and the Northeast Ohio Regional Sewer District. By providing electric power to these public utilities, CPP helps to keep sewer and water rates lower.

Other public facilities among CPP's top 20 consumers include the Cleveland Convention Center, the Justice Center, City Hall, the Cleveland Metroparks Zoo, the Cleveland Board of Eduction, the main branch of the Cleveland Public Library, and the Cuyahoga County Juvenile Court. Since these facilities are tax supported, having less expensive electrical power available means less tax money is required for their support.

In the past decade CPP has changed significantly, switching from a generator of power to a wholesale purchaser and distributor of power. This strategy has been assisted by favorable legal rulings that resulted in two high-voltage interconnects between CPP and its for-profit competitor. These interconnects have made it possible for CPP to purchase less-expensive wholesale power from areas as far away as New York and Kentucky and have it delivered to its facilities through other power company transmission lines.

In addition to obtaining reliable, low-cost power through the new interconnects, CPP has also embarked upon a major capital improvement and expansion program. Higher capacity substations to handle electrical power transfer are replacing older ones. Also, while Cleveland Public Power presently supplies electricity to more than 40 percent of the neighborhoods in Cleveland and serves more than 44,000 homes, improvements begun in 1987 will expand the service area to more than 70 percent of the city by 1992. This will put lower-cost electrical power

Cleveland Public Power's Lake Road substation provides service to the downtown area, including Cleveland Municipal Stadium and the North Coast Harbor.

within reach of many industrial plants in the southeast section of the city and make it available for more residential customers as well.

As CPP moves into new sections of the city, new substations and line equipment are being added. A $50-million bond issue is financing these improvements. Revenue from sale of electrical power, not tax revenue, is repaying the bonds.

Computers have been added to help CPP's staff stay on top of daily events and monitor system operation, as well as to provide customers with instant answers on billing and service questions. An in-house computer enables CPP to apply modern financial management techniques to every facet of operations. The computer also monitors all CPP's capital improvement programs and projects. The use of computers, combined with an increased emphasis on customer service, has resulted in more rapid solutions to customer billing and service problems, and has enabled new residential hookups to be quickly processed.

Management and operations people at CPP are an effective and highly skilled resource. Many employees have been with the division for more than 15 years, meaning that the system can count on seasoned and well-trained workers. Management efforts to strengthen human resources are based on careful selection of applicants, solid in-service training, and good internal communications that keep employees focused on the system's strategic customer service goals.

The Cleveland Public Power system is now a reliable source of electrical power for a large portion of the city of Cleveland. Plans for the future include continued investment into upgrading and expanding the system until it reaches throughout the entire city.

Cleveland Public Power is a strong force in stimulating economic growth in the city. Its commercial customer rates are about 17 percent less than those of its for-profit competitor. The availability of lower priced CPP electricity is a strong incentive for new industry to locate within Cleveland's city limits. The Populist legacy continues to serve Clevelanders well.

Cleveland Public Power was selected to provide electricity to the Nautica entertainment complex, located on the west bank of the Cuyahoga River, including the new Powerhouse project.

CLEVELAND WATERWORKS SYSTEM

Lake Erie gives Cleveland a wonderful and diverse recreational resource. It also provides a reliable source of good water that continues to play an important role in the area's economic growth while enhancing the area's quality of life.

This abundant raw and potable water makes Northeast Ohio attractive to industrial and commercial users, service companies, and residents of the greater Cleveland area. As might be expected, water service is provided to customers at relatively low cost because of the enormous supply of water available from Lake Erie, estimated to contain 127 trillion gallons.

The Cleveland Division of Water, part of the city's Department of Public Utilities, operates as a self-supporting regional utility providing water service to the city of Cleveland and 70 surrounding communities. The division has more than 1,000 employees.

The system, placed in service in 1856, supplies water to approximately 375,000 homes and businesses. The service district encompasses a 640-square-mile area and serves more than 1.5 million people. Producing an average of 320 million gallons of potable water per day, the Division of Water has a production capacity in excess of 500 million gallons per day. The division generates approximately $115 million annually in metered sales revenue.

Lake Erie is an inexhaustible reservoir estimated to contain 127 trillion gallons of water. Far out in the lake, like a ship at anchor, is massive crib No. 3, one of four intake conduits drawing raw water to help meet the consumption demands of greater Cleveland's residents, hospitals, educational facilities, businesses, and industry. The steel crib, built in 1895, consists of two concentric steel cylinders 50 and 100 feet in diameter, with the circular space filled with concrete, set on a solid timber base. Crib No. 3 is connected to the Kirtland Pumping Station by a nine-foot circular, brick-lined tunnel measuring 26,047 feet long. Average daily intake from the crib is 119.5 million gallons, with 200 million gallons per day being the design capacity. Photo by Mort Tucker Photography, Inc.

A $1.5-million, state-of-the-art Supervisory Control and Data Acquisition (SCADA) system has replaced outmoded dials and gauges in the monitoring of 12 secondary pumping stations' data, such as pressures, flows, and tower elevations. The SCADA computer system also provides for the remote starting and stopping of pumps by means of telecommunications, as well as records pumpage levels, pressures, and flows from the four treatment plants. Photo by Ron Hare Photography

Four water treatment plants in the system produce the potable water sold and distributed throughout the area. Each plant has its own intake, filtration, and treatment equipment, and pumping facilities used in the production process.

Water is distributed throughout the service area by means of almost 5,000 miles of water mains, a complex system of reservoirs, water towers, above-ground storage tanks, and primary and secondary pumping stations. The system is divided into

The $113.5-million rehabilitation of the Division Avenue Filtration Plant, placed in service in 1917, is the most significant single project currently in the Cleveland Division of Water's $350-million capital improvement program. As the oldest of the four water treatment plants, the Division Avenue Plant had deteriorated significantly during its existence. Work is under way to ensure the plant's structural soundness, improve the water treatment process, and install wastewater disposal facilities. Photo by Ron Hare Photography

four operational service districts that are generally defined by elevation above lake level, as well as by distance from Lake Erie. In addition, these service districts form the basis for the division's water rate structure.

The four water treatment plants are designed to produce uniformly high-quality, potable water. Treatment standards maintained by the Division of Water meet or exceed the requirements prescribed by both federal and state environmental protection agencies. Water quality is continually monitored by a laboratory staff of chemists, biologists, and technicians.

During the past few years the Division of Water has undertaken a multiyear, multimillion-dollar capital improvement program of updating the system so it will be able to meet the ever-changing needs of the area. The most significant project in the program is the reconstruction of the Division Avenue water treatment plant at a cost of $113 million. Completion of this project is scheduled for late 1990.

Other significant projects in the program include the construction of numerous supply mains to carry more water to the growing suburban areas, construction of additional secondary pumping and storage facilities to further distribute the increased available supply, the cleaning and lining of selected existing mains to restore them to their original capacity, as well as numerous improvements at the production facilities themselves.

It should be noted that although various capital improvement projects are under way, the system is well maintained and more than meets the needs of its customers.

For example, even though 1988 was a drought year—breaking all previous records for the number of days when the temperature rose above 90 degrees in Northeast Ohio, with only sparse amounts of rainfall—the system met the demands of all customers with only minimal inconvenience to them. This was accomplished even while the Division Avenue plant was operating at one-half of capacity during reconstruction. This is a good indication of the degree of operational efficiency maintained by the Division of Water.

Greater Clevelanders can be proud of the level of performance attained by their waterworks system. They can also be confident that the Cleveland Division of Water will continue to meet their needs for water service in the future.

Maintenance employees throughout the Cleveland Division of Water system perform both preventive and predictive maintenance on equipment that seasonally supplies anywhere from 250 million to 475 million gallons of water per day to 1.5 million greater Clevelanders. The maintenance employees work on pumps, motors, chemical feeders, chlorine equipment, heating systems, piping systems, electrical systems, and small and large valves up to 72 inches in diameter. Photo by Ron Hare Photography

WUAB-TV, CHANNEL 43

ABOVE: The studios and offices of WUAB-TV, Channel 43, located at 8443 Day Drive in Parma.

On Sunday, September 15, 1968, at 5:20 p.m., a group of broadcasting executives watched with pride as WUAB-TV, Channel 43, signed on the air. This moment was the culmination of many months of planning and hard work to create Cleveland's sixth television station.

Although broadcasting had begun, construction of WUAB's studio and office building was not finished, so for its first few months of operation, the WUAB staff worked under trying circumstances—in five different places. Transmission was housed in the transmitter building, production in a bowling alley next door to the main building, and the studio in a trailer parked beside the bowling alley. The program, art, and film departments were set up in an office in a nearby shopping center. The administration offices were 17 miles away in a downtown Cleveland office building. None of this could be detected by viewers, and WUAB immediately saw its audience grow.

The station's original appeal has continued throughout the years, and WUAB is considered an industry leader and ranked as one of the top UHF independent television stations in the country.

A combination of sports, movies, and off-network programs built WUAB into a successful programming alternative. It is still the foundation for the station's programming strategy today. The station's promotional slogan in 1968, "Channel 43 Plays Favorites," is still very applicable in 1989.

Although it is located in Parma, a Cleveland suburb, and serves all of Northeast Ohio, the station is licensed to the City of Lorain. That city is the focus of weekly public affairs programs "Uniquely Lorain" and "Lorain Conversation," which was hosted for nearly 20 years by Alice Weston. The first woman to host a television show in Cleveland,

BELOW: Channel 43's Ten O'Clock News debuted in January 1988. Providing the Cleveland area with its only full-hour newscast at 10 p.m., "The Right News At The Right Time" has proven to be very successful.

Weston was inducted into the Ohio Senior Citizens Hall of Fame in October 1987. Linn Sheldon's "Barnaby" character has entertained youngsters in the Cleveland area for more than 40 years, including 15-plus years at WUAB. And Marty Sullivan's "Superhost" has kept people of all ages chuckling at his Saturday-afternoon antics.

The station was originally owned by the Transamerica Corporation and flew the flag of the United Artists Broadcasting, but became part of the Gaylord Broadcasting Company family in August 1977. This change helped WUAB grow in size, prestige, and dominance, because Gaylord provided funds for new projects.

WUAB took a successful step forward in January 1988 with the introduction of "The Ten O'Clock News." Having already accomplished goals to improve the station's signal strength to 5 million watts, convert to stereo audio, and convince the Arbitron rating service to install meters in the Cleveland market, former general manager Michael E. Schuch set upon his fourth and boldest project.

Facilities such as this state-of-the-art production control room give Channel 43 its polished look.

Planning for "The Ten O'Clock News" began in June 1987, when the station committed more than $2 million in capital expenditures, including a live remote truck and state-of-the-art electronic newsroom. In addition, a news department of 24 full-time people was assembled. The hour-long newscast has been successful in attracting viewers and advertisers.

Sports has always been a part of Channel 43's programming lineup. The station has become synonymous with Indians baseball, and 1989 will mark the 10th year the Tribe's games can be seen on Channel 43.

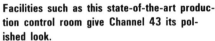

The future of WUAB-TV, Channel 43, looks bright. The television business is changing, as independent TV stations and cable give the viewing public more choices.

WUAB will continue to develop innovative programming. The station has been the television home of Cleveland Indians baseball since 1980. WUAB now airs many first-run programs, premier movies, and live prime-time specials to augment its popular lineup of off-network programs, including "The Cosby Show," "M*A*S*H," "Night Court," "Cheers," "Who's The Boss," and "Growing Pains."

WUAB is extremely proud of its pleasant working atmosphere. The enthusiastic and dedicated team of broadcast professionals has been instrumental to the success enjoyed by the station.

Says vice-president and general manager Bill Scaffide, "This is an exciting time for independents, because independents control their own destiny." At WUAB, "destiny" means continued success and growth in Cleveland market.

CHAPTER 11

Manufacturing

Producing goods for individuals and industry, manufacturing firms provide employment for many Cleveland area residents.

Photo by Roger Mastroianni

LTV STEEL COMPANY

The city of Cleveland and the Terminal Tower serve as a backdrop for LTV Steel's No. 5 blast furnace, shown here at dusk. Located just two miles from Public Square, LTV Steel's Cleveland Works employs more than 6,500 residents of Cleveland and its surrounding communities.

LTV Steel Company is one of America's largest steelmakers, with annual sales of nearly $4 billion, shipments approaching 9 million tons, and approximately 18,000 employees. The company was created in 1984 when the steelmaking operations of Republic Steel Corporation were joined with those of Jones & Laughlin Steel, a wholly owned subsidiary of The LTV Corporation, following the merger of LTV and Republic.

Jones & Laughlin's story began in 1853, when Benjamin Franklin Jones purchased an interest in a small Pittsburgh ironworks owned by B. Lauth & Brother. The new organization was called Jones, Lauth & Company. James Laughlin bought out Lauth's interest in the firm in 1862, but 40 years passed before the company incorporated as Jones & Laughlin Steel Company.

Jones & Laughlin began its association with LTV in 1968, when The LTV Corporation purchased controlling interest in J&L. The steelmaker became a wholly owned LTV subsidiary six years later. After acquiring Youngstown Sheet and Tube Company through a merger of LTV and Lykes Corporation in 1978, J&L was the nation's third-largest steel company.

Republic Steel Corporation dates back to 1899. Its principal forerunner, Republic Iron and Steel Company, was organized by an amalgamation of 35 small companies. It expanded through acquisitions in the late 1920s and changed its name to Republic Steel Corporation in 1930. Republic's general offices were established in Cleveland in 1936. The company grew steadily during the next 40 years, and in 1984 ranked as the fourth-largest integrated steel manufacturer in the United States.

Cleveland is LTV Steel's corporate headquarters and home of the company's Cleveland Works. On the banks of the Cuyahoga River, the Cleveland Works is one of LTV Steel's most modern flat-rolled steelmaking facilities. There the firm produces steel for the automotive, appliance, manufacturing, energy, building, and electrical equipment industries.

The Cleveland Works is the largest flat-rolled steel production complex in North America, with both basic oxygen- and electric-furnace steelmaking capacities. This fully integrated facility is a high-volume steel supplier with extensive experience in meeting critical product requirements. Its modern continuous-slab caster significantly increases the quality of its engineered steels, primarily ultra-low-carbon, high-strength, and electrogalvanized sheet.

LTV Steel at Cleveland, and at its other facilities located in Ohio, Indiana, and Illinois, produces more continuously cast flat-rolled steels than any other domestic steelmaker and has the industry's greatest capacity in modern hot mills, cold-rolling mills, and coating lines.

In order to meet its objective of 100-percent customer satisfaction, LTV Steel has implemented a system of scientific process management throughout the company called Integrated Process Control (IPC). Incorporating modern management tools such as statistical process control, participative management, and analytical troubleshooting, Integrated Process Control is an LTV Steel concept designed to produce consistently high

LTV Steel's Cleveland Works is the largest flat-rolled steel production complex in the United States. Here a coil of high-quality engineered flat-rolled steel is readied for shipment.

quality in all aspects of the firm's operations—from raw materials to customer service.

The IPC system of total process management has a clearly defined objective: "To bring world-class quality at competitive cost to every product line within LTV Steel, and to do it in such a way that improvement is a never-ending discipline."

The key target is that of reducing variability by utilizing a methodology that breaks down seemingly difficult and complex processes into small, simple parts that can be routinely managed. Implementation of this total process management philosophy has enabled LTV Steel to become the only domestic integrated steel manufacturer to offer an across-the-board steel Quality Guarantee on its full line of prime flat-rolled products.

LTV Steel's continued investment in modern steelmaking facilities in Cleveland and at its other producing locations, and its commitment to quality through Integrated Process Control, have set the standard for excellence and customer satisfaction in the industry.

LTV Steel ultimately depends on its employees to give it the competitive edge needed in today's global economy. The firm knows that good employees come from communities that provide a satisfactory quality of life for all their citizens. LTV Steel supports employees' volunteer efforts and contributes through the nonprofit LTV Foundation to various community projects in which its employees are active. One such project is the adoption of Cleveland's South High School, where LTV employees volunteer in a program that prepares students to enter the work force. The Cleveland Toys for Tots program, in which LTV employees have participated for 20 years, makes more than 35,000 children a lot merrier every Christmas.

In addition, LTV Steel is a strong supporter of United Way. More than half of its employees participate in United Way, steadily increasing their support each year. LTV executives lend management skills to United Way campaigns in their communities, and the firm provides the United Way with "loaned executives," who oversee campaigns of other companies.

With investment in modern manufacturing facilities, excellent employees, an innovative process control system, and commitment to its community, LTV Steel Company is positioned to be an efficient integrated steel producer well into the future.

BELOW: LTV Steel sponsors numerous community activities, including the Cleveland public school system's Adopt-A-School program, through which LTV Steel has "adopted" South High. The students shown here have been recognized for their achievements in the areas of academia, citizenship, athletics, music, and class attendance at a recent year-end awards assembly.

ABOVE: The continuous-slab caster at LTV Steel's Cleveland Works produces steel destined for the automotive, appliance, manufacturing, energy, building, and electrical industries. The caster sets North American production records with regularity.

VAN DORN COMPANY

It started with the sale of a wrought-iron fence in 1872.

Today the Van Dorn Company, headquartered in Cleveland, is a recognized leader in the manufacture of containers and plastic injection-molding machinery. It is composed of several divisions and operates 14 plants.

One of the world's largest producers of drawn aluminum containers, Van Dorn's container divisions are also major manufacturers of metal, plastic, and composite material containers for the paint, petroleum, chemical, automotive, food, pharmaceutical, and household products industries.

The plastic machinery division of Van Dorn produces injection-molding machinery with from 40 to 3,000 tons of clamp force to meet the needs of industries as diverse as the automotive, appliance, electronic, container, housewares, computer, medical, toy, communications, and construction industries. Through large investments in research, state-of-the-art manufacturing facilities, and quality-assurance programs, Van Dorn maintains a leadership position in machine and computer control technology and manufacturing techniques.

The company's management philosophy is one of decentralization. Each of Van Dorn's divisions is autonomous and has total responsibility for its own marketing and product development. The parent company provides centralized financial management and capital for growth. In this way each division can exploit its strengths and knowledge of the market to develop new products.

Anticipation of new and changing markets and an ongoing commitment to new product development supported by extensive research and development have put Van Dorn at the technological forefront with advancements as diverse as the first drawn aluminum can with easy-opening lid for processed foods and a high-speed, co-injection blow-molding machine to manufacture plastic bottles and wide-mouth jars.

The plastic machinery division of Van Dorn Company produces injection-molding machinery for a wide range of industries.

Although many businesses speak of innovation and meeting customer needs, the Van Dorn Company's 117-year history exemplifies how dedication to these tenets can make a small iron fence company into a major industrial corporation.

In the early 1870s James H. Van Dorn built a new home in Akron. The iron fence he designed and erected to surround his new property was much admired by his neighbors, who wanted to purchase one like it. In 1872 Van Dorn sold his first iron fence and shortly thereafter purchased the Spring Shoe Forge in Akron to increase the production capacity of his new business.

In 1878 Van Dorn moved his business to Cleveland, which was close to raw materials and larger markets. He named it the Cleveland Wrought Iron Fence Works. That same year Van Dorn was bidding on a job in Milwaukee when he heard that someone needed a jail. Deciding that jails were just "fences built indoors," he bid on the job and returned to Cleveland with two orders. Soon the Van Dorn Iron Works Company was the largest jail manufacturer in the world.

The company continued to ex-

Van Dorn maintains a leadership position in machine and computer control technology and manufacturing techniques.

pand its product line throughout the late 1800s and early 1900s. It made parts for streetcars, switchboards, and bicycles; fabricated steel cases and map drawers; steel frames for building construction; railroad equipment and mailboxes; container systems for freight hauling; truck parts; and metal office furniture.

Despite Van Dorn's production versatility, the Great Depression brought financial difficulties to the company. Then, in 1939, N.T. Jones, a successful executive in a fastener and welding business, was hired to direct the company. Following World War II Jones saw that Van Dorn needed to diversify and move away from its concentration in the heavy metalworking industry. In 1944 Jones identified containers and plastic injection-molding machinery as two fields that promised growth. Further, the combination of these fields provided a balanced mix of disposable consumer products and capital equipment in a new industry that, as Jones foresaw, was destined to grow.

The steady 45 years of growth and the positions of leadership the Van Dorn Company has achieved in these fields attest to the wisdom of N.T. Jones' decision and the philosophy of innovation and meeting customer needs with which the company has been run.

This growth has been accompanied by unswerving loyalty to the Cleveland area. In 1970 Van Dorn made a conscious decision to keep its headquarters and some manufacturing plants in the city. A major factor in this decision was the firm's desire to create jobs in the area around its main plant on East 79th Street. The area was depressed, and economic development was high on the community's list of priorities. Van Dorn also became active in the Woodland East Community Organization, which encourages companies to remain in or move into the East 79th and Woodland area. With Van Dorn's support, the neighborhood and the local economy have become stronger.

Another reason that the organization decided to remain there is that Cleveland has tremendous human resources. The Van Dorn Company is proud to be headquartered in Cleveland, which can count among its assets outstanding colleges and universities, a wealth of cultural institutions, and fine outdoor recreation facilities. "The best thing about Cleveland, however, is its people," says L.C. Jones, chairman and chief executive officer. "They're the city's greatest natural resource and have been so important in making Van Dorn what it is today."

LEFT and BELOW: One of the world's largest producers of drawn aluminum containers, Van Dorn also manufactures metal, plastic, and composite material containers.

WARNER & SWASEY COMPANY

Warner & Swasey designs and produces precision machine tools. For more than a century manufacturers have relied on Warner & Swasey for products that are durable, versatile, and productive. The firm is recognized as a world leader in machine tool technology because of its experience, innovation, and commitment to customers. These characteristics can be traced directly to the founders, Worcester Warner and Ambrose Swasey.

Warner and Swasey first met when they were apprentices in a machine shop in Exeter, New Hampshire. They worked and boarded together and became close friends. Both men were self-taught mechanical geniuses, quite willing to study subjects that interested them far into the night. Swasey was fascinated with architecture and learned enough about it to design Warner & Swasey buildings. He also influenced the design of many Cleveland buildings. Warner's early interest in astronomy led to his study of higher mathematics and telescopes, interests later reflected in the company's products.

When they finished their apprenticeships, the two men were hired by Pratt & Whitney. Warner soon attracted attention by greatly reducing the time required to manufacture a piece of machinery. And Swasey distinguished himself by inventing two new machines for cutting accurate gear teeth.

In 1880 the two friends moved to Chicago, taking four highly skilled co-workers with them, and founded Warner & Swasey, precision machine tool manufacturers. The company moved to Cleveland the following year and began to expand rapidly. Many of Warner & Swasey's early machines were custom developed to meet individual customer requirements. But after Warner & Swasey incorporated in 1900, it began to specialize, concentrating on the production of turret lathes and the design and production of precision telescopes.

One hundred years after its founding, Warner & Swasey went through several rapid ownership changes. In 1980 it was purchased by the Bendix Corporation; three years later Bendix was purchased by Allied Corporation. Finally, in 1984, Cross & Trecker purchased Bendix Automation, including Warner & Swasey, from Allied.

Although the Cross & Trecker companies operate as separate business units, they share resources and technology, creating a corporate capability that far exceeds the sum of its parts. Together they produce a broad array of technologically sophisticated and highly productive machine tools, systems, controls, metrology equipment, presses, and automated material-handling equipment.

Warner & Swasey manufactures horizontal and vertical CNC turning centers in Ohio, England, Japan, and India. The international locations of Warner & Swasey production facilities illustrate the global nature of today's machine tool business.

During the past 15 years Warner & Swasey suffered from international competition, as did the entire machine tool industry in the United States. Emulating its founders, Warner & Swasey responded by launching an aggressive research and development program. A reflection of the importance of the research and development program to the company's future is the fact that 82 percent of all products shipped by

An earlier product model in the foreground provides a setting for a Warner & Swasey executive discussion.

The turning division manufacturing floor where quality products are assembled for satisfied customers.

Consultation and coordination work to benefit the customer.

Warner & Swasey in 1988 did not exist in 1987.

A multimillion-dollar research and development effort produced the Titan series of CNC turning centers, first introduced in late 1986. The Titan offers exactly what the industry is demanding—flexibility, automation, and reliable operation. There are more than 50 variations on the basic model, including slant bed, vertical, and horizontal machines in two- and four-axis configurations. Customers such as Caterpillar, Mack Truck, and Nordson will use the new Titan series to increase their manufacturing productivity.

Contributing to Warner & Swasey's success are traditions from its early history: good people, a concern for the needs of the customer, and a desire to do the job right the first time. Warner & Swasey hires the finest engineers, system integrators, innovators, craftspeople, and marketing experts. The company asks customers what they need and supports research to develop the products they demand. Warner & Swasey also offers an extensive customer support program, including training, preventive maintenance, complete on-site service, and a large inventory of parts.

Warner & Swasey is optimistic about the future. The company is competing successfully worldwide and developing partnerships with international firms. Its connection with Cross & Trecker enables it to satisfy the full range of customer needs from machine tools to peripheral products. With its broad base of large and small customers in the automotive, aerospace, agricultural, and appliance industries, as well as in government, Warner & Swasey Company expects to continue to be an important corporate citizen in Cleveland and around the world.

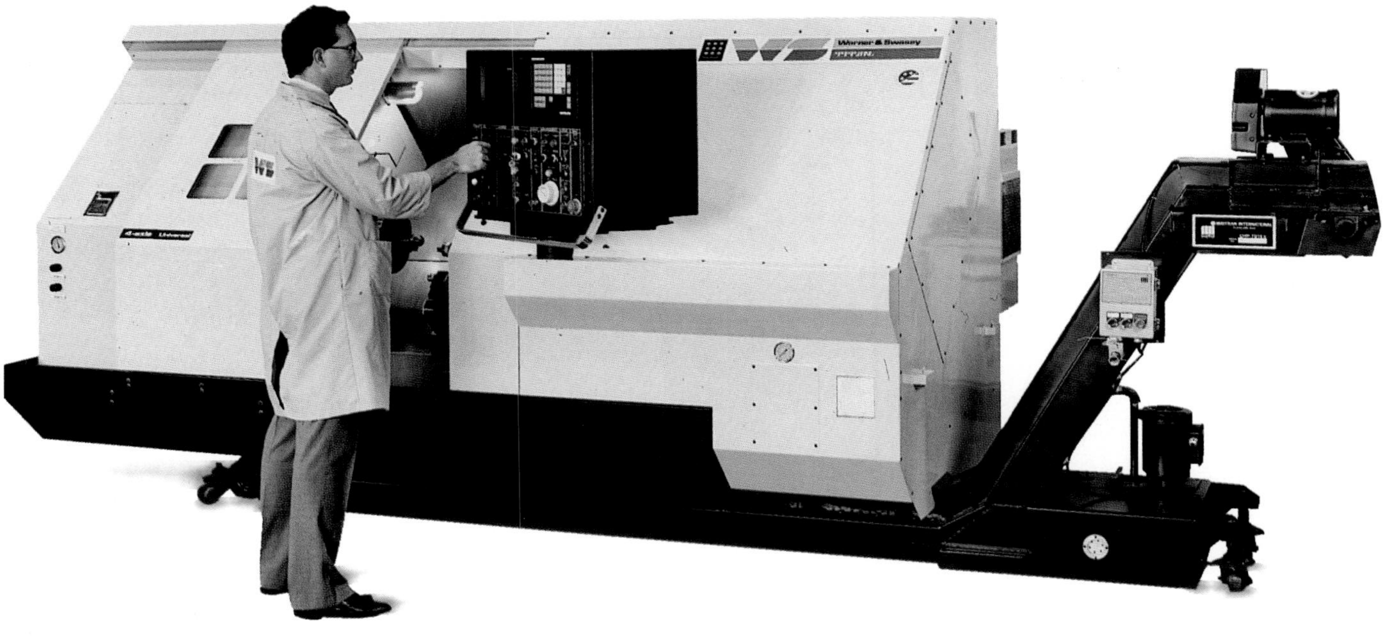

The latest in turning technology.

BP AMERICA

The prominence of BP America's headquarters on Cleveland's skyline is fitting, considering the role played here by the company and its predecessor, John D. Rockefeller's original Standard Oil Company.

With more than 4,000 employees in the Cleveland area, BP America has long been a contributing force in the city—economically and through support of nonprofit organizations.

The company is best known locally and throughout Ohio for its Sohio® service stations (which are being changed to the BP® brand). But it is much more than an Ohio gasoline marketer.

It is the largest producer of crude oil in the United States and refines and markets gasoline and other petroleum products through almost 8,000 service stations in 26 states.

It produces chemicals and manufactures composite materials and advanced ceramics used in automobiles, electronics, defense, and aerospace. Its Purina Mills Company is the largest domestic producer of branded animal feeds.

With 40,000 employees and assets of more than $20 billion, BP America is one of the largest industrial companies in the United States. It represents almost one-half the assets of its parent, London-based British Petroleum Company p.l.c. (BP), which operates in more than 70 countries and is the third-largest oil company in the world.

The BP America of today was formed in 1987 after BP, which already owned 55 percent of Standard Oil's stock, acquired the outstanding shares. BP then merged its U.S. operations with Standard Oil's.

John D. Rockefeller, 1839-1937. Courtesy, Western Reserve Historical Society

BP America headquarters.

But the histories of Standard Oil and BP started with two men who represent the drive and spirit that contributed to the world's rapid industrial growth in the late nineteenth and early twentieth centuries.

One of the more notable industrial leaders of that era was Rockefeller, who joined with partners to build his first refinery in Cleveland's industrial Flats section in 1863. He founded Standard Oil in 1870 and three years later moved the fledgling company into an office that stood on the site of BP America's present headquarters.

Standard Oil thrived under Rockefeller's direction. By 1882 the company was one of a group of affiliates. Operations were organized under a New York-based trust that dominated the petroleum business in the United States. Under legal attack, the trust was replaced by a holding company in 1889. But that did not prevent its ultimate dissolution.

In 1911 the Supreme Court divided the Standard Oil combination into 34 independent companies. The original Ohio-based Standard Oil was left with a refinery and a few tankwagons. But the firm grew rapidly.

As part of a change to a unified brand name at BP America stations in 26 states, Sohio® outlets—long familiar in Cleveland and throughout Ohio—are being replaced by green, BP®-branded stations.

By 1924 it operated more than 400 Sohio service stations in Ohio. Over the next two decades it captured a third of the Ohio gasoline market. Then the company—which itself had come to be called Sohio—began to diversify.

A discovery by company scientists of an improved method to make acrylonitrile—a key ingredient in artificial fibers and plastics—launched Sohio into the chemicals business in 1954. By the early 1970s the company was a regional refiner and marketer with interests in coal, chemicals, and plastics. And it was poised to embark on a multimillion-dollar venture that would begin its affiliation with BP and transform it into one of the nation's largest energy firms.

BP's history, too, started with a visionary: William Knox D'Arcy, a British attorney who had made a fortune from gold mining in Australia. In 1901 D'Arcy sought a concession from the Shah of Persia to explore for oil in that country (now Iran). In 1908, on the verge of pulling out his exploration team after years of fruitless searching, D'Arcy saw his luck changed when one of his wells "came in a gusher." The Anglo-Persian Oil Company was incorporated the following year.

Its fortunes were changed in 1914 by Winston Churchill, who, as Great Britain's First Lord of the Admiralty, sought a secure source of oil for the Royal Navy. At Churchill's urging, the British government paid $2 million for a 51-percent interest in the company.

With its finances assured, Anglo-Persian began the international expansion that would eventually bring more than 70 nations into its fold. It opened new oil fields in the Middle East, Africa, and Europe and markets in five continents. In 1954 it renamed itself The British Petroleum Company (BP). It later diversified into chemicals and other businesses and established operations in the United States.

In 1969 BP confirmed a major oil strike in Alaska's Prudhoe Bay. Further studies of the Prudhoe field revealed the firm held under its leases more than 4 billion barrels of recoverable reserves—half the field's total expected output.

BP decided its U.S. interests, including the Prudhoe Bay reserves, could be best managed through an established U.S. oil refining and marketing company. Standard Oil was widely known as among the best. It was a perfect match. BP wanted an American-managed, domestic refining and marketing business and crude-short Standard Oil wanted its own source of oil.

On January 1, 1970, in exchange for portions of its stock, Standard Oil acquired from BP rights to about half the 10 billion barrels of oil at Prudhoe Bay in Alaska. Standard Oil also acquired other properties, including service stations on the East Coast.

Then came seven years of enormous investment as the Prudhoe Bay field was developed and the 800-mile Trans-Alaska Pipeline was constructed. Standard Oil put together a fleet of chartered tankers to carry oil to markets in the Lower 48 states. The 1977 start-up of the Prudhoe field and the pipeline signaled for Standard Oil a new period of expansion financed by earnings from the huge investments in developing and delivering Alaskan oil.

Scientists at BP America's research center in Cleveland's Warrensville suburb conduct research in areas such as advanced oil recovery techniques and environmental protection systems. Here a researcher uses a CAT scanner, which produces extremely refined X-ray images, to analyze a core of rock taken from an oil well.

BP prospered, too—and searched for ways to invest profits from Alaska and the North Sea, the company's other main oil-producing areas. BP acted to take advantage of one of the best opportunities in 1987 by offering to buy Standard Oil's remaining publicly held shares. The offer went through, and BP America was created.

Today the company operates under the following groups:

—BP Exploration explores for and produces oil and natural gas onshore and offshore in Alaska, western states, and the Gulf of Mexico. It owns 51 percent of the Prudhoe Bay field and major interests in other Alaska fields, including Endicott, the first offshore oil field in the Arctic. It also owns 50 percent of the Trans-Alaska Pipeline. Its BP Gas unit gathers and markets natural gas to distributors and small industries.

—BP Oil refines crude oil and markets petroleum products via a wholesale and retail marketing network concentrated in 23 states east of the Mississippi and in Oregon, Washington, and Northern California. It operates five refineries, two of them in Ohio (Toledo and Lima). Its retail network includes full-service, ProCare® auto centers in Ohio and Pennsylvania and more than 40 truckstops. The company also provides jet fuel at more than 40 airports and marine fuel at major U.S. seaports.

—BP Chemicals produces or licenses the production of more than 90 percent of the world's acrylonitrile, a key ingredient in plastics and artificial fibers. It is a major domestic producer-marketer of acetic acid (latex paint, solvents, and fibers) and produces and/or markets other plastics and chemicals for agriculture, packaging, pharmaceuticals, and other uses. Units under BP Chemicals manufacture a diverse array of products, from polymer coatings for electrical wire and cable (BP Performance Polymers Inc.) to composite materials for defense and aerospace (HITCO) and advanced ceramics for automotives, aerospace, and electronics (the Carborundum Company).

—BP Nutrition's Purina Mills, the leading U.S. supplier of branded animals feeds, markets feed and health products for livestock, poultry, and pets. Other units breed and market poultry (Pilch, Inc.), and salmon (Anadromous, Inc.), and produce seed corn (E.J. Funk and Sons, Inc.).

The company has mined and marketed coal for many years, as well. But in 1989 it announced that it was selling its coal properties, which operated under BP Coal, in Illinois, West Virginia, and Indiana.

In the Cleveland area, in addition to its headquarters, BP America has a BP Oil terminal and operations center on East 49 Street and, in the Flats, a laboratory dedicated mainly to fuels and lubricants research. At a major research center in Warrensville Heights, company scientists conduct research in areas such as advanced oil recovery techniques, environmental protection, and new product development. A regional petroleum products marketing center is located in Independence.

Fulfilling its responsibilities as a corporate citizen, the company reinvests in Cleveland in several ways.

An Alaska drilling rig. BP America, the largest producer of domestic crude oil, gets most of its oil from Prudhoe Bay and other oil fields on Alaska's North Slope.

As part of its national corporate contributions program, it contributes millions of dollars annually to Cleveland-area nonprofit organizations and programs. These include groups that strengthen public education, bolster neighborhood businesses, and rebuild deteriorated urban housing. Hospitals, homes for the aged, youth groups, and other social service organizations receive support directly or indirectly through company and employee donations to the United Way. Other grants underwrite art and dance education, community theater, galleries, and cultural treasures such as the Cleveland Symphony and Cleveland Ballet.

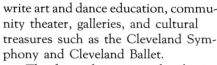

The firm often joins other businesses, foundations, civic leaders, and neighborhood organizations to develop programs that tackle pressing social problems—how to improve urban education, for example. It supplements its grants by directly investing in urban-renewal projects. Employees contribute, too, through memberships on nonprofit boards and through volunteer work.

BP America also helps enliven the Cleveland area by sponsoring and helping to direct events such as free art shows and concerts. A major example is RiverFest. Sponsored by BP America and its BP Oil unit, the festival draws hundreds of thousands of Clevelanders to the Flats to enjoy food, music, and boating events on the Cuyahoga River.

ABOVE: Other BP America facilities in Ohio include BP Chemicals' plant in Lima.

BELOW: BP America community support includes serving as the major sponsor for Cleveland's annual summer RiverFest in the Flats. The company underwrites many nonprofit organizations in Cleveland in education, housing renewal, health and human services, and the arts.

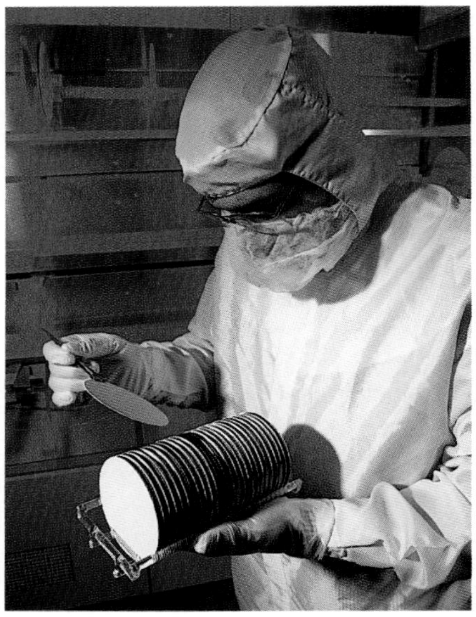

A technician of The Carborundum Company examines a ceramic disk produced for makers of computer microchips. Carborundum, based in Niagara Falls, New York, makes products including advanced ceramics for electronics and automotives. In addition to crude oil and natural gas, petroleum products, and chemicals, other BP America companies produce animal feeds, wire and cable coatings, and composite materials for aerospace and defense.

ALCAN ALUMINUM

Cleveland's Galleria and Tower at Erieview is home to Alcan's U.S. headquarters.

Cleveland has been the U.S. headquarters city for Alcan, the leading international aluminum company, since 1965. As the firm began to build and acquire fabricating operations in the United States in the 1960s, Cleveland was chosen as the administrative center because of its central location in America's industrial heartland and its convenience to the world headquarters of the parent, Alcan Aluminium Limited, in Montreal. Alcan executives charged with selecting a U.S. headquarters were also impressed with the quality of life and cultural assets offered by the Cleveland metropolitan area.

Internationally, Alcan has 45 major subsidiaries and related companies in 19 countries and more than 56,000 employees engaged in all phases of the aluminum industry, including bauxite mining, alumina refining, aluminum smelting, recycling, and the fabrication and sale of semifinished and finished products.

With more than 200 Alcan employees in downtown and suburban locations, Cleveland is home to headquarters offices for six Alcan units:

Alcan Aluminum Corporation, the principal U.S. subsidiary and an Ohio-chartered corporation, provides administrative services—legal, personnel benefits, financial, and auditing—for Alcan's organization in the United States and is responsible, through a business development office in Cambridge, Massachusetts, for the origination, acquisition, and growth of new business ventures in aluminum-related fields.

Alcan Rolled Products Company is the largest fabricating unit of the Alcan Group in North America. With eight plants strategically located to serve major domestic as well as export markets, it is one of the industry's leading producers of aluminum sheet, plate, and foil products for beverage and food cans; semirigid containers, household foil, and commercial packaging; building and construction; heat exchangers; automotive and transportation applications; industrial distribution; and many other consumer and industrial products. Multimillion-dollar investments in recent years have made Alcan's sheet rolling facilities among the industry's most sophisticated and technologically advanced.

Alcan Ingot & Recycling, the company's aluminum producing and ingot marketing organization for the United States, has a primary smelter in Kentucky and two plants for recycling in Kentucky and Georgia. For many years Alcan Ingot & Recycling has been the largest supplier of primary aluminum ingot to independent fabricators, particularly extruders, in the United States. Major markets include the building and construction and transportation industries. As an important recycler of used beverage containers, Alcan's recycling plants produce sheet ingot that is rolled again into quality aluminum sheet for beverage containers.

Alcan Chemicals is the division re-

For many years Alcan has been the leading supplier of aluminum ingot to independent fabricators, particularly extruders, in the United States.

sponsible for the production, marketing, and sales of alumina and other aluminum-related chemicals used in the manufacture of ceramic products such as spark plugs, refractory bricks, computer substrates, dinnerware, and catalytic converters for automobiles. It also markets products used in the production of water-treatment chemicals, antiperspirants, glass, plastics, and flame retardants.

Alcan Aerospace is the sales organization for Alcan products directed to the aerospace and defense markets: sheet, plate, extrusions, and advanced structural materials developed by Alcan such as Lital® aluminum-lithium alloys. Customers include builders of commercial and military airframes and armored military vehicles, space vehicle contractors, and subcontractors to those groups.

Alcan Extrusions USA is the newest Alcan division, created following the acquisition in early 1989 of Jarl Extrusions, a leading producer of aluminum extrusions with plants in New Hampshire and Tennessee. The division produces and markets extrusions to original equipment manufacturers who use them for end uses such as sailboat masts, light poles, highway and bridge guard rails, and architectural/building products.

In addition, Metal Goods, Alcan's nationwide chain of metal service centers, has one of its 24 locations in the greater Cleveland area. It specializes in the distribution of corrosion-resistant metals, including aluminum, stainless steel, nickel alloys, titanium, brass, and copper, in a variety of forms.

Alcan Building Products, a major manufacturing and marketing organization for residential and commercial building products, has its headquarters in nearby Warren, Ohio.

In Cleveland, Alcan participates in maintaining the special quality of life and cultural assets of the area by actively supporting a variety of social, civic, educational, and arts organizations such as United Way, public television station WVIZ, and Junior Achievement. It has also served as an original sponsor of Cans For Kids, a program to recycle aluminum cans for the benefit of Cleveland Children's Services and the aid it provides abused and abandoned children.

Alcan companies and operations in other U.S. locations are leaders in the production and marketing of household and packaging foil products, metal powders and pigments, electrical wire and cable, and pipe for irrigation.

Internationally, Alcan is a leader in developing new technology and applications for aluminum and aluminum-related products. Important examples include Alcan's Aluminum-Structured Vehicle technology, which allows the production of adhesively bonded aluminum automobile bodies on conventional production lines; Anotec™ separation devices capable of filtering particles as small as a virus from human blood; high-performance automotive engine components; and advanced materials such as structural ceramics and Duralcan™ silicon carbide reinforced aluminum.

Aluminas and other aluminum-based chemicals from Alcan are used in products ranging from spark plugs and dinnerware to computer substrates and flame retardants.

The rolling mills of Alcan Rolled Products, a major producer of aluminum sheet for a variety of markets, are among the most technologically sophisticated in the industry.

BEARINGS, INC.

From left: president and chief executive officer George LaMore and chairman John R. Cunin.

American in ingenuity, American in integrity—Bearings, Inc., has become the nation's largest bearings distributor because it remains dedicated to its credo: "Integrity in distribution." Bearings, Inc., plans to stay the leader in the industry just as it plans to stay in Cleveland.

Such deep-felt commitment and tenacious application of ethical business practices is fostered throughout the 3,137-employee firm, from the top down. Sustained growth has become an annual occurrence for Bearings, Inc., mostly because of the leadership of John R. Cunin, chairman of the board, who started as a shipping clerk in 1948, and George L. LaMore, president and chief executive officer, who boasts of 48 years with Bearings, Inc. As LaMore explains, "We're very proud of our company and our heritage, so we are especially concerned with where we are going and how we get there."

Perhaps these men and their employees remain close to such lofty business ideals and practice them sincerely because of the company's roots in a truly American success story. Founder Joseph M. Bruening set the pace when he opened the tiny storefront operation of the Ohio Ball Bearing Co. on a downtown Cleveland street in January 1923. He remained sole chairman until he retired in 1983.

The story goes that the fledgling entrepreneur had moved to Cleveland from Cincinnati to get married. Living in the YMCA before the wedding, on the evening of his first day of business, he went to take a shower, and when he returned to his room, someone had purloined his wallet and clothes. He literally started the company without the shirt on his back. He went on to borrow $5,000 and started selling replacement parts for cars and trucks. As the firm evolved into a profitable distribution business, Bruening never found the need to manufacture a single bearing.

From Bruening's early expansion into Youngstown, Cincinnati, and Akron, Bearings, Inc., now maintains 267 branches throughout the United States and Puerto Rico, with eight regional, four special distribution centers, and two service centers. From a first-year sales total of $80,000, the company has become a more than $640-million-per-year international operation, with more than 100 major suppliers, some 450,000 stockkeeping units, and approximately 160,000 customers throughout the United States alone. Customers represent every industry, and none of them contributes more than 2 percent of Bearings' business.

No matter how large the inventory, the customer list, or the revenue figures grow, Bearings, Inc., remains first and foremost a customer-service-oriented firm. The company prides itself on employing salespeople who know the manufacturers, the inventory, and their customers' needs. Believing extra service saves customers' money and encourages return business, Bearings' employees recently recorded, in one year, 25,000 after-hours emergency calls for customers. Each of the 267 branches has a customized inventory so that each customer can quickly receive the exact part needed. The firm has also discovered that making this extra-special brand of quality service "typical" generates a certain enthusiasm among employees as well.

Bearings, Inc., distributes antifriction ball bearings, power transmission, and equipment-maintenance products to all types of industries, including primary metals (rolling mills for steel and aluminum); pulp, paper, and wood; food (farm and processors); petrochemicals; mining; and aircraft. To fully stock its diverse product line, the company relies upon and supports several key local and regional suppliers, including

SKF USA, Goodyear, Torrington Fafnir (power transmissions), Reliance Dodge, Rexnord, Emerson Power Transmission, Chicago Rawhide (seal manufacturers), and, its oldest single supplier with whom it has grown as businesses, Timken Co. in Canton.

In fact, the company has established a strong reputation for promoting American manufacturers and products as much as possible. Bearings, Inc., works closely with various organizations such as the Bearings Specialist Association and the Anti-Friction Bearing Manufacturers Association to bolster domestic competition and free enterprise. Says George LaMore, "Our business depends on viable working operations in the United States. We can't sell to closed plants."

The corporate headquarters of Bearings, Inc., at 3600 Euclid Avenue.

That commitment to America starts right at home, in the backyard of the Bearings, Inc., world headquarters. At John Cunin's instigation, the firm was one of the first members of the MidTown Corridor, an organization formed to revitalize an entire section of Cleveland's commercial and industrial area that had become somewhat dilapidated in the post-industrial period experienced by many major cities. That commitment continues still further into the local community via the involvement of the corporate officers and many of the employees in such organizations as the American Heart Association, the American Cancer Society, United Cerebral Palsy Association, Boy and Girl Scouts of America, Cleanland, Achievement Center for Children, Cleveland Tomorrow, and the Playhouse Square Foundation.

Bearings, Inc.'s, efforts to promote quality service, interests in American business, and extensive participation in community development have not gone unnoticed. T.E. Bennet, president of the Torrington Company, a division of Ingersol Rand, captured the importance of the firm's influential position when he said: "Five or 10 years from now, as the next generation of managers look back on these days, they will recognize that Bearings, Inc., management was way ahead of the times."

SUNARHAUSERMAN

SunarHauserman designs and manufactures furniture, systems, storage, seating, and textiles for the office environment. Interior designers use SunarHauserman products to design office environments, such as reception areas, conference rooms, management and executive offices, and administrative and professional/technical areas.

The firm's history began in 1913, when E.F. Hauserman was a salesman for a steel window sash company. Steel window sash was new and wasn't installed like wooden sash, so it was not readily accepted by contractors. Hauserman thought the window would sell better if the company took responsibility for installation. His employer disagreed, so Hauserman started his own business, E.F. Hauserman, Inc., to install the windows. This way, he could do the job the way customers needed it to be done. This gave birth to SunarHauserman's most important business principle: The company is responsible for customer satisfaction.

Hauserman also believed that there was no substitute for doing work right and on time. These philosophies contributed to the firm's rapid growth. Soon Hauserman had installation contracts for most companies east of the Mississippi using the steel sash.

Customers began to request that Hauserman install new metal window sash inside buildings in interior factory walls. As the demand for interior installations increased, the company was often called upon to reinstall windows during factory renovation after windows were removed, their support walls torn down, and new walls built somewhere else. Hauserman decided there was a market for movable walls that assembled and disassembled easily as factory owners' needs changed. In 1917 his company began to design and manufacture the world's first movable steel wall. In doing so, Hauserman contributed more than a new product to commercial interior design; he created a new interior construction method and along with it a new industry.

By 1923 the firm was manufacturing the first movable wall designed for the administrative office, rather than the factory environment. Hauserman walls were installed in the most celebrated buildings of the day: the Empire State Building, the Chrysler Building, and Rockefeller Center.

RIGHT: E.F. Hauserman, founder.

BELOW: SunarHauserman designed the world's first movable steel wall and created a new industry. Photo circa 1920

The company's wall products evolved to include interior lining, soundproofing, and walls that were compatible with suspended ceilings and recessed lighting. As offices became more attractive, Hauserman's company was changing from one primarily focused on construction techniques to one in which design was becoming more important.

E.F. Hauserman and the movable wall business expanded nationwide. During the next several decades the business continued to create improvements with its movable walls to meet the changing needs of building construction and office design.

The company had grown into international markets by the 1950s, acquiring customers in Canada and Europe. In the next decade Hauserman introduced Signature and Delineator walls, the first mass-produced, design-oriented, movable wall systems. DoubleWall was another new product designed to compete with plaster wall construction, concealing duct work, wiring, plumbing, and cables, but making them easily accessible by the use of removable panels.

In the 1970s Hauserman, Inc., a holding company, was formed, and E.F. Hauserman became a principal operating division. E.F. Hauserman continued its construction industry orientation and introduced the Design Option Panel system, becoming the first manufacturer of both full-height movable walls and open-plan panel systems. It provided office designers with single-source, flexible solutions to increase office productivity.

As the company grew to recognize that an important element of building design was helping people work better, it decided to add a line of office furniture to complement its wall products. There it met an entirely different industry culture—one that emphasized design and the use of space. It also discovered a different buying system that depended on a dealer network rather than direct sales to customers.

The company decided it needed to acquire expertise in the office furniture industry. In 1978 it purchased the Sunar Company, a Canadian firm with a reputation for world-class design and manufacture of high-quality steel and wooden office furniture. Three stunning showrooms, designed by architect Michael Graves, were opened by the end of the decade to display new Sunar furniture products. Four more showrooms soon followed. Hauserman also opened two designer showrooms to display its wall products: one by Japanese architect Arata Isozaki in Chicago and another by Massimo Vignelli and neon artist Dan Flavin in Los Angeles. The concept that offices could be not only functional but also works of art began to catch on.

E.F. Hauserman and Sunar Company were merged in 1983 to form SunarHauserman. The mission state-

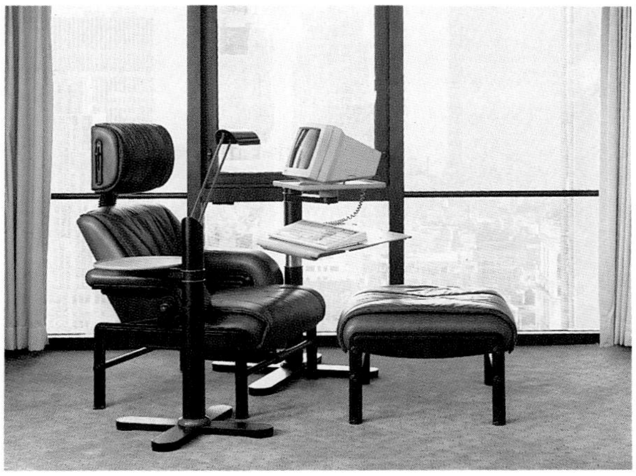

LEFT: What every computer operator dreams of—a comfortable workstation. Shown is the Jefferson chair and ottoman designed by Niels Diffrient.

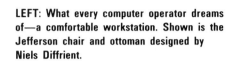

BELOW: The Acorn™ chair (in front of desk) and the Rotonda™ chairs (against the wall) were designed by Lella and Massimo Vignella; the Helena™ desk chair's designer is Niels Diffrient; and the designer of the Cameron furniture (desk, workwall, and storage cabinet) is Douglas Ball. Photo by Elliott Kaufman, NYC

The Race® system designed by Douglas Ball.

ment of the new corporation says, "The company will be the leader in providing innovative products of design excellence and outstanding quality that help people work productively in pleasing and integrated office environments." E.F. Hauserman's conviction that the firm should take responsibility for customer satisfaction had expanded to include not only the purchaser of its products but also the user.

Writing the mission statement was the easy part of joining the two firms into SunarHauserman. When the two companies merged, they had four different computerized inventory and ordering systems. Product distribution networks and sales techniques were different; there was too much production capacity for the more limited product lines; and many of the manufacturing plants were not equipped to make the new SunarHauserman product line.

A massive restructuring process began in 1983 that was not completed until the end of the decade. Many products that did not represent the mission statement were eliminated, a furniture-dealer distribution system was developed, and plant capacity was significantly reduced to fit the needs of the remaining product offering. In the process three business units, including product and plant, were sold. The wall business and the Cleveland plant continue to operate, concentrating on the construction wall market.

Finally, due for introduction in the early 1990s is a new furniture system to complement the company's existing furniture system and provide a response to the furniture customer's needs for a movable wall that is part of this system.

Today the SunarHauserman product line beautifully enhances office productivity from highly automated general offices to the executive suite—and it does so in a variety of ways.

Race®, designed by Douglas Ball, is a beam-based system that plans horizontally and provides superior wire management with wood and laminate workstation components.

Cameron, a wood system that is visually compatible with Race®, is a freestanding solution to the task requirements of today's offices.

Supporting these systems are four chair lines that reflect the company's commitment to good design that functions well, two filing and storage systems, and a collection of lounge seating, tables, textiles, and executive furniture created by a number of prominent architects and designers.

SunarHauserman is now focused on products for the office environment that offer quality construction, flexibility, and excellent design. The company stresses customer service, including shorter manufacturing lead times and ease of ordering. The firm strives for leadership in its market niche, where outstanding quality and innovative design set this company apart from competition.

A Uniwall™ filing system.

SunarHauserman has grown and evolved its product line since 1917, but its emphasis on innovation to satisfy customers needs has never changed.

CLEVELAND-CLIFFS INC

Cleveland-Cliffs Inc traces its roots to 1845, when enterprising businessmen opened iron ore mines in Michigan. The new mines supplied a growing steel industry and helped forge a vital link in the chain supporting the nation's growing economy.

Members of Massachusetts' illustrious Mather family founded Cleveland-Cliffs and Pickands Mather & Co. in Cleveland. Both firms provided iron ore for more than a century to the nation's steel mills. The two companies became one in late 1986, when Cleveland-Cliffs acquired Pickands Mather.

Because they were socially conscious, the Mathers encouraged cultural developments in the communities around their mines as well as in Cleveland. Cleveland-Cliffs has long been responsive to human needs and to environmental issues as well.

Control room operators at the concentrator of Hibbing Taconite Mine on Minnesota's Mesabi Iron Range watch screens that are part of an automated system to supervise activity at the mine's primary crusher. From this room operators monitor systems processing iron ore through the plant as well as the beginning of the crusher process outside. Computerized and automated systems such as these assure efficient operations and reliable pellet quality.

Planned maintenance such as this inside a 32-foot-diameter grinding mill at Tilden Mine in Michigan's Upper Peninsula is among cost-control measures Cleveland-Cliffs uses to retain its century-old leadership position in the production of iron ore used in making steel. Each Tilden mill is shut down every 14 weeks so one-third of the metal plates lining the inside can be replaced. The mills grind crude ore to face-powder fineness so iron particles can be liberated. The fine material is rolled into marble-size pellets and heat hardened.

Cleveland-Cliffs is the world's largest producer of iron ore pellets and manages about 50 percent of the active pellet capacity in North America. The company owns iron ore reserves in North America and Australia, and sells iron ore pellets worldwide.

Cliffs learned early that to compete successfully, it must be technologically efficient and innovative. Its pioneering spirit has been recognized worldwide in many aspects of iron ore mining, processing, and mine management. Today quality is monitored precisely with the aid of computers.

Low-grade crude ore is mined and processed to produce a high-quality iron ore pellet. In 1988 about 40 million gross tons of iron ore pellets were expected to be produced from Cleveland-Cliffs' North American mines.

In response to customers' needs to reduce costs, much iron ore pellet production in the past two years has included the addition of limestone or dolomite to create "fluxed" pellets. These pellets enable steelmakers to introduce both ore and limestone simultaneously into their blast furnaces. Researchers are at work on other technological innovations to keep Cliffs a supplier of choice to steel mills.

Today Cleveland-Cliffs is undergoing a dramatic economic turnaround after several years of rationalization in the iron and steel industries. The company's future is directly linked to the steel industry's integrated plants, which rely mainly on North American iron ore pellets because they have the advantages of low cost, quality, accessibility, and security.

The steel industry is experiencing a strong resurgence due to increased competitiveness, the closing of obsolete facilities, and other factors. Cleveland-Cliffs Inc is ready to capitalize on the industry's recovery.

THE EXCELLO SPECIALTY COMPANY

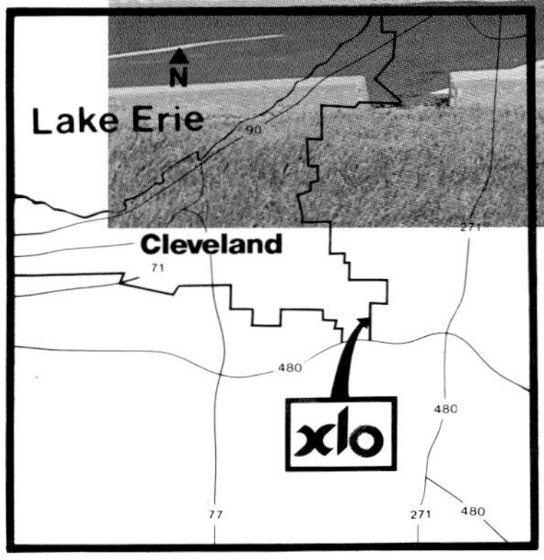

Excello's headquarters is located in Cranwood Industrial Park, combining easy access to major highways with a parklike setting.

The Excello Specialty Company was formed in 1934 to manufacture pennants and banners, automobile spare tire covers, and other related advertising specialities. The firm survived the Depression years and continued to grow by specializing in two major market areas: water-applied decalcomanias (decals that use water to activate an adhesive) and silk-screen processed fluorescent posters and billboards.

In late 1955 two sons of one of the original owners inherited the business. It was clear to them that to achieve growth for the company, they must seek new ways of responding to its markets and proceeded to operate on that basis.

By 1964 Excello had developed a highly flexible manufacturing facility and was producing not only extremely small decals with fine printing and intricate die cutting, but also large decals suitable for applying logos to truck-trailers.

In 1978 the firm began to need more room, and that same year it moved to its present location. A full-time designer was added to the staff, and a full-size prototype room was set up in the new headquarters. The operation made pressure-sensitive decals and paint-masking systems for a variety of uses, including the application of logos and decoration for trucks and aircraft, heavy construction machinery, and automotive use.

In 1979 the firm dramatically changed how it was managed. When the older brother retired, Excello purchased all of his stock, and key employees were invited to purchase shares, joining in company management. Eight employees are now owners and six serve on the board of directors, with the remaining brother, Wallace R. Jones, retaining controlling shares and serving as chief executive officer.

The newly formed team honed in on Excello's research into adhesives, film, and protective liners, and improved the firm's ability to meet precise customer specifications with consistent high quality. Excello proceeded to create a new concept in the masking and protective-covering materials market by developing a selectively placed adhesive-coated plastic product that is supplied in pad form and is used for a variety of applications, one of which is moisture barriers for the interior of automobile car doors.

In addition, all employees are involved in quality-assurance and product/process improvement. Employees are regularly invited to share their ideas and experiences directly with management. Better products, better customer service, and more innovative product development have been the result. The firm now holds 15 patents for the processes used in its products and has won many industry quality awards.

As Excello has grown, the jobs it creates for community residents have continued to multiply. The firm employs more than 170 people and has sales in excess of $12 million. Since 1980 people have been the key to the organization's success and to its nearly 40-percent-per-year growth rate. The Excello Specialty Company will continue to encourage and support employee involvement to maintain its competitive edge in quality production and product innovation.

At Excello, employees make the difference. Here (clockwise, from upper left) employees gather for a problem-solving session; the research and development staff hard at work; the design team mulls over a problem; and the quality-assurance staff uses a computer to track performance.

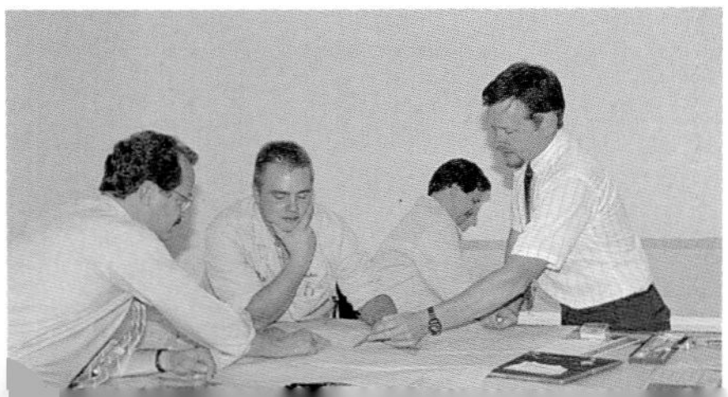

OGLEBAY NORTON COMPANY

From mine to mill, Oglebay Norton Company supplies iron ore (shown here), silica, coal, and other minerals to the steel, ceramic, electric-utility, construction, recreation, and oil- and gas-well service industries.

"Find it, mine it, bring it to market." This has been the operating principle of the Oglebay Norton Company for more than 130 years.

Oglebay Norton is a Cleveland-based firm that supplies raw materials for a variety of industries. These raw materials include iron ore, coal, quartz sand, silica, pumice, perlite, and fluorspar. It also operates a Great Lakes marine transportation company that transports iron ore, coal, limestone, and other dry bulk cargoes and runs coal-loading terminals on the Ohio River.

Oglebay Norton anticipates the raw material needs of the nation 20 years into the future and invests accordingly. In 1981 the company spent more than $50 million to build the 1,000-foot-long *Columbia Star,* one of the largest ore boats on the Great Lakes. The *Star* can unload its own cargo and needs a crew of just 30. These features, plus the long life expectancy of freshwater boats, promise a good return on the company's huge investment.

The 1,000-foot *Columbia Star* is one of 13 self-unloading vessels in the Oglebay Norton fleet, plying iron ore, limestone, and coal between Great Lakes ports.

Oglebay Norton began in 1854, when Isaac Hewitt and Henry Tuttle, Cleveland commission agents, saw that a vast market existed for the iron ore in Michigan's Lake Superior country. They began bringing the Michigan ore to Cleveland as agents for the Lake Superior Iron Company. By 1869 the firm was transporting 650,000 tons of iron ore per year and had become H.B. Tuttle & Company.

Henry's son, Horace Tuttle, and Earl Oglebay, whose father was in the iron manufacturing business, met in Cleveland and decided to form Tuttle, Oglebay and Company in 1884. The firm became the agent for the Lake Superior Iron Company and expanded to include the management of several iron ore mines in Michigan's Upper Peninsula.

These were rough and ready times. As Harrie S. Taylor, president of Oglebay Norton, said at the company's centennial, "These were men used to weighing risks, willing to pay the price; if they lost, there'd be no whimpering; if they won, they'd press their advantage . . . It's no wonder they built America."

In early 1890 John D. Rockefeller also bought iron rangeland. He asked a friend, David Norton, to find a partner to mine and transport his ore to market. Norton chose Earl Oglebay, then managing and selling one million tons of ore annually from mines in Michigan's Upper Peninsula. The two men joined forces and formed Oglebay, Norton & Co.

Growing as the nation has grown, the Oglebay Norton Company has persevered for more than a century to discover, mine, and bring to market the raw materials essential to the nation's progress.

LUCAS AEROSPACE POWER EQUIPMENT CORPORATION

Utilizing advanced technology, a test technician at LAPEC checks the final product.

Lucas Aerospace Power Equipment Corporation (LAPEC) is the world's leading manufacturer of DC starter-generator systems for turbine-powered helicopters, general aviation aircraft, and commuter transports. The company pioneered the concept of using a single electric motor for both starting turbine engines and generating electrical power on aircraft once the engines are started.

LAPEC has more than 40 years' experience in the development, application, and production of electric power-generating and electromechanical actuation systems for commercial and military aircraft. The firm manufactures three types of products: AC and DC air- or oil-cooled electric generating systems; DC starter-generator systems; and electromechanical servo and actuation systems.

Today its systems fly on aircraft such as the de Havilland Dash 8, Saab 340, Embraer 120, Beech 1900, Cessna Citation series, Fairchild Metro series, British Aerospace Jetstream 31, as well as the F-15 and F-16 fighters. LAPEC also serves world helicopter needs with electric systems on board Bell, McDonnell Douglas, Sikorsky, Boeing Vertol, MBB, and Agusta products. New electric systems are currently being designed for the U.S. Air Force Advanced Tactical Fighter and the U.S. Navy's Advanced Tactical Aircraft.

LAPEC's electromechanical and servo-actuation systems are used on missile, aircraft, and ground applications. The firm's capability for innovative mechanical designs has produced actuation systems that power control surfaces on missiles. This expertise has also been applied to surface-to-air missile launchers. The LAPEC actuation system raises and rotates the launch platform upon command from the ground launch controller.

LAPEC has been a member of the greater Cleveland community since 1940, when, as Jack and Heintz Inc., it produced engine starters and aircraft instruments during World War II.

In 1961 the Siegler Corporation purchased the company. The following year Lear and Siegler merged, and it became known as the Power Equipment Division of Lear Siegler Inc.

Lucas Industries Inc. acquired the division in 1988 and renamed it Lucas Aerospace Power Equipment Corporation. Lucas, the parent company, is a strong believer in research and development, employee training, and doing what it takes to be competitive in the world marketplace. These beliefs are shared by the LAPEC management team, which meets with all employees quarterly to inform them of progress made in sales, research projects, financial performance, and other timely subjects. Employees are trained in technical skills, supervisory management, and problem solving.

LAPEC plans to become more competitive in the world marketplace through the implementation of problem-solving task force teams and cellular manufacturing concepts. New facility construction is under way. The firm will take an active role in the community, because, says LAPEC president Donald L. Mottinger, "You can't isolate the company from the community. The quality of our community affects the quality of our workers."

At Lucas Aerospace Power Equipment Corporation, the company and its employees are still committed to innovation, and second best is still unacceptable.

Designed and manufactured by LAPEC, this AC generating system is currently in use on the F-15E fighter aircraft.

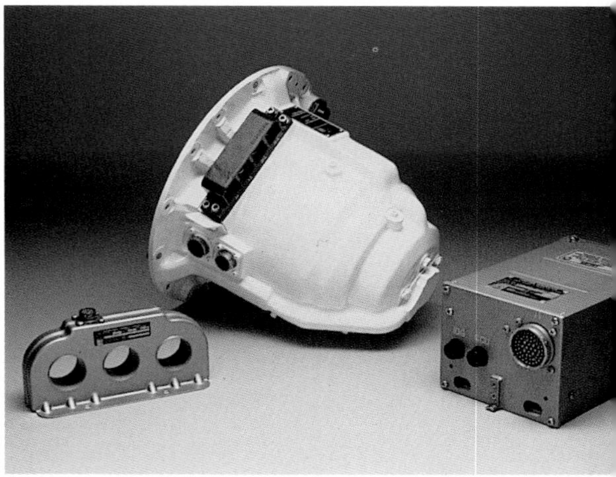

PREFORMED LINE PRODUCTS

Shown here is an application with fiber optic cable of the PREFORMED™ Splice Case with FIBERLIGN® Fiber Optic Organizer in Gig Harbor in the Washington service area.

Tucked away in a Cleveland suburb is the world's leading cable dynamics and vibration laboratory. There, at Preformed Line Products (PLP®), engineers simulate windstorms and ice conditions to test products that protect power and telecommunication cables. The firm's research helps utilities and telecommunications companies ensure steady, reliable transmission of energy and communication—the lifelines of modern civilization.

Since 1947 PLP has been the recognized leader in the industry it founded: overhead line vibration control. In the early 1940s a customer complained to Thomas Peterson, an electrical engineer with U.S. Steel and Wire Company, that high-voltage cables strung between transmission towers often broke at their point of support. Electric companies wrapped these lines in several feet of soft aluminum wire and clamped the ends, but the wires eventually loosened, and the cables still snapped.

In response to this problem, Peterson invented PREFORMED™ armor rods—strong aluminum alloy rods manufactured in a spiral shape. He found that if rods of a certain diameter were wrapped around a power line, they held tightly to the conductor and protection was better.

Peterson started a business to sell his new invention. More products soon followed, including ties that attached conductor cables to insulators, spacers that prevented cables from slapping together, dampers that quelled vibration, and a variety of anchoring devices.

These products found markets all over the world. Preformed Line Products has 17 plants in 11 countries and 1,800 employees worldwide. The company's world headquarters and research center remain in the Cleveland area.

PLP has stayed a step ahead of its competitors through an aggressive research and development program. It has also expanded into new areas, entering the vibration-measurement business and developing underground products, largely for the telecommunications industry.

In recent years the telecommunications industry has been making the transition from copper and aluminum wire to fiber optics. Preformed Line Products responded by investing in its own fiber optics company and pursued a rapid expansion in fiber optics technology. Telecommunications now makes up nearly half its sales, with the main product being stainless-steel Splice Cases to protect spliced copper or fiber optic cables from water, dirt, and other contamination.

The firm's products can solve many cable and line problems, and so can its people. Preformed Line Products' technicians and engineers go on site to solve difficult line construction problems. Whether wide-span cables are threatened by high winds or underground systems by the elements, PLP will tackle the problem. The business of Preformed Line Products is longer and safer cable life—in the air and underground.

Thomas F. Peterson (left), founder of Preformed Line Products and originator of "preforming" rods into a helix with inside diameter smaller than outside diameter. Shown is a bending machine forming aluminum dead-ends at original factory on 5349 St. Clair Avenue in Cleveland.

C-P-C GENERAL MOTORS PLANT

The 291-acre C-P-C General Motors facility in Parma, southwest of Cleveland, employs more than 4,500 people.

The C-P-C General Motors plant in Parma, southwest of Cleveland, consists of two buildings with approximately 3.2 million square feet of manufacturing space spread across 291 acres of land. This Chevrolet-Pontiac-Canada Group facility employs more than 4,500 people and carries out several manufacturing processes.

Construction of the Parma plant began in 1947 at a cost of $11 million and was designed for the production of pressed metal stampings and components for the assembly of a Chevrolet light car. When this project was cancelled, production of truck and commercial stampings was begun in November 1948.

In 1949 Parma began producing Powerglide transmissions and, in 1950, truck and commercial propeller shafts. In 1954 propeller shaft production was expanded to include passenger car models. Today it is the largest supplier of propeller shafts in the United States, producing 130 different assemblies.

Growth continued into the 1960s with expansions in the Pressed Metal and Transmission plants. In 1969 ground was broken for a new Prop Shaft Plant, which was occupied in 1970.

As Parma acquired the seat business of the former Fisher-Coit Road facility in 1982, it began a joint process with the local union to review its relationship and competitiveness. This review resulted in an innovative local agreement in 1983 wherein a commitment was made to change to a participative environment that supported greater employee involvement through the implementation of Team Concepts. This joint commitment paved the way for a Chevrolet-Pontiac-Canada Group (C-P-C) announcement in 1985 of a $580-million major press room modernization project. This modernization and the Joint Commitment to Team Concept and Competitiveness resulted in Parma receiving pressed metal work for the 1987 Corsica and Beretta and the 1988 Pontiac Gran Prix, Buick Regal, and Oldsmobile Cutlass.

Since 1984 Parma has, under the auspices of a Joint Human Resource Group, provided 485,000 hours of intensive training. This training included group dynamics, team building, quality improvement, technical and specific equipment training, as well as the upgrading of skills and knowledge of the firm's employees.

Because of Parma's past success and renewed commitment to providing components for cars and trucks in a joint effort, it was awarded all of the pressed metal parts for the 1990 GM-200 (Chevrolet Lumina, Pontiac Transport, and the Oldsmobile Silhouette). Never before has one press plant been responsible for the pressed metal components associated with one vehicle. This is the largest project ever undertaken by Parma and is an important part of its business.

The future shows signs of continued success for the people of C-P-C Parma and the surrounding communities. Parma is dedicated to providing "great components for great cars and trucks," embracing the beliefs and values of the Quality Network. Truly Parma is Teamed up for Tomorrow—Today.

Pressed metal components for General Motors vehicles are produced at the C-P-C Parma plant.

INLAND FISHER GUIDE EUCLID PLANT

This GM facility is located in Euclid just minutes from downtown Cleveland. Photo by Maria Sugar-Marin

The Inland Fisher Guide trim plant, which employs approximately 1,400 people, has a long and varied history. The facility was constructed in 1942-1943 by the Cleveland Pneumatic Aerol Company under government contract to build landing struts for aircraft as part of overall World War II production program. Purchased by the Ferguson Tractor Company after the war, the facility was sold to Fisher Body in 1947 and converted to an automobile assembly plant. From 1948 to the end of the 1970 model year, 1,907,568 automobile bodies, which included all of GM's nameplates, were assembled there.

The 1970 model year was the last in which Euclid employees built automobile bodies. That same year conversion to trim plant operation began. For the next 19 years—first as a Fisher Body trim facility, then as an Inland plant, and more recently as an Inland Fisher Guide—the Euclid facility has specialized in Cadillac products. Employees presently produce interior trim (seat cushion, seat back, armrest, and headrest) for the Cadillac DeVille, Cadillac Fleetwood Brougham, Buick Century, Buick Electra, Pontiac Bonneville, Pontiac 6000, Oldsmobile Ninety-Eight Regency, and Oldsmobile Custom Cruiser.

Trim production does not require high levels of automation; however, technology has been incorporated where appropriate. Out of 1,250 sewing machines in daily operations, about 50 percent are automatic or programmable. This percentage continues to increase each year.

The Euclid plant is operating under the team concept/synchronous manufacturing—a total production system that emphasizes teamwork, simplicity, getting back to basics, and a common-sense approach to manufacturing, with the flexibility to meet changing customer needs on a just-in-time delivery. To meet these requirements, employees are provided with the training and skills needed to build some of the best products on the market today. They are trained in decision making, problem solving, communication skills, quality principles, and inventory reduction.

Euclid's hourly work force is represented by the United Automobile Workers union. Labor and management have come a long way in their working relationship since 1949, when UAW formed Local 1045 in Euclid. Today employees at all levels are becoming involved in the total process of production, including quality review, cost, inventory reduction, and the examination of new business opportunities.

In order to build on the more cooperative relationship between management and employees, UAW-GM Quality Network is being implemented as the focal point of ongoing efforts to become a high-quality, low-cost manufacturer of the products that customers value most. The network represent a joint effort by GM and UAW to draw all GM people—both hourly and salaried—into the process of maintaining quality and productivity.

In order to provide cut stock on a just-in-time basis, computer-programmed cutting tables such as this one are strategically placed within the sewing areas. This minimizes the inventory and eliminates the possibility of cut parts being delivered to the wrong location. Photo by Maria Sugar-Marin

SIFCO INDUSTRIES, INC.

SIFCO Industries, Inc., which has undergone a dramatic restructuring over the past few years, celebrated its 75th anniversary in 1988.

The company has built a worldwide reputation on its ability to deliver exemplary quality products and services over the years. With that heritage as a base, the firm's increased focus on the rapidly expanding aerospace industry will enable it to enhance its quality reputation and maximize potential for future growth and profitability. SIFCO has emerged as a global manufacturer and marketer, focusing on metalworking products and services and the remanufacturing of jet engine components for the commercial airlines of the world.

Charles H. Smith, Jr., chairman of the board, and Kevin O'Donnell, president and chief executive officer, have provided farsighted leadership at SIFCO and moved the company into the international market. Smith was named one of the Ten Most Outstanding Men in America in both 1954 and 1955. He has had a long association with the International Labor Organization, an agency of the United Nations, and currently serves as the U.S. representative to this body.

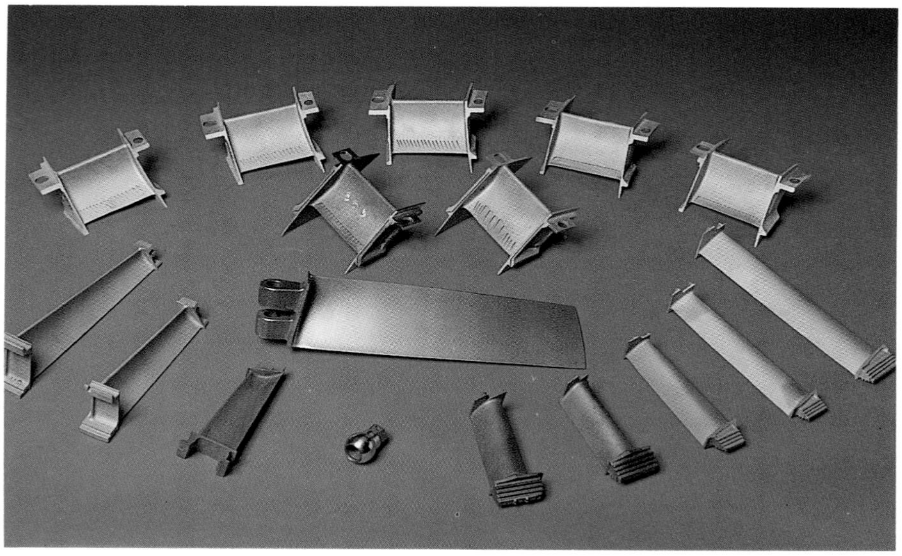

These jet engine vanes and blades are among the components repaired for commercial airlines worldwide by SIFCO's Turbine Components Group.

Kevin O'Donnell was director of the Peace Corps in the early 1970s and now serves as chairman of the Cleveland Council on World Affairs. He is also a trustee or member of many Cleveland civic and cultural organizations.

SIFCO's long-standing commitment to research and development in the metals industry and its dedication to service have helped make it the internationally successful company that it is today.

SIFCO has weathered the transition from manufacturing to service in part because of its personnel policies. Participatory management and management/worker communication had high priority at SIFCO long before "quality circles" became popular. All of SIFCO's new manufacturing and service facilities are salaried rather than hourly operations; employees are informed monthly about the company's progress. The result is a flexible, productive work force.

When SIFCO was founded in Cleveland in 1913, it was called the Steel Improvement Company because it applied the scientific principles of heat treating to improving the physical properties of metals, primarily steel. Three years later SIFCO merged with the Forest City Machine Company and added forging capabilities. The organization was renamed the Steel Improvement & Forge Company.

During the early 1900s steel forging became the primary means of automobile parts production, so the auto industry became the young company's biggest customer. Forging steel and other metals became even more crucial with the onset of World War I. There was a critical need to develop forging techniques

The Cleveland headquarters of SIFCO Industries, Inc., a global manufacturer and marketer focusing on metalworking products and services and the remanufacturing of jet engine components for the commercial airlines.

A 3,200-ton hydraulic screw press. SIFCO's forge operation has been a pioneer in forging technology throughout its 75-year history.

for stronger and more lightweight steel alloys. SIFCO responded to these challenges, and by the end of the war the company had established itself as a leader in research that resulted in the production of previously hard-to-forge alloy metals.

One of Charles H. Smith, Sr.'s, first actions as sales manager in 1920 was to end the company's dependence on the auto industry. He believed that many metals in addition to steel could be forged with scientific knowledge, proper equipment, and instruments to control processing. His pioneering vision led to several forging firsts credited to SIFCO, including Monel metal, high-temperature austenitic stainless steels for turbo supercharger, turbine wheels, titanium, commercial forging of molybdenum alloys for the missile industry, and copper beryllium for undersea communications. The company's expertise in forging special alloys and producing complex shapes to precision tolerances made it the ideal supplier of many new industries, most important of which turned out to be the aircraft industry.

In the 1950s SIFCO expanded into the international market by helping to build a production forge in Canada. The firm has since done design consulting, equipment purchase, training, and financial investment for new forging plants in Brazil, Argentina, Japan, and India. Currently the company is also providing sales and marketing assistance to Korea and the People's Republic of China.

SIFCO also entered the electrochemical field by purchasing the rights to a French process called Dalic electroplating, which selectively adds metal to a metal surface. A wide variety of pure metals and alloys can be applied by hand to repair worn surfaces, eliminating the expense of dismantling equipment and sending it to a tank electroplater. The process has been certified for a growing list of aircraft engine and marine applications.

In 1967 SIFCO was certified by the government to remanufacture airplane engine turbine components, a process that enables airlines to rebuild rather than replace worn engine parts. By 1977 SIFCO had acquired companies that gave it the capabilities to cold forge steel and manufacture large-diameter bearings.

SIFCO was not untouched by the economic downturn in the early 1980s. Restructuring was necessary to achieve growth. Many of SIFCO's more traditional operations were sold and assets redeployed. Press forging operations were shut down, and the cold forging and bearings facilities, as well as the company's Brazilian holdings, were sold.

While some areas of the business were pared down, others expanded. SIFCO began to shift its emphasis from original parts manufacturing to servicing and remanufacturing. Repairing and rebuilding jet engine parts is presently a major component of the business. New plants were built in Tampa, Florida, and Cork, Ireland, to handle this growing operation.

The success of SIFCO's restructuring over the past few years, which has gradually sharpened the focus of its energies on the aerospace industry, is dramatized by the fact that currently there are more than 150 commercial and military aircraft for which the divisions of SIFCO either produce airframe and engine forgings, repair or remanufacture engine components, provide precision machined parts, or offer plating repair services.

Kevin O'Donnell, SIFCO president and chief executive officer, summed up the company's attitude when he recently stated, "Having just finished our 75th year, we are looking forward to the final quarter of our first century with confidence and excitement." The outlook for SIFCO Industries, Inc., is bright as it moves into challenging areas of expansion under dynamic leadership.

Plating repair of a jet engine component. SIFCO selective plating solutions and equipment are used in a broad range of aerospace and marine applications.

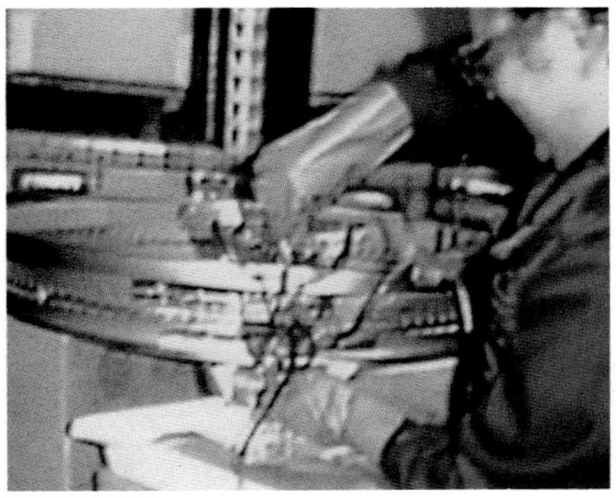

PICKER INTERNATIONAL, INC.

With more than 70 years of experience, Picker International, Inc., headquartered in Highland Heights, continues to be a leader in medical equipment manufacturing, boasting a complete line of diagnostic imaging equipment from conventional X-ray to magnetic resonance imaging. Picker employs more than 7,000 people worldwide and has annual sales approaching $700 million. A multinational network of sales and service professionals enables Picker to keep its promise to improve health care worldwide.

James Picker, the founder of Picker X-ray, was a Russian pharmacist who emigrated to New York. He provided physicians with supplies for a new diagnostic modality that had been developed in 1895 in Germany by Wilhelm Conrad Rontgen, a renowned German physics professor. Supplying the chemistry to develop the image and film, Picker realized he was working only half the business equation—the consumable side. To meet the manufacturing side of the equation, he purchased the Waite Bartlett Manufacturing Company in Cleveland, which had the technology to manufacture X-ray systems. Merging the two companies, he began developing and selling equipment.

In 1981 Picker International was formed by the merger of Picker X-ray, General Electric Company Medical of Great Britain, and Cambridge Medical Instruments. Today Picker continues as a growing subsidiary of the General Electric Company (GEC), plc, one of the largest corporations in the world, with more than 140 companies and nearly 200,000 employees. Backed by the resources of GEC, Picker invests heavily in research and development, enabling it to produce innovative products that open new possibilities for medical science and improved health care.

Few technologies have advanced as rapidly as medical diagnostic imaging with recent technological advancements revolutionizing examination of the human body. Picker continues as a leader in world markets, offering a complete range of equipment in magnetic resonance, computed tomography, digital imaging, X-ray, and nuclear medicine.

The newest of the diagnostic imaging techniques, magnetic resonance (MR), is a noninvasive method that explores the human body without the use of harmful ionizing radiation. Because MR is able to discriminate between types of tissue and can image structures surrounded by bone, it is especially useful in diagnostic evaluation of the brain, spinal cord, heart, and lungs.

MR uses a strong magnetic field that reacts with the hydrogen atoms in human tissue to produce radio frequencies that are reconstructed into visual images with the use of a computer. The magnetic field used in MR may be 5,000 to 40,000 times greater than the earth's magnetic field yet cannot be seen, touched, felt, or heard.

Rather than forming images directly from an X-ray beam as in conventional X-ray procedures, computed tomography (CT) is a multistep process where X-ray beams pass only through the section of the body being imaged. The radiation passes through the body's internal structures and is intercepted by a solid-state detector. The information gathered by the detector is reconstructed in a digital computer to produce a gray-scale image of a section layer or slice of the body.

Picker's ultrafast CT system, FASTRAC™, with scan speeds more than 15 times faster than conventional CT, which requires one to three seconds per scan, greatly improves image quality where patient motion was previously a problem and is especially significant for imaging the beating heart. FASTRAC™ provides excellent images of joints in motion and blood flow in the brain, and its .20-second scan time is able to freeze cardiac motion.

As clinical partners, Tulane University Medical Center and Picker In-

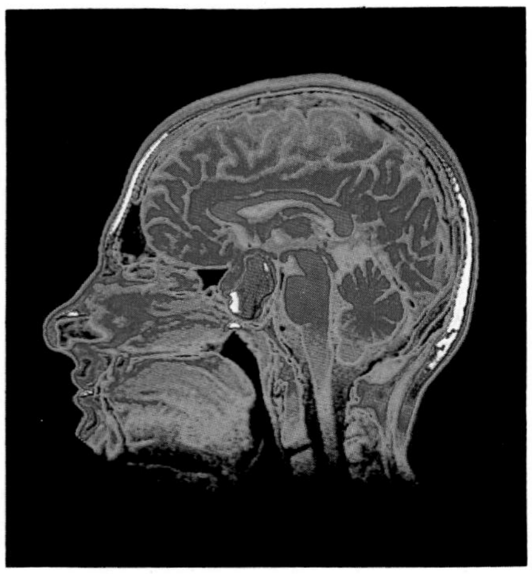

This image, obtained on a Picker VISTA® magnetic resonance imaging system, shows a 10-millimeter slice through the skull clearly indicating a cystic brain tumor.

Picker International world headquarters.

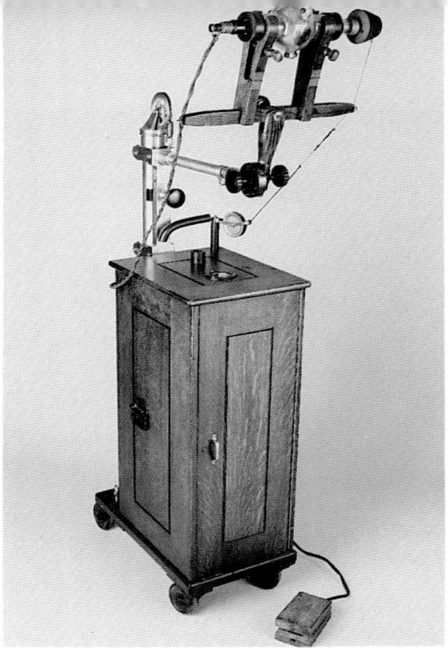

Picker's military involvement dates back to 1914 with the development of the Army field hospital X-ray unit.

ternational reached a milestone in CT research through trials with a CT scanner, which, for the first time, shed some light on sickle cell disease, a blood disorder primarily affecting children. Valuable input such as this provides the basis for future product development at Picker.

The quality of Picker's current digital X-ray equipment has vastly improved over equipment made only five years ago. Cameras linked to digitized image intensifiers make it possible for physicians to instantly review images on a video monitor as they are acquired, allowing for quick diagnostic evaluation.

Acknowledging the importance of early detection in the fight against breast cancer, Picker's mammography systems provide high-quality images needed to identify early breast cancer. Picker images are sharp enough to display clear anatomical detail, providing physicians with the ability to differentiate soft tissue fibers, all at a safe dose.

Nuclear medicine systems, in contrast to the other modalities, study the radiation emitted from a patient rather than striking the body with radiation. In a nuclear medical exam, an extremely small amount of a radioactive isotope is injected into the patient's blood stream and is imaged as it perfuses through the specific body part under evaluation. A camera detects the gamma rays emitted from the patient to create the image that depicts function of the body part. Nuclear medical imaging is excellent for assessing brain, heart, liver, kidney, and bone function.

Picker has maintained a long and successful historical military involvement that began in 1914 and continues today. In 1914 the Department of the Army asked Picker to develop the first military bedside field unit deployed by U.S. military organizations during World War I. It was relatively primitive by current standards, with no insulation on the high-voltage wires or radiation protection. In 1938, under contract to the Department of War, Picker supplied a military field X-ray unit that could be easily deployed and utilized in wartime conditions.

In 1989 development of specialty imaging products continues with a $38-million research and development contract with the U.S. government for the design of a military transportable radiographic fluoroscopic system. A $10.5-million Department of Defense (DOD) contract awarded to Picker in 1989 for 10 computed tomography systems is the largest DOD contract ever awarded a Cleveland company.

The Health Care Products Division of Picker International is the largest manufacturer and supplier of film, chemistry, and accessories to the diagnostic imaging and health care marketplace, with major distribution centers throughout the United States. Picker's Service Division, a team of highly trained service specialists in diagnostic imaging, is on call 24 hours per day to ensure that diagnostic imaging departments run smoothly.

All divisions of Picker International share the goal of improving health care around the world. Their dedication is seen throughout the firm's rich 70-year history and is evident in the research and development challenges they have ambitiously established for the future.

The Picker I.Q.™ computed tomography scanner, the most financially and medically efficient scanner available, uses the latest state-of-the-art technology to provide uncompromised image quality in the most compact CT on the market.

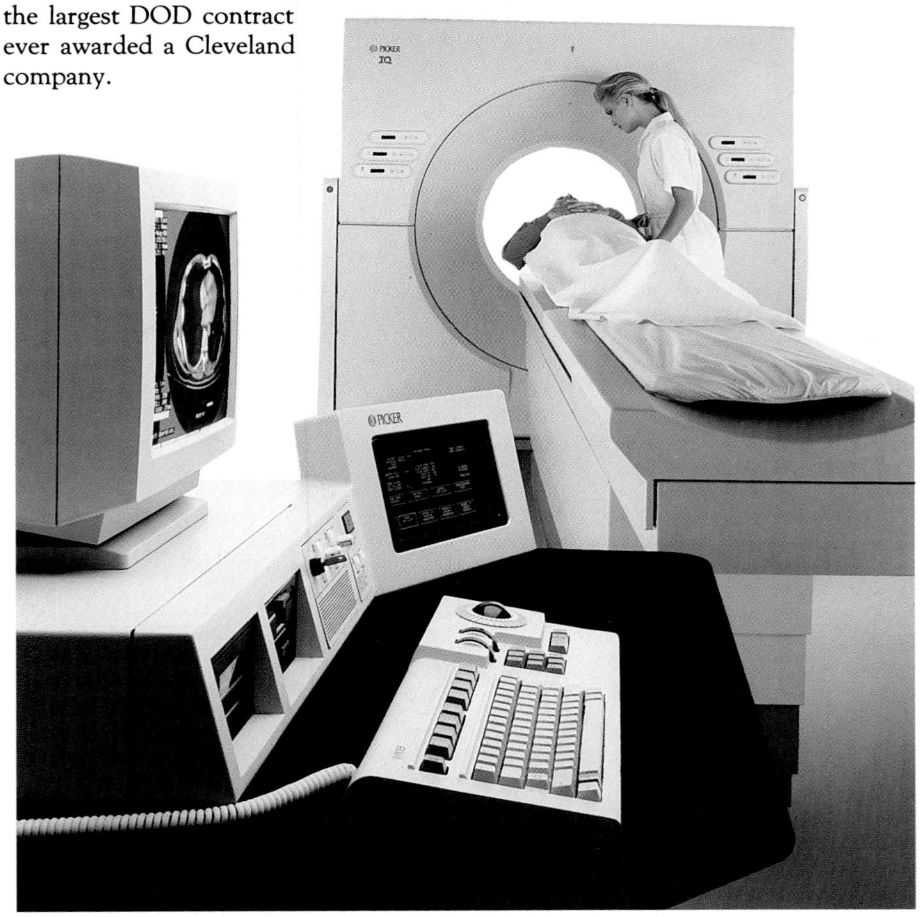

RELIANCE ELECTRIC COMPANY

For more than 80 years the people of Reliance Electric Company have built competitive success on an intimate understanding of the processes and businesses of their customers. Reliance people select the best technology, envision its advantage to real-world problems, mold it into world-class products, integrate these products with existing systems, and achieve dramatic improvements in customers' operations. This process is applied technology—people solving problems through technology. It is a continuous commitment to individual and team achievement with one overriding objective—delivery of superior value to industrial, commercial, and telecommunications customers. At Reliance Electric, applied technology starts with people.

Reliance Electric's presence and commitment to Cleveland began in 1907, when inventor John Lincoln and industrialist Peter Hitchcock formed a corporation with headquarters and manufacturing operations concentrated in Cleveland. Reliance's dedication to innovation began with the development of the world's first variable-speed DC motor. This technological breakthrough revolutionized industry, laying the foundation for the electrical motor-driven industrial processes of today and helping to establish Cleveland as a center of industrial technology development.

With its roots in the electrical equipment industry based on DC motor technology, Reliance became a major AC motor supplier during the 1930s and served as a leading supplier of motors to the United States Navy during World War II. The firm again led technology application by commercializing the world's first packaged electronic drive in 1938, extending the state of the art in industrial control.

As Reliance's electrical products business maintained its lead in applied technology, Reliance moved into a range of new businesses during the 1950s, 1960s, and 1970s. The company became an industry leader in rugged and dependable mechanical power-transmission products and systems with its acquisition of the Reeves Pulley Company, the Master Electric Company, and the Dodge Manufacturing Company. These three businesses now form Reliance's Mechanical Group, recognized the world over as a premier competitor and producer of mechanical industrial products from mounted bearings to gear reducers, gear motors, mechanical adjustable-speed drives, and mechanical components.

During the 1970s Reliance moved into the telecommunications industry through the acquisitions of three companies, each with a long history of innovation, quality products, and responsive service to the telecommunications industry. Lorain Products of Lorain, Ohio, manufactures power products for telephone operating companies. Reliable Electric/Utility Products builds connection, termination, and protection hardware and products for central office telephone installations, subscriber loops, and customer premise applications. R-TEC Systems manufactures sophisticated communications electronics and line-testing systems. Together these three businesses form Reliance Comm/Tec, one of the leading suppliers to America's vitally important telecommunications network.

Rouge Steel Company selected the flexibility, programmability, and reliability of Reliance Drive Systems to provide sophisticated process drive control.

Three different business segments—electrical motor and control products, mechanical power-transmission products, and telecommunications equipment—all focus on delivering superior customer value with the effective application of technology. Each brings the right human and capital resources to bear on customers' needs with quality, effective products, and market-responsive service. A common commitment to value benefits the diverse industries served by Reliance.

After seven decades as an independent company, Reliance was acquired by Exxon Corporation in

1979 in one of the largest corporate acquisitions in history at that time. Under Exxon ownership during the early 1980s, Reliance invested hundreds of millions of dollars to reinforce the already-strong technology base and to restructure manufacturing capabilities in response to international competition. These strategic investments have enhanced the firm's stature as a formidable global competitor in each of its target businesses.

State-of-the-art graphics enhance Reliance Electric Systems that control sophisticated web processes and other production operations throughout the industry.

In December 1986 Reliance regained its independence when a group of investors, led by senior Reliance management, demonstrated their confidence in the future of the company by purchasing Reliance from Exxon. As an independent company once more, Reliance remains dedicated to the principles and ideals that guided the business through its first eight decades.

Today Reliance Electric is a global enterprise. With 13,000 employees worldwide, the firm serves industrial, commercial, and telecommunications markets on five continents with international technical, manufacturing, and service resources. In Canada, Mexico, Brazil, Germany, Switzerland, the United Kingdom, Australia, Japan, and the United States, Reliance is executing a global strategy to identify the best of the world's technology, develop world-compatible designs, and manufacture the highest-quality, most market-responsive products available anywhere.

Reliance has a strong and continuing presence in Northeast Ohio. Reaffirming its belief in the future of this region, the company anchored its corporate headquarters in Mayfield Heights, a Cleveland suburb. The Electrical Group, headquartered nearby, directs the worldwide operations of the industrial motor and control businesses. Other Cleveland-area facilities include the principal motor and control research center, a sophisticated process drive systems manufacturing plant, and service, sales, and graphic arts facilities. Lorain Products, a Reliance Comm/Tec company, is one of the largest employers in Lorain, a nearby city west of Cleveland. Just to the east, in Ashtabula, Reliance operates a major industrial motor plant.

In all, more than 2,500 Reliance Electric Company people in Northeast Ohio bring a personal sense of dedication to the goal to be the "best of competition," built on the knowledge that Applied Technology Starts with People.

The Lorain® S.M.A.R.T.® microprocessor control/monitoring unit reports power system status by telephone on touchscreen CRT.

Dodge® Para-Flex® elastomeric couplings, installed between two speed reducers on this run-out table, eliminate continuous pivoting wear and prevent shaft breakage. Dodge Mounted Bearings provide smooth-running performance.

Engineered AutoMate® programmable controllers in use synchronizing the restart of hundreds of chemical refining motors following power disruptions.

FORD MOTOR COMPANY

When a sand system operator monitors quality control at Ford's Cleveland Casting Plant, he does not simply check components for defects. He goes through a comprehensive system of statistical process control that includes elaborate control charts, defect prevention measures, and extensive analysis.

Statistical process control training is provided for all key employees—from top management to production employees and maintenance personnel. Mere conformance to specifications is not enough; there must be continual improvement in casting quality, waste reduction, productivity, and costs.

At Ford, quality is not just a goal, it is a way of life, and this philosophy has guided the automotive giant to unparalleled success in the 1980s. In 1988 Ford sold 6 million cars and trucks worldwide and claimed 21.7 percent of the U.S. automotive market, its highest share in 10 years. That same year the company's earnings surpassed its previous industry record level profits by 14 percent.

An automatic D.C. rocker arm cover rundown machine on the eight-cylinder assembly line at the Engine Plant.

Ford's four Cleveland manufacturing plants have been instrumental in this latest success story. Employing more than 9,500 people, the plants have made the Cleveland area Ford's most important base of operations outside of Michigan.

Ford has introduced sweeping changes that have dramatically altered its corporate culture over the past decade. While other automobile manufacturers adopted a wait-and-see attitude during the economic slump and fuel crisis of the early 1980s, Ford management invested in quality improvements and new product development. The goal was to produce a series of all-new vehicles and components that would achieve "best in class" standards for quality and operating efficiency. The result has been several extremely popular car and pickup truck models, including Aerostar, Sable, Taurus (*Motor Trend* magazine's Car of the Year for 1986), Thunderbird Turbo Coupe (1987 Car of the Year), and Thunderbird Super Coupe (1989 Car of the Year).

A six-cylinder engine assembly leaving final dress up and on its way to hot test at the Engine Plant.

The company also invested heavily in its employees. In a bold, new participative management approach, Ford has moved decision making closer to the people who are actually involved in manufacturing. In support of this process, Employee Involvement (EI) groups have been formed to resolve a variety of issues, from improvements in the work place to quality and operational effectiveness. In Ford's Cleveland Casting, Stamping, and Engine plants, a modern "team approach" gives members the chance to make decisions on how tasks are to be performed by their specific team.

At all Cleveland plants, innovative internal communication programs keep employees apprised of the latest company developments and solicit their ideas to improve quality and work-related issues. Each Cleveland plant has its own employee newsletter and monthly up-

ABOVE: At the Casting Plant, the computerized control room for the new flaskless molding line is a state-of-the-art system.

RIGHT: Dimensional accuracy is checked with a computer-controlled measuring machine at the Casting Plant.

dates that report on the state of the plant, including production and sales statistics, costs, quality, and areas for improvement. Closed-circuit TV systems broadcast news about the entire automotive industry and other Ford operations.

Ford is working more closely than ever with the United Auto Workers (UAW) on several employee education and benefit programs. For example, the Education and Training Assistance Plan provides tuition for employees interested in furthering their college-level educations, and the Successful Pre-retirement Planning Program assists employees to plan for the financial, health, and other aspects of retirement.

Safety—always an important concern of the Cleveland plants—continues to be a top priority. Where accidents were once analyzed after they occurred, accident prevention is now the primary goal. Near accidents are not simply reported, they are used as training opportunities for avoiding such incidents in the future.

The company first came to Cleve-

Computer-aided design equipment is used for both tooling and plant facilities at the Casting Plant.

land in 1906, when it established a sales and services office downtown, but almost a half-century passed before the firm built manufacturing plants in the area. In the early 1950s' postwar auto industry boom, four Ford plants opened within a few years of each other—the Cleveland Casting Plant, Cleveland Engine Plants Nos. 1 and 2, and the Walton Hills Stamping Plant.

CLEVELAND CASTING PLANT (CCP)

Every day approximately 3,000 tons of iron are melted in this plant to cast the cylinder blocks, heads, crankshafts, and other metal parts used in Ford engines, transmissions, and axles. The castings are then shipped to plants in Ohio, Michigan, Canada, and Mexico for final machining and assembly.

When CCP first opened, it immediately achieved worldwide recognition as a showcase foundry, incorporating the latest technology in industrial plant construction, equipment design, and operations layout. But Ford did not rest on its laurels: Over the years the plant has undergone several modernizations and expansions. Ventilation and environmental control equipment have been maintained at state-of-the-art levels.

In addition, core making, molding, melting, and finishing have been upgraded. A new Learning Center, including computer training facilities and conference rooms, now provides training programs for both hourly and salaried employees.

Ford's commitment to manufacturing world-class castings has not stopped there. During 1987 a $180-million capital improvements program—part of a $300-million modernization program for four casting plants nationwide—was allocated for new state-of-the-art manufacturing systems within the Cleveland Casting Plant.

Today the plant occupies almost 1.6 million square feet—60 percent more floor space than the original facility. The plant's 3,700 workers produce castings for almost 11,000 engines per day.

CLEVELAND ENGINE PLANT NO. 1

This plant manufactures six- and eight-cylinder engines, as well as stampings, camshafts, crankshafts, water pumps, and many other parts used in Ford vehicles. Built in 1951, the plant has been enlarged several times since then and now encompasses 1.9 million square feet on a 72-acre site.

The plant's 2,600 employees pro-

A 2,500-ton harmonic drive, quick die set computerized transfer press at the Stamping Plant. The 270-by-108 bed size press runs mainly cross members and lower back panels for passenger cars.

duce 3,700 engines per day—a total of 890,000 engines every year. Together, Engine Plants 1 and 2 account for more than $1.2 billion in annual sales.

CLEVELAND ENGINE PLANT NO. 2

Constructed in 1955 on 80 acres, this 1.8-million-square-foot plant produces engine components to be used by Plant No. 1 and by other Ford engine plants, including Lima, Ohio; Dearborn, Michigan; and Chihuahua, Mexico, on a just-in-time basis. Instead of stockpiling large inventories of parts and supplies, the plant produces them just in time to arrive at their machining and assembly destinations when needed. Supported by new electronic communications links among all Ford plants and independent suppliers, this process has saved millions of dollars in production expenses for the company.

WALTON HILLS STAMPING PLANT

Located in southeast Cuyahoga County in the village of Walton Hills, this plant employs more than 2,400 personnel and processes some 1,000 tons of steel daily to produce the body panels for the Ford and Lincoln-Mercury car and truck lines.

Originally opened in 1954, the Walton Hills plant has been the focus of five expansion programs over the years. In addition, the facilities have been upgraded with the latest advances in computer-integrated management, quality-assurance technology, metallurgical processes, and production machinery.

As is the case for all of Ford's Cleveland facilities, the impact of the Walton Hills plant on local communities cannot be overestimated. With an annual payroll of $110 million, the plant pays almost $3 million in annual personal property and real estate taxes, significant additions to the coffers of local governments. More than $30 million is spent on goods and services obtained from local firms, contributing to the stability of local economies.

* * *

The Ford Motor Company has always believed in returning the support given to the firm by the communities in which it has facilities. Every year Ford returns $1.5 million to greater Cleveland in the form of donations to United Way, civic and cultural organizations, hospitals, colleges, chambers of commerce, and manufacturing associations. The company donates automobiles, power-train components, and sheet-metal parts to local schools with vocational training programs, and conducts plant tours for schools interested in the automobile manufacturing process. Ford also has committed $3 million to Cleveland Tomorrow to help revitalize the downtown area and neighborhoods.

As a worldwide leader in automotive products and services, as well as in aerospace, communications, and financial services, Ford Motor Company is proud to have played such a vital role in the renewed economic vigor in Cleveland. The firm views its history in Cleveland as a platform on which to build future success in the twenty-first century. Along the way it expects to be a full partner in Cleveland's future as a major center of automotive manufacturing technology.

A high-density blank storage area at the Stamping Plant.

The destacker loader on a transfer press at the Stamping Plant.

THE FERRY CAP & SET SCREW COMPANY

The Ferry Cap & Set Screw Company, in Cleveland's Industrial Flats district, was started in 1906 by William C. North. It originally manufactured standard hardware bolts. In the late 1960s the company dropped the hardware line and began to specialize in the manufacture of high-strength, heat-treated bolts for diesel engines used in off-the-road equipment, trucks, and buses. These bolts can withstand extremes of stress and heat.

The firm got its name this way: North wanted to entice Thomas Ferry, a local tooling genius, to come into the business. Ferry agreed, on the condition that the business be named after him. Thomas Ferry became president shortly after joining the company upon the retirement of William C. North and remained president until his death in 1931. He then was succeeded by Harold D. North, Sr., William's son. The Ferry Cap & Set Screw Company is now run by William North's grandsons, Harold D. Jr. and William H. North.

Thomas Ferry is responsible for an invention that revolutionized the bolt-making industry. Bolts used to be made by taking a metal rod the diameter of the bolt head, then cutting it down to form the shaft. This process wasted a great deal of metal. Ferry Cap's solution was cold upsetting, which involves taking a piece of metal rod the size of the bolt shaft, then hammering the end to form the head. This not only saves metal, but also makes a stronger bolt.

Not satisfied with revolutionizing bolt manufacturing, Ferry Cap has taken initiative in two other areas of its business—quality control and management style.

The company's quality-control system is very precise. A data sheet is sent with each shipment that tells the chemical makeup of the steel, the name of the operators that machined the bolts, and the history of the manufacturing process. Each step in the entire process can be traced. Because bolt failure could destroy an entire engine, the firm's ability to certify quality is crucial to its customers.

The company changed its management style in the late 1970s. Top management was reduced, and managers covered several areas, backing up each other and making their jobs more interesting. Better communication between management and production staff was established by holding thrice-monthly meetings.

The result is a company in which all employees enjoy their jobs, respect one another's work, and take pride in manufacturing high-quality products.

The Ferry Cap & Set Screw Company, founded in 1906, is located in Cleveland's Industrial Flats district.

THE JOSEPH & FEISS COMPANY

The Joseph & Feiss Company is America's oldest tailored clothing manufacturer and Cleveland's oldest manufacturing company. It can trace its beginnings back to a small general store in Meadville, Pennsylvania, opened in 1841. Four years later the company, named Koch & Loeb, moved to Cleveland and established itself as a wholesale men's apparel firm.

The firm was using jobbers to manufacture men's and boys' clothing, but at the end of the century it opened its own small production shop. It rapidly became the largest clothing house to do all its own manufacturing under one roof.

In the early 1900s the company adopted the name Joseph & Feiss. It expanded its plant and began a new label, Clothcraft, which soon gained distinction in the industry as "the best suit for the money."

By 1920 the firm had opened a nine-acre plant that is still its headquarters today. The plant initially served as both social center and work place for many of its employees. The company offered recreational and health facilities far ahead of its time—a bowling alley, handball courts, a swimming pool, medical and dental care, and classes in English and citizenship for its predominantly immigrant work force.

Modern methods of brand marketing and advertising for wide retail distribution were pioneered by Joseph & Feiss during those years. One of its most popular styles, a blue serge suit sold and advertised as No. 5130, was so successful it became known as the Model T of the clothing industry. By 1925 more than 235,000 serge suits were sold annually by the company.

After World War I the firm invested in other plants and developed new ways to cut, sew, baste, and press. Quality controls were introduced to preserve and improve the standards already tested over time.

As styles changed and fashion became an important factor in the clothing industry, Joseph & Feiss acquired the Samuel Spitz Company, maker of Cricketeer. This line soon became the firm's flagship label. All other brands were incorporated under it, and a line of women's business suits was added.

In 1966 The Joseph & Feiss Company became a wholly owned subsidiary of the Phillips Van Heusen Corporation. Joseph & Feiss continued to demonstrate that it was more profitable to make an excellent garment than to cut corners.

In 1987 the firm was purchased by a group of Joseph & Feiss employees. The Joseph & Feiss Company now employs more than 2,200 people in its plants in Ohio, New York, and Kentucky, and has offices in New York City, Los Angeles, Chicago, Dallas, and Atlanta. Its motto remains the same: "We will deliver the best product for the money, on time, and with the best service."

In addition to the main manufacturing facility on West 53rd Street in Cleveland, the company has plants in Brooklyn, Ohio (shown here); Utica, New York; Harrodsburg, Kentucky; and Lorain, Ohio.

The Joseph & Feiss Company manufactures under the labels Cricketeer, Country Britches (shown here), Geoffrey Beene, and Cricketeer for Her.

INVACARE CORPORATION

While the greater Cleveland area is generally recognized as one of the world's premier medical centers, it also is home to the world's leading manufacturer, marketer, and distributor of home health-care products—Invacare Corporation. Headquartered 30 miles west of Cleveland in Elyria, Ohio, Invacare's product line includes prescription and standard wheelchairs, respiratory equipment, hospital-type beds for the home and nursing homes, patient aids, continuous passive motion devices, and cardiovascular exercise equipment.

In December 1979 A. Malachi Mixon III, Invacare's current chairman, president, and chief executive officer, and a group of Cleveland area investors purchased the company from Johnson & Johnson. Annual sales at that time were $19 million; net income was about $100,000; the company employed 350 people; and products consisted of standard wheelchairs and a limited line of patient aids.

Since then Invacare has become one of greater Cleveland's outstanding entrepreneurial success stories: Sales have climbed to $160 million in 1988—an eight-fold increase; net income has grown to approximately $5 million; and worldwide employment numbers 1,700 individuals, with about 1,100 of those employed locally. Six manufacturing facilities and 31 North American distribution centers produce and distribute the world's broadest line of home health-care products. From a virtually nonexistent export business in 1979, some 20 percent of Invacare's revenues in 1988 came from international operations.

Invacare's industry leadership is perhaps best evidenced through the results of a 1987 health-care industry survey conducted by *Medical Products Sales,* a leading trade publication. When asked which manufacturers routinely provide the best field support, sales managers for dealers and distributors nationwide named 90 different companies. Invacare ranked number one ahead of industry giants Johnson & Johnson and 3M—a real tribute to Invacare employees and confirmation of the company's commitment to service.

Invacare's growth has been fueled by a combination of socioeconomic and demographic conditions, as well as the company's own efforts to address these conditions.

The chief external factor influencing Invacare's success is the trend toward home health care. This trend has been accelerating for the past decade, due to a combination of events, including aging of the population in all developed countries; continuing medical advancements that prolong life; increased population of disabled children brought about by improved pre-, neo-, and postnatal

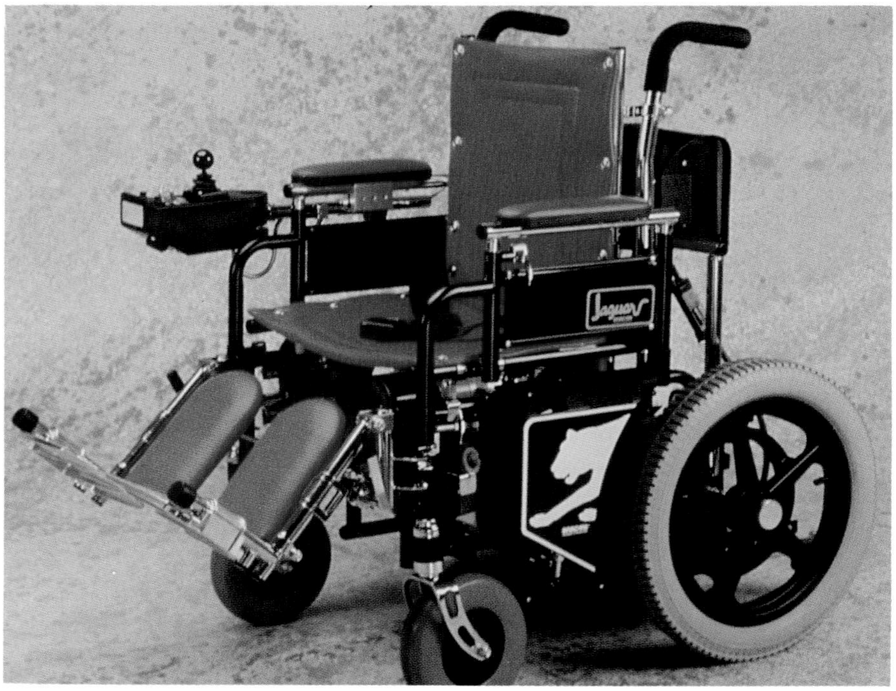

Product innovation is one of Invacare's hallmarks. Invacare was the first company in its industry to design a motorized wheelchair specifically for children. The Jaguar (shown here) is one of the firm's wheelchairs for children.

A. Malachi Mixon III, Invacare chairman, president, and chief executive officer, and a group of Cleveland area investors bought Invacare in December 1979. Sales have increased eight-fold since then. Photo by Bruce Zake

Invacare designs and manufactures virtually all of its electronic componentry internally. A new microprocessor-based controller was introduced recently. The computer program allows easy changes to a power wheelchair's performance characteristics to meet an individual's special needs.

care; economic pressures on hospitals forcing them to discharge patients earlier in the recovery process; greater integration into society of disabled individuals; more stable government regulatory conditions; and the increasing burden of care for AIDS.

To address these trends, Invacare has adopted a five-part corporate strategy that includes offering the industry's broadest product line and continuing to expand it, providing the highest levels of customer service in the industry, employing the largest and most highly compensated direct sales force in the industry, providing industry leadership in product innovation, and ensuring a competitive cost structure.

Through its broad product line, Invacare can supply as much as 50 percent of a home health-care equipment dealer's needs through one contact point, with unmatched convenience and cost savings to the dealer.

In customer service, 90 percent of the company's core products can be delivered on the next day or receive same-day pickup by dealers, due to the firm's extensive distribution network. In fact, in addition to Invacare products, the network is now being utilized to distribute home-care products manufactured by other high-quality companies.

Invacare is recognized widely as a product innovator in its industry. Over the past decade the company has played the leading role in reducing weight and improving performance of standard wheelchairs, redesigning the home-care bed to make it easier to install, and developing from scratch the industry's best performing and most reliable power wheelchairs. Recent innovations include a microprocessor control and a new drive system that doubles the range of a motorized wheelchair on a single battery charge. In the home-care industry, these improvements compare to the changeover from black and white to color television in the consumer electronics industry.

Invacare has invested heavily over the past five years to ensure its competitive position, with record or near-record capital spending every year since 1985. Consolidation of operations in Elyria from four plants to two resulted in a substantial cost reduction while preserving all jobs. The company has carried out a similar effort in the United Kingdom. Late in 1988 the firm opened Invamex, a new 78,000-square-foot manufacturing facility in Mexico just across the border from McAllen, Texas. The plant offers an extremely competitive hourly wage structure, and products are manufactured to meet or exceed U.S. standards.

Invacare has shared its success both with Cleveland and Elyria and especially in support of programs involving the physically challenged. Recently supported events have included Cleveland's Week on Wheels, the Invacare Cup Racing Series in conjunction with the National Wheelchair Association, and a number of other wheelchair athletic teams.

Invacare Corporation plans to continue this high level of community involvement as it continues its growth—currently running at double the industry average. The company expects to achieve the $250 million in sales threshold by the early 1990s by continuing and enhancing its strategic approach to the market through product line breadth, advanced customer service, product innovation, and cost competitiveness.

Standard wheelchairs made up most of Invacare's product line in 1979. While standard wheelchairs are but one component of the broadest product line in the home-care industry today, they continue to be an Invacare strength. The two models shown here are light in weight, with updated design and use of modern materials such as composite wheels.

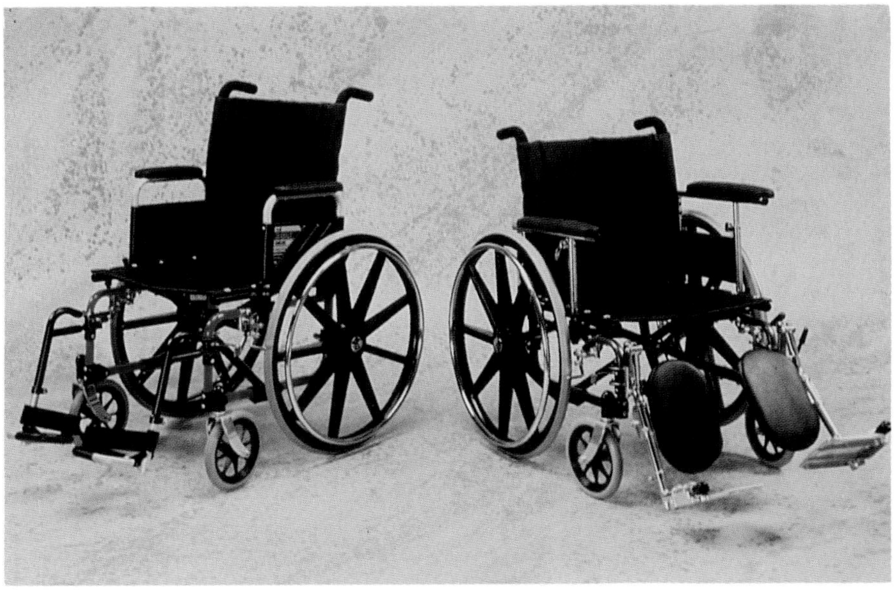

OHIO MATTRESS COMPANY

The Stearns & Foster Dynasty Emerald pillow-top mattress has a super-soft quilted pad attached to the firm-support mattress.

There is nothing sleepy about the Ohio Mattress Company, a *Fortune* 500 company that has a 25-percent market share and is the world's largest bedding manufacturer.

Through its Sealy operations, Ohio Mattress produces Sealy mattresses and box springs, which it licenses worldwide. According to industry figures, Sealy is the leading brand of conventional bedding, with 21 percent of market share, almost equal to the second- and third-most popular brands combined.

Ohio Mattress also owns the Stearns & Foster Bedding Company, one of the oldest and largest premium-brand manufacturers in the United States. Its bedding sells at a higher price than other brands and usually comes with a 15-year warranty. Ohio Mattress also owns operations that make and distribute waterbeds, waterbed furniture, and convertible sofas.

Unlike others in the conventional bedding industry, Ohio Mattress has grown phenomenally. In 12 years, from 1976 to 1988, while the rest of the industry grew 127 percent, Ohio Mattress grew 1,475 percent, from annual sales of $32 million to $540 million.

The company was founded in 1907 by Morris Wuliger, whose grandson Ernest Wuliger is current chairman. In 1924 Ohio Mattress became a Sealy then-licensee, one of eight companies licensed to manufacture and sell Sealy bedding; the corporations paid Sealy a royalty for the use of the Sealy name, and Sealy used the funds for national advertising and promotion campaigns to establish Sealy as a national brand. In 1950 Sealy introduced its Posturepedic® mattress, which it developed in conjunction with orthopedic surgeons to provide firm support as well as comfort. The Posturepedic® became the world's largest-selling premium mattress.

Since bedding was becoming a brand-name business, Ohio Mattress decided to buy other Sealy licensees. Besides, the company was looking for ways to expand and grow. To fund the acquisitions, the firm became publicly owned in 1970. Soon Ohio Mattress was Sealy's largest licensee, with 25 percent of Sealy sales in the United States. In 1971, however, Sealy exercised its right of first refusal to let Ohio Mattress buy licensees in Florida and Philadelphia. A 16-year period of litigation began.

In the meantime, Ohio Mattress continued to grow. In 1983 it acquired the Stearns & Foster Company, a 140-year-old firm recognized as a top-quality producer of premium mattresses with a lasting reputation for fine craftsmanship and distinctive product features.

Next, Ohio Mattress acquired Lifetime Foam Products, a supplier to Sears. Ohio Mattress is also one of the nation's largest waterbed suppliers. In recent years it has acquired both Monterey Manufacturing and Wavecrest, two companies that make waterbeds, and Woodstuff Manufacturing, which produces waterbed furniture. In addition, Ohio Mattress has Sealy and Stearns & Foster divisions that produce sofa beds.

In 1986 the Ohio company won judgments totaling $77 million, plus interest, against Sealy. This prompted a number of Sealy licensees to offer their firms to the Ohio company, which soon acquired 100 percent of Sealy stock as well as all Sealy bedding licensees in the United States, except one in New Jersey.

As a result of the 1986 purchase of the Sealy brand name and the right to license it, Ohio Mattress had an enormous growth spurt. In 1987 the company doubled its sales. Ohio Mattress reorganized its expanded Sealy bedding operations into six regions and converted a San Diego subsidiary into a Sealy plant, resulting in lower delivery costs and better customer service.

In the spring of 1989 the Ohio Mattress Company was acquired by Gibbons, Green, van Amerongen.

Today Sealy enjoys the best consumer recognition in the industry: In an independent study, Sealy was perceived as the best quality and the best value. Sealy also has a broad-based product line, ranging from luxury king-size models that retail at $2,200 per set to promotional twin-size sets at $200.

RIGHT: Ohio Mattress is a leading producer of waterbeds and waterbed furniture. The Monterey-brand Ultrafirm watermattress represents an advance in waterbed technology.

BELOW: Sealy's new Posturepedic® bedding line appeals to a broad consumer base. It features new styling, improved components, a more luxurious appearance, and attractive colors and covers. Shown is the upscale Ultra Premium Grandeur Acclaim pillowtop.

Stearns & Foster has a reputation as an innovator with continual product advances, such as its foam-encased mattresses and a unique tradition of handmade eight-way hand-tied springs, a feature nobody else has offered for the past 50 years.

To stay on top in its industry, Ohio Mattress constantly monitors buying patterns and other consumer needs. Most consumers who have recently bought a mattress chose one of higher quality than before. Larger sizes, which became available in 1961, were popular in the 1970s—a fact more readily appreciated when one realizes that the traditional full-size mattress is 54 inches wide, equal in width to two crib mattresses laid side by side.

More consumers are also buying waterbeds. A consumer survey revealed that 9 percent of those polled had one, and 18.5 percent were considering the purchase of one. Ohio Mattress is one of the nation's largest waterbed suppliers. It recently introduced a line that offers a choice of firmness. This was a first in the waterbed industry, which usually characterized waterbeds by motion (waveless, etc.).

Waterbeds aside, most mattresses sold today consist of two parts: the foundation, or box spring, and the mattress, or inner springs, with a cover of quilting and fabric.

Sealy is a leading supplier of contemporary sleep sofas, such as the Savannah, pictured here.

The box springs and the mattress work together to support the body. The more body weight put on the mattress, the more the coils push back, with the box springs coming into play more and more as weight increases.

With time, mattress wear becomes visible; unseen, the box springs wears out to a corresponding degree. For that reason, both the mattress and box spring must be replaced: Putting a new mattress on top of an old box spring would be like building a new house on a deteriorated foundation.

Research and development figure prominently in Ohio Mattress' operations. Ohio Mattress has the most extensive products testing laboratory and research and development center in the home furnishings industry.

The research facility serves several purposes: to test new materials to improve mattress durability, to train personnel, and to compare the quality of company products with those of competitors.

In 1983 Ohio Mattress introduced a new way to test its mattresses for support and comfort: DataMan. A computerized model of an adult, DataMan precisely measures the mattresses' surface pressures and compares them with the levels of firmness and comfort that are essential for a good night's sleep.

Computers are also used to analyze the stress levels a component of a mattress will encounter over a lifetime of normal use. Tests can accurately predict how long and how well mattress components will perform.

Even in a comparatively few years, considerable changes are made in mattresses and box springs as a result of research findings. Ohio Mattresses' product has been almost totally changed—transformed by new materials, new ways of achieving support, and new configurations of old materials and techniques.

Literally 100 changes are made in just five years. The angle of the torsion coil is changed to eliminate squeaks, and the coil is also coated, again to prevent squeaks, the main source of complaints. The staples are cut longer or differently to hold better. The thread in the quilting is changed for more durability.

The goals of all these changes are reducing returns from very few to zero, and producing a superbly attractive mattress that provides support and long wear. Modern mattresses are quite different from early ones. Anyone with a long memory can recall button-tufted mattresses—now .1 percent of the market—and the ubiquitous ticking mattress cover. Cover ticking isn't even manufactured any longer.

The Ohio Mattress Company is well on its way to achieving its goal of zero returns. The firm is growing much faster than the bedding industry itself, indicating that the mattress maker is wide awake and convincing more and more people to buy its product.

Like its products, Ohio Mattress Company looks forward to a long life. Ernest Wuliger, chairman, believes that Ohio Mattress' people are ordinary people capable of extraordinary performance and that they make the firm's success possible. The company looks back on 80-plus years of tremendous growth—and forward to even more growth in the future.

THE STANDARD PRODUCTS COMPANY

In 1920, when Dr. James S. Reid left the Public Health Service to doctor automotive gas caps instead of people, a new era in Cleveland industrial history began. Today his Standard Products Company averages sales of more than $500 million annually. The company manufactures rubber and plastic parts for the automotive original-equipment industry, rubberized track for military vehicles, and tread rubber for tire retreading. Moreover, the firm has invested millions of dollars in plants, equipment, and technology, and has reached out to the community through the Standard Products Foundation.

The operation officially became The Standard Products Company at incorporation in 1936. In early decades automobile manufacturers purchased the small firm's patented door locks, window channels, and weatherstripping. Their unique design and production methods contributed to the company's success. Later, over the years, these were improved even more, and sales steadily increased. The management team also invested in Canadian and British companies that were to become part of the company's capacity.

In recent decades, under president James S. Reid, Jr., Standard Products has developed a sophisticated extrusion manufacturing technique. That and its electrostatically flocked rubber process help meet customer demand for lighter-weight, less-costly automotive window and door seals and for decorative automotive trim. In the 1950s the firm also began to produce most major military tracks used by U.S. defense forces.

New construction, acquisitions, and collaborations position Standard Products well in the international market. The company's production facilities, joint ventures, and licensing agreements in the Americas, Europe, Australia, and Asia allow it to supply original equipment to automobile manufacturers anywhere in the world. Its Oliver Rubber subsidiary manufactures precured and conventional-tread rubber for the tire-retreading industry.

This growth has benefited stockholders who have seen their stock value and dividends rise significantly. Moreover, greater Clevelanders have benefited too. The Standard Products Foundation improves the quality of life in Northeast Ohio through contributions to educational and charitable causes. It exemplifies the goals of service and excellence that have guided Standard Products since its inception.

Thus, as The Standard Products Company approaches the new century, its emergence to a significant industrial enterprise is part of Cleveland corporate history. The firm's success demonstrates the level of competence, dedication, and planned creative competitiveness that characterize the new Cleveland.

Manufacturing rubber weatherstripping and decorative vinyl trim for automobiles has fueled Standard Products' growth into a premier supplier of parts for the worldwide automotive industry. Standard Products also produces military track shoe assemblies, while its Oliver Rubber subsidiary is a major manufacturer and marketer of tread rubber for retreading truck tires.

THE CLARK-RELIANCE CORPORATION

ABOVE: An architect's rendering of the new Clark-Reliance headquarters offices and manufacturing complex in Strongsville, occupied in 1988.

LEFT: This building on Carnegie Avenue in Cleveland was the home of Reliance Gauge Column Company at the time it was merged with Clark Manufacturing Company in 1963.

The Clark-Reliance Corporation has grown from roots put down more than 100 years ago by the makers of the first alarm water column ever offered to boiler operators. In 1884 Jackson Allen and Frank Bort produced and marketed that unique alarm system, which became standard equipment with the nation's boiler manufacturers in a few years, at their Reliance Gauge Column Company in Cleveland.

Clark-Reliance, acquired in 1962 by seventh-generation Cleveland industrialist Harry E. Figgie, Jr., now produces a variety of measuring, control, alarm, separation, and energy-conservation equipment for the processing and power industries. The company has grown seven-fold in the last half of the 1980s.

Dr. Harry E. Figgie III, president and chief executive officer of the company, attributes this recent growth to an aggressive sales force, vigorous product development and redesign, and advanced manufacturing techniques. A surgeon at University Hospitals of Cleveland who specializes in total joint replacement, Dr. Figgie uses similar advanced principles such as computer-aided design and custom fitting of joints in his practice of medicine.

Also instrumental in the company's growth has been a series of mergers and acquisitions. Reliance Gauge was merged with Clark Manufacturing Company to form the present organization in 1963. The merger joined Reliance's monitoring expertise with Clark's steam specialty products, such as steam traps, pressure-regulating valves, steam separators, and strainers. In 1982 Clark-Reliance purchased Anderson International's line of steam traps, adding air-release valves, float and thermostatic traps, and combination thermostatic-inverted bucket traps to its product mix.

Three more acquisitions occurred in 1986—Jacoby-Tarbox Corporation of Yonkers, New York, a leader in the design and manufacture of sight-flow indicators; Anderson International's line of entrainment separators and purifiers; and Jerguson Gauge and Valve Company of Burlington, Massachusetts. These moves positioned Clark-Reliance as a single-source, full-service supplier of fluid-control products and services.

To provide for the growth resulting from these acquisitions, the corporation erected a new headquarters building and consolidated manufacturing complex in Strongsville, just south of Cleveland. The production facilities are advanced and produce the entire range of the company's varied product line.

The new plant is a leader in automated material handling, flexible manufacturing, and rigorous quality control. Dr. Figgie describes it as visible proof of the company's resolve to provide its markets with the most efficient, reliable, and cost-effective products possible.

The Clark-Reliance product mix now includes steam traps, liquid level gauges, remote reading indicators, water columns, turbine water-induction protection devices, sight windows, flow indicators, entrainment separators, pressure-reducing and pressure-regulating valves, and pipeline strainers. Twenty percent of total sales are to overseas customers.

Dr. Figgie says the company is committed to its people and to the city that is its home. His father, Harry E. Figgie, Jr., chairman of Figgie International Inc., carried on the family business begun in Cleveland by his father, Harry Figgie, who was one of the founders of Rockwell International and the Eaton Corporation. "We are committed to the personal and professional growth of our people and to the growth of our corporation," Dr. Figgie says.

In addition to his surgical practice and his executive duties at Clark-Reliance, Dr. Figgie is an assistant professor of orthopedics at University Hospitals, assistant professor of biomechanics at Case Western Reserve University's School of Medicine, and visiting scientist at the Hospital for Special Surgery in New York. The demands on his time have led to a philosophy of participatory management at Clark-Reliance. "Department heads seek the involvement of their people," he says. "Decisions are made at the lowest competent level. But everyone adheres to our combined strategic and financial plan."

The philosophy has obviously paid dividends. Clark-Reliance has been a recipient of Arthur Andersen's Greater Cleveland 100 Award for top area corporations. And it has a compounded annual growth rate of more than 20 percent since 1963.

In addition to its Strongville headquarters and manufacturing facility, the company has a large service center and stocking warehouse in Houston, Texas, and sales offices nationwide and in 24 foreign countries.

The overriding objectives of the company remain as constant today as over a century ago, when Jackson Allen and Frank Bort came up with their first alarm water column: to blend innovative engineering with performance-proven concepts to best meet the requirements of its customers. Dr. Figgie believes the best place to meet this goal is Cleveland.

"It's our hometown," he says, noting that his children are ninth-generation Clevelanders. "Cleveland has good people, a good work force, and a good work ethic. We've had great success here."

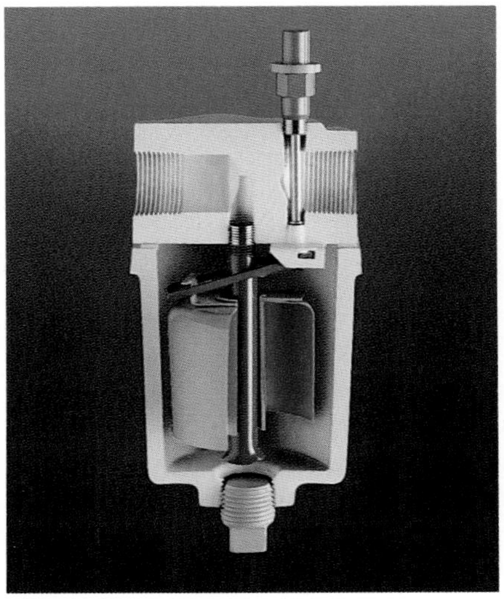

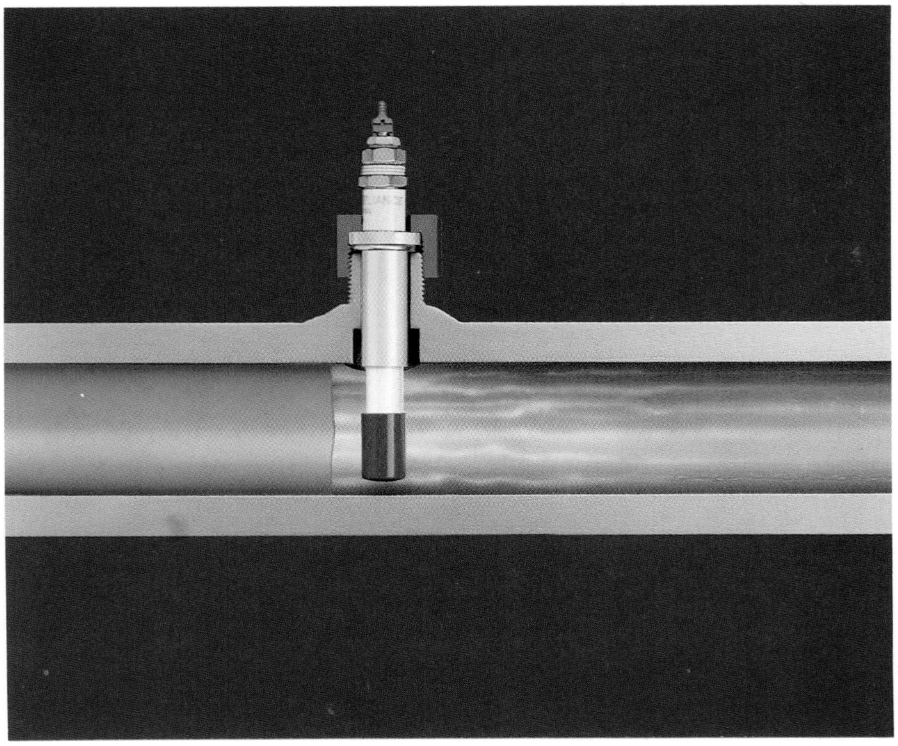

ABOVE: The Clark-Reliance ENDURATRAP® inverted bucket trap (cutaway view shown here) is part of the broadest line of steam traps and fluid controls available from one source.

RIGHT: Clark-Reliance pioneered the use of conductivity probes in boiler controls with its probe-type water column (pictured here in cutaway form) and Electro EYE-HYE® remote-reading water-level gauge. This was a major step forward in boiler control technology.

ESSEF CORPORATION

Essef Corporation of Chardon has helped establish greater Cleveland as a world leader in composite engineered plastics. Incorporated in Bedford, Ohio, in 1954, by James A. Horner, the company was then known as Structural Fibers, Inc. It pioneered the production of fiberglass-reinforced plastic products used in place of cast, forged, or other formed parts normally made of metal. The new parts were corrosion-free and weighed much less than the metal parts they replaced.

Horner, chief executive officer of Essef, moved his company to Chardon, a semirural community east of Cleveland, in 1958. He credits Cleveland's commercial banking community with making the decision to invest in the area an easy one. He says he walked into a bank with a plan for a 10,000-square-foot plant and walked out with a commitment.

The big breakthrough for the company came after it set up shop in Chardon. Structural Fibers began producing fiberglass-reinforced, plastic pressure vessels based on design criteria and developed in the engineering laboratories at Cleveland's Case Institute of Technology. Dr. Harry R. Nara, a professor of engineering at Case, was instrumental in developing pressure vessel standards. He became a director of the company in 1959, as did fellow researcher and faculty member Edward G. Bobalek, a polymer scientist.

"We created the world of thermoplastic and thermoset pressure vessels," Horner says. "No one else was making them in large quantities from scratch with zero defects to various standard specifications."

At the core of Essef's business was the development of a proprietary molding process—internal bag molding. The firm initially produced defense-related plastic products such as components for the Polaris and Hercules missiles. The internal bag-molding process led to the type of seamless pressure vessels that are now the principal components of water-treatment equipment products worldwide. Other products followed, including pumps and filters, as well as custom-molded plastic cabinets and subassemblies for computers and business machines. Two of Essef's largest customers are IBM and Xerox.

The move into swimming pool products came in 1971 with the acquisition of Pacific Fabrication, Inc. It had a nucleus of international distribution for product lines fabricated of stainless steel, bronze, and iron. This subsidiary, now known as Pac Fab, Inc., was the first step toward diversification through product development and acquisition. Pac Fab produces complete systems for pools, including pumps, valves, and filters manufactured of composite engineered products.

Two years later a subsidiary, Structural Fibers International, GmbH, was organized in West Germany. It provided distribution to support entry into the European water-treatment and swimming pool markets. Then, in 1976, a third subsidiary, sa SFC nv, was formed in Belgium to broaden the company's manufacturing base for European customers.

Essef bought FAME Plastics, Inc., in 1981 to gain a custom injection molder specializing in precision engineered plastic parts for the business machine and computer industries. The FAME and Pac Fab subsidiaries are both headquartered in North Carolina, but Structural Fibers division and the parent firm remain in the Cleveland area.

The company changed its name to Essef Industries, Inc., in 1982 and simplified it to Essef Corporation three years later, to reflect the firm's growing diversity. It retained its former name, Structural Fibers, to identify the original core business engaged in the manufacture of water-treatment products.

Aside from Cleveland's progressive commercial banking services, Horner lists tooling resources, polymer research, legal and accounting services, availability of skilled trades, and what he calls "the quality of personnel" as major factors in his decision to base his company in greater Cleveland.

"The people are hardworking, highly skilled, and fair," Horner says. Dedicated and experienced personnel are thoroughly trained in the use of Essef's sophisticated equipment. They are committed to the most stringent quality-assurance programs in the industry. And they are committed to the company. Essef employees—235 in Chardon and approximately 1,200 worldwide—own stock in their firm. When Essef went public in 1987, approximately 250 employees were shareholders in the company.

"Today Cleveland remains the center for plastic tooling," says Horner. He attributes the availability of local expertise to experience gained in the development of tire-making molds in Akron.

"You've got skilled trades passed from generation to generation," Horner says. "Immigrants who were exposed to the Industrial Revolution in Europe brought the Industrial Revolution with them to Cleveland. It's the kind of thing that you find in Northeast Ohio. You would have a very difficult time in other parts of the country finding similar skilled trades."

Horner's belief in local resources prompted him to build a new plant on property adjacent to the present facility on Essef Corporation's 50-acre holdings in Chardon. Already in production at the new plant is a large thermoplastic container, the OverPac™, designed to hold 55-gallon steel drums of leaking hazardous waste. Horner sees another new market for large items about to blossom in molded plastic gasoline tanks for automotive applications.

"We're investing in a modern plant and in state-of-the-art technology," Horner says. "When this plant is done, we will begin modernization of the original plant with entirely new process technologies. We're planning to stay in the Cleveland area."

Essef Corporation of Chardon is a world leader in composite engineered plastics.

KEITHLEY INSTRUMENTS, INC.

Keithley Instruments, Inc., is a leader in the design, manufacture, and marketing of both electronic test and measurement instrumentation and software used for data acquisition and analysis. Its products and systems are found in universities, industrial research laboratories, engineering development departments, and quality-control areas of industrial electronics companies worldwide. Keithley provides highly accurate and sensitive data about electricity, temperature, and periodic phenomena. Keithley has a particular expertise in measuring very small electrical signals. In fact, the company has developed an instrument that can measure less than one-millionth of one-millionth of an ampere of electrical current.

Joe Keithley set up his own electronic instrument company in Cleveland in 1946, and he was pretty lonesome for the first year. His shop, which consisted of one room off a back alley, had a table, two benches, a drill press, some basic instrumentation, and a leaky roof. Since he hadn't yet connected with Cleveland's technical community, he was forced to solve his design and development problems himself.

Why did Keithley choose Cleveland for his business? He felt Cleveland was a good place to live and was a day's drive from other large cities with potential customers for his products. There was also a lot of electronic development happening in Cleveland at Brush, Victoreen, Ward Antennas, and Radiart. In addition, Cleveland had significant business and scientific resources at local universities.

His first product was a Phantom Repeater, an amplifier that magnified an electronic signal for oscilloscopes and voltmeters. The Phantom Repeater was built in a friend's manufacturing facility and shipped from Keithley's basement.

From the company's inception, Keithley established his attitude toward doing business: quality, service, innovation, integrity. The company has been known ever since for outstanding product quality and excellent service, both before and after sales. Some of this, admits Joe, was "learned through adversity." He still recalls his most embarrassing moment 30 years ago, when a piece of equipment that had been returned for service was accidentally shipped out as a new product. The error was corrected, and the shipping/receiving system was overhauled to prevent another such occurrence.

In 1950 a friend of Keithley's suggested that he build an electrometer, applying his expertise in low-level measurements to a relatively new type of instrument. After learning that another company made a single-range unit, Keithley decided to develop a two-range device. That first electrometer, the Model 200, and all its descendants established Keithley as a leader in sensitive measurement technology. As the product line expanded, the business grew. In 1956 the firm signed on its first overseas distributor, Toyo of Japan, a business relationship that is still going strong.

J.F. Keithley (left), founder and chairman of the board, with Thomas Brick, president and chief executive officer of Keithley Instruments, Inc.

Keithley Instruments designs, manufactures, and markets electronic test and measurement instrumentation. Shown here is a Superconductivity Test System.

ABOVE: Using real-time output of a model 194A.

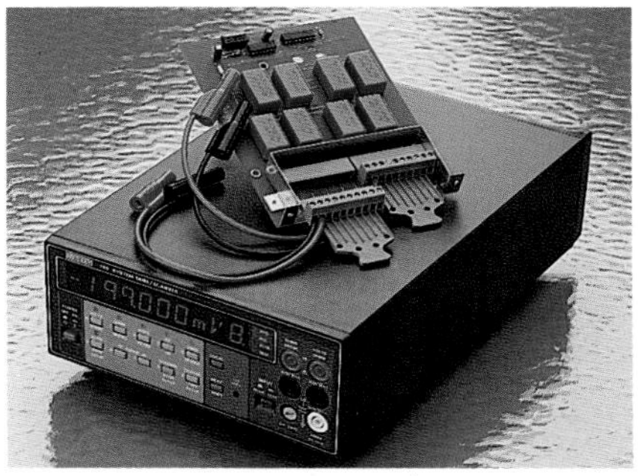

RIGHT: A model 199 System DMM/Scanner.

The 1960s revolutionized the electronics industry and Keithley Instruments. That decade saw the development of solid-state electronics, which led to more reliable instrumentation and digital readouts. Keithley took advantage of the improved component technology to improve and expand the product line. The firm was so successful that it grew from 25 employees working in 20,000 square feet of space and producing $1.325 million in sales to 206 people working in a new, 90,000-square-foot headquarters building in suburban Cleveland producing $5 million in sales. A digital multimeter, introduced in 1970, sold three times more units than the company predicted in its sales forecasts.

Foreign sales played an important part in the firm's dramatic growth during that period. Keithley sold $80,000 worth of instruments overseas in 1960, doubled that in 1961, and continued rapid overseas sales growth for the next 10 years. Keithley opened its first overseas office in Switzerland in 1963, established a subsidiary in Munich in 1966, and formed a subsidiary, Keithley Instruments, Ltd., in Reading in 1967.

The growth of the semiconductor industry, and with it personal computers, has created new market opportunities for Keithley to sell to engineering and scientific customers. Keithley designed and produced instruments that interact with one another and with computers to control experiments and acquire research data. The firm entered the software market, producing specialized research software for use with personal computers.

The company has received 10 IR-100 awards, which are given by *Industrial Research Magazine* to the 100 most significant new technological products developed each year. In addition, photographs of the 1985 and 1987 winners of the Nobel Prize in Physics show the scientists in their laboratories with Keithley instruments. The firm stays ahead of the game by working with area research facilities to develop ideas for products and to share new product advances.

Keithley Instruments owes its success to focusing on market niches, the rapid growth of the electronics industry, and its employees. Keithley Instruments demands a lot of its employees but also offers ample rewards. Employees know they are producing something positive and useful; they know their work is valued. The company's decentralized management approach places decision making close to those who are doing the job and to the customer. Keithley hasn't laid people off when times are tough, and it has a strong policy of promoting from within. It also pays 100 percent of educational costs for employees.

The result is a firm with a consistent 10- to 20-percent growth rate since its founding, one that has never had an unprofitable year, and one that continues to invest 9 to 12 percent of its sales revenue in research and development. Keithley Instruments, Inc., is a company that continues to succeed at being the absolute best at what it does.

A Model 617 programmable electrometer.

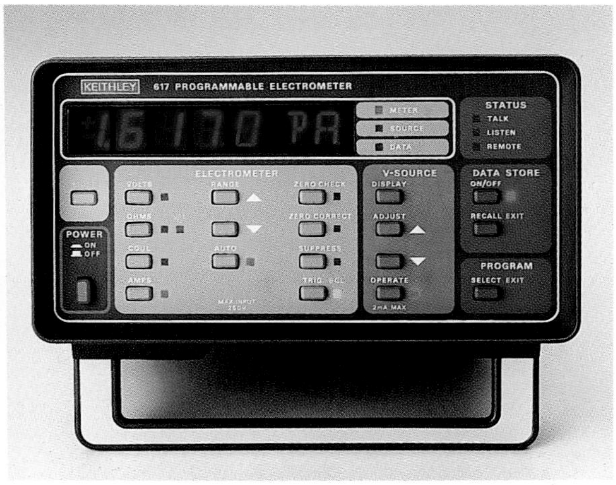

55
Marlboro
Lights

CHAPTER 12

Business And Professions

Greater Cleveland's business and professional community brings a wealth of service, ability, and insight to the area.

Photo by Roger Mastroianni

GREATER CLEVELAND GROWTH ASSOCIATION

(From left) William J. Williams, chairman and chief executive officer of the Huntington National Bank and chairman of the Greater Cleveland Growth Association; George V. Voinovich, former mayor of the City of Cleveland; and Thomas Vail, publisher and editor of *The Plain Dealer* and chairman of the New Cleveland Campaign.

The Greater Cleveland Growth Association is the largest metropolitan chamber of commerce in the country—and an active force behind Cleveland's economic turnaround. Working with business, professional, and institutional leaders, this nonprofit association is dedicated to three goals: economic development, community betterment, and direct service to members.

The chamber's history dates back to 1848, when the Cleveland Board of Trade was created to promote the city's commerce and civic welfare. Now, with more than 9,000 corporate members and nearly 12,000 individual members, the Greater Cleveland Growth Association is recognized nationally for innovative programs that are shaping the city's future.

The Association increases job opportunities in Greater Cleveland by attracting, expanding, and retaining business investment, and by creating an environment conducive to economic development.

In recent years particular growth industries have been a focal point of the Association's efforts. Target groups include headquarters and back office operations, health care and medical equipment, printing and publishing, equipment and manufacturing, and polymers.

Small business has an effective friend and advocate in the Association's Council of Smaller Enterprises. With some 8,400 member companies, COSE is the largest organization of its type in the United States and a significant contributor to Cleveland's national reputation as a hotbed of entrepreneurship.

To meet the needs of its members—both large and small—the Association provides business development, expansion and financing assistance, business advocacy at all levels of government, and a wide range of targeted educational programs.

The Association also is an umbrella organization for many projects and programs targeted directly at specific community needs. These include: Leadership Cleveland, which creates a network of informed, involved community leaders; the Cleveland World Trade Association, which helps local firms compete in the global marketplace; the Cleveland Regional Minority Purchasing Council, which fosters partnerships between minority and majority businesses; and the Build Up Greater Cleveland program, which has secured more than $600 million over five years to repair and maintain the area's infrastructure.

Because of its size, the Association can provide added services to its members and the community. The organization's research department, for example, provides corporations, media, and the public with timely and relevant economic data on the Cleveland area. Through its management of the Ohio Industrial Training Program, the Association has secured more than $5 million in state funds to upgrade the skills of nearly 60,000 area workers. And, through its Marketing and Communications Division, the Association promotes Greater Cleveland's economic development advantages locally, regionally, and nationally.

"The work of the Greater Cleveland Growth Association has paid off in record levels of investment, a lower unemployment rate than the national average, and a city firmly positioned for tremendous growth," notes president William H. Bryant.

Photos by Don Snyder

Greater Cleveland Growth Association staff officers (left to right): Carol Rivchun, vice-president, marketing and communications; K. Michael Benz, executive vice-president; John Polk, vice-president, Council of Smaller Enterprises; William H. Bryant, president; William R. Plato, vice-president, economic development; Raymond Kappenhagen, controller and assistant treasurer; and Carole F. Hoover, senior vice-president, government and community affairs.

ARTHUR ANDERSEN & CO.

Established in 1913 in Chicago as the Andersen, Delaney & Co., Arthur Andersen & Co. has offices worldwide and in almost every major U.S. city. It provides accounting, auditing, tax, financial consulting, management information consulting, and professional education services. The story of the firm is the story of many outstanding individuals.

The firm's founder, Arthur Andersen, was a maverick who defied turn-of-the-century convention by hiring college-educated accounting professionals. Leonard Spacek, the firm's second managing partner, campaigned for higher standards in the accounting profession and sought clients more aggressively than was sometimes considered genteel in the late 1940s through the 1960s.

The tradition of innovators at Arthur Andersen has continued, especially in the Cleveland office, where managing partners have always distinguished themselves by serving the Cleveland community and by becoming leaders in the firm's international organization.

Donald Erickson opened the Cleveland office in 1946. Arthur Andersen was one of the first major accounting firms in the area to offer specially designed services to smaller and privately owned businesses.

The accounting professionals at Arthur Andersen & Co. have made a major contribution to small and emerging businesses in Cleveland since 1946.

Many of these clients have grown with the firm, becoming major public corporations. Arthur Andersen is now one of the largest providers of accounting and auditing services to privately owned businesses in Cleveland.

Harvey Kapnick was Cleveland's managing partner from 1962 to 1970. He saw the firm become the second-largest of Cleveland's Big Eight accounting firms. Kapnick was a colorful figure in the city's business and cultural community. He gave generously to the arts and convinced other executives and corporations to do the same. Kapnick went on to serve as the firm's chairman and chief executive officer from 1970 to 1979.

Fred Brinkman was managing partner of the Cleveland office from 1970 to 1978. A native of Cleveland, Brinkman went on to head the firm's operations in many parts of the world including Asia during the firm's most formative years in that area.

Forrest Hayes, managing partner of the Cleveland office beginning in 1978, saw opportunities for positioning the firm to participate in the technological advances that have dominated the 1980s. Arthur Andersen has been a major player in Cleveland's transition from old-line, labor-intensive manufacturing to more automated techniques and in the increased merger and acquisition activity of the 1980s. The firm is a major provider of management information consulting services in Northeast Ohio. As systems integrators, the Arthur Andersen consulting professionals play a leading role in the implementation of information technology in a broad range of industries, including manufacturing, distribution, financial services, and healthcare.

One of Arthur Andersen's greatest contributions to Cleveland has been professional service to small and emerging businesses. The high quality of the firm's work has enabled clients to grow and prosper, providing steady growth and fueling the area's economic comeback. These accomplishments, along with the firm's volunteer efforts, make Arthur Andersen & Co. a major player in Cleveland.

BAKER & HOSTETLER

COUNSELLORS AT LAW

Baker & Hostetler is one of the oldest and largest national law firms in the United States. It was founded as Baker, Hostetler & Sidlo in 1916. One of the founders, Newton D. Baker, was a two-term Cleveland mayor, Secretary of War under President Woodrow Wilson, and, in the words of Justice Oliver Wendell Holmes, "the outstanding lawyer of his generation."

Baker returned from Washington in 1921 to run the law firm. Along with the firm's co-founder, Joseph C. Hostetler, he developed a philosophy for practicing law that continues today at Baker & Hostetler. The firm has always worked to create long-term, personal relationships with clients, serving the full range of their legal needs, whether they are individuals, families, or corporations. Baker & Hostetler has developed a reputation for dealing with privately held companies, some of which have grown into some of today's largest corporations.

In the 1920s, through Baker's guidance, the firm attracted large and influential clients across the country. Following Baker's death in 1937, Joseph C. Hostetler stayed to assemble an outstanding group of lawyers and increase the firm's client base. Most of the firm's growth has occurred since the early 1970s, and it now employs more than 430 lawyers.

The firm was founded in 1916 by (from left) Newton D. Baker, Thomas L. Sidlo, and Joseph C. Hostetler. Baker was a two-term Cleveland mayor who served as Secretary of War under President Woodrow Wilson.

Baker & Hostetler is among the nation's 20 largest law firms and has offices in Cleveland and Columbus, Ohio; Denver, Colorado; Orlando, Florida; and Washington, D.C. It is organized and managed as a single partnership; staffed by teams of talented, hardworking legal experts; and aided by the latest information management and communications systems.

Baker & Hostetler is a full-service firm, with lawyers practicing in virtually every area of civil law, including business and corporate, tax, employment relations and employee benefits, environmental, trade regulation, creditors' rights, litigation and trusts, and estates law.

The firm has special expertise in media and communications; sports; food, drug, and health care; and intellectual property licensing and enforcement. As an example, Baker &

LEFT: Baker & Hostetler's corporate practice includes many of the nation's major corporations and institutions, as well as several emerging businesses.

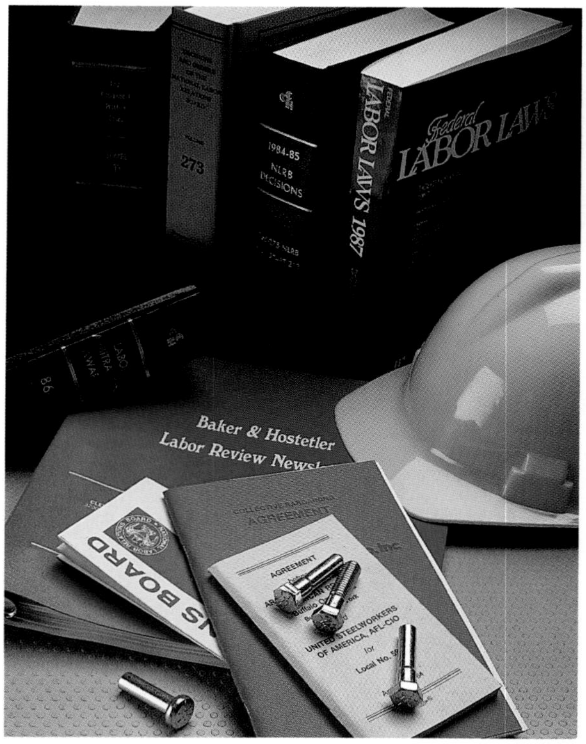

RIGHT: The Employment Law and Employee Benefits lawyers counsel clients in diverse industries across the nation.

Baker & Hostetler lawyers bring a multidisciplined approach to solving client problems.

Hostetler has grown to be a leader in representing the communications industry since 1922, when E.W. Scripps became a client. Scripps Howard, with its many newspapers and broadcast stations, is still a client today. Its New York-based United Media subsidiary works closely with Baker & Hostetler's intellectual property experts in guiding the licensing and enforcement of copyrights and trademarks for United Media's "Peanuts" and "Garfield" comic strip characters. The firm represents many other newspapers and broadcasting companies, including *The Chicago Sun-Times* and *The Plain Dealer*, Cleveland's daily paper.

Baker & Hostetler has been in the forefront in matters involving technological advances in the communications industry, such as securing new frequencies for cordless telephones and pagers. *Fortune* magazine termed the firm's work in communications law as "excellent."

As professional sports in America has changed from a national pastime to big business, aspects such as franchise ownership, team management, and game telecasting have become more complicated and the stakes higher. Baker & Hostetler has represented the American League of Professional Baseball Clubs since 1928, when the firm wrote the league's reorganization agreement and constitution. In 1986 Baker & Hostetler helped the Jacobs brothers, major developers in Cleveland, acquire the Cleveland Indians baseball team, ensuring that the club would remain in the city. Baker & Hostetler has also counseled the National Football League Management Council and the Bert Bell NFL Player Retirement Plan.

With health care emerging as one of the nation's fastest growing industries, Baker & Hostetler has again been a leader in serving the needs of that industry. In addition to representing individual physicians and group practices, the firm has handled many hospital mergers nationwide and assisted several regional Blue Cross/Blue Shield insurance systems in Ohio and New York to merge as well. Research institutes, PPOs, HMOs, and the world-famous Cleveland Clinic Foundation are all among Baker & Hostetler's clients.

In the end, it is appropriate to recall words that Newton Baker once wrote about democracy—words that are equally true of the style that Baker & Hostetler has always sought to bring to its work: Men and women should "cooperate to study and solve their problems, without envy or personal ambition, and find their reward in a handsome aggregate result in which their touch can be felt but from which their grasp is absent."

Baker & Hostetler—"a partnership of quality counsel and personal commitment to our clients, our profession, and our communities." Seated in the first row (from left) are John Lewis Smith III, Washington, D.C., managing partner; John H. Burlingame, executive partner; and standing (from left) G. Thomas Ball, Orlando managing partner; James A. Clark, Denver managing partner; and Gary L. Bryenton, Cleveland managing partner.

McKINSEY & COMPANY, INC.

Managing director James E. Bennett (right) stands with directors A. Steven Walleck (center) and Robert A. Garda in front of a directory of McKinsey's offices worldwide.

McKinsey & Company, Inc., is an international management consulting firm serving top management in businesses and organizations worldwide on matters of strategy, organization, and operations. The firm's mission is to help clients make positive, lasting, and substantial improvements in their performance. To carry out this mission, it places great emphasis on building an organization that is able to attract, stimulate, develop, and retain exceptional people.

McKinsey employs more than 3,000 consultants and support staff in 42 offices worldwide. About one-half of the firm's work is done in the United States, one-third in Europe, and the balance in Japan, Australia, Canada, and Latin America.

The company was founded by James O. McKinsey in 1926 in Chicago. He soon had a flourishing practice based on an approach that put business problems in the context of industry structure, competitive possibilities, and functional department integration. The firm expanded in the United States and overseas under the guidance of Marvin Bower, who played an important role in defining the consulting profession as we know it today. Bower, an attorney formerly with the law firm that is now Jones, Day, Reavis & Pogue in Cleveland, was the principal molder of McKinsey as it is today. He applied legal thinking and ethics to the business of advising corporations. This evolved into a conviction that the interests of the client must come first, and the firm must remain completely independent and objective. These are guiding principles at McKinsey today.

The Cleveland office of McKinsey & Company was founded in 1963 with a professional staff of eight—three principals and five associates. By the late 1980s the Cleveland office and its satellite office in Pittsburgh had grown to about 100 professionals.

Much of McKinsey's practice is devoted to helping clients develop and implement strategies at the corporate and business-unit levels. When organizational problems hamper a company, McKinsey is asked to determine the changes needed in key management systems, management style, corporate culture, and structure. If operational effectiveness concerns top management, McKinsey works on functional problems, such as research and development, finance, marketing, manufacturing, distribution, human resource management, planning, and control.

McKinsey's clientele consists of

Study teams from McKinsey's Cleveland office work with area corporations to increase their ability to compete successfully. Here, Jeffrey C. Sinclair, Kenneth J. Ostrowski, Richard C. Gridley, and Kristin A. Hayes are analyzing a client situation.

Research by McKinsey consultants into new and emerging problems in the business world has led to a number of widely acclaimed books.

organizations in all types of private enterprise—manufacturing, transportation, banking, insurance, retailing, and utilities—and public-sector and nonprofit organizations, as well. Although most of McKinsey's clients are *Fortune* 500 companies or their equivalents in other countries, the firm has also developed expertise in serving smaller, fast-growing companies.

The Cleveland office client base reflects this diversity. The office serves manufacturing companies, as well as businesses involved in consumer durables, energy, aerospace, and financial services. Cleveland's industrial clients include machinery, automotive, and steel producers, as well as distribution firms. Nearly one-half of *Fortune* 500 companies headquartered in Cleveland, Detroit, and Pittsburgh are or have been clients of McKinsey & Company.

McKinsey helps its clients increase their ability to adapt to abrupt changes in the business cycle, more sophisticated customers, and shifting distribution channels and to compete successfully in the global marketplace. This means, in large part, enabling clients to compete with foreign producers by increasing productivity and marketing effectiveness.

The Cleveland office has played a key role in McKinsey's manufacturing, marketing, and organizational effectiveness practices, and has also contributed expertise on the financial services, steel, automotive, and aerospace industries. In addition, some consultants have developed special expertise in corporate, business unit, and merger/acquisition strategy.

In addition to direct work with clients, all McKinsey offices have extensive internal research and development programs. It was research of this sort that led to the best-selling book *In Search of Excellence.*

McKinsey's contributions to the Cleveland community have been extensive. It conducted a study that led to the creation of Cleveland Tomorrow, an organization of chief executives from the city's largest corporations who are committed to revitalizing the city. When the Regional Transit Authority needed management assistance, McKinsey made one of its senior directors available to serve as interim general manager and carried out a study that resulted in major changes in the governance and management practices of the organization. Other pro bono work has included studies for the City of Cleveland, the Cleveland Orchestra, the Cleveland Ballet, the Playhouse Square Foundation, Big Brothers and Big Sisters of Cleveland, and several universities and secondary schools.

All McKinsey offices have a strong commitment to a one-firm policy. "One-firm" means that the firm can draw—with remarkable ease and efficiency—on the expertise of professionals worldwide. McKinsey & Company, Inc., employs the same approaches to work everywhere, constantly exchanging people and ideas among offices. A common mission, guiding principles, and strategy bind the firm and its people together. It is a truly global operator at a time when the world is moving toward a global economy.

McKinsey recruits only people who have a chance for a successful long-term career with the firm. Those who join the company have excellent academic records and generally have managerial or professional experience. The majority of the people on the Cleveland office consulting staff have M.B.A.s; others have Ph.D.s, J.D.s, and master's degrees in such diverse areas as engineering, industrial administration, psychology, and the humanities.

Jim Bennett, managing director of the Cleveland office of McKinsey & Company, Inc., notes, "Cleveland continues to offer ample opportunity for interesting work with forward-looking companies. Our commitment to quality service for our clients is uncompromising. The people who embark on a career with us will find their work challenging and stimulating."

NATIONAL CITY BANK

National City Bank has been in Cleveland a long time. Its predecessor, City Bank of Cleveland, was founded in 1845. The discovery of iron ore in northern Michigan, railroad expansion, and the discovery of oil at Titusville, Pennsylvania, all contributed to rapid growth in Cleveland. City Bank played a major role in financing that growth.

In 1865 the state banking system was abolished and a national currency was established. City Bank became National City Bank. The institution grew steadily, and in 1901 its assets totaled $2 million. It maintained a conservative policy and avoided speculative loans during the 1920s and was the only bank in Cleveland that never restricted payments to depositors during the Great Depression.

At the end of World War II, the bank opened its first suburban branch office. In 1973 National City Corporation, a bank holding company, was formed. It has grown to super-regional status with assets of $22 billion and banking offices throughout Ohio, Kentucky, and southern Indiana. National City Bank serves 500,000 people throughout Northeast Ohio and has a branch network of 82 offices.

Deregulation of the banking industry, interstate banking, and technological advances, such as electronic funds transfer, have created more challenges and opportunities for National City Bank than ever before. One challenge the bank has met head-on is that of maintaining quality in the face of tremendous growth. Quality in service to customers and in the caliber of employees is one of the institution's top priorities. In 1987 the retail banking group formed a Performance Quality Advisory Committee to codify corporate values. Mutual respect among employees and sensitivity to the needs of customers were determined to be the cornerstones of quality. The committee advocates courtesy, efficiency, and promptness for employees at all levels.

National City Bank's reputation as a high-quality bank rests in part on its excellent training programs that include employee cross-training, management development, and employee recognition. The Corporate Banking and Commercial Banking Management Development programs prepare employees for management positions in corporate lending, corporate services, and retail banking. Other internal training programs include internal audit development, trust development, and training in operations and systems management.

The same cautious approach that served National City Bank so well in the 1930s will benefit both the bank and its customers in the 1980s and 1990s. The bank has traditionally been receptive to new technology if it meant better service for customers. However, National City is conservative about offering new products until it's certain people want them and will benefit from them. In 1960 magnetic ink sorters were introduced and ushered in the computer age at National City Bank. By 1970 the institution had an automated customer information file and a Money Manager

National City Center, headquarters complex of National City Bank, in the heart of Cleveland's financial district.

The quality of National City's cash management services, such as state-of-the-art lockbox processing, earned the bank a unique designation of excellence from corporate clients.

Plan that provided customers with combined monthly statements. In 1972 a Money Manager cash machine was installed at National City's Westgate branch in Rocky River, becoming the first such ATM in Cleveland. Today National City Bank's Money Center ATMs are part of Money Station, one of the nation's largest regional electronic funds transfer networks.

The bank recently added Direct Link, a service that enables customers to call a computer 24 hours per day for fast, accurate information about checking and savings accounts. This service handles about 5,000 inquiries per day. In 1987 National City Bank introduced the In Touch program, which offers computer-based financial information to owners of small and medium-size businesses.

National City Bank has always been one of Cleveland's most active and generous corporate citizens. The bank's commitment to the community is expressed in several ways. First, its conservative lending policy benefits the local economy by encouraging sound business ventures. However, if a business customer encounters difficulty repaying a loan, the bank works with the customer to make the business profitable. National City Bank knows that a thriving small business community is essential to the health of Cleveland's economy.

National City Bank also works with neighborhood organizations, such as the Citywide Development Corporation and Neighborhood Housing Services, to rehabilitate houses, businesses, and apartment buildings. Because even helping agencies need help sometimes, National City Bank contributes to many of Cleveland's health and human service agencies, such as the Benjamin Rose Institute, the Phyllis Wheatley Association, and the Square Meals Hunger Program, to name just a few. The bank also supports a program that helps nonprofit agencies reduce operating costs.

National City Bank adds significantly to the quality of life in Cleveland by supporting the arts. A grant from National City Bank made possible the Cleveland Ballet's holiday classic production of *The Nutcracker*. The bank continues to fund this annual production and helps the Playhouse Square Foundation's redevelopment effort with financial contributions and personal involvement. National City's sponsorship of the Cleveland Museum of Art's Paul Klee exhibit set a record for corporate support of a single exhibit.

National City Bank, one of Cleveland's oldest and most respected corporate citizens, will continue to play an important part in the city's business, social, and cultural life well into the future.

The increasingly technological face of banking is symbolized by the $22-million annex to National City Bank's operations center.

A $2.5-million automation project, completed in 1989, significantly strengthened National City's position in the forefront of the retail banking market.

ROBINSON-CONNER OF OHIO, INC.

Account service teams are responsible for the delivery of professional services to clients.

Robinson-Conner of Ohio, Inc., is part of one of the largest national independent general insurance agencies in the United States. Its purpose is to solve customers' business and personal risk problems. Formed by the merger of the Workers' Compensation Service Company and Insurance Management Services, Incorporated, Robinson-Conner of Ohio is one of the few Ohio insurance brokers capable of providing a full range of workers' compensation services, insurance and risk management services, and life/group health-related services.

Robinson-Conner is most helpful to firms experiencing claims and losses and those with a high potential for claims and losses. Because Robinson-Conner deals with all aspects of risk management, the firm is of particular value to any company examining alternatives to conventional insurance. Its services include consultation on the design of risk-management programs, supported by claim management, loss-control service, and management of insurance services as appropriate.

Service accountability is provided by a professional staff with a broad range of education and experience. Computer analysis is used to forecast losses, analyze conditions causing those losses, project future losses, and develop realistic alternatives designed to fund future losses.

Robinson-Conner has access to an unlimited number of insurance companies and negotiates contracts tailored to a client's needs. The firm acts as an advocate for its clients, designing contract terms that match client need, rather than purveying off-the-shelf packages.

Robinson-Conner provides its clients with complete insurance claims management service. It handles the administration of workers' compensation claims, as well as employee benefit plans and unemployment compensation claims. It has the technical expertise to link its computers to the computer systems of the State of Ohio and private insurance providers, enabling the rapid reception and transmission of insurance information. The firm has built a reputation for professionalism among insurance providers and other agencies with whom it does business.

An example of Robinson-Conner's customized insurance management is its claims management service for hospitals. By prescreening claim forms, managing paperwork more efficiently, and ensuring that claims get to the correct desk in the provider agency, the firm has greatly increased cash flow for several hospitals throughout Ohio. Clients have come to realize how fully the company is committed to understanding their businesses, solving their problems, and communicating solutions in plain English.

Maintaining protection in the event of loss is critical to the success of every American business. Today total and complete protection is not available in off-the-shelf insurance contracts. It requires finding and identifying potential problems and developing appropriate solutions; developing solutions for clients is what Robinson-Conner of Ohio, Inc., is all about.

State-of-the-art microcomputer systems provide immediate access to client risk information and claim data.

MIDDOUGH ASSOCIATES, INC.

Middough Associates provided the architectural/engineering services for the renovation of, and additions to, this office and component testing facility for large construction vehicles.

Middough Associates, Inc., opened for business as a consulting engineering partnership in March 1951. The company consisted of W. Vance Middough and four associates. It operated out of a small downtown Cleveland office and had a client list of one: J&L Steel. The company grew slowly but steadily. By 1970 Middough employed more than 40 engineers and designers. Nearly 20 years later the firm has grown to more than 250 employees.

Initially the firm focused its engineering services in the steel and other heavy-metal industries. Cleveland was an ideal location—at the center of the Midwest's industrial region. But as other types of jobs became available, Middough decided not to specialize, choosing instead to let the firm grow in directions that challenged its engineers and designers. In fact, Middough's willingness to design based on client need, rather than precedent, remains one of its significant attractions to many clients.

The firm has taken on diverse and geographically widespread projects—from constructing an airplane engine overhaul facility in Singapore to converting Great Lakes tugboat engines from steam to diesel. It designed the propulsion system for three of New York City's Staten Island ferryboats in 1965 and a complete steel mill for the Atlantic Steel Company of Georgia in 1974.

Middough's client services reflect the changing requirements of industry. These services now include architectural design; machine and machine control design; instrumentation; materials handling; civil, industrial, structural, and environmental engineering; and electrical and piping system design.

As the company and its services steadily expand, a conscious effort is being made by Middough to incorporate new technology into its internal operation as well as its engineering and design work. Record-keeping and word-processing functions are automated. Telecommunication equipment enables information and designs to be transmitted to customers over the phone. Computer-aided design capabilities streamline production of designs and drawings.

To help keep its clients on the leading edge, Middough has developed expertise in process control—designing computer-controlled manufacturing facilities in which the entire process, from raw materials to finished product, is automated. This makes manufacturing more efficient and consistent than traditional methods and makes the final product more competitive.

Middough has the experience and expertise to produce a simple one-page engineering drawing or to manage the installation of an entire $100-million facility. From Singapore to South America, the company has designed manufacturing facilities while handling new equipment, speaking new languages, and adapting to the metric system. Whether a client needs a full range of engineering services or just one, Middough Associates, Inc., has what it takes to get the job done.

The waste-heat recovery system on the crude-oil heater at this major Ohio oil refinery was a Middough project. The recovery system preheats combustion air to 600 degrees Fahrenheit and in the process saves $7,000 per day in fuel consumption.

THIRD FEDERAL SAVINGS AND LOAN ASSOCIATION

Third Federal is a mutual savings and loan whose goal is to help people realize the "American dream"—owning a home. It's a simple goal but one that has kept Third Federal strong, through the nation's economic ups and downs, since it was founded in 1938.

The Great Depression of the 1930s caused mortgage foreclosures to increase from 75,000 in 1928 to 275,000 in 1932. In response to the deepening economic crisis, Congress passed several laws that shaped today's savings and loan industry and paved the way for the founding of Third Federal Savings and Loan Association. The Federal Home Loan Act of 1932 established guidelines for savings and loans; the 1934 National Housing Act provided insurance for home mortgages. Soon after, the Federal Savings and Loan Insurance Corporation was established to ensure the safety and stability of savings and loan institutions such as Third Federal.

The history of Third Federal parallels the dreams of its co-founders, Gerome R. and Ben S. Stefanski. As early as 1934 the Stefanskis pondered the feasibility of obtaining a federal charter for a new savings and loan. With a small group of civic-minded citizens from the southeast section of Cleveland, they requested a charter to establish a federal savings and loan near 70th and Broadway. There were obstacles, including a statistical report that said the neighborhood could become a slum area. However, the Stefanskis persisted, the charter was granted, and on May 7, 1938, the first office of Third Federal Savings and Loan opened at 6875 Broadway. The initial capital of the organization was $50,000.

Business grew steadily, and by 1940 Third Federal needed more office space, so it moved to larger quarters nearby. The new building had once been a bank and had a large vault, but it had been occupied by other businesses during the Depression. A tavern had been the most re-

Mr. and Mrs. Ben S. Stefanski, co-founders of Third Federal Savings and Loan Association.

cent occupant, but the wine was moved out and the money moved in.

On the organization's 10th anniversary in 1948, its assets were $9 million and it was paying a 2-percent dividend on savings. Third Federal was getting a reputation for paying good returns on savings and needed more outlets to accommodate the increase in business. Third Federal's first branch opened in a Cleveland suburb in 1957. Mergers with other savings institutions resulted in a second branch in 1958 and a third in 1961.

When the association celebrated its silver anniversary in 1963, it opened four branches—more than in any other year. Third Federal had 66,127 customers, 8 offices, assets of $150 million, and reserves of more than $12 million.

Although Third Federal continued to grow, the business was still based on providing people with a safe place to deposit savings and on investing earnings into the community. On its 30th anniversary a new branch building was erected in a western suburb, where statistics showed that every third person was a Third Federal customer.

The 1970s were boom years. Through mergers, Third Federal acquired 17 offices by the end of the decade. These mergers were profitable for the savings and loan and for the stockholders of the acquired companies. In each merger, all employees were retained, benefits continued, and customer services improved.

Third Federal was known for maintaining the largest general reserves of any savings and loan in the greater Cleveland area. Ben Stefanski, a survivor of the Great Depression, built up cash reserves "for a rainy day."

The rainy day arrived in the early 1980s, with high inflation and volatile interest rates. Because it had maintained large cash reserves, Third Federal was able to keep its mortgage rates a few points below the local market rates and pay depositors a slightly higher rate than other institutions. Despite the industry setback, Third Federal topped one billion dollars in assets at the end of 1982.

In the mid-1980s federal legislation gave the thrift industry more latitude. Savings loans were allowed to make limited commercial loans, offer trusts, accept demand deposit accounts, and invest in government securities. A decision about Third Federal's direction had to be made. Stefanski and Third Federal directors decided that the company should continue to do what it did best—make home mortgage loans. By not diversifying when other savings and loan companies did, Third Federal was able to expand its niche in the single-family mortgage market. Third Federal now serves the individual home-mortgage market in Cuyahoga and surrounding counties.

Ben Stefanski retired as chief executive officer of Third Federal in October 1987. His youngest son, Marc A. Stefanski, became chief executive officer, director, and chairman of the board at the October 1987 board meeting. He plans to continue his father's "plain vanilla" approach. According to Marc, Third Federal offices are utilitarian—"serviceable, but not fancy."

Third Federal Savings and Loan Association will continue to expand, first into the eastern suburbs of Cleveland and perhaps later into Columbus and Cincinnati. It will continue to reinvest in the communities it serves and maintain large cash reserves because these factors have made the company a success. Marc says he's going to follow his father's advice: "Just keep your sights on your objectives and your ideals."

Marc A. Stefanski was elected chairman of the board and chief executive officer in October 1987. He succeeded his father, who retired after 50 years of service.

THE HUNTINGTON NATIONAL BANK

The Huntington National Bank's magnificent office in the Huntington Building contains the largest banking lobby in the world. Constructed in classic Greek Revival style, the lobby has two main wings that come together in the shape of the letter "L." The Euclid Lobby (above) extends 224 feet, including the rotunda, which forms the intersection of the two arms of the "L" shape.The third-floor balcony (opposite, top) has an elegant coffered ceiling around its entire length.

The truly inspiring lobbies spread 50 feet wide between Corinthian columns made of Italian marble, which rise to a height of 38 feet. Each lobby area is surmounted by an arched skylight roof, five floors above the banking level. A transparent dome rises 84 feet above the rotunda. The Chester Lobby (opposite, bottom) stretches 310 feet along Chester Avenue. There are four massive Jules Guerin murals. The mural at the top of the grand staircase includes a figure representing Pierce Anderson, of Graham, Anderson, Probst & White, the architect who designed the building.

In the early 1970s a major restoration project was undertaken, which by 1975 had earned the bank a number of awards, including the prestigious President's Award from the National Trust for Historic Preservation.

For more than 120 years The Huntington National Bank has been a financial leader in Ohio, committed to providing innovative services and banking products to its customers and supporting civic and cultural life in the communities in which it operates. It brought that same commitment to Cleveland when it acquired the Cleveland-based Union Commerce Bank in 1982.

The Huntington National Bank is a subsidiary of Huntington Bancshares Incorporated, one of Ohio's oldest and largest bank holding companies. Headquartered in Columbus, the holding company's banking, commercial and residential mortgage, trust, and investment banking subsidiaries currently operate more than 246 offices in 11 states.

The bank's Cleveland office is headquarters for the northern Ohio region, which includes Cleveland, Akron, and Toledo.

Founded in 1866 by Pelatiah Huntington, The Huntington National Bank originated as an investment bank called P.W. Huntington & Company. In 1922 it obtained expanded trust powers from the Federal Reserve System, including the authority to act as a trustee, executor, and administrator for estates, and registrar for stocks and bonds.

In 1958 The Huntington National Bank opened its first branch office; its first suburban office was opened three years later. The bank doubled its assets between 1958 and 1966, when it was established as a bank holding company, and in 1979, when state banking laws changed, its 15 affiliates merged into one fully integrated institution. By 1982 Huntington was Ohio's fourth-largest bank holding company, with assets of more than $5 billion.

That same year Huntington made a strong impression on the Cleveland market by acquiring the $1.3-billion Union Commerce Corporation and its principal affiliate, Union Commerce Bank, which had Cleveland roots going back to 1853. The bank's downtown Cleveland office, located in the Huntington Building at the prestigious corner of Euclid Avenue and East Ninth Street, is one of the most architecturally dramatic and historically significant in the city. Opened in 1924, the banking office houses the world's largest banking lobby. A restoration program in the mid-1970s earned the bank a number of awards, including the National Trust President's Award for Historic Preservation. In 1988 Huntington announced a major renovation program for the Huntington Building and completed an extensive redecoration project of the banking lobbies.

With the acquisition of Union Commerce, the bank broadened its services, offering a mix of commercial and consumer banking services. Innovative products were made available to the Cleveland market, including simple-interest lending and personal credit lines. In addition, contracts and other lending documents were rewritten to make them easier for consumers to understand.

banker concept allows each customer to have a primary bank contact for all traditional banking needs, such as personal credit, student loans, and savings plans. If the customer has special needs for trust or investment services, the personal banker acts as the conduit to the appropriate person or department.

Both these programs are guided by a commitment to "precision" banking, an approach by which the bank maintains the highest standards of customer service.

Relationship banking and per-

The Huntington National Bank has been an important corporate citizen, participating fully in Cleveland's civic and cultural life. For example, the bank has played a leading role in United Way's Small Business Campaign and has made a significant commitment to education in Cleveland. Bank officers are active in numerous community organizations, including those designed to improve educational opportunities for the city's youth, such as Youth Opportunities Unlimited (a summer jobs program), Cleveland Initiative for Education, and the Adopt-A-School program. Through the latter two programs, the bank works directly with Nathan Hale Intermediate School and South High School, providing tutoring and other assistance, and recognizing students for attendance and academic achievements. One example of the bank's support of the arts is its major sponsorship of the Cleveland Ballet's production of *Romeo & Juliet.*

The Huntington National Bank's mission is to provide the best customer service and to introduce new products that will distinguish the bank in today's competitive banking environment. Because banking is built on relationships, the institution introduced Relationship Banking for business customers in 1984. Each customer is assigned to a relationship banker, who handles all of the customer's banking needs. Through their relationship banker, commercial customers have access to all of the bank's resources. Designed to help a business at every stage of growth, commercial banking services include cash management, planned expansion lending, and working capital support to international banking and specialized credit.

Responding to the success of the commercial relationship banking program, the bank introduced the Personal Banker program in 1986 for its retail customers. The personal sonal banking are a return to the days when people had a special rapport with their banker. Perhaps Pelatiah Huntington said it best when he said, "The Huntington National Bank aims to unite what is best in modern practice with strict adherence to ethical standards." This is Huntington's corporate philosophy, which is in operation even today—to combine the personal touches of the past with the technological conveniences of the present and future.

TOWERS PERRIN

Towers Perrin brings together the strength and skills of three consulting firms that have been serving clients for more than 70 years:

TPF&C, whose consulting practice began in 1917 in Philadelphia, was formally established as Towers, Perrin, Forster & Crosby in 1934. TPF&C specializes in total compensation (pay and benefits), actuarial, communication, and related human resource consulting services.

Cresap, which began in 1946 as Cresap, McCormick and Paget, merged with TPF&C in 1983. Cresap helps many of the world's leading organizations improve performance and enhance capabilities in strategy, marketing, organization, operations, and information systems.

Tillinghast, formerly known as Tillinghast, Nelson & Warren, dates back to 1962. It merged with TPF&C in 1986. Tillinghast provides actuarial services and management counsel to life and casualty insurance companies and related enterprises. It also provides risk management services to businesses, institutions, and government agencies.

Tillinghast led the evolution of universal life insurance, and TPF&C is credited with designing the first pension plans in the United States. Nationwide, Towers Perrin has more than 50 clients who have been clients for 30 years or longer, ample evidence of its solid expertise and long experience.

The Cleveland office, the fifth of Towers Perrin's 52 offices worldwide, opened in 1958. The city's strong business base made Cleveland attractive as a regional office. Cleveland TPF&C began with three employees and served a territory that included all of Ohio and eastern Michigan. That same area is now served by three Towers Perrin offices with a combined staff of more than 150 people. The Cleveland office has more than 65 employees.

The Cleveland office has a history of helping clients devise better, more effective pay systems and benefit programs, as well as helping them explain these changes to their employees. In recent years the firm has broadened its human resource consulting, helping companies design internal development, succession, and recruitment programs. The firm also does annual salary surveys in the Cleveland area and shares this information with its clients to help them maintain a competitive compensation structure.

The office has a firm commitment to enhancing the city's quality of life. It has consistently taken a leadership role in United Way and is a longtime sponsor of the Cleveland Orchestra. As part of its 30th anniversary in 1988, the office sponsored a special performance at Blossom Music Center, the Cleveland Orchestra's summer home.

Backing the Cleveland office is the Towers Perrin international consulting organization. It serves more than 8,000 businesses and organizations, including 90 percent of the *Fortune* 100 industrials, 65 percent of the *Fortune* 500 industrials, 50 percent of the *Fortune* 500 service companies in the United States, and almost 20 percent of the 500 largest companies outside the United States. However, Towers Perrin continues to treat each business as though it were

Secretary Beverly Bogacki discusses a scheduling need with office administrator Gay Dean as secretary Brenda Burston looks on.

From left: actuarial specialists Chris Garrett, Tim Swintek, and Henry Wu make extensive use of computers in solving client problems.

Practice leaders discuss how recent legislation will affect the firm's clients. They are (from left) Bill Napoli, Paul Mee, Paul Gewirtz, and Jim Reeves.

the firm's only client. In 1987 Towers Perrin quietly overtook its competitors and emerged as the second-largest management consulting firm in the United States.

The firm has a total staff of some 5,000 internationally. Because it has such a large network of offices, Towers Perrin can serve clients in their own geographic area. Nonetheless, Towers Perrin is a single company owned by active employees. A single standard of performance prevails worldwide—an absolute commitment to quality. Quality, for Towers Perrin, encompasses: objectivity in identifying, analyzing, and fulfilling client needs; providing practical solutions that can be put into action efficiently and cost effectively; establishing and maintaining good working relationships with clients; integrity; complete independence, allowing the firm to offer counsel and guidance based solely on the issues involved; ability, demonstrated by the high caliber of the consulting staff and the results of their work, the professionalism of technical and support staff, and the effectiveness of its computer resources; and curiosity, satisfied by a search for broader and deeper knowledge.

Effective communication is what holds Towers Perrin together. The exchange of information and ideas, in all directions, enables the organization to bring diverse experience and skills to clients' problems. This interchange is facilitated by a centralized training system that encourages networking. The firm also encourages employees to work on projects with people from other locations to get to know these people and their working styles, and to share their knowledge and experience. A computerized information system keeps client assignment records so that a solution that worked for a company in Cleveland can be reviewed for application to a problem in Paris.

The sheer size of the firm gives it an advantage over its competitors, enabling it to draw on experienced people and information sources from around the world. Towers Perrin is also able to attract highly qualified, productive people. The firm is structured to reward success; of 5,000 employees, 600 are owners. Ownership is by invitation, based on performance and contribution.

Surveys have shown that employees at Towers Perrin have a high degree of respect for one another. So all of them—both professional staff and support personnel—believe their work is valued.

Continued growth is Towers Perrin's plan for the future. Whether expanding geographically, diversifying services, or broadening its information base, Towers Perrin's efforts will have as its cornerstone—as it was in the past—serving clients' needs.

Employee benefits consultant Bob Hardin outlines the agenda for a client seminar with information specialist Sue Vitt.

BACIK, KARPINSKI ASSOCIATES INC.

To accept all challenges is the operating principle of Bacik, Karpinski Associates Inc., an aggressive Cleveland consulting engineering firm formed in 1983. Dale A. Bacik and M. James Karpinski were both well-known, experienced engineers when they decided to get more involved with their clients by starting their own business. The firm has expanded rapidly. It employs more than 40 people in Cleveland and 16 in the New York office, which opened in 1985.

The firm specializes in providing complete mechanical and electrical engineering services for health care, educational, commercial, and industrial facilities. Cleveland has been a particularly good location for this technological business. The city is a health care leader, and its economic renaissance has generated both renovation and new construction work requiring high-tech, professional engineering services.

Bacik, Karpinski Associates works closely with architects and building owners in new construction and remodeling. The firm designs heating, ventilating, air conditioning, plumbing, piping, electrical, lighting, security, fire-protection, power-distribution, and communication systems. It conducts energy-use-analysis studies and does site investigation, as well as providing contract administration services, such as cost estimating and construction management. Some of the more visible projects in which the firm has been involved are the $45-million renovation of the Stouffer Tower City Plaza Hotel on Public Square, the North Point Tower office building, and the extensive remodeling of Cleveland City Hall.

Bacik, Karpinski Associates strives for excellence, creativity, and dependability in both service and quality of work. The firm requires that clients' work be done both economically and according to the highest standards. It emphasizes the use of innovative methods to meet mechanical and electrical engineering challenges. Staff are reminded not to approach new projects with preconceived ideas, but to analyze them in terms of work requirements and budget constraints. "A team approach to projects takes advantage of the synergy that occurs when people work together on problem solving," says Jim Karpinski, vice-president.

The principals of the firm: Dale A. Bacik (left) and M. James Karpinski.

Bacik, Karpinski Associates' extensive experience with building renovations includes Stouffer Tower City Plaza Hotel.

The primary objective of the firm is to complete projects on time and within budget. It has established a strong reputation for living up to this promise. "Cost overrun" is not in Bacik, Karpinski's vocabulary, but "on time and within budget" is standard usage. Proof of the firm's success is referrals and repeat business from satisfied clients. For example, its first client, Kaiser Foundation Hospitals, has come back to Bacik, Karpinski Associates with more than 40 significant projects.

Part of what makes a consulting company successful is the ability of its staff to establish relationships with people: clients, fellow employees, contractors, distributors, and city officials. Because Bacik, Karpinski needs people with good technical and interpersonal skills, employee satisfaction has a high priority at the firm. "We continue our process of growth as our people grow with us," says president Dale Bacik. "Each individual on our staff represents the firm, therefore everyone is important."

The policies and practices of the firm give employees a great deal of latitude and, at the same time, foster effective operation. The firm prefers to promote from within, and if a

The firm has expertise in a wide variety of projects such as North Point Tower, a 20-story high-rise office complex.

staff member develops a special expertise needed by the company, a position is created. All employees get help with planning their careers, establishing personal and professional goals, and implementing them. Bacik, Karpinski is a good place to work, with competitive salaries, a merit raise system, excellent employee benefits, and a family atmosphere. Extras, such as company-paid parking, help with college tuition, and a profit-sharing plan, tell employees that they are valued by the firm.

Living up to its commitment to professional development, the firm helps employees pay for continuing education and supports their involvement in professional organizations. These activities keep staff abreast of changes in technology and in the consulting business. Bacik, Karpinski employees have been recognized for their contributions to professional journals and periodicals.

Bacik, Karpinski Associates holds professional registrations in more than 20 states. Membership in the National Council of Engineering Examiners provides immediate access to registration in other states. Dale Bacik serves on the executive committee of the Cleveland Consulting Engineers Association. Dennis Wessel, a principal with the firm, has served as president of the Cleveland Chapter of the American Society of Heating, Refrigeration, and Air Conditioning Engineers. Jim Karpinski has also been active in this organization. The other principal of the firm, Anthony Bledsoe, is recognized for his building code expertise and is a leader in this area.

The firm's participation in the Organizational Peer Review Program within the consulting engineering profession is another way it accepts all challenges. Bacik, Karpinski has received valuable feedback from the peer review process. The findings of peer review and subsequent implementation of the results were aimed at enhancing the firm's professional practice and its service to clients.

The firm is also involved in the engineering co-op program at Cleveland State University. This program gives engineering students field experience by alternating one quarter of classwork with real-world work. The program takes one year longer to complete, but its students are already experienced engineers when they graduate.

Bacik, Karpinski Associates Inc. is committed to the Cleveland community because it has fostered the firm's growth. Not only does the firm believe that teamwork solves engineering problems, it also believes that by working together the greater Cleveland community can solve any challenges that lie ahead.

The engineers at Bacik, Karpinski Associates are highly skilled professionals who specialize in state-of-the-art technology as demonstrated at Sherwin Williams Technical Research Center.

CUYAHOGA SAVINGS

Cuyahoga Savings was founded in 1893 as the Cuyahoga Savings and Building Company to provide customers with a safe place for savings and a convenient home purchase plan. It ended its first year of operation with $89,667 in assets. By 1918 the company had shortened its name and accumulated assets of more than one million dollars.

In 1936 Clarence P. Bryan joined Cuyahoga Savings as a teller. He worked his way up steadily, becoming assistant secretary in 1941 and treasurer five years later. By 1954 he was president and remained in that position until 1971, when he became chairman of the board.

Under his leadership, executives at Cuyahoga Savings were encouraged to be active in Cleveland's civic affairs. Bryan set the pace, serving on many civic and welfare boards in the Cleveland area. He was also a leader in the finance industry, both locally and nationally. An early proponent of corporate commission, purchase, and display of art, Bryan adorned the public areas and corporate offices of the Cuyahoga Savings Building with sculptures, paintings, prints, and wall hangings. Artists from Cleveland and Ohio are strongly represented. The collection also includes some of the great giants of the century, such as Miro, Segal, and Bertoia.

Clarence's son, William R. Bryan, followed in his father's footsteps. He joined the Cuyahoga Savings staff in 1962, was elected president and managing officer in 1975, and became chairman of the board in 1987. William Bryan has continued his father's encouragement of community service activities.

William R. Bryan, president and chairman of the board, at the entrance to the main office housed in the company's building in downtown Cleveland.

The main headquarters of Cuyahoga Savings, built in 1965, won the Cleveland Chamber of Commerce Building Award that year. It was the second private funds building to be erected in Erieview and set the pace for the outstanding development for downtown.

Cuyahoga Savings has been in downtown Cleveland since it first opened its doors on the fifth floor of the old Arcade. Eventually, it moved to the Arcade's first floor, and in 1946 it left the Arcade for East Ninth Street and Prospect. Twenty years later Cuyahoga Savings was the first Cleveland-based company to commit to investment in Erieview, one of Cleveland's early downtown revitalization projects.

Cuyahoga Savings is an extremely strong savings and loan company; assets are in excess of $260 million, and its net worth to assets ratio is 6.7 percent. This is 2.5 times the federal requirements.

It has distinguished itself by providing superior customer service and innovative mortgage and savings plans. Cuyahoga Savings promises customers personal service, product communication, and skilled employee training. Visiting branches, monitor-

Informative, educational, and timely material is available to customers and the community.

ing telephone calls, and doing frequent customer surveys enable the company to deliver on these promises.

Customers' comments reflect the success of this strategy:

"If I were a millionaire and doing all my business with you, I couldn't be treated any better. I feel that when I go into your bank, I am a person, not a number. Everyone takes an interest. You know everybody, and they know you. I enjoy doing business with your bank. With regards to service, you have it all."

Cuyahoga Savings combines customer service with community service. It raises as much as $12,000 per year for each of more than 30 nonprofit agencies by marketing charitable organizations' Christmas cards at the company's branch offices. It is also active in Cleveland Action to Save Housing (CASH), which makes home improvement money available to needy Cleveland residents.

An innovator, Cuyahoga Savings, in 1973, was the first financial institution in greater Cleveland to introduce adjustable-rate mortgages. Most other financial institutions did not start using adjustable rates until 10 years later. When interest rates began to rise in the late 1970s, 80 percent of Cuyahoga Savings' portfolio was adjustable. This allowed it to remain profitable when other financial institutions were experiencing difficulties.

Cuyahoga Savings continues to emphasize the advantages of an adjustable-rate mortgage to consumers. Such a mortgage is assumable by a new buyer of a home. It is expandable, eliminating the need to apply for second mortgages for such things as home additions or repairs. It is also portable—that is, once a consumer has been approved for a mortgage, there is no need to make a new application if he or she buys another house. All Cuyahoga Savings mortgages can also be paid early without penalty.

Cuyahoga Savings offers traditional savings products, such as passbook accounts and certificates of deposits. Anticipating the need for a broader line of financial services, the bank offers its customers checking accounts and MasterCard and Visa credit cards. In 1983 an affiliate, Cuyahoga Financial Services Agency, Incorporated (CFSA), was formed. CFSA is a broker/dealer and an insurance agency, offering mutual funds, tax-deferred annuities, tax-free bond unit trusts, and life and nursing home insurance. But the most important function provided by CFSA is advice. Financial counselors, using basic financial information provided by the consumer, explain financial choices. Clients are provided with strategies to reduce taxes, increase earnings, discover financial peace of mind, or all three. There is no charge for this service.

In the future, Cuyahoga Savings will continue to be very good at what it does—remaining financially strong and serving the community. It plans to develop new services as needs arise. Since it has such an excellent system of customer communication, Cuyahoga Savings will continue to create new programs well ahead of its competitors.

Financial seminars are given regularly for the firm's customers and the public. Close to 40 such educational sessions are conducted yearly. Shown here is Chet Kermode, senior vice-president/marketing for Cuyahoga Savings and president of Cuyahoga Financial Services Agency, Inc.

BLUE CROSS & BLUE SHIELD MUTUAL OF OHIO

America was mired in the Great Depression, but Clevelander John R. Mannix, a pioneer in prepayment health care, was optimistic in 1934, when the Cleveland Hospital Service Association first opened its doors. Mannix was so optimistic, in fact, that he bet a colleague a straw hat that the new hospital insurance plan would have 10,000 subscribers by 1939. Mannix, however, was wrong. It took the association just one year to win 10,000 subscribers.

Today Blue Cross & Blue Shield Mutual of Ohio, the descendant of the Cleveland Hospital Service Association, has far more than one million policyholders and pays out hundreds of millions of dollars each year. Moreover, it is at the forefront of helping to keep the region's health care costs down.

But cost containment has always been an integral part of Blue Cross' historic fabric. It was in the 1920s that Mannix, a Cleveland area hospital administrator who would eventually head Blue Cross in Cleveland, came to a simple but important realization: If the annual hospital cost of an area was to be divided by the population and applied to individuals, residents would only have to pay a minuscule amount for hospital needs.

With similar efforts sprouting up nationwide, Mannix' dream of prepaid hospitalization became reality on March 30, 1934. It was then that the nonprofit Cleveland Hospital Service Association, with the support of everyone from local hospital presidents to labor leaders, was incorporated. Giving it teeth, the association wielded the Cleveland Inter-Hospital Agency Contract, which, in essence, was a guarantee that local hospitals would go along with the plan.

Indeed, prepaid hospital care was an idea whose time had come. At first, only individual subscribers were covered, and even then they had to be part of a private company's group plan. But as the sub-

John R. Mannix

Ohio Hospital Association in 1935 (left to right): John A. McNamara, first director, Cleveland Hospital Association; Monsignor Maurice Griffin, pastor of St. Philomena Church, East Cleveland, a trustee of the American Hospital Association; Judge Brenner of Akron; Michael A. Kelly, assistant director of CHA; and Arden Hardgrove, superintendent of Akron City Hospital.

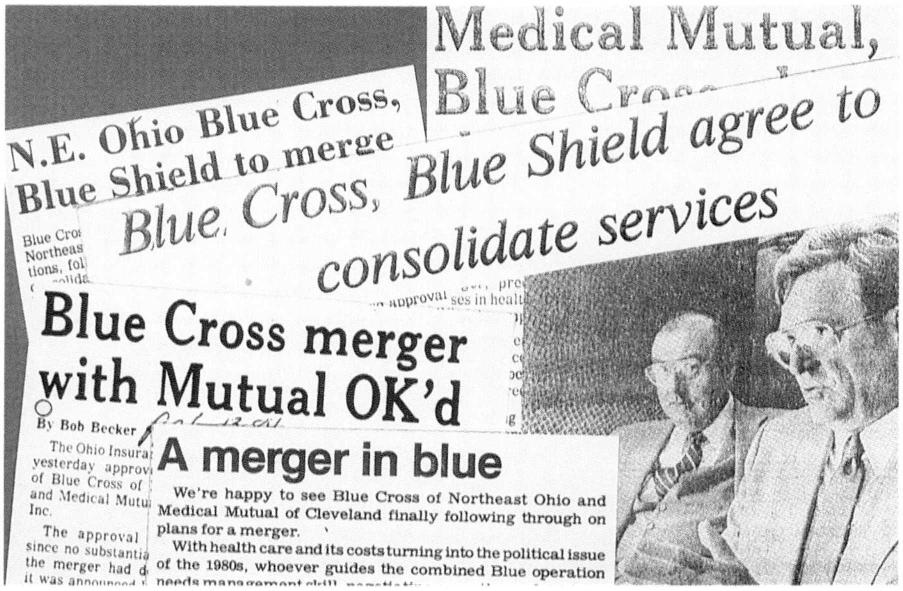
Medical Mutual,
N.E. Ohio Blue Cross, Blue Shield to merge
Blue Cross, Blue Shield agree to consolidate services
Blue Cross merger with Mutual OK'd
By Bob Becker
A merger in blue
We're happy to see Blue Cross of Northeast Ohio and Medical Mutual of Cleveland finally following through on plans for a merger.
With health care and its costs turning into the political issue of the 1980s, whoever guides the combined Blue operation

Newspaper articles reporting the merger between the Cleveland plan and the Toledo plan.

Blue Cross & Blue Shield Mutual of Ohio corporate headquarters.

scriber roles in Cleveland grew even larger, plan improvements came one after another, from including entire families to adding maternity care coverage. By September 1941 enrollment reached 500,000.

While Cleveland Hospital Service Association grew, a related move was afoot that would take health care insurance in Cleveland one step further—payment of doctors' fees. And while the short-lived Cleveland Medical Service Association sought to fill that role in 1941, it was not until Medical Mutual of Cleveland, Inc., was created in 1945 that the public had the benefits of prepaid doctors' fees.

Although separate entities, the Cleveland Hospital Service Association and Medical Mutual had strong ties, including numerous shared subscribers. Over the years, of course, both organizations burgeoned and, because of their respective high standards, were approved as affiliates of the nationally known Blue Cross and Blue Shield plans.

The years would bring other changes, too. In 1947, for example, the Cleveland Hospital Service Association left its original headquarters in the 1900 Building on Euclid Avenue and settled into the Rose Building at East Ninth Street and Prospect Avenue. A decade later that site became headquarters of Blue Cross of Northeast Ohio, the resulting corporation of the merger between the hospital association and its nearby counterpart, the Akron Hospital Service. And, in June 1984, when the merger of Blue Cross of Northeast Ohio and Medical Mutual of Cleveland was approved by the state, the Rose Building became home to Blue Cross & Blue Shield Mutual of Northern Ohio.

To enhance the efficiency of the companies, the Cleveland-based plan and the Toledo-based plan merged on April 8, 1986. The resulting corporation, Blue Cross & Blue Shield Mutual of Ohio, is the 13th-largest health insurance company out of 700-plus carriers in the country.

Formed as a "hospital service organization," the plan's Blue Cross components (the part that covers hospital bills) was required, under state law, to contract with all hospitals within its service area. As part of its efforts to contain the increase in health care costs, Blue Cross & Blue Shield of Ohio sought the aid of the Health Insurance Reform Act, which the state legislature passed in 1987.

The selective contracting legislation, which went into effect October 1, 1987, allows Blue Cross & Blue Shield plans in Ohio to contract with those hospitals judged to provide health care at reasonable prices.

The names and faces of the leaders would change also as men such as Arthur D. Baldwin, the Cleveland Hospital Service Association's first president, and Eugene L. Martin, Medical Mutual's first director, passed the mantle on to others. But through it all—changes in leadership, good economic times and bad—serving the policyholders remained paramount.

Still there remain challenging times for Blue Cross & Blue Shield Mutual of Ohio; the battle against high medical costs no doubt will continue into the 1990s and beyond. But people such as chairman and chief executive officer John Burry, Jr., remain optimistic. "I look forward to the next 10 to 15 years," Burry said on the occasion of Blue Cross' 50th anniversary. "No one knows the health care business better than we do. And we have the best health care system in the world, much of it right here in Ohio. The Blue Cross and Blue Shield Plan has played an important part in making all this possible, and I don't see our role going away."

Similar sentiments, no doubt, are what won John Mannix a straw hat a half-century earlier.

SOCIETY NATIONAL BANK

Since its founding in 1849, Society National Bank has been an integral part of the economic vitality of Cleveland and has prepared itself to play an even larger role in this city's—and the Midwest's—renaissance into the twenty-first century.

Samuel Mather established the Society for Savings, a mutual savings bank, at 4 Bank Street in what was then Cleveland's warehouse district. His and his colleagues' intent was to create a financial institution where wage earners could deposit their money and provide for their families' future. One measure of their success was the rapid growth of deposits and loans that allowed depositors to lead a better life and secure their children's future.

Another measure was the continuous need to obtain more office space to serve their growing number of depositors. The Society for Savings moved four times in 40 years, in 1890, relocating into Cleveland's first skyscraper, a 10-story building at 127 Public Square.

Designed by the architectural firm Burnham & Root of Chicago, the structure was completed in 1889. (It was designated a national historical landmark in 1976.)

Society prospered and served the people who worked in Cleveland's heavy industries, fully meeting their needs—even during the Great Depression. In 1925, at the request of the Cleveland Board of Education, Society initiated a School Savings Program that encouraged students to save their money and also taught them the rudiments of how a bank works.

Times changed, and Society's leadership recognized the need to respond to a changed marketplace. In 1956 Society National Bank was incorporated as a subsidiary of Society for Savings so the institution could provide commercial banking services.

Two years later Society for Savings reincorporated as a one-bank holding company, Society Corporation, a move that heralded a period of vigorous expansion. Between 1958 and 1979 Society acquired 12 community banks that served 16 Ohio counties. These institutions were located in northeastern Ohio, the Youngstown area, and in the Columbus and Dayton regions.

In the early 1980s Society refocused its attention on downtown Cleveland. The merger with Central Corporation resulted in the city's third- and fourth-largest banks becoming a much more competitive institution with improved earnings and streamlined operations.

Society effectively doubled in its assets in less than five years to become a $10-billion (in assets) institution and today operates more than 200 offices throughout Ohio.

Society National Bank is a major full-service bank that remains as responsive as ever to the needs of its local retail markets. On the corporate and trust sides, Society has gained the sophistication to meet the needs of these more specialized markets.

Society National Bank belongs to the Green Machine shared automated teller machine network and offers its customers access to their accounts through Money Station, another regional shared ATM network, and PLUS, an international shared ATM network.

Always an innovator in customer service, Society, in 1971, was the first commercial bank in Ohio (and one of the first in the nation) to use the on-line teller terminal, a sophisticated electronic data-processing system that immediately posted a customer's transactions.

Recognizing that anticipating the customer's needs and exceeding the customer's expectations are two keys to providing quality service, Society encourages its employees to outperform the competition by delegating considerable responsibility to its managers. They are on the front line and therefore best understand the specific needs of individual markets.

Ever since it effected the School

An artist's rendering of Society Center as it will appear when it opens in 1991.

Savings Program, Society has recognized the need for and value of a strong public school system. Realizing that good schools underpin a healthy community and a healthy economy, Society National Bank has been very active in Cleveland's Adopt-A-School program since its inception earlier this decade.

In a move that underscores its commitment to downtown Cleveland and optimism about the city's future, Society Corporation, parent of Society National Bank, will return to Public Square after Society Center is completed in 1991. Society Center will consist of a 55-story office tower that will be connected to its former headquarters building at 127 Public Square. The old headquarters building will be renovated to preserve its architectural heritage while meeting the needs of today's customers.

Society Corporation and Society National Bank will be the primary tenants of Society Center. Robert W. Gillespie, chairman and chief executive officer of both the corporation and the bank, says, "We're returning to our roots in Public Square."

Restoration of the old Society building includes removing a 41-year-old addition, major structural and mechanical renovations, and extensive cleaning. The banking lobby, with its entrance on Public Square, will retain its historic flavor.

The architect for the 850-foot-plus tower, a slender spire of light-colored stone, is Cesar Pelli & Associates. The tower will complement its neighbors on the square, the BP America Building and Terminal Tower. In addition, the complex will link Public Square and the Mall, two of downtown Cleveland's most important public spaces.

Says Gillespie, "Society Center is another realization of our commitment to Cleveland. By preserving the historic Society building and constructing a significant new property, we've combined the best of the past with a vision for the downtown's future."

Society's vision for the future is built on six values shared by its employees as well as steel, stone, and glass. Those six shared values are:

—A belief that quality should pervade all their activities and endeavors.

—An emphasis on initiative and innovation.

—Service to the customer.

—Commitment to fellow employees.

—Concern for the communities of which the corporation is a part.

—Dedication to shareholders.

"Taken together," Gillespie states, "these values form a durable framework for ensuring a productive and enriching environment in which to conduct our business. As long as we adhere to them, Society should continue to grow and prosper with Cleveland."

Chairman and chief executive officer Robert W. Gillespie (far right) meets with Society bankers from throughout Ohio as part of the follow-up of an employee attitude survey.

BOOZ•ALLEN & HAMILTON INC.

Booz•Allen's Cleveland office is the heart of the firm's worldwide expertise with manufacturing companies and in operations and strategy consulting. Much intellectual capital is developed here that is used to assist clients all over the globe.

Booz•Allen & Hamilton ranks among the world's largest and most widely respected international management and technology consulting firms. Headquartered in New York City, the firm serves its worldwide client base from permanent offices in the United States, Europe, Latin America, and the Asia Pacific region. Among these offices is the one in Cleveland, where some 60 staff members serve clients from the Midwest to the Far East.

Since the firm was founded in 1914, its professionals have conducted more than 55,000 assignments for 10,000 clients in more than 75 nations. These clients include more than 70 of the 100 largest companies in the world, more than 400 of the 500 largest industrial corporations in the United States, and 60 percent of the world's largest banks. Some 85 percent of its engagements come from companies the firm has served before.

Booz•Allen's professionals serve the top tier of management of the world's outstanding corporations and institutions—as problem solvers, independent analysts, and experienced counselors—in functions critical to their clients' strategic and operating success. Whatever the assignment undertaken, the firm's objective remains the same: to enhance total client performance by providing the insight, objectivity, judgment, and expertise required for the resolution of complex corporate and public policy issues. Booz•Allen is also committed to the design of realistic, achievable recommendations and plans of action. In more than one-third of its assignments, the firm is asked to assist in the implementation of strategies and recommendations.

Booz•Allen is a privately held corporation wholly owned by more than 175 partners, all of whom are officers of the firm and are actively involved in client assignments. To meet the dynamic, complex needs of its clients, Booz•Allen draws on the diverse backgrounds, skills, experience, and creativity of more than 2,600 talented professionals selected on the basis of both their prior accomplishments in industry and/or government and their achievement in leading academic institutions.

To meet the increasingly specialized needs of its clients, the firm has established numerous worldwide practices, each focusing on a specific function or industry. The firm's function-specific practices spearhead its work in strategy, information systems technology, and operations. The firm's industry-based practices focus on the financial sector, including banking and insurance; manufacturing; the aerospace industry; electronics; chemicals; consumer products; the information industries; the energy industry, including oil and gas and utilities; the health care industry, including hospitals, pharmaceuticals, medical equipment, and related businesses; the automotive industry; and the retailing industry.

Booz•Allen is especially oriented toward providing a global perspective on business issues, a viewpoint increasingly critical as the world economy becomes knit together and competition quickens on an international scale. Operating from offices in world centers of trade, Booz•Allen serves clients seeking new opportunities for growth around the globe. Local partners and staff throughout Europe, Latin America, and the Asia Pacific region handle assignments involving multinational issues.

Booz•Allen's approach to every assignment is precisely tailored to the specific needs of each client. In preassignment discussions, a Booz•Allen officer works closely with client management to define the scope and objectives of the project being undertaken. The firm then assembles a project team whose specialized skills match the assignment's require-

Booz • Allen's commitment to Cleveland dates from the early 1950s, when the firm began serving the top tier of the area's corporations and institutions. The firm's partners—long-term area residents—are strong contributors to the community, active in numerous civic endeavors.

ments. Each team is directed by an actively involved officer-in-charge. During all phases of an assignment, the Booz • Allen team maintains close contact with the client, holding frequent meetings to brief management, test preliminary findings, allow mid-project evaluation, and discuss emerging solutions. This collaborative approach is integral to Booz • Allen's consulting strategy.

Booz • Allen adheres to a strict code of professional standards and ethics that includes a mandate to avoid conflicts of interest. The firm ranks the confidentiality of the information it gathers and the proprietary interest of its clients among its highest priorities.

To maintain its standards of professionalism, Booz • Allen invests continually in the research and evaluation of marketplace trends, new management techniques, and emerging technologies. The nonproprietary results of these knowledge-building programs are often shared with the firm's clients through reports on Booz • Allen-initiated surveys and multiclient studies, through the firm's extensive publications program, and through frequently held conferences and executive briefings.

In today's fast-paced, unforgiving environment, management must move beyond simplistic categorizations and quick-fix solutions if it is to foster innovation, strengthen long-term performance, and sustain competitive advantage. Booz • Allen shares management's concern with—and stake in—the challenges confronting the international business community and is committed to working with its clients to frame insightful, realistic solutions to their most demanding and high-impact problems. Equally important, Booz • Allen's worldwide resources—developed and refined over 75 years of service—have positioned the firm to help its clients take the critical extra step from analysis to action and, in doing so, to close the achievement gap between strategic planning and strategic performance.

Booz • Allen's objective on every assignment is the same: to enhance total client performance. Through expertise-based consulting, the firm makes recommendations grounded upon rigorous analysis; provides insight, objectivity, and judgment relative to the issues at hand; and ensures a successful program of implementation.

ERNST & YOUNG

Shortly before press time Ernst & Whinney and Arthur Young combined to form Ernst & Young. The newly formed firm has 70,000 people in more than 100 countries.

The reception lobby in the firm's Cleveland office.

The belief that accounting could be more than mere bookkeeping is the bedrock on which Alwin C. Ernst built his practice that was to become the global professional services giant, Ernst & Whinney.

It cost A.C. Ernst and his brother, Theodore, $40 per month to lease their first office in Cleveland's Schofield Building, beginning July 1, 1903. Today that office is just across the street from the 1,100 people in the Ernst & Whinney Cleveland office, as well as the North-Central Region headquarters and the majority of national office departments. The firm now has 35,000 people in 450 offices in 80 countries worldwide.

Through the lean early years A.C. Ernst stuck to an idea that was novel for that time; he believed one of accounting's most important functions was to produce information that could be used to interpret and manage the operations of a business.

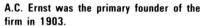

A.C. Ernst was the primary founder of the firm in 1903.

In 1908 he formed the special services department to facilitate his business counselor and management concept. It was the forerunner of a staff that now exceeds 2,000 management consulting specialists who provide business problem-solving capabilities to nearly every type of organization in the United States.

Today Ernst & Whinney offers clients professional service in audit, tax, and management consulting. The consultants range from merger and acquisition and information systems specialists to those with expertise in cost management, productivity, and strategic planning. The tax specialists work in many complex compliance and planning areas to help minimize tax payments for both corporations and individuals. The firm's industry areas of expertise include manufacturing, health care, financial services, insurance, retailing, real estate, transportation, and energy for both publicly held and privately owned businesses. The firm also serves state and local governments.

Ernst & Whinney's growth mirrored the explosive twentieth-century growth of Cleveland as a manufacturing and transportation center and was partially driven by the city's vitality. For example, such early clients as Cleveland Cap Screw Company and Cleveland Trust Company grew into today's TRW Inc. and Ameritrust Corporation.

Today it would be impossible to separate Ernst & Whinney from the greater Cleveland community. The firm is auditor for more than one-third of the public companies in Northeast Ohio. It is also the acknowledged national and local leader in serving the health care industry, a major Cleveland resource.

The firm has long supported virtually every major cultural and charitable institution in the community and is auditor for most of them. They include the Cleveland Orchestra, the Cleveland Museum of Art, United Way Services, the Jewish Community Federation of Cleveland, the

The basic philosophy of Ernst & Whinney.

Cleveland Museum of Natural History, the Cleveland Playhouse, the Cleveland Ballet, Case Western Reserve University, and John Carroll University.

The Ernst & Whinney Foundation provides matching gifts and grants that support special business programs at the university level. Another asset to the community is the firm's national training facility, the Richard T. Baker Education Center, designed specifically to meet modern needs for delivering high-quality, continuing professional education.

The international character of Ernst & Whinney can be traced back to its founder. In 1920 the firm had 28 offices and was looking to expand beyond the United States because A.C. Ernst knew he would need international ties to serve his clients and attract new ones. Three years later he got his opportunity when he went to London for discussions with Sir Arthur Whinney and Mr. (later Sir) Charles Palmour.

His new contacts were partners in the venerable firm later known as Whinney, Murray & Co. A working agreement reached during these talks would one day evolve into Ernst & Whinney International.

By the time A.C. Ernst died in 1948, the firm had grown to a total of 52 offices nationwide. His successor was Hassel Tippit, who continued the expansion domestically and internationally. In 1964 Richard T. Baker was elected to head the firm. He established its leadership in such key areas as health care and insurance.

In 1978, one year after Baker retired, chairman Ray J. Groves merged Ernst & Ernst with the New York-based firm of S.D. Leidesdorf & Co. The following year the formation of Ernst & Whinney International unified the firm's practice areas globally, and on July 1, 1979—76 years to the day after A.C. Ernst opened his Euclid Avenue office—the new name of Ernst & Whinney was adopted all over the globe.

Ernst & Whinney's worldwide revenues now top $2 billion, and the upward trend is continuing. "Our firm's excellent momentum becomes readily apparent when you consider that just five years ago, our revenues were only about one-half what they are today," Groves points out.

The key to maintaining Ernst & Whinney's competitive edge has been adherence to the Quality of Service philosophy articulated by A.C. Ernst at the turn of the century.

Quality in Everything We Do has become the watchword of Ernst & Whinney. Groves says it "means consistently putting forth our personal best. This involves drawing on all of our individual talents and capabilities—plus those of other E&W people as needed—to accomplish the task at hand. It is being able to say when we complete a job, 'I am satisfied and proud that I did my best.'"

The Richard T. Baker Education Center is Ernst & Whinney's national training facility.

KEEVA J. KEKST ARCHITECTS

Eastland Mall, Tulsa, Oklahoma. Photo by Peter Renerts

In the work of Keeva J. Kekst Architects, the disciplined expression of a fine art form converges with the deadlines and budgets of the business world.

Kekst has a rare expertise and specialty: designing developments for the investment real estate community. The firm designs single buildings and multi-use developments. In doing so, it draws on skills honed over 28 years in the design of office buildings, general retail space, shopping malls, hospitality buildings, and entertainment complexes.

Based in Cleveland, Kekst is national in scope. The firm is registered in 42 states and has an office in Los Angeles to serve western clients. Clients include Forest City Enterprises, Inc. (Cleveland); Homart Development Company (Chicago), a division of Sears, Roebuck and Co.; and Melvin Simon & Associates, Inc. (Indianapolis).

Kekst has completed projects in California, Oregon, Florida, and Washington, D.C., as well as in the Midwest. One complex includes a 400-suite hotel, an 850,000-square-foot general office building, a regional shopping mall, an entertainment complex, and parking garages.

In 1960 Keeva J. Kekst, licensed just one year, was fired from his first job. A speculative developer hired him on a contingency basis to design an apartment building, then the largest between New York and Chicago. A second job quickly followed, and soon several architects were working for Kekst.

Over the years Keeva J. Kekst has focused on creating a remarkable environment where architects pursue a double commitment to product and service: the highest quality of architecture and full understanding of the client's perspective and business needs.

Commitment to quality involves such factors as creating an excellent design, selecting superior materials, producing clear documents for contractors, and meeting regulatory code requirements, while creating a building that will serve its purpose and please those who use it. Keeva J. Kekst Architects is sensitive to the styles and values of each project's community and has won many awards.

In 1987 National Mall Monitor named the Kekst-designed Mall at Victor Valley (Victorville, California) the best-designed mall in the United States and awarded honorable mention for Ross Park Mall (Pittsburgh) in the one-million-square-foot category. That year the International Council of Shopping Centers named Kekst's Eastland Mall (Tulsa, Oklahoma), the best-refurbished mall in the United States. In 1988 National Mall Monitor named the Great Northern Mall addition (Cleveland) the best remodeling addition to an existing mall.

Clients want a satisfying building, but top priorities are at the busi-

Mall of Victor Valley, Victorville, California. Photo by Peter Renerts

ness level: meeting deadlines, working with budget constraints, and knowing other requirements, such as zoning regulations. Kekst creatively brings all these factors together. The service aspect of the firm is seen in its total client focus. To achieve that, Kekst assigns each project to a partner in charge, who becomes the client's personal architect and contact throughout the project. At any one time Kekst may have 100 projects; each lasts for 12 to 36 months, with different amounts of activity and intensity in each phase.

During each phase the partner in charge draws the architects needed from the firm's four major departments: design, technical documents, regulatory needs, and business. Each architect brings a specialized expertise and perspective. The senior designer, for example, sees the project in the context of design, aesthetics, and function; another team member may be an expert in structural steel; another may spend 90 percent of his or her time on regulatory concerns. The partner in charge coordinates the project within the context of the client's total needs.

Keeva J. Kekst sees the development of an extremely competent team as the key to growth, and the firm has grown almost continuously. In the past five years it has tripled as it took on more projects, including more complex ones. Of all U.S. firms, few have more than 60 architectural personnel. Kekst has about 180 devoted strictly to the discipline of architecture—more than any other Cleveland firm.

Spectrum Office Building, Independence, Ohio. Photo by Peter Renerts

Ross Park Mall, Pittsburgh, Pennsylvania. Photo by Peter Renerts

One key to Kekst's success is its mix of large, mid-size, and small jobs. Current jobs range in size from one with a construction cost of $4 million to one costing $60 million. Only a few national architectural firms can handle projects with a construction cost of $50 million to $60 million.

A major factor in Kekst's success is its pursuit of excellent architects in a wide range of specialties. Kekst recruits in many major cities and attracts the highest quality designers and young architects. Keeva J. Kekst calls them "a pinprick in the side of complacency."

Keeva J. Kekst is proud of adopting the firm's policy of transition of ownership. All 11 of the firm's present owners have worked their way up in the firm. As the first generation of owners retires, the firm will be managed by a second generation, also with many years of experience in the firm.

Today Kekst sees his mission as the creation of timely, timeless architecture, working within the constraints of the pragmatic world. In the firm he has built, the practice of architecture is a highly developed art.

LAVENTHOL & HORWATH

Laventhol & Horwath is an innovative accounting and consulting firm with a commitment to excellence and superior client satisfaction. This has been the firm's approach since it was founded in 1913, and it has prospered as a result.

Laventhol & Horwath's Cleveland office opened in 1918. It was relatively small until 1976, when Kerry C. Dustin, an accountant from another major accounting firm, was hired to expand the practice. Instead of stressing services in which the firm had expertise and then identifying customers who needed them, Dustin asked clients and potential clients what services they needed.

He hired professionals with the necessary skills and resources to meet client needs, including such nontraditional backgrounds as lawyers, appraisers, psychologists, and writers. This strategy has succeeded: The Cleveland office now employs more than 150 people. Through a strategic plan of internal growth, a steady flow of new clients, and selective mergers, L&H has grown to become the seventh-largest accounting firm in the nation and the seventh largest in Cleveland.

"Our strength is serving the entrepreneurial market," says managing partner Dustin. "We like to be involved in client businesses where the owners are still active and want to see the business expand. Our approach is to understand their needs, solve their problems, and create growth opportunities. We are client advocates, not sellers of canned solutions.

"Laventhol & Horwath also has been a catalyst in Cleveland's economic recovery. The firm has played an important role in many of the high-profile business developments in the greater Cleveland area, including the expansion of LTV Steel, the relocation of Figgie International to Cleveland, and the selection of Cleveland for the Rock 'n' Roll Hall of Fame and Museum. We also helped to start another $200 million in new business projects."

Laventhol & Horwath's philosophy is to provide services other accounting firms do not so that L&H is in a position to act as a true business counselor. These services are tailored to meet client needs in many ways:

The firm provides customized services in job training, insurance consulting, information systems consulting, appraisals, litigation support, special investigative services, as well as feasibility studies and operational consulting for nursing homes, hotels, medical service groups, and commercial/retail projects. Its client base includes companies involved in manufacturing, services, distribution, banking, insurance, and transportation.

Through its networking efforts, L&H contributes to clients' internal growth. Many of the firm's partners specialize in mergers and acquisitions, financing, and human resource development.

L&H also offers all the traditional services of an accounting firm: auditing, accounting, tax compliance and planning, estate planning, and business and personal financial planning.

By expanding organizational consulting/planning, health care, mergers and acquisitions, information systems, insurance, and nursing home and retirement community services, Laventhol & Horwath plans to continue growing in Cleveland into the twenty-first century. In fact, it has taken three floors of the gleaming new Renaissance Center at Playhouse Square, which will open in 1990.

Jack Burry (left), president, chief executive officer, and chairman of the board of Blue Cross & Blue Shield of Ohio, and Vince Campanella, L&H senior principal, discuss the major insurance company's dramatic increase in profitability and the creative consulting projects L&H has undertaken for the company.

The beautiful, new Renaissance Center on Playhouse Square, home of Laventhol & Horwath's Cleveland office.

HORIZON SAVINGS

Founded in 1920 as a neighborhood mutual savings and loan, the East Cleveland Savings and Loan Company became Horizon Savings in 1982. It became a publicly held financial institution in 1986, a change that positioned it to respond aggressively to the opportunities of a deregulated banking environment, including strengthening its presence in the greater Cleveland market. Horizon's recent expansion to the western suburbs demonstrates its support of the revitalization of the metropolitan area.

Horizon offers a variety of financial services through its growing number of branch offices. Among them are new savings instruments and investment vehicles to expand both customer services and corporate profitability. On the other side of the savings and loan equation, conventional residential mortgages make up a major portion of its loan portfolio; however, Horizon also specializes in financing luxury homes, autos, boats, and low-risk, mid-size, commercial real estate.

Believing that there is a finite amount of business available in the savings and loan arena, Horizon has planned an aggressive growth strategy based on superior customer service and strategic management. "We're very concerned that customers receive what they consider added value for their investment," says Horizon's president and chief executive officer, Lynn L. Fritzsche.

To let customers know their business is appreciated, Horizon provides traditional services innovatively. For example, once a week Horizon tellers go to the Council Garden Retirement Home so residents can do their banking without worrying about transportation or safety. Valuing customers also means that Horizon's loan officers will take papers to a customer's home, instead of requiring him or her to come to a Horizon branch office.

Community involvement is an integral part of Horizon's mission to serve its customers and communities. Managers and staff alike take active roles in demonstrating their willingness to help others. Whether it is conducting educational presentations on banking and financial services for high school classes and community groups or participating in fund-raising activities for local charities, Horizon's people are ready to show their commitment to serving their communities.

With net worth (assets minus liabilities as a percentage of assets) far in excess of requirements for either savings and loans or banks, Horizon is recognized as one of Ohio's strongest publicly traded financial institutions. Its sound financial base and its emphasis on caring for the customer are building a firm foundation for future growth and expanded services. As a participant in the economic resurgence of Cleveland, Horizon Savings looks forward to making additional contributions to and benefiting from this renewed vitality.

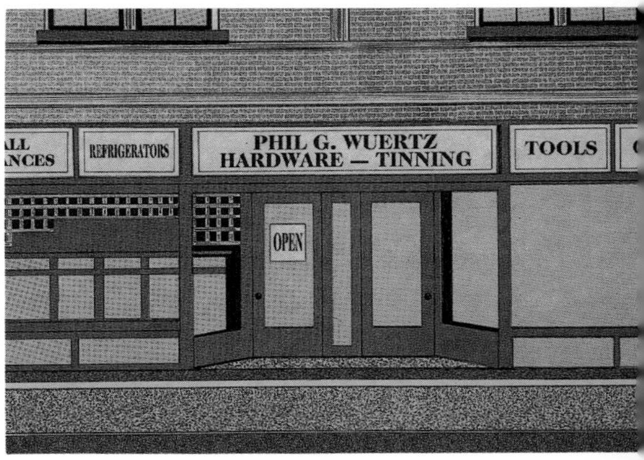

Originally founded in 1920 as East Cleveland Savings, Horizon had its beginnings in the back of a hardware store.

Horizon Savings, serving the greater Cleveland suburbs, is headquartered in Beachwood.

TOUCHE ROSS

Cleveland's Flats area houses LTV Steel blast furnaces. Don de Camara is in the foreground of a furnace site.

Clevelanders admire commitment. They appreciate hard work, dedicated people, and sound results. That is why the Cleveland business community values Touche Ross, the multinational Big Eight accounting and consulting firm that gives its clients a competitive edge.

Touche Ross was one of the first companies to recognize Cleveland's tremendous growth potential during the early 1970s. Impressed with Cleveland's strong industrial base and expanding technology and service sectors, Touche Ross realized that the city represented an attractive opportunity for growth investments. In 1976 Touche Ross made a commitment to Cleveland by acquiring the large, well-respected local accounting firm of Schultz, Krahe, Martin and Long, whose services enhanced those already provided by the existing Touche Ross Cleveland office.

During these early years Touche Ross represented small manufacturers, developers, and retailers, serving their basic needs for record keeping, accounting, auditing, and tax return preparation. With the help of Touche Ross, many of these clients grew rapidly, went public, and diversified. Meanwhile, Touche Ross was also growing and diversifying, entering into more sophisticated service areas, including advanced management techniques, mergers and acquisitions, corporate reorganizations, and computer systems development.

In the 13 years since Touche Ross first recognized the dynamic growth potential of Cleveland, the firm's practice has expanded tenfold. Today a staff of more than 200 professionals and administrative support people are serving hundreds of northeastern Ohio companies in virtually every industry. The firm's specialty areas include real estate, manufacturing, retailing, and entrepreneurial businesses. Many of the original Touche Ross clients continue to expand and prosper with the firm's assistance, increasing the city's expanding reputation as an attractive place for people to work and live.

One such relationship is with the premier Cleveland real estate developer Jacobs Visconsi & Jacobs (JVJ), which has been transformed from its origin in the 1950s as a small, private, real estate partnership into a billion-dollar enterprise. As JVJ's service needs evolved, Touche Ross specialists kept pace. Today, as JVJ explores new opportunities for shopping malls, office buildings, hotels, parking garages, housing, and other urban developments in Cleveland and elsewhere, Touche Ross assists JVJ with economic impact reviews to ensure cost-effective implementation of development projects that will provide the highest-possible economic benefits to their communities.

The Stouffer organization is another example of the Touche Ross ability to provide a comprehensive network of support services to assist clients in aggressive growth programs. Although the Stouffer foods and hotels operations have long been headquartered in Cleveland, they are today part of the multinational Nestlé Enterprises. Through acquisitions and new product development, Stouffer's Cleveland-based operations have grown substantially, requiring an increasingly sophisticated, international level of service support. With an in-depth understanding of Stouffer's business operations, Touche Ross professionals provide continuity in this high-growth environment. Recent contributions have included the firm's detailed review of

Stouffer's Frozen Prepared Foods building is in the background of this photograph of Ed Hicks of Touche Ross and Ken Jalen of Stouffer Corporation.

Stouffer's plans for rehabilitating a downtown historic structure. Ultimately, with Touche Ross assistance, Stouffer's received $8 million in rehabilitation tax credits for the project, close to one-third of its total costs.

Both Touche Ross and its clients benefit from the firm's ability to attract and retain high-caliber national talent. The excellent quality of life in Cleveland has attracted many Touche Ross professionals to the city from other locations. Many have been recruited nationally from outstanding accounting, M.B.A., and J.D. programs. All have been attracted by the unique opportunities for personal and professional growth that Touche Ross and Cleveland provide.

Touche Ross recognizes the importance of employee training and support in providing clients a continuity of quality services. The firm's partners and managers play a personal role in developing the skills of the newest members of the Touche Ross team.

In addition, all members of the professional staff participate in ongoing educational programs, including courses in their specialty areas. By encouraging personnel to develop strong skills in special areas of interest, Touche Ross is able to offer clients professional expertise in the broadest possible range of services.

The Touche Ross environment promotes creative thinking and an entrepreneurial spirit. Partners, senior managers, and staff brainstorm informally in search of innovative solutions to client problems. Anyone who is enthusiastic about an idea is encouraged to pursue its development. One such idea has developed into a firm-sponsored chapter of Toastmaster's.

A Touche Ross Community Task Force matches the interests of individual employees with professional, arts, and civic organizations in Cleveland, encouraging active involvement in the community. Many Touche Ross families participate in volunteer activities together, from the Shaker Lakes Nature Center programs to the volunteer activities supporting the Cleveland Orchestra and Blossom Music Center. The firm also supports United Way and many human service organizations with financial contributions and with the hard work of Touche Ross professionals. There is a Touche Ross employee working for the success of nearly every arts, civic, and trade group in Cleveland, repaying the community for the many opportunities that the city has afforded Touche Ross' professional growth and development.

The success of Touche Ross in Cleveland has been a reflection of the success of the city itself. As Cleveland approaches the challenges of a new decade, Touche Ross reaffirms its commitment to fostering growth and expansion in the community's business sector, and to nurturing new industries that will guide the city into the twenty-first century.

Jim Deiotte, Mary Ellen Rodgers, and Beverly Blazek (seated) at Health Hill Hospital for Children, a United Way Agency.

The Galleria is a downtown mall developed by Jacobs Visconsi & Jacobs. Pat Mullin shows the beauty of the lighted mall area in the evening.

SQUIRE, SANDERS & DEMPSEY

Squire, Sanders & Dempsey has represented Cleveland State University throughout its years of growth.

Squire, Sanders & Dempsey is the oldest law firm in Ohio operating continuously under the same name. Founded in 1890 by Andrew Squire, James H. Dempsey, and William B. Sanders, it begins its second century as a national and international law firm with more than 400 lawyers in offices in Cleveland and Columbus, Ohio; Washington, D.C.; New York; Phoenix, Arizona; Jacksonville and Miami, Florida; and Brussels, Belgium.

One of the nation's largest firms, Squire, Sanders & Dempsey remains committed to the core values espoused by its founders: a single firmwide operating philosophy, a diverse practice and a true partnership atmosphere, and the conviction that its legal work must never be less than its best.

The firm's practice is built around a double core of corporate and public-sector clients—from multinational public companies to emerging private companies and hundreds of federal, state, and local governmental agencies. This broad and diverse public and private sector representation is the hallmark of the firm.

By 1992, to better serve clients and meet the growing demands of its international practice, the firm will leave the building that has been its national headquarters for more than 60 years. When Squire, Sanders & Dempsey moves to the new 56-story Society Center Tower on Public Square, in the heart of Cleveland's downtown, it will settle in one of the most advanced law offices in America, with state-of-the-art library, telecommunications, and conference facilities.

The first commitment of Squire, Sanders & Dempsey is to its clients. To provide quality representation over the long term, the firm recruits the top graduates from leading law schools and offers them challenges as compelling as any law firm in the United States. Firm lawyers come from more than 34 states and 12 foreign countries. They represent more than 60 different schools, with backgrounds as diverse as journalism, music, education, engineering, and the Peace Corps, and they are encouraged to become proficient in more than one aspect of the law.

Corporate clients of Squire, Sanders & Dempsey include Centerior Energy Corporation, which the firm incorporated almost a century ago as the Cleveland Electric Illuminating Company; BP America, one of the world's largest oil companies; Bridgestone; USX; Union Carbide; Ferro Corporation; LTV Steel; Harris Corporation; General Electric; Lubrizol;

and the Ford Motor Company. Mergers and acquisitions, leveraged buy-outs, and tender offer transactions are standard services for both the firm's domestic and foreign corporate clients.

From its earliest days the firm has been recognized nationally for its representation of governmental bodies at all levels. Each year Squire, Sanders & Dempsey offers legal opinions on some 1,200 separate issues of bonds, notes, and other tax exempt securities worth some $2 billion. These offerings have included $101 million in Jacksonville, Florida, airport bonds; Cleveland Clinic construction bonds of almost $250 million; and Metropolitan Washington Airport Authority bonds of more than $200 million.

Among the professional organizations that Squire, Sanders & Dempsey represents is the highly visible National Collegiate Athletic Association. Educational clients include local school districts and major universities that receive counsel on a range of matters, including finance, collective bargaining, sexual harassment, and employment matters.

The firm also has a highly regarded estates and trust practice that includes estate and personal business planning, the representation of individuals in the control and transmission of wealth, estate trust administration, and the representation of businesses operated through trusts, charitable trusts, and private foundations.

The firm has more than 100 lawyers in its litigation department. At any one time they are involved with more than 2,000 cases in virtually every state in the country, encompassing the full range of matters that affect business today. The firm represents the Federal Home Loan Bank Board and the Federal Savings and Loan Insurance Corporation in numerous lawsuits arising out of savings and loan failures. There is an active practice in takeover contests, securities litigation, shareholder derivative actions, and first amendment cases. Squire, Sanders & Dempsey also handles a wide range of corporate and commercial disputes, anti-trust litigation, product liability, intellectual property, and toxic tort cases.

Squire, Sanders & Dempsey is one of the nation's leading environmental law firms. The U.S. Environmental Protection Agency retained Squire, Sanders & Dempsey to train personnel in implementing the State Revolving Fund Program created by the Water Quality Act of 1987 to stimulate construction of wastewater treatment facilities.

With more than 30 lawyers, the firm's labor practice is one of the largest of any national law firm. In addition to the traditional representation of corporations, its labor lawyers also counsel more than 200 municipalities, school districts, and other public bodies.

The firm's Washington-based federal regulatory practice represents large public and private companies, trade associations, and state and local governments through the entire spectrum of matters from energy to telecommunications to government contracts before all major governmental agencies.

Since its earliest days pro bono service has been integral to the life of the firm. In 1988 alone, Squire Sanders' offices devoted pro bono time valued at almost $.75 million. Since 1968 Squire Sanders' lawyers have staffed a full-time position at the Legal Aid Society of Cleveland.

Squire, Sanders & Dempsey performed legal work for BP America to help make possible the TransAlaska Pipeline.

Squire, Sanders & Dempsey is also involved in its community. It is a leader among local law firms in United Way giving. In recent times Squire, Sanders & Dempsey lawyers have led two of Cleveland's most ambitious community efforts—the $38-million Playhouse Square Center theater restoration, the largest project of its kind in the world, and the Cleveland Initiative for Education, the $16-million public-private effort to motivate inner-city students to remain in and graduate from school.

THE OSBORN ENGINEERING COMPANY

The motto, "Designing Tomorrow Since 1892," exemplifies Osborn's activities over the past century. Osborn-designed facilities are located worldwide. Each is specifically tailored to meet the needs of the time for manufacturing, transportation, sports, research, office, warehouse, and space-related activities.

When Frank C. Osborn founded the company, Clevelanders needed tires for their automobiles and bridges to drive over. Osborn engineers responded by designing structures over the Cuyahoga River and tire plants in the Akron area. They continued to apply new engineering technology as they designed other landmarks important to Cleveland history. The Union Club, Public Hall and Music Hall, Grays Armory, and the original Cleveland Trust domed building were but a few of their projects.

ABOVE: The Osborn Engineering Company designs corporate office buildings for clients worldwide.

LEFT: Osborn's staff of engineers and architects meets the challenge of the most exacting design specifications for projects such as this NASA Power Systems Facility.

In the early decades of the twentieth century, Osborn also became known for its expertise in sports facilities. Babe Ruth may have "built" the Yankees, but Osborn designed Yankee Stadium. Some of Osborn's other early projects included League Park and Municipal Stadium in Cleveland, Comiskey Park in Chicago, the Polo Grounds in New York, Fenway Park in Boston, Tiger Stadium in Detroit, and Lambeau Field in Green Bay. On college campuses, the firm designed stadiums for the University of Michigan, West Point, Notre Dame, and many facilities elsewhere.

As the United States economy grew, so did Osborn's services. Sensing that its clients needed more diverse expertise and would benefit from "one-stop shopping," the engineering firm added architects and landscape designers. Clients needed to come to only one office to find civil, architectural, process, electrical, structural, mechanical, and environmental help under one roof.

Clients also benefit from Osborn's involvement in professional organizations. Since founder Frank Osborn started the Civil Engineers Club, forerunner of the Cleveland Engineering Society, Osborn principals have actively sought to update technological knowledge. Their service on committees and as officers of state and national professional organizations has brought international recognition to Cleveland talent.

The size and diverse skills of the firm also enable Osborn to react quickly to problem situations. When a client's Arkansas subsidiary was damaged by a tornado, an Osborn team was on its way within hours, prepared to assess damage and plan repairs.

In the 1980s, under chairman George R. Shilling and president Robert M. Namen, changing political, economic, and environmental conditions made new demands on Osborn's technological competence. Designs had to be energy efficient, meet special ventilating and air-cleaning requirements, and resist earthquakes and explosions. The company employed the latest computer-aided drafting and design capabilities to deliver its

ABOVE: This collegiate coliseum reflects the firm's expertise in designing sports facilities from Municipal Stadium in Cleveland to Three Rivers Stadium in Pittsburgh.

LEFT: Corporate office interiors are specifically tailored to meet the needs of Osborn's clients for ease of utility, comfort, and beauty of surroundings.

multifaceted services. During this time Osborn also expanded as an international leader in new institutional concepts, renovations and restorations, food-service facilities, industrial and recreational complexes, stadiums, computer facilities, laboratories, and research centers. Its projects circled the globe and even helped the space effort.

Osborn's newer stadiums, such as Three Rivers in Pittsburgh and Robert F. Kennedy in Washington, D.C., were results of this advanced technology. At RFK, the partial roof has no vertical structural members obstructing the view from seating areas. It also has a continuous pressbox, a special mezzanine seating section, and a movable area that converts 6,000 seats from baseball to football use.

When the lights came on at Wrigley Field in Chicago, Osborn was there, too. In its lighting designs, it used computers not only to satisfy needs on the field but also to accommodate the surrounding neighborhoods. The massive floodlights illuminate the field without blocking the view of neighbors who watch the game from their rooftops.

The same kind of care and exacting service is extended to all Osborn clients. Whether *Fortune* 500 or small in size, the company's clients keep coming back. Many current clients seek renovations or restorations of earlier projects. The restoration and the conversion of Akron plants to corporate headquarters are examples.

Other clients want revolutionary concepts never before tried. At NASA's Lewis Research Center, Osborn designed a building for developing the power system of the proposed space station. The firm also has worked on perfecting retractable roofs for stadiums.

Because so many of the projects are challenging new ventures, Osborn personnel tend to stay with the company for many years. They also stay because they own the company. All stock is held by personnel actively engaged in the operation of the business. At retirement or separation, that stock must be sold back to the firm to be resold to other company personnel.

This intimacy with the firm imbues all Osborn employees with a sense of purpose and pride. Clients see this commitment as the Osborn family turns client problems into working solutions. Knowing that the future is only as good as the structure it is built on, clients continue to choose architects and engineers with a record of demonstrated success. For multifaceted processes in a multinational world, they know they can count on The Osborn Engineering Company, the firm that has been "Designing Tomorrow Since 1892."

ROULSTON & COMPANY, INC.

Roulston & Company attracts professional researchers and provides the freedom and resources to creatively pursue financial intelligence.

Ask most Americans to identify the headquarters of central intelligence, and they will say Washington, D.C. Ask many financial specialists, and they will say Roulston & Company, Inc., in Cleveland. As an internationally respected fundamental research firm, Roulston & Company has gathered reliable intelligence for more than 25 years. Furthermore, it has used that intelligence in the successful management of millions of dollars in investment portfolios for pension funds, profit-sharing trusts, foundations, institutions, and individuals.

The role of a fundamental research firm has been unique to Roulston and to Cleveland. Most other financial researchers use their data to support activities such as selling stocks, underwriting, or investment banking. Roulston has no such interests; its research serves as the basis for making investment decisions for its clients.

Roulston believes that basic researchers must have no conflict of interests. For that reason Roulston officers do not serve as directors of companies on which they publish research, nor does Roulston & Company buy or sell securities for its own account. Buy and sell decisions are made by the research department, not by salesmen or portfolio managers. The company's remuneration is based solely on a percentage of the market value of each portfolio. Thus, an increase in market value results in an increase in profit.

Because that increase in market value is a direct result of accurate economic intelligence, Roulston aggressively pursues its intelligence gathering. The firm specializes in approximately 200 companies headquartered in the industrial Midwest bordered by Pennsylvania, Michigan, Illinois, and Kentucky. Every day the firm has at least two dozen researchers visiting offices, plants, warehouses, sales operations, suppliers, and competitors worldwide. In any given year they travel well over one million miles.

Roulston's medium is person-to-person contact. The company believes that printed statistics and reports are less reliable than information gathered from face-to-face conversation and observation. Company policy states that researchers must have personal contact at least once a month with every company that the firm follows.

In analyzing the tire industry, for example, Roulston researchers visit major manufacturers in the United States every month. In addition, they visit every manufacturer in the world on a regular basis and contact 150 of the largest tire dealers in the United States every month. This consistent pursuit is what sustains the company's leadership in economic intelligence.

It also sustains leadership in analyzing the major industries of the Midwest. Throughout its history, Roulston & Company has been the respected authority on numerous industries, including the steel, appliance, retail, trucks, automotive, rail, ma-

A fundamental research firm, Roulston & Company, Inc., has successfully managed millions of dollars in investment portfolios for more than 25 years.

chine tools, chemical, and aluminum industries. Moreover, as the economic strengths of the Midwest have expanded, so has Roulston's ability to identify new trends and to track the region's changing economic base.

This dedication to gathering pure intelligence is nothing new to founder and chairman Thomas H. Roulston. From his experience on the Hanover, New Hampshire, police force while a student at Dartmouth College and his military service as chief of police in the federal territory of Alaska, he learned the techniques of good research. Accurate results require skilled manpower and sufficient funding.

Roulston applied those principles to Roulston & Company when he founded the firm in May 1963. Since that time he has attracted experienced, successful personnel and has given them the freedom and resources to creatively pursue financial intelligence that can be turned into actionable investment ideas. The corporate expectation is and has been that the research will produce a consistent 15-percent or better annual compounded rate of return on recommended investments.

The order desk at Roulston & Company.

The research capacity has increased the visibility of Roulston & Company and of Cleveland in the international marketplace. Roulston's London office opened in the 1960s and its Hong Kong office in 1987. In addition, every five weeks, the firm distributes to institutional customers worldwide a published report on each of the companies that are of interest to the institution.

Along with meeting the persistent demands of increasing international responsibilities, Roulston works tirelessly to improve the quality of life and economic viability of the Cleveland community. One of the firm's most significant contributions has been in neighborhood revitalization. In the early 1980s Roulston co-founded Midtown Corridor, a program to rehabilitate a wide geographic area on the east side of the city. Its leadership in renovating and landscaping a new corporate headquarters there earned design honors for the firm. Its renovation of the University Club, one of the city's historic buildings in the corridor, provided incentive for neighboring property owners to invest significantly in their own properties.

Most members of the firm are involved in civic and charitable endeavors. Participation in the annual United Way campaign is a condition of employment. Individual and collective efforts on behalf of numerous charitable organizations help enhance many areas of the city.

This civic involvement is just another example of Roulston's across-the-board pursuit of excellence. Throughout its history the company has demonstrated its dedication to an economically vital, attractive environment. Moreover, the firm's success at setting and meeting goals has demonstrated the importance of combining extraordinary commitment with exceptional resources. In the world of tomorrow, these commitments will become even more important. Thus, greater Clevelanders are justifiably proud of the leadership of Roulston & Company, Inc., the central intelligence agency of the North Coast.

Morning meetings provide a free flow of information among the professionals at the firm.

CONVENTION & VISITORS BUREAU OF GREATER CLEVELAND

Its business is to sell Cleveland—the hotels and convention centers, entertainment and shopping, friendliness and service. The Convention & Visitors Bureau of Greater Cleveland is an independent marketing and sales organization that aggressively promotes Cleveland to the convention, trade show, and tourism industries.

Tourism is big business. Nationwide, it is an increasingly important source of income and employment: Conventions and trade shows are a $15-billion industry with an annual growth rate of 4.6 percent.

And in Cleveland, a city that has just begun to tap tourism's economic potential, service to visitors provided the equivalent of full-time employment for more than 28,000 people. Visitors—people from at least 100 miles away—spend $1.25 billion in greater Cleveland in just one year.

How has Cleveland become a destination for convention-goers and travelers? The bureau's president, Dale R. Finley, enumerates several key factors: Cleveland's coastline, its major-league sports and entertainment, its easy accessibility, its friendliness and affordability, and its economic and social turnaround.

As a major city on America's North Coast, Cleveland offers attractions such as a now-clean and sparkling Lake Erie and 90 miles of urban coastline, plus the Cuyahoga River. The Flats offers prime riverfront entertainment on a working waterway; nearby is the development of the North Coast Harbor.

Greater Cleveland's high ranking as a metropolitan area—it has a buying income of $34 million—gives it the economic clout to demand the best in entertainment, sports, recreation, cultural institutions, and dining.

Cleveland has emerged as a major entertainment center. Visitors can begin the evening with a performance in Playhouse Square, which boasts three magnificently renovated theaters, or at Front Row, and continue into the wee hours of the morning in the lively atmosphere of the Flats.

Highlighting Cleveland's annual events are the Cleveland National Air Show and the Budweiser-Cleveland Grand Prix, a CART-sanctioned Indy car race. Other annual events range from the Mid-America Boat Show to the National Rib Cook-Off.

The beautifully landscaped grounds of the Cleveland Museum of Art welcome art lovers to many outstanding exhibits such as the paintings by Spanish masters, the medieval Guelph treasure, and the Oriental and Middle Eastern works of art.

A major city on the now-clean sparkling Lake Erie, Cleveland is a prime choice for trade shows, conventions, and tourists lured by the successful promotional efforts of the Convention & Visitors Bureau of Greater Cleveland.

As the population looks for travel destinations close to home and easier on the pocketbook, Cleveland has come into its own: 50 percent of the population of the United States and Canada is located within 500 miles of Cleveland. Added to that are Cleveland's affordability compared to other big cities, its ethnic diversity, and its reputation for friendliness and hospitality.

To promote Cleveland and its attractions, the bureau has seven salespeople—five focus exclusively on conventions and trade shows and two focus on the travel and tourism industry. Other bureau staff include a membership public relations and communications division, convention services, and other support staff.

What goes into an organization's selection of Cleveland as a convention site? The bureau maintains active files on 4,000 national and international organizations. To sell

Cleveland, a salesperson determines the next open convention date for each organization, identifies the specialized needs and attractions for that organization, maintains contact with the organization's central office, identifies members in greater Cleveland and makes sales calls to them, and invites the organization's meeting planners to Cleveland for an on-site inspection tailored to their needs.

After Cleveland has been selected as a finalist for a convention site, the bureau's staff sells Cleveland's advantages over its contenders and prepares a presentation for the meeting where members will vote on the convention location. In marketing to conventions and trade shows, the bureau promotes facilities and services geared to the scope and nature of the client's needs, whether those needs are education or entertainment oriented.

Chief among these facilities are the Convention Center, which has undergone a $28-million renovation, and the International Exposition (I-X) Center, noted in the *Guinness Book of World Records* as the largest single-building exposition facility in the world. Incidentally, the bureau is independent of these centers and all other Cleveland services and attractions it markets.

The bureau's sales effort to the convention and trade-show audience is supported by advertising in trade publications, promotional literature and publications, media kits, personal presentations, audiovisual programs, and on-site inspections.

In addition to providing extensive information on Cleveland attractions and events, the bureau produces the Destination Planning Guide detailing services and accommodations available. The bureau also provides a full complement of services to make the convention run as smoothly and pleasantly as possible. Bureau staff members provide promotional literature to build convention attendance and assist with program planning and publicity. The organization also provides coordination of hotel reservations, registration services at the convention, and official visitor guides listing attractions for convention-goers to see and do.

For all Cleveland visitors, the bureau staffs information centers at several sites, including the Tower City Center and Nautica. It also provides calendars of monthly events to hotels; official visitor guides; a recorded, fun phone; a visitor information line; and maps.

The Convention & Visitors Bureau also attracts pleasure travelers to the greater Cleveland area. Two salespeople focus exclusively on tour planners, motorcoach operators, travel operators, and travel writers, educating them on greater Cleveland's many advantages.

The bureau offers group tour op-

ABOVE: The bureau staffs information centers at several sites, including Tower City Center and Nautica.

LEFT: Playhouse Square and its three magnificently remodeled theaters is part of a revitalized downtown Cleveland.

Polar bears beg for handouts at the Cleveland Metropark Zoo, one of the finest in the country.

erators a city with many attractions: a big city with the best in entertainment, cultural institutions, sports, recreation, and dining. To market these attractions, the bureau represents Cleveland at major travel industry meetings for domestic and international tour planners.

The bureau also publishes a comprehensive planning manual for motorcoach tour operators, helps companies develop travel packages to the Cleveland area, and conducts familiarization tours. It also helps coordinate and promote area activities, events, and attractions for U.S. and international brokers.

According to Finley, the bureau is a business no different from any other business. A widget company has a product, advertising and sales, service, and research and development. The bureau's widget is the facilities and attractions of Cleveland.

The Convention & Visitors Bureau is very much a business, a point dramatized by its recent move into the corporate-type surroundings of Tower City Center. Indeed, the Terminal Tower was the bureau's first home.

Founded in 1929 as part of the chamber of commerce, the bureau was incorporated in January 1934 as an independent, not-for-profit organization. Its chairmen over the years constitute a who's who of Cleveland, with names such as Louis Seltzer, Tom Vail, Jim Carney, Lee Howley, Sr., Bill Boykin, Ruth Miller, and William N. Hulett.

The bureau today is owned by 200-plus members. Each year its chairman appoints a nominating committee to name 84 board members. Nine are public officials: Cleveland's mayor, the president of the city council, and all county commissioners. The other 75, who serve a three-year term, represent the community's corporations, banks, hotels, and suppliers.

Among the services and benefits of membership is a hospitality training program that reflects well on the member's organization as well as on Cleveland in general. The bureau helps set the tone for how visitors are treated, helping improve the perception of Cleveland. The bureau wants visitors to take away and leave behind very specific things: to take a positive impression of Cleveland and to leave dollars here . . . to have such a good time that they return to Cleveland, and tell friends, relatives, and associates how great Cleveland is.

The bureau's success in bringing a convention to the city is intimately related to the quality of the product. Whether a convention comes depends on the presence of the right hotel and convenient accommodations downtown. It depends on how the organization's planners perceive Cleveland and ultimately on how the organization's members perceive Cleveland.

Likewise, the history of the bureau is directly related to the changes in Cleveland. For many years the bureau was run by a tiny staff headed by Ed Brennen, who was not only chief operating officer but also one of the bureau's only two salespeople.

For years Cleveland enjoyed national prominence: It had one of the

Severance Hall is the home of the Cleveland Orchestra, conducted by Christoph von Dohnányi. Reputed to be one of the finest in the world, the orchestra has toured the United States and abroad.

first convention centers in the United States and a vital core city with 5,000 downtown hotel rooms. Then began a very slow, imperceptible slide typical in the Midwest: Activity moved to the suburbs; downtown hotels and theaters closed; and no new taxes or revitalization occurred. At the same time other cities enjoyed growth and revitalization.

Cleveland's comeback as a convention and tourist city depended on the revitalization of the city: the construction of new downtown hotels, $2 billion worth of downtown construction, the revitalization of Playhouse Square and the Flats, and projects such as Nautica and the North Coast Harbor.

In addition to these changes, all essential to the bureau's activity and development, there was another factor especially important for the bureau's funding. Ohio enacted a law in 1980 that allows county commissioners to pass a countywide hotel-motel occupancy tax of up to 3 percent. That bed tax put the bureau into position for the twenty-first century: The bed tax paid by visitors accounts for 92 to 95 percent of the bureau's budget, which now totals $3.1 million per year; most of the balance comes from membership fees.

In 1983 the bureau made a 25-year commitment of $1.2 million per year to underwrite the amortization costs of renovating the Convention Center. By the time the renovation was complete, several other significant events had also occurred, most notably the construction of large hotels downtown, the revitalization of Playhouse Square, and the activity in the Flats. Today Cleveland's turnaround is well under way.

The bureau itself has undertaken a comprehensive plan with several key goals. One goal is to increase business, government, and general awareness of the importance of convention and tourism business. Another goal of the bureau is to increase future convention bookings more than the national rate of growth.

Greater Cleveland's reputation has not caught up with the positive reality—the reverse of what is true for other convention cities whose reputation is greater than the reality. Finley looks forward to the not-so-distant future when the media and the public in other cities will perceive Cleveland as an outstanding city. He believes Cleveland can become one of the nation's first-tier cities, with all the accompanying benefits for both visitors and Cleveland.

Business is booming at the Galleria, one of the many shopping centers that has aided in the economic growth of the greater Cleveland area.

Cleveland Municipal Stadium is a favorite spot for baseball and football fans of the Cleveland Indians and Cleveland Browns.

NEW YORK LIFE INSURANCE COMPANY

LEFT: From left (standing): Sidney G. Halpern, agent, New York Life Insurance Company, with clients Jon Munson, Tom Munson, and (seated) Robert Munson, all of Phillips/Day & Maddock, Inc.

CENTER: Craig W. Koenig (seated) and Brian E. Koenig of Koenig Sporting Goods.

RIGHT: Edwin Arsham (right), CLU, agent, New York Life Insurance Company, with Sheldon G. Adelman of Blue Coral, Inc.

Cleveland was on the western frontier when New York Life Insurance Company began selling insurance in the city, paying off on several claims involving policyholders killed by arrows.

The first New York Life policyholder in Ohio was Israel S. Converse, a 40-year-old Clevelander who bought a $10,000 policy in 1845. A more famous policyholder and greater Cleveland resident was President James A. Garfield.

Today the value of New York Life's total life insurance on Ohioans amounts to more than $5 billion.

The insurance company's investment in Cleveland, spearheaded by its Shaker Heights and northern Ohio general offices, is much more than a collection of insurance policies. The firm supplied the financing for the National City Center building and other city projects such as the Diamond Shamrock building and the Ohio Savings Plaza.

On a more personal level, executives from both the Shaker Heights and northern Ohio office have taken part in Junior Achievement/Project Business Programs and one, Robert Cromar, served as president of the Cleveland Playhouse. In the past 10 years the company and its employees have contributed more than $100,000 to United Way in Cleveland.

The Cleveland area has been one of the most profitable for the firm, ranking fifth in the nation for insurance sold. It has produced five of the leading agents of the company, including Sid Franklin of the northern Ohio office. In fact, Ben Feldman of Youngstown is one of the leading insurance agents in the industry worldwide.

New York Life and its financial affiliates market life insurance and a range of financial services—including mutual funds, real estate, gas and oil limited partnerships, and unit investment trusts—to middle-to-upper-income-market families.

The firm has its two general offices, and one of New York Life's six central service offices, in greater Cleveland. The central service office handles claims from Ohio, Michigan, Indiana, western Pennsylvania, and most of New York.

New York Life, one of the first mutual life insurance companies in the nation, has deep roots in Ohio. Of the first 1,000 policies it sold, nine were on the lives of Ohio residents. The firm opened its Ohio office in 1845, and during the California Gold Rush of 1849, it paid death benefits on 12 Ohioans who died seeking a fortune in gold dust.

The company's investment in Cleveland's redevelopment now totals $95 million in commercial mortgages. "We look for projects that make a statement in the community we are in," says Larry Gordon, general manager of the Shaker Heights office. "New York Life will grow with the community."

Seated (from left) are Marion Burns, associate general manager, and Lawrence Gordon, general manager, with the Shaker Heights management staff—Timothy M. Babbert, Jeffrey S. Polunas, Therese C. Schmidt, Patrick J. Crean, and Michael G. Zorio.

JONES, DAY, REAVIS & POGUE

Jones, Day, Reavis & Pogue, Cleveland's largest law firm, has evolved along with, and beyond, the city to provide counsel for corporations, institutions, and individuals on a global basis.

Tracing its origins to a small office opened in Cleveland in 1893, the firm now has more than 1,050 lawyers in 16 offices worldwide—10 domestic and 6 overseas.

The legal empire is based in the new North Point Building at East Ninth Street and Lakeside Avenue in downtown Cleveland. The twin triangular towers provide 270,000 square feet of space that is home to 300 lawyers and 600 other employees.

While Cleveland has grown from the world's busiest iron ore port into a multifaceted industrial and service hub, Jones, Day, Reavis & Pogue's practice focuses on five major areas: corporate, government regulation, litigation, real estate/construction, and tax.

The lawyers are supported by advanced technology that provides the most complete information possible. The heart of the system is the North Point Information Systems Service Center. The center has more than 10 billion bytes of computer space and disk capacity to hold more than a half-million documents simultaneously. The attorneys also are linked via a desk-top computer network to clients, other attorneys and offices, internal and external information retrieval systems, and electronic mail. In addition, the center has video capabilities designed to assist attorneys in associate and expert witness training. Backing up the electronic data banks are the 33,000 volumes in Jones Day's legal library.

Jones Day's investment in technological assets serves clients' needs and also serves as an inducement for top-notch legal talent to join the firm. Approximately 125 of the firm's lawyers held prestigious judicial clerkships upon completion of law school. The talent flows in the opposite direction as well—a chief legal adviser of the U.S. State Department, a White House aide, and other top national advisers came from the Cleveland office alone.

Jones Day has established a strong national and international presence. The firm began by opening a Washington office in 1946, following the trend of its clients toward national and international expansion. It has continued to grow in size and influence through mergers and strategic growths. The firm's 1986 merger with Surrey & Morse opened up the international arena for Jones Day by establishing offices in London, Paris, and Riyadh, Saudi Arabia. The most recent merger, with Atlanta-based Hansell & Post, established Jones Day as the second-largest law firm in the world. The firm recently operated an office in Tokyo and will establish a presence in Brussels prior to year-end, significantly enhancing its global capabilities.

Despite its status as one of the nation's largest law firms, Jones Day has maintained its structure as a single integrated partnership, and each office takes its lead from the Cleveland headquarters.

"Jones Day's leadership also serves Cleveland well," says Richard W. Pogue, the firm's managing partner. "Members of the firm sit on committees and boards for a wide range of corporations, hospitals, civic and social service organizations, foundations, colleges and universities, and school systems in the greater Cleveland area.

"We hope that we return to the community that which Cleveland has given us—solid backing."

A presence in Cleveland since 1893, Jones, Day, Reavis & Pogue now provides legal counsel for corporations, institutions, and individuals worldwide. The firm is headquartered in the prestigious North Point Building at East Ninth Street and Lakeside Avenue in downtown Cleveland.

AMERITRUST

The bold, new statement being made on downtown Cleveland's Public Square—Ameritrust Center—is the latest expression of both the banking company's nearly century-old commitment to Cleveland and its interest in the city's unfolding renaissance.

The 60-story office tower and hotel project is the new home of Ameritrust's corporate headquarters. The bank sold its former headquarters, the Ameritrust Tower, to the developers of the new complex, Richard E. and David H. Jacobs.

Remaining in the Ameritrust family is its main bank building, a national historic landmark famous for its stained-glass dome by Tiffany. It has been the home bank of the company since it opened in 1908. But the firm's history reaches back to much more modest beginnings.

The Ameritrust Rotunda building, which was declared a national landmark in 1973 by the National Register of Historic Places. Rising behind it is the 29-story Ameritrust Tower, opened in 1971, and designed by Marcel Breuer.

Ranking today as one of the largest bank holding companies in the Midwest—with $10.5 billion in assets, 6,000 employees, banks in Indiana and Michigan, and more than 75 branches, Ameritrust evolved from a safe deposit business in a rented basement.

It began in 1893 as the Security Safe Deposit & Trust Company in the old Garfield Building, and the following year it adopted the name that served it until the late 1970s, The Cleveland Trust Company.

Cleveland Trust received its first deposit on March 9, 1895, and 15 days later J.G.W. Cowles was elected the first president of the company. By the time the main bank building opened in 1908, the same year F.H. Goff became the company's third president, Cleveland Trust already had 15 branches. Since those early days there has been spectacular growth marked by a steady involvement in the community.

Goff led the company until he died in 1923, enlarging the number of branches to 52 and building the business to 397,000 depositors and $176 million in resources. However, Goff is best remembered for his contribution to the community.

In 1914 he founded the Cleveland Foundation, the first community charitable trust in the nation. Goff and Cleveland Trust supplied the funds to operate the foundation during its early years, but by the time he died the foundation was well established with assets of more than $367,000.

Today the Cleveland Foundation has assets in the hundreds of millions of dollars and distributes grants throughout the Greater Cleveland area. In recent years the foundation has undertaken major commitments in the fields of education and neighborhood revitalization.

Another company pioneer was Harris Creech, who succeeded Goff and guided Cleveland Trust through the troubled waters of the Depression. Creech single-handedly stopped a run on the bank on April 26,

The lobby of the Ameritrust Main Office Rotunda building. Adorning the walls are 13 murals painted by Francis D. Millet, an acclaimed artist who perished in the sinking of the *Titanic*. The stained-glass dome by Tiffany measures 61 feet across. The inner dome is made of leaded, stained glass. Fifteen feet above is the wired-glass outer dome, fashioned after the Pantheon of Rome, which protects the inner dome and allows daylight to illuminate the stained glass.

1933. He climbed up on a desk in the middle of the main bank, clapped his hands to get the attention of the growing throng of customers who wanted their money, and told them: "Unfounded rumors about The Cleveland Trust Company have resulted in depositors coming into the bank to secure their money. It is our wish that accommodation be made for

One example of Ameritrust's commitment to the community was its corporate sponsorship of the grand opening of the new North Coast Harbor. The major civic celebration, called Ameritrust Harbor Expo, launched a new 21-acre inner harbor and stands as a significant testimonial to the renaissance of Cleveland. Several hundred Ameritrust employees, such as the two shown here, served as hosts and hostesses for the three-day festivities, which drew more than 200,000 proud greater Cleveland citizens.

them to secure their money if they want it, and we are keeping our doors open until 5 o'clock instead of 3 o'clock. We will open tomorrow at 9 o'clock."

The crowd dispersed and the guaranteed total payout policy saw the company through the crunch. Cleveland Trust inaugurated a consumer credit department for making small loans, payable on the installment plan, in 1938.

The same spirit that Cleveland Trust exhibited in the early part of the century, by helping to develop much of greater Cleveland's residential area through aggressive mortgage lending, prompted Ameritrust to inaugurate one of the most innovative services in community banking. In 1986 the firm opened the Ameritrust Development Bank, an institution whose assets work only in local development projects.

The Development Bank is a full-service, commercial bank offering a full range of services and products, including small business loans and commercial and residential real estate mortgage loans. It was created to allow institutions and large investors to earn a substantial return on their investments while fueling community development.

One of the bank's first projects was Lexington Village, a $13-million rental development in Cleveland's near east side Hough area. Another was the first new Cleveland neighborhood development in 50 years, the Central Villa cluster of homes near St. Vincent Charity Hospital. The Development Bank has been used as a model by banks nationwide.

The philosophy behind the Development Bank is simple; Ameritrust believes local institutions and individuals who believe in the city's future should be able to play a part in Cleveland's growth and development. Every penny invested in the bank stays in Cleveland to stimulate economic growth in the city.

Ameritrust, owner of the biggest bank in Ohio and the 20th-largest trust department in the nation with more than $30 billion under its management, is also big in terms of community involvement on an individual basis. The company's employees have established the highest per-capita contribution to United Way in Cleveland.

In many ways, whether it involves putting together the financing for downtown Cleveland's Galleria shopping center or supporting Ohio's Thomas Edison Program for rebuilding the state's industrial base, Ameritrust backs up its belief that it has an obligation to support the community that nurtured it.

This 60-story Ameritrust Center will be the new home of Ameritrust's corporate headquarters, due to open in late 1993, on Cleveland's historic Public Square. Designed by Kohn, Paderson and Fox, it will be the tallest buillding in Ohio.

THE EMERALD HEALTH NETWORK, INC.

The Emerald Health Network was founded in 1984 as a network of six area hospital and physician-based Preferred Provider Organizations. The EHN was actually one of the first health care organizations in the country to combine the resources of a number of hospitals and physicians to implement the PPO concept of appropriate utilization of services, facilities, and physicians in a "network."

This first generation of The Emerald Health Network was comprised of hospitals and physicians with proven track records for cost efficiency and for providing quality care. The EHN was also one of the first health care programs to initiate a utilization review process using on-site medical directors within each of the PPOs, to help ensure quality care in the right setting at the right price.

This decentralized review process, coupled with the convenient locations of the EHN hospitals and the choice of thousands of physicians, all contributed to the early success of The Emerald Health Network.

Today The Emerald Health Network continues to adhere to the PPO concept of cost-efficient providers upon which it was founded. Now in its second generation, the EHN has developed and strengthened that concept, evolving into a market-driven system responsive to the ever-changing needs of the businesses it serves.

To complement its on-site utilization review process, the EHN now incorporates central utilization review and quality-assurance processes. These enable the EHN to provide employers with qualified data derived from hospital pre-admissions, length of stay comparisons, and other review procedures. To help make health care even more affordable, the EHN also offers inpatient hospital reimbursement options to fit employers' needs.

The Emerald Health Network's ability to adapt to the needs of the market over the past five years and its openness to innovation continue to make it one of the most viable, cost-saving health care products in the market. Proof is in the network's growth. In October 1983 the EHN was incorporated with six PPOs and 2,000 members. Today The Emerald Health Network includes 23 hospitals and 3,500 physicians serving more than 170,000 members in an 11-county northeastern Ohio area.

Quality care in the right setting at the right price is the goal of The Emerald Health Network. Today the Network includes 23 hospitals and 3,500 physicians serving more than 170,000 members in an 11-county northeastern Ohio area.

Photo by Roger Mastroianni

CHAPTER 13

Building Greater Cleveland

From concept to completion, Cleveland's building industry and real estate professionals shape tomorrow's skyline.

Photo by Barbara Durham

CRAGIN • LANG, INC.

Cragin•Lang, Inc., one of Cleveland's first and most prestigious business real estate firms, has played a vital part in the development of Cleveland and northern Ohio. A cityscape of downtown Cleveland's Lake Erie skyline is pictured here.

Cragin•Lang, Inc., one of Cleveland's first and most prestigious business real estate firms, has played a major part in developing the shape and face of the city as it is known today. Commercial real estate brokers with origins to 1867, Cragin•Lang has brought together Cleveland's buyers and sellers of land, retail property, office buildings, and industrial plants as the city has grown and diversified through the years.

Today, over a century since founder Daniel Taylor first opened for business and began the Cragin•Lang story, the firm continues to thrive at the heart of the city's growth by attracting new industry to the area and by providing comprehensive real estate services to meet the needs of northern Ohio businesses. Just as the city has changed and grown, business real estate has grown into a sophisticated, high-technology, analytical service that is integral to informed commercial real estate decisions. Six specialized service groups that make up the Cragin•Lang organization include: Industrial Sales and Leasing, Office Sales and Leasing, Investment Services, Property Management, Appraisal, and Financial Services.

Cragin•Lang clients range from *Fortune* 500 companies to small, rapidly growing businesses. The firm assists these clients by using its vast network of information about properties to guide them through business expansion or moves. Clients seek out Cragin•Lang because of the firm's ability to help developers, buyers, and sellers of commercial property to make real estate decisions based on the best information available.

A close look at Cragin•Lang's six specialized service groups follows here.

Industrial Sales and Leasing: Industrial real estate brokerage is the art of successfully bringing together those who have space available with those who need space. Every day the business community calls upon the Cragin•Lang Industrial Sales and Leasing Group for its experience, persistence, and creativity in bringing together industrial property owners with companies needing space.

With comprehensive knowledge of industrial real estate, constant research of the market, and the ability to get to the heart of a company's needs, the Cragin•Lang industrial brokerage team helps businesses capitalize on the right opportunities.

Office Sales and Leasing: Every business has a set of unique characteristics that determines its needs for office space. The role of Cragin • Lang's Office Leasing Group is to quickly assess those needs and help clients find just the right fit with their environment.

Market savvy, the latest real estate software, and a vast up-to-the-minute data base enable the Cragin • Lang Office Leasing Group to analyze clients' needs and instantly survey all available property to match those needs.

From suggesting office efficiency plans to executing subleases and lease buyouts, Cragin • Lang brokers are there with the type of solutions that can only come from experience. It's this experience and dedication to clients that keep Cragin•Lang the leading source for office space referrals year after year.

Investment Services: A successful real estate investment is built upon a complete and accurate business analysis of an opportunity. At Cragin • Lang, the Investment Services Group possesses the level of knowledge and expertise needed to serve its broad base of business and individual investors.

As part of a full-service business real estate firm, the Investment Services Group has access to the most immediate market information available. Cragin • Lang's comprehensive data base, advanced software, and direct pipeline to the market increase the Investment Services Group's ability to better analyze investment opportunities and counsel its clients accordingly.

Property Management: The industry has tagged it property management, but at Cragin • Lang the focus is asset management. Complete responsibility for the property's short- and long-term value is the Property Management Group's charge.

From administration through hands-on operations, Cragin • Lang's Property Management professionals monitor every activity at the property. In addition, timely monthly financial reports provide owners with accurate information pivotal to their planning.

Appraisal: A professional real estate appraisal is a balanced blend of quantitative data analysis and the objective discovery and evaluation of tangible characteristics of a property.

At Cragin•Lang, the appraisal professionals have an impressive background in a variety of appraisal assignments. Aside from their many years of experience, they are members of the prestigious American Institute of Real Estate Appraisers (MAI) and the American Society of Appraisers (ASA). These professional associations set the highest standards for the industry, requiring member certification and adherence to a strict code of ethics. These memberships also give Cragin • Lang the ability to call upon a nationwide network of qualified appraisers for assistance anywhere in the country.

Financial Services: True effectiveness in mortgage brokerage hinges on a clear understanding of both the lender's and borrower's investment objectives. Since an opportunity exists for both parties to benefit from the relationship, a mortgage broker's task is to apply his expertise to satisfy both sets of objectives and expedite a mutually beneficial transaction. At Cragin • Lang Financial Services, Inc., that expertise is the result of years of experience on both the lending and borrowing sides of the equation. That's what enables Cragin • Lang Financial Services, Inc., to adeptly and quickly establish common grounds for satisfying a diverse set of investment objectives.

In addition, Cragin • Lang Financial Services, Inc., has the ability to utilize the vast data base and resources that Cragin • Lang, Inc., its sister full-service real estate firm, offers. This experience and the staff's constant interaction with the market ensure that up-to-the-minute data is used throughout each phase of financial structuring.

The Cragin • Lang, Inc., portfolio of services and the property and clients it represents combine to position it as the second-largest business real estate firm in Ohio. A member of the New America Network, the world's largest business real estate network, Cragin • Lang is proud to be a part of the success story that features the renaissance of Cleveland and the growth of Ohio.

Corporate headquarters for Cragin • Lang, Inc., is located in the First Federal Savings and Loan Building in the heart of the financial district.

MK-FERGUSON COMPANY

Cleveland-based MK-Ferguson Company is a major engineering and construction subsidiary of the Morrison Knudsen Corporation of Boise, Idaho, one of the world's largest engineering and construction firms. Founded in Cleveland on August 5, 1918, by Harold Kingsley Ferguson under the name The H.K. Ferguson Company, it became a wholly owned subsidiary of Morrison Knudsen Corporation in 1950. The firm then became MK-Ferguson Company in 1985 to emphasize its expanding role as a major Morrison Knudsen subsidiary, supplying engineering and construction services to industrial, energy, and government markets. Since 1918 the company has completed thousands of projects for many of the world's largest concerns in all 50 states and more than 55 foreign countries. Today it numbers more than 1,200 employees at its Cleveland headquarters and more than 5,000 total employees domestically and internationally.

Throughout its history the company has continued to refine and advance its technology. The firm has earned repeat business through its interest in improving the client's productivity, as well as by staying on schedule and within budget. Its rapid growth has paralleled the growth of the companies—and industries—it serves.

Over the years the company also has established many "firsts." By combining design engineering and construction services in one company, it became one of America's first "total responsibility" builders. MK-Ferguson was the first to build synthetic rubber plants in the United States. It served as designer and constructor of the first full-scale nuclear thermal diffusion plant for the Manhattan Project, a project that marked the beginning of a long and continuing involvement in the nuclear energy field. The company has participated in the design and/or construction of more than 25 percent of the United States' basic oxygen furnace steel-making capacity. MK-Ferguson built one of the first steel mills in the nation to combine three major processes under one roof: basic oxygen steel making, vacuum degassing, and continuous casting. It is also the first company in the world to perform decontamination and decommissioning services for a commercial nuclear power plant. This tradition of innovative involvement in traditional and emerging industries continues.

Today MK-Ferguson Company successfully tackles the construction and engineering of manufacturing, process, power, and research and development facilities for a variety of industries and government. These markets include aerospace, cement, chemicals, metals, food and beverage, electronics, general manufacturing, paint and resins, pharmaceuticals, plastics and rubber, steam and power generation, cogeneration, and energy

The application of advanced technology to enable basic industries to be more competitive is another MK-Ferguson strength.

MK-Ferguson's automation capabilities include the design, engineering, and installation of high-speed bottling lines for the food and beverage industry.

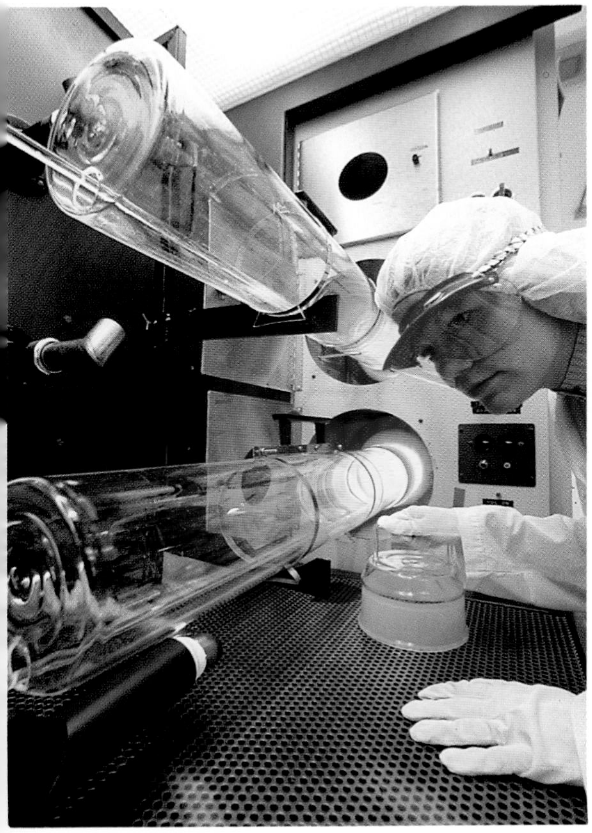

The company provides engineering and construction services for a range of high-tech industries, including electronics manufacturing, research and development facilities, pharmaceutical, and aerospace.

from municipal waste.

And, as American industry has increasingly focused on high technology, MK-Ferguson has paved the way with increasingly sophisticated capabilities. The firm has erected clean rooms for manufacturing and testing solid-state electronics, installed state-of-the-art instrumentation and control systems, supplied planning in environmental control and energy conservation, and developed automated systems approaches in computer-integrated manufacturing, robotics, material handling, logistics, and communications and monitoring. MK-Ferguson also has kept pace with environmental concerns through its environmental expertise and expanding hazardous waste remediation activities.

The company today applies this innovative expertise to a variety of market niches, as well as in long-term client relationships and "partnering" programs. For Anheuser-Busch, Inc., America's largest beer maker, the firm has engineered and built six grass-roots breweries in addition to major expansion, renovation, and modernization projects at seven other Anheuser-Busch breweries.

MK-Ferguson is a major long-term partner with E.I. du Pont de Nemours in a variety of engineering and construction projects domestically and internationally. In the nuclear and fossil energy sectors, MK-Ferguson has constructed numerous power plants and today serves as a major contractor for the modification, retrofit, and maintenance of operating facilities.

For the Department of Energy, the company is a major contractor in the area of high- and low-level nuclear waste storage, disposal, and remedial action. In the alternate energy field, MK-Ferguson is an active leader in project development activities for municipal solid waste-to-energy conversion as well as research and pilot plant projects.

Finally, MK-Ferguson has been and continues to be a provider of services for government agencies on the local, state, and national levels. The company today performs work for the Department of Energy, the Department of Defense, the Department of State, the National Aeronautics and Space Administration (NASA), and numerous other state and local governments and agencies.

Today, with headquarters in downtown Cleveland, offices in San Francisco and Boise, and operations throughout the country, MK-Ferguson Company has completed its seventh decade of achievement and looks forward to building new worlds in the decades ahead.

Heavy construction capabilities include this government defense nuclear waste processing facility in addition to fossil electric generation facilities.

THE ALBERT M. HIGLEY COMPANY

Since its founding by Albert M. Higley, Sr., in 1925, The Albert M. Higley Company has become one of the largest construction managers and general contractors in northern Ohio. Its growth is a result of the founder's belief that the company should undertake only those projects it was qualified to do well. Today, because of its continued reputation for quality and integrity, 90 percent of all contracts are from repeat clients—proof that the firm's original philosophy has worked well.

From the time of its founding until the end of World War II, The Albert M. Higley Company built such notable landmarks as the Cuyahoga County Airport, the Cleveland Skating Club, the Cleveland Coast Guard Station, and Cleveland Pneumatic Aerol in Euclid, the largest defense plant built in this area during the war.

The impressive headquarters building and reception area for Broadview Savings and Loan Company is a showcase for the quality workmanship of The Albert M. Higley Company.

After the war's end Cleveland embarked on a period of industrial, institutional, and commercial growth, and numerous projects built by The Albert M. Higley Company could be seen throughout the area. These ranged from major projects for 12 of the local area hospitals; suburban retail stores for JCPenney, May Company, Sears, Roebuck and Co., and Higbee's; and educational facilities for the many universities located in the area.

During the 1970s The Albert M. Higley Company completed more than 2,000 projects and showed its flexibility by being involved in many widely diversified projects, including a major portion of the Justice Center Complex, eight major parking structures, many large industrial facilities, and Sea World of Ohio in Aurora.

As the decade of the 1980s comes to a close, the company's work includes such energy- and ecology-related projects as the Cleveland Electric Illuminating Company's Perry Nuclear Power Plant, sewage treatment facilities for the Northeast Ohio Regional Sewer District, and water treatment facilities for the City of Cleveland. Other notable projects in the process of completion include the Red Cross headquarters, W.O. Walker Rehabilitation Center, The Renaissance in North Olmsted, and the revitalization of Cain Park. The amount of work under contract has grown to approximately 75 million yearly, and 10,700 projects have been completed since its founding in 1925.

The Albert M. Higley Company prides itself in its flexibility, and it continues to be dedicated to excellence, doing only that work that it can do well. This philosophy has helped it grow in the past and will continue to be the cornerstone of future expansion.

REALTY ONE

Realty One is the eighth-largest, and one of the fastest-growing, independent realty companies in the United States. The story behind this growth is one of steadfast commitment to the notion that the quality of greater Cleveland's housing stock, and the city's amenities, make the community a superior place to raise a family.

Realty One, a full-service real estate company, has 50 residential realty offices serving 12 counties. It handles residential and commercial sales, property management, new-home sales, nationwide relocation, home warranty protection, and homeowners insurance. It also provides financial services, including mortgages, to home buyers.

A new corporation was formed in January 1987 by the merger of two leading Cleveland real estate firms: HGM Hilltop, Realtors, and Miller-Bishop & Associates, Realtors.

Realty One's corporate philosophy is to have a team of self-motivated and dedicated people committed to business excellence in real estate service and to develop a superior working and motivational climate for its employees and sales associates. The firm relies on a sophisticated management style to encourage the ongoing development of every member of the organization in order to chart their future growth, market share, and profit year after year. Realty One's long-term plan includes adding more offices and expanding its extensive real estate services.

Realty One's willingness to embrace the newest technology has also contributed to its rapid growth. The company uses a mainframe computer system to keep track of real estate transactions and business management information. All Realty One staff are trained to use the computer to assure fast and accurate communications.

Realty One's business is based on people. With more than 1,600 sales associates and 350 employees, the company maintains a family atmosphere and open lines of communication to management. Realty One is full of dynamic people who are excited about the real estate business and are working hard to provide quality service to customers.

These people also work hard in community volunteer programs. Every office is involved in some volunteer effort, such as the March of Dimes, the Achievement Center for Children, the American Cancer Society, or the company's HUG'UM the Bear Safety Program. Vincent Aveni, chairman of the board and chief executive officer of Realty One, provides a strong role model for his staff. He serves on the boards of trustees of several community service organizations and is highly involved in the real estate industry on local, state, and national levels.

Realty One has invested in Cleveland because it believes in Cleveland. So far, it hasn't been wrong.

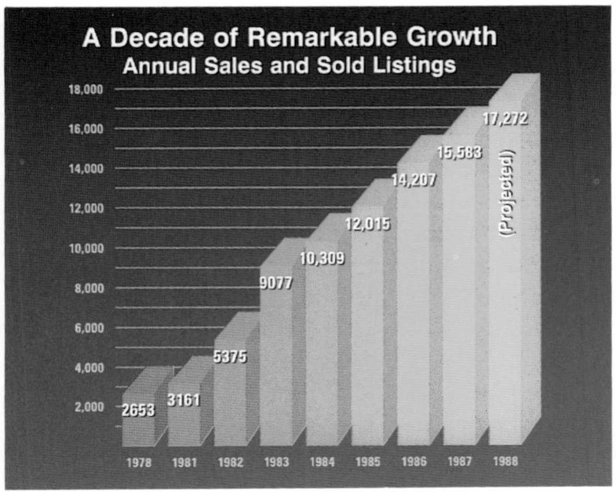

LEFT: A real estate giant emerges from the catastrophic recession of the early 1980s. Realty One grew from a local company serving only Cleveland's eastern suburbs to the leading Realtor in Ohio and the eighth-largest independently owned company in the nation.

BELOW: Vincent T. Aveni (seated), chairman of the board and chief executive officer of Realty One, with the firm's two other owners (from left): James C. Miller, president, and Joseph T. Aveni, vice-chairman.

BISKIND DEVELOPMENT COMPANY

Great Northern Corporate Center has established a reputation as the most prestigious office building on Cleveland's west side.

Biskind Development Company has been an integral part of the greater Cleveland community since 1949. A full-service real estate development, construction, and management company, Biskind Development has an established reputation for innovation and a high standard of excellence in all phases of real estate development.

One of Biskind Development's best known projects is Great Northern—a 400-acre, multiuse development located in North Olmsted, a western suburb of Cleveland.

Fueled by the vision of Biskind Development's founder, Saul S. Biskind, Great Northern began evolving in the mid-1950s. At that time the city of North Olmsted was a sleepy rural community with a scattering of small businesses, farms, older homes, and developed streets. But Saul Biskind looked beyond the strawberry and blackberry patches as he slowly assembled and purchased more than 300 acres for commercial development. The close proximity to Cleveland Hopkins International Airport and talk of a major freeway linking east and west made the area ripe for development.

In 1957 ground was broken for the first phase of the planned complex: Great Northern Shopping Center, a 330,000-square-foot retail/community center. Acknowledged as the major catalyst for an explosion in area population growth and business development, Great Northern Shopping Center grew steadily through the 1960s and 1970s.

When Daniel E. Biskind, president and chief executive officer, took the company reins from his father in 1974, planning began in earnest to fulfill the original Great Northern vision. Dan Biskind instituted a strategic planning process into the company's day-to-day and long-range operations. Under his leadership both the firm and Great Northern experienced phenomenal growth. By the late 1980s the Great Northern Complex contained more than 225 retail merchants, services, restaurants, and entertainment facilities within a 1.5-million-square-foot shopping complex; a half-million square feet of office space; more than 250 hotel rooms provided by two hotels, The Hampton Inn and a full-service Pierre Radisson Inn; and 1,000 housing units.

The Great Northern complex is a success story in the greater Cleveland area. Great Northern Shopping Center has established and maintains a dominant position in the state of Ohio and is one of the top 50 retail centers in the United States. Great Northern Mall is the number-one retail center in the Northeast Ohio region based on sales volume.

Biskind Development has received numerous awards and honors for office buildings within the Great Northern campus. Great Northern Corporate Center is heralded as the "most prestigious office address" on Cleveland's west side. The buildings have attracted a wide variety of tenants, the majority of which are members of *Fortune's* 1,000 top companies

In the late 1980s Great Northern employed about 5,000 people in more than 2 million square feet of retail, office, and hotel space. Exciting plans into the twenty-first century include an additional one million square feet of office space, hotels fur-

nishing 600 guest rooms with attendant conference/meeting/ fitness facilities, and an additional department store at Great Northern Shopping Center. Upon completion Great Northern will be a $500-million venture and will employ approximately 15,000 people.

The ability to create successful, multifaceted developments such as Great Northern requires vision and a long-term commitment to planning that vision. It requires adaptability in an ever-changing marketplace. It demands uncompromising quality and attention to every detail.

In addition to developing multiuse environments, Biskind Development Company provides comprehensive build-to-suit services and creates mutually beneficial joint ventures. The company's experience also includes suburban multiuse projects; single and multifamily developments; office, industrial park, and retail developments; and downtown multiuse redevelopment.

Biskind Development is organized into two divisions: retail and commercial. The company employs 150 people with highly experienced professionals in all aspects of development—planning, design, construction, finance, leasing, marketing, and management. In-house capabilities ensure efficient, cost-effective, responsible, and responsive service from a single source. Under the direction of Dan Biskind, the firm's approach to each project is user oriented—tailored to meet and exceed individual needs and expectations.

Headquartered at Great Northern, Biskind Development Company is actively involved in economic development in the Northeast Ohio region. As the firm's president and chief executive officer has expressed, "We believe Cleveland will be a star in the 1990s, and we look forward to continuing to play an integral role in the renaissance of the greater Cleveland area."

Great Northern's mall expansion opened in 1987. The central atrium, shown here, rises to a domed skylight.

MANAGEMENT REPORTS, INC. (MRI)

MRI's PC-based software is used by more than 1,000 property managers and exceeds IREM's tough standards.

Management Reports, Inc. (MRI), is the pioneer of the automated property management industry. This industry began in Cleveland in 1971, when MRI developed accounting and property management software for several large Northeast Ohio real estate developers. The unusually high concentration of influential developers in the Cleveland area sparked MRI's initial growth and enabled the firm to become the industry pacesetter.

In addition to local developers, Management Reports, Inc., has serviced some of the nation's largest real estate syndicators, developers, asset managers, and corporate real estate departments. The privately owned company offers a comprehensive range of management information products and solutions tailored to the needs of either commercial or residential property managers. Services that distinguish MRI from others in the industry include training on site and at regional offices, implementation and value-added consulting services, custom programming, system integration, and modem and toll-free telephone support.

Rather than concentrate on solving just one specific problem, MRI provides full-service solutions for property managers. Two such full-service options are Information Processing Center services and stand-alone software.

Information Processing Center (IPC) services provide access to mainframe reporting for managers who desire unlimited growth potential but want to avoid data-processing overhead costs and possible hardware obsolescence. Low-cost telecommunications and laser-printed reports are just two of IPC's benefits. Whether it is one or 1,000 rental properties, IPC services simplify a property manager's task for lease management, tenant accounting, accounts payable, financial reporting, budgets, and marketing analysis.

MRI introduced stand-alone software in 1984 to meet the needs of customers preferring in-house data processing. The software will run on a variety of hardware configurations. While an unlimited number of hardware arrangements are possible, three scenarios commonly accommodated by MRI's software packages are: single-user microcomputers in client offices, multiuser local-area networks, and multisite systems at property and/or regional offices integrated to a central-based host computer. Stand-alone software is available for work order maintenance and HUD reporting as well as some of the same things available from IPC (lease management, tenant accounting, accounts payable, financial reporting, budgets, and marketing analysis).

Information Processing Center services and stand-alone software are the two principal "products" of MRI. Both exceed industry standards established by the Institute of Real Estate Management. Recently Coldwell Banker installed MRI's system to manage its extensive commercial portfolio. Coldwell Banker manages more than 25,000 commercial leases nationwide.

Achievements such as this demonstrate that Management Reports, Inc., continues to advance industry standards, and the city of Cleveland has been—and will remain—instrumental in that progress.

With MRI's Information Processing Services, mainframe computer power is available to clients in their offices at a fraction of the cost.

FOREST CITY ENTERPRISES, INC.

Forest City Enterprises, Inc., is a major national real estate company that develops and manages mixed-use properties, shopping centers, office buildings, hotels, apartment complexes, and land. With its beginnings in the lumber retail business 68 years ago, Forest City is now devoted almost exclusively to real estate.

The company now has more than one billion dollars of completed properties at cost in its real estate portfolio and more than $5 billion of projects currently in construction or development.

In the early 1980s Forest City set as its goal to become a nationwide developer of major real estate projects. It sold its retail division, a longtime leader in the Cleveland home-improvement store market, to Handy Andy in March 1987.

Today Forest City is active in real estate in 20 states and the District of Columbia. Its current portfolio is comprised of 18 shopping centers (12 million square feet), 11 office and mixed-use projects (4 million square feet), 35 apartment complexes containing 14,877 living units, and four hotels containing 1,337 rooms. The firm has more than 22 million square feet of projects under construction or development.

Forest City not only builds and develops real estate, but as a vertically integrated company it also manages and maintains its buildings. As an owner-manager, the firm achieves greater value on its investments. Through its Residential Development Division it builds high-rise residential housing, using the company's patented modular building method.

Forest City's goal is to seek out unique projects of large size that will make a major impact in the communities they serve. Two examples of long-term urban mixed-use projects stand out:

—Tower City Center, a billion-dollar, 6.5-million-square-foot, mixed-use project located in downtown Cleveland, is one of the largest mixed-use urban redevelopment projects in the nation. Tower City Center will feature new and renovated office buildings, including the 52-story landmark Terminal Tower building, a Ritz-Carlton Hotel, a Neiman-Marcus store, and a 336,000-square-foot shopping mall containing 125 retail stores, movie theaters, a food court, and parking for 3,000 cars. The first phase of Tower City Center is scheduled to open in early 1990.

—MetroTech, a 4.7-million-square-foot, mixed-use project located in downtown Brooklyn, New York, is a billion-dollar commercial, high-tech, and academic development on 16 acres adjacent to the nationally renowned Polytechnic Institute of New York. This project, when complete, will comprise 11 buildings. Among its anchor tenants are Chase Manhattan Bank, Brooklyn Union Gas Company, the Securities Industry Automation Corporation, and the New York Telephone Company.

Forest City also operates a Wholesale Lumber Division that trades lumber in the United States and Canada and sells lumber and building materials to contractors in Northeast Ohio. It is the largest wholesale lumber brokerage company in the nation.

Forest City Enterprises, Inc., is a member of the American Stock Exchange.

Looming above the construction at the billion-dollar Tower City Center is the Terminal Tower, the landmark office building complex in Cleveland. Tower City Center and its three major company-owned existing properties—the 52-story Terminal Tower, Post Office Plaza, and retail mall—are leading the rejuvenation of Cleveland. In 1990 a new Tower City Center will be unveiled that will include the first regional shopping mall built in Cleveland in more than 12 years, a new rail rapid transit station, a luxury Ritz-Carlton Hotel and office building, the Post Office Plaza, and the Skylight Office Tower. A Neiman-Marcus store is expected to open in 1992 at the center.

One Pierrepont Plaza, the first major office building constructed in downtown Brooklyn, New York, in more than 25 years, is a $150-million, 19-story structure that is among the most technologically advanced buildings in the world, incorporating building and operating systems at the leading edge of the office development business.

SYSTEMATION

ABOVE: Systemation's forward-thinking management team—executive vice-president Milo Chelovitz, president Bill Stilson, and executive vice-president Steve Spaeth—has provided direction for the company since 1967.

RIGHT: Vice-presidents John Bianco and Pat Frey review a recently accepted proposal with Integrated Manufacturing Technologies manager John Kluchar.

Systemation provides high-quality computer software services to business and industry. Widely recognized for its professional approach to information system needs—including systems integration planning, design, programming, implementation, and consultation—Systemation prides itself on delivering prompt, cost-effective, client-centered solutions.

Software is behind almost every important function in today's society. It regulates computers in cars and traffic lights, evaluates stock for Wall Street traders, analyzes loans for banks, routes telephone calls and truck fleets, and paces factory production. Banks, distribution companies, and factories depend heavily on computers to manage paperwork and payroll. Ensuring that these information systems work, and work efficiently, is what Systemation is all about.

Systemation is one of the oldest, largest, and most successful software service companies in Northeast Ohio. It was formed in 1967, shortly after computers began to be widely used in businesses. Bill Stilson, president and a founder of the company, had been in computer sales. He saw that businesses purchasing computers needed help in designing systems to make them work for their business. Systemation was created to meet this need.

In April 1989 Systemation was acquired by CAP GEMINI AMERICA, an international professional services firm. Systemation continues to operate as a division with its current management and staff.

Today many executives see the advantages to using Systemation consultants: The company puts its clients' needs first; it has diverse systems and industry experience; it provides innovative, reality-tested solutions to business problems; and it stands behind its work. Each project is monitored so that conformance to both Systemation's and the client's standards for quality is ensured.

Systemation has grown steadily, keeping pace as the business world's need for software assistance has burgeoned. The company has maintained an average growth rate of 20 percent per year since its beginning, largely generated within its home Cleveland market area. The demand for its services within the Cleveland area has grown so rapidly that Systemation has only recently expanded beyond the Northeast Ohio market. It now has offices in Columbus and Youngstown, Ohio, and Pittsburgh, Pennsylvania.

The firm actively recruits and attracts senior computer and software professionals. Employee turnover is extremely low—unusual for the information systems industry—and there is virtually no turnover at the management level. Because it is such a stable company, clients can rely on Systemation for help tomorrow with a system installed today. The firm offers its clients the most talented people and best service in the marketplace.

Currently Systemation has more than 500 employees. As a group they average 12 years' experience in computer systems, including extensive work in applications development, software packages, systems software, and hardware. This experience extends from the mainframe environment to personal computers. Staff members continually update their skills and keep current with new applications, techniques, and standards.

When hiring, the company looks at a potential employee's ability to adjust to a client's business environment, as well as his or her technical skills and experience. Systemation's computer specialists become an extension of the client's own staff, but are backed by Systemation's experienced management team and an extensive technical support network.

While employees' experience and ability to work well in the client environment are important, Systemation also believes that employees should lead balanced lives and spend time on interests and responsibilities outside the company.

ABOVE: Systemation's professional consultants average more than 12 years' experience each in every type of systems application and technology.

LEFT: Responsive to clients' individual needs, Systemation draws on its large, diversified staff of systems professionals to provide just the right team for each project.

Another Systemation strength is that it has developed broad client relationships in health, finance, distribution, manufacturing, transportation, and education. Systemation can meet the needs of companies of all sizes with a complete range of professional services. It is large enough to handle big assignments, yet gives full attention to small ones as well. Because the firm is not affiliated with any hardware or software vendor, it remains objective and flexible in solving problems for clients. Systemation's recommendations are based solely on its expertise and on customer input.

Says Bill Stilson, "What a client needs is what Systemation will provide—even if we have to train or hire to meet that need. However, in most cases, our staff will already have experience with something we know will work for a client, because it has worked successfully for another business."

This means that Systemation is client driven. It develops solutions that work because it looks at problems from the client's perspective and uses methods that fit the client's operation. Systemation observes and evaluates solutions from the perspectives of management, end users, and the information systems department. As a result, it can develop a software system that will perform efficiently and effectively for everyone who uses it. Having worked with more than 2,000 clients, from *Fortune* 500 corporations to small businesses, the company has accumulated design and implementation experience at all levels of systems sophistication.

No matter what kind of problem a client has, someone at Systemation has the experience and expertise to solve it. Companies that contract with Systemation for assistance receive more than a consultant. They enjoy the benefit of working with a corporation committed to maintaining its position as the largest, most successful software services firm in the region.

DUNLOP & JOHNSTON, INC.

When John Dunlop and Frank Johnston emigrated from Scotland to Cleveland, they brought little more than their skills and carpentry tools. However, since Cleveland was growing rapidly, there was a demand for new houses, factories, and churches. Dunlop & Johnston formed a partnership in 1910 and became carpentry contractors. Gradually they assumed responsibility for entire projects. By the time Dunlop & Johnston, Inc., incorporated in 1930, the company had a reputation for reliability as a general contractor.

What began as a partnership of carpenters is now a general contracting firm producing $25 million to $30 million of service billings per year. Dunlop & Johnston (D&J) employs more than 200 people during the peak building season and has between 25 and 40 percent of its own labor on any given project. The firm specializes primarily in hospitals and industrial and commercial buildings.

One of the primary factors in D&J's success is that the partners understood the needs of building owners. They gave personal attention to the details that ensured quality construction and on-schedule completion. These factors play a major role in the company's success today. When D&J finishes a building, the clients are pleased with the construction, and a long-term personal relationship is established. Because developing this type of personal relationship depends on people, D&J's first priority has always been to maintain an organization of experienced, professional, and conscientious people who manage the firm's resources for maximum benefit to the client. "People make us what we are," says Dunlop & Johnston's president, William H. Spencer.

ABOVE: Master Builders' world headquarters.

LEFT: The atrium at North Point, a premier Dunlop & Johnston project.

Dunlop & Johnston provides a broad range of construction and real estate development services. As general contractor, it takes total responsibility for a project—from site preparation to interior finish and landscaping. Dunlop & Johnston works on a design-build basis or with the owner's architect. By undertaking a substantial portion of most projects with its own work force and subcontracting the remainder to qualified firms, D&J ensures scheduling and quality performance.

The company can serve as construction manager, assisting the owner in selecting a site, choosing a design team, and preparing budgets and cost estimates. Dunlop & Johnston not only helps the owner review design concepts, materials, and construction methods but also value engineers the project. The firm then

acts as the on-site manager, coordinating and expediting the project.

When working as a general contractor, subcontractor, or project manager, D&J maintains control of each project by assigning a manager who is familiar with the estimate and the requirements of the job. This manager works directly with the owner and the design team to ensure good communication as the project moves forward. Management duties include purchasing, scheduling, coordinating, expediting, and quality control.

The manager also works with a support team of other D&J staff that may include structural, civil, architectural, and mechanical engineers and field superintendents. Team craft foremen lead groups of journeymen carpenters, cement finishers, masons, operating engineers, and construction laborers.

Because D&J was an experienced concrete subcontractor long before concrete was used widely as a building material, it can provide specialized expertise in structural and architectural applications of poured-in-place and precast concrete.

A special projects division at D&J continues the personal services performed by the company's original founders. It concentrates on smaller, more detailed projects, where D&J craftsmen can minimize the inconvenience associated with remodeling a home or retrofitting an office.

Unlike most other general contracting firms, D&J maintains a fairly large research and development department that studies and evaluates building materials and construction methods. It often erects experimental structures on company property.

A large inventory of equipment and tools, including cranes, concrete pumps, hi-lifts, and other material-handling equipment, supports all these activities. The firm's fleet of radio-equipped cars and trucks ensures not only delivery of materials on schedule but also a quick response if special tools are needed in an emergency.

Not content to provide excellent construction services, D&J has taken an active role in its community. Several officers have served in a local neighborhood development organization called Miles Ahead. This organization works with the city and neighborhood groups to attract new business and jobs into the Miles Avenue area. It also works with existing businesses to beautify the area through landscaping and building maintenance.

Dunlop & Johnston is also preparing for the future by adding engineering and management students from Case Western Reserve University and the University of Akron to its staff. Says William Spencer, "We are getting excellent people with good training from our local colleges." The company works closely with these and other schools in the area to help students develop a real picture of what construction careers involve. One such program is Constructor for a Day, which takes students on a one-day field trip to a construction site and explains the construction process.

Dunlop & Johnston, Inc., is committed to Cleveland, its development, and its people. It believes that people build buildings from the craftsman to the contractor to the architect to the owner. Each must perform his task in cooperation with the other for the project to be a success. The firm's employees bring that same attitude to all projects and are proud of the quality of work that results.

The reception center for Jones, Day, Reavis & Pogue at North Point.

RESERVE SQUARE

Scheduled for completion in the spring of 1990, Cleveland's downtown address for upscale urban living will be Reserve Square, a multimillion-dollar development housing a luxury first-class Radisson Suites Hotel, a retail shopping arcade, a first-class health club, restaurants, and the largest apartment complex and the only gourmet supermarket in the downtown area.

Within walking distance of the redesigned complex are the Galleria, Cleveland Municipal Stadium, Public Square, Tower City, the Warehouse District, Playhouse Square, and the Flats, many of downtown Cleveland's main attractions. Additional good restaurants, many serving dinner and late suppers, are nearby.

Opened in 1973 and known as the Park Centre, the original twin-tower residence was built with the downtown worker in mind. Located in the middle of everything, Reserve Square enables residents to walk to their downtown job, saving hours of stress-packed commuting time every weekday. And on weekends, residents can leave for the theater 15 minutes before curtain time.

ABOVE: This spectacular granite porte cochere will welcome all to Reserve Square, a multimillion-dollar, twin-tower commercial and residential development within walking distance of many of downtown Cleveland's main attractions.

RIGHT: The shopping arcade will have the only supermarket, Bockwinkle's, in the downtown area.

A reconfiguration of The Park's existing high-rise apartment, shopping, and recreation complex, Reserve Square contains 750 apartments, 254 hotel suites, and 300,000 square feet of retail/office space.

The Chicago-based Equity Financial and Management Company, principal owner of the property bounded by East 12th, Chester, Superior, and 13th streets, created a "retail street" or shopping arcade directly through the center of the property from 12th to 13th streets. Specialty retail shops and services were chosen to meet the needs of the residents, hotel guests, and downtown commuters.

As the only supermarket in the downtown area, the 20,000-square-foot Bockwinkle's offers a rich array of gourmet food for the multitude of people living in and passing through the complex.

A spectacular granite porte cochere will provide an impressive grand portal to all who enter. The dramatic entrance is comprised of a three-story steel-and-glass canopy highlighting the hotel and shop signs using Tivoli lighting. The adjacent boulevard shops have complementary canopies and window displays. The top of the complex is dramatically lit in the spirit of Cleveland's skyline and is capped at the summit with a neon band. There are separate entrances for the apartments, shopping arcade, and hotel to enhance privacy and security.

Responding to the growing demand for quality hotel accommodations in downtown Cleveland, the Radisson Hotel Corporation brought its expertise in the development, management, and operation of restaurants and hotels to the upscale Reserve Square. Radisson's affiliate, the Carson Travel Agency Company, offers the resources of the largest travel agency in the United States.

The Radisson Suites Hotel converted a portion of the West Tower into 254 suites offering spacious meeting rooms and first-class food, beverage, and health facilities. The Radisson features a luxurious fifth-floor lobby with a cocktail lounge and executive conference rooms.

In the 23-story residence tower, the exterior walls of each unit are all window from the ceiling to about three feet from the floor. Textured concrete was chosen as the main surface treatment to give Reserve Square an unmistakably urban character. There are 34 penthouse suites, 28 three-bedroom suites, 675 one-bedroom suites, and 28 efficiency suites.

Between the towers on the fifth-floor level is the fitness center and recreation area. It is a two-story, freestanding building accessible by glass-enclosed tunnels from either tower. The building stands directly over the enclosed garage. The fitness center includes an indoor pool, sunbed, men's and women's locker rooms with showers and saunas, and a large workout room. A deck on the north side of the pool leads to stairs that access the wooded and landscaped sundeck and park. Residents make good use of the fitness center, especially before work and at the end of the day. However, since Reserve Square is located downtown, some residents even use the fitness center during their lunchtime.

On the first floor, or just below the fitness center, is a comfortably decorated resident lounge. To the south of the fitness center building are two lighted omnicourt tennis courts.

The history leading to the creation of Reserve Square has not been an easy one. No amount of amenities was able to spare The Park from the downturn that hit Cleveland and the rest of the Midwest. Five years after The Park opened, it was purchased by First Property Management in foreclosure. It had suffered from high vacancies and delinquencies because it was designed for a life-style concept that was ahead of its time. Cleveland had long since reached its nadir, and the downtown was nearly dead after 5 p.m.

From 1973 to 1983 there was a steady erosion of the city's industrial base and consequent loss of jobs. The market of The Park was soft and, as a result, the property had to struggle to keep the vacancy level low and the prices high enough to maintain the profile of high repute.

Crucial to the success of The Park and now Reserve Square was the local economy's rebound, which helped fuel the spectacular rebirth of the downtown area as exemplified by the development of the Flats and Playhouse Square. During the rebound The Park was spending heavily in advertising and promotion to ensure positive exposure and to attract the maximum number of residents.

From 1983 to 1985 major discounts and promotions of specific suite types enabled The Park to keep close to 90-percent occupancy. The turning point seemed to occur in

RIGHT: Residents in Reserve Square's high-rise apartments enjoy the amenities offered within the complex and the close proximity of downtown Cleveland.

BELOW: The fitness center and recreation area is a two-story, freestanding building between the towers on the fifth floor. It includes an indoor pool, sunbed, locker rooms with showers and saunas, and a workout room.

1985 when the economy was improving, inflation had leveled, and The Park was finally perceived as a good place to live.

Suddenly buildings were rising everywhere in the downtown area, and the morale of Clevelanders in general was high. In 1986 The Park began to minimize its deals and incentives and was able to maintain an

ABOVE and LEFT: The luxurious first-class Radisson Hotel offers quality accommodations to business travelers and tourists visiting downtown Cleveland.

occupancy level in the mid-90-percent range. The property was tailored to meet the needs of long-term renters, and flexible lease plans were added to satisfy corporate tenants who wanted short-term, furnished suites.

Next came a decision to discontinue all rent deals and gradually raise rents and upgrade the property and the service package. Aesthetic updating was undertaken to continue to attract a more upscale and professional tenant.

The tenant profile shows a steady increase in professionals, rising from 42 percent in 1982 to 68 percent in 1988. Other aspects of the profile have remained nearly constant; about 60 percent of the tenants are male and 80 percent are single.

The tenants—many of them young professionals such as lawyers and investment bankers—have a great opportunity to get to know each other. They may end up in line together at the supermarket on the first floor or get acquainted through a wide variety of in-house activities. There are concerts, fashion shows, barbecues, and parties. There are also rowing teams, a volleyball team, and a softball team.

All of the sports teams continue to help maintain Reserve Square's high level of involvement in the community. For example, the rowing teams compete on the Cuyahoga River in the Flats Rowing League, and Reserve Square hosts an annual volleyball tournament that has attracted 30 teams from corporations. The tournament has raised more than $10,000 for the Citizens Mental Health Assembly's Teen Stress and Suicide Prevention Program.

Reserve Square likes to think of itself as a neighborhood. It even has a caroling group that tours the downtown area during the holidays to spread good cheer. The complex is also a regular point—No. 62—on Cleveland's popular sightseeing tours on Lolly the Trolley.

Because of the attractions of city life, some people who work in the suburbs and could live close to their jobs have chosen to live at Reserve Square. The prospects for more tenants going the same route are high because many corporate offices are locating on the fringe of urban areas.

Life-style is the main reason tenants choose Reserve Square. Living downtown offers convenience, friendliness, and excitement. Those who transfer to Cleveland from New York, Chicago, and other major urban areas say Reserve Square is a bargain. They point out that suites cost considerably less than what they paid for comparable apartments in other cities, and the service package includes a concierge and doorman. All the amenities one could want are also at their fingertips.

Reserve Square, which covers a full city block, has a choice location in the center of a business district that has undergone dramatic growth with the addition of One Cleveland Center and other new buildings. More development in the area, part of the Erieview revival undertaken by Richard E. and David H. Jacobs with their Galleria shopping mall as the flagship, will make the location even more desirable.

As downtown development continues to evolve, Reserve Square stands poised to take advantage of every improvement and new attraction.

KING JAMES GROUP

When four research engineers at the National Aeronautics and Space Administration (NASA) decided to go into real estate development in 1954, they changed their focus from outer space to inner space. After starting in traditional sublot home building, their first major venture was constructing luxury homes in a subdivision they created in Westlake.

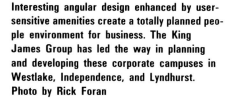

From the mid-1950s to the early 1970s housing construction was the major focus of the company. The King James Group (KJG) built more than 2,800 homes and condominiums and developed more than 500 acres of land. Then, in 1973, KJG expanded into the commercial development market with the construction of its first office building—the first office condominium in the state of Ohio. This was followed by four more rental office buildings in a planned office park. Today KJG has grown to a major presence in the three leading suburban office markets—Westlake, Rockside, and Cedar/I-271 (west, south, and east).

What has set KJG apart from other office developers is its emphasis on features that tenants want. In a highly competitive office market such as greater Cleveland, this kind of attention leases space. Pocket parks and common areas for workers' break times, zoned climate control, security, and proximity to restaurants, shopping, and entertainment are things tenants appreciate. In addition, the firm has formed tenant advisory boards. These groups meet quarterly to discuss any building problems and suggest ways that KJG can meet tenants' changing needs.

A typical KJG office park contains such amenities as outdoor balconies, landscaped jogging/walking paths, professionally staffed fitness centers, a restaurant or cafe, and a day-care center.

"What we are attempting to do," says Rick Foran, KJG's marketing director, "is to create the total office environment that we think will give us, and our tenants, a long-term competitive edge."

In KJG buildings there is a thermostat for every 800 square feet. If the accounting department wants it warmer and the sales department wants it cool, they can both be comfortable in a KJG building. Conference rooms used by all tenants, quarterly newsletters, outdoor picnic areas, and an on-site team of property management professionals who make certain that businesses are not disrupted by mechanical breakdowns make KJG buildings especially attractive. Open floor plans allow tenants the flexibility in designing their office layouts, an option many businesses find appealing.

KJG has more than 1.5 million square feet of office park space under management or construction, and plans to begin construction on an additional 250,000 square feet before the end of 1991. For the King James Group, amenities have spelled success.

Interesting angular design enhanced by user-sensitive amenities create a totally planned people environment for business. The King James Group has led the way in planning and developing these corporate campuses in Westlake, Independence, and Lyndhurst. Photo by Rick Foran

King James Group creates a sense of arrival with three-story entryways that feature landscaping and impressive waterfalls in the glass lobby. Shown here also is the walk-out balcony for executives and staff on the fourth floor. Photo by Tom Abel Photographics

Total planning of office parks includes nature trails for thinking or breaks from the office tedium. The King James Group also includes amenities such as fitness centers, auditoriums, atriums, after-work parties, and restaurants right in the office park. Photo by Rick Foran

LINCLAY CORPORATION

Linclay's 40-acre development in Mayfield Heights—the proposed seven-building project will be developed during the period from 1989 to 1994.

Constructing and managing office buildings that provide beautiful, comfortable working environments is what Linclay Corporation is all about. This Missouri-based development firm opened its Cleveland division in March 1988.

The company is a general partnership development firm, nationally recognized for original architectural designs and high-caliber construction. It has developed a reputation for excellence by providing reliable basic systems (heat, light, air, and water) and by planning projects in minute detail.

Basic building systems are the heart of any building. No matter how stunning a building looks, occupants become irritated if the windows won't open, the air conditioning dies, the heat becomes apparent only after lunch, or the drinking fountains act like a sprinkling system. Linclay's insistence on good, basic systems design frees occupants to concentrate on their work, not their survival.

Planning is another recognized strength of this company. Before any construction begins on a project, Linclay and its client know exactly how the building will look, inside and out. Linclay plans every detail from ground breaking to the selection of artwork for the lobby. The client also knows precisely how long it will take to build it. Planning eliminates surprises during construction and enables equipment and materials to be delivered when needed. There are no delays on a Linclay project while builders wait for an air conditioning unit to arrive, for pink Italian marble to be cut and shipped to the United States, or for a supplier to receive the correct wall covering. On a Linclay project, there are no delays at all. The company has not missed a scheduled opening date since it was founded in 1963.

Linclay's development efforts are focused in three main areas: office and industrial development, retail development, and design/build projects for individual clients. The firm's completed development projects stretch from Presque Isle, Maine, to Winnemucca, Nevada, and include properties in St. Louis, Cincinnati, Columbus, Dayton, Memphis, Chicago, Omaha, Kansas City, and Denver. In the past 25 years Linclay has developed more than 19 million square feet of office, industrial, and retail space, valued at more than $1.2 billion, in 14 states and 32 cities.

Linclay began as a development firm, but it has gradually grown to include total commercial real estate services, such as property management, ownership, and investments. The company manages more than 6 million square feet of property. In addition to its own buildings, it provides management services for clients such as The Prudential, New York Life, Aetna, and Allstate insurance companies. Linclay-managed properties are consistently less expensive to operate than the national average for properties because of the company's de-

The 55,000-square-foot corporate headquarters of Reliance Electric in Mayfield Heights.

Eastmark, a 92,000-square-foot, Class A, multitenant office building, is the centerpiece of Linclay's Landerhaven Corporate Center in Mayfield Heights.

tailed operating standards, ability to take advantage of economies of scale, and attention to preventive maintenance.

The asset management staff at Linclay is composed of property specialists trained in building energy-management computer technology. Its goal in managing a building is to maximize owner income and reduce owners' building management time.

Linclay Investments, a joint venture with New York Life Insurance Company that is currently projected for $80 million in public offerings, is housed in the Denver office. Linclay will be responsible for purchasing, managing, and selling property on an exclusive basis for New York Life.

Linclay's operation is decentralized. Each division is fully staffed to provide all services needed by its clients, including asset management, construction, design, development, and financing. Each division is also capable of handling all phases of development—from securing property, through construction, to managing completed buildings. Legal services, computer information systems, accounting, and human resource management are centralized to support division offices. The firm employs more than 200 people nationwide.

The company was founded in 1963. Its first development project was on a 25-acre tract of land near the intersection of an interstate highway and a major cross street in St. Louis, Missouri. This site was developed into the Progress West Business and Industrial Park, which combines prestigious office buildings, light industry, and warehouses in a park-like setting.

The early growth of the corporation came from designing and building projects for individual business clients, such as the company's work on the Reliance Electric corporate headquarters in Cleveland. In the late 1970s Linclay opened divisions in several other cities and expanded its development activities. Today Linclay has offices in Columbus, Cincinnati, Denver, and its national headquarters in St. Louis. It has more than $200 million in projects under development nationwide.

Linclay was drawn to Cleveland because it has made the transition from an economy based on heavy industry to one based more on services and high technology. It has tremendous natural recreational resources and is an excellent location from which to serve the business needs of the Midwest. Linclay's Cleveland office will serve as a base for the company's development activities throughout Northeast Ohio.

Linclay is an entrepreneurial firm, maintaining a balance between development activities and asset management growth. Noted for high-caliber people, strong ethics, aggressiveness in the marketplace, attention to detail, and client service, Linclay Corporation has created superior business environments nationwide. The company's development approach has positioned it to take on the challenge of providing excellent service to its user and investor clients, both now and in the future.

The entryway to Eastmark features a full-height vaulted glass atrium. Interior finishes and design are befitting a Class A office building, combining the attention to quality and detail that is the hallmark of every Linclay development.

THE SPOHN CORPORATION

The Spohn Corporation, headquartered in Cleveland, is one of the largest mechanical systems contractors in the Midwest. By reputation it is one of the nation's finest. Plumbing, heating, ventilation, air conditioning, power, and process piping—all these mechanical systems have been installed by Spohn.

The company began in Cleveland in 1911, when George W. Spohn began doing repair work and residential heating. George P. Nachman, a Lehigh University mechanical engineer, joined Spohn in 1917, and they incorporated The Spohn Heating and Ventilation Company. During the 1920s and 1930s the firm worked on schools, apartments, and offices, and added plumbing and air conditioning to its list of services. World War II brought a considerable volume of work to the company in many defense plant installations, including the Ravenna Arsenal.

In 1964 the corporate name was shortened to The Spohn Corporation, since the thrust of the firm's business had expanded beyond heating and ventilation.

The Spohn Corporation records show it has performed in excess of 400 mechanical contracting installations in the northeastern United States, with gross earnings up to $25 million annually. Spohn has literally helped shape Cleveland's skyline by providing mechanical contracting services to The Cleveland Clinic Foundation, the State Office Building, Erieview Plaza, National City Center, the Palace Theatre, Western Reserve Historical Society, WJW TV-8, and many other facilities. Surrounding suburban communities have Spohn buildings, too: Stouffer Food Corporation (Solon), Union Carbide (Westlake), FAA facilities (Oberlin), Parma schools—and the list continues.

The Spohn Corporation attributes its business success to many factors. One unique concept that sets it apart is the assignment of an individual project manager to each project. That person assumes total responsibility for the project, regardless of size. Lines of communication are direct and uncomplicated because the project manager has all necessary information.

Another unique aspect of The Spohn Corporation is the use of a computer-aided estimating and project control system. This state-of-the-art hardware and software system is twice as fast as the older, seat-of-the-pants estimate procedure, and it assures a greater degree of accuracy and control. As technology changes, The Spohn Corporation changes to improve services to its customers.

The Spohn Service Corporation, the firm's service arm, ensures that all Spohn-installed equipment and systems work. A fleet of trucks provides 24-hour maintenance to the installations that depend upon trouble-free service.

From small remodeling jobs to Cleveland's larger skyscrapers, The Spohn Corporation continues to help the city shape its skyline, making a lasting contribution to Cleveland's industrial and commercial growth.

The Spohn Corporation has been responsible for the mechanical systems installations in some of Cleveland's larger skyscrapers, such as The Eaton Center (below) and National City Bank (right).

Photo by Jennie Jones

CHAPTER 14

Quality Of Life

Medical, educational, religious, and entertainment institutions contribute to the quality of life of Cleveland area residents.

Photo by Barbara Durham

THE MT. SINAI MEDICAL CENTER

The Mt. Sinai Medical Center is a major teaching hospital located in University Circle, which is the heart of Cleveland's health, educational, and cultural institutions.

As Cleveland's only Jewish-sponsored hospital, Mt. Sinai has a long tradition of dedication to teaching, research, family-centered medical care, and state-of-the-art technology.

Affiliated with the Case Western Reserve University School of Medicine, Mt. Sinai maintains an extensive array of teaching programs, including the only residency program in emergency medicine in the city.

Mt. Sinai also is proud to be the hospital of choice for so many of Cleveland's community-based physicians. More than 500 doctors are on the Mt. Sinai staff, directing the care of about 20,000 inpatients and 100,000 outpatients. Mt. Sinai is one of few area hospitals to see a continued rise in patient admissions over the past several years.

Founded in 1903, Mt. Sinai is known nationally for being an innovator in the health care field.

The world-famous Optifast weight-control program was born at Mt. Sinai out of research into the life-threatening diabetes and hypertension that often accompany obesity. Doctors found that by taking off weight, patients who were critically ill often were able to resume normal lives without medication. There are now 450 Optifast programs worldwide, including the original--Mt. Sinai's Lifeprints weight-control center on Chagrin Boulevard in Beachwood.

Budding artist Tracey Green paints in the Pediatrics playroom.

BELOW: Neonatologist Carmen Hines, M.D., with one of her patients from the Special Care Nursery at The Mt. Sinai Medical Center.

BELOW, RIGHT: Surgeons at Mt. Sinai combine expertise and state-of-the-art technology in the operating room.

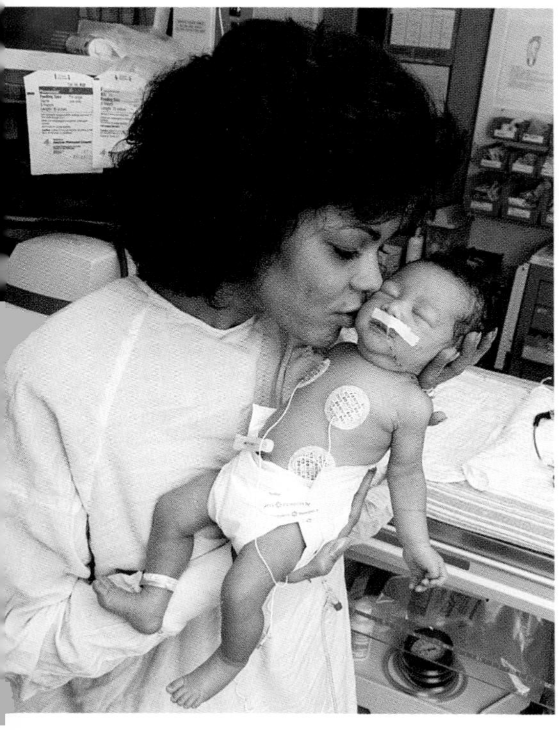

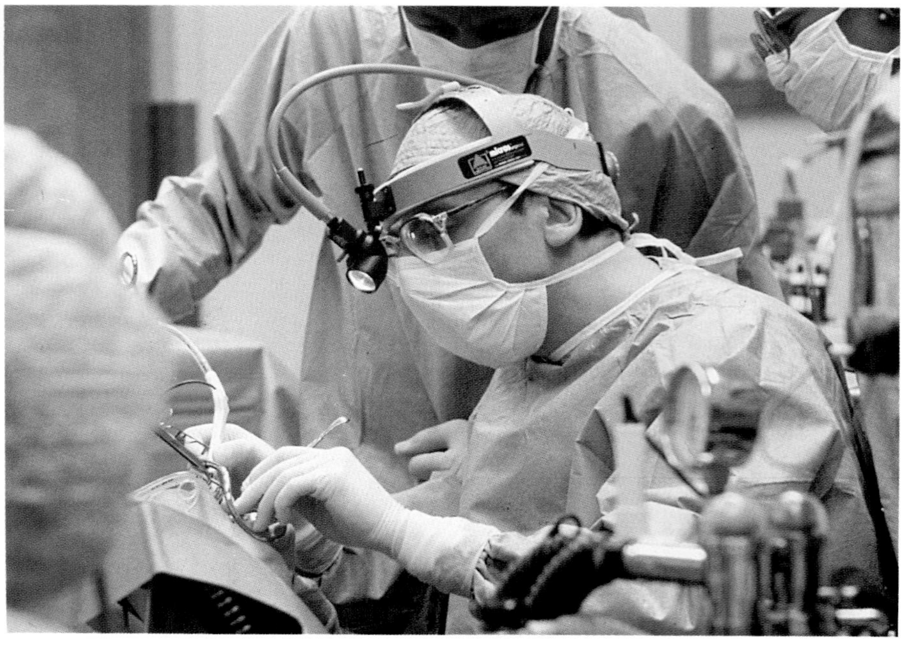

Susan Biasella, R.N. (left), manager of The Mt. Sinai Medical Center's Maternity Matters Center, plays with the newborn son of Maternity Matters Center clients Jeffrey and Nancy Polster of Beachwood, Ohio.

Mt. Sinai's expertise in the field of nutrition, dating back to the development of Optifast, has also led to the medical school's Department of Nutrition relocating to Mt. Sinai. It is the first time a university department has moved into an affiliated hospital.

Mt. Sinai was a national leader in the field of in-vitro fertilization. The world's first surrogate baby born to a genetically unrelated mother (fertilized with the sperm and egg of the adopting couple) began in a Mt. Sinai laboratory.

A strong program in obstretrics and gynecology is spearheaded by the Mt. Sinai Maternity Matters Center, an education and information center for expectant parents located in suburban Beachwood. Mt. Sinai also is proud of its innovative efforts in a number of other fields, including pediatrics, gerontology, and its extensive heart program.

Mt. Sinai is leading the field in the area of Sports Medicine. Mt. Sinai's Sports Medicine Institute opened a new Sports Rehabilitation Center inside the Mandel Jewish Community Center in Beachwood. The area's only rehabilitation program located inside a fitness facility, the center's goal is to return all athletes to their sport as soon as is safely possible.

Mt. Sinai is affiliated with Laurelwood Hospital, one of the area's most prominent psychiatric and substance-abuse hospitals. In 1988 Laurelwood opened two outpatient centers to serve the populations of Lake County, and eastern and western Cuyahoga County.

Mt. Sinai doctors specialize in 30 disciplines. And, through its teaching programs, Mt. Sinai extends its commitment to excellence into the future. With 150 interns and residents participating in 13 different programs, around-the-clock medical expertise is available to all patients.

In nursing, too, Mt. Sinai strives for excellence. It is affiliated with and is pioneering unique programs to enhance nursing professionalism.

The Mt. Sinai Medical Center's mission is to create the finest possible environment in which medical and allied health professions can join forces to enhance, protect, and extend human life.

Gary Calabrese, licensed physical therapist and coordinator of Mt. Sinai's Sports Rehabilitation Center at the Mandel Jewish Community Center, assists an amateur athlete.

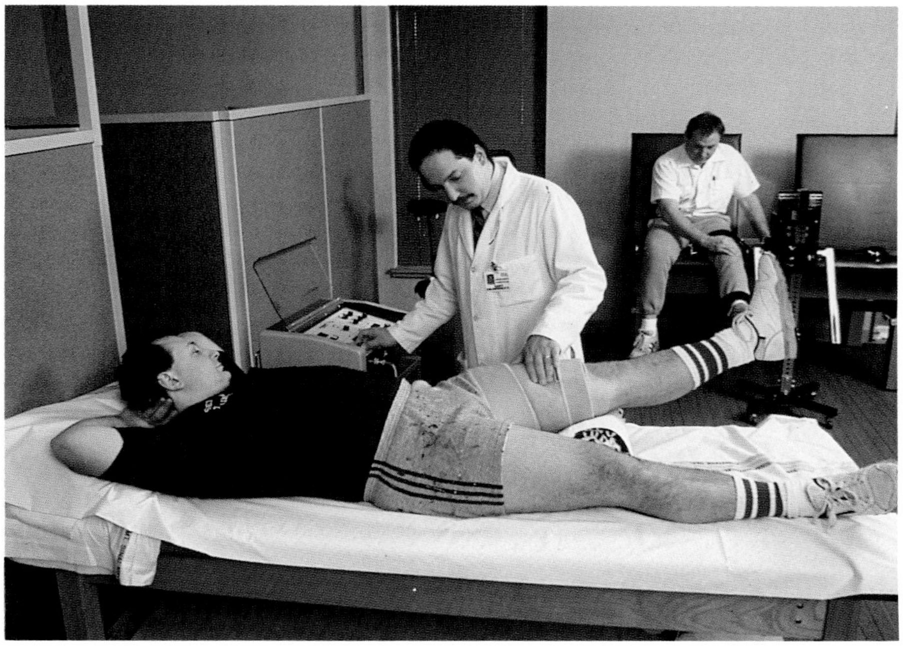

SAINT VINCENT CHARITY HOSPITAL & HEALTH CENTER

Saint Vincent Charity Hospital & Health Center—the "Downtown Hospital."

Saint Vincent Charity Hospital & Health Center, located in the heart of Cleveland, first opened its doors in 1865. Bishop Amadeus Rappe, a group of French nuns, and a small group of civic leaders worked together to establish Saint Vincent Charity as one of the first private general hospitals in Cleveland; it had a bed capacity of 80 when it opened. Captain James Lewis, wounded in the Civil War, was the first patient admitted, but he was rapidly followed by many other wounded veterans. Now, almost 120 years later, Saint Vincent Charity Hospital & Health Center continues to give concerned, caring, quality health care to patients in the Cleveland area and beyond.

The hospital is uniquely situated within Cuyahoga County. On one side is the downtown Cleveland business district, and on the other is an inner-city residential neighborhood. Its location at the interchanges of all the city's freeways makes it one of the most centrally accessible hospitals in the county. For this reason it draws a broad mix of patients, from trauma patients to those seeking cosmetic surgery, from adolescents to senior citizens, and from the seriously ill to those interested in preventative health care techniques.

Saint Vincent is sponsored by the Sisters of Charity of Saint Augustine. In addition to Saint Vincent Charity Hospital & Health Center, the Sisters also sponsor St. John and West Shore hospitals in the Greater Cleveland area, Timken Mercy Medical Center in Canton, and Providence Hospital in Columbia, South Carolina.

The Sisters of Charity have consistently looked to the future, planning the hospital's role in a constantly changing health care environment. In 1872 Saint Vincent Charity opened Cleveland's first surgical amphitheater for the demonstration of clinical and surgical procedures to medical students. As early as 1894 the Sisters were practicing creative medical service management. Realizing that many patients needing medical care did not require hospitalization, they set up an "outdoor" department, one of the earliest hospital outpatient programs in the United States.

In 1898 the Saint Vincent Charity Hospital School of Nursing was founded. In 1919, using money given to the hospital by the National Conference of Catholic Hospitals, the hospital opened one of the first hospital social service depart-

Saint Vincent Medical Office Building is the site of the Occupational Health & Wellness Center.

ments in the country.

The beginning of specialized work in heart disease began at Saint Vincent Charity with the opening of the Cardiovascular Laboratory in 1950. This research led the way to successful open-heart surgery at the hospital in 1956. The operation was the first of its kind in Cleveland and the third in the world. A new patient wing, Tower A, was added in 1965 to handle the increasing number of patients. Another tower was added in 1976, bringing the hospital's full capacity to 442 beds.

Since 1972, when the staff and administration reaffirmed their belief in Cleveland by deciding to remain at the hospital's East 22nd Street location, Saint Vincent Charity Hospital has been known as the "Downtown Hospital." In 1982 the Sisters of Charity again brought their hospitals forward by establishing the Sisters of Charity of Saint Augustine Health and Human Services Corporation to oversee their operations and to facilitate their collaboration. The corporation has allowed the Sisters of Charity to continue their sponsorship role and their tradition of caring for all persons regardless of race, creed, or ability to pay. This tradition of caring is reflected in Saint Vincent Charity's logo, a cross formed by four hearts clustered around a central heart. The logo represents charity, the core of all the hospital's services, surrounded by the work essential to the hospital: caring, research, health promotion, and education.

Innovative approaches to medical care and a commitment to treat the whole person, not just the injury or illness, have marked the delivery of health care services at St. Vincent. The hospital is one of only three in the area operating a Trauma Center. This means the hospital is staffed and equipped to offer the most sophisticated emergency services for critically injured people, 24 hours per day, seven days per week. The Trauma Center, which enlists support from every major area of the hospital, is staffed with highly skilled and certified physicians. These physicians are prepared to address a patient's every need, from paramedic support in the streets through stabilization efforts in the Emergency Room, to the expert trauma surgeons in the operating rooms and intensive care units.

In addition, Saint Vincent Charity participates in a Critical Care Transport Network with University Hospitals of Cleveland, providing emergency transport, in any kind of weather, via ground, helicopter, or jet aircraft. Any of the modes of transport can be in service with a full medical team in a matter of minutes,

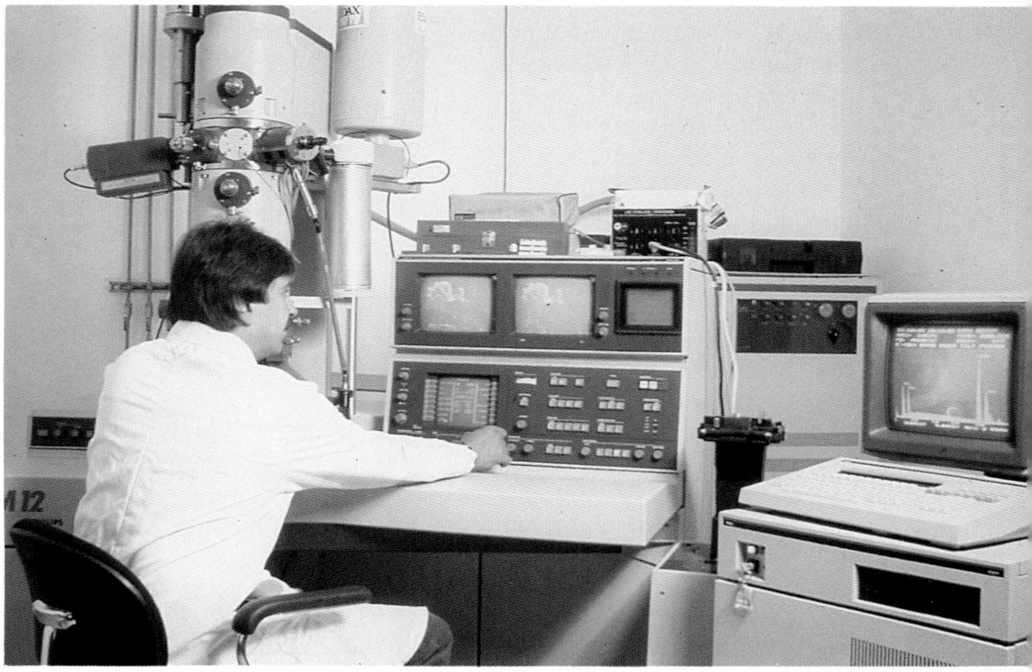

Electron microscopy at the Cleveland Research Institute.

LifeStar Mobile Intensive Care Emergency Transport Vehicle.

offering a faster response time, enhanced service, excellent back-up capabilities, and skilled medical expertise.

Nonemergency medical care for many residents of the community is provided through Saint Vincent Charity's Ambulatory Care Center. This center is an outpatient facility with many separate clinics that serve more than 20,000 patients per year.

Another area in which Saint Vincent Charity has been a leader is in mental health. Ohio's largest general hospital psychiatric program is available through Saint Vincent's Woodruff Pavilion. Working in cooperation with the Cuyahoga County Community Mental Health Board, Woodruff provides northern Ohio's only psychiatric emergency center. It operates a professionally staffed emergency hotline, offering counseling and support for emotional and psychiatric problems 24 hours per day, every day. Saint Vincent Charity is the only medical facility in northern Ohio to offer such round-the-clock crisis intervention.

Woodruff Pavilion also treats eating disorders, offers geriatric psychiatry services, and has a complete general psychiatric medical program. Its award-winning adolescent psychiatric program provides counseling and treatment for young people who have been victimized, as well as those with alcohol and substance-abuse problems.

Saint Vincent's nationally recognized Rosary Hall alcohol and drug rehabilitation program, one of the finest in the United States, has been of direct help to more than 30,000 men and women, offering an outpatient service as well as an in-house facility.

Saint Vincent Charity reinforces its strong commitment to serving the whole patient through a pastoral care team, whose members visit patients and assess their spiritual needs upon entering the hospital. Pastoral care team members also visit patients daily to give comfort and discuss specific concerns.

In addition to its downtown location, Saint Vincent Charity operates satellite health care centers that provide medical care closer to patients' homes.

Quality medical care goes hand in hand with excellence in medical research. In 1980 Saint Vincent's commitment to research was reaffirmed with the opening of the Cleveland Research Institute (CRI) as a hospital subsidiary. This independent corpora-

Medical residents with the hospital's director of Pulmonary Disease.

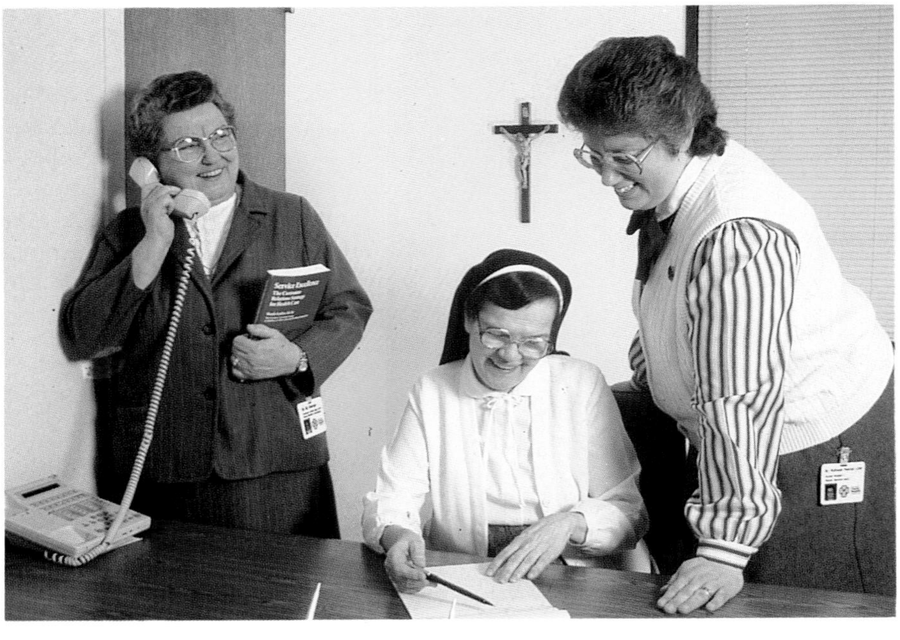

The Sisters of Charity of St. Augustine, the hospital's sponsors, are integral to ongoing patient care.

A laser is used here in peripheral vascular angioplasty.

tion coordinates all facets of medical research at the hospital. Building on previous accomplishments in orthopedic research, the scientific staff of Saint Vincent Charity's Cleveland Research Institute is involved in many facets of scientific investigation, expanding studies into such important areas as heart disease. Currently researchers are directing their cardiovascular research studies toward the early detection and prevention of atherosclerosis.

Hand in hand with ongoing research is the program of continuing education that keeps staff updated on the latest medical breakthroughs. Saint Vincent Charity's residency programs provide young doctors with the highest levels of training and experience covering many clinical services. This, coupled with other continuing educational programs, reflects the commitment to education, placing significant value on Saint Vincent as a major teaching hospital in the Cleveland area.

In keeping with its mission to promote health as well as heal the sick, Saint Vincent Charity's EXCELLE™ Programs offer a wide variety of health promotion opportunities that emphasize techniques necessary to help people return to health or stay well. These programs include Cardiac Renewal, Corporate Programs, Culinary Arts, Pulmonary Rehabilitation, Respiratory Renaissance, Smoking Cessation, Sports Excellence, Stress Management, and Weight Management, to name a few.

Not content to be a leader only in the medical arena, Saint Vincent Charity has also taken a prominent role in revitalizing its own neighborhood. In 1983 the hospital, along with Cleveland State University and Cuyahoga Community College, established the St. Vincent Quadrangle, a consortium of institutions and businesses surrounding the hospital. The purpose of this organization is to improve the quality of life and promote the economic revitalization of the area. Since its formation, the Quadrangle has beautified and strengthened the local community through new business development, building renovation, and the addition of flower gardens and miniparks. It has developed a Quadrangle police force through in-kind contributions of staff and resources of its member organizations. This force provides an additional security presence in the area to supplement existing law enforcement professionals.

Saint Vincent Charity Hospital & Health Center is more than a historical legacy. It began as a downtown urban hospital in 1865, and today it is recognized as an outstanding health and wellness center, a leader in bringing unique, innovative medical services to the people of northern Ohio and beyond.

The St. Vincent Quadrangle is a symbol of unified community efforts.

PARMA COMMUNITY GENERAL HOSPITAL

Parma Community General Hospital was founded in 1961 by a six-city consortium. The political leaders of Brooklyn, Brooklyn Heights, North Royalton, Parma, Parma Heights, and Seven Hills combined efforts to make financing the hospital possible. Today Parma Hospital is a major regional hospital, with a service area that extends into the southern and southwestern suburbs of Cuyahoga County.

Parma Hospital has always provided its service area with the finest health care at the most reasonable cost. Outpatient surgery, especially laser surgery, has converted expensive inpatient admissions to less expensive, outpatient visits. Under the hospital's new FasTrack emergency room urgent-care system, patients with minor injuries can be treated quickly, with full hospital service as a backup. In addition, a new short-term rehabilitation unit aids patients recovering from strokes, heart attacks, and severe trauma.

It's a well-known fact that preventing illness by educating people is the most cost-effective medical service a health institution can provide. Parma Hospital does its part to keep medical costs down through comprehensive health education programs. Its separate health education facility offers 150 varied wellness classes and reaches more than 20,000 people per year. Courses cover prenatal instruction, nutrition, senior health issues, and cardiac rehabilitation, to name a few. Regular seminars on topics such as plastic surgery give potential patients the opportunity to learn about elective and reconstructive surgery procedures and costs.

Since Parma Hospital is a community hospital, patients can be seen by their own physicians in their own neighborhood. However, because Cleveland is a health care mecca, with teaching clinics and tertiary services at other large hospitals, Parma Hospital's patients can take advantage of services throughout the city. If specialized care is needed, patients can be transferred for treatment, then returned to Parma Hospital for follow-up. In addition, Parma Hospital draws its staff from Cleveland's highly skilled pool of professional health care providers.

Parma Hospital established the 55Plus program to meet the needs of older people in its service area. This program provides free transportation to and from the hospital, reduced rates for homemaker services when patients are recovering from an illness, assistance with insurance forms, free health screening, and a free subscription to a newsletter for seniors.

Parma Hospital's service community is an area of rapid development and steady population increase. The hospital is anticipating the needs of its patients by building a medical campus that will include laboratories and multispecialty physicians' offices. Satellite facilities in other suburban locations will function as both doctors' offices and diagnostic clinics.

Parma Community General Hospital has a history of innovative health care and is dedicated to providing excellent, cost-effective community health care services in the future.

The modern entrance to Parma Community General Hospital welcomes patients and visitors alike.

SEA WORLD OF OHIO

Shamu shows off his best behavior for a young Sea World visitor. Performances by Shamu, sea lions, seals, and dolphins help youngsters become enthusiatic students of marine life.

Sea World of Ohio is one of the region's most popular places for family fun. This beautifully landscaped, 90-acre marine life park attracts visitors from Ohio, neighboring states, and Canada. Since the park opened in 1970, 23 million people have passed through the entrance gates.

When people think of summer recreation, they think of Sea World, dolphins, and Shamu, the majestic killer whale. Sea World's ever-expanding summer entertainment also includes a Summer Nights program, with marine animal shows, speedboat races, laser shows, and fireworks.

Sea World of Ohio is part of Sea World Enterprises, which includes three other Sea World parks in California, Florida, and Texas, as well as other entertainment parks in Florida.

Sea World of Ohio is home to 19 different kinds of marine mammals, more than 350 types of fish, nearly 100 specimens of reptiles, and one of the largest waterfowl collections in the world. Since 1963 Sea World Enterprises has made these animals and their marine environments available for study to qualified research organizations through the Hubbs Marine Research Institute in San Diego.

Education is another important activity at Sea World of Ohio. Almost 2 million children have learned about the marine environment through hands-on classes during the school year. In addition, Sea World's outreach projects take educational programs to students who can't visit the park.

Sea World offers other community services, including a year-round catering service for receptions, proms, weddings, and civic luncheons. It has served as a unique site for some of Cleveland's most exciting fund-raising events. These have helped raise money for the Cleveland Ballet, the Boys and Girls Clubs of Greater Cleveland, Ronald McDonald House, and the Diabetes Association of Greater Cleveland, to name just a few.

Sea World provides a significant boost to the local economy. The park employs more than 1,200 people during the summer season and 100 people year round. Since it opened in 1970, it has purchased more than 5.5 million pounds of fresh, restaurant-quality fish to feed its marine animals. It has purchased enough meat to make 4 million hamburgers and 4 million hot dogs for hungry park visitors. Half of all visitors to Sea World come from out of town, so the park also boosts the area's restaurant and lodging business.

Throughout the past two decades Sea World of Ohio has become a unique and exciting place in the family entertainment business, providing the Great Lakes region with fun, education, and community service.

HEALTH CLEVELAND

Fairview General Hospital has a panoramic site, high above the Valley Parkway of the Cleveland Metroparks System.

Health Cleveland, Inc., is the parent organization created in 1986 by the affiliation of Fairview General Hospital (FGH) and Lutheran Medical Center (LMC). In terms of inpatient admissions, Health Cleveland is the largest provider of hospital services in the western greater Cleveland area.

Working together, while maintaining their separate corporate structures and boards of trustees, has had a number of advantages for the hospitals and their patients. For one, the affiliation, by opening the doors of each hospital and its satellite service facilities to patients from the other, has increased the number of locations where patients can receive services. For another, more services are available to more patients, since specialized programs that previously existed at only one of the hospitals are now offered at both. Also costs are being reduced through activities such as joint purchasing, sharing of administrative staff, and coordination of new and existing programs.

FGH and LMC have a distinguished history in health care. Fairview began serving the Cleveland community in 1892. Lutheran first opened its doors four years later. Both hospitals are church affiliated and were founded on the conviction that the sick and needy should be given the best, most compassionate care society could muster. While medicine has grown and changed, compassion still forms the basis of all the care offered by Health Cleveland.

For example, the system sponsors a Senior Circle program that has won national recognition because of the specialized services it provides in the hospital and throughout the community. With the graying of America, the service needs of older persons are increasing dramatically, and Fairview and Lutheran have positioned themselves as caring institutions, ready and able to meet this demand through the innovative Senior Circle program.

The major ingredient in Health Cleveland's success is people. Both hospitals have exceptionally fine staffs, including volunteers, physicians, nurses, and other health care professionals. The medical staffs include a number of the city's leading practitioners, some of whom have achieved national renown.

Both hospitals have long traditions of support and involvement by the community's business, professional, and civic leaders. The rosters of the boards of trustees of the two hospitals and related organizations contain the names of many who rank among Cleveland's most notable and successful citizens.

Similarly the hospitals would not be the excellent institutions they are today were it not for the generosity of many of the city's leading families and businesses. Recognition plaques throughout the two complexes are testimony to the important role charitable contributions have played in the hospitals' development.

Together Fairview and Lutheran offer virtually any health care service a patient could need, from comprehensive inpatient and outpatient divisions to a rapidly growing home care capability. In all, the two institutions provide medical services to approxi-

FGH has developed a comprehensive pediatrics service to complement its maternity program, the largest in Northeastern Ohio.

mately 1,500 patients daily.

The patient care program at FGH involves highly specialized tertiary inpatient units for coronary and post-surgical cases, obstetrics (perinatology), and newborn intensive care as well as a full range of primary care services.

FGH is particularly well known for its maternity service, which is as comprehensive as any currently available. More babies are born at FGH's Birthing Center than anywhere else in northeastern Ohio. More than 4,000 births are recorded in some years.

FGH has been the leading center for heart care on the far west side for many years. The hospital's special 16-bed cardiac intensive care unit was the first in Cleveland. FGH's heart care capabilities include the latest diagnostic technology, open-heart surgery, angioplasty, and ongoing patient support programs.

Fairview is a citywide leader in surgery, ranking among the top five hospitals in annual volume of cases performed. An $11-million Surgery Center has extended the hospital's ability to meet increasing demand for outpatient surgery, while also providing state-of-the-art facilities for highly complex inpatient procedures.

Lutheran Medical Center has long focused on four cornerstones of health care: aging, cancer, occupational health, and medical education.

Its medical geropsychiatric program provides inpatient evaluation and treatment of the medical, social, and emotional problems that prevent the elderly from living normal, independent lives. Thousands of patients have been helped since the program's inception.

Lutheran is also known for its comprehensive cancer program. It is one of a network of strong medical and surgical services maintained by LMC and supported by excellent ancillary services, such as radiology, anesthesiology, and laboratory medicine.

Lutheran Medical Center is also complete with coronary and intensive care units, and specialized labs for cardiovascular services and andrology (infertility) studies.

A leader in occupational health, LMC operates Downtown Healthcare Services (DHS) at 1313 Superior Avenue. DHS offers downtown residents, businesses, and their employees a variety of medical services, including urgent care.

Medical education, LMC's fourth cornerstone, has been strengthened by this affiliation. FGH and LMC maintain residency training for internal medicine, surgery, and family practice physicians. FGH also has a School of Nursing, and its graduates regularly rank among the top scorers of all applicants taking the state R.N. licensing examinations.

Health Cleveland claims areawide leadership in health education for the general public. The Center for Health Education, housed in a free-standing facility in Rocky River, offers a course schedule that is among the most extensive of any hospital-based program nationally.

Health Cleveland, by pooling the resources and expertise of Fairview General Hospital and Lutheran Medical Center, has taken a major step toward providing high-quality, cost-effective health care and related services. The corporation continues to explore ways to bring even more improved health care to the people of the greater Cleveland area.

Lutheran Medical Center serves the entire near West Side community from its location in historic Ohio City.

LMC has long been known for the strength and scope of its radiology services.

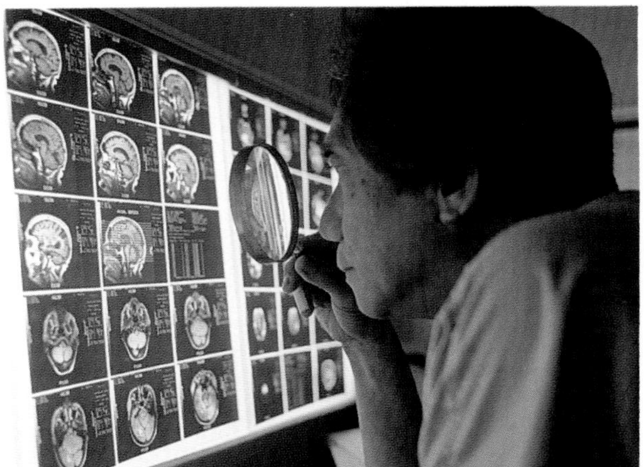

KAISER PERMANENTE

The Ohio Region of Kaiser Permanente is directed by the management-medical leadership team of Kathryn A. Paul, vice-president and regional manager, and Ronald G. Potts, M.D., president and medical director of the Ohio Permanente Medical Group, Inc.

Kaiser Permanente pioneered the prepaid group practice approach to health care more than a half-century ago. Today Kaiser Permanente offers its more than 5.5 million members in 16 states and the District of Columbia quality, comprehensive medical care at a reasonable, predictable price. Kaiser Permanente members don't have forms to fill out or bills from doctors, hospitals, or laboratories to pay.

The traditional medical community once criticized Kaiser Permanente because members' choices of physicians were limited. Today members may choose from among a wide selection of Permanente physicians practicing in the Ohio Region. A Kaiser Permanente member's personal physician will arrange for specialty care when needed. Members need never delay seeking medical care because of its cost. Their monthly dues and their broad benefits cover nearly all necessary care.

Kaiser Permanente is attractive to physicians because it offers them important benefits, too. Permanente physicians practice together as a group dedicated solely to treating Kaiser Permanente members. This group practice arrangement enables each physician to focus on his or her specialty while relying on the advice and expertise of trusted peers.

Kaiser Permanente's success springs from a joint endeavor between the professions of business and medicine. Business managers handle day-to-day functions such as enrolling members and arranging for all aspects of their health care delivery so that Permanente physicians can concentrate fully on meeting members' health care needs. The Kaiser Permanente system allows physicians to teach, conduct research, and develop methods of delivering health care more effectively and efficiently.

As the marketplace has responded to climbing health care costs and attempts by business and government to reduce their share of these costs, more hospitals and physicians have affiliated with managed-care health plans to secure patients and revenue. But many consumers are concerned that physicians, under pressure to control costs, may compromise the quality of the medical care they provide.

Permanente physicians have no economic incentives to overtreat and no pressures from fellow physicians or any third party to undertreat. Permanente physicians are paid on a capitation basis. This means that for a fixed, monthly payment for each enrolled member, the physician group provides for all covered and necessary medical services. This arrangement encourages timely, appropriate, cost-effective care. And Kaiser Permanente's emphasis on prevention and early detection of illness is a far more cost-effective approach than the traditional medical model of treating patients after an injury or illness.

In January 1969 the Community Health Foundation of Cleveland (CHF), a community-sponsored prepayment plan launched in 1964, merged with Kaiser Permanente and was renamed the Kaiser Community Health Foundation. Shortly thereafter, the new health plan purchased a skilled nursing facility in Parma for conversion into the area's first Kaiser Permanente hospital and medical center. Kaiser Permanente's Ohio Region now serves more than 200,000 members in Cuyahoga, Geauga, Lake, Lorain, Medina, Portage, Stark, Summit, and Wayne counties. In the greater Cleveland area, Kaiser Permanente hospitalizes patients at its own expanded medical center in Parma, at Saint Luke's Hospital on the east side, and at Fairview

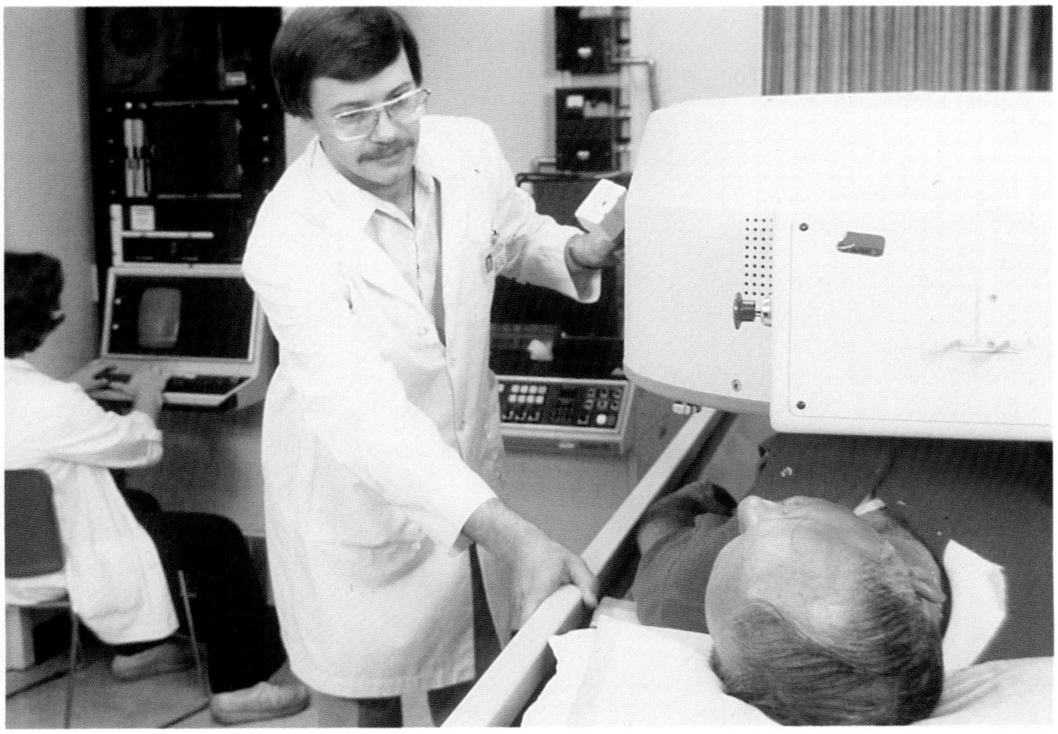

Kaiser Permanente medical coverage includes diagnostic procedures as well as routine office visits and hospitalization.

General Hospital for maternity care on the west side, and refers patients requiring certain highly specialized procedures to MetroHealth Medical Center and The Cleveland Clinic Foundation.

Kaiser Permanente actively promotes health in the Northeast Ohio community by sponsoring health education and physical fitness programs. It has built physical fitness courses on the campuses of several of its medical facilities and sponsored senior citizen baseball teams, the annual Frost Belt Classic (a cross-country ski race), and a summer Health Run. It also offers the Professor Bodywise Traveling Menagerie to elementary schools as a community service. This live theatrical show uses costumed characters and puppets to teach elementary schoolchildren about healthful behavior. Kaiser Permanente also supports a wide variety of other community programs related to health and the arts.

Kaiser Permanente began in 1933, when Dr. Sidney Garfield established a small hospital in the Southern California desert to provide health services for workers building the Los Angeles Aqueduct. He started a plan in which employers paid a portion of their workers' compensation premium to provide care for industrial illnesses and injuries. He also offered workers a chance to enroll in the prepayment plan for nonindustrial-related health care. Dr. Garfield's success and workers' praise for the plan attracted industrialists Henry and Edgar Kaiser. They asked him to set up a similar plan for workers building the Grand Coulee Dam in 1938.

During World War II Dr. Garfield and the Kaisers established prepaid group health care plans at Kaiser shipyards in the San Francisco Bay Area and Vancouver, Washington, and at the Kaiser steel mill in Fontana, California. Today's Kaiser Permanente program grew out of these earlier industrial medical care plans. More than 30,000 employers, large and small, offer their employees a chance to enroll in Kaiser Permanente.

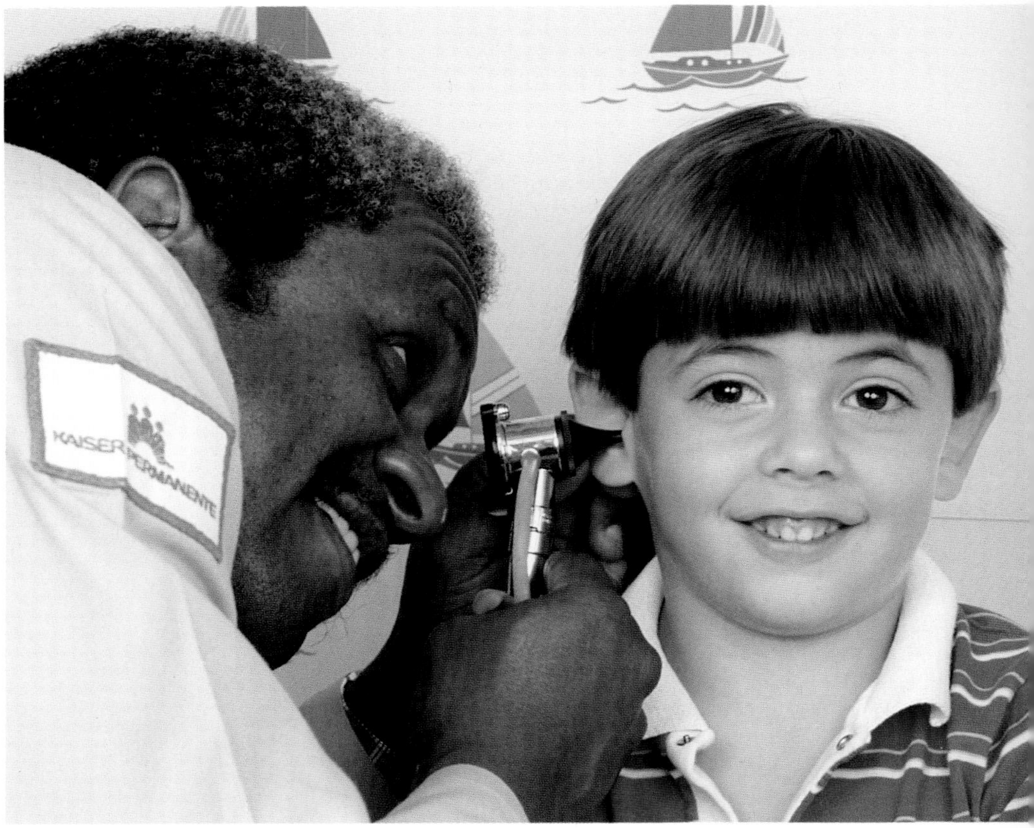

CUYAHOGA COMMUNITY COLLEGE

Cuyahoga Community College (CCC) is Ohio's first and largest community college serving nearly 24,000 students each quarter and more than 40,000 annually. These students receive affordable, quality education in more than 60 career fields in health, business, engineering, and public service technologies and in more than 30 liberal arts areas that enable them to transfer to four-year baccalaureate programs.

Since opening its doors in 1963, CCC has touched the lives of more than 400,000 students. Today students are more mature, with the average age nearly 30. More than 70 percent are part-time students, and more than 60 percent are female. Students range from recent high school graduates to displaced homemakers, laid-off factory workers, and business managers learning new skills. Eighty-nine percent of CCC's graduates remain in Cuyahoga County, adding to the area's trained work force and its economic growth and vitality.

As a comprehensive community college district accredited by the North Central Association of Colleges and Schools, each of CCC's three campuses—downtown Cleveland, Parma, and Warrensville Township—reflects the diversities of the communities it serves. The new Unified Technologies Center (UTC) also exemplifies CCC's commitment to responding to a changing economic environment in business and industry.

Founded as "the people's college," CCC has throughout its history offered services and programs that set a community college apart. These include special services for the disabled, Vietnam veterans, senior adults, and youths. While the commitment to traditional higher education remains strong, CCC has assumed a larger role in the social and economic fabric of greater Cleveland by participating in vital partnerships.

The UTC gives business and industry a unique public/private opportunity to draw upon advanced technology resources that will help them to compete successfully in a radically changed economic environment. Through its partnership with the Cleveland Advanced Manufacturing Program, the UTC has teamed up with Case Western Reserve University and Cleveland State University in a program of applied research, technology applications, and high-quality education and training to improve manufacturing productivity among area companies. The UTC is also home to the recently completed Louis B. Stokes Telecommunications Center.

CCC takes a leadership role in using the arts to build the bridges between the campus and community. The internationally recognized Tri-C JazzFest, the Cultural Arts Series, and Showtime at High Noon Series bring outstanding music, dance, theater, and art events to the greater Cleveland area.

The college is also a founder of the St. Vincent Quadrangle, a consortium of businesses and institutions working together to improve conditions in the neighborhood surrounding CCC's Metropolitan Campus, Cleveland State University, and Saint Vincent Charity Hospital & Health Center.

Cuyahoga Community College is an ever-changing, responsive institution that contributes significantly to Ohio's economic development. Supported by state allocations, county tax levies, and student fees, CCC has become an institution with a proven success record in Ohio.

Program offerings at Cuyahoga Community College range from the practical arts to the fine arts, with associate degree concentrations including art, dance, music, and theater arts.

The expanding health care area means increasing popularity for Cuyahoga Community College's health career programs. The college offers 27 programs, the largest number of health career programs in Ohio.

ST. JOHN HOSPITAL

St. John Hospital, a 225-bed health care facility on Cleveland's West Side, is part of a multihospital system sponsored by the Sisters of Charity of St. Augustine Health & Human Services, Inc. Equipped with the latest technology, emphasis is also placed on patients' social, psychological, and spiritual needs as well.

All good hospitals fight disease with the latest technology, but St. John Hospital has something else in its arsenal—compassion. At the same time that patients' visible illnesses are treated at St. John, their social, psychological, and spiritual needs are also met. The hospital regards family support and social relationships as vital to the emotional well-being of the patient. Doctors, nurses, psychiatrists, counselors, nutritionists, and social workers all help plan each patient's treatment program.

Established in 1890, St. John is a 225-bed Catholic hospital on Cleveland's west side and a co-owner of St. John & West Shore Hospital in Westlake. It is part of a multihospital system sponsored by the Sisters of Charity of St. Augustine Health & Human Services, Inc. The hospital specializes in four areas: kidney disease, cancer, mental health, and geriatric care.

St. John has operated a kidney treatment center since 1964; almost 30 patients per day receive hemodialysis. In addition, it is one of only two hospitals on Cleveland's west side to offer an alternative to hemodialysis—Continuous Ambulatory Peritoneal Dialysis (CAPD). This self-administered dialysis enables patients with kidney disease to be more active and independent.

Long a leader in radiology, St. John Hospital was the first in Ohio to treat cancer with radiation therapy equipment. It continues to be a leader in radiology and radiation therapy, and offers other sophisticated cancer treatment as well.

St. John's mental health service is the largest on the west side, providing both a care plan for the patient and support for the family. Through education, the hospital is also helping to erase the stigma attached to mental disease.

St. John was among the first hospitals to focus on the special medical problems of the elderly with a complete network of services called the Senior Health Connection. Through the hospital's outpatient assessment center, a complete physical examination is performed on older adults. The mental state of the patient and the well-being of the family are considered in the assessment of the older adults' health status.

For St. John, improving the quality of life is as important as extending life itself. Several innovative programs ensure that both patients and their families are fully served. The Mobile Medical Care program provides visits from a doctor or nurse at the elderly patient's home. Hospital Rounds is a free shuttle service that takes patients to and from the hospital. The REFRESH program provides respite for caregivers and a home away from home for dependent persons, as well as overnight hotel accommodations for surgery patients.

St. John is more than a hospital—it is a community that cares. The hospital provides not only high-quality health care, but also a healing atmosphere.

THE CLEVELAND CLINIC FOUNDATION

The Cleveland Clinic Foundation has a reputation as one of the finest medical research and treatment facilities in the world. It is dedicated to providing children and adults with specialized medical care in an environment of highly regarded research and education programs. Close cooperation among physicians on difficult cases is a tradition. More than 100 researchers are working on projects at the Foundation to better understand disease and develop practical solutions.

The Cleveland Clinic Foundation (CCF) is ranked in the top one percent of U.S. hospitals according to case complexity; it has the resources to treat rare and very serious diseases and conditions. The Foundation is also one of the largest and most productive hospitals in the United States. Staff physicians manage 700,000 outpatient visits and 32,000 hospital admissions per year. It is the first medical facility in the United States to qualify as a National Referral Center. This status is conferred by Congress and is intended to safeguard the nation's advanced medical centers that serve large geographical areas.

The Foundation is an international health resource. Patients come from all over the world seeking the sophisticated, interdisciplinary care for which The Cleveland Clinic Foundation is famous. Eighty-five percent of the Foundation's patients are from outside the immediate community—from all 50 states and 78 foreign countries. Eighty-six percent of new patients come to the Foundation after receiving medical attention at another facility. Even though patients come from all over the world, CCF takes very seriously its responsibility to meet the medical needs of people in Northeast Ohio.

Patient care has always been the driving force behind The Cleveland Clinic Foundation. In fact, it was founded by four physicians who started a group practice to improve patient care. Group practices were not common in 1921, when Frank Bunts, George Crile, Sr., William Lower, and John Phillips banded together for "better care of the sick, investigation of their problems, and further education of those who serve."

Because medical knowledge was burgeoning and patient care was becoming complex, they pooled their resources and specialized. Dr. Bunts was the senior surgeon; Dr. Crile, also a surgeon, advanced the cause of research; Dr. Lower was a urologist; and Dr. Phillips founded the medical division. Despite setbacks, such as the stock market crash in October 1929, the Foundation expanded, continuing to make history in patient care, medical research, education, and management.

Today there are 1,000 full-time physicians at The Cleveland Clinic Foundation. They are salaried employees of a not-for-profit group practice. The Foundation is physician governed, but has an independent board of trustees that represents the community. This arrangement ensures that the Foundation's direction will be determined by the public good, and that it will operate with

The Foundation's two-square-mile campus is a Cleveland landmark. More than 1,000 full-time physicians offer state-of-the-art specialized care.

full fiscal integrity. The board oversees the Foundation's unique combination of research and education programs and makes sure they are integrated with outpatient and hospital service delivery.

The Cleveland Clinic Foundation operates Centers of Excellence that address the major health concerns of our time. These centers treat patients, develop innovative programs, and conduct research. Their multidisciplinary approach combines the professional expertise of physicians, nurses, and allied health, technical, and administrative personnel. Among the Centers of Excellence are:

—Cardiovascular Center. This is one of the largest heart centers in the world, recognized as a pioneer in coronary angiography and bypass surgery. It offers a comprehensive range of medical and surgical services for cardiovascular and cerebrovascular disease.

—Cancer Center. Ohio's largest cancer treatment center has developed less radical surgery for thyroid, breast, bone, and larynx cancer; introduced 24-hour discharge for mastectomy patients; and tested new chemotherapy and radiation techniques.

—Musculoskeletal Center. Design of replacement joints for knees, wrists, and hips; development of new treatments for rheumatoid arthritis; and refinement of tendon-releasing surgery for cerebral palsy patients are among this center's accomplishments.

—Neurosciences Center. This is one of the nation's foremost epilepsy diagnosis and treatment centers for stroke, tumors, degenerative nerve disorders, and epilepsy. The Mellen Center for Multiple Sclerosis has enabled establishment of a health-maintenance program for MS patients.

—Digestive Center. With electronic-chip technology that enables physicians to view the gastrointestinal tract on a video monitor, The Cleveland Clinic Foundation has improved diagnosis and treatment of inflammatory bowel disease, ulcers, polyps, and tumors.

—Urogenital and Reproductive Center. In addition to in vitro fertilization, innovative programs include home dialysis, surgery to correct impotence, and a Kidney Transplant Clinic.

The Cleveland Clinic Foundation also contributes to the economic health of the greater Cleveland area. With 9,000 employees, it is the city's largest employer at a single site and the city's largest nongovernment minority employer. Employees, as well as patients and their families, spend millions of dollars locally every year. In addition, The Cleveland Clinic Foundation annually generates $350 million in new dollars for the area's economy through patient care, research, and education, with an economic impact of $2.6 billion. The Foundation's expansion and construction program has provided work for people in 100 specialty trades and is helping to revitalize the surrounding neighborhood.

Commitment to the community is also expressed by meeting the health needs of the indigent. According to Cleveland's Center for Health Affairs, the Foundation ranks fifth among 31 area hospitals in providing indigent care. The Foundation also contributes laboratory services to the City of Cleveland, helps with a neighborhood health center, and provides support for a senior citizens' outreach program.

The Cleveland Clinic Foundation is a medical treasure, renowned worldwide, yet firmly committed to Cleveland.

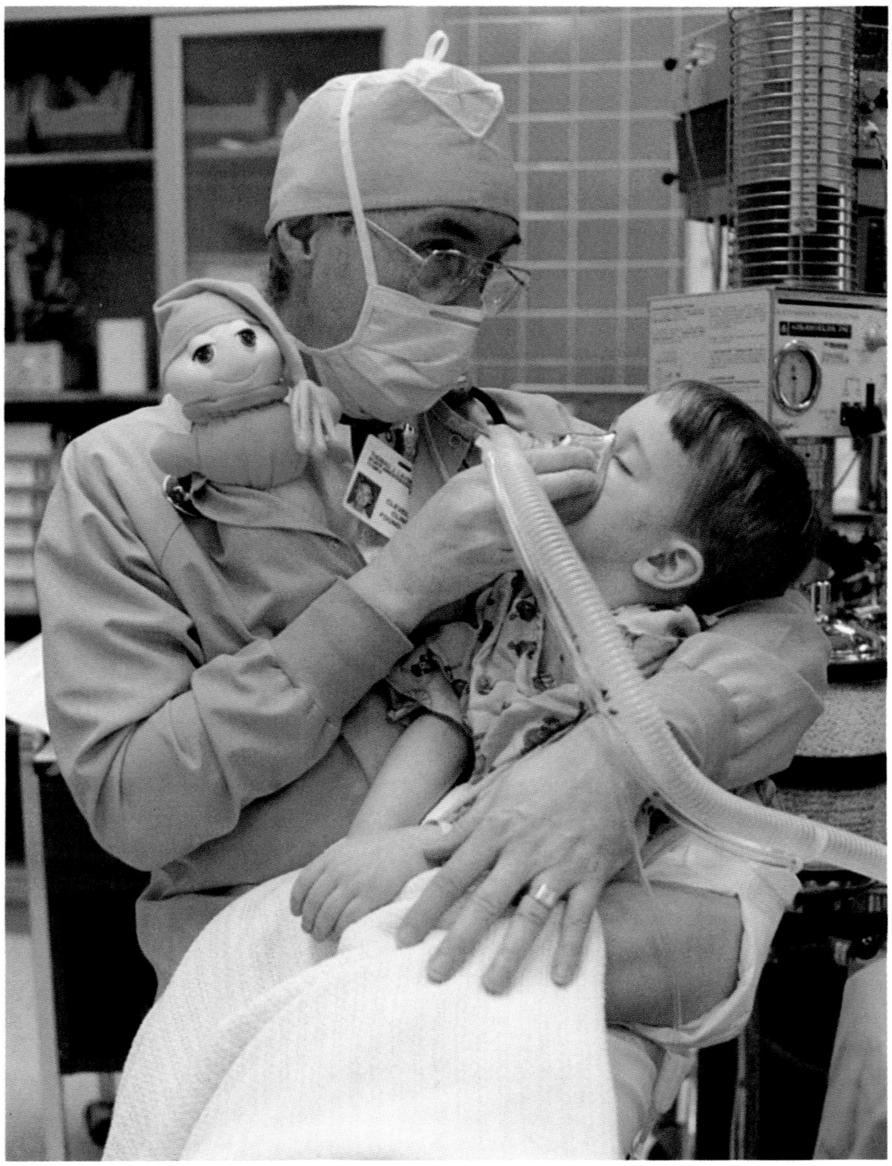

Compassionate patient care is a hallmark of The Cleveland Clinic Foundation.

CATHOLIC DIOCESE OF CLEVELAND

Ohio's rapid population growth spurred statehood for the territory in 1803. The number of Catholics in the area was growing, too. The Diocese of Cincinnati, which included all of Ohio, Michigan, and Wisconsin, was created in 1821 to meet their needs.

The Ohio Canal, which connected Cleveland with the Ohio River and which brought many Irish workers to northern Ohio, was completed in 1832. Then the Commodore Vanderbilt Railroad, connecting Cleveland with Chicago and New York, was finished in 1849. Cleveland's future as an industrial center and a mecca for immigrants was assured. Many German Catholic immigrants settled in the area and began farming, adding to the need for a new diocese. In April 1847 the Diocese of Cleveland was carved out of the Cincinnati Diocese.

The Cleveland Diocese included all of northern Ohio, from Lake Erie south to the 41st parallel. Father Louis Amadeus Rappe, a French-born missionary who had worked with canal workers in Toledo, was appointed the first bishop.

Originally, there was only one church for all the Catholics within the city limits of Cleveland. Dedicated as Our Lady of the Lake in 1840, it became popularly known as St. Mary's on the Flats. The parishioners of St. Mary's reflected the waves of immigration that swept across the United States from Europe. In just 40 years St. Mary's was the mother church of the German, Irish, Bohemian, French, and Polish communities. Each group survived

LEFT: Honors chemistry students Maridi Borszcz and Ed Sarnowski perform a tricky experiment at Holy Name High School under the watchful direction of teacher Marylyn Frohwerk.

BELOW: Mary James, Cleveland's first lay pastoral administrator, and Father Dan Begin distribute Holy Communion at Cleveland's Epiphany Parish.

Bishop Anthony M. Pilla shares the history of Cleveland's first Catholic church, St. Mary's on the Flats, with Enrique Carrion, member of St. Josephat Parish.

the difficulties of starting life in a new country by working together and holding on to a common faith. Eventually, St. Mary's fell into disrepair and was finally torn down in 1886.

When Bishop Rappe resigned his office in 1870, the diocese served more than 100,000 Catholics. During the years of his service, he founded schools, hospitals, orphanages, and homes for the aged and indigent. He also founded St. Mary Seminary, which still flourishes today.

During Bishop Rappe's tenure, Cleveland's St. John Cathedral was built. The exterior was designed by Bishop Rappe and his chief contractor, John B. Wigman. On October 22, 1848, the cornerstone of the cathedral was laid. The foundation was completed by the end of the year, and the walls were begun the following spring. The interior of the cathedral was the first one designed by Patrick Charles Keeley, who went on to design and build 16 cathedrals in other cities nationwide. The St. John Cathedral interior was done in the Gothic style, with a carved oak altar and statues made in France. Financial difficulties slowed progress, but in 1852 the brick ornamental Gothic edifice was finished. It was 170 feet long, 75 feet wide, and could seat 900 people.

Today the eight-county Cleveland Diocese includes Cleveland, Lorain, Painesville, and Akron and their surrounding communities. The diversity of the diocese means it must minister to the needs of urban, suburban, and rural communities. Urban and suburban parishes have ways of sharing resources through a program called Parish to Parish Sharing.

The Cleveland Diocese continues to be a haven for immigrants. It contains more than 50 nationality parishes that serve a diversity of people in the diocese. There are more than 240 parishes in the Cleveland Diocese, including the nationality parishes. Most of the work of the church goes on at this level. Each parish attempts to meet the needs of the people in its area. A parish council, made up of men and women of the parish, works with the pastor to resolve parish issues.

The lay people take a very active role in the decision making of the Catholic Church. A diocesan vision and goals process is under way, which attempts to involve as many people as possible in determining priorities for the rest of the century. The lay people are involved in decisions about fund raising. They also make up the majority of Catholic school faculties.

A trend in the church is to appoint more local priests as bishops in their home dioceses. The Bishop of Cleveland, Anthony M. Pilla, is the first native Clevelander to be named to that post, although Cleveland has provided bishops for many other dioceses nationwide.

The Catholic Church's emphasis on social action—constructive responses to war, poverty, and racism—is an important part of its community ministry. The Social Action Office of the Cleveland Diocese works with community organizations and parishes on social action issues, such as housing or community relations problems.

Teacher Mary Pittinger shares a favorite book with first graders Kionna Steele, David Perez, and Amy Chan at Immaculate Conception School.

One of the major institutions of the diocese is the system of Catholic schools. It is the largest system in Ohio and the seventh-largest private system in the United States. In the City of Cleveland alone, the diocese operates 45 elementary schools and seven secondary schools. In Cleveland's 13 inner-city schools, nearly 90 percent of children enrolled in Catholic schools are not Catholic. This reflects the church's commitment to serve the wider community and to minister to the whole person.

The commitment to the whole person is also demonstrated by the Catholic Charities Corporation of Cleveland. This fund-raising and financial agency supports a wide range of service programs.

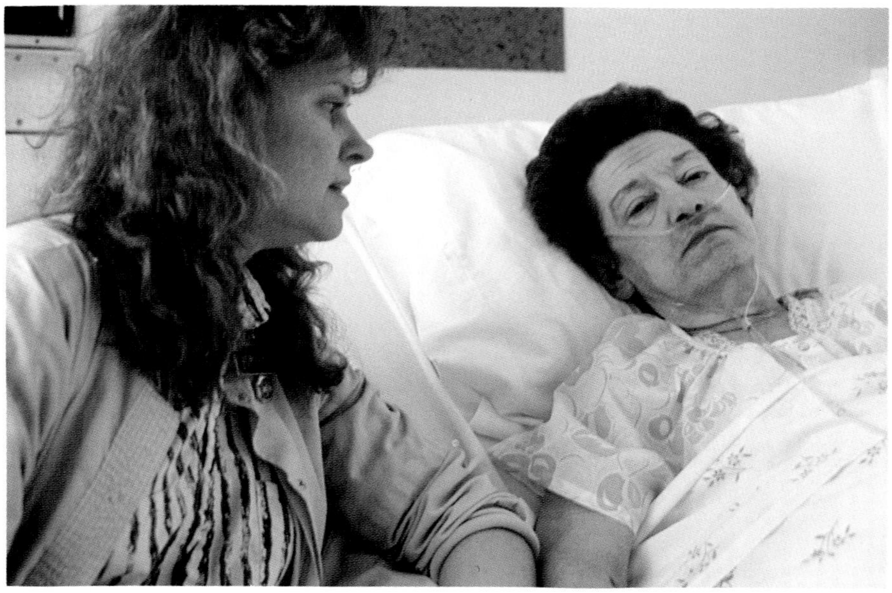

ABOVE: Sister Rose Mary Hoge, O.S.U., offers tutorial support to Sarah Lee Collins at the Martin de Porres Center in Cleveland's Glenville community.

LEFT: Joy Broucek, L.P.N., offers Doris Walker a special touch of encouragement at St. Augustine Manor, a skilled nursing facility.

The history of Catholic Charities as a fund-raising organization goes back to 1918 and a meeting between Father Charles H. LeBlond, first Diocesan Director of Catholic Charities, and Herman J. Trenkamp, a prominent Cleveland Catholic businessman. The two men discussed the importance of the services being provided and the problem of raising funds to support them. At that time the Catholic Church's charitable work was funded by a parish district collection system, street fairs and raffles, and fund-raising efforts by nuns engaged in charitable work.

Father LeBlond explained that the gap between funds collected and money needed was widening every year. A more reliable source of funds had to be found if new buildings were to be constructed or old ones renovated. Trenkamp was impressed with the number of services Catholic Charities provided on such uncertain sources of income. He suggested that the story of these good works should be told with greater vigor throughout the diocese. He decided what was needed was a dynamic group of Catholic laymen organized to raise money.

Trenkamp was a man of action. In April 1919 the Catholic Charities Corporation was incorporated by the State of Ohio. The trustees were all volunteers. Their social and economic backgrounds were varied, and they represented the entire geographic area of the diocese. Their first organized fund-raising appeal netted $72,000 from 20 parishes.

The Catholic Charities Appeal has been very successful and has steadily expanded. Between 1922 and 1945 from $200,000 to $300,000 was raised annually, except during the height of the Depression. By 1957 the million-dollar mark was attained, and in 1970 the $2-million mark was passed. By the mid-1980s the Appeal was raising more than $6 million per year to support a broad range of community services.

LEFT: Director of Family Services Ellen Benoit conducts a family therapy session at Parmadale Village.

BELOW: John Wallace, with the advice of teacher Melissa Messmer, works on a computer puzzle at OLA/St. Joseph Center for developmentally handicapped children.

Less than 10 percent of all money raised goes to pay for fundraising expenses and administration. The rest is used to serve more than 300,000 families and individuals who ask for help from agencies and programs supported by the Catholic Charities Appeal.

In addition, the Catholic Charities Corporation and the Diocesan Director of Catholic Charities, trustees and staff of the Federation of Catholic Community Services, and members of advisory boards review the budgets and requests from each program or institution. These reviews give Catholic Charities information to develop funding priorities and appropriate appeal goals.

The mission of this arm of the Catholic Church is to translate the gospel message into programs that serve people directly, to confront the root causes of injustice, and to affirm and promote the dignity of every person. Catholic Charities is dedicated to eliminating social injustice and providing human service programs that help the entire community, especially the poor. These programs are characterized by enablement, advocacy, and building a caring Christian community. They include:

—Institutions and services for disturbed, neglected, or handicapped children; the elderly; mentally retarded adults; runaway youth; alcoholics; the poor; the homeless; and the hungry.

—Counseling centers that provide individual, family, and group counseling; psychiatric consultations; and outpatient psychiatric services to children, youth, and their parents.

—Regional service bureaus to provide social services to the various counties that make up the diocese.

—Special service offices to focus on the specific needs of children and youth, the aged, married couples, the mentally retarded, the deaf and hard of hearing, and the blind.

—Information and referral services linking people in need with diocesan and community human services.

Catholic Charities also endeavors to promote shared responsibility, accountability, and stewardship among the agencies it supports and a spirit of cooperation with other community services. The agencies funded by Catholic Charities recognize their responsibility to manage their resources and evaluate their services carefully.

To improve service delivery, the Federation of Catholic Community Services was formed in 1972. This organization has member agencies for which it provides services such as bookkeeping, collections, and audits. It also provides technical assistance in grantsmanship, management, periodic program review, program consultation, development of priorities, and budget management. The federation works to enhance the charitable activities of the Diocese of Cleveland for the benefit of people from all walks of life, regardless of religion, race, sex, or financial condition.

Catholic Charities has placed an increasing emphasis on "A Legacy of Caring," a long-term financial support program that suggests people establish living endowments or consider leaving money or other worldly goods to Catholic Charities. In this way, they will contribute to the development of a more consistent source of support for the church's human services work.

Bishop Anthony Pilla has written: "The history and tradition of the Diocese of Cleveland, along with its present-day wealth of cultures and peoples, is a rightful source of pride for us all. In spite of ever-present problems and shortcomings, when we see all that has been done in the past, we can take courage in the present, and with the help of our God, hope in the future."

JEWISH COMMUNITY FEDERATION

Each year some 500 community volunteers turn out for "Super Sunday," the all-day dialathon that realizes more than one-fourth of all commitments to the annual Jewish Welfare Fund Appeal.

A cornerstone of Jewish life in Cleveland is the Jewish Community Federation. Founded in 1903 as the Federation of Jewish Charities, the organization was created to eliminate competing fund drives by uniting several local campaigns into one comprehensive appeal. Today, while development of financial resources continues to be central in the federation's mission, the organization has a complex, far-reaching agenda that dwarfs the original vision.

The Jewish Community Federation responds to the needs of the Jewish community locally, nationally, and overseas through organized leadership, cooperative action, and coordinated fund raising. Although it strives to blend varying elements in the community into a strong and cohesive Jewish force, part of the federation's vitality stems from the differing viewpoints represented and expressed by the thousands of men and women who participate in it. The objective has always been unity, not uniformity.

The final authority of the federation is its membership, which consists of some 20,000 people who make contributions of at least $10 to the annual Jewish Welfare Fund Appeal. Members elect a board of trustees at each annual meeting, and the board, in turn, elects federation officers. But the key to the organization's success is the legions of devoted volunteers who commit themselves so thoughtfully and energetically to the federation's wide range of humanitarian activities.

After operating out of various downtown locations for 62 years, the federation erected its own four-story structure at 18th and Euclid in 1965.

Although hundreds of community volunteers serve on various federation committees, it is the annual Jewish Welfare Fund campaign that galvanizes almost 2,000 men, women, and young adults into voluntary action. Their dedicated participation helps achieve yearly campaign goals that exceed $25 million.

These contributions, realized from a community of 65,000 Jews, place Cleveland at the top of all major American Jewish communities in per capita giving. Moreover, as a result of the great number of volunteer hours and overall efficiency of the drive, campaign and collection costs are less than 6 percent.

Transcending Jewish Welfare Fund statistics is the meaning of the Jewish Welfare Fund. It supports counseling, home-delivered meals, day care, Jewish education, resettlement services, and scores of other vital programs in Cleveland, Israel, and around the globe. It means heightened Jewish consciousness for every individual who participates in a campaign mission to Israel or Washington or who hears a campaign speaker. And it means "community," owing to the extraordinary way the Jewish Welfare Fund Appeal unifies and mobilizes Cleveland Jewry.

A quite different financial resource is the federation's Endowment Fund, created in 1955 to meet emergencies and help launch promising experimental projects. Of hundreds of local grants, some of the largest have supported imaginative programming in Jewish education, family life, and the capital needs of several Jewish agencies. An innovative mortgage assistance program, the Heights Area Project, received Endowment Fund support in the 1970s and continues to promote integrated communities today. The Endowment Fund has also participated in community-wide projects such as the Playhouse Square Foundation's revitalization program, Cleveland Initiative for Education in the city's public schools, Greater Cleveland

Endowment Fund support of the Cleveland Initiative for Education's Scholarship-in-Escrow program exemplifies the federation's commitment to the total community.

Community Food Bank, and the Child Day Care Planning Project of the Federation for Community Planning.

The federation's Mandel Human Resources Development Program promotes broader community involvement and a higher caliber of both volunteer and staff leadership. Especially successful undertakings are annual leadership development courses—effective pathways to major leadership roles for young men and women.

Hand in hand with developing financial resources, federation volunteers guarantee that contributor dollars are used as efficiently as possible. Budget and social planning volunteers must stay intimately aware of community needs and agency programs designed to meet those needs. That constant process includes conducting demographic research, setting community priorities, helping develop new services, taking advantage of government funds, and looking ahead to facility needs. The budgeting and planning arms also link the federation with a major partner in boosting quality of life in the Cleveland area—United Way Services.

In recent years social planners have devoted considerable attention to programs for persons with disabilities, older persons, and single parents and their children. Particularly high on the federation's planning agenda are issues of Jewish identity, as the community seeks to ensure that the next generation will live as committed, informed Jews.

The federation's deep commitment to combating anti-Semitism and discrimination, preserving human rights, clarifying church-state issues, keeping the public informed about Israel, heightening awareness of the Holocaust, maintaining a harmonious Jewish community, stabilizing neighborhoods, and strengthening Cleveland Jewry's relationship with the general community fills the challenging arena known as community relations. Volunteers in that vital arm of federation activities organize rallies in support of Soviet Jewry, sponsor study missions to Israel, work with schools to promote Holocaust studies and to smooth religious frictions related to holiday celebrations, and reach out to other religious and ethnic groups.

While the Jewish Community Federation is a progressive, contemporary organization always planning for tomorrow, it also is shaped by its beginnings and the ancient tradition of *tzedakah*—social justice. Although the meeting minutes of today may be typed on a word processor and duplicated on a high-speed photocopier, they still deal with the same Jewish ideals and deeply human concerns that led to the federation's creation in 1903. Those ideals will continue to guide the organization in the years ahead.

With the 85 and older segment of the Cleveland Jewish community nearly doubling during the 1980s, and the 65 and older population approaching 20 percent, programming for the elderly is a major thrust of the federation's work with its family of local agencies.

UNIVERSITY HOSPITALS OF CLEVELAND

Helicopter blades pierce the night air—a child with a dangerously high fever arrives at University Hospitals. She is one of 27,500 patients who will receive medical care at University Hospitals (UH) in one year. This child was sent to UH because the hospital offers world leadership in patient care, research, and teaching.

Cleveland is a medical mecca, and University Hospitals is at the center of it. The hospital's roots go back to 1863, when volunteers established a "home for the friendless Civil War refugees." This grew into a medical care facility that affiliated with Western Reserve University well before 1900.

The affiliation distinguishes UH to this day. The principal difference between University Hospitals and other health care providers is its teaching function. Each year more than 500 residents train there. In addition, only members of the Case Western Reserve University schools of Medicine, Dentistry, or Nursing are eligible to be on staff. Thus, patients continually have access to the latest medical diagnoses, procedures, and equipment.

The finest medical technology is available in emergency situations through the use of University's Air Service helicopters.

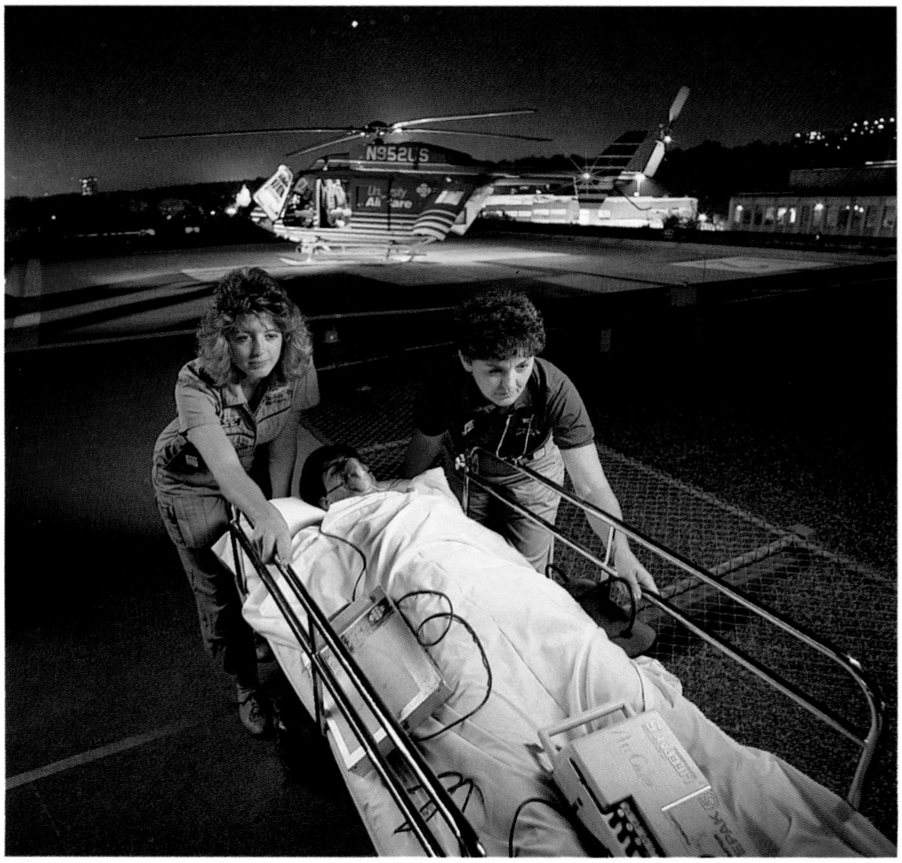

This affiliation has other advantages. Promising medical research is conducted. In fact, the combined projects at University Hospitals and the university form Ohio's largest biomedical research center.

The combination of focused research with exceptional patient care has resulted in many firsts for University Hospitals. The world's first blood transfusion, gas anesthesiology, and mitral valve operation were performed there. The UH staff first developed a mechanical respirator, removed a heart tumor, and isolated thiamine and Vitamin B.

The hospital was the first in Ohio to own a Positron Emission Tomography (PET) Scanner. The child in the helicopter will benefit from the powerful diagnostic capabilities of this equipment.

University Hospitals of Cleveland offers leadership in patient care, research, and teaching.

This long list of triumphs attests to University Hospitals' ability to treat the most complicated medical problems known. Yet patients at the five campus buildings often are unaware of these accolades. They see the hospital through its caring, personalized staff. At Lakeside and Hanna House, general medical facilities; McDonald Hospital for Women; Rainbow Babies and Children's Hospital; and Hanna Pavilion psychiatric hospital, the patient and the family are the focus of attention. The hospitals' 874 beds are almost always occupied. The Emergency Room and Ambulatory Services are used by thousands more. They come to take advantage of the hospitals' internationally known expertise in pediatrics, geriatrics, high-risk maternity care, cancer, Alzheimer's disease, orthopedics, and other specializations.

University Hospitals has the greatest array of biomedical research in Ohio. It also trains the doctors who will be the future of medicine. However, its principal focus, both now and in the future, is to make its patients well.

CLEVELAND STATE UNIVERSITY

Cleveland State University is located on Euclid Avenue in downtown Cleveland. Its student body comes from all levels of study and all walks of life in Cleveland and the surrounding area to fulfill their educational goals in a stimulating urban environment.

Cleveland State University (CSU) is proud to be in downtown Cleveland, right in the middle of business, politics, and large-scale developments. Students are not in a sylvan setting, removed from real life; they're at a truly urban university. "We're part and parcel of the community," says Dr. John A. Flower, president of CSU. "Our intent is to be woven into the fabric of greater Cleveland."

The students affirm that goal. They are black, white, rich, poor, from prep schools, from city schools, all ages, all levels of study. Almost all of them come from Cuyahoga County or the six surrounding counties, and most of the 51,000 graduates have remained in the Cleveland area. Among them are local judges who attended CSU's Cleveland Marshall College of Law, the largest law college in the state.

When Cleveland State University opened in the 1960s, it offered mostly bachelor's degrees, but gradually, as the demand for postgraduate education increased, it established many graduate programs. Now, one-fourth of CSU students are at the graduate level.

Cleveland State University works with area manufacturers through the Advanced Manufacturing Center (AMC), a part of Cleveland Advanced Manufacturing Program (CAMP). The goal of CAMP, according to Robert G. Brown, its president, is to promote international competitiveness for manufacturers by bringing advanced technology into their production systems.

Improving Ford's feeder bowl systems was one of AMC's early successes. Feeder bowls shake small parts until they line up facing the same direction; then they spit them out one-at-a-time into automated assembly operations. Sometimes, however, there are problems with the manufacturing process. CSU's researchers identified the vibration patterns in the feeder bowls and discovered how to make them operate at peak efficiency by using vibration sensors, called accelerometers. Because of this breakthrough, Ford now has an advantage over its competitors. This particular application of accelerometers might be original enough to qualify for a patent.

Cleveland State University has been an active part of city life for more than 20 years. CSU's diverse student population, academic programs that train professionals to serve the community, and collaboration with area industry all fulfill the university's mission to be part of the city that surrounds it.

"Cleveland State University is moving into a period of maturity," Flower says. Doctoral degree offerings are expanding, including a doctorate in Business Administration, added in 1988. "The university is becoming more well rounded, so that CSU is not only woven into the fabric of greater Cleveland, but is also making that fabric stronger."

MERIDIA HEALTH SYSTEM

Meridia Health System was founded in December 1984. Its mission is to become the health system of choice in greater Cleveland by providing high-quality, essential health services at competitive prices in convenient, attractive surroundings.

Meridia is now the largest inpatient health-care system in Northeast Ohio. It began with the merger of Huron Road, Euclid General, and Hillcrest hospitals. In 1986 Suburban Community Hospital joined the system. Meridia, however, is much more than four cooperating hospitals.

"We are a multihealth system, not a multihospital system," says Richard J. McCann, president and chief executive officer of Meridia Health System. "We have a common mission and purpose, and we are developing a management philosophy that is unique to Meridia."

The multihealth network maintains 11 facilities in 40 communities on Cleveland's east side and covers more than 300,000 households. More than 1,100 physicians in 40 specialties work in the Meridia Health System. Along with nearly 5,000 other health professionals, they serve more than 40,000 inpatients and 100,000 outpatients each year.

Meridia Euclid Rehabilitation Center is a 48-bed center dedicated to the restoration of people, disabled by disease or injury, to their maximum physical function, through a comprehensive, integrated program of medical and social services. Accredited by the Council on Accreditation of Rehabilitation Facilities (CARF), the center offers a multidisciplinary team approach to the care and treatment of patients. The center is adjacent to Meridia Euclid Hospital.

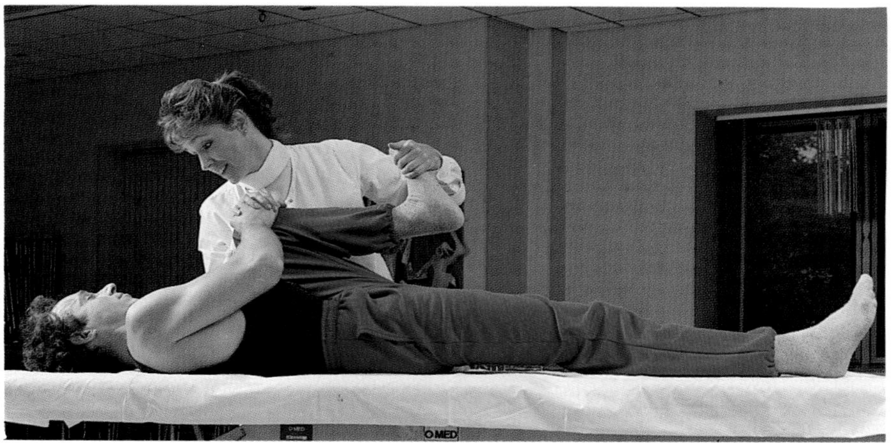

The Meridia system also includes a school of nursing, a rehabilitation center, a psychiatric facility, a drug and alcohol treatment center, a physician referral and appointment service called Medline, home health care and home IV therapy, two medical buildings, and a radiology imaging and therapy center.

Meridia is a single health-care resource working to improve the range and quality of services. To meet the need for emergency and walk-in health care, Meridia operates four hospital-based emergency departments, fast-track urgent care, and an emergency medical ambulance service headquartered at Meridia Huron Hospital. An agreement with the Cleveland Clinic was signed in 1988, facilitating future cooperation between Meridia and the clinic for specialized services.

All the "creature comforts" of home are at hand in Meridia Hillcrest Hospital's labor, delivery, recovery (LDR) suites, providing an enlightened approach to childbirth that fosters increased family participation in the birthing experience. Birthing suites are also available at Meridia Euclid Hospital.

Meridia Institute and Meridia Health Ventures are separate business units within Meridia Health System, responsible for developing outpatient services, such as home health care and other nonacute care. These services address the growing need for posthospital support.

Meridia's strength lies in its ability to adapt to change. The trustees of the four hospitals—the architects of the merger—foresaw some trends that would affect health care nationwide toward the end of the century. The challenges included too many beds, rising costs, reduced subsidies

Meridia Suburban Hospital's remodeled intensive/coronary care unit provides private, glass-enclosed rooms for close monitoring of patients. All four Meridia hospitals offer intensive/coronary care units.

for indigent care, nursing shortages, a growing demand for geriatric services, and a transition from fee-for-service to contract reimbursement programs. Meridia is currently the only multihealth system in Northeast Ohio, and it is flexible enough to weather changes in health care.

Another unique aspect of Meridia's corporate structure is that each facility operates independently in matters of health-care delivery; however, one benefit of the merger is the consolidation of fiscal controls, marketing, human resources, and risk management. Linked management information systems now in the implementation phase will also cut overall costs significantly. Cost savings resulting from centralized purchasing, self-insurance, and reduced legal fees are about $3 million annually.

Because of its purchasing clout, Meridia can invest in the latest technology, such as the system-wide laser surgery centers or the new intensive/coronary care unit at Meridia Suburban. In addition, the corporate staff functions as the research and development arm for the system, planning new programs and services. This arrangement enables Meridia to reposition itself in response to the changes in the health-care environment.

In keeping with its goal of providing the full range of essential health services, Meridia offers many specialized community programs. One such service is the Senior Circle program, with special health education activities for seniors, help with medical and insurance forms, and discounts through area merchants. Exercise programs, such as Get Off Your Rocker and Walkersize offer fun, companionship, and an incentive for seniors to stay active. Other community programs meet the special needs of women; people recovering from heart attacks and cancer surgery; those living with diabetes or other chronic conditions, such as chronic pain; and people who need nutrition counseling and help with weight problems.

Employees as well as patients have benefited from the creation of the Meridia system. It is Meridia's goal to practice the service excellence philosophy by fostering an environment that encourages all employees to do their best work and to be satisfied with their jobs. Employees also have better career advancement and skill-building opportunities within the Meridia network than they did at the separate hospitals. For example, the Meridia Huron School of Nursing recently opened an evening registered nurse program to accommodate many daytime employees interested in advancing their careers. In addition, Meridia operates a two-year radiologic technology program.

Meridia Health System will continue to respond to new health-care challenges with innovative and cost-effective services aimed at improving the quality of life and preserving and restoring health.

Meridia Huron Hospital's cardiac catheterization laboratory features the latest in diagnostic technology for detecting and analyzing heart problems. Cardiac catheterization is also offered at Meridia Euclid Hospital.

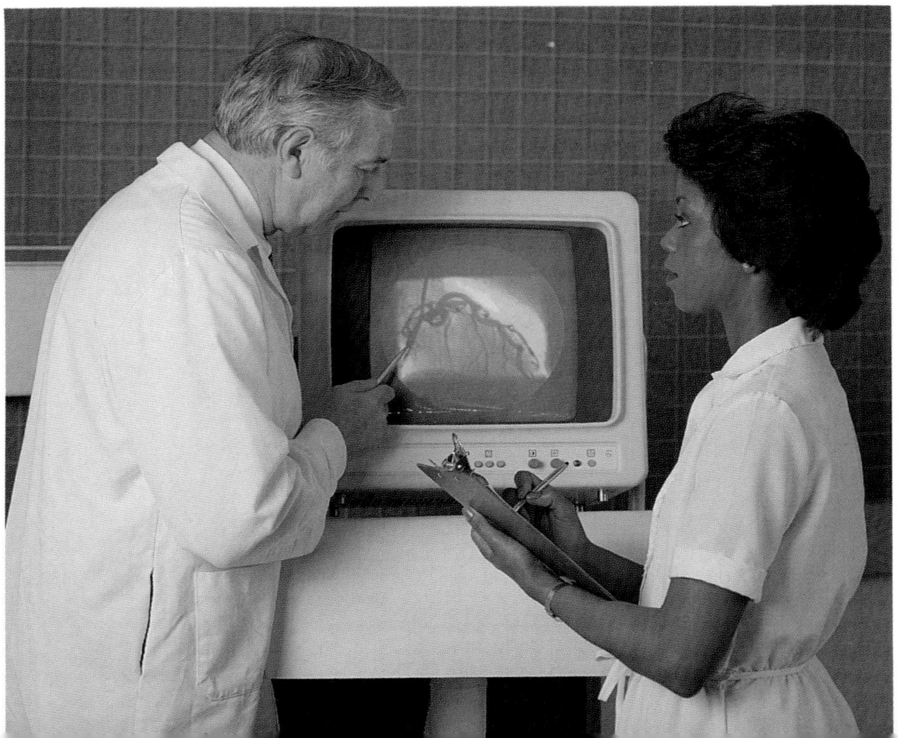

CIGNAL
EXIT

C H A P T E R **15**

The Marketplace

Cleveland's retail establishments, service industries, products, and sporting events are enjoyed by residents and visitors to the area.

Photo by Jim Baron. Courtesy, Image Finders, Inc.

CONCORD HOTELS, INC.

In 1985 Bert Moyar, Andrew Kartalis, and Mark Laport formed a new Cleveland business partnership and created the Concord Companies, a hotel group now ranked among the country's leading hoteliers. The organization, made up of Concord Hotels, Inc., Concord Development Co., and Concord Hospitality Enterprises, boasts an impressive portfolio of hotels representing respected national chains, including Clarion, Holiday, Days, Hampton, and Comfort.

Since its formation in 1985 Concord has developed and acquired a strong network of limited-service and full-service hotels. In the Cleveland area, Concord Hotels include the Clarion Hotel and Conference Center (Eastlake), The Holiday Inn (Beachwood), The Holiday Inn (Mayfield), and the Days Hotel (North Randall).

With expertise in every phase of hotel site selection, design, development, construction, and total management—Concord does it all.

The Concord track record speaks for itself. Its hotels have been built at sites that have proven the wisdom of their selection. With the experience gained from its acquisition and development activities, Concord has perfected its expertise in designing hotels that lend themselves to easy and efficient operation. Concord understands the necessity to correlate the development effort to the management process—to build facilities that can operate efficiently, while responding to each guest's needs and wants.

Concord's vision for the future includes growth, expansion, and continued success, with development of selected new sites and the acquisition of well-positioned existing facilities. The Concord game plan also includes management of properties owned by others and unbundling services to provide sophisticated accounting help to other owner-managers.

What sets the Concord Companies apart? What is the basis for their success? Knowledge, commitment, a team approach, and vision play a major part. But determination is Concord's most important collective corporate strength. The Concord team is not afraid to go the distance. In every project, it assumes responsibility for success with persistent attention to detail. Concord creates opportunities from the day-to-day challenges that may hold others back. With determination and drive, experience, and growth orientation, Concord arrives at a winning combination.

Concord Hotels, Inc., and its sister companies stand for quality service, good business, and a commitment to success. That commitment has built the Concord organization as it has brought business and jobs to the area and become a vital part of the Cleveland lodging economy.

The Clarion Hotel and Conference Center in Eastlake, Ohio, is a flagship hotel in the Concord Hotel chain. Ample rooms and extensive conference facilities are complemented by fine dining in Mantel's restaurant (inset).

PIERRE'S FRENCH ICE CREAM COMPANY

How does a company make hundreds of thousands of people happy? It's easy: make gourmet ice cream. At least, that's what Pierre's French Ice Cream Company has been doing for more than 50 years. And people in Ohio, Pennsylvania, and Georgia are grateful.

When Sol J. Roth, Pierre's president, opened his ice cream company in 1947, he decided to run his business on one simple principle, "Quality, above all else, with a fair price." In 1947 there were 22 ice cream producers in the Cleveland area. Today Pierre's is the only independent ice cream plant in Cleveland. Roth's simple principle turned out to be the formula for success.

Pierre's ice cream continues to meet premium standards because it is made with only the finest ingredients: real cream, fresh-roasted nuts, tree-sweetened fruit, and melt-in-your-mouth chocolate chips. In addition to ice cream, Pierre's makes sherbets, sorbets, and frozen yogurt.

Introduced in April 1988, Pierre's Lite, was created in response to the growing number of health-conscious consumers seeking a nutritious and satisfying alternative to higher-fat, higher-calorie ice cream. Pierre's Lite is 95-percent fat free, has one-third fewer calories than regular ice cream, and, because it is calcium enriched, provides 50 percent of the U.S. RDA of calcium in each four-ounce serving. The line's success has prompted the addition of several flavors and a new pint-size package.

Following Pierre's Lite, the company expanded its selection of healthful desserts to include a soft frozen yogurt. Lower in cholesterol with 30 percent fewer calories than ice cream, Pierre's Soft Frozen Yogurt demonstrated immediate consumer acceptance. The company credits its success to an incomparable smooth and creamy recipe, nine mouth-watering flavors, and sizable calorie and cholesterol reductions.

THE EDWARD J. DEBARTOLO CORPORATION

From shopping to thoroughbred racing, The Edward J. DeBartolo Corporation plays an active role in the economic growth and expansion of the Cleveland area. The firm, which is recognized as one of America's top real estate development and management firms, operates 3 regional malls, 2 community centers, 14 department/specialty stores, several business parks, and a thoroughbred racetrack within the region. Currently more than 6,000 people are employed at these DeBartolo-owned entities.

Great Lakes Mall, opened in 1961, was the first major suburban mall in Ohio and the corporation's first venture into the infant industry of enclosed retail complexes. Great Lakes Mall became the cornerstone for DeBartolo's extensive portfolio, which encompasses more than 86 million square feet of commercial space including more than 77 malls and community centers. Today the 1.5-million-square-foot Great Lakes Mall has undergone a comprehensive renovation and expansion program, which ensures its ability to service generations of shoppers.

An integral link in the DeBartolo retail chain is Randall Park Mall in North Randall. With more than 225 shops, the 2-million-square-foot mall was the largest in the world when it opened in 1976. Richmond Mall, in Richmond Heights, is another corporately owned and operated property that has provided quality merchandise to area residents for more than two decades. Great Lakes Plaza and Maple Leaf Plaza are also part of the holdings. Each mall's overall plan includes provisions for community-oriented programs such as Frequent Shopper, Spotlight, and Million Dollar Machine.

Aside from its retail interests, The Edward J. DeBartolo Corporation is one of America's top investors in sports enterprises with ownership of three thoroughbred racing facilities, the Pittsburgh Penguins of the National Hockey League, and the NFL's "Team of the 1980s," the San Francisco 49ers (owned by Edward J. DeBartolo, Jr.). Thistledown in North Randall was the first of these ventures. In 1960 DeBartolo purchased the facility and then

ABOVE and TOP: Thistledown is one of Ohio's top thoroughbred racing facilities.

LEFT: Randall Park Mall is one of more than 66 shopping malls operated by The Edward J. DeBartolo Corporation.

embarked on a modernization program that transformed the 1920s-style track into one of the top operations of its kind in the state.

In 1986 the completion of a $25-million renovation gave Thistledown an enclosed grandstand, new dining facilities, and the first Diamond Vision color display board in the Midwest. The Ohio Derby, one of the state's most prestigious thoroughbred events, and the Rose DeBartolo Memorial Handicap (presented in honor of Mr. DeBartolo's mother) are hosted at Thistledown annually.

The Higbee Company has serviced Northeast Ohio for more than 125 years. In 1988 DeBartolo, in partnership with Dillard Department Stores, Inc., purchased the 14-unit department store/specialty chain. Recognized as Ohio's largest sales volume retailer of upscale merchandise, Higbee's specializes in bringing the finest quality goods and services to area shoppers. Each of the stores are actively involved in supporting community-oriented programs.

The Edward J. DeBartolo Corporation was founded in Youngstown in 1944. Under the direction of Edward J. DeBartolo, chairman and chief executive officer; Edward J. DeBartolo, Jr., president and chief administrative officer; and Marie Denise DeBartolo, executive vice-president of personnel and public relations, the firm continues to strengthen its leadership role in real estate development and management. Currently 82 projects are in the planning and development stages. These innovative developments and planned expansion through acquisitions will allow DeBartolo to provide continued economic growth through the region and across America.

The Higbee Building on Public Square in downtown Cleveland.

ABOVE and LEFT: Higbee's department stores have served Northeast Ohio for more than 125 years.

INTRANS, INC.

When Brian Hall started college, he planned to be an architect. However, after working for a summer in his father's trucking company, Industrial Transport, Inc., he decided to be the architect of a business rather than of a building. Now, with undergraduate and graduate degrees in business behind him, Brian Hall is president of both Industrial Transport, Inc., and InTrans, Inc., a company he founded in 1985 with his cousin, Carmen Hall. The firms are among the 10 largest black-owned trucking companies in the United States, employing more than 140 people in Ohio, Michigan, and Illinois.

Industrial Transport was involved in over-the-road trucking (moving goods across the state and the country) and trailer switching (moving trailers on and off railroad cars and in and out of assembly plants). Today Industrial serves seven assembly plants in three states. InTrans purchased the over-the-road segment of Industrial Transport's business and has added other services. In addition to freight hauling, InTrans now trains and leases vehicle drivers to other companies and does small-package delivery. The firm also has a separate division that installs cable for cable TV services.

President Brian E. Hall with Horace Hall, vice-president of Industrial Transport, Inc.

Headquartered in Cleveland, Ohio, InTrans, Inc., has a strong commitment to Cleveland's black community. It works closely with the Job Training Partnership Act (JTPA) and veterans' programs to train and employ people to whom job skills and steady work mean a substantially better life.

Hall believes Cleveland offers excellent opportunities for entrepreneurs, especially enterprising minorities. There are many good role models, most of whom are very active in the Minority Purchasing Council of the Greater Cleveland Growth Association and in the Cleveland Business League, a business association for minority entrepreneurs.

In addition to running two trucking concerns, Hall is active in the Ohio Trucking Association, the Council of Smaller Enterprises, and Big Brothers. Brian Hall inherited his desire to serve the community from his father, William Hall, who is president of the Cleveland Business League and active in the Greater Cleveland Growth Association and the Northeast Ohio Area Coordinating Agency.

During the Carter Administration, William Hall lobbied for deregulation of the trucking industry, believing it would open the industry to minorities. But when deregulation of the trucking industry finally became reality, it almost undid the company. A license from the Interstate Commerce Commission is required to operate as a contract or common carrier. Before deregulation it wasn't easy for any company to obtain such a license, but it had been impossible for minority trucking firms. With the assistance of Westinghouse Electric Corporation, which supported Industrial Transport's application to the Interstate Commerce Commission, the company became one of the first black-owned trucking firms to be awarded a 48-state general commodities license.

Brian E. Hall, president of InTrans, Inc.

The license was such a valuable commodity that it could be used as collateral for loans to purchase trucks and other capital expenditures. When the industry was deregulated, this license no longer gave the firm any advantage, and the Halls had to look elsewhere for capital development funds. In addition, deregulation ushered in fierce competition with larger, more established motor carriers who reduced prices to maintain market share.

To cut costs and streamline operations, InTrans turned to computers,

Industrial Transport's Ford Motor Company switching operation in Lorain.

Frank Hall, InTrans dispatcher.

devising an automated information system that revealed both the company's profit centers and its financial weaknesses. Using this information, InTrans and Industrial switched their focus from interstate to intrastate operations and developed a strong regional service network. InTrans also diversified, moving into expediting, consolidation, and warehousing.

A major benefit of deregulation is that, in a competitive atmosphere, shippers are most concerned about finding a transport service that offers the best deal, the most knowledgeable service, and the best performance. InTrans excels in all these areas. So, despite initial difficulties, in the long run, deregulation has had a positive effect on this resourceful company.

InTrans' high standards and commitment to meeting customers' special needs are important reasons for its success. It knows that efficient transportation and excellent service lead to satisfied customers. Excellent service is an InTrans tradition, evident in every phase of its operations. The company initiated in-house driver training to ensure a professional attitude and appearance for all its staff. It operates a diverse fleet of modern equipment, including dry and refrigerated vans, flatbed trucks, and specialized equipment. The internal truck maintenance program guarantees that all this equipment is always available and in good working order when customers need it.

InTrans' computers track long-haul shipments so that tightly scheduled runs can be planned and executed for customers. Long-haul transportation, warehousing, and small-package delivery enable InTrans to provide a shipping service that combines long-haul economy and local convenience. InTrans also has expertise in moving oversize loads. The management team at InTrans has real-world experience in the transportation industry because

JoAnn Reed, comptroller.

they have come up through the ranks. They understand the daily challenges of the business and know how to get the job done.

The future looks bright for InTrans, Inc. Plans to expand into the Baltimore area are in the works. More diversification is being considered. Eventually Brian Hall dreams of expanding internationally into developing countries worldwide. So far, all of his dreams have come true.

THE INTERNATIONAL EXPOSITION CENTER

Hot air balloons, hundreds of boats and cars, and thousands of people—it never feels crowded inside the High-Bay Exhibit Area.

The International Exposition Center, adjacent to Cleveland Hopkins International Airport, is the largest single-building exposition facility in the world, according to the 1988 *Guinness Book of World Records.* With 2.5 million square feet of indoor space, this building offers a variety of exhibition spaces that can be used separately or combined, and each with special technical features exhibitors require.

At the International Exposition (I-X) Center, the marketing strategy is "flexibility." The I-X Center is a facility that can host any event, from the largest to the most intimate. It is proud of its ability to accommodate not only public and industry trade shows, but also sporting events, business conferences, and special events of all sizes.

The I-X Center is home to such popular events as the Mid-America Boat Show, the Greater Cleveland Auto Show, and the Great Lakes Recreational Vehicle Show. In addition, it plays host to the American and Canadian Sport, Travel, & Outdoor Show, one of the largest shows of its kind in the country, attracting more than 300,000 visitors from Ohio, surrounding states, and Canada to the Cleveland area.

At the I-X Center, it is important to think big. The Main Exhibit Hall has 800,000 square feet of exhibition space that can be divided for simultaneous events or used in its entirety. It has a maximum ceiling clearance of 80 feet, with 300-foot clear spans and heavy floor loading capacities. Semitrailer trucks, massive construction equipment, and an Olympic-size running track appear small in the Main Exhibit Hall.

Access to the Main Exhibit Hall is provided by two 300-foot by 45-foot, clear-span, hanger-type doors. Oversize equipment and machinery, including boats and commercial airplanes, can be easily moved in, unloaded, and erected for display and demonstration. In addition, there are 24 loading docks around the building, 15 drive-in truck doors, an 800-foot inside rail spur, and interior truck ramps connecting the building's Main Exhibit Hall to other exhibit levels in the building.

Low Bay and Mezzanine Exhibit halls each have 400,000 square feet of display space with an additional 25,000-square-foot hall available for small groups and displays. The 20,000-square-foot Conference Center is ideal for seminars and meetings. Outdoors there is a half-million-square-foot exhibit area, a 50-acre truck marshalling area, and extensive storage space. "Big" also describes the I-X Center's ample 10,000-space parking area and 40-foot electronic billboard at its entrance.

The sun always shines at the I-X Center thanks to its state-of-the-art, metal-halide, multivapor lighting system, which provides light that closely approximates daylight. The quality of illumination is an ideal enhancer for color telecasting and for capturing eye-catching highlights on displays at the center's shows and events. In addition, the flexibility of

LEFT: The I-X Center gleams with pride even after the crowds have gone home for the night.

BELOW: Parking at the International Exposition Center is plentiful and close.

this lighting system enables the I-X Center to customize and tailor individual lighting for each show.

In addition to space, service is a key factor in the I-X Center's success. An extensive utility distribution system provides electricity, telephone service, compressed air, and water to all exhibitors who need them. In addition, the entire building is wheelchair accessible.

The center's location—adjacent to Cleveland Hopkins International Airport—could not be more convenient for exhibitors. Van Dusen Air Services, a corporate aviation terminal (FBO), is located just a few yards from the Exposition Hall. The Van Dusen Terminal is luxuriously equipped inside, while outside, planes take advantage of the 24-hour maintenance, refueling, and security services.

From the exhibitor's standpoint, professional services provided by the I-X Center are as important as the size and flexibility of the exhibit space. The I-X Center provides complete decorating, layout, and design services in house, and I-X Center marketing and public relations personnel offer assistance to show producers.

The I-X Center sits on 188 acres of land, and the center's owners have big plans for it. Its proximity to the airport and to the NASA Lewis Research Center gives its owners the opportunity to spearhead economic development in the area.

The center's development plans include the addition of a full-service, 300-room hotel connected to its Main Exhibit Hall by an enclosed walkway. An office complex and retail center will be developed in conjunction with the hotel. Long-range development plans include the creation of a permanent international trade mart. The center is designated as a duty-free trade zone, which means items can be received and stored until they are sold in the United States or are returned to the country of origin.

Whether it is a meeting for 200 people, a small trade show, or a world-class exhibit, the International Exhibition Center has the space, the staff, the parking, and the services to handle it.

STOUFFER FOODS CORPORATION

Serving American families good food has been Stouffer's mission since 1922, when Abraham and Mahala Stouffer opened a dairy counter in Cleveland. Wholesome buttermilk, fresh-brewed coffee, and Mrs. Stouffer's Dutch apple pies brought customers back again and again.

With a dedication to quality and a keen understanding of customer need, the Stouffers and their sons, Vernon and Gordon, opened their first restaurant in 1924. By 1926 the Stouffer name was on a chain of restaurants throughout the Midwest. Despite hard times during the Great Depression and World War II, the restaurants prospered by providing good food and good service at a fair price.

In the late 1940s Vernon Stouffer noticed a new trend, an increase in take-out orders. At Stouffer's Shaker Square restaurant, so many customers asked for take-out food that Stouffer chefs tried freezing popular items to meet this demand.

The Stouffer Foods Division was officially christened in 1954, when Stouffer's opened its first frozen-food-processing facility in Cleveland. Stouffer's began to concentrate seriously on filling the expanding consumer need for good, tasty, easy-to-prepare frozen foods. Since then the company has had three main operating characteristics: innovation, quality, and a people philosophy.

Stouffer's entire product line is innovative. The concept of frozen "convenience foods" was novel in itself when the only available frozen foods were traditional "TV dinners." Stouffer's saw a market for unusual dishes—spinach souffle, lobster Newburg, Welsh rarebit—offering value, convenience, and, above all, good taste.

Stouffer's introduction of French bread pizza was a complete departure from the frozen pizza of the day. By combining crisp French bread with traditional pizza toppings, Stouffer's created a truly original frozen pizza.

When Stouffer's Lean Cuisine was launched in 1981, the frozen-food business was changed forever. With its low calorie count, great taste, variety, and convenience, Lean Cuisine appealed to the growing number of busy, health-conscious consumers.

Stouffer's scored another frozen-food success in the 1980s as sales of its frozen entrees to the food-service industry took off. With the same attention to quality and taste, these products enable restaurants and other institutions to serve good food at low cost, and to serve it as their own.

In 1968 Stouffer Foods opened a 42-acre facility in Solon, one of Cleveland's eastern suburbs.

Several quality-assurance programs maintain the company's high standards. Comprehensive testing of finished products ensures quality and purity.

In 1986 the company entered the complete frozen dinner category with an eight-product line called Dinner Supreme. That same year it also introduced a dual-oven tray that maintained taste, texture, and appearance in both microwave and conventional ovens.

Today Stouffer Foods are available through supermarkets and grocery stores nationwide. Stouffer's manufactures more than 100 different items, including entree, side dishes, French bread pizza, Lean Cuisine entrees, and Dinner Supreme complete meals. Regular entrees and side dishes account for almost one-third of the firm's sales, and Lean Cuisine, for another third. French bread pizza alone accounts for nearly $100 million in annual sales.

The primary reason for Stouffer's success is its unswerving dedication to quality. The company's founders insisted that their first restaurant focus on good food, and their high standards have continued to influence Stouffer's product development.

Stouffer's always begins with good food, then experiments with producing it in larger quantities without sacrificing taste. The firm only automates food preparation if it is an improvement over hand preparation. Once Stouffer's develops a good product that can be made in large quantities, it goes into production.

The first step in production is selecting the ingredients. The company's purchasing staff works closely with vendors to assure that ingredients meet its criteria. Ingredients are subjected to stringent laboratory tests. Aspects of packaging, such as the color and wax coating, are also scrutinized.

Stouffer's uses the most advanced preparation and packaging techniques available. First, the food is prepared for processing—meats are cooked, cream and milk are blended, and macaroni, spaghetti, and lasagna noodles are made from only the finest specially ground flour. The ingredients then move to a production line where finished products are created, many of them by hand. All Stouffer products are quick frozen and then stored in a mammoth 120-foot-tall, minus-five-degrees-Fahrenheit, high-rise freezer.

Several quality-assurance programs maintain the company's high standards. Comprehensive testing of finished products ensures quality and purity. These standards are so high that Stouffer products have been chosen by the National Aeronautics and Space Administration

(NASA) for the quarantined feeding of astronauts after their trips into space. The Apollo 11, 12, and 14 astronauts dined on Stouffer's for four good reasons: purity, flavor, quality of ingredients, and variety.

Innovation and quality don't become reality unless a company attracts and keeps good employees. Stouffer's owes its success to a loyal and dedicated team of more than 4,000 employees, many of whom have been with the firm for 10, 20, and even 35 years. The company has never had a layoff and promotes from within, encouraging individual initiative. Its open-door management policy means that any employee can take a concern to the company president and get a hearing. Other special employee benefits include free meals at plant cafeterias and discounts at Stouffer-affiliated hotels and restaurants.

What is noticeable about Stouffer's is the encouragement each employee receives to take responsibility for the quality of the product. Production staff join the quality-control team in testing food as it comes off the line. More than 90 times a shift, samples are tested. Is the rice over or under cooked? Is the macaroni too soft or too hard? Does the sauce taste right? Are the vegetables cooked enough? Are they cooked too much? One employee who thinks something is not Stouffer's quality can reject a batch. For example, one year, a quality-control employee did not think the Jonathan apples used in Stouffer's escalloped apples were up to the company's normal quality standards. Even after adjustments were made in the production recipes, she felt the finished product was just not "Stouffer's." She took her complaint to the president, and that year's entire production of escalloped apples was canceled.

In 1968 Stouffer Foods opened a 42-acre facility in one of Cleveland's eastern suburbs. Since this new location did not have bus service, and a great many of Stouffer's employees did not have cars, the company announced the move a year ahead of time. It offered to pay for driving lessons and to underwrite car loans for any employees who needed cars to work at the new location. When the move was complete, not one employee was left behind.

Since 1968 the firm has continued to expand almost every year, opening facilities in South Carolina and Utah to meet the growing demand. In 1973 Stouffer's became part of Nestlé, the world's largest food corporation, but it still holds to its original purpose. Says Dave Jennings, president of Stouffer Foods Corporation, "We develop foods that taste good, foods you would make or serve at home. And we don't sell truckloads, we sell individual packages to individual consumers. Every package has to be good."

While Stouffer Foods Corporation will continue to be an innovator in the development and production of frozen convenience foods, it will also explore ways to deliver good foods to consumers in other convenient forms in the future. In the past few years significant research has been done to develop products that will take greater advantage of the speed and convenience of the microwave oven. Stouffer's will always offer good-tasting, innovative foods in which quality and convenience are the Stouffer standard.

When Stouffer's Lean Cuisine was launched in 1981, the frozen-food business was changed forever.

HOLZHEIMER INTERIORS, INC.

Dedication to design excellence and a firm commitment to client satisfaction has made Holzheimer Interiors, Inc., one of the largest and most sought-after design studios in northern Ohio.

Holzheimer's outstanding design concepts and craftsmanship have created a nationwide clientele. "Our policy has always been to cater to clients needs, giving more than the contract requires," says chairman Harry Holzheimer. "We take responsibility for the outcome, not just to the letter of the contract. We do whatever extras it takes to make the contract work." This policy has resulted in a very loyal clientele. The firm has designed everything from small vacation homes to palatial country estates and corporate headquarters. An interesting note is that more than 98 percent of Holzheimer clients are repeat customers or referred by other Holzheimer clients.

Located in the heart of Cleveland's cultural center at University Circle, Holzheimer Interiors is one of the city's design leaders. It all began in 1902, when John Holzheimer opened the company that specialized in interior and exterior residential painting. His son, Frank, added quality wall coverings. All five of Frank's sons worked in the business and rapidly expanded the firm to include old-world craftsmanship in furniture, cabinetmaking, and upholstery.

Today Holzheimer's fifth generation is extremely diversified. Whether it be a traditional residence or a state-of-the-art, high-tech medical facility, the designers are skilled in achieving maximum results.

Located in the heart of Cleveland's cultural center at University Circle, Holzheimer Interiors is one of the city's design leaders.

Throughout the extensive in-house research library, the design staff has easy access to detailed information on more than 3,000 manufacturers plus more than 350,000 imported and domestic wall covering, fabric, wood, marble, and carpet samples.

Located just a few blocks from the Holzheimer main studio and showroom is Holzheimer's custom shop. There skilled craftsmen excel in all phases of cabinetry, mill work, finishing, antique restoration, upholstery, and specialty construction. These old-world talents, combined with new technology, enable the company to maintain strict quality control. From initial design concept to final installation, the designers and craftsmen work hand in hand to obtain the desired results.

Being sensitive to client needs and living requirements has made Holzheimer Interiors, Inc., a respected name in the design industry.

ORLANDO BAKING COMPANY

"We're either the largest small bakery or the smallest large bakery in the area," smiles Nick Orlando as he bites into a warm crusty roll just out of the oven at the Orlando Baking Company. Finished loaves, with crunchy golden crusts, are removed from the ovens, inspected, cooled, and packaged. Boxes of bread are loaded into vans and whisked to the top restaurants and grocery stores in Cleveland. This is a typical morning at Orlando Baking Company, maker of the "finest breads since 1872," according to its company logo.

Orlando specializes in hearth-baked breads, which are slowly baked without a pan. These are made from old-world recipes passed down through the Orlando family, some for more than five generations. Orlando works on a "fresh every day" philosophy, so nothing goes into its bread but basic ingredients.

The company provides daily delivery to restaurants and most grocery stores in Northeast Ohio with more than 125 different breads and rolls, including Kaiser rolls, Jewish rye, French bread, Italian garlic bread, old-world round bread, steak and sausage rolls, and Orlando's Ciabatta® bread.

Orlando's first delivery "vehicle" when the Cleveland bakery opened in 1904 was a horse and buggy.

Orlando's sales have been growing steadily in recent years, assisted by consumers who are shunning soft white bread with a lot of sugar and preservatives in favor of specialty breads with more flavor, texture, and no additives. The irony is that Orlando has always provided the flavorful, hearty bread that consumers now demand. "We haven't changed, it's the market that has come around to our way of thinking," says Nick Orlando, the company's president.

Another factor in the firm's recent expansion is its excellent service record. If a restaurant manager runs out of rolls, a quick call will result in an emergency delivery, even if Nick Orlando has to bring it in the back seat of his car.

Says Orlando, "We make our bread the way the best restaurants would do it if they baked it themselves. That's why we sell to many of the finest restaurants in northern Ohio."

The bakery's newest facility, built in 1979, is located in Cleveland's near east side.

The Orlandos opened their first bakery in 1872 in Castel Di'Sangro, Italy. This bakery is still operated by a branch of the Orlando family. In 1904 Guiseppe Orlando brought his family to Cleveland and began making the same delicious, hearth-baked bread the Orlandos made back in Italy. Only the best ingredients were used, and each loaf was baked slowly for full flavor, hearty texture, and golden crust.

Nick Orlando recalls that Guiseppe Orlando's son was killed in World War I. "Guiseppe needed more help, so he sent for his brother's son, my grandfather, in 1920." In 1922 Nick's grandfather purchased the business, and over the years his four sons joined him. Five generations after it was founded in Italy, the Orlando Baking Company is still owned by the Orlando family and still baking top-quality ethnic breads.

One of the specialty breads recently introduced to the Cleveland area is Ciabatta®, a slipper-shaped bread from Italy's Lake Como region. This distinct bread has been a tradition there for centuries and is one of Italy's most popular breads. If Orlando has anything to do with it, Ciabatta® will take over the Cleveland market as well. It's a very simple bread, containing no sugar, shortening, or preservatives, yet Cia-

batta® is extremely difficult for most bakers to produce. Each loaf takes Orlando nearly two days to mix, proof, and bake.

The resulting loaf has a crusty outside and moist inside with a delicious slightly sour flavor. Because of its unique shape and texture, Ciabatta® not only enhances any entrée, it is also ideal for pizza, sandwiches, and hors d'oeuvres. Ciabatta® is the perfect bread for the creative palate. Ciabatta® has already become a big hit in specialty gourmet stores in New York (famous Balducci's for one), Washington, D.C., Philadelphia, and Pittsburgh.

Orlando is delivering Ciabatta® fresh to restaurants and frozen to grocery stores, which is something new for the company. In the past Orlando has produced only fresh-baked bread and rolls, but the firm began to explore the frozen food market in 1987. By partially baking bread then quick freezing it, Orlando can deliver frozen bread that will give consumers "baked today" flavor without resorting to preservatives or artificial ingredients. Customers finish baking the bread when they are ready to use it. Orlando has already expanded its frozen Italian garlic and Ciabatta® breads into the remainder of Ohio and has plans to expand into Michigan, Pennsylvania, and other nearby states.

The bakery has moved several times, but it has always been located on Cleveland's east side. The latest move, in 1979, was accomplished with help from the Woodland East Community Organization and an Urban Development Action Grant through the City of Cleveland. Woodland East Community Organization, a group of local businesses, encourages other businesses to settle in the east side community, providing jobs for residents and stabilizing the area. The land on which the bakery now stands was once an area of empty lots and abandoned houses. Now the City of Cleveland and the Woodland neighborhood can count on tax revenues from a thriving business with an annual payroll of more than $3 million.

With a younger Orlando generation already in the business and more new product ideas in development, it looks like the Orlandos plan on adding at least another 100 years to their history of baking the finest breads.

LEFT: Orlando is the only wholesale bakery in the country making Ciabatta® bread.

BELOW: Bread, fresh from the oven, is carefully inspected daily.

THE L.J. MINOR CORPORATION

The L.J. Minor Corporation was founded in Cleveland in 1951 by Lewis J. Minor, Ph.D., a food scientist honored by the U.S. government for developing special foods for World War II ration kits.

Dr. Minor foresaw that restaurant operators in postwar years would need new ways to make large quantities of stock and broths that are essential ingredients for the soup, sauces, and gravies on a restaurant's menu. In 1951 chefs needed fresh beef bones and vegetables, plus lots of cheap heating energy and several hours of cooking time, to make a small amount of soup or sauce stock.

Using Dr. Minor's new fresh flavor bases, the same chef could make five gallons of comparable stock in four to five minutes. He simply mixed a concentrated beef or chicken base with boiling water and stirred. Cost and labor savings made possible through use of Dr. Minor's new bases created a new food-service market.

At the outset, Dr. Minor made a sales decision that proved an immediate success and still pays off today. He hired retired professional chefs as sales support and product development consultants. Each chef was an outstanding individual. Each had unmatched professional experience and knowledge. These prestigious chefs were able to convince other proud culinarians that the new Minor bases deserved a working role in even the finest hotel and restaurant kitchens.

Because Minor's bases fulfilled their quality flavor claims, word spread and sales increased. By 1966 Minor's bases were in national demand by restaurants, hotels, schools, hospitals, catering firms, colleges and universities, even steamship and airline companies.

And as soon as company finances permitted, Dr. Minor began to repay the obligation he felt he owed to the American chefs who placed their faith and business with his new company. He commenced donations of money and services—both in his company's name and from himself and Mrs. Minor—that have made the name "Minor's" synonymous with generous support for culinary professionalism.

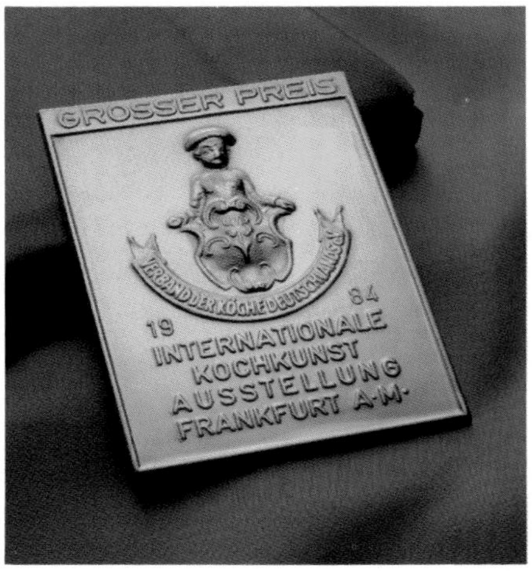

LEFT: At the 1984 International Culinary Competition (World Culinary Olympics) in Frankfurt, West Germany, The L.J. Minor Corporation culinary team won The Grand Prize In Gold in its category, the first time in the history of the event this highest-possible award was won by an American food company.

BELOW: Minor's chicken and beef bases are sales leaders for the company's extensive line of 13 premium-quality natural meat, poultry, and seafood fresh flavor bases.

Michael L. Minor, CEC, AAC, vice-president and corporate executive chef.

Shown at the dedication of the Lewis J. Minor Technical Center in Cleveland on December 18, 1986, are (from left) Dr. Lewis J. Minor; Mrs. Ruth Minor; Cleveland Mayor George Voinovich; company president retired U.S. Army Lieutenant General John D. McLaughlin, and Cleveland Councilwoman Helen Smith.

In 1974 one of the company's most significant employees, Thomas A. Ryan, passed away. Tom Ryan was Dr. Minor's second cousin, an attorney, and business manager since the early years. In large measure he had guided Minor's dynamic growth and, in 1973, persuaded retired U.S. Army Lieutenant General John D. McLaughlin to join the firm.

Prior to retirement, General McLaughlin headed the U.S. Army Support Command in Europe and earlier commanded the U.S. Army Quartermaster Center at Fort Lee. Known in the U.S. food industry for positive innovations in military feeding practice, General McLaughlin received the Silver Plate Foodservice Operator of the Year Award in 1973.

General McLaughlin expedited programs to reorganize the changing family company into a modern, market-sensitive business firm staffed by career professionals, supported with computer information systems, research and development, and state-of-the-art technology.

In 1983, for health and retirement reasons, Dr. Minor sold his company to a private group avowed to preserve Minor's outstanding industry image for quality products and service. General McLaughlin, president since 1979, became board chairman, president, and chief executive officer, while Dr. Minor continued as chairman emeritus and senior scientific consultant.

In October 1986 William F. McLaughlin was elected president. He had joined the company in 1982 as vice-president and controller, later becoming executive vice-president and chief operating officer. Under his direction Minor's continued impressive sales growth and capital expansion programs.

On December 29, 1986, Minor's was acquired by Nestlé Enterprises, Inc., parent company of 11 U.S. food-related companies owned by Nestlé S.A., based in Switzerland. Today the L.J. Minor Corporation has facilities in three greater Cleveland areas: corporate headquarters in a brand new building in Solon; manufacturing and technical center on Cleveland's near West Side and the main distribution center in Brecksville. Minor's also owns and operates a special products plant in Celina, Ohio, acquired in 1987.

Shortly after Dr. Minor started his company in 1951, he published these Business Aims to guide its growth: "I believe that honesty, integrity, accuracy, punctuality, courtesy, kindness, friendliness, helpfulness, and cleanliness are the tenets upon which my business shall be built.

"I will endeavor always to be helpful, not only to employees, my management team, and stockholders but also to customers, government agencies, and competitors.

William F. McLaughlin, president, The L.J. Minor Corporation.

"My experience in the food industry indicates that there will always be room for a company that sells quality products that are consistently controlled to ensure uniformity at a fair price that will result in a normal profit.

"Service will be the keynote of our business, and every effort will be put forth to give the customer exactly the product that he specifies."

Today these principles are alive and in practice at The L.J. Minor Corporation, a significant, growing contributor to the food-service and food-processing markets in the categories of stocks, natural meat flavors, soups, sauces, and gravies.

NESTLÉ ENTERPRISES, INC.

Nestlé Enterprises, Inc. (NEI), is the parent company for 11 food, beverage, and hospitality operations in the United States owned by Nestlé, S.A., Vevey, Switzerland. The NEI companies in the Cleveland area are Stouffer Restaurant Company, a nationwide chain of specialty restaurants founded and headquartered in Cleveland; Stouffer Foods Corporation, a producer of premium frozen foods; Stouffer Hotel Company, a major hotel and resort company; and L.J. Minor Company, producer of soup bases for the food-service and food-processing industries.

NEI also owns Nestlé Foods Corporation, Hills Bros. Coffee, Inc., Beech-Nut Nutrition Corporation, Wine World, Inc., Sunmark, FreshNes Foods Corporation, and Nestlé Puerto Rico, Inc. These companies manufacture more than 800 products and services. Most brands are either first or second in sales in their market, or gaining share on the leaders.

NEI has had outstanding, consistent growth: Sales have increased by more than 50 percent since 1982, when the companies were brought under the NEI umbrella. This growth has been achieved by specializing in quality products and services and by building each business internally.

Says James M. Biggar, chairman and chief executive officer of NEI, "The major thrust of Nestlé Enterprises will continue to be built around quality, food-oriented businesses striving to remain ahead of the competition by providing true value to the American consumer."

Biggar also emphasizes that Nestlé became the largest food company in the world through a combination of aggressive new product development and strategic acquisitions. And all companies Nestlé has acquired in the United States are still run by the same management people who were there when the companies were acquired.

Each Nestlé acquisition has been a strategic move followed by an influx of quality-improving technology by heavy marketing investment. Stouffer Foods is the best example of a successful Nestlé acquisition. Since 1973, when Nestlé acquired Stouffer Foods, the firm's sales have increased 12 times. The other Stouffer companies also have grown, and there are now 40 Stouffer hotels and 72 Stouffer restaurants nationwide.

Nestlé firmly believes in quality and value, which is achieved through strong marketing, advanced technical research, efficient manufacturing facilities, and commitment to the community.

The NEI companies also excel in community involvement. Nestlé believes a successful business has benefited from the community—resources, people, and sales—and it has a responsibility to give something back. The NEI companies do this in a variety of ways.

In the Cleveland area, the Stouffer companies alone give more than one million dollars per year for charitable contributions. Nationally, NEI contributes to some 43 different United Way organizations. Grand openings of Stouffer hotels are usually accompanied by gala benefits for local charities. NEI also has made corporate gifts to colleges for nu-

Stouffer's founder Vernon Stouffer is shown in one of his most familiar poses—tasting Stouffer's food in a test kitchen. Stouffer tasted reheated frozen prepared foods and freshly prepared entrées side by side and insisted that they taste and look alike and have the same quality before the frozen products could be shipped to the stores.

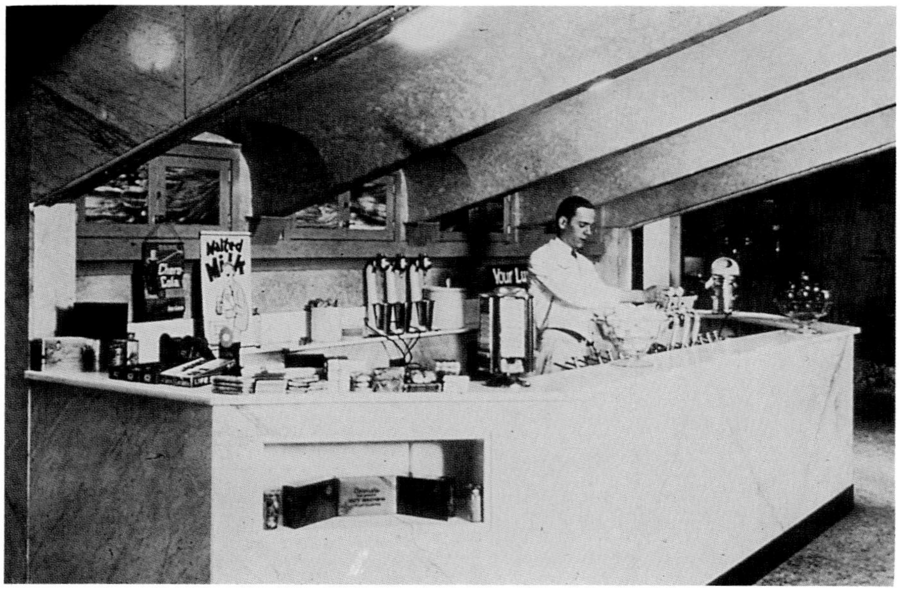

Abraham Stouffer's original buttermilk stand opened in 1922 in the lower level of Cleveland's historic Arcade and gave rise to the first Stouffer Restaurant, which opened in 1924 in Cleveland. Dairy products from the Stouffer farm, unique sandwich combinations, and Mrs. Mahala Stouffer's deep dish apple pie made the buttermilk counter a popular place.

In 1866 in Vevey, Switzerland, Henry Nestlé found a way to create nourishing infant food from whole milk that resulted in a reduced infant mortality rate. In the same village, Daniel Peter was making milk chocolate. Nearby in Cham, Switzerland, Charles Page, an American, developed an excellent condensed milk. The companies formed by these three men were merged into what is now Nestlé.

Today the firm is devoted to processing the finest ingredients into high-quality food. Its products include chocolate, instant tea and coffee, culinary products, frozen prepared foods, ice cream, dairy products, and infant foods. Nestlé also is represented in the cosmetics business with L'Oreal and in pharmaceuticals with Alcon. Nestlé products are now made in more than 50 countries and distributed on five continents.

tritional research and education, underwritten scholarships for culinary training, and consistently supported community programs for feeding the poor and hungry through Hunger Task Forces, food banks, Salvation Army kitchens, and others. NEI also supports many civic and cultural organizations.

A characteristic common to all NEI companies is an emphasis on people and communication. Employee information meetings presided over by top executives are generally held quarterly, and the sky's the limit on questions. Employees may ask anything about the company and its policies. People feel as if they are part of the action because managers listen to their concerns. If a manager is unable to answer a question or explain a procedure on the spot, he or she gets the answer and relays it to the employee.

NEI managers try to maintain a family feeling with fellow employees about the corporation. NEI companies also invest in employee training and development, promoting from within whenever possible. All NEI employees are made to feel their jobs are valuable. The firm's longstanding reputation for making top-quality products instills pride in its employees. This approach has created tremendous employee loyalty; most NEI companies have a large percentage of employees with 20 to 30 years' service. This is an achievement, especially in the restaurant and hotel industry where turnover is typically high. Caring about employees extends to all parts of the work environment and even includes the landscaping around NEI company facilities.

Nestlé S.A., parent to the Nestlé U.S. companies, was founded more than a century ago in Switzerland as a milk-processing company by three men who had all been independently experimenting with food processing.

The Stouffer Corporation and Nestlé Enterprises' headquarters building in Solon, outside of Cleveland, was completed in 1979 and also serves as headquarters for Stouffer Hotels and Resorts. A new Nestlé Enterprises building was completed at the end of 1989.

James M. Biggar, chairman and chief executive officer of Nestlé Enterprises, Inc., and president and chief executive officer of the Stouffer Corporation. Nestlé Enterprises consists of nine Nestlé-owned U.S. companies, including Stouffer Foods Corporation, Stouffer Hotels and Resorts, Stouffer Restaurant Company, L.J. Minor Corporation, Nestlé Foods Corporation, Beech-Nut Nutrition Corporation, Hills Bros. Coffee, Wine World Inc. (Beringer Vineyards), and Nestlé Puerto Rico, Inc.

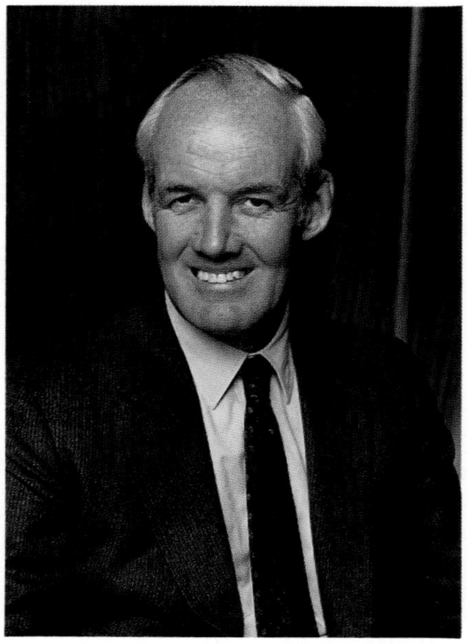

WARNER STORAGE, INC.

"Here today and here tomorrow" is the Warner Storage promise. Its history shows just how reliable this promise is. Warner Storage, Inc., has deep Cleveland roots that go back to its founding by the Warner family in 1895. It became one of the first agents of North American Van Lines in 1935. When Thomas A. Keefe, Sr., bought Warner Storage in 1960, the Warner name had such an excellent reputation that the new owner chose not to change it.

Under Keefe, Warner has maintained a steady annual growth rate of about 15 percent. It is now the largest North American Van Lines agent in Northeast Ohio. To accommodate the company's rapid expansion, a warehouse and office facility was built in 1981. The 25,000-square-foot warehouse is large enough to store the furniture and household goods of 600 families. Another 8,000 square feet of bonded warehouse space is available for containers waiting to be inspected by customs agents. The entire warehouse is protected by 24-hour climate-control, security, and fire-prevention systems.

Warner has more than 40 full-time employees, with an average of more than 12 years of service with the company. "This is a happy, professional type of environment—a good place to work," says Kathleen Soeder, administrative vice-president of Warner Storage and Tom Keefe's daughter.

Warner Storage can handle all types of moves: commercial and residential, in-town, across the country, or around the world. Warner has moved many of Cleveland's corporate offices to new locations within the city. It also handles most of the Cleveland deliveries for several large computer manufacturers.

The bottom line for any corporate move is the cost of the move plus the cost of employee and equipment downtime, damage, and disruption. Warner's commercial relocation specialists help plan office moves that minimize downtime, provide security for documents, and coordinate tasks ahead of the move. Warner's files are full of letters from enthusiastic customers. Special projects, such as relocating Cleveland's classical music radio station's record library or moving the law library of Cleveland's largest law firm, have won Warner special praise.

Moving families is the firm's greatest challenge. People often arrive in an unfamiliar city feeling frightened and overwhelmed. Says Kathleen Soeder, "Sometimes you have to be a psychiatrist, a babysitter, a counselor, and the Welcome Wagon all in one." It doesn't take long, though, for the enthusiasm that Kathleen and others at Warner Storage, Inc., feel about Cleveland to rub off on newcomers. Families soon settle in and wonder why they didn't move to Cleveland earlier.

Operation of Warner Storage, Inc. is under the direction of (from left) Robert M. Weaver, vice-president/sales; Andrew T. Keefe, operations manager; Kathleen Soeder, vice-president; and Thomas Keefe, president.

etc. EXECUTIVE SUITES

A new concept in business services—etc. Executive Suites—has evolved from what began as a modest typing service with a bigger office than it needed. When they moved into a lease office in 1985, Gayle Oust and Diane Fistek only wanted to pick up overflow typing jobs. They were disappointed that no small, quality offices were available in Independence, a rapidly growing commercial district south of Cleveland.

That was their first clue on the way to establishing a new business. When one of their clients indicated that it was too bad he could not move into their office to take advantage of their secretarial services, the idea took shape. And when a real estate broker asked if they had thought of renting out executive suites, they decided to take the plunge.

Diane Fistek (left) and Gayle Oust, partners in etc. Secretarial Company, say hands-on management has made their leasing of executive suites a success.

Gayle and Diane moved from their original office to 3,000 square feet of prime office space. They divided the space and offered new clients a desk, telephone, and secretarial and receptionist services, all for a monthly lease payment. After 18 months they were ready to expand to 13,000 square feet and 63 offices.

Among the companies that used etc. Executive Suites was Coldwell Banker, the real estate giant, which set up its first greater Cleveland office there. Tenants get a receptionist to greet their visitors, telephone answering, typing and word processing, access to telex and facsimile transmission facilities, a small private meeting room, a conference room, a kitchen, daily janitorial service, and complimentary coffee. They also get expert help from Gayle and Diane, who have a staff of two part-time and three full-time employees.

"We are hands-on owner-operators," says Gayle. "There is not one aspect of this business we have not done. And we teach our employees every aspect, including that clients deserve the extra personal service that we provide as owner-operators. At least one of us is always here to help."

Their clients are lawyers, accountants, start-up businesses, and out-of-state companies testing the waters in the Cleveland market. A typical client is a start-up business that outgrows the executive suite once it starts to grow.

"The cost today for an individual or small company to establish a presence is very high," says Diane. "We give new businesses a chance to establish credibility. They come to us and then they leave us, but that's good."

The next move for etc. Executive Suites will be no farther than downtown Cleveland or the city's east side, where Diane and Gayle will offer new businesses another place to hang their hats until everything is up and running.

Etc. Executive Suites boasts more than 12,000 square feet of individual office and meeting space.

DEXTER WATER MANAGEMENT SYSTEMS

World headquarters for Dexter Water Management Systems is located in Chagrin Falls.

Dexter Water Management Systems, formerly the Mogul Division of Dexter Corporation, has been a water-management specialist since 1915. With division headquarters located in Chagrin Falls, the company provides total water-management programs for industrial, commercial, and institutional users. Its products and services save customers thousands of dollars every day in energy costs for manufacturing, processing, and comfort-related applications.

Dexter Water Management Systems (DWMS) sells products that include additives for water and fuel treatment, testing kits, and automated chemical feeding and control systems. Additives help prevent corrosion, deposit formation, and microbial growth in water-cooling and -heating systems. They also cut fuel consumption by improving combustion efficiency and reducing post-combustion deposits. Testing kits offer a fast, economical way for customers to monitor conditions in their water systems. In addition, automated chemical feeding equipment improves efficiency and extends equipment life in water-handling systems by delivering water-treatment dosages at proper feeding levels.

The company's research continues to make important contributions to the advancement of water- and fuel-treatment technologies, and to the development of environmentally acceptable additives. DWMS has moved aggressively into environmental health and safety, recognizing that water is a precious resource. At the beginning of the 1980s the company received the prestigious Vaaler Award, which recognizes technical breakthroughs in the chemical industry, for creating an all-organic product to inhibit corrosion, deposit formation, and microbial growth in cooling systems.

Dexter Water Management Systems is also known worldwide for its services. These include complete water-treatment management services, analysis of water-management systems, technical consultation on the design and manufacture of water-treatment systems, and general technical services for solving many water- and energy-management problems. The company's salespeople are technical experts, able to monitor systems, make engineering recommendations, conduct energy audits, and help customers start up new facilities.

Typical DWMS services include a thorough survey of the water-heating or -cooling system; implementation of a customized treatment program; regular service, including laboratory analysis of samples; periodic energy profile studies of water-using equipment to maximize heat-transfer efficiencies; and comprehensive training programs for client system technicians.

The company operates internationally through a network of 26 offices. Each location provides the full complement of the company's products and services. Continuous development of chemicals, equipment, and testing/service facilities, including air and water environmental controls, enable each office to provide fast, reliable service to every customer.

In addition, a complete customer support program assures continuing after-sale assistance. Sales representatives regularly monitor customers' programs and keep them informed of new formulas and techniques. They supply special operational charts and forms, and lend a hand whenever it

Dexter Water Management Systems specializes in results-oriented treatments for cooling towers.

is needed.

Dexter Water Management Systems, formerly the Mogul Division of Dexter, started in 1915 as the North American Fibre Products Company, founded by Henry G. Tremel. It employed 15 manufacturing representatives and sold building products. Continual innovation and improved technology led to the development of a highly durable waterproof material to seal building roofs. The material was called Hornblende, and it was Mogul's bread and butter for years.

During the Great Depression North American Fibre needed additional products. One of its first water-treatment products, Boiler Coat, was used to decrease heat loss through cracks in a boiler setting. A few years later a new product called Everclean Boiler Process revolutionized boiler maintenance by decreasing the need to manually clean deposits and sediment from boiler tubes.

One of the company's first salesmen, Mike Mohrman, realized the sales potential of this new product, but needed a way to demonstrate its effectiveness. He filled a glass jar with mud and water, then boiled the mixture, and added a few drops of Everclean to show how it separated the impurities from the water. The first demonstration kit was born. Soon all the salesmen had a demo kit, and Everclean rapidly became a success.

Tremel decided he wanted to distinguish Everclean from the Hornblende line, as well as conquer the boiler maintenance market. Moguls were well known as the largest Indian elephants. They were often decorated in colorful tapestry and used to lead circus parades. Tremel thought Mogul was an excellent symbol for a product line he knew would eventually lead the company to financial success. The Mogul water-treatment line became so successful that the company's name was changed to Mogul.

In the 1960s Mogul began to expand through acquisitions, guided by C.C. Tippet, a young entrepreneur who bought 70 percent of the firm's stock in 1955. His first purchase was General Chemicals, which manufactured Mogul's water-treatment products. Mogul continued to grow rapidly in this decade through increased sales and acquisitions. In 1977 Mogul merged with Dexter Corporation, the oldest continuously listed company on the New York Stock Exchange.

Founded in 1767, Dexter initially produced industrial specialty papers, but began to diversify in the mid-1950s into other chemical-related products. It has traditionally been characterized by young leadership and an emphasis on research and development. Its commitment to bringing new and better products to the marketplace and paying the substantial price demanded of product leadership parallels Dexter Water Management System's long history of product and service excellence.

Operator training is just one of many support services available to Dexter Water Management Systems customers.

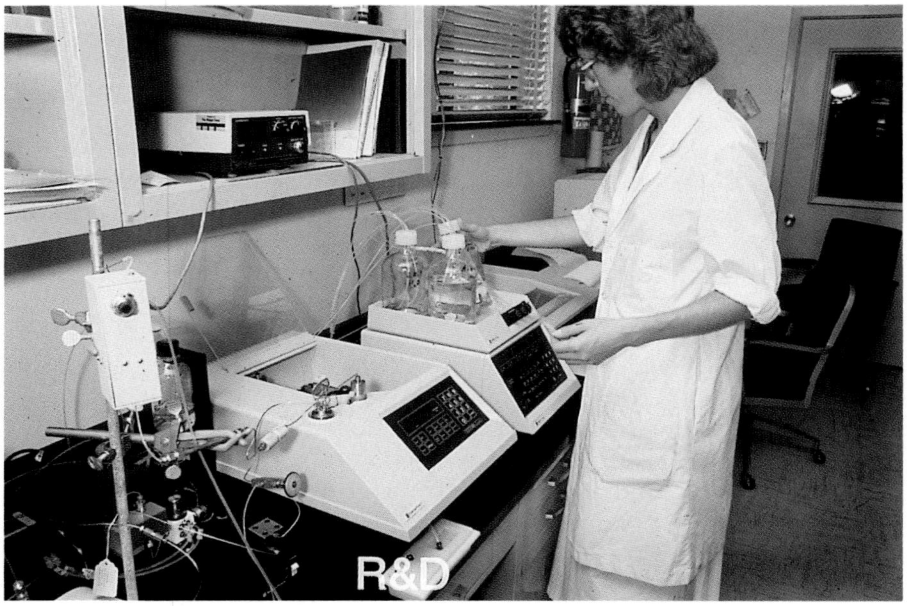

Research and development activity is intensive and ongoing as Dexter Water Management Systems seeks more alternatives for effective systems management.

HOLIDAY INN LAKESIDE

The Holiday Inn Lakeside is surrounded by the splendor of downtown Cleveland.

The Holiday Inn Lakeside boasts a superb location right on Lake Erie, in the fastest-growing part of downtown Cleveland. Its guests are within a few blocks of the Convention Center, Public Square, government and corporate offices, the theater district, and the Galleria Mall.

Managed by National Hospitality Corporation since 1980, Holiday Inn Lakeside has been a leader in Cleveland's hotel industry. It was the first hotel in the area to establish "executive floors" that offer the finest services and amenities. Guests on these floors enjoy many extras, including free stretch-limousine service within the downtown area and airport, key-accessed elevators, personalized service, spacious rooms, executive boardroom, and a private lounge where complimentary continental breakfast is served (with morning newspaper) and, in the early evening, cocktails and hors d'oeuvres are provided.

Another valuable service available to businesses and organizations using Holiday Inn Lakeside is a teleconferencing facility that connects with more than 1,000 other Holiday Inns nationwide, enabling firms to train employees, announce products, and share speakers, all from the comfort and convenience of downtown Cleveland.

When Joel Mason, the owner of National Hospitality Corporation, first visited Cleveland, he saw tremendous potential and a bright future. He decided to invest in the Holiday Inn Lakeside because of its location. And he wanted to transform the hotel into one that would appeal to Cleveland's most discriminating visitors.

Believing that people and the services they provide are what make a hotel first class, National Hospitality Corporation has filled key management positions with professionals who have worked in some of the world's finest hotels. Then, after asking customers about services they expect from a hotel, National Hospitality instituted those services at Holiday Inn Lakeside.

More than $3 million has been spent to redecorate the hotel and broaden its services. It has a formal restaurant that serves continental cuisine, a casual dining room, and a bar featuring complimentary daily hors d'oeuvre specials with live jazz music. Four hundred tastefully remodeled guest rooms feature individual climate control, color TV, and panoramic views of Lake Erie and the city skyline. A heated indoor pool and a fitness center, complete with exercise equipment and a sauna, keep guests in shape during their visits.

"First-quality hotel facilities are essential for a city to grow," says Christer Holtze, general manager of Holiday Inn Lakeside. "When people are traveling, they expect to be able to obtain the same level of service and quality accommodations they receive in their home cities. We believe that Holiday Inn Lakeside now offers the finest services to its guests. People who use our facilities will want to return to Cleveland to do business."

Holiday Inn Lakeside has also combined innovation and service in creating the 18th floor conference center. Eleven additional rooms on the

Continental cuisine is served in the beautifully appointed Rockefeller formal dining room.

18th floor, including an executive boardroom, can be used as breakout rooms or for smaller meetings. The grand ballroom is perfect for large banquets. It can hold 400 people, but it can also be divided into three rooms for luncheons or seminars.

Holiday Inn Lakeside prides itself on providing a personal touch to groups using its facilities. When an organization schedules a meeting, the hotel staff tailors every aspect of the meeting to the organization's requests. Flowers in company colors, special menus, extra telephones and electrical outlets, and a complete line of audiovisual equipment are available.

If an organization wants to make a lasting impression on meeting attendees, the hotel can provide an elegant ice-sculpture centerpiece for a special touch. On more lighthearted occasions, the "King-Kong" treat (chocolate-covered bananas on a stick, rolled in peanuts, served by the Holiday Inn's own "gorilla") is just the ticket.

After its meeting is over, every group is asked to fill out an evaluation form. Food and beverage quality, room appearance, employee attitude, and the client's response to the facilities are all rated. This information is then used to upgrade and expand conference and hotel services.

Holiday Inn Lakeside does more than provide top-notch lodging, dining, and meeting facilities; it also is involved in Cleveland. The hotel employs more than 250 area residents. It works closely with area colleges, enabling students to participate in internships and cooperative education programs. In conjunction with the Ohio Rehabilitation Services Commission, Holiday Inn Lakeside trains people with learning disabilities or emotional problems, or those recovering from accidental injuries for hotel jobs. Two full-time rehabilitation specialists are based at the hotel, training people to be housemen, floor maintenance workers, maids, and kitchen workers.

The inn's management staff participates in the Greater Cleveland Growth Association and the Cleveland Waterfront Coalition, an organization dedicated to developing Cleveland's downtown lakefront. Holtze serves on the vocational committee of the Cleveland Rotary Club and is president of The Greater Cleveland Hotel/Motel Association. Holiday Inn Lakeside has served as campaign headquarters for several local political candidates. Central operations for the Revco Marathon and the National City Bank Triathlon also have been housed there.

Of course, due to its immediate proximity to Lake Erie, Holiday Inn Lakeside is also a great place to watch annual lakefront events such as the Budweiser 500 Auto Race and the Cleveland Air Show.

Cleveland Browns and Indians fans can take advantage of Holiday Inn Lakeside's Sports Special package available during football and baseball seasons. The hotel also features romantic specials, such as Champagne Weekends, Pampered Honeymoons, and Anniversary Packages. These include champagne, a continental breakfast, dining, free parking, and use of the pool, sauna, and exercise room.

Holiday Inn Lakeside symbolizes the new spirit of Cleveland, which thrives on the rich assortment of cultural institutions in and around downtown—new businesses, fine shopping, sparkling nightlife, and a rapidly growing residential community.

John D's Cafe provides a moderately priced breakfast and lunch buffet in a fun atmosphere.

STATLER OFFICE SERVICES & EXECUTIVE SUITE

Executives working temporarily in Cleveland and businesses run by one person both face the difficult task of locating and staffing an office. They need not only a full-time receptionist, a secretary, a part-time bookkeeper, and someone to handle meeting preparations, but also a copier and a facsimile machine. This sounds like a tall order, but it is all provided by Statler Office Services, Inc.

Early in 1980 Barbara Bloom saw the need for office services and facilities in Cleveland and decided she could provide them. In 1981 she opened Statler Office Services, Inc., in the Statler Office Tower. Her research told her that this hotel-turned-office-building was the perfect place for her business. In the heart of downtown Cleveland's financial district, at East 12th and Euclid, it is on a major bus line and on Cleveland's main thoroughfare. The Statler Office Tower is just across the street from the Union Club and the Cleveland Athletic Club, two prestigious gathering places for Cleveland's business leaders. In addition, the building has a restaurant, airline ticket counters, and steady pedestrian traffic.

The firm's location is in the heart of Cleveland's business district, within walking distance of the city's leading banks, athletic and social clubs, theaters, department stores, and an assortment of restaurants. There is indoor parking, and the location is central to all industrial parks and 15 minutes from the airport by auto or rapid transit.

Bloom began her company by offering word-processing services, but she never lost sight of her long-range goal to offer complete executive offices. In 1983 Statler Office Services added a public telex service and a facsimile bureau. Then, in 1985, Statler Executive Suite opened its doors, providing staff, space, and services for a total executive office environment.

The handsome offices have all the amenities of a large corporation. These include personalized telephone answering, a receptionist, word-processing/typing services, a 24-hour facsimile machine, computers, voice-

Barbara Bloom, president, whose foresight saw the need for Statler Executive Suite services in Cleveland—professionals providing individual offices and support services to business.

Individual offices in a beautiful corporate environment are only part of the services offered by Statler Executive Suite.

mail messaging, mail handling, phone-in dictation, utilities, a lobby listing of client-company names, and limousine, messenger, and janitorial services.

In addition, Statler Executive Suite helps clients with bookkeeping, proposal design, printing business cards and stationery, and formatting letters. A conference room is available for meetings, and there is always a pot of fresh coffee. Barbara Bloom believes a client has a right to expect perfection, and she intends to supply it.

The private offices, complete with all communications and support services, are perfect for representatives in sales, banking, finance, and a host of related businesses. There is even a conference room available for multimedia presentations.

It is an ideal solution for attorneys, accountants, and consultants, as well as the business headquartered elsewhere that wishes to put a satellite office in Cleveland or just "test the waters." The short-term lease and turnkey facility makes it perfect for new entrepreneurs or the short-term needs of large, out-of-town companies.

Statler Executive Suite is a member of Global Office Network—the leading business centers of the world and an international referral network designed for qualified executive suites. Only through a network conforming to set standards of excellence can quality be assured on an international level. As a result, tenants of Statler Executive Suite can "branch out" with confidence within the Network. Statler also belongs to Executive Suite Network, the largest association of executive suites providing professional development as well as the largest Network database available in the industry.

Statler Executive Suite rapidly became a financial success and plans to add other locations in Cleveland and across Ohio.

Barbara Bloom has a unique relationship with her staff. She respects her employees, never asking them to do tasks she wouldn't do herself. On the other hand, she expects them to meet her client-service objectives. She rewards loyalty and good service, as exemplified by her promotion of a seven-year employee of the firm to the position of vice-president in early 1988.

Bloom, who was a downtown booster long before it was popular, saw businesses such as hers as a key to restoring life to downtown Cleveland. She typifies the new spirit of business in Cleveland, investing in the city when revitalization was more dream than reality. Now, as new shopping centers, restaurants, apartments, and office buildings spring up all over downtown, Barbara Bloom's vision is being realized.

Complete office services available include private offices, conference facilities, and such technical support services as word processing, telex, and facsimile. The company's motto: "We run the office while you manage your business."

STOUFFER TOWER CITY PLAZA HOTEL

In a city enjoying a rich renaissance, Stouffer Tower City Plaza Hotel stands out. As part of an emerging chain of world-class hotels and resorts, the historic downtown hotel is one of Cleveland's established jewels, for almost a century hosting and embracing Cleveland's most significant social, civic, and cultural occasions.

Built in the grand European style, Stouffer Tower City Plaza Hotel has 492 rooms, 49 suites, and more than 60,000 square feet of meeting and conference room space. Following a remarkable restoration and renovation program, the hotel currently offers the most luxurious accommodations in the area, as well as state-of-the-art meeting facilities.

The Public Square site of the Stouffer Tower City Plaza Hotel has a long history, starting in 1815, when Cleveland's first hotel, Mowrey's Tavern, opened there. This log tavern's dining room hosted Cleveland's first theater performance in 1820. Later it was renamed Cleveland House, and the hotel's barn was the depot for Cleveland's first railroad.

After a fire in 1845 that destroyed the hotel, a new owner built Dunham House, a four-story brick hotel. The building was later enlarged into one of the finest facilities of its kind in the Midwest. Renamed Forest City House, it was the site of Marcus Hanna's announcement, in 1895, of William McKinley's candidacy for president.

Forest City House was torn down and replaced by the magnificent 1,000-room, $4.5-million Hotel Cleveland, which opened in 1918. The innovative building was E-shaped, so that each guest room had a window. The hotel was next door to the new, electrified Union Terminal, and it advertised that "A Redcap can bring you from your train to our front desk in two minutes; no taxis, no out-of-doors." It is still a two-minute indoor walk from the Rapid Transit station to the hotel's front desk.

The hotel was acquired in 1959 by a national chain. It was closed in 1977 and placed in receivership. Under the leadership of Cleveland Browns' owner Arthur Model, seven leading Cleveland corporations, including Chessie System, Eaton, Diamond Shamrock, Higbee's, TRW, and the Stouffer Corporation, along with Steve O'Neill, stepped in to restore the hotel to its original grandeur. In 1978 the refurbished hotel opened as the Stouffer Inn on the Square.

William N. Hulett (left), president of Stouffer Hotel Company, and James M. Biggar, chairman and chief executive officer of Nestlé Enterprises Inc., in the Presidential Suite of Stouffer Tower City Plaza Hotel.

Stouffer Tower City Plaza Hotel is in the heart of downtown Cleveland on Public Square.

The Stouffer Hotel Company, headquartered in Cleveland, has a history of community involvement, starting with its purchase of the hotel. Since 1978 the firm has been involved in nearly every one of Cleveland's major civic events. In 1986, to signal its faith in the city's vitality, the Stouffer Hotel Company announced a three-year, $35-million renovation plan for its landmark downtown hotel. "This program reflects our ongoing commitment to the highest levels of service and standards of quality, and to the continued revitalization of downtown Cleveland," said William N. Hulett, president of the Stouffer Hotel Company.

As part of the program, the name of the hotel was changed to Stouffer Tower City Plaza Hotel, emphasizing its prominence as part of the massive Tower City Center redevelopment complex. Renovation was highlighted by the introduction of Club Floors at the hotel, which in-

LEFT: Guests staying on the Club Floors at Stouffer Tower City Plaza Hotel have the exclusive use of the bilevel Club Lounge and the Cleveland Library of Commerce, a special information facility in the lounge created in cooperation with the Greater Cleveland Growth Association.

BELOW: The newly renovated Grand Ballroom is one of the largest hotel banquet facilities between New York and Chicago, and has always been the elegant setting for the city's most celebrated social events and meetings.

clude special service features designed for the executive traveler. All 492 guest rooms were refurbished, meeting rooms were remodeled, and the Grand Ballroom, the largest hotel ballroom between New York and Chicago, underwent complete renovation.

Club Floors, the top three floors of the hotel, comprise 145 guest rooms, the Presidential Suite, and 11 luxury suites with parlors. Each room has remote-control color TV, a refrigerator stocked with drinks and snacks, and desk-top and bedside telephones, and each bathroom features a TV, telephone, and hair dryer. Two floors are joined by a bilevel Club Lounge, which has a sitting room, conference room, and library. The library was created for executive travelers in cooperation with the Greater Cleveland Growth Association to provide information on the city and its businesses.

The Club Floors have set a new standard of personalized service and accommodations in Cleveland. Guests have their own concierge services, express check-in and checkout, and private access to their floor by personal key. Complimentary continental breakfast is served daily in the lounge, complimentary hors d'oeuvres each evening from 5 p.m. to 7 p.m., and beverage service is available throughout the day.

Building a world-class hotel and conference facility depends as much on the staff as on the building. Stouffer Tower City Plaza Hotel recruits excellent people and provides continuous Spirit of Hospitality training. Customer relations are a major focus at the hotel, with guest comment cards receiving a personal reply from the president.

While a large portion of the hotel's midweek business comes from executive travelers and corporate meetings, on weekends Stouffer Tower City Plaza Hotel is a very popular "getaway" spot. It's just minutes from Cleveland's Playhouse Square and the nightlife of the Flats and Warehouse districts, and a 10-minute walk from Cleveland Municipal Stadium (home of the Cleveland Indians and the Cleveland Browns) and the Convention Center. The hotel is also home to one of Cleveland's finest restaurants—the French Connection. Weekend packages built around these attractions and other downtown events, such as the RiverFest and the Square to Square Festival, are always popular.

The hotel is a charter member of the Historic Hotels of America program recently developed by The National Trust For Historic Preservation.

It has also earned the prestigious Four-Diamond Award from the American Automobile Association. Stouffer Tower City Plaza Hotel expects to continue to be Cleveland's premier luxury hotel, focusing on service and on state-of-the-art facilities in a historic landmark setting.

MICELI DAIRY PRODUCTS COMPANY

The teenager eases his beat-up Model-T pickup truck into the maze of hilly, red-brick streets that knit themselves into the tight pattern of Cleveland's east side Italian neighborhoods. He's not sure this is going to work.

John has been up since 4 a.m., but sleep is the farthest thing from his mind. His early-morning message, "fresh scamorze and ricotta," brings curious housewives out onto porches and third-floor balconies. Used to a variety of early-morning

Technicians work 24 hours per day in the Miceli laboratory developing natural products that use no preservatives.

vendors, they wonder who this new voice is. The same question crosses the minds of startled shopkeepers, stopped mid-crank beside their half-opened awnings.

Minutes later the smiling young man lowers the tailgate and hauls out a pair of scales and his fresh batches of ricotta and scamorze (now called mozzarella) cheeses.

John Miceli is in business.

John Miceli was only 15 years old when he began tailgating traditional Italian cheeses into the city. His immigrant father, Anthony, had taught the boy old-world methods of cheese making at the family farm in Newbury, Ohio, 20 miles east of Cleveland.

Their few dairy cows provided more than enough milk for the family so that the little extra could be sold to local dairies. But shortly after World War I that market dried up, and John decided to make and sell the cheese himself.

John's enterprise paid off with a steadily growing clientele within Cleveland's Italian community, but was considerably slowed during World War II as he worked long hours in a defense plant.

After the war John Miceli returned to making cheese full time, now renting plant space from three local dairies for his newly founded Miceli Dairy Products Company. And the business took off. Independently owned grocery stores throughout the Cleveland area wanted the same excellent ricotta and mozzarella that they could order only from John Miceli.

In 1949 Miceli Dairy Products Company moved into its own plant on East 90th Street, and the next 40 years would see three generations of Micelis dedicated to their fast-growing product lines and markets.

Miceli's four children, Rosemarie, John Jr., Carol, and Joe, are all active in the day-to-day operations of the business. Sharing the same values as their father, they continue to stress consistency of product and high-quality service to the customer.

"I am not surprised at my children's success in the business," says John Sr., who has seen Miceli Dairy Products Company grow from local Model-T tailgate deliveries to distribution in 50 states via a modern semi-trailer fleet. Miceli Dairy is now a recognized leader in the fresh, Italian cheese market nationwide.

Unlike nearly all its competition, Miceli Dairy remains family owned and operated. Known for extraordinary product innovation, the Micelis have always responded to their consumers by expanding their line of authentic Italian cheeses over the years. More recently new products have included soft-style mozzarella, Parmesan, Romano, string cheese, and blue cheese. The company is also prominent in the rapidly growing ricotta market, producing whole milk, traditional, part skim, and lite.

It was Miceli Dairy that developed the innovative 15-ounce sealed container for ricotta cheese, extending shelf life to 90 days without using preservatives. The company has also taken the lead among Italian cheese manufacturers in packaging shredded cheeses. Miceli was one of the first Italian cheese companies to get Kosher certification on its ricotta and one of the first to volunteer for USDA approval, a certification it has had for more than 20 years.

Today, with a state-of-the-art plant and equipment, the most impor-

Miceli's fifth plant expansion, completed in 1989, includes an ultramodern warehouse/cooler.

tant part of the Miceli Dairy operation remains authentic old-world craftsmanship and flavor in its products. Technicians work 24 hours a day in the Miceli laboratory, developing natural products that use no preservatives. They also create nutritional recipes with a focus on part-skim and lite products.

Miceli Dairy Products Company is proud of its tradition of fine products, and proud to be an integral part of its growing Cleveland community. Miceli is involved in many civic projects, including the Woodland East Community Organization (WECO), the Greater Cleveland Growth Association, and the Cleveland and Akron Food Banks.

Miceli is one of the leaders in the growing ricotta market, producing four types: whole milk, traditional, part skim, and lite.

When hard times hit the firm's inner-city neighborhood, many businesses abandoned the area. But the Miceli family remained at their original site, not only adding buildings and beautiful landscaping, but, more importantly, providing much-needed jobs.

Today, with the latest plant expansion completed in 1989 and a brand-new fleet of trucks rolling, Miceli Dairy Products Company continues its search for new ways to foster company and community growth by developing new products and introducing traditional Italian cheeses heretofore unavailable on the American market.

Miceli Dairy Products Company takes great pride in its Ohio and Pennsylvania milk suppliers. Indeed, without their fine-quality milk, superior Italian cheese would be impossible to make. Authentic flavor inspires the advertising programs that have boosted the company's and community's growth.

The young man in the pickup truck needn't have worried; it worked out fine.

Miceli Dairy Products Company produces a variety of all-natural, authentic Italian cheeses for the retail and foodservice markets.

STOUFFER RESTAURANT COMPANY

Located atop tall buildings in major American cities, Stouffer's "Top" restaurants, including Cleveland's Top of the Town in Erieview Plaza, feature fine dining with spectacular views.

Stouffer Restaurant Company began as a tiny buttermilk stand back in 1922; now it's a national chain of more than 70 specialty restaurants. The high-quality food and dedication to service that was a Stouffer family requirement soon transformed the buttermilk stand into a restaurant and into a national chain of restaurants by 1928. The company continued to grow steadily for the next 40 years by operating family-oriented restaurants.

In the 1960s Stouffer Restaurant Company moved in a new direction by establishing the elegant "Top" restaurants. Located atop tall buildings in major American cities, these restaurants, including Cleveland's Top of the Town in Erieview Plaza, feature fine dining with spectacular views.

The 1970s brought rapid growth and several popular new concepts. Among them was J.B. Winberie, a down-to-earth, cozy restaurant where fresh pasta, seafood, and signature dishes are featured. This concept has emerged as the primary focus of the firm's growth. In 1987 Stouffer's acquired the Borel Restaurant Corporation, owner of the Rusty Scupper chain, and nearly doubled in size.

At the same time changes were made to other restaurants. One traditional Stouffer's restaurant became the Chicago Bar & Grill and The Whole Grain. Stouffer's now operates four Bar & Grill restaurants. All combine good food with people-watching—great places to dine and make new friends. The Whole Grain is a health-food-oriented restaurant that offers quick take-out or eat-in service.

The 1980s brought Parker's Lighthouse restaurants into the Stouffer Restaurant Company. These restaurants combine mesquite-grilled seafood and regional specialty dishes with dramatic waterfront views. Stouffer Restaurants also operates three Cheese Cellars, informal restaurants with a wine cellar theme; six James Taverns, featuring old-fashioned American home cooking; and two Piers, which feature seafood.

In the Cleveland area, the Stouffer Restaurant Company operates eight restaurants and two fast-food outlets, and plans to add another two locations before the end of the decade.

Stouffer Restaurants emphasize well-prepared fresh foods. While many restaurants depend on their liquor business to keep profits high, Stouffer's focuses on good food. Test kitchens are always experimenting with new dishes that appeal to changing tastes and fit requirements for more healthful food. Stouffer's pioneered "The Look of Lean," high-quality, tasty meals under 300 calories. It has now developed more than 100 recipes in this category. Menus include more fish and poultry, fewer fried foods, less cholesterol and salt, and more flavor. Stouffer's was the first restaurant chain to introduce oat bran muffins, which combine hearty flavor with high bran content.

Since its first restaurant opened in 1924, the Stouffer Restaurant Company has been providing customers with reliable, consistent, high-quality service, products, and value. Stouffer restaurant managers stay in touch with food trends by listening to customers, studying the competition, and knowing when to make changes. They've been trained to stay on top of new ideas.

Stouffer's provides the training, tools, and encouragement to keep restaurant staff growing. Managing a restaurant is a complex job. In addition to ordering, preparing, and serving food, a good restaurant manager must have initiative and a talent for dealing with people. Providing efficient, friendly service is just as important as offering good, wholesome food.

The company's management training program is eight weeks long. Trainees work in every restaurant position: They cook, they serve, and

they train. Traditional topics, such as financial management, time management, and employee relations, are covered, along with specific restaurant skills, such as food, dining room, and bar management. Each trainee is assigned to a restaurant, where he or she spends a week "shadowing" an experienced manager before taking over responsibilities for a shift; however, training does not end there. The first training session is the beginning of a long-term development process that includes field training seminars, biannual performance reviews, and career discussions.

At Stouffer Restaurants, all employees are encouraged to view their jobs as careers. The company is working nationwide to position the job of server as an important career by developing recognition events for excellent service and by training its managers to understand and respect how important good service is to the success of the business.

Stouffer Restaurants offer some of the best employee benefits of any major restaurant chain: dental and health care, life and accident insurance, disability, and retirement. Management personnel are also reimbursed for the costs of continuing education. Because the firm operates restaurants in more than 20 states, it offers a choice of location and opportunities for advancement.

Stouffer Restaurants' parent company, the Stouffer Corporation, was acquired by Nestlé, S.A., in 1973. In 1982 it became a separate operating company under the umbrella of Nestlé Enterprises, Inc. (NEI). There are nine food-related NEI companies in the United States. In Cleveland,

they are (in addition to Stouffer Restaurants): Stouffer Foods, Stouffer Hotels, and the L.J. Minor Company. With Nestlé behind it, the Stouffer Restaurant Company has expanded, as well as maintained research and development efforts to refine and refresh its menus.

The Stouffer Restaurant Company is solidly positioned as a national chain of specialty restaurants—the place to go for America's favorite foods.

CLEVELAND COCA-COLA BOTTLING COMPANY, INC.

Cleveland Coca-Cola Bottling Company, Inc., opened in 1905 and now employs more than 200 people at its near east side plant. Coca-Cola has always been a strong Cleveland supporter. In 1986 that support was renewed with the company's decision to invest millions of dollars in renovating its Cleveland plant. Improvements included replacing equipment, building a new loading dock, completing a million-dollar exterior face-lift, and computerizing most of the operations. The decision to make such a substantial investment was based, in part, on Cleveland's recent economic rebirth, which brought new business to Coca-Cola. Cleveland also has a trained work force and a good location, key ingredients in the company's success.

Both nationally and locally, Coca-Cola is dedicated to providing excellent products to its consumers and the very best service. To achieve these goals, Coca-Cola emphasizes three areas: employees, customers, and community.

Coca-Cola fosters employee growth by providing company-sponsored training, underwriting part of college tuition expenses, encouraging personal development, recognizing individual performance, and promoting from within.

Customer support is also a key element in Coca-Cola's success. The firm not only supplies a variety of products that appeal to many people but also helps retail customers merchandise these products. National and local media advertising campaigns are launched. Company sales managers help store owners build imaginative, attention-getting product displays and provide display and promotional materials, such as giant inflatable Coca-Cola cans, banners, and tote bags.

Coca-Cola also gets involved in the community. In 1988 the national Coca-Cola/Boy Scouts program, "Drugs: A Deadly Game!" won the prestigious "C" Flag from the President's Citation Program for Private Sector Initiatives. The program was the largest antidrug-abuse education campaign in history, reaching more than 5 million members of the Boy Scouts and the general public.

In Cleveland, Coca-Cola has worked with Cleveland Browns players as resource people in the antidrug campaign. The company sponsors summer one-on-one basketball clinics, featuring professional players who encourage youngsters to stay in school and set healthy goals for themselves. Coca-Cola contributes to college scholarships for underprivileged students and is a major Cleveland-area sponsor of the United Negro College Fund's golf tournament. In addition, the company cosponsors such community events as the Cleveland Air Show and the Cleveland Grand Prix.

Between 1978 and 1988 Cleveland Coca-Cola Bottling Company, Inc., doubled its business in the Cleveland area and it expects to do the same in the next decade. Employee support, customer service, and community involvement have been a winning combination for Coca-Cola.

The economic rebirth of Cleveland inspired Cleveland Coca-Cola Bottling Company, Inc., to invest substantially in a renovation of its near East Side plant.

PATRONS

The following individuals, companies, and organizations have made a valuable commitment to the quality of this publication. Windsor Publications and the Greater Cleveland Growth Association gratefully acknowledge their participation in *Cleveland: Shaping the Vision.*

Advancement Corporation
Alcan Aluminum*
Alexander & Alexander of Ohio
American Asset Management Co.
American Gas Association Laboratories*
Ameritrust*
Arthur Andersen & Co.*
Bacik, Karpinski Associates Inc.*
Baker & Hostetler*
Bank One, Cleveland, N.A.
Bearings, Inc.*
Biskind Development Company*
Blue Cross & Blue Shield Mutual of Ohio*
Booz•Allen & Hamilton, Inc.*
BP America*
Catholic Diocese of Cleveland*
Chicago Title Insurance Co.
The Clark-Reliance Corporation*
Cleveland-Cliffs Inc.*
The Cleveland Clinic Foundation*
Cleveland Coca-Cola Bottling Company, Inc.*
Cleveland Electric Illuminating Company*
Cleveland Public Power*
Cleveland State University*
Cleveland Waterworks System*
Computer Task Group, Inc.
Concord Hotels, Inc.*
Convention & Visitors Bureau of Greater Cleveland*
C-P-C General Motors Plant*
Cragin•Lang, Inc.*
Cuyahoga Community College*
Cuyahoga Savings*
The Edward J. DeBartolo Corporation*
Dexter Water Management Systems*
Dunlop & Johnston, Inc.*
The East Ohio Gas Company*
The Emerald Health Network, Inc.*
Ernst & Young*
Essef Corporation*
etc. Executive Suites*
The Excello Specialty Company*
The Ferry Cap & Set Screw Company*
Ford Motor Company*
Forest City Enterprises, Inc.*
GE-Reuter-Stokes*
The Greater Cleveland Regional Transit Authority*
Health Cleveland*
The Albert M. Higley Company*
David G. Hill & Assoc. Co. LPA
Hinkley Lighting Co.
Holiday Inn Lakeside*
Holzheimer Interiors, Inc.*
Horizon Savings*
The Huntington National Bank*
Inland Fisher Guide Euclid Plant*
The International Exposition Center*
InTrans, Inc.*
Invacare Corporation*
Jewish Community Federation*
Jones, Day, Reavis & Pogue*
The Joseph & Feiss Company*
Kaiser Permanente*
Keeva J. Kekst Architects*
Keithley Instruments, Inc.*
King James Group*
Laventhol & Horwath*
Linclay Corporation*
LTV Steel Company*
Lucas Aerospace Power Equipment Corporation*
McKinsey & Company, Inc.*
Management Reports, Inc. (MRI)*
Meridia Health System*
Miceli Dairy Products Company*
Middough Associates, Inc.*
The L.J. Minor Corporation*
MK-Ferguson Company*
The Mt. Sinai Medical Center*
National City Bank*
Nestlé Enterprises, Inc.*
New York Life Insurance Company*
Oglebay Norton Company*
Ohio Bell*
Ohio Mattress Company*
Orlando Baking Company*
The Osborn Engineering Company*
Parma Community General Hospital*
Picker International, Inc.*
Pierre's French Ice Cream Company*
Preformed Line Products*
Realty One*
Reliance Electric Company*
Reserve Square*
Robinson-Conner of Ohio, Inc.*
Roulston & Company, Inc.*
St. John Hospital*
Saint Vincent Charity Hospital & Health Center*
I. Schumann & Co.
Sea World of Ohio*
SIFCO Industries, Inc.*
Society National Bank*
The Spohn Corporation*
Squire, Sanders & Dempsey*
The Standard Products Company*
Statler Office Services*
Stouffer Foods Corporation*
Stouffer Restaurant Company*
Stouffer Tower City Plaza Hotel*
SunarHauserman*
Systemation*
Third Federal Savings and Loan Association*
Touche Ross*
Towers Perrin*
Union Carbide Corp.-PARMA
University Circle, Inc.
University Hospitals of Cleveland*
Van Dorn Company*
Warner & Swasey Company*
Warner Storage, Inc.*
WUAB-TV, Channel 43*

*Participants in Part Two of *Cleveland: Shaping the Vision.* The stories of these companies and organizations appear in chapters 10 through 15, beginning on page 294.

BIBLIOGRAPHY

Campbell, Thomas F., and Edward M. Miggins, eds. *The Birth of Modern Cleveland*. Cleveland: Western Reserve Historical Society, 1988.

Condon, George E. *Cleveland: Prodigy of the Western Reserve*. Tulsa, Okla.: Continental Heritage Press, Inc., 1979.

Goulder, Grace. *John D. Rockefeller: The Cleveland Years*. Cleveland: Western Reserve Historical Society, 1972.

Herrick, Clay, Jr. *Cleaveland's Rich Heritage*. Cleveland: The Early Settlers Association, HKM Press, 1976.

Rose, William Ganson. *Cleveland: The Making of a City*. Cleveland and New York: The World Publishing Company, 1950.

Sunshine, Linda, and John W. Wright. *The Best Hospitals in America*. New York: Henry Holt & Co., 1987.

Van Tassel, David D., and John J. Grabowski, eds. *The Encyclopedia of Cleveland History*. Cleveland: Case Western Reserve University; Bloomington and Indianapolis: Indiana University Press, 1987.

INDEX

CLEVELAND'S ENTERPRISES INDEX

GENERAL INDEX

Italicized numbers indicate illustrations

A

B

C

D

E

F

G